MODERN IMPERIALISM AND COLONIALISM

A GLOBAL PERSPECTIVE

Trevor R. Getz
San Francisco State University

Heather Streets-Salter
Washington State University

Prentice Hall

Boston   Columbus   Indianapolis   New York   San Francisco   Upper Saddle River   Amsterdam
Cape Town   Dubai   London   Madrid   Milan   Munich   Paris   Montreal   Toronto   Delhi
Mexico City   São Paulo   Sydney   Hong Kong   Seoul   Singapore   Taipei   Tokyo

Executive Editor: Jeff Lasser
Editorial Project Manager: Rob DeGeorge
Editorial Assistant: Amanda Dykstra
Senior Marketing Manager: Maureen E. Prado Roberts
Marketing Assistant: Marissa O'Brien
Production Manager: Meghan DeMaio
Creative Director: Jayne Conte
Cover Designer: Karen Noferi
Manager, Cover Visual Research & Permissions: Karen Sanatar
Cover Photo: "The Beheading of Atahualpa," Accession # lat01019/Courtesy of San Jose State University CSU IMAGE Project.
Full-Service Project Management/Composition: Aparna Yellai/GGS Higher Education Resources, PMG
Printer/Binder/Cover Printer: R.R. Donnelly & Sons
Text Font: Times-Roman 10/12

Credits and acknowledgments borrowed from other sources and reproduced, with permission, in this textbook appear on appropriate page within text.

Library of Congress Cataloging-in-Publication Data

Getz, Trevor R.
  Modern imperialism and colonialism : a global perspective / Trevor R. Getz,
Heather Streets-Salter.—1st ed.
        p. cm.
  Includes bibliographical references and index.
  ISBN-13: 978-0-321-42409-9
  ISBN-10: 0-321-42409-3
  1. Imperialism—History. 2. History, Modern. I. Streets-Salter, Heather. II. Title.
  D208.G48 2011
  325'.3—dc22

                                                        2010010005

10 9 8 7 6 5 4 3 2 1

Prentice Hall
is an imprint of

www.pearsonhighered.com

ISBN 10:   0-321-42409-3
ISBN 13: 978-0-321-42409-9

CONTENTS

MAPS

PREFACE

WHY STUDY IMPERIALISM? A PERSPECTIVE FROM THE UNITED STATES IN 2010

We have lived through, or are living through, an age of American empire, or so we're told. As early as the 1820s, the United States began to understand itself as the pre-eminent power on the American landmass, a status that was represented partly by the linguistic mapping of the proper adjective "American" to decribe solely U.S. projects. In 1941, as the industry and military of the United States geared up for the Second World War, publisher Henry Luce predicted an "American century" in which the formal European empires would crumble before the onslaught of the financial, cultural, and corporate imperialism of the United States.[1] Certainly some of Luce's forecasts proved correct. In the post-war period, and especially since the collapse of the Soviet Union in 1991, the United States has become the world's pre-eminent military power, the only nation-state truly able to exert its will around the globe through a network of client-states and semi-permanent bases on every continent. On the other hand, American hegemony has never been unchallenged, and has almost always been carried out in cooperation or through negotiation with other states. In the decade of the 1990s, there were many charges of American imperialism in Latin America, Asia, and the Middle East, but rarely did U.S. involvement in these regions take the form of large-scale military intervention or the formal occupation of overseas territories.[2]

In the wake of the September 11, 2001 attacks on the United Stated by al Qaeda terrorists, American imperialism became once again a leading theme of both popular and scholarly debate. In a search for the motives behind such a terrible operation, some commentators put the blame on American foreign policy.[3] The architect of the attack himself, Osama bin Laden, who described American operatives abroad as *crusaders*, wrote that "What America is tasting now, is something insignificant compared to what we have tasted for scores of years. Our nation [the Islamic world] has been tasting this humiliation and this degradation for more than 80 years. Its sons are killed, its blood is shed, its sanctuaries are attacked, and no-one hears and no-one heeds. . . . When the sword comes down [on America], after 80 years, hypocrisy rears its ugly head."[4]

The administration of President George W. Bush responded to the 9/11 attacks with a vigorous and global campaign that culminated in the invasion of Afghanistan and Iraq. In preparing the American and global public for these campaigns, the administration avidly sought to avoid any imputation that they were seeking to build an American empire. The elected officials, bureaucrats, and generals involved in planning the operations scrupulously avoided the public use of terminology that smacked of imperialism, consistently stating as their objectives the restoration of global stability and the protection of America's borders.[5] The President himself explicitly avowed

---

[1] An excellent evaluation of the extent of limitations of the "American century" is David Reynolds, "American Globalism: Mass, Motion, and the Multiplier Effect," in *Globalization in World History*, edited by A.G. Hopkins (London: Pimlico, 2002).

[2] See, for example, Subcommondante Marcos, "The Fourth World War," *In Motion Magazine*, November 11, 2001.

[3] For early coverage of this debate, see Walter Lafeber, "The Post September 11 Debate Over Empire, Globalization, and Fragmentation," *Political Science Quarterly*, 117 (2002), 1–17; and Benjamin Ross, "In Search of Root Causes," *Dissent*, 49 (2002), 40–43.

[4] Text of Osama bin Laden's statement of October 7, 2001. Translation supplied by the Associated Press.

[5] Kevin Baker, "The Fear in Ideas: American Imperialism, Embraced," *New York Times Magazine*, December 9, 2001, 53.

that the United States "has no empire to extend" and no "territorial ambitions."[6] Rather it was the administration's critics who introduced the terminology of empire. Among the first were politicians, like British Liberal Democrat party leader Charles Kennedy, who denounced what he called the Bush administration's new American imperialism.[7] Soon, a flood of influential scholars, pundits, and government leaders worldwide were railing against American "imperial ambitions" or "imperial delusions."[8] In response, supporters of the war in Iraq began to appropriate the vocabulary of empire, defending the notion of an American empire rather than arguing that it did not exist. Policy analyst Max Boot wrote in May 2003: "If we want Iraq to avoid becoming a Somalia on steroids, we'd better get used to U.S. troops being deployed there for years, possibly decades, to come. If that raises hackles about American imperialism, so be it. We're going to be called an empire whatever we do. We might as well be a successful empire."[9] Meanwhile Niall Ferguson, the centrist scholar of the British Empire, warned Americans to shake off their imperial denial: "deny it who will, empire is as much a reality today as it was throughout the 300 years when Britain ruled, and made, the modern world."[10]

The defeat of the Republican party in 2008 ushered in the prospect of a less unilateral and aggressive foreign policy, and proponents of a bellicose U.S. foreign policy like Victor Davis Hanson at the conservative Hoover Institute bemoaned "the omnipotent influence of Obama's multicultural creed: Western civilization is unexceptional in comparison with other cultures, and history must be the story of an ecumenical, global shared brotherhood."[11] Yet President Barack Obama has not managed to unravel the sinews of foreign entanglement that critics call *imperialism*, and even in the midst of a domestic recession U.S. troops are based or involved in conflicts around the world.

The passions ignited by the debate over American empire, both at home and abroad, do not merely reflect current U.S. foreign policy. Instead, they arise from a world shaped by the collective memories of centuries of imperialism and colonialism. Formal empires may no longer cover the globe to the extent they once did, but their after-effects are all around us. This is nowhere more obvious than in the relationship between the secular/Christian-majority states of the United States and Europe (along with Jewish-majority Israel) on the one hand and the Muslim-majority states of Asia and North Africa on the other. Their relationship today is complex, in large part because the history of that relationship is messy and multifaceted. Islamic and Christian empires of the medieval and early modern eras co-existed both peacefully and fractiously, as crusaders and as traders. Africans, Europeans, and Asians of both religions were for centuries not only enslaved to labor in each other's colonial fields and to fight in each other's imperial armies, but also often experienced tolerance and even welcome in states that thrived on religious diversity. For a time, the great Muslim empires ruled over millions of Christian subjects, and some Muslim-majority states still do. However, in the last two centuries much of the Islamic world came to be formally ruled by or informally subject to vast maritime empires based in Europe. In the context of these shared imperial experiences, modern notions of race and class and contemporary structures of expansion and oppression with global significance

[6] Michael Ignatieff, "America's Empire is an Empire Lite," *New York Times*, January 10, 2003.
[7] Andrew Woodcock and Jane Merrick, "Kennedy Warns of 'Imperialism' over Bid to Oust Saddam," *Press Association*, September 23, 2002.
[8] G. John Ikenberry, "America's Imperial Ambition," *Foreign Affairs*, September/October 2002; Eric Hobsbawm, "America's Imperial Delusion," *Guardian*, June 15, 2003; Noam Chomsky, *Imperial Ambitions: Conversations on the Post 9–11 World* (New York: Metropolitan Books, 2005); and Igor Gedilaghine, "Iranian FM blasts US 'Imperialism' as He Visits Russia," *Agence France Presse*, April 4, 2002.
[9] Max Boot, "American Imperialism? No Need to Run Away from Label," *USA Today*, May 5, 2003.
[10] Niall Ferguson, "America: An Empire in Denial," *Chronicle of Higher Education*, 49 (March 28, 2003), B7.
[11] Victor Davis Hanson, "Just Make Stuff Up," *National Review Online*, June 12, 2009, http://article.nationalreview.com/print/?q=OTAyNzFjMmMwOWJjYmFmMTA2ODdjODZmZmQ0MWE1Mzg=

were formed.[12] The events of 9/11 and the U.S. invasions of Iraq and Afghanistan cannot be understood outside of these experiences.

But it is not merely the events of 9/11 and the occupation of Iraq that have an imperial past. No part of the world was untouched by empires over the past half-millennium, and very little of importance that happens today can be divorced from an imperial context. Conflicts in Ireland, Israel–Palestine, the Balkans, and elsewhere are rooted in the legacies of empire. It was as subjects of modern empires that the world's populations re-arranged themselves. The movements of Africans to the Americas, Europeans to Oceania, and Asians to the Caribbean were often compelled or facilitated by imperial technologies and policies. Less obviously, imperialism also constrained the movements of peoples, as when East Asians were excluded from Australasia and North America. Stretching across continents, these empires helped to shape the movement of not only humans but also species of plants, animals, and pests. These organisms were carried across seas and land to new places, along with languages, religions, and cultures. Diplomacy, commerce, and war between empires shaped global boundaries. Moreover, imperialism served as the foster parent of both globalization and nationalism in the modern era. As with any parent and its children, the relationship between these three trends has not always been a smooth one, but it is not possible to understand them separately.

The purpose of this book is to explore imperialism and colonialism: an inter-related series of trends that have embraced much of the human experience in the last half-millennium. The building of modern empires—once treated as the ascendancy of one part of the world over the others—was in fact a shared, global experience that tied together the world's regions as never before. Under the rule or influence of great intercontinental empires, diverse populations expanded their political, economic, military, and social links and exchanged ideas, human populations, plant and animal species, and technology. This is not to suggest that empire created an even, equal exchange between societies; by definition, it did not. Nevertheless, for better or for worse, these great empires have been among the most important institutions in shaping modern history.

This textbook addresses modern imperialism and colonialism from a truly global and holistic perspective. From the formation of centralized gunpowder empires in Eurasia and parts of Africa to the demise of the bi-polar Cold War world, this book investigates our evolving understanding of the origins, nature, mechanisms, and demise of modern empires. As well as evaluating empires as structures, it explores the doctrines, ideologies, and practices of imperialism and colonial rule. This approach is relatively novel. Conventionally, texts that deal with these topics either focus on a single empire or component of empire, such as a colony or metropole, or investigate imperialism across several empires but for a tightly defined period. Almost all histories of modern imperialism begin in Europe, and few contextualize European empires within global imperial networks and systems. Many are comparative, but none so far has managed to tell the story of modern empires from a truly integrated perspective. In this era of increasing globalization, such approaches are increasingly inadequate.

ACKNOWLEDGMENTS

Heather would like to thank her colleagues at Washington State University and in the World History Association for supporting and encouraging her to look at the world's past through a wide-angle lens. She would also like to thank Trevor for inviting her to join this project, and for his patience and support throughout its writing. Her students who have taken her Global Imperialism class since 1999 also deserve thanks, as their questions and insights have deeply informed this book. Finally, she wishes to thank her family and friends for their continued love, support, and fellowship. She especially thanks her husband, Steven Salter,

---

[12] A peace-maker's view on this can be found in Imam Feisal Abdul Rauf, *What's Right with Islam Is What's Right with America: A New Vision for Muslims and the West* (San Francisco: Harper San Francisco, 2004), 1–9.

for leaving Kuala Lumpur on a Monday instead of a Friday. The consequences of such an act have made all the difference in her life.

Trevor would like to extend his thanks to colleagues at San Francisco State University and throughout the Bay Area, especially Chris Chekuri, John Corbally, Richard Hoffman, and Ugo Nwokeji. He also extends his apologies to students in his Modern European Imperialism and History of Africa courses who have been guinea pigs in the development of this project. He expresses his gratitude to Heather for transforming so readily from a critical reviewer to a contributing partner early in the process of proposing this book. Last but not least, he thanks his family and friends for their support and wishes Bafana Bafana good luck in the FIFA World Cup.

Both authors would particularly like to thank the editorial staff at Pearson, and especially Rob DeGeorge. Finally, we extend our appreciation to the following reviewers for their insights and suggestions: Heather J. Abdelnur, Blackburn College; Gayle K. Brunelle, California State University, Fullerton; John Corbally, Menlo College; Corrie Decker, University of California, Davis; Stephen Englehart, California State Polytechnic University; Benjamin Grob-Fitzgibbon, University of Arkansas; Thomas D. Hall, Depauw University; John McNeill, Georgetown University; Mark Ruff, Saint Louis University; Peter Stamatov, Yale University; Theodore R. Weeks, Southern Illinois University; Kenneth Wilburn, East Carolina University; and Louise B. Williams, Central Connecticut State University.

Introduction

WHY DEFINE?

The purpose of this chapter is to define the terms used in the title of this book: *empire*, *imperialism*, *colonialism*, *global,* and *modern.* The definitions that we give here are not authoritative because meaning is transitory: even when the same words are used by people across the world or throughout time, the meanings they signify are often very different to different authors and audiences. In other sections of this book, we will study many of the scholars who have defined empire, imperialism, and colonialism in their own terms: John Hobson, Immanuel Wallerstein, Hannah Arendt, Rosa Luxemburg, Ronald Robinson, Aimée Césaire, Wolfgang Mommsen, Vladimir Lenin, David K. Fieldhouse, Joseph Schumpeter, Franz Fanon, Eric Hobsbawm, Anthony Hopkins, Peter Cain, and many others. We will also meet many groups who used these terms for their own purposes, and others who lived under imperial rule or in colonial situations without making use of these words. In this chapter, however, we define each of these words as they are used in this volume. Our definitions are shaped by our thesis. We propose that imperialism and colonialism in the modern period were shared experiences in a global context. We believe that empires in different parts of the world over the past 500 years can be effectively compared, and moreover are linked to each other in such ways that they share certain attributes. Therefore, our definitions are more *global* than many that came before. Additionally, we believe that imperialism and colonialism were total experiences. They were not just political or economic, but also influenced social organization and cultural formation. Similarly, we argue that empires were so integrated that the experiences of the inhabitants of the imperial core and the imperial periphery were closely linked and helped to shape each other. Therefore, our definitions are meant to reflect the *totality* of these experiences.

The definitions provided in this chapter balance the need for useful explanations of important concepts with an acknowledgment of their complexity. They are intended to be practical tools both for deconstructing primary sources written in the vernacular and for interpreting secondary sources. They are designed to acknowledge the values ascribed to these words while at the same striving for objectivity. Finally, they are constructed as keys to decoding both the real-life experiences of empire and the scholarly debate about them.

EMPIRE

Depending on how the term is used, the existence of empires can be said to predate the evolution of the terms that describe them. Most experts agree that the Akkadian confederacy of Mesopotamian city-states under a single ruler achieved the shape and structures of an empire around 2350 BCE, although scholars disagree as to how that empire was understood by its architects and inhabitants. The western European word *empire* has been traced back only as far as the Latin verb *imperare*, which means "to command." In the period of the Roman monarchy that preceded the establishment of the republic, Roman rulers possessed *imperium*, or the ability to execute the law, lead the army, hold public assembly, and make sacrifices. Following the elimination of the monarchy in 509 BCE, this right was transferred first to the elected *Consuls*, and later as the state expanded to the *Praetors*, or magistrates. Thus from its inception, the term *empire* was related to notions of rulership and sovereignty. This interpretation survived the fall of Rome and was resurrected in the European early modern period. King Henry VIII of England, for example, used the term to express his independence from both the Church in Rome and the continental powers following his divorce from Catherine of Aragon in 1534. With the Union of the Crowns in 1603, King James I named his composite kingdom of England, Wales, Scotland, and Ireland "the Empire of Great Britain."[1] By doing so, James claimed absolute sovereignty over all four territories. This history cemented the place of sovereignty at the center of the definition of empire, and correctly so. Among the most important processes in the development of the empires described in this book were the consolidation of power, authority, and legitimacy in the persons of a monarch or dynasty and their courts and supporting bureaucracies.

Yet there was an alternate understanding of the term *empire* that also emerged from the Roman period: the notion of political and military expansion beyond the homeland or ethnic community into other regions. For the Romans, this elaboration began with the conquest of Sicily in 241 BCE. In order to govern this new province, Rome sent out a treasury official. However, this officer had not been granted imperium by the Senate, and he therefore had difficulty executing laws and resolving local disputes. Accordingly, the treasury official was replaced by a praetor, who carried imperium overseas for the first time. As Rome's territory expanded in the late Republic period, Romans began to think of their new

provinces as the *imperium Romanum*: those places to which Roman authority extends. From both conquered people and undefeated opponents they learned new techniques and technologies that they could put to use in administering their far-flung territories. Mesopotamia, especially, had a long history of large empires such as the Akkadian, Assyrian, and Persian. Roman generals campaigning in this region rapidly adopted the techniques and the finery of Mesopotamian rulers and brought them back to Rome. By the time of Caesar Augustus, c.31 BCE, Romans were willing to accept the accession of a hereditary emperor. Upon seizing power, Augustus styled himself *princeps,* or "first person," and ruled almost unchallenged both in Rome and throughout what was now, properly, an empire.[2] In the centuries following the fall of the Roman empire, various successor states claimed to have inherited the mantle of its imperial power—notably Byzantium, the Carolingian Empire of the Franks, and the Germanic Holy Roman Empire. In each case, ruling elites made use of the notion of imperium, and in some cases the term itself, thus providing channels by which both the word and the idea of empire were brought down to the modern era.

The modern terms *empire* and *imperialism* emerged within Romance and Germanic European languages, including English, in the fifteenth century as a result of three widespread trends. The first was the emergence of increasingly centralized powerful states in Europe, a trend shared with parts of Asia and Africa. The second, related, trend was the increasing competition between these expanding states. Finally, there was the emergence of maritime empires that brought the monarchs of western Europe to rule over subjects who were culturally and ethnically distinct from themselves. Thus, seventeenth-century monarchs like James I of Britain, in styling themselves emperors, were

---

[1] Nichaolas Canny, "The Origins of Empire: An Introduction," in *The Oxford History of the British Empire*, vol. I, *The Origins of Empire*, edited by Nicholas Canny (Oxford: Oxford University Press, 1998), 1.

[2] See, for example, Frank Tenney, *Roman Imperialism* (New York: MacMillan, 1914). See also A.P. Thornton, *Doctrines of Imperialism* (London: John Wiley, 1966), 29–31.

asserting sovereignty both at home and overseas. The meaning they ascribed to these claims still inform our understandings of empire as

> a large political body which rules over territories outside of its original borders. It has a central power or core territory—whose inhabitants usually continue to form the dominant ethnic or national group in the entire system—and an extensive periphery of dominated areas. In most cases, the periphery has been acquired by conquest.… Empires, then, must by definition be big, and they must be composite entities, formed out of previous separate units. Diversity—ethnic, national, cultural, often religious—is their essence. But in many observers' understanding, this cannot be a diversity of equals. If it is, if there is no relation of domination between "core" and "periphery," then the system is not an empire.[3]

This consensus understanding of empire is fundamentally a *structural definition* of empire. In other words, it seeks to explain what an empire looks like, largely by suggesting that empires possess certain key features that separate them from other models of social and political organization. The important features of this definition are that the term *empire* describes relationships between polities or states, that one or more of these states exhibit certain types of control over the others, and that they possess inequality and differentiation within the empire. Each of these features is derived from the core principle of state sovereignty at home and abroad.

We can see, therefore, that modern western definitions of empire are chiefly applied to certain types of states or polities. Admittedly, as the term has become more widely used, it has also come to be applied to supra-national orders, individuals, and monopolistic businesses.[4] In these cases, however, the user is merely implying that the business, group, or individual possesses the unchallenged power and perhaps extensive holdings commonly imputed to imperial states. Most scholarly critiques of empire, while debating, elaborating, and limiting this power, continue to accept state authority and power as the key features of empires. In the popular textbook *The Dynamics of Global Dominance*, for example, political scientist David B. Abernethy argues that empire is defined not only by the strictly legalistic notion of sovereignty but also by the very real exertion of control. Like Howe, Abernethy depicts empires as having a core state or "mother country" (the **metropole**) and dominated states outside of the core that are claimed as possessions (**colonies**). The metropole, he asserts, exerts both legal and physical control over the colonies. For Abernethy, as for many political scientists, whether or not a state is an empire can be empirically determined by assessing whether or not it fulfills certain conditions: not only that the metropole formally claims sovereignty over the colonies and has this claim recognized by other great powers, but also that the metropole establishes structures of control in the colonies.[5]

For Abernethy, the only empires that exist are those that both formally claim sovereignty over the domestic and external affairs of a colony and exert real control over those affairs. However, for decades, scholars have recognized a looser definition of empire that encompasses situations in which a dominant state exerts some control over the economic and political institutions of another state without claiming sovereignty. Often termed **informal empire**, this situation has been widespread during various periods of the last two centuries (and perhaps earlier) and arguably exists in

---

[3] Stephen Howe, *Empire: A Very Short Introduction* (Oxford: Oxford University Press, 2002), 14–15. Howe describes this as a consensus definition and goes on to develop a somewhat more complex definition of his own.

[4] Perhaps most significant is the recent publication of Michael Hardt and Antonio Negri, *Empire* (Cambridge: Harvard University Press, 2001). Hardt and Negri define the "new" empire as an unguided and acephalous process of globalization.
[5] David B. Abernethy, *The Dynamics of Global Dominance: European Overseas Empires, 1415–1980* (New Haven, CT: Yale University Press, 2000).

today's world as well. German historian Jürgen Osterhammel describes informal empire as a situation in which

> The weaker state remains intact as an independent polity with its own political system. It can conduct its own foreign policy and regulate routine domestic affairs. There is no colonial administration, but occasionally—especially in the area of finance—a mixture of foreign and indigenous administration.... Nonetheless, the weaker state is only sovereign to a limited extent. "Big Brother" guarantees privileges for himself in "unequal treaties" as the result of selectively applied pressure ("gunboat diplomacy").... "Big Brother" is represented by consuls, diplomats or "residents," all of whom intervene in domestic policy in an "advisory" capacity, particularly in conflicts over succession, and underscore their "advice" with the threat of military intervention when it appears warranted.... Informal empire ... presupposes a distinct economic superiority of Big Brother.[6]

Definitions of informal empire, like this one, tend to remain focused on issues of control rather than legal sovereignty, and occasionally control is exerted by corporations or groups without sovereign authority acting in lieu of a state. This has led some scholars to reject the term as "unacceptably vague" because it seems to cover all kinds of situations in which a party or institution exerts control over a state without claiming to be sovereign.[7] Indeed, the line between informal empire and mere influence is vague. That the term remains in wide use, however, indicates its usefulness to scholars seeking to reconcile differences between the clearly defined sovereign reach of formal empire

on the one hand and evidence of imperial control that extends outside the metropole and the formal colonies on the other. This includes **dependencies** (semi-autonomous states with ambiguous sovereign status), **protectorates** (polities in which indigenous authorities and occupying forces share sovereignty and authority), and sometimes **dominions** (a specific twentieth-century term for British overseas territories heavily settled by British emigrants). It also includes client-states over which the empire claims no sovereignty at all, but still extends some control. Together with formal colonies, these states form a continuum that is often termed the *imperial periphery*.

It is the relationship between the periphery and the metropole that differentiates empire from other forms of political and social organization. Specifically, empires are characterized by an internal inequality of status and treatment. Inhabitants of the periphery are generally not considered citizens, but rather subjects, without political freedom or rights to the extent these are enjoyed by inhabitants of the metropole. Often the distinction between citizen and subject is based not only on location of residence but also on a sense of ethnic or cultural difference. There are economic and political components to this discrimination as well; empires are largely implemented and maintained for the benefit of one or more classes or factions in the metropole, often at the cost of inhabitants of the periphery. In order to maintain the empire, the distinction between citizen and subject must be constantly policed and re-established, often through the use of violence. The result is that empire has come to be explicitly linked with the oppression of periphery populations.

However, it is important to note that the relationship between the various units of the empire is usually multifaceted and reciprocal, if admittedly uneven. This is a relatively recent discovery for scholars, and is partly a result of the flourishing of studies of colonialism in the period following the demise of European formal overseas empires in the 1960s and 1970s. In these decades, a new wave of researchers—many former colonial subjects themselves—began to focus on colonized peoples not only as victims but also as actors in pursuit of

---

[6] Jürgen Osterhammel, *Colonialism: A Theoretical Overview* (Princeton, NJ: Markus Wiener, 1997).

[7] Winifred Baumgart, *Imperialism: The Idea and Reality of British and French Colonial Expansion, 1880–1914* (Oxford: Oxford University Press, 1982), 6.

their own goals. This focus helped lead to the recognition that inhabitants of the imperial peripheries helped to shape empires, operated both within and against them, and ultimately brought them down. In the process, they reshaped the societies of imperial metropoles as well. As two leading historians of colonialism, Ann Laura Stoler and Frederick Cooper, have asserted

> Europe's colonies were never empty spaces to be made over in Europe's image or fashioned in its interests; nor, indeed, were European states self-contained entities that at one point projected themselves overseas. Europe was made by its imperial projects, as much as colonial encounters were shaped by conflict within Europe itself.[8]

In this interpretation, empire is more than just an uneven political grouping in which one polity exerts control over others. Empire is, instead, the product of innumerable interactions between the metropole and the periphery. It is produced from the connective tissue of laws and lawyers, orders and administrators, agents, pressure groups, traders, missionaries, students, scholars, soldiers, and servants that bind the periphery and the metropole together. The identities of various groups within the empire are also constructed in part through the power that they have over each other and their views of each other. Thus, literary scholars and historians from Edward Said to Catherine Hall and Mary Renda as well as anthropologists such as Jean Comaroff and John Comaroff have shown how our sense of who we are in the United States and Europe was largely shaped through discussions of the ways in which we are not like Africans, Haitians, Indians, or Arabs.

Empire is therefore located within each of the colonies, protectorates, dependencies, and dominions as well as the metropole. It is also, however, to be found between and among the political and geographic designations. This conception of empire, which has come to dominate the field of imperial studies, thus views empire as a single reality. Its practitioners examine the relationships and connections established and shaped by forces from all over the empire. They explore these relationships from a variety of perspectives: not only those of policy makers but also colonial and metropolitan populations, imperial migrants and transients, and the many individuals whose identity and background was mixed.

The same emphasis on perspective has led to a reinterpretation of empire as a process with a beginning and an end. Certainly, empires are impermanent. But how are they formed, and why and to what extent do they disintegrate? The idea that the formation and collapse of empires is observable leads us to view empire not only as a set of structures but also as processes that unfold on a global stage. Empires are born by a process by which one polity comes to exert control over other states or peoples without fully integrating them. Empires collapse when either this control ends or full integration is achieved thus terminating the dominance–subordination relationship. In some cases, however, the end of empire is caused by the defeat or eclipsing of one empire by another. In these cases, very often, imperial structures and relationships are transferred and transformed, rather than destroyed.

By assimilating these new, more globalized and reciprocal definitions of empire with older but still relevant strands, we arrive at a definition of empire that is informed not only by issues of sovereignty and control but also by interaction and that not only explains imperial structures but also reflects imperial processes.

Empire, then, is an agglomeration of multiple polities and diverse populations bound together in an uneven relationship in which one polity exercises significant control over the others and, in many cases, claims sole sovereignty over all of the polities. This relationship is characterized by an intricate network of political, economic, cultural, legal, communication, and demographic ties. An

---

[8] Ann Laura Stoler and Frederick Cooper, "Between Metropole and Colony," in *Tensions of Empire: Colonial Cultures in a Bourgeois World*, edited by Frederick Cooper and Ann Laura Stoler (Berkeley: University of California Press, 1997), 1.

empire is born when disparate polities or peoples become suborned to a dominant polity. It can be said to have ceased to exist when the constituent polities re-establish sovereignty over themselves or become so integrated into the dominant polity that there is no longer any significant difference between them either by law or in practice. In many cases, however, one empire segues into another, a process that is denoted by the transfer of the imperial metropole to a new location.

IMPERIALISM

The origins of the Anglo-French term *imperialism* are well established. Like *empire*, it is an adaptation of the Latin word *imperium*, resurrected to serve a specific purpose. It first appears in documents emanating from the court of French King Louis-Philippe, who applied it to express his power within France—a purpose similar to Henry VIII's use of *empire*.[9] The term was subsequently popularized by the supporters of the Bonapartist Emperor Napoleon III in the 1860s, and they too used it to signify the French monarch's domestic power and authority. It rapidly crossed the channel to Britain, where the term *empire* was already being used to describe Britain's vast overseas possessions. Here it came to signify patriotism and support for the intercontinental empire, two sentiments that were increasingly interlinked. Used in this way, however, it did not necessarily imply expansionist inclinations, but rather a sense of kindred spirit or community across the oceans with the British expatriates settled in Canada, Australia, and other parts of the empire.[10]

Thus by the last decades of the nineteenth century, the word *imperialism* had come to be understood in English as an expression of the conviction that Britain and its overseas colonies were one and the same. It was therefore intertwined with domestic patriotism and a sense of ethnic nationalism. In the 1880s, however, a series of economic crises rooted in increasing competition against other major powers for colonial markets and raw materials mobilized British public opinion in support of renewed imperial expansion into new areas, many of which had not been previously settled by Anglophone Europeans. Proponents of this rekindled expansionism came to be labeled imperialists as well, and imperialism came to be affixed to a universe of ideas tied together by their common application as justifications for the acquisition of colonies. The term thus used was equally applicable to humanitarian concepts of a civilizing mission, to extreme racialism, and to patriotic jingoism.

By the early twentieth century, when J.A. Hobson began to describe the post-1880 scramble for colonies and influence as a "new imperialism," the term had assumed its modern form.[11] Most subsequent definitions of imperialism agree that it refers to an ideology or set of doctrines, that it implies domination, that it reflects international affairs, and that it involves actions and ideas in support of expansionism and the maintenance of empire. Nevertheless, the term is still somewhat differently interpreted by specialists working on domestic studies of the major imperial powers, by historians and political scientists seeking to understand global events and trends, and by scholars who focus on empire as a unit.

A logical starting place for understanding imperialism is in the internal affairs and social organization of imperialist metropoles. The term never really lost its domestic connection, in part because of the close relationship between the development of modern imperialism and modern nationalism, two contemporary worldviews that are inextricable. Some regional specialists have even defined imperialism simply as the "extension of national policies into active world policies."[12] Indeed, although this definition is not sufficient, it

[9] Heinz Gollwitzer, *Europe in the Age of Imperialism 1880–1914* (New York: W.W. Norton, 1979), 10. First published 1969.
[10] Philip D. Curtin, ed., *Imperialism* (New York: Walker and Company, 1972), ix.

[11] John A. Hobson, *Imperialism: A Study* (London: George Allen & Unwin, 1954), 71–93. First published 1902.
[12] Gollwitzer, *Europe in the Age of Imperialism*, 10.

is accurate to argue that imperialism cannot be understood without reference to the domestic sphere. Simply put, the strategies employed by governments to establish order and authority at home are often adapted to the role of ruling new populations in the imperial periphery—so much so that sometimes the two processes hardly seem distinct from each other.

Imperialism doesn't just describe the policies and actions by which the empire is ruled in the metropole and abroad, however. It also describes the thoughts, doctrines, and ideologies that cause and justify imperial expansionism. In some contexts, these ideas culminated in **cultures of imperialism**, which are characterized by the espousal, by large segments of society, of a sense of duty or desire to establish an empire. Such cultures of imperialism encompass economic, social, cultural, demographic, environmental, and political factors. They are often intensely wrapped up in conceptions of identity including race, class, ethnicity, and gender. Religion, also, is harnessed to imperialism and can even feature as the main theme of imperialist sentiment. When a culture of imperialism exists, fervor for imperial expansion periodically sweeps the populace, especially at moments of economic or political crisis. It is usually at these moments that cultures of imperialism can become manifest in governmental policies as governments seek to harness popular sentiment by overseas adventure and the exertion of power over territorially distinct states and peoples—in other words, the creation of an empire. The influential British historian of empires D.K. Fieldhouse stresses intention as the key to identifying acts and policies that emerge from imperialist agitation. Imperialism, he argues, is a *deliberate* act of aggression that results from factors found within the society of the metropole.[13] Once a culture of imperialism exists, the urge to build empires usually achieves fruition in external acts of violence or acquisitiveness. Empires are not, however, always the result of imperialist agitation. Historically, some empires have been constructed despite the relative absence of a culture of imperialism in the metropole, usually as the unforeseen results of war, through a gradual process of settlement and commercial exploitation, or in response to agitation from settlers and agents overseas.

A.P. Thornton's *Doctrines of Imperialism* is one of the classic studies charting the melding together of ideologies and sentiments into a set of imperialist principles. Thornton's principal contribution is the assertion that "imperialism is less a fact than a thought. At its heart it is the image of dominance, of power asserted; and power is neither used nor witnessed without emotion."[14] Thus for Thornton, imperialism is not found in the *acts* of imperial dominance, but rather in the popularization and encoding of thoughts and ideas that precedes and invokes it. These he divides into doctrines of power, civilization, and profit. Each doctrine can be found expressed in historical sources of all natures as a motive for empire-building. They are also, Thornton avers, symptomatic of wider, commonly held worldviews within imperialist societies. However, Thornton's work must be applied with care. Doctrines of imperialism may well have existed and may continue to be identifiable and even to dominate certain public, popular, and intellectual spaces within societies for a period, but they are never hegemonic. Large numbers of individuals and interest groups may at times collectively embrace imperialism, but they often do so for diverse motives and with different understandings of what imperialism meant. Thus while imperialism is often a shared sentiment, in practice it is expressed in different ways by different actors.

In embracing this complex explanation of imperialism, Thornton explicitly rejects the much simpler and more concrete definition of imperialism as the process of building an empire, a definition favored by political scientists like David Abernethy.[15] Yet the connection between doctrines of imperialism and acts of empire-building is obvious and causative. Although

---

[13] D.K. Fieldhouse, *Colonialism 1870–1945: An Introduction* (Basingstoke: Macmillan, 1988), 3.

[14] Thornton, *Doctrines of Imperialism*, 2.
[15] Abernethy, *The Dynamics of Global Dominance*, 21.

empire can exist without imperialism, cultures of imperialism almost invariably lead to attempts to construct empires. For Abernethy and his social science colleagues who look at empire—rather than metropoles—as a unit of study, these acts are far more obvious and significant than the ideologies that inspire them. For these scholars, imperialism and empire are closely linked terms. If empire is characterized by the control of a periphery by a metropole, it follows that imperialism is the term that describes that process of control. Tony Smith, a political scientist, expresses this connection simply: "Imperialism may be defined as the effective domination by a relatively strong state over a weaker people whom it does not control as it does its home population, or as the efforts to secure such domination."[16] Nor is the connection between imperialism and dominance made solely by political scientists. Sociologists have explored the links between the two as well, the most significant being Joseph Schumpeter. For Schumpeter, imperialism arises from the aggressive urges of militarized ruling classes, who dominate others not in pursuit of concrete rewards but rather as a manifestation of objectless institutionalized violence that begins within societies, and is subsequently turned outward.[17]

Such definitions of imperialism as a specific form of domination, closely tied as they are to structural definitions of empire, are comfortingly concise, and have their uses. Yet they are far from complete. Neither Schumpeter's attempt to define imperialism within patterns of human nature nor Smith's view of it as a process of control by one state over separate peoples considers the precise historical context from which imperialism emerges at specific times and places in human history. Imperialism, after all, describes a *deliberate* process of empire-building, and thus studies of imperialism must seek to understand

why people *choose* to pursue empire in a defined setting. As Thornton puts it, "To consider imperialism as the direct control of one area and its inhabitants by the government of another is certainly to deal in a manageable idea, but to do this at all asks for a detachment neither found nor wanted on the hustings, or in the basement rooms where conspirators gather."[18] Moreover, while imperialism is a useful term for describing processes of domination on the level of the empire, the way those acts are manifested within the colonies and dependencies is more often described by the term *colonialism.*

Thus, imperialism must be located by scholars *both* in the metropole and in the empire generally. It is also, however, a term that describes the global relationships *among* competing metropoles and empires. Imperialism as a term was popularized in an era of intense competition between industrialized powers, and imperialism as a process was part and parcel of that struggle. It is therefore impossible to consider imperialism without looking at the international context. This was a fact recognized immediately by theorists who wrote during the apex of formal imperialism. The German progressive Heinrich Friedjung, for example, combined nationalist expansion and great-power politics in his definition of imperialism as policies arising from tension between the major European states.[19] This concept of imperialism as the embodiment of national rivalry has gone on to inform a wide range of contemporary theories seeking to explain specific examples of imperialism described in this volume. Marxist historians may focus on economic competition and access to global markets, political and diplomatic historians on power politics and strategic position, and social historians on politicians' mobilization of nationalist sentiment, but all agree that imperialism is linked both to international

---

[16] Tony Smith, *The Pattern of Imperialism: The United States, Great Britain, and the Late-Industrializing World Since 1815* (New York: Cambridge University Press, 1981), 6.
[17] Joseph A. Schumpeter, *Imperialism and Social Classes* (Oxford: Blackwell, 1951). Schumpeter first published this theory in German in 1918/1919.

[18] Thornton, *Doctrines of Imperialism*, 5.
[19] Heinrich Friedjung, *Das Zeitalter des Imperialismus 1884–1914*, 3 vols (Berlin: Neufeld & Henius, 1919–1922); and Wolfgang J. Mommsen, *Theories of Imperialism* (Chicago: University of Chicago Press, 1982), 4. Translated by P.S. Faller.

realities and to public and governmental perception of the threat of rival states to internal stability and security in the metropole. Thus the development of a great-power system is a feature of periods of intensifying imperialist sentiment, and in these cases, the empire is commonly depicted as a source of strategic materials and positions, a defensive buffer, and a collection of bargaining chips for use in diplomatic dealings with other industrialized states. The inevitable exaggeration of such periods of high tension is what leads to otherwise unexplainable acts of imperial expansion, such as the late-nineteenth-century Anglo-French struggle to occupy barren stretches of the Sahara desert and Germany's occupation of faraway Pacific Islands.

Imperialism, therefore, is an ideology or doctrine in support of the creation and maintenance of empire. When held by significant and opinion-forming segments of society, often within the context of tension between great powers, it can become inextricably intertwined with other economic, social, cultural, demographic, environmental, gendered, and political aspects of society so that it is relevant both to domestic politics and foreign affairs. When political decision-making bodies translate imperialist sentiments into action, it is expressed as an aggressive set of policies culminating variously in formal dominion or informal control over external polities or peoples (i.e., empire), as well as being characterized by belligerence toward rival expansionist powers.

COLONIALISM

Colonialism is a much younger term than either empire or imperialism, and one that has been used largely to fill perceived gaps left by the two older terms. Initially, the term referred to the Mediterranean practice of establishing overseas communities. In the long history of the Mediterranean world, seafaring peoples such as the Greeks, Phoenicians, and Romans established physically separate but culturally interlinked communities for a variety of regions. Some of these colonies were established by the exiled losers of civil conflicts, while others were trading entrepots, and still others were formed by refugees from overpopulation in areas of limited natural resources. The Greeks knew these overseas communities by two names: *apoikiai* were autonomous city-states established outside of the Greek peninsula, while *emporia* were dependent trading positions scattered around the eastern Mediterranean. Such diasporas were common in the Mediterranean, where populations encouraged by the small size, elongated shape, diversity of trade goods, and relatively consistent ecology and climate of the region surrounding the inland sea to embark from their homelands and scatter themselves liberally around the hinterland. Such colonies could sometimes eclipse their homelands. Carthage—Rome's great rival—was a Phoenician colony that survived the Assyrian occupation of the Levant to become a great Mediterranean power. At its height, Carthage, like many pre-modern Mediterranean states, was populated by a multi-ethnic mélange of Libyans, ethnic Phoenicians, Celts, Greeks, and transients from across the Mediterranean and North Africa. The Romans, too, came to possess many cosmopolitan territories. However, these were not called *colonies*. In Latin, the label *colinae* was reserved solely for communities for Roman citizens planted in the Italian and overseas provinces as a garrison.

Colony, the English revival of the Roman term *colinae*, was popularized in the vernacular language in the seventeenth century to describe the newly formed English settlements in the Americas. Thomas More had first revived the Latin term to describe communities transplanted from the fictional island of Utopia in his 1516 book of the same title (he spelled it *colonia*), but it only gradually came into common usage.[20] In the cosmopolitan context of industrializing Britain, colony came to be applied largely to expatriate British communities as they came into existence, first in North America and later in Australia, New Zealand, and to some degree the Caribbean and the Cape Colony of South Africa. As such it

---

[20]David Armitage, "Literature and Empire," in Canny, *The Origins of Empire*, 108.

remained closely linked to the classical denotation of emigrant settlers transplanted to a new location. In the nineteenth century, however, the term had to be adapted as new forms of domination and strategies of administering overseas colonies came into existence. To overseas settlements were added maritime enclaves and colonies of exploitation only thinly staffed by citizens from the metropole.[21] It took some time for colony to replace "imperial possessions" as the accepted expression for these new territories, but as it did the term *colonialism* similarly came to refer to the process of domination of the indigenous populations of the colonies of exploitation rather than the translocation or administration of metropolitan settlers. This older process, conversely, came to be labeled **colonization**. By the 1950s, anti-colonial figures took the lead in using *colonialism* as a precise term to explain imperial processes that took place in the periphery, rather than the metropole, and scholars largely followed.[22] Problematically, however, the term gradually came to assume numerous dimensions and has since become almost as amorphous in common use as *imperialism*.[23] Thus, the limits and shape of colonialism need to be carefully defined to be serviceable.

At the heart of a usable definition of colonialism is the matter of location. Certainly, colonialism takes place in colonies, but the synchronization between the two terms is not complete. One of the most significant modern theorists of colonialism, Jürgen Osterhammel, begins his definition of colonialism by stating that it is "a relationship of domination between an indigenous (or forcibly imported) majority and a minority of foreign invaders."[24] By this definition, colonialism is present only in localities where immigration from the metropole is limited. This is almost the opposite of the Roman definition of *colonae* and suggests that colonialism does not exist in colonies of settlement at all. Osterhammel is far more comfortable in stretching the definition to encompass situations where formal colonies do not exist, but where the limited control defined as informal empire does. In applying the label of colonialism to these regions, Osterhammel recognizes the similarities in forms of oppression and dominations both within formal colonies and in de facto regions of the empire. It was in order to simplify the treatment of these similar processes in the two sets of regions that D.K. Fieldhouse coined the umbrella expression *imperial periphery* in 1973.[25] For the purposes of this book, however, Osterhammel's exclusion of settlement colonies is not useful: the practices and effects of colonial oppression are present both where the proportion of settlers is high and where it is low, although they may be differently expressed.

Colonialism, therefore, can be located throughout the periphery: within colonies, protectorates, dependencies, and in the informal empire. Conversely, and unlike imperialism, colonialism is not normally understood as being located in the metropole. Indeed, at its most basic and concise, colonialism can be defined as the implementation of imperialist policies in the periphery, a definition adopted by many political scientists. David Abernethy, for example, writes that "[c]olonialism is the set of formal policies, informal practices, and ideologies employed by a metropole to retain control of a colony and to benefit from the control."[26] Stephen Howe asserts that colonialism is "strictly political," and describes "systems of rule by one group over another, where the first claims the right ... to exercise exclusive sovereignty over the second and to shape its destiny."[27]

Yet these visions of colonialism have been criticized in recent decades as too limited in scope and too centered in the metropole. The influence of scholars from the humanities, many

---

[21] A superior typology can be found in Osterhammel, *Colonialism*, 4–12.

[22] D.K. Fieldhouse identifies President Sukarno of Indonesia as an important manipulator of the term in his anticolonial rhetoric. Fieldhouse, *Colonialism 1870–1945*, 6.

[23] Howe, *Empire*, 25.

[24] Osterhammel, *Colonialism*, 17.

[25] Mommsen, *Theories of Imperialism*, 102; and D.K. Fieldhouse, *Economics and Empire 1830–1914* (London: Weidenfeld and Nicolson, 1973).

[26] Abernethy, *The Dynamics of Global Dominance*, 22.

[27] Howe, *Empire*, 30–31.

of whom have adopted the designation postcolonial scholars, has broadened the political scientists' definition through the recognition that politics and culture are intensely intertwined, not least because authority, power, and force are often used to construct and maintain "ideas, cultures, and histories."[28] These scholars still acknowledge that as the product of the processes of empire-building, colonialism is a political relationship between a state and its subjects. However, they also argue that as the product of cultures of imperialism, colonialism is a cultural relationship of domination and subordination among metropolitan citizens and colonial subjects. They further suggest that because empire is defined by "control" and "difference," colonialism as a set of policies and actions is largely about dividing the population of a colony into categories (through taxonomies of ethnicity, race, class, gender, and religion), defining the status of and policing the boundaries between the different groups, and then controlling them.[29] Moreover, these categorizations are often constructed through overlapping schemes—for example, many conquering metropoles conceive of themselves as holy and masculine nations, and construct their colonial subjects as feminine and pagan as well as racially or ethnically inferior.

Moreover, to treat colonialism as a purely political expression of imperialism carried out in the periphery ignores the basic reality that the blueprint of domination implied by imperialism has never successfully been implanted wholesale in the colonial periphery. The reality is that imperialism as a set of strategies and policies formulated first in the metropole has always historically been proven to be flawed in its conception for two reasons. As noted earlier, imperialism as an ideology was never entirely unified, and internal divisions among imperial agents led to many different manifestations of colonialism. Missionaries, military

men, corporate officers, civil servants, and their spouses brought with them different ideas as to their task, different concepts of their own identity, and different plans of action. As the Africanist and theorist of colonialism Frederick Cooper argues, they came with "not so much 'colonialism'—a coherent set of practices and discourses intended to dominate conquered people while maintaining their distinctiveness—as a series of hegemonic projects."[30] With this turn of phrase in the highly influential 1997 anthology *Tensions of Empire*, Cooper shattered the concept of a single imperial blueprint for any empire. Instead, he urged scholars to re-envision colonialism as a whole series of projects, changing over time and space and according to the character of their instigators and participants, that added up to a whole when seen from afar.

Diverging visions and projects of imperial agents are not the only differences between imperialism and colonialism, however. Even more important were the ideas and actions of colonial subjects. Imperialist doctrines did not initially take into account indigenous and cosmopolitan populations, who weren't supposed to possess freedom of action. Yet they quickly demonstrated they did, in a variety of ways. Each location within the periphery was populated by indigenous peoples as well as migrants and transients from around the world. Some of these individuals became important collaborators, enabling colonial rule. Other segments of the population resisted that rule or infiltrated its offices. Arguably most individuals, most of the time, sought merely to survive and thrive and thus accommodated the presence of imperial agents and rules when necessary and avoided them when possible. At times, they were able to force the colonial administration to renegotiate the terms of their authority and power. Of course their relationship to colonial institutions and officials remained unequal. Structures of racial and ethnic hierarchy, disparities in the law, discrepancies in military power and civil authority, and financial inequality all

---

[28] This is one of the foundational ideas of postcolonialism, as expressed by Edward Said in his 1978 classic. Edward W. Said, *Orientalism* (New York: Vintage Books, 1978), 5.

[29] This important tenet of postcolonialism is very well expressed in Partha Chatterjee, *The Nation and Its Fragments: Colonial and Postcolonial Histories* (Princeton, NJ: Princeton University Press, 1993).

[30] Frederick Cooper, "The Dialectics of Decolonization: Nationalism and Labor Movements in Postwar French Africa," in Cooper and Stoler, *Tensions of Empire*, 409.

conspired to limit the agency of colonized peoples vis-à-vis the citizens of the metropole. Nevertheless, in all cases colonial authorities had to take into account the opinions and needs of segments of the local population in formulating and implementing policy. This difference in context between periphery regions and the metropole made it inevitable that colonialism (in action) in every case differed from the theories and doctrines of imperialism.

Colonialism, then, refers to the set of practices and policies implemented by imperial agents to obtain and maintain control, stability, economic objectives, and social engineering in the constituent polities of the imperial periphery. These projects may be formulated by metropolitan agencies, colonial officials, or in rare cases local groups. In every case, however, the manner in which they unfold is heavily influenced by decisions undertaken by locally stationed agents of the imperial power and by the actions of the inhabitants of these overseas regions. Thus, while colonialism is related to imperialism, it is tied much more closely to events within the colonized regions and among colonized peoples and becomes therefore somewhat different in practice. The study of colonialism by necessity takes into consideration the manner by which populations, groups, and individuals accommodated, negotiated, resisted, infiltrated, cooperated, and tried to manage colonial rule.

GLOBAL AND MODERN

The terms *empire*, *imperialism*, and *colonialism* are useful tools for historians conducting comparative studies. By defining these terms concisely yet flexibly, it is possible to evaluate the similarities and differences between the Inca, Roman, and British empires. Yet this exercise is of limited use. In the first place, the contexts in which these geographically and chronologically diffuse empires operated were wildly different. Additionally, these empires represent largely unconnected human experiences in space and time. On the other hand, it is very useful to study the British, French, and German empires of the early twentieth century together, or

equally the Ottoman, Mughal, and Habsburg empires in the setting of the sixteenth century. Even while acknowledging vast differences between the societies from which these empires arose, it is possible to extract certain significant commonalities within these groupings. Most of these similarities are a result of the singular fact that these empires were connected to one another. They commerced in goods, traded ideas, exchanged plant and animal species, and exchanged subjects and citizens and were in some cases territorially contiguous. Thus, while it is possible to study each empire separately, it is even more useful to see them as part of a global context, in which the actions of and transformations within each society impacted others.

This book is really a global study of the world in the modern age. Other historians have studied this period on a global scale, but most have used nation-states rather than empires as their unit of analysis. By choosing to focus on modern empires in a global context, we make three core arguments. First, we argue that empires are an appropriate unit by which to study global interaction as well as local phenomena, although certainly not the only useful unit. Second, we contend that it is impossible to suitably analyze empire and imperial and colonial processes in the modern period without consideration of global contexts. Finally, we aver that the modern era is an appropriate period in which to consider these processes. Of the key terms in these arguments, we have already defined imperialism, colonialism, and empire. It remains for us to address the issue of scope in terms of the *modern* period and the *global* setting.

Scope may seem to be an issue easily defined and then dismissed, but in fact the scheme by which we divide up the past chronologically—like the manner in which we divide it up geographically—tells us a lot about the way we conceptualize history. Consider, for example, the notion of a modern era. The term *modern* carries with it a great deal of baggage. Like imperialism and empire, in the nineteenth century, the expression was generally seen as having positive connotations. Modernity was associated with progress—industrialism, capitalism, technology, and advances in all areas of human policy, culture, and activity. At a time when western

Europeans were increasingly coming to regard themselves as leaders in all of these areas, modernity was associated with a certain "European-ness," and by extension other peoples of the world were generally regarded as stagnating or backward. Historians working in this setting used the word to describe Europe's recent past, beginning with the European Renaissance in the fifteenth century. Later, some scholars separated this era into the *early modern period* that preceded the seventeenth- to eighteenth-century Enlightenment and the *contemporary period* that post-dated it.[31] Before these periods lurked the pre-capitalist Dark Ages. Thus, modernity was a concept that gave scholars the ability to divide European historic and contemporary population into modern people who lived like them ("us") and pre-modern people who were seen as living very different lives ("others"). However, Europeans' ancestors were not the only people "othered" by this use of the term. So too were peoples considered not to be in the modernizing mainstream: not only Asians, Africans, Americans, and Oceanians but also Europeans on the fringes of society such as Celtic and Balkan peoples and at times even women and rural-dwellers. It is no wonder that many groups and classes of people around the world came to challenge, redefine, re-claim, and at times reject the concept of modernity, as we will see in later chapters.

Thus, *modern* at first referred to what was thought of as an entirely internal set of developments within Europe.[32] Since the 1960s, however, a host of critics composed of anti-colonial and civil rights activists, area studies specialists, and dissident scholars began to challenge this conceptualization, a process that culminated in new periodizations and global history narratives. In 1996, Jerry H. Bentley, the author of a well-known world history textbook, proposed to re-periodize world history based on interactions between societies rather than evolutionary internal processes within

societies. Building on a wide body of scholarship that recognized inter-continental and trans-regional links stretching far back into the past, Bentley accepted 1500 as the beginning of the modern period but because of global rather than merely European transformations.[33] For Bentley, the modern era was defined partly by the re-opening of Old World (Asian, European, and African) commerce and exchange following a period of collapse in the fourteenth century.[34] Connected to this was the expansion of this commercial, biological, and intellectual exchange to encompass the Americas, and thus the emergence of a truly global system. As Bentley puts it

> By the early fifteenth century, Western Europeans had borrowed, invented, accumulated, and refined a technological complex that enabled them to become much more prominent than before on the world stage … partly as a result of their technological advantage, and with the unexpected aid of diseases that ravaged populations in the Americas and the Pacific islands, Western Europeans embarked on campaigns of expansion that vastly magnified their influence in the world. These campaigns opened a sixth era of world history—the modern age, extending from 1500 to the present, a period during which all the world's regions and peoples ultimately became engaged in sustained encounter with each other, thus a period that inaugurated a genuinely global epoch of world history.[35]

This notion of a historical fissure at the end of the fifteenth century, ascribed alternately to internal

---

[31] Dietrich Gerhard, "Periodization in European History," *American Historical Review*, 61 (1956), 903, 906.

[32] Consider, for example, the use of the term by political theorists as outlined in Dante Germino, " 'Modernity' in Western Political Thought," *New Literary History*, 1 (1970), 293–310.

[33] Among the most significant texts in establishing early periods of cross-cultural interaction is Andre Gunder Frank and Barry Gills, eds., *The World System: Five Hundred Years or Five Thousand* (New York: Routledge, 1994).

[34] The seminal text in proposing a fourteenth-century Eurasian collapse is Janet Abu-Lughod, *Before European Hegemony: The World System A.D. 1250–1350* (New York: Oxford University Press, 1989).

[35] Jerry H. Bentley, "Cross-Cultural Interaction and Periodization in World History," *American Historical Review*, 101 (1996), 768–769.

European or to global causes, has become deeply embedded in the study of empires and imperialism. In this discourse, it manifests itself as a division between older "land-based" empire and newer "maritime" empires. It divides Stephen Howe's book *Empire: A Very Short Introduction* into two parts, for example. It is similarly essential to David Abernethy's thesis that the maritime European empires of the fifteenth through twentieth centuries were distinct from empires elsewhere and in previous periods.[36]

There is certainly some validity to the use of the late fifteenth century as a benchmark in human history, if only because it was the moment at which extensive, sustained, and reciprocal integration between the Old World (Europe, Asia, and Africa) and the New World (the Americas) began. Even if we refuse to entirely discount arguments that African seafarers washed up in Central America or that Ming Dynasty fleets touched the Pacific coast before 1492, and even taking into account medieval Viking and perhaps Basque familiarity with the Atlantic coast of North America, it was not until the voyages of Columbus that the widespread and sustained exchange of humans, plant and animal species, technologies, and ideas between these two great landmasses began within the context of newly established inter-continental empires. The impact of that exchange was and continues to be of enormous depth and on a worldwide scale.[37] Thus, if the word *global* is read literally, 1492 seems to indicate the beginning of a new era that could conveniently be labeled the modern age.[38] In this sense, the dawn of the modern world refers not to the technological sophistication or cultural attitudes of certain peoples, but rather to the joint experience of a truly global world—one in which empires played a leading role.

There are, however, critics of this periodization. For the purposes of this book, the most significant are those who refute the idea that the transcontinental empires that emerged from European metropoles in this period represented a significant break with the past. William H. McNeill perhaps the earliest scholar to tentatively place European maritime empires within a historical context that was wider than Europe, was one of the pioneers of world history. In a short booklet entitled *The Age of Gunpowder Empires, 1450–1800*, McNeill suggested a Eurasian system in which interlinked states and empires shared certain common attributes just prior to the voyages of Columbus. He included in this system not only major European states such as England, France, and the Iberian powers of Portugal and Spain, but also Russia, the tri-continental Ottoman Empire, and the Mughal Empire in central Asia and India. McNeill identified within these states two related trends of particular importance: the development of cannon and the centralization of power under a monarch. These trends enabled these states to become powerfully expansive under royal authority. For McNeill, the Iberian empires in the Americas were born of pretty much the same processes as Mughal expansion in south Asia and Ottoman conquests in North Africa and the Balkans.[39]

McNeill's analysis challenges the contention that the post-1492 European empires were distinctive in that (in Abernethy's words) "not one but several empires were [being] constructed at about the same time and administered in parallel."[40] In fact, as early as 1400, both the development of imperial forms of state sovereignty and expansionist empire-building processes were already underway in some regions of Eurasia, driven by a resurgence in population, the development and diffusion of new technologies, and an inter-continental trade renaissance. None of these processes was centered in western Europe. Instead, they were shared across large regions of Eurasia and Africa that were increasingly

---

[36] Abernethy, *The Dynamics of Global Dominance*, 6–12.

[37] Probably the most significant text on this topic is Alfred Crosby, *The Columbian Exchange: Biological and Cultural Consequences of 1492* (Westport, CT: Greenwood Press, 1972).

[38] William A. Green, "Periodizing World History," *History and Theory*, 34 (1995), 99–101. Green writes that "prior to 1492, history at its grandest level could only be hemispheric."

[39] William H. McNeill, *The Age of Gunpowder Empires, 1450–1800* (Washington: American Historical Association, 1989).

[40] Abernethy, *The Dynamics of Global Dominance*, 9.

integrated with each other. In less than half a century, the Americas would join them as well. In telling the history of the modern world from an imperial perspective, the histories of these regions from these dates forward are inseparable.[41]

One of the modes of interaction among these far-flung societies over the last 600 or so years has been that of the empire. In fact, many of the defining cultural feature of modernity are at least partly products of imperialism and colonialism. These include the globalization not only of products but also ideas: notions of race, gender, self, and "otherness" that seem to have homogenized what were previously a wide diversity of conceptualizations of these how the world worked. Through the workings of power, some understandings of the world (largely those of powerful imperial states) have come to be shared around the world while others (especially those of colonized peoples) have been submerged. As you will see in this book, the application of the term *empire* is an example of this. Although this word comes to us out of a European heritage describing specific types of state and power constructions, it is now applied to a wide diversity of situations across time and around the world. In some cases, this application is apt, but in others less so, but in any case the term itself is an example both of the lingering powers of empire and the concurrent creation of "modernity."

Yet while we use the term *modern* in this book to refer to a period of time in which the world seemingly became smaller, we must warn against blithely accepting the idea that there is a single kind of modernity and that modernity is necessarily the same as "western-ness." While the world since 1400 has increasingly a pattern of homogenization, and while Europe and the United States have at least since the 1850s been the dominant actors in setting the pattern of global experiences, by its nature modernization has involved actors from around the world and

still allows space for a variety of alternative viewpoints and perspectives.

In this book, the *modern period*, therefore, refers to a phase in world history of increasing but often uneven cross-cultural interaction that began in Eurasia and North Africa in the early fifteenth century and that is marked in part by competition between empires on a global stage. Modern empires are characterized by their high levels of interaction, by the possession of certain technology, by relatively centralized state structures, and by their ability to integrate rural and urban as well as metropolitan and peripheral regions. Modern empires are heavily informed by their *global* context, compete and interact with distant societies, and may even possess territories or trading positions on multiple continents. Modern imperialism is informed by and operates within multi-continental international politics. Modern colonialism is a highly interactive process that involves not only citizens of the metropole and inhabitants of the colonies but also immigrants and transients from often far distant origins.

Questions

1. Look at the definitions of *empire*, *imperialism*, and *colonialism* in this chapter together. Is it possible to have an empire without imperialism or colonialism? Is it possible to have imperialism without colonialism? Is it possible to have colonialism without imperialism? Defend your answer.
2. Where in the contemporary world or recent past do we see states are *not* empires? Give examples (don't try to be exhaustive). What makes these state forms different from empires?
3. One of the defining factors of empire is the relationships between the metropole and the periphery. What kinds of "relationships" do you think this might mean?
4. Based on these definitions, would you characterize the United States as an imperial metropole today? If not, why not? If so, how would you define its culture of imperialism? Where is its periphery? Who are its primary agents of empire?

---

[41] A superior text that captures pre-1492 Eurasian interaction is David P. Ringrose, *Expansion and Global Interaction, 1200–1700* (New York: Addison Wesley Longman, 2001).

CHAPTER 1

Empire: The Emergence of Early Modern States and Empires in Eurasia and Africa

The world of the nineteenth and twentieth centuries was shaped by "modern" empires that spanned the globe or dominated great regions of it. Emerging from industrial societies such as Britain, the United States, France, Japan, the Soviet Union, and more briefly Germany and Italy, these states were constructed and maintained by vast armies and navies with military superiority over the peoples they conquered. Their empires were sustained by enormous industrial economies whose managers and profiteers benefited from empire. They were justified by contemporary ideologies of race, technology, and religion that proclaimed a duty to dominate and to "civilize" other peoples.

These empires have often been studied as part of a "new" imperialism that resulted from great transformations in the nineteenth century. They are described as the products of the changes wrought by modernity upon Europe: industrialization, new sciences and scientific racialism, liberalism. In future chapters, we will explore exactly these connections. However, the nineteenth- and twentieth-century empires were, in fact, rooted in long-term trends that connected them to earlier eras of history and to the history not just of Europe but of the entire world. Perhaps most significantly, the empires of our recent past faced remarkably similar challenges to those of the fifteenth, sixteenth, and seventeenth centuries. These empires of the *early modern period*—as it is often termed—also struggled to centralize power in the hands of the state, to convince merchants and the general populace of the metropole to support their policies of imperialism, and to find ways to rule the culturally, spiritually, and economically diverse people of their empires and to bind them together.

Can we connect the technologies and strategies of these early modern empires with those of the nineteenth- and twentieth-century empires? Geographically, the imperial cores of the two periods do not match up. The largest empires of the early modern period were centered in Asia and North Africa: the Mongol state, Ming China, Tīmūrid (Mughal) India and Central Asia, and the Ottoman Empire. The only comparable European empires were those of the Spanish and Austrian Habsburgs and Portugal. The great imperial centers of the modern era in northern Europe, Japan, and the United States were either politically fragmented or politically peripheral in this earlier period. The longest direct geographical continuity that existed was the Russian state centered upon Muscovy, which expanded almost unceasingly from the fifteenth to the twentieth century.

Yet as the first four chapters of this book will show, the early modern era was a period of increasing globalization and the building of economic and intellectual connections between regions of the world. This rising interconnectedness made it possible for states like England (later Britain) to begin to learn techniques of colonial rule from established powers like the Mughals. The migration of peoples and expanding trade gradually enriched established states like France and built new nations like the United States. The flow of technologies spread military expertise and equipment to regions like Japan where they could become tools of empire.

In this chapter, we explore the rise of early modern empires in Eurasia and North Africa during the period 1380–1650. We suggest that a number of large, cohesive imperial states emerged during this period—partially as a result of a sharing of ideas and technologies, which itself was made possible by the Eurasian system created by the Mongol Empire. We then go on to explore several ideas about the ways in which these empires came into being and operated: the rise of gunpowder military economies, the emergence of alliances between different sectors of society, and the development of unique but interestingly interconnected cultures of imperialism. This leaves for chapter 2 the larger issues of early modern imperial interaction and colonialism. Alone, however, these chapters do not give a global picture. Thus in chapters 3 and 4 we expand our scope to include the Americas, sub-Saharan Africa, and the Polynesian Pacific: early modern imperial systems that themselves grew from earlier Eurasian and North African roots.

THE EMERGENCE OF THE EARLY MODERN STATE SYSTEM

Beginning in the late fourteenth century, a rush of empire-building washed across the world. The largest of these empires blossomed first in Eurasia: the Iberian Peninsula (Portugal and Spain), eastern Europe (Russia and the Austrian Habsburgs), Central Asia (the Ottoman and Tīmūrid Empires), and China. Together with a constellation of smaller states, their emergence reversed a period of political and economic fragmentation following the Black Death of the 1340s–1380s and the collapse of the Mongol Empire. Within a century, for the first time in human history, they began to connect all of the world's continents in commercial, intellectual, and biological ties. Although each empire was unique, and each emerged in the context of distinctive local events, nevertheless their expansion reflected similar attempts to control the resurgent inter-continental commerce of the fifteenth and sixteenth centuries and to mobilize new technologies and equipment.

These great Eurasian empires were merely the largest manifestations of a trend of state-building that stretched across Eurasia and parts of Africa from the end of the fourteenth century onward. At the beginning of the early modern period, for example, Europe possessed 500–600 co-existing polities. By the late nineteenth century, this number was reduced to 25. Across eastern Europe and Central Asia in the same timeframe, Russia swallowed 30 independent states and khanates. In mainland South-East Asia, 22 independent states that existed in 1350 were reduced to 3 by 1823.[1] Similar consolidations took place in South Asia, where large states like Vijayanagar and especially the Mughal Empire rapidly overcame fragmented princedoms. On Eurasia's southern fringe, the Ottoman Empire came to span three continents, fusing together South-West Asia, the Balkans, and North Africa. Nearby, the Horn of Africa was consolidated in the hands of a few large states of which the most expansive was Abyssinia (Ethiopia). Gradually,

---

[1] Victor Lieberman, "Transcending East-West Dichotomies: State and Culture Formation in Six Ostensibly Disparate Areas," *Modern Asian Studies*, 31 (1997), 463–546.

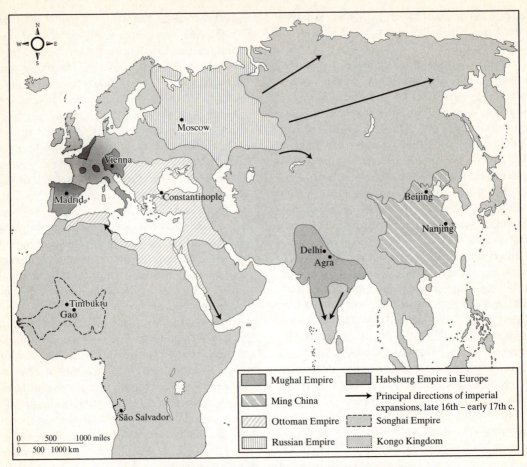

Early Modern Empires of Eurasia and North Africa, c. 1550

the process was extended to areas beyond the older Eurasian trading zone to new regions of sub-Saharan Africa. There, however, the independent consolidation of large states was overtaken by the extension of European maritime empires and especially by the effects of the Atlantic slave trade. In the Americas, the large states and independent communities that had formed a political and commercial network of their own were overcome by European armies, settlers, and diseases after 1492.

While the political regimes of each state were unique, they were all characterized to varying degrees by three linked processes. The first was *centralization*, by which both power and authority tended to become consolidated under a single state authority, usually a ruling monarch or dynastic family and a royal or imperial court. The second was *rationalization*, by which authority and power in the state became increasingly subject to a permanent, organized bureaucracy at the center of the state. The third was *expansion*, by which states increased in size and in some cases developed imperial institutions and relationships.

The context in which these processes took place was the disintegration of the Mongol Empire.[2] From about 1220 to well into the late fourteenth century, the great bulk of Eurasia had come under the control of this single political entity. Only the fringes of the landmass—Europe, Japan, South and South-East Asia, and North Africa—had remained independent. The result of this unique unification had been a flowering of "cultural and artistic achievement" and long-distance trade.[3] These developments were catalyzed by the Mongol rulers' ability to safeguard overland trading routes and to provide relative safety and stability across vast stretches of Eurasia.[4] Cities in a band across Eurasia and surrounding the Indian Ocean and the Mediterranean and China seas—London, Bruges, Genoa, Venice, Constantinople, Cairo, Bukhara, Samarkand, Hormuz, Kilwa, Cambay, Calicut, Malacca, and Guangzhou—flourished in these conditions forming a vast "archipelago of towns."[5] Each city was a center of commerce and production, connected to surrounding agrarian regions and to long-distance trading partners by economic, political, and social links.

The causes of the mid-fourteenth-century collapse of this network are debated, but the very nature of its connectedness may have been one key culprit. Like a two-edged sword, the connections that enabled societies across the Old World to share wealth and innovations also made them dependent upon each other. The collapse of one prop of the system was bound to affect the others. In this context, a series of diseases, bad harvests, and political upheaval across the Mongol domains signaled the beginning of a commercial decline. Perhaps the most significant was the outbreak of epidemics that stretched far beyond the borders of the empire. The best known of these was the dreaded Black Death, which spread rapidly along both overland and maritime trade routes, devastating both commercial towns and the surrounding countryside from China across the vast expanse of Eurasia and North Africa to England.[6] The effects of the epidemic were exacerbated in some regions of Asia by a series of bad agricultural years.[7]

---

[2] Some scholars argue that commercial integration of Eurasia and North Africa goes back much further. See, for example, Andre Gunder Frank and Barry Gills, eds., *The World System: Five Hundred Years or Five Thousand* (New York: Routledge, 1994).

[3] This phrasing is taken from the influential modern pan-Eurasian work of Janet Abu-Lughod, *Before European Hegemony: The World System A.D. 1250–1350* (New York: Oxford University Press, 1989), 4.

[4] One of the best short treatments of the Mongols comes in the David P. Ringrose's superb survey of global interaction. Ringrose, *Expansion and Global Interaction, 1200–1700* (New York: Addison Wesley Longman, 2001), 5–24.

[5] Fernand Braudel, *Civilization and Capitalism, 15th–18th Century*, vol. III, *The Wheels of Commerce* (New York: Harper & Row, 1984), 30.

[6] William H. McNeill, *Plagues and Peoples* (New York: Anchor Books, 1976), 132–146. Admittedly, McNeill's work remains controversial and some scholars have suggested that contemporaneous plagues in various parts of the world may have been caused by a variety of epizootics.

[7] K.N. Chaudhuri, *Asia Before Europe: Economy and Civilisation of the Indian Ocean from the Rise of Islam to 1750* (Cambridge: Cambridge University Press, 1991), 246–268.

Moreover, Black Death may have come at a period of great vulnerability for the Old World economic network, as there is some evidence that parts of Eurasia were already experiencing a commercial downturn as early as the 1330s.[8]

The economic depression of the mid-fourteenth century was hard on many societies, but it was devastating to the Mongol leadership that relied heavily on income from trade to run their vast empire. In Asia, insurgents began to see this weakened condition as an opportunity to challenge their Mongol rulers, and these challenges form the context for the origins of four early modern empires: Ming Dynasty China and the Ottoman, Russian, and Mughal Empires.

China was in the early fourteenth century the head—if not the heart—of the Mongol state. Chinggis Khan had begun the assault on China in 1210, and his grandson Khubilai had defeated the last rulers of the Chinese Song Dynasty in a 12-year campaign that ended in 1279. Calling themselves the Yuan dynasty, Khubilai and his successors ruled China from approximately 1271 to 1368. Yet Yuan leadership began to decline as early as the 1330s, as factional intrigue weakened the central government and rebel movements emerged in the provinces.[9] The most significant of these movements was the Daoist Red Turban movement, whose leader Zhu Yuanzhang captured the Yuan capital at Beijing in 1368, took the title the *Hongwu Emperor*, and established the Ming dynasty, with authority over all of the core provinces of China.[10] This massive polity thus became the first of the major states to assert its independence from the Mongols.

The first half of the fourteenth century also witnessed a decline of Mongol power in South-West Asia (the Middle East). Here the most significant challenger was a small Turkic-speaking state ruled by the Bey Osman (Bey 1281–1299, Sultan 1299–1326), which had for decades paid tribute to the Mongol emperors. In 1299, Osman declared his (then still small) state independent from Mongol Rule, and it came afterward to be named in his honor the "Ottoman" state.[11] Osman and his successors rapidly claimed territory not only from the Mongols, but also from the Byzantine Empire to the west, from whom they acquired Greece, Bulgaria, Macedonia, southern Serbia, and in 1392, Albania.[12] They briefly lost ground again in the fourteenth century to the brilliant Mongol warrior-lord Tīmūr (known in the west as Tamerlane), but upon his death in 1405 his empire immediately contracted, enabling the Ottomans to re-establish themselves. By mid-century, Anatolia (modern Turkey) was reconquered and the Ottomans were able to advance again in Europe. The accession of Mehmed II (1451–1481) to the Sultanate opened a new period of expansion and the development of a truly imperial Ottoman state. The descendents of Tīmūr maintained hold only of Persia, until they were defeated in 1501 by an alliance of Persian religious and military figures led by a soldier who crowned himself Shah Ismā'īl I (1501–1524). This Safavî (or Safavîiyya) state quickly became the Ottomans' main rival in the east.[13]

Arising to the east of Persia, the great Mughal Empire is most often associated with northern India. In fact, however, it too emerged out of the Tīmūrid upheavals of the late fourteenth century. The founder of the Mughal emperor, Zahir-ud-din Muhammad Babur (hereafter known as Babur, 1526–1530), claimed descent both from Tīmūr and Chinggis Khan.[14]

[8] Frank and Gills, *The World System*, 179–180.

[9] F.W. Mote, *Imperial China 900–1800* (Cambridge: Harvard University Press, 1999), 518–528.

[10] Ibid., 563–564. See also the English or Chinese versions of *The Cambridge History of China*, vols. 7 and 8, *The Ming Dynasty*, edited by Denis C. Twitchett and Frederick W. Mote (Cambridge: Cambridge University Press, 1998).

[11] See Halil Inalcik, *The Ottoman Empire: The Classical Age 1300–1600* (London: Phoenix Press, 1994). First published 1973.

[12] Ringrose, *Expansion and Global Interaction*, 44.

[13] H.R. Roemer, "The Safavî Period," in *The Cambridge History of Iran*, vol. 6, *The Timurid and Safavî Periods*, edited by Peter Jackson and Laurence Lockhart (Cambridge: Cambridge University Press, 1986), 190–193.

[14] John F. Richards, *The New Cambridge History of India*, vol. 5, *The Mughal Empire* (Cambridge: Cambridge University Press, 1993), 9, 44–47.

Babur led his followers to northern India from Central Asia in the 1520s, and in 1526 he defeated the Muslim rulers of Delhi, the Lodi family. Gradually, they extended their sway over Afghan and Hindu rivals. Under Akbar (1556–1605), the Mughals occupied much of northern India including the rich and fertile region of Bengal. By the end of Akbar's reign, the Mughal state comprised a vast, multi-ethnic, and still expanding empire.

The Mughals, Ottomans, and Safavîs shared an Islamic identity with the Mongols, but a Christian successor to the Mongols also came into being in the western portion of their domain. The Slavic state of Russia began as the Grand Duchy of Muscovy, which for much of the thirteenth century was a leading tributary to the Mongol Khanate of the Golden Horde. As the power of the Mongol state waned in the fourteenth century, that of Muscovy increased, allowing the Grand Dukes to flex their muscles on the margins of the Khanate. In 1478, Grand Duke Ivan III conquered his once-powerful neighboring city-state of Novgorod.[15] By the mid-sixteenth century, allied to other former subjects of the Mongols, the Muscovite Russians were powerful enough to take on two Muslim-dominated Mongol successor states located to their east—the Khanates of Kazan and Astrakhan. Kazan was conquered in 1552 and Astrakhan in 1556. The conquest of Kazan and Astrakhan decisively turned Russia into a truly multi-ethnic empire, under a self-proclaimed czar (emperor).[16] It also opened up the steppe lands of Central Asia and the sparsely populated reaches of Siberia to the expansion of the Russians, who were limited in the west by emerging European rivals.

These European peoples, located at the extreme western limit of Mongol strength, had never been conquered by them. In any case,

Europe's fragmented geography—its islands, peninsulas, and mountain chains—has throughout history made it difficult for any single state to rule the continent effectively. The exception was the Habsburg Empire, which at its height included Spain, the Low Countries, Burgundy, Austria, Bohemia, parts of Hungary, and positions in Italy and North Africa as well as a growing empire in the Americas. Yet even this vast domain proved too large to rule effectively. Its territories could not be effectively mobilized for unified action, it only gradually developed a unified state bureaucracy, and it dissolved quite quickly under pressure.

The Habsburg Empire was formed largely through marriage, and it's worth briefly listing the weddings that built their dominion. The Habsburgs were descendents on the male side of a leading German aristocratic family, the Dukes of Austria. In the fifteenth century, members of the Habsburg family were regularly elected Holy Roman emperors, although this latter title gave them little real additional authority or power outside of their ancestral lines. Their horizons became greatly widened by the wedding of Maximilian Habsburg (Holy Roman Emperor Maximilian I, 1486–1519) to Mary, heiress of Burgundy, in 1477. This added to his ancestral domains not only the territory of Burgundy in eastern France, but also Mary's family possessions in the Netherlands. A second wedding— that of Maximilian's son Philip the Handsome to Joan of Aragon-Castile—doubled the size of the Habsburg inheritance. As the heir to Ferdinand of Aragon and Isabella of Castile, Joan gave Philip claim to Spain as well as territories in Italy and the Americas. Maximilian also arranged a double wedding for himself and for his daughter that sealed an alliance with the rulers of Bohemia and Hungary (Vladislav Jagellon) and of Poland-Lithuania (Sigismund Jagellon) in 1515.[17] Following the death of

---

[15] Andreas Kappeler, *The Russian Empire*, translated by Alfred Clayton (Harlow: Longman Press, 2001), 14–16.

[16] Michael Khodarkovsky, *Russia's Steppe Frontier: The Making of a Colonial Empire, 1500–1800* (Bloomington: Indiana University Press, 2002), 105–110. See also Kappeler, *The Russian Empire*, 14–22.

---

[17] Victor S. Mamatey, *Rise of the Habsburg Empire 1526–1815* (New York: Holt, Rinehart and Winston, 1971), 1–7.

Vladislav while fighting the Ottomans at the battle of Mohács in 1526, Bohemia became a Habsburg domain, while Hungary was partitioned between the Habsburgs, Ottomans, and an independent Transylvania.

Upon Maximilian I's death, therefore, his grandson Charles was not only elected Holy Roman Emperor Charles V (1519–1556), but also inherited an enormous domain stretching across much of Europe. Yet he almost immediately recognized that his inheritance was too vast for one individual to rule. Choosing to focus on Spain and its dependents, Charles therefore turned the administration of the eastern territories including the Austrian hereditary lands over to his brother Ferdinand in 1521. In 1555, Charles abdicated as Holy Roman Emperor in Ferdinand's favor (1555–1564) and, in the following year, turned the Spanish division of the Empire over to his son Philip II (King of Spain, 1556–1598). The Habsburg domains were now permanently divided, although the two branches of the family remained intertwined and allied.

Philip II inherited the throne of an increasingly wealthy, largely unified Spain with extensive colonies in the Americas (discussed in chapters 3 and 4) as well as in the Philippines and with dominion over the Netherlands. It was at this point that the Habsburg Empire in Spain transformed itself into a Spanish Empire. In the years prior to the Habsburg marriages, Ferdinand and Isabella of Spain had forged from their domains both a Spanish identity and a unified Spain, largely through wars with the Muslim rulers of southern Spain known as the **reconquista** (or reconquest).[18] The dual monarchs also sponsored overseas adventures such as that of Christopher Columbus. Ferdinand and Isabella were succeeded by the Habsburg Charles V, child of Philip the Handsome and their daughter Joan. Yet throughout his reign, Charles saw Spain as merely one of his domains, and visited it only intermittently.[19] His son Philip,

by contrast, recognized Spain as the center of his empire, and its overseas colonies as an imperial periphery.

The reconquista produced not one but two great early modern maritime empires. Spain shared the Iberian Peninsula with Portugal, as well as with several Islamic states, and their histories are intertwined with each other. In the late medieval period, the peninsula was a zone of intense intermingling and interaction between Muslims, Christians, and Jews. Yet relations were not always friendly, and the two Christian states of Spain and Portugal became unified largely out of a struggle to evict their Islamic rivals. The smaller, more westerly Portuguese state coalesced earlier than the larger Spanish state, and by around 1250 it was virtually territorially complete. Thus in the fourteenth and fifteenth centuries, the task of the Portuguese monarchs was not to expand the state within the peninsula but to subdue alternate power centers—the nobility, the church, and the military orders. All of these remained useful tools, as we will see, but had to be subverted to the monarch's authority. This task was largely completed by 1410.[20] For the remainder of the modern period, Portugal under its kings would be an expansionist independent state, except for a brief period of unification with Spain between 1580 and 1640.

In the fifteenth and sixteenth centuries, Portugal and Spain took the energy that had built them into powerful states and turned it outward. Neither had neighboring territory, but both had Atlantic coastlines and access to favorable ocean currents. Thus, both states turned their attention to Atlantic Islands such as the Canaries. Portuguese monarchs Dom João II (1481–1495) and Dom Manuel I (1496–1521) sponsored commercial expeditions along the West African coast and the establishment of fortified positions meant to dominate the gold trade with West Africa, of which the most important was São Jorge da Mina, built in

[18] Henry Kamen, *Empire: How Spain Became a World Power 1492–1763* (New York: HarperCollins, 2003), 16–17.
[19] Ibid., 49–67.

[20] See Sanjay Subrahmanyan, *The Portuguese Empire in Asia, 1500–1700: A Political and Economic History* (Harlow: Longman, 1993), 30–36.

1482 on what came to be known as the Gold Coast.[21] Successive voyages brought Portuguese expeditions further down the coast, culminating in Bartholomeu Dias's "doubling," or passing and returning, of the Cape of Good Hope in southern Africa. By 1498, a squadron under the command of Vasco da Gama entered the Indian Ocean, connecting the Iberian states to the vast Indian Ocean trading zone.[22] A second wing of Iberian overseas acquisition brought sailors flying Spanish and Portuguese flags across the Atlantic to the Americas, a story told in chapters 3 and 4.

The great empires of the early modern era were in constant interaction with other, smaller emerging states. In North Africa, for example, Spain, Portugal, and the Ottomans interacted with a variety of local Muslim authorities. Some, like the Barbarossa brothers Arrudj and Khayruddin, accepted Ottoman suzerainty in return for aid against the Spanish. In this way, the areas comprising coastal Libya, Algeria, and Tunisia were brought informally into the Ottoman **tributary** system.[23] In Morocco, on the other hand, the Sa'ādi family managed to play the Ottomans, Spanish, and Portuguese against each other and in this way to build an independent state.[24] In North-East Africa, the development of the independent Christian Ethiopian (Abyssinian) state similarly put it in a position to preserve its independence from the Ottomans by seeking an alliance with Portugal in the fifteenth and sixteenth centuries.

In Asia as well, small and medium-sized states gradually coalesced in the early modern period. The unification of Japan was one significant example. Split by feuding factions of feudal lords, or daimyo, Japan lacked anyone who could claim to represent a centralized authority until 1615, when Tokugawa Ieyesu eliminated his final

rival for the position of *shogun*, or state warlord, in 1614.[25] In South-East Asia, a small number of cohesive states emerged in the fifteenth century linked economically to China. These included both trading city-states such as Melaka and Aceh and larger agglomerations such as Burma, Siam, and Vietnam. While China was economically intertwined with South-East Asia, it interfered militarily with its southern neighbors only twice—intervening in Vietnamese (Annamese) politics in 1406–1427 and in Burma in the mid-1440s.[26] It was following the Chinese withdrawal after 1427 that the local Le dynasty established itself as the rulers of Vietnam.

Vietnam and other emerging South-East Asian states rapidly built commercial links to South Asia trading partners. These included not only the Mughal Empire but also a number of emerging states at the tip of the Indian sub-continent such as the Hindu state of Vijayanagar. These in turn were linked to maritime towns such as Hormuz and Aden on the Arabian Peninsula, to the emerging Ottoman Empire, and to a string of East African city-states that shared a set of cultural and linguistic attributes that we now know as Swahili. These Swahili polities—including the important port-cities of Mogadishu, Malindi, Sofala, and Mombasa—were connected to resource-rich states of the African interior. Several of them experienced significant population expansion in the fifteenth century, as Indian Ocean trade revived.[27]

Between the east coast of Africa and South-East Asia, the Indian Ocean formed a vast and multi-national maritime zone of exchange—the richest in the world—with the Mughal Empire as its central pivot. Chinese merchants participated as well. In the first part of the fourteenth century,

[21] John Vogt, *Portuguese Rule on the Gold Coast 1469–1682* (Athens: University of Georgia Press, 1979), 21–34.
[22] J.H. Parry, *The Age of Reconnaissance* (London: Phoenix Press, 2000), 131–148. First printed 1963.
[23] "Algeria, Tunisia and Libya: the Ottomans and Their Heirs," in *UNESCO General History of Africa*, vol. 5, *Africa from the Sixteenth to the Eighteenth Century* (Berkeley: University of California Press, 1999), abridged edition, 120–134.
[24] "Morocco," in *Africa from the Sixteenth to the Eighteenth Century*, 104–119.

[25] George Sansom, *A History of Japan 1334–1615* (Stanford: Stanford University Press, 1961), 397–406.
[26] Jung-pang Lo, "Policy Formulation and Decision-Making on Issues Respecting Peace and War," in *Chinese Government in Ming Times*, edited by Charles O. Hucker (New York: Columbia University Press, 1969), 41–72.
[27] See Derek Nurse and Thomas Spear, *The Swahili: Reconstructing the History and Language of an African Society, 800–1500* (Philadelphia: University of Pennsylvania Press, 1985), 80–98.

the great maritime cities of the Indian Ocean from Melaka to Mombasa were visited by the vast Chinese fleets of the Muslim eunuch-admiral Zheng He. These great convoys ended in 1433, yet less ostentatious but equally significant commercial networks continued to tie the entire region together in annual trade circuits.[28] The Ottomans, too, participated in this trade following Sultan Selim I's (1512–1520) 1516 conquest of Egypt. Ottoman control over this strategic link between east and west helped to drive the Portuguese toward an alternate route into the Indian Ocean around the southern tip of Africa. The wealth of the Indies was a major attraction for Europeans, and the Portuguese were only the first of a number of states to support voyages of exploration and piracy that aimed to possess at least part of it. Portuguese and Spanish expeditions were rapidly followed by others mounted by French, British, and multinational groups.[29]

The parallel developments of large empires and centralizing states in many parts of Asia, Africa, and Europe in this period should not obscure differences among them. Some of the states described earlier were vast agrarian empires with powerful landed gentry and religious or scholarly elites. Others were small, principally commercial, and dominated by merchant elites. Some were built and maintained largely through conquest, others more through dynastic marriage, religious and national identity-building, and alliance. Yet beneath these differences was a shared history that can be highlighted by investigating the origins, forms, mechanisms, and functions of the state across this vast region of the early modern world. Within this shared history we can locate the development of modern imperialism, empires, and colonialism. This is the task

to which we now turn, by considering three inter-linked sets of analyses proposed by scholars to explain the emergence of these new large states and empires.

A GUNPOWDER REVOLUTION?

The principal theory advanced to explain this sudden efflorescence is called the *gunpowder revolution*. Wrapping technology, economy, and culture together, this theory begins by positing that Eurasian and some African societies in the early modern period jointly participated in the recovery of local, inter-regional, and long-distance trade following the subsidence of the mid-fourteenth-century depression. This resurgence in trade facilitated the spread of new transportation and military technologies—particularly firearms, but also ship-building and navigation techniques. Together, these trends intensified the power and authority of those rulers who could afford to participate in the expensive technological arms race, and allowed them to enhance their power especially with respect to feudal lords, community leaders, and nomadic peoples. The resulting decrease in the number of viable militaries was a critical factor in the development of early modern states. In order to maintain these costly armies and navies, however, states had to compete to control and to tax greater shares of global production and commerce. What this meant was that states that wanted to maintain their power had to continue to expand. To do this, governments created alliances with merchants, which then competed with rival state-merchant alliances to control natural resources, commercial entrepots, and production centers. Such increased competition in turn drove the need for larger and more expensive weapons and armies. It was partly this search for new sources of income and trade routes that led to the "voyages of exploration" that established connections among previously separated regions of the world.

The centralized governments that evolved through this process shared certain characteristics to varying degrees. These included the use of gunpowder technologies, the mobilization of

---

[28] For a primary account of one of Zheng He's voyages, see Ma Huan, *Ying-Yai Sheng-Lan* [The overall survey of the ocean's shores], edited by Feng Ch'eng Chun and J.V.G. Mills (Cambridge: Hakluyt Society, 1970), 179–180. For more on Indian Ocean commerce in this era, see Andre Gunder Frank, *ReORIENT: Global Economy in the Asian Age* (Berkeley: University of California Press, 1998).

[29] A venerable work on the subject is Joseph R. Strayer, *On the Medieval Origins of the Modern State* (Princeton, NJ: Princeton University Press, 1970).

religious and secular heritage in a search for **legitimacy,** and the development of alliances with merchants and religious leaderships as well as landed elites. In many states, these trends helped to create fledgling cultures of imperialism. From some of these states emerged true empires. In most of these empires, some types of modern colonialism emerged.

In 1983, the pioneering world historian William McNeill put together a unified theory that proposed that the development of gunpowder and firearms was the key factor leading to the formation of early modern world empires.[30] Gunpowder was probably discovered or invented only once in world history, by tenth-century Chinese alchemists. During the Song dynasty, weapons were developed that made use of this gunpowder, including "fire arrows" and cylinders that spewed perforated iron balls. The Mongol Yuan emperors further elaborated these weapons and built the first guns probably around 1288. The spread of gunpowder technology from China was facilitated by the vast Mongol hegemony.[31] There is evidence that Arab armies were making use of gunpowder-filled rockets and fireworks around 1240 and of Syrian "fire lances" around 1280. The earliest European recipes for making gunpowder appeared around the same time.[32] Unlike gunpowder, the cannon may have been developed in several places independently. The earliest Chinese cannon dates to about 1332. In Europe, a type of cannon was used to defend Florence in 1326, and later at the Hundred Years War Battle of Crécy in 1346. However, the cannon remained largely underpowered until the early fifteenth century. The debut of truly powerful cannon occurred at the 1451–1453 Ottoman siege of Constantinople, where the Sultan Mehmed II commissioned a Hungarian metallurgist to cast enormous firearms capable of blasting down the walls of that great city.[33]

Aside from turning the tide of some set-piece sieges, however, this evidence does not make it clear why cannon, and later personal firearms, had such a decisive effect in world history. After all, early firearms were enormous, liable to explode and kill their operators, and in the case of muskets were often less powerful than existing bow-and-arrow technology. Yet the rapid spread and utilization of gunpowder technology suggests that it was indeed significant. McNeill proposes that this might have been because gunpowder weapons—and especially cannon—reversed the power balance between monarchs and local authorities in many regions of Eurasia and Africa.

In the late medieval period across most of Eurasia and North Africa, the balance of power and authority generally resided in the relationship between rulers and land-owning elites. These landowners, who can perhaps be titled *feudal* or aristocratic classes, held a great deal of power largely because of their military contribution and strength. Often, they held sway over large areas from fortified castles that were difficult to destroy. These aristocrats used proceeds from their land to arm themselves heavily and to equip and maintain entourages of skilled cavalrymen (knights, samurai, *sipahis*) and footmen. The introduction of the cannon, however, shattered the power of these elites. In the first place, cannon were specifically designed to destroy fortifications such as castles, thus eliminating their only real advantage over the larger forces of the monarch. In the second place, cannon were so expensive that most landowners could not afford them. This gave certain authorities—usually monarchs and central governments—a monopoly on the new weapon. The introduction of personal firearms also contributed to the weakening of these local authorities. States could equip peasant armies, or professionals, with muskets. Although the musket was not in early years as effective as

---

[30] William H. McNeill, *Pursuit of Power: Technology, Armed Force, and Society Since 1000 A.D.* (Chicago: University of Chicago Press, 1983). See also by the same author, *The Age of Gunpowder Empires, 1450–1800* (Washington, DC: American Historical Association, 1989).
[31] Jack Kelly, *Gunpowder: Alchemy, Bombards, and Pyrotechnics* (New York: Basic Books, 2005), 2–15.
[32] Ibid., 22–25.

[33] One eyewitness account is Nicolo Barbaro, *Diary of the Siege of Constantinople 1453*, translated by John Melville-Jones (New York: Exposition Press, 1969).

the bow, it was easy to learn to use and therefore gave the state the ability to arm a force of amateurs to fight the experienced henchmen of the landed elites.

The result was threefold. First, the new weapons shifted the balance of power (and consequently the ability to tax populations) from local to central authorities, thus enabling state centralization and rationalization. Second, they increased the power of the first states in the region to adopt this technology against surrounding states and nomadic/pastoral peoples, thus facilitating the integration of states noted in this period. Finally, the new technology increased the financial needs of the state, thus leading to competition for resources and for control of inter-regional commerce.[34]

These effects can be seen in every region to which gunpowder technology spread in the early modern world, but especially among the great early modern empires. As we have seen, the Ottoman Empire first used firearms to great effect. Although the cannon that destroyed the walls of Constantinople were designed by a Hungarian, the Ottoman Sultans subsequently sponsored an indigenous bronze cannon industry controlled by the state alone. Equally significantly, Sultan Murad I (1359–1389) financed a state army manned largely by slaves that served as a counterpoint to aristocratic power. By the mid-fifteenth century, this force, known as the Janissary Corps, was largely armed with muskets. Throughout much of the sixteenth century, Ottoman military engineers, artillerymen, and musketeers were feared from Europe to East Asia, while Ottoman galleys controlled much of the Mediterranean and, periodically, the western Indian Ocean as well.[35]

Similarly, the founding of the Mughal Empire by Babur rested on his effective use of muskets and cannon against the cavalry of his nemesis the Sultan of Delhi at the 1526 Battle of Panipat. Yet his successor, Humayun (1530–1556) was almost undone by the rulers of Gujarat who possessed a large army of cannon and Turkish and Portuguese gunners. Partly as a result, the great Emperor Akbar undertook a campaign of military innovation and reorganization that included developing a centralized army, an over-arching system of military ranks, and a prohibition against the possession of artillery by any force other than that of the emperor. His large, professional army enabled him to conquer most of central India. Most assessments suggest, however, that military technology stagnated and finally declined under the rule of Shah Jahan (1628–1658).[36]

The Russian ascendance over the successor Khanates in Central Asia depended in part on its transition from a cavalry-centered, feudal society into a musket-and-cannon centralized power. The first steps were taken by Ivan III (1462–1505) and Vasilii III (1505–1533). In 1571, Russian cannon defended Moscow from the besieging army of the Khanate of Crimea and marked the inability of Central Asian rulers to take fortified cities armed with gunpowder weapons. In 1532, a second invasion turned back when it encountered Russian units defending the Oka River with arquebus (early muskets) and cannon.[37] Nevertheless, the Russian military forces remained dominated until the seventeenth century by middle-class cavalry armed with edged weapons and bows, many of whom were soldiers given land in the newly conquered territories in return for service.[38]

In many regions of Eurasia and Africa, several competing gunpowder-armed states arose simultaneously. This was true, for example, in continental South-East Asia, where Burma, Siam,

[34]McNeill, *The Age of Gunpowder Empires*, 1, 8, 10, 27–28, 34, 38, 39. See also Marshall Hodgson, *The Venture of Islam*, vol. 3, *The Gunpowder Empires and Modern Times* (Chicago: University of Chicago Press, 1974), 17. First published 1961.
[35]John F. Guilmartin, Jr., "The Military Revolution: Origins and First Tests Abroad," in *The Military Revolution Debate: Readings on the Military Transformation of Early Modern Europe*, edited by Clifford Rogers (Boulder, CO: Westview Press, 1995), 300–305.

[36]Richards, *The Mughal Empire*, 42–43, 57, 60, 68, 80, 142–143.
[37]Khodarkovsky, *Russia's Steppe Frontier*, 19–21.
[38]Richard Hellie, "Warfare, Changing Military Technology, and the Evolution of Muscovite Society," in *Tools of Hegemony*, edited by John Lynn (Chicago: University of Illinois Press, 1990), 75–99.

and Vietnam used personal firearms and cannon to subdue surrounding states and to resist Chinese incursions and later Portuguese interventions. Island states such as Melaka and Aceh also proved themselves capable of developing sophisticated cannon and gun-wielding ships.[39] This was also true in Europe, where the brief period of dramatic cannon superiority over masonry came to an end rather rapidly in the late fifteenth century with the development of the *trace italienne*, a new form of fortification resistant to cannon. This innovation helped to halt the consolidation of Europe and facilitated a balance of power among many, mid-sized states. It halted the development of a truly hegemonic Habsburg Empire based on Spain and Austria in the sixteenth century and resulted in an era of almost constant warfare that included the struggles of the eastern Habsburgs against the Ottomans, the Spanish–French wars, the revolt of the Netherlands, and the Thirty Years' War (1618–1648). This competitive environment spurred further, even more costly military developments that culminated in the sixteenth and seventeenth centuries in large and professional standing armies, new types of military organization, heavier financial burdens, and thus higher levels of taxation, as well as more brutal and lengthy wars.[40]

Equally significant was the effect of this sustained burst of military diffusion and innovation on western European maritime technology. Before the early modern period, the principal naval vessel of competing states in both the Mediterranean and the Indian Ocean was the oar-driven galley. Indeed, even in the sixteenth and seventeenth centuries, galleys retained some advantages over sail-driven ships because of their maneuverability in coastal areas. However, the galley had several key disadvantages. Its large crew made it difficult to operate over long distances, cargo space was small, and perhaps most importantly the ranks of oars made it difficult to carry large numbers of cannon.[41] Before the fifteenth century, however, it faced little competition from sail-driven ship designs. From China to England, most sailing ships were smaller and more fragile than large galleys and could not stream against the wind. This situation was transformed, however, between the fifteenth and seventeenth centuries through a complex and long process of diffusion and innovation. First, ship-building techniques using strong internal frames were developed in the western Mediterranean. These formed the base for a new sail configuration that mixed Arab lateen (or triangular) rigging with Breton square rigging. This arrangement allowed the new ship—called the *caravel*—to travel both fast and against the wind.[42] By the early sixteenth century, these caravels were mounting small numbers of guns in rear-pointing gunrooms. Although useful for bombarding ports such as the Swahili cities of East Africa, these were initially of limited use in gun-battles. Only after 1545 were long rows of broadside-mounted cannon introduced in England, where cheaper iron cannon were also replacing brass guns. The combination vastly increased shipboard firepower.[43] These types of innovations, which spread gradually around maritime Europe, slowly led to European domination of the seas. There is a great deal of scholarship, however, that suggests that for the sixteenth and early seventeenth centuries the naval gap between Europe and other regions should not be overstated.[44]

---

[39]Lieberman, "Transcending East-West Dichotomies," 516–517; and A. Reid, *Southeast Asia in the Age of Commerce, 1450–1680* (New Haven, CT: Yale University Press, 1990), 220–226.

[40]This is the heart of Michael Robert's famous assertion of a sixteenth- and seventeenth-century military revolution that effectively propelled European military organization and technology to the global forefront. However, one of his critics, Geoffrey Parker, argues that it was based on the fifteenth-century developments. Clifford Rogers, ed., *The Military Revolution Debate: Readings on the Military Transformation of Early Modern Europe* (Boulder, CO: Westview Press, 1995).

[41]Parry, *The Age of Reconnaissance*, 56, 120.

[42]Ibid., 57–65; and N.A.M. Rodger, "Guns and Sails in the First Phase of English Colonization, 1500–1650," in *The Oxford History of the British Empire*, vol. I, *The Origins of Empire*, edited by Nicholas Canny (Oxford: Oxford University Press, 1998), 80–81.

[43]Rodger, "Guns and Sails," 85–91.

[44]P.J. Marshall, "Western Arms in Maritime Asia in the Early Phases of Expansion," *Modern Asian Studies*, 14 (1980), 13–28; and John Thornton, *Africa and Africans in the Making of the Atlantic World* (Cambridge: Cambridge University Press, 1992), 40–42.

One of the great mysteries of the gunpowder empire theory is why the Ming emperors of China, the home of gunpowder, largely chose not to equip their armies with muskets and the new types of cannon. The answer certainly isn't a lack of ability. Zheng He's fifteenth-century vast fleets of enormous ships, which towered over the Portuguese caravels of later centuries, were equipped with firearms.[45] Moreover Japan, China's neighbor, developed an advanced musket industry in the 1560s. Indeed, it was the effective use of these weapons by Nobunaga and the Tokugawa's descendants that led to the island's unification.[46] Under Hideyoshi, Japan even turned these weapons against the Choson (Korean) state. Significantly, however, the musket-equipped Japanese armies failed to defeat the Choson and Ming forces that came to their aid. Such evidence, which suggests that firearms were not in all cases decisive, makes the Ming Emperor's decisions more understandable.

In fact, the search for some type of exceptional "otherness" in Ming China, popular though it is among western academics, is a misguided one. Simply put, the types of battles that were of most concern to the Ming emperors—fought against mobile nomadic armies—rendered heavy cannon useless. Ming weaponry was, in fact, sufficient for their needs, although in the long run sitting out the next stages of the gunpowder revolution would prove to be a mistake. A similar situation existed in much of Africa, where, for example, Portuguese firearms proved useless in the dense forests of Angola against bow and spear-wielding forces.[47]

SECTORAL ALLIANCES

For those states that did adopt them, however, the new weapons were not cheap—a fact that leads us to a second set of analyses concerning the rise of large states and empires—in this case combining politics, economics, and culture. Simply put, the expense of all of this new technology and the expertise needed to operate it made it necessary for sovereign rulers to turn to other segments in society who could help pay these costs. These allies could also assist the state in developing bureaucracies and in ruling new populations. Both the financial and the logistical requirements of maintaining the empire thus facilitated the formation of partnerships between the state on one hand, and merchants and religious authorities on the other. Moreover, existing land-owning elites also often remained an important part of the equation. In short, rulers turned to these groups in search of money. In return, each group demanded certain concessions, often asking to have a say in the making of laws. Political scientists describe the resulting collaboration between governments on the one hand and financial, religious, and military elites on the other as an alliance of several sectors.[48]

Nowhere was the relationship between imperial ruler and sectors of society more complex than in the Mughal state under Akbar. The Tīmūrid Emperor was backed up by a sophisticated set of institutions that centralized power in his hands. The most obvious were the class of military commanders, or **Mansabdari**, who owed allegiance to the emperor. This multi-ethnic martial aristocracy included Iranians, Central Asians, and Indians; Hindus, Sikhs, and Muslims. The mansabdari were ranked according to importance, and some of the most significant had personal relationships with the emperor as disciples in a royal cult that transcended religion, ethnicity, and family identity.[49] The emperor and his military officials alike were sustained by a system of

---

[45] Kuei-Sheng Chang, "The Maritime Scene in China at the Dawn of Great European Discoveries," *Journal of the American Oriental Society*, 94 (1974), 347–359.

[46] Conrad Totman, *A History of Japan* (New York: Wiley-Blackwell, 2005), 205–209.

[47] John K. Thornton, "The Art of War in Angola, 1575–1680," *Comparative Studies in Society and History*, 30 (1988), 360–378.

[48] These have been remarked upon in early modern Europe frequently, but existed elsewhere to similar degrees. David B. Abernethy, *The Dynamics of Global Dominance: European Overseas Empires, 1415–1980* (New Haven, CT: Yale University Press, 2000), 35–38, 61–63.

[49] J.F. Richards, "Formulation of Imperial Authority Under Akbar and Jahangir," in *The Mughal State 1526–1750*, edited by Muzaffar Alam and Sanjay Subrahmanyan (Delhi: Oxford University Press, 1998), 21–22, 151–153.

landed gentry, or **zamindari**, who held title to both vast and in some cases quite tiny cultivated lands.[50] Many of the mansabdari and zamindari invested heavily in both internal and long-distance commerce, and by the seventeenth century a type of royal trade in which the state invested in commerce also developed.[51] At the same time, Akbar relied for both religious and legal advice upon Sufi Muslim leaders from Central Asia and India. He sponsored orthodox Muslim orders, but at the same time was generally tolerant of the variety of faiths within his state.[52] This brought Akbar into conflict with *ulamâ*, or religious magistrates, and his successors would eventually abandon this broad-mindedness.

The Ottoman state, as well, combined a potent mix of religious, land-owning, and commercial elites. At its heart was the feudal *timar* system, by which the Sultan granted rural landholding rights to feudal knights, or **sipâhîs**, in return for military and administrative service. However, in the fifteenth and sixteenth centuries, the Ottoman Empire was also a center of global commerce. Thus, the Ottomans specifically sponsored the development of commercial society, including welcoming Jews evicted from Christian Europe. Sultans such as Bayezid I (1389–1403) and Mehmed II used their control of important trade routes as a foreign relations tool. Internally, they carefully regulated the guilds, or *hirfet*, and also protected them from external threats.[53] Both Muslims and non-Muslims could be members of guilds, but despite this general tolerance the Sultan's identity as the champion of Sunnî Islam and supreme representative of Sharî'a law was central to his power and authority. The Ottoman ulamâ were more closely integrated into the state than in the Mughal Empire. Many served as *kâdîs* (religious magistrates who also served as the state's legal system) and were closely aligned

with the army.[54] Both institutions were seen as extensions of the Sultanate, and helped to enforce his will within the empire and without. This alliance gave a flavor of religious crusade to Ottoman expansions, both against the Shî'i Safavî and against Christian states. The complex motivations for Ottoman expansions thus often combined elements of military aspiration, pursuit of economic gain, and militant Islamic objectives. However, both the Ottoman emperors and the religious authorities were generally pragmatically broad-minded.[55] Non-Muslims were organized into special communities, or **millets**, and enjoyed tolerance in return for special duties.

Religion similarly played an important role in the development of Christian-dominated imperial states. This was particularly true of societies that bordered Muslim competitors, especially Russia, Spain, and Ethiopia. Russian imperialism contained a very strong sense of an Orthodox Christian mission, especially after the fall of Constantinople to the Ottomans.[56] After 1589, Russian czars even appointed their own independent patriarch of the Orthodox Church. Although this militant Christianity had to be tempered by the realities of ruling large numbers of Muslims, it remained an important aspect of Russian imperial rhetoric, and Orthodox priests remained among the most vocal proponents of expansionism. Other proponents included the sons of middle-class and aristocratic families seeking land of their own. In annexing Novgorod in 1470, Ivan III expropriated all of the land owned by local landlords and turned it over to these young men. In return, they committed themselves to serve in the military in times of war, and thus increased the Russian central government's ability to wage war and mobilize resources.[57] Commercial interests contributed to empire-building as well. As the Russians expanded into Siberia, family firms such as the Stroganovs set up vast

[50] S. Nural Hasan, "Zamindars under the Mughals," in Alam and Subrahmanyan, *The Mughal State*, 284–300.
[51] Alam and Subrahmanyan, *The Mughal State*, 26–28.
[52] Richards, *The Mughal Empire*, 30–33, 34–36, 60, 153–158.
[53] M.A. Cook, ed., *Studies in the Economic History of the Middle East* (London: Oxford University Press, 1970), 207–218.

[54] Hodgson, *The Gunpowder Empires*, 101–109.
[55] Inalcik, *The Ottoman Empire*.
[56] Khodarkovsky, *Russia's Steppe Frontier*, 2, 34, 103–104.
[57] Dominic Lieven, *Empire: The Russian Empire and Its Rivals* (New Haven, CT: Yale University Press, 2002), 240.

economic networks and even employed Cossack mercenaries to defeat the Siberian Khanates. Imperial soldiers and forts soon followed.[58]

For the Catholic rulers of the Spanish and Austrian Habsburg empires, Islam was not the only religious foe—Protestantism too threatened the foundations of the Church *and* the state. To fund the fight against Protestant "heresy" and Muslim states at the same time required a complex balancing act. The Spanish crown controlled two of the most significant mercantile regions in the Low Countries (Spanish Netherlands) and in portions of Italy, but silver from the Americas was increasingly important as a source of income as well. The Castilian nobility could be counted upon to pay taxes regularly, but the Aragonese and other subjects could not. In the east, the German states of the Holy Roman Empire contributed little to the Austrian Habsburg emperors, who relied mostly on revenue from the wealthy provinces of Bohemia.[59] Both sets of Habsburg monarchs were closely affiliated with the Catholic Church, and their intolerance of Protestantism gradually increased during this period. Rudolf II of Austria (1576–1612) was militantly anti-Protestant and allied himself closely with the clergy in persecuting Protestants during and after the Thirty Years' War.[60] The Church's support was also a significant prop to royal authority in the continuing conflict against the Ottoman Empire in Hungary and elsewhere.

The consolidation of Spain by Ferdinand and Isabella and of the Portuguese state in the fifteenth century mobilized Church, landed gentry, and merchant-bankers, even while the sovereigns of both states sought to control these various groups. Spain's 1482–1492 conquest of the last Muslim state on the Iberian Peninsula, Granada, was funded by the Church as well as Italian and Jewish financiers.[61] Subsequently, the Castilian Cardinal Cisneros promised to turn over the income of his entire diocese to the King if he would invade Muslim Africa. Spanish aristocrats also supported the reconquista or elimination of Muslim states from the Iberian Peninsula, not only out of ideology but also as a way to acquire new tracts of land. Yet landowners, too, were important components of Iberian overseas expansion. Before 1492, the gradual acquisition of formerly Muslim territories had meant that new land had periodically become available to Spanish and Portuguese aristocrats and their sons. After the fall of Granada, however, this process came to an end, and new land became scarce. Thus, aristocrats—and especially second and third sons who stood to inherit little—looked to the overseas empire as a place to acquire lands and wealth.[62] This combination of Church, bankers (many of them foreign), militarized aristocrats, and a growing body of merchants became even more important as Spain and Portugal turned their attentions overseas. The Church also provided an ideology of the ongoing crusade against Islam and the duty of converting non-Christians overseas, while financiers helped fund state-sponsored voyages of exploration and conquest in hopes of high profits, and soldier-aristocrats of the reconquista quickly became *conquistadors*. At the center of these webs were the royal courts of Spain and Portugal, which developed and disseminated across their two states the sense of a royal prerogative and a Christian duty to create an empire.

The integration of state, Church, finance, and military was, in fact, never entirely completed in either Spain or Portugal. Religious orders—like the Jesuits—and knightly orders often pursued their own goals, as did the merchants who often competed with royal trading monopolies. Yet the sectoral alliances in Spain and Portugal were mutually supportive of an aggressive, outward looking set of policies emanating from the monarchies. Scholars have often compared this Iberian culture of exploration with that of Ming China,

---

[58] Kappeler, *The Russian Empire*, 34–35.
[59] Charles Ingrao, *The Habsburg Monarchy 1618–1815* (Cambridge: Cambridge University Press, 1994), 11–13; and Paul Kennedy, *The Rise and Fall of the Great Powers: Economic Change and Military Conflict from 1500 to 2000* (New York: Vintage Books, 1989), 43–44.
[60] Ingrao, *The Habsburg Monarchy*, 36–38.

[61] Kamen, *Empire*, 15–18.
[62] Parry, *The Age of Reconnaissance*, 20.

which seemed after 1430 to turn inward and even become isolationist. Thus, they have created the idea of a vibrant, innovative culture in the west and a stagnating culture in the east. In fact, the turn inward in China was a result only of government policies, rather than any cultural shift away from commerce. Even as the Ming emperors refused to sponsor overseas commercial and military endeavors, Chinese merchants continued to be as entrepreneurial as those of any other region. In the fifteenth and sixteenth centuries, Chinese merchant-family networks built strong and lasting ties with South-East Asia, Japan, the Philippines, and other regions. In South-East Asia, some even came to assume important political roles as key supporters of commercially oriented regimes. Around these family firms, communities of Chinese traders and migrants developed in states across the western Pacific, and as a result a China-centered economy continued to dominate the region. Thus, sixteenth- and seventeenth-century China was perhaps the greatest consumer of silver from the Spanish colonies in the Americas, and the producer of what were arguably the finest consumer goods in the world.[63]

Why then did the Ming emperors choose not to support these ventures with state resources? One compelling argument has to do with the special sectoral alliances that formed under the Ming emperors. China's exploding population and dynamic economic growth in this period is startling, but little of this money reached the Ming emperors, who were isolated from the increasingly commercial urban population of China by a powerful class of land-owning aristocrats and imperial bureaucrats that sought to maintain power by excluding the growing merchant class.[64] The power of the land-owning families was based largely upon their ability to address the government's need to feed and manage the largest, most populous of the early modern states largely from resources found within the state. As a result, not only were merchants' interests not strongly represented in the court, but those trading

overseas were especially sidelined. While this unique alignment may indeed highlight the differences between the expansionist policies of Spain and the internally concentrated policies of the post-1433 Ming emperors, these differences merely reflect the manner in which two early modern states responded to different local realities. For China, these included the fact that the Ming dynasty ruled a territory that was already perhaps as large as was manageable using early modern technology, whose internal trade was larger than that of Europe as a whole, and that was culturally and historically cohesive. Such considerations are evidenced by Ming decisions not to intervene in neighboring states or actively support Chinese merchant communities overseas.[65]

The Ming example, while unique, demonstrates that the formation of sectoral alliances was a shared strategy of empire-building states across Eurasia in this period, and not one unique only to Europe. These alliances were significant not only in strengthening the state, but also because they gave different groups within society the ability to shape the ways in which empires expanded and functioned in this period.

THE SEARCH FOR LEGITIMACY

The third set of arguments about the connected nature of these early modern states and empires is that they all had to seek ways to get their populations to acknowledge the **legitimacy**—or right to rule—of their ruling families and elites. Armies of soldiers, bureaucrats, and merchant fleets were the most obvious agents of the imperial state, but they could not alone convince the general populace of the legitimacy of the state. Thus beneath them, empires mobilized intellectual, historical, and religious claims of sovereignty and legitimacy aimed at their own people, at potential challengers, and at competing states. Most often, these claims represented popular ideologies adapted to the service of the state. Because of the multi-sectoral alliance structure of gunpowder

---

[63] Mote, *Imperial China*, 717–721.
[64] Ringrose, *Expansion and Global Interaction*, 168–172.

[65] An interesting study on this topic is Lo, "Policy Formulation and Decision-Making."

states, these ideologies usually incorporated elements that could serve the interests of important commercial, religious, and sometimes land-owning elites, as well as the monarch and his court. In the case of the great empires of the early modern world, they were also linked to worldviews that had expansionist or outward-looking components and that amounted essentially to *cultures of imperialism.*

Portugal is an excellent example of the development of this type of culture. In their struggle to dominate powerful political, military, and religious groups and to defeat the Muslim Almoravids in southern Portugal, the Portuguese kings had in the twelfth and thirteenth centuries developed a crusading ideology. This sense of a religious duty bound the nobility to the king and also increased the sovereign's popularity. Therefore, rather than abandoning the crusading ideology following the expulsion of the Muslims from the Iberian Peninsula, Dom Manuel I developed it into a form of royal messianism, through which he came to believe that he had been chosen to liberate Jerusalem. His strategy for achieving this goal was the unification of European and Ethiopian Christians, which helps to explain both his support for expeditions to the east and the aid Portugal gave to Ethiopia in its struggle against Muslim rivals. However, Manuel's religious goals by no means conflicted with Portugal's commercial objectives: the struggle against the Egyptian Mamlûks and later the Ottomans not only reflected Portugal's sense of a religious duty but at the same time helped to establish a Portuguese monopoly of the pepper and spice trade from Asia to Europe by blocking an alternate trade route through Egypt to Venice. Both Portuguese and foreign merchants at Manuel's court lobbied for state funds to be committed to eastward exploration and overseas expansion, and Manuel's support for these ventures marks their ascendance over land-owning aristocrats.[66]

Portugal was not the only state to incorporate Christianity into its sense of an imperial mission. Spanish identity, too, was bound up in the reconquista and the subsequent expulsion of Jews and Muslims, and later in the struggle of Philip II against both Protestantism and rebellion in the Netherlands. The Austrian Habsburgs, as well, used their status as champions of the Catholic Church both to promote their struggle against the Ottomans and to justify their suppression of regional autonomy and local authorities in Bohemia and Hungary during the Thirty Years' War.[67] The Habsburgs also employed a second claim to legitimacy—their designation as Holy Roman emperors. Although the Holy Roman Empire was entirely dysfunctional after the fifteenth century, and although its German states were in effect wholly autonomous, the Habsburgs' claim to the title asserted their right to rule as heirs to the Roman emperors.

Russian imperial identity, too, asserted the czar's position as defender of the Church and heir to the Roman emperors. The title *czar* itself is a derivation of the Roman title Emperor, or *Caesar*, and its assumption by Ivan IV (1530–1584) in 1547 indicated the maturity of the Russian sense of an imperial mission. Although Ivan II had also called himself czar, few foreign rulers of his day had recognized the title and Vasilii III had abandoned it. By reclaiming the title czar, Ivan IV declared his sole *imperium* over Russia. By proclaiming it without the Pope's explicit consent, he declared his independence from the Pope and laid his claim to the position of defender of Christianity. His coronation also asserted his right to rule all of the lands of the Khanate of the Golden Horde. His subsequent invasion of Kazan and Astrakhan backed his grandiose coronation with actions, but the Christian identity of the imperial mission necessitated that the Muslim population of his empire be ruled as subjects, rather than citizens.[68]

---

[66] Subrahmanyan, *The Portuguese Empire*, 49–51; and Luís Filipe Thomaz, "Factions, Interests, and Messianism: The Politics of Portuguese Expansion in the East, 1500–1521," *Indian Economic and Social History Review*, 28 (1991), 98–109.

[67] Many of the Spanish and the Austrian Habsburg monarchs clearly took this role very seriously. Mamatey, *Rise of the Habsburg Empire*, 8, 38–57.

[68] Khodarkovsky, *Russia's Steppe Frontier*, 34, 40, 103–104; and Kappeler, *The Russian Empire*, 14.

Like the Russians, the Mughal emperors combined religious and historical claims to legitimate their sovereignty over a vast and multi-ethnic empire. Because, however, they relied on Hindu and Sikh as well as Muslim elites to hold the empire together, their ideology was, at least initially, far more focused on dynastic heritage than religious mission. Under Akbar, the expanding empire was bound together by imperial mythology that held the emperor to be the infallible heir to Tīmūr, and essentially a divine figure at the center of a wide ring of discipleship, by which leading officials, zamindari, and mansabdari bound themselves in a solemn commitment ceremony—incorporating aspects of different faiths—to obey and to serve him.[69] Subsequent emperors, however, turned toward a stricter Muslim ideology. Aurangzeb (1658–1707) completed this transition by embracing the idea of an imperial duty to spread Islamic law, by elevating the power of the ulamâ, and by discriminating against non-Muslim subjects of the empire.[70]

Ottoman claims to imperial legitimacy matured in the sixteenth century through the dual processes of autocratic centralization and assumption of religious authority as inheritors of the mantle of the Prophet. Although the authority of early Sultans was heavily restricted by powerful soldiers-turned-landowners—the *ghâzîs*—the development of the Janissary corps, a ranking system for all civilians and military officials, and a ceremonial royal court under Mehmed II gave the Sultan a type of imperial sovereignty. This development of autocratic rule was supported by an absolutist ideology, which declared that all officials were ritually *slaves* of the Sultan, who represented both religious and temporal authority.[71] This trend peaked under Selim I, who built up the Janissaries to defeat the Mamlûks, and thus elevated his personal power at the expense of the ghâzîs. By capturing the holy cities of Medina and Mecca from the Mamlûks, Selim was also able to use Islam as a central prop of his authority to a greater degree

than his predecessors. He added to his titles the designation Caliph—the chosen successors to the Prophet—and the Sunnî ulamâ of the empire, at least, accepted this claim.

Unlike the other major early modern empires, Ming China was based on a historically cohesive and coherent Chinese state that had pre-existed under a number of dynasties culminating in the Song period immediately prior to Mongol rule. Zhu Yanzhang carefully designed his imperial ideology to capitalize on the existing Chinese identity even before he became the Hongwu Emperor. The doctrine of the Red Turban sect of which he was a principal leader was openly anti-Mongol, and it therefore embraced a somewhat xenophobic ethnic Chinese sentiment. During the early years of his struggle for power, he rapidly attached himself to the "Little Prince of Radiance," who was claimed to be a descendant of the last Song emperor. Yet he abandoned both his pledged loyalty to the "restored" Song and to the Red Turbans after he had built a large following among Chinese landowners and scholar-bureaucrats and came into possession of sufficient authority to claim the throne for himself in 1367. Nevertheless, Zhu found it expedient to name his new dynasty Ming, or "radiance," after the "Little Prince" in recognition of the people's sentiments.[72] As the Hongwu Emperor, Zhu claimed to have restored Chinese rule to China and asserted that his victories were proof of the God's approval, or "mandate of heaven." These two ideas remained intertwined as the principal ideological props of the Ming emperors' rule.

SUB-SAHARAN AFRICAN EMPIRES?

While the revival of trade and the gunpowder revolution helped to spur the growth of large states in Eurasia and North Africa during the period from the late fourteenth to the early seventeenth century, not all regions of the world necessarily experienced similar trends. Indeed, the populations of much of sub-Saharan Africa, Australasia, and the Americas as well as some parts of Europe and Asia

---

[69] Richards, "Formulation of Imperial Authority," 151–153.
[70] Richards, *The Mughal Empire*, 171–178.
[71] Hodgson, *The Gunpowder Empires*, 100–104.

[72] Mote, *Imperial China*, 558–532, 559.

were outside of the Eurasian and North African zone of state-building. Nevertheless, this does not mean that states and empires did not develop and exist in these regions during this period. In subsequent chapters, for example, we will explore the large states of the fourteenth-century meso-America and the Andean zone of South Africa. But it is appropriate here to discuss whether sub-Saharan Africa had empires during this period.

We have already seen that much of coastal Africa was very much part of the story of reviving global trade in the fifteenth and sixteenth centuries. The Swahili city-states, Senegambians, Ethiopians, the peoples of the Gold Coast and even regions further south traded and otherwise interacted with Ottoman, Portuguese, and Mughal subjects as well as each other. However, because of the obstacle of the vast Sahara desert and because of distance, wind patterns, and ecological differences events within Africa tended to dominate the ways in which states formed in these regions.

In most contemporary world history textbooks, it has become common to label a number of early modern African states as empires. These include the West African states of Ghana, Mali, and Songhai along with Central Africa polities such as Luba, Lunda, and Kongo and of course Ethiopia. There are numerous reasons why this has happened. In the first place, later rulers of these areas claimed descent from early emperors. Similarly, early North African and European explorers and missionaries often applied to the states they encountered titles such as "kingdom," "empire," and "caliphate" in an attempt to understand them in familiar language. Lastly, modern scholars of Africa seeking to reverse the idea of the continent as "backward" and "tribal" have often endorsed these titles. Yet are they correct? Did empires in fact exist in sub-Saharan Africa in the early modern period?

Certainly, numerous states existed in Africa south of the Sahara during this time. Yet African historian John Thornton has pointed out that most of them were relatively small.[73] Simply put, most of sub-Saharan Africa did not experience the

same trends of centralization and expansion as Eurasia and North Africa during this period. This does not prove, however, that there were no early modern sub-Saharan African empires. In fact, we have plenty of evidence of several very large states in the West African region just south of the Sahara after 1250 including Mali and Songhai, both of which may have controlled up to 1 million square kilometers. While not as large as the Ottoman Empire at its height (4 million square kilometers) or the Mughal state (almost 2 million square kilometers), these are nevertheless sizable states. Similarly, large states existed south of the vast Congo rain forests including after 1390 Kongo, which figures heavily in the story of Portuguese expansion discussed in the next chapter.

Were these large states in fact empires? Size alone cannot prove anything. In going back to our definition of empire used in this book, we must look at questions of authority and control, of differentiation between metropolitan citizens and subjects, and of networks of exchange between metropole and periphery. Thornton, for example, would probably argue that most sub-Saharan African states in this period were more like confederations—alliances of small states tied together—than empires.[74] In this section, we will explore whether the title *empire* applied well to the three most likely candidates in this region and period—Mali, Songhai, and Kongo.

It makes sense to begin with the state Thornton knows the most about: Kongo. This long-lived state on the west coast of Central Africa seems to have formed around 1390 and to have existed at least until the late seventeenth century, when it fragmented under both external and internal pressures.[75] There is a debate about the origins of the state that is important to our understanding of its configuration. We have no written sources from this area for the late fourteenth century, and most local oral sources suggest that its leaders were descendants of invaders who had conquered the peasants who made up

---

[73] Thornton, *Africa and Africans*, 103–104.

[74] Ibid., 9.

[75] Another state later formed in about the same region, but in a different configuration and under different leadership.

most of the rural population. This story has been used to explain the dualism of Kongolese society, which in the sixteenth and seventeenth centuries seems to have been split into a rural peasantry and an urban nobility in the capital of São Salvadore who lived off the peasants' surplus as well as luxury goods produced by slaves on plantations around the capital city.[76] Yet Thornton doubts this explanation. Instead, he argues, this division obscures the origins of the Kongolese state as a confederation. Although later kings seem to have sponsored stories of earlier military prowess as a means of legitimizing their rule, there is evidence in these stories that the urban nobility of the sixteenth and seventeenth centuries were descended from many lineages (families) who were rulers of multiple small states that fused by marriage with the rulers of Kongo.[77] Only some peripheral provinces seem to have been added by conquest, and many of these remained nominally independent so long as they paid an annual tribute.

Nevertheless, it could be argued that Kongo had a metropole–periphery configuration, if a rather different one than most Eurasian empires. The metropole in this case was the capital, where almost the entirety of the nobility lived and which had an economic system based on slave labor. By contrast, the rural provinces largely produced food through communal or family-based labor systems. These provinces were ruled by nobles temporarily dispatched from the interior, whose main job was to collect food surpluses for the capital. The stability of the state was based on the fact that there was only really one prize for any power-seekers: the capital. Whoever controlled São Salvadore controlled the state. Indeed, arguably, the reason it finally broke up in the seventeenth century was that Portuguese trade helped to revive several provincial towns, which then became centers for dissidents to gather in

order to challenge the central authorities.[78] Based on the difference between the urban center and rural periphery of Kongo, the argument could be made that Kongo was a confederation that at some point turned into a sort of an empire.

Was this a common process in sub-Saharan Africa? Certain similarities seem to exist in the so-called Sahelian region just to the south of the Sahara Desert. There, a series of states succeeded one another beginning with Ghana (Wagadou), which emerged from a small base in the tenth century to control the important trading centers of the Niger bend for about a century, followed by Mali (c.1235–1550), which gradually ceded power to a rival to the east called Songhai (c.1390–1591). Both Ghana and later Songhai were apparently the victims of invasions from Morocco in 1054 and 1591, although neither of these resulted in a long occupation by North Africans.

Although typically now described as a sequence of empire, the situation in the Sahel seems to have been rather more complex. Unlike in much of Eurasia, populations in this part of Africa were relatively sparse, especially away from the river. As a result, control over land was less important than control over people. Less powerful groups often affiliated with their more powerful neighbors through negotiated relationships, through the payment of annual tributes, or sometimes through forced enslavement. Relationships among the more powerful were characterized by shifting patterns of extended family alliances and at times warfare. The object of this maneuvering was to control the gold and salt trade between North and West Africa and especially the trading centers of Timbuktu, Gao, and Jenné. Safe (or isolated) from the effects of the Mongols and the spread of gunpowder armies, these patterns provided continuity from the Ghana period into the era of Songhai ascendancy.

---

[76] John Thornton, "The Kingdom of Kongo, ca. 1390–1678: The Development of an African Social Formation," *Cahiers d'Études Africaines*, 22 (1982), 326–329.

[77] John Thornton, "The Origins and Early History of the Kingdom of Kongo, c.1350–1550," *International Journal of African Historical Studies*, 34 (2001), 102, 104, 111.

---

[78] Much of this paragraph is based on Thornton, "The Kingdom of Kongo," 326–329, 338.

One example is that of the best-known Sahelian states: Mali. Conventional histories of this state depict it as an empire created by a Mande-speaking king named Mārī-Djāta or Sundiata (c.1235–1255), who was the creator of an empire that reached its height during the rule of the glorious and expansive Mansā (king) Mūsā I in the late fourteenth century. These Mansā and their successors ruled their vast empire, including the important trading from a capital called Mande Kaba (modern Kangaba), using imperial administrators to rule a core area that was culturally Mande and armies (*sofas*) to conquer non-Mande speakers and incorporate them into the empire.[79]

However, recent scholarship suggests that the Malian state was more of a confederation than a centralized empire. Jan Jansen, for example, has suggested that imperial Mali was really a "segmentary" society of relatively equal and allied extended families (*kafuw*) and that Mārī-Djāta was just a temporary war leader.[80] The "empire" was thus built by a core group of kafuw who were allied over long periods of time, and occasionally spun off groups who conquered outsiders and ruled them as essentially independent polities. Similarly, Kathryn L. Green suggests that Mande Kaba was not really an imperial capital or seat of an empire. Instead, the idea that it had been was introduced by much later rulers of a much-reduced Mali state to legitimize their own rule.[81]

Yet this formulation does not exclude the possibility of Mali being an "empire" of a somewhat decentralized sort. At least by the time of Mūsā I, there existed a Mande-speaking metropole of shared language and cultural values, whereas many non-Mande-speaking groups from the Gambia River area all the way east to the middle Niger River were ruled as subordinates by Mande-speaking elites who had trade and cultural ties to the core. The rebellion of some of these groups, including the inhabitants of Songhai, helped to fragment this large state in early sixteenth century.

The sixteenth-century Songhai, which succeeded Mali as the largest Sahelian state, similarly ruled many different groups including (as defined by their languages) Fube, Soninke, Tuareg, Dogo, Bambara, and Bozo. Equally importantly, like Mali they came to control the major trading center of Timbuktu. Under the rule of the Askia dynasty, the Songhai ruling class became increasingly Muslim, and Islam became a defining feature of citizenship. This essentially created a colonial underclass of "traditionalists," non-Muslims in the provinces who were not forced to convert but were nevertheless restricted from entering the ruling elite. Most Muslims were concentrated in Timbuktu and the 11 core provinces of the state, while further provinces that were mostly not Muslim were ruled by imperial governors.[82] Perhaps because of its economic importance and its Muslim majority, Timbuktu seems to have enjoyed an intermediate status with local administrators (kâdîs, as in the Ottoman Empire, but loyal to the local population more than the state) and imperial officers sharing power.[83]

Were these sub-Saharan African states actually empires? The difficulty in answering this question comes largely from the problems of applying a Eurasian term to African situations. As we discussed in the introduction, our understanding of "empire" is shaped by the western empires more familiar to us, many of which were much more centralized than these African states. Yet this does not necessarily mean that there were not

[79] The father of the study of this region using Arabic sources is Nehemia Levtzion. See especially Nehemia Levtzion, *Ancient Ghana and Mali* (London: Metheun and Co, 1973).

[80] Jan Jansen, "The Representation of Status in Mande: Did the Mali Empire Still Exist in the Nineteenth Century?" *History in Africa*, 23 (1996), 87–109; and "Polities and Political Discourse: Was Mande Already a Segmentary Society in the Middle Ages?" *History in Africa*, 23 (1996), 121–128.

[81] Kathryn L. Green, " 'Mande Kaba' the Capital of Mali: A Recent Invention," *History in Africa*, 18 (1991), 127–135.

[82] John O. Hunwick, "Songhay, Borno and the Hausa States, 1450–1600," *History of West Africa*, vol. I, 3rd ed., edited by J.F.A. Ajayi and Michael Crowder (New York: Columbia University Press, 1985), 323–371.

[83] Michael A. Gomez, "Timbuktu Under Imperial Songhay: A Reconsideration of Autonomy," *Journal of African History*, 31 (1990), 5–24.

similar processes at play in both sets of states, which may be enough to convince us that the term *can* appropriately be applied to Songhai, Kongo, and/or Mali.

Conclusion

In Eurasia and North Africa, early modern empires were created out of the context of the economic revival of the early modern era. The wealth generated by this revival drove commercial rivalries, and new weapons technologies were adopted to fight these conflicts. However, only large, centralized states could afford to compete at this level, and thus commercial conflicts drove imperial expansion and interaction at several levels. The conquest of new territories increased the tax base, whether by acquiring taxable farmers or by gaining control of trade. In their drive to acquire these new territories, monarchs often sought funds from other sectors of their societies, and imperial expansion thus often came to serve *their* needs—whether economic, evangelical, or political. Finally, in order to maintain control over both powerful sectors of society and the general population, rulers devised ideologies and notions of a national mission that amounted to cultures of imperialism. This process differed somewhat but not entirely from other parts of the world such as sub-Saharan Africa, where distinctive processes were at work.

As we shall see in the next chapter, this process created a competitive environment that promoted imperialism on a global scale. It also ushered in exploitative systems of colonialism. The linking of Eurasia and North Africa with sub-Saharan Africa, the Americas, and Polynesia expanded and extended these trends. Together, these regions participated in the development of early modern forms of empires, imperialism, and colonialism that were analogous, but not identical, to those of later centuries.

Questions

1. Why did so many empires and large states form in Eurasia and North Africa in this period? What factors enabled or caused this transformation to happen? What was the role of commerce and technology?

2. Explain how strategies of centralization, rationalization, and expansion characterized the states in the Habsburg Empire, the Russian Empire, Ming China, Tīmūrid (Mughal) India and Central Asia, and the Ottoman Empire in this period.

3. Compare and contrast the operation of sectoral alliances in the Habsburg Empire, the Russian Empire, Ming China, Tīmūrid (Mughal) India and Central Asia, and the Ottoman Empire.

4. What tools, messages, and agents did the Portuguese kings, the Habsburg emperors, the Rurik and Romanov (Russian) czars, the Ming emperors of China, the Tīmūrid (Mughal) emperors, and the Ottoman sultans use to legitimize their rule in this period? What, if any, general conclusions can you draw from this?

5. Consider the information presented about Mali, Songhai, and Kongo. Given the definition used in this book, would you define these states as empires at their height? Why or why not?

CHAPTER **2**

Imperialism and Colonialism: Imperial Interaction and Nascent Colonialism in Early Modern Eurasia and North Africa

We have seen in chapter 1 that expansive, competitive centralized states developed across large areas of Eurasia and Africa between 1380 and 1650. In looking back, historians refer to only some of these polities as empires. However, their application of the label is inconsistent: historians often disagree whether individual states were empires, and what the term even means for this period. In this chapter, we employ the term as it is applied throughout the book. Only certain states in this period can accurately be said to have exhibited the discrimination among internal territories and populations that marked them as empires complete with policies and practices of colonialism. A number of Eurasian states in this period are commonly called *empires*—specifically the Russian, Habsburg Austrian, Spanish, Portuguese, Ottoman, and Mughal empires. Yet other states emerging in this era—such as France, Burma, and Morocco—are more typically described as emerging "nation-states." Although they sometimes found themselves populated by groups with separate identities and senses of belonging, their strategies for dealing with these internal divisions were usually aimed at fully assimilating these various peoples into the general population, and thus in developing a "national" identity. Were the Russian, Habsburg, Spanish, Portuguese, Ottoman, and Mughal states somehow different? And if so, can they be said to have developed cultures of imperialism, to have pursued policies of colonialism, and to have employed imperial modes of interaction?

In attempting to answer this question, we must first admit that any division of early modern polities into "nation-states" and "empires" is somewhat misleading. For one thing, some scholars still doubt that the labels *colonialism* and *imperialism* are really applicable to any states in this period. Additionally, many borderline cases existed, such as England, Ethiopia, Safavî Persia, Ming China, and Vietnam. These states sometimes employed policies of colonialism before 1650, but tended to absorb and assimilate the population groups of their early conquest. For the vast empires of early modern Eurasia, however, such policies were not practicable. These sprawling territorial and maritime empires—the Portuguese and Spanish empires, the domains of the Austrian Habsburgs, the Ottoman Sultanate and the Mughal Empire, and Russia—found it impossible for a variety of reasons to entirely absorb their many, multi-ethnic, and often unwilling subjects. In this chapter, we will discuss these empires through two themes: the origins and development of early modern colonialism and the development of a global imperial system of interaction.

Scholars have usually avoided using the term *colonialism* to describe the strategies by which early modern empires ruled non-metropolitan populations, preferring to reserve it for the nineteenth- and twentieth-century overseas empires. In the first two sections of this chapter, we break that division by presenting evidence that early modern empires experimented with and pioneered modern forms of colonialism. In the first section, we look at colonialism as it developed in each of the great early modern empires in turn. In the second section, we compare these narratives and suggest several commonalities and themes. Perhaps the most fundamental of these is the importance of local as well as metropolitan factors in shaping the relationship between the imperial government and its colonial subjects. The narratives also suggest that, as in later periods, early modern empires ruled through a wide variety of official and unofficial agents and by employing a diversity of strategies including settlement, negotiation, and force.

Externally, the great multi-ethnic empires found themselves interacting with each other and with other states and peoples in an increasingly competitive and interlinked global context. Much of the attention scholars have showered upon this early modern "globalization" has come from economic historians, who have endlessly debated the size and implications of inter-regional trade in this period. Viewed from a political perspective, however, early modern globalization can arguably be understood as a story of imperial rivalry, characterized by interlocking alliances, political-economic competition, and open warfare. This global imperial interaction is the topic of the third and fourth sections, discussed first in economic and then in political terms.

In the fifth section, we explore the Portuguese maritime empire in Africa and Asia as a variation on both trends of colonialism and imperial interaction.

As in the previous chapter, the peoples of the Americas and the European empires being established there are discussed only peripherally, largely because these are the topics of chapters 3 and 4. It is important to remember, however, that the stories of early modern Eurasia and Africa on the one hand, and the Americas and the Atlantic on the other, were closely intertwined during this period.

MODELS OF EARLY MODERN COLONIALISM

Why did some early modern states turn toward structures and policies that appear imperial, whereas others evolved in the direction of nation-states that stressed a single, national identity? Scholars have sometimes searched for answers to this question within individual societies or by comparing two or more states. They have sought to find cultural, political, or economic differences that distinguish Mughal and Ottoman societies, for example, from early modern French and English societies. However, no national characteristic has been found to satisfactorily explain the differences between them. Our alternate explanation is both more global and more local. In the first place, empire was *mutually constructed*. In other words, imperialism and the imperial metropole came to exist alongside colonialism and the imperial periphery. Without colonialism, there could be no empire. The question thus becomes why some states became more assimilative, while others turned more to policies of colonialism. The answer is largely a matter of local conditions. While technological, bureaucratic, economic, and logistical advances that were shared across North Africa and Eurasia made it possible in the early modern era for centralized states to expand to a vast size and for centralized governments to control a vast population, in reality most states found their expansion potential was limited. The Ming emperors in 1500 may have ruled 100 million subjects with some efficacy, but no other state approached that population. Significantly, Ming China after c.1500 is notable in that it did not strive to expand formally, but rather to encourage neighboring states to pay tribute while remaining independent. Perhaps this was because its rulers knew or believed that they had hit the demographic and geographical limits of effective governance given the technology at their disposal.

Most states were halted in their ability to expand by neighboring states or by regional geography. This was true in western Europe, the Horn of Africa, and South-East Asia, for example, where the fragmented nature of the environment and the rough parity of a number of states led to consolidation of power in several hands, rather than one.[1] In Central Asia, on the other hand, the wide-open spaces and the disparity of arms and organization between Russia, the Ottomans, and the Mughals on one hand and less technologically sophisticated neighboring populations on the other facilitated the rise of empires. And size did matter. Where states remained smaller, populations were generally less heterogeneous or diverse, and as a result the state was able to concentrate on assimilating outlaying populations to the culture of the core regions. This is exactly the process that best characterizes early modern England, France, Vietnam, Burma, and Morocco, for example.[2]

States that expanded more widely, however, soon found themselves in control of vast populations that were both culturally distinct and geographically distant. Thus, situations arose in which the state was unwilling and/or unable to bring those groups to the same status as the inhabitants of the core state: the metropole. In order to rule these regions, the state and its agents formulated formal policies or haphazardly developed approaches toward the peoples of some territories that set them off as different, and usually inferior, subjects. It was this demarcation of the status of some provinces and peoples from others that defined these empires from other, more nucleated states, and that gave rise to early modern colonialism.

One important factor in the way colonialism developed was the states' sectoral alliances with metropolitan religious, land-owning, and commercial sectors described in chapter 1. Each of these groups had an agenda to pursue: landowners often expected to be able to claim additional lands in the newly acquired territories, religious elites sometimes hoped to convert conquered populations or to establish their own version of orthodoxy, and merchants generally anticipated increasing their profits at the expense of commercial and productive classes in the newly acquired territories. Thus, each sought to shape the way the newly acquired territories and populations were ruled and the rights extended to them. Meanwhile, local populations also sought to define their relationship with the state and with the population of the metropole.

Whether we search for causes in the metropole or in the imperial periphery, the fact is that in the Rurik and Romanov (Russian), Habsburg, Tîmûrid (Mughal), Ottoman, and Ming (Chinese) states certain territories came to be delineated as separate from the metropole and marked off for special treatment. Within these territories, colonial policies came to be formulated. Officials from the metropole were appointed to govern the territory and its populace. On the state's behalf, they entered into negotiations with certain local elites to win their support or at least acquiescence to the new order. Sometimes settlers were brought in from the metropole or older territories to strengthen the hand of the state. Institutions were set up to control the local populace: armies and police, churches, and sometimes schools. But control was never complete—the cooperation or at least acceptance of portions of the local population were required in order to maintain imperial rule.

We will see later that the structures and strategies of sixteenth and seventeenth century were models for subsequent empires. Yet early modern imperialism differed from that of later era. In the early modern period, for example, racism was not

---

[1] This argument is made by Paul Kennedy in *The Rise and Fall of the Great Powers: Economic Change and Military Conflict from 1500 to 2000* (New York: Vintage Books, 1989) and also by Jared Diamond, but only for Europe. See Jared Diamond, *Guns, Germs, and Steel: The Fate of Human Societies* (New York: W.W. Norton & Co., 1997), 403–425.

[2] See Victor Lieberman, "Transcending East-West Dichotomies: State and Culture Formation in Six Ostensibly Disparate Areas," *Modern Asian Studies*, 31 (1997), 476–477, 481.

yet the dominant ideology of "difference" that could be used to justify the differential rule of peoples of the imperial periphery. The dissimilarities in technology and sophistication between metropole and periphery were usually minor as well, leading at the most extreme to only very weak colonial models. Finally, the state apparatus was not yet as highly developed as it would become in future years. Thus, the type of peripheral administration we usually see in this period was haphazard, sometimes incompletely executed, and constantly evolving. Can it still be argued that these were examples of colonialism?

The forms of rule that developed under the Austrian Habsburg emperors are an instructive example. When Charles V handed over the administration of the eastern portions of the empire to Ferdinand I in 1521, his dominions included only the family's hereditary lands in Austria (the *Erblande*) and a segment of Croatia. Ferdinand also inherited Bohemia (Czechoslovakia), a small strip of Hungary following the death of their Jagellon King Louis II at the Battle of Mohács in 1526. In addition, the Habsburgs rulers were generally elected Holy Roman emperors, although functionally this was an empty title.

The main task facing Ferdinand in the sixteenth century was to weld the Bohemian, Austrian, and Hungarian lands he had inherited into a single, viable state. The task was a difficult one. Although Habsburg rule was firmly entrenched in Austria (which served as a sort of metropole for the empire), Ferdinand faced well-established and quite diffuse power structures in Bohemia and Hungary. Bohemia, which included the districts of Lusatia and Silesia, was peopled largely by ethnic Czechs, Sorbs, and relatively recent German immigrants. Under the Jagellon kings, the Bohemian *estates*—political bodies largely composed of land-owning aristocrats, knights, and in a separate college the representatives of royal towns—had enjoyed a great deal of autonomy, including the right to elect a king. Hungary was even more diverse and independent-minded. Here, Ferdinand technically inherited the state as a whole, but after the Battle of Mohács about one-third of it had fallen under Ottoman control, while the

Transylvanian region became independent. The portion to which Ferdinand managed to lay claim was peopled largely by ethnic Magyars, Slovaks, Ruthenes, Croats, and a sprinkling of Germans in the towns. The Hungarian *diet* (or parliament) consisted of two chambers. In the upper chamber sat the great land-owning aristocrats, or magnates, along with the high officers of the Church. In the lower chamber sat lower aristocrats, along with one representative from the royal towns collectively. Even in the Austrian parliament, the Erblande, Ferdinand's power was limited by the local elite of the many small districts, principalities, and church lands, some of which remained largely autonomous until 1665. Here, as in Hungary and Bohemia, the "estate" assemblies that represented the aristocrats, clergy, and large towns were in practice quite powerful. The situation in all three of these regions was further complicated by religious diversity. Although Ferdinand had inherited authority over few Muslims, both the Eastern Orthodox tradition and Protestantism were practiced within his domains.[3]

The task of unifying this decentralized agglomeration required that Ferdinand and his successors undercut the existing authorities in each region. Their biggest challenges were in Bohemia and Hungary, which were particularly independent and which possessed non-German ethnic and national identities. The estates in each were too strong and independent-minded to allow easy assimilation, and both the constant Ottoman threat and the emperor's reliance upon Bohemian taxes for the bulk of his income forced Ferdinand to compromise more than he would have liked with the landowners and city-dwellers who were the main military force and tax payers. Thus, for example, when Ferdinand attempted to restrict the Bohemian estates' rights to pass legislation, they forced him to back down by refusing to vote

---

[3] See Charles Ingrao, *The Habsburg Monarchy 1618–1815* (Cambridge: Cambridge University Press, 1994), 9–14; and Robert A. Kann and Zdeněk V. David, *The Peoples of the Eastern Habsburg Lands, 1526–1918* (Seattle: University of Washington Press, 1984), 24–28, 57–58.

the taxes he needed.[4] A similar crisis emerged in Hungary in 1530, when Ferdinand tried to replace the Hungarian *Palatin* (an official elected by the diet to administer the realm) with a royal lieutenant chosen by the emperor. The diet resisted, and Ferdinand was forced to acquiesce to a compromise by which the diet was allowed to elect a *palatinal* lieutenant to serve under the royal lieutenant and control certain judicial functions.[5]

Ferdinand and his successors did find other ways to assume control of some local political authorities in Bohemia, however. Their most important step was the suppression of local *circuit assemblies*, by which the aristocrats of each locality met to discuss politics and to implement decisions of the diet. These the emperor gradually outlawed between 1528 and 1547. An abortive uprising in 1547 also provided the justification by which he took away the autonomy of some Bohemian towns and imposed on them royal administrators and judges.[6] The continuing Ottoman threat, however, halted him from doing the same in Hungary.

Partly in reaction to the policies of Ferdinand and his successors, Protestantism in Bohemia began in the sixteenth century to take on something of the flavor of an anti-colonial movement. With many (although not all) Protestants opposed to the Habsburgs, some Protestant sects such as the Unity of Czech Brethren took on a vaguely nationalistic air. Protestantism helped to inspire and justify the 1547 uprising, which was nevertheless quickly crushed by Ferdinand. However, Bohemian Protestant resistance remerged in 1616, with the *defenestration* (ejection out of a window) of three Catholic delegates in Prague. The result was the Thirty Years' War.

The Thirty Years' War fundamentally changed the power equation in Bohemia, although less so in Hungary. In response to the defenestration and to the growing affiliation between Protestantism and anti-imperial dissidents, Emperor Ferdinand II (1619–1637) mobilized all loyal sectors of imperial society against the rebels. In 1620, imperial troops defeated a rebel army at the battle on the White Mountain, and Ferdinand rode triumphantly into Prague. He gutted the Bohemian estates, replaced their rights to "elect" Habsburgs as king with hereditary succession, and allowed loyal aristocrats to purchase at cut prices the land of fleeing Protestant landowners. Ferdinand also brought in Catholic churchmen, and especially Jesuit priests, who took over local schools and undertook a campaign of forced education, book-burning, and the re-education of peasants.[7] All officials and administrators became servants of the emperor, rather than the estates.[8] These new positions were largely occupied by ethnic Germans. In Austria and Hungary, as well, Protestantism was suppressed, but nowhere was the operation so clearly colonial as in Bohemia, where the Czechs were reduced to a "submerged nationality" of peasants, without official representation or leadership. By contrast, when Hungarian Protestants also rose against the Habsburgs the threat of Ottoman involvement aid allowed them to bring the emperor to the negotiating table, and to win certain concessions affirming their rights and religious freedoms.

Habsburg rule in both Hungary and Bohemia during the sixteenth and seventeenth centuries can be said to have had certain characteristics of modern colonialism. Throughout this period, Habsburg emperors attempted to centralize authority and imperial bureaucracy in Vienna, the capital of their Austrian metropole. Although the emperors were technically elected (and later hereditary) kings of Hungary and Bohemia, these states were treated differently than their Austrian hereditary domains. Yet the two examples of Hungary and Bohemia also point out the very different forms colonial rule could take. In Bohemia, the relative weakness of the local estates, and the position away from the military border with the Ottomans, allowed the Habsburgs to gradually reduce local autonomy. The Battle of White Mountain was merely one event in the process

---

[4] Kann and David, *The Peoples*, 27.
[5] Ibid., 61.
[6] Ibid., 31–33.

[7] Ingrao, *The Habsburg Monarchy*, 34–36.
[8] Kann and David, *The Peoples*, 104–114.

that resulted in the Habsburgization, Germanization, and Catholicization of Bohemia. The continual militarization of Hungary, by contrast, empowered the Hungarian estates, and allowed them to avoid this fate, at least so long as the Ottoman threat remained present. These differences highlight the tension between colonialism as force and oppression on the one hand, and as negotiation and accommodation on the other.

Ottoman rule of the empire's peripheries was equally complex. While most of the Ottoman provinces were administered under the timar system as districts of the metropole, several special relationships evolved between the state and conquered populations that led to the development of an imperial periphery made up of numerous, often unique arrangements. The military strength of the Khanate of Crimea forced the Ottoman rulers to extend it some autonomy. Similarly, the status of Mecca as a holy city meant that it continued to be largely autonomous under its *sharif*, a local and hereditary official. A somewhat different situation existed in the North African provinces of Algeria, Tunisia, and Tripoli, where janissary garrisons were established, but for financial and logistical reasons authority was left largely in the hands of local elites. A similar level of autonomy evolved in Egypt, Baghdad, and Basra, and along the African coast of the Red Sea where royal governors and judges (*kâdîs*) ruled the province without the aid of timar-possessing *sipâhîs*, and the local administration merely paid an annual tribute to the Sultan. The Christian, European provinces of Moldavia, Wallachia, Dubrovnik, Georgia, Circassia, and for a period Transylvania were again different.[9]

Ottoman rule was, in fact, quite flexible in accommodating local realities. Following the 1516–1517 Ottoman defeat of the Egyptian Mamlûks, for example, Ottoman Sultan Selim I installed a janissary garrison in Egypt but retained the services of a Mamlûk defector, Khãyr Bey, as the province's governor. In 1524,

Egypt was reorganized as a tributary province, with power split between janissary officers and the governor, and characterized by the retention of a number of Mamlûk administrative techniques. The janissary officers became increasingly powerful into the late sixteenth century, eventually adopting the grandiose style of the Mamlûk generals who had ruled before them, and in 1631 they even managed to replace an imperial governor with one of their own. These officers were thus able to act as almost totally independent colonial agents, so long as they paid the annual tribute to the imperial treasury. As a result, they largely became integrated into local elite circles. The same was true in the Maghreb states of Tunisia and Tripoli, where soldiers sent to aid the corsairs in their struggles against Christian fleets rapidly became entirely interlocked with the local leadership.[10]

The Ottoman administration of the largely Christian European provinces was somewhat different. Several of these provinces, for example in the Balkans, were acquired as early as the mid-fourteenth century by Sultan Murâd I (1362–1389). Eastern Hungary, conquered in 1526, was the last such acquisition. From the beginning, Ottoman rule accommodated local culture. Murâd recognized the Orthodox Church, co-opted feudal knights into the timar system, and established a uniform tax code. On the other hand, the Catholic Church was (at least in principle) abolished, and Ottoman kâdîs did impose some aspects of Sharî'a law.[11] In the fifteenth century, however, the growth in the proportion of Ottoman subjects who were Muslim led to the reorganization of non-Muslims in the Christian provinces and elsewhere into *millets*, or religious communities. In 1453, two millets were formally recognized for Orthodox and Armenian Christians, and another for Jewish subjects came into de facto existence. The leaders of these millets were often religious officials, and the Sultan co-opted them as legal authorities, responsible to a large degree for

[9]Halil Inalcik, *The Ottoman Empire: The Classical Age 1300–1600* (London: Phoenix Press, 1994), 104–118.

[10]*UNESCO General History of Africa*, vol. 5, *Africa from the Sixteenth to the Eighteenth Century* (Berkeley: University of California Press, 1999), abridged edition, 72–77, 124–126.
[11]Inalcik, *The Ottoman Empire*, 13.

civil and criminal matters, as well as consultants on taxation and public safety.[12]

While the Balkan territories were largely brought under the timar system—their Muslim and non-Muslim rural populations alike organized under *sipâhî* landowners—the more distant territories of Moldavia, Wallachia, Transylvania, Georgia, Circassia, and Dubrovnik enjoyed a status similar to that of the Khanate of Crimea. While occasionally occupied by Ottoman armies, these states were essentially independent. Thus although their rulers often acknowledged the Sultan's sovereignty and were thus regarded by the Ottomans as vassal states, they in fact acted opportunistically and sent tribute to the imperial treasury only when threatened or when it suited them. The Transylvanian princes, for example, used the threat of an Ottoman alliance to maintain their independence from the Habsburgs, but were never forced to accept an Ottoman governor. The Sultans generally accepted this relationship, since these provinces were too distant to control or even to campaign in annually.

The relationships between gunpowder empires and smaller polities in eastern Europe/western Asia were especially complex because they occurred at the intersection of Ottoman, Habsburg, and Russian spheres of influence. Transylvania, as we have seen, loosely attached itself to the Ottoman Sultans in order to maintain their independence from the Habsburgs, and the khans of Crimea similarly hoped the Ottomans would shield them from Russian expansion. Russia, in fact, was fast becoming in the sixteenth century the overlord of large numbers of Muslim subjects, just as the Ottomans ruled many Christians. This created some difficulties for Russian czars whose imperial ideology was bound closely to Orthodox militancy. While the notion of a religious mission might play well in Moscow, it did not suit the realities of ruling vast, ethnically diverse, and religiously disparate populations. Russia's early conquests—the surrounding

Slavic principalities and Novgorod—had been small, nearby, and ethnically related. Thus, the local elites could be either incorporated or, in extreme cases, replaced entirely by Russian Orthodox priests and the sons of Russian nobles.[13] In the case of Kazan and Astrakhan in the 1550s, this was clearly not possible, and as a result the surviving Muslim aristocracy in both of these states were confirmed in their lands. Their taxes, and those of the peasants, remained the same as they had been under the khans, but were redirected to the Russian treasury. The khanates were also given a special status in the central government, and administered by a separate department, the *Prikaz Kazanskogo Dvortsa*. At the same time, a chain of forts was built across the khanates and manned by imperial soldiers, and any revolts were put down with great force, as in 1570–1572 and 1581–1582. The lands of the khans and their leading followers who had died resisting the Russians or who had fled were turned over to aristocrats, and the government supported the settlements of Russian merchants in the towns of Kazan and Astrakhan.[14]

From the 1580s onward, Russia also came to exercise increasing authority in Siberia. The inhabitants of this vast area were immensely diverse and spoke a number of languages, many of them unrelated. These included Manchu, languages related to Mongolian, Urgik, other Turkic languages, and even Arabic. Although most of the inhabitants of this region lived in smaller kinship-based societies, they were capable of fierce resistance. However, their populations were decimated both by diseases and by the eradication, by Russian and European trappers, of the fur-bearing animals upon which they relied. Throughout their territories the Russian army built forts that by 1639 reached to the Pacific. This line of fortresses underpinned Russian authority in the region, but here again the czars' agents

---

[12]Peter F. Sugar, *Southeastern Europe Under Ottoman Rule, 1354–1804* (Seattle: University of Washington Press, 1977), 44–47.

[13]Dominic Lieven, *Empire: The Russian Empire and Its Rivals* (New Haven, CT: Yale University Press, 2002), 240; and Andreas Kappeler, *The Russian Empire*, translated by Alfred Clayton (Harlow: Longman Press, 2001), 18–19.

[14]Michael Khodarkovsky, *Russia's Steppe Frontier: The Making of a Colonial Empire, 1500–1800* (Bloomington: Indiana University Press, 2002), 114–115; and Kappeler, *The Russian Empire*, 18–19, 28–31.

found that they could only achieve their principal goal—the collection of furs—by recruiting local collaborators. Clan and tribal chiefly officeholders were, as a result, brought into government and charged with the collection of taxes, in the form of furs. In return, the colonial administration recognized their status as chieftains. Military administrators and unofficial agents of empire—fur-traders and adventurers—also took advantage of the patchwork nature of identity and politics in the region. Communities were frequently recruited to conquer or dominate neighbors who resisted, and many did so either for pay or because of long-standing feuds. Yet the independent trappers, merchants, and adventurers almost as frequently undermined Russian rule by their corruption and brutality toward even co-operating local populations, especially animist and clan-based societies.[15]

While western European scholars have made much of the brutality carried out in the name of the Russian Empire toward the Siberian population, the Romanov czars more frequently recognized the need to reach an accommodation with local elites, and at times peasants, in order to secure their rule. This reality is underscored by the special status granted to peasant-farmers in Kazan and Astrakhan. While the rural population of the Russian metropole was being enserfed in the sixteenth century—and thus turned into unfree laborers bound to the land—Muslim farmers in Kazan were granted the right to remain free peasants so long as they paid traditional taxes, usually through pre-existing Islamic aristocrats, to the imperial treasury. This is one of the great ironies created by the overall weakness of colonial rule in the early modern era.

The Muslim Mughal empire under Akbar similarly found ways to accommodate the vast number of Sikh and Hindu subjects who came under their rule. They did so largely through a sophisticated, bureaucratic system that balanced strategies of co-opting local elites as *mansabdari* military officials and land-owning *zamindari*, on the one hand, with the establishment of centralized imperial administrations in the provinces on the other. Underpinning this strategy was Akbar's conscious cultivation of a tolerant and integrative imperial ethos.

The most significant and possibly richest provinces of the empire were the Hindu Rājpūts of the Gangetic plain, and it was their acquisition in the 1560s and 1570s that truly transformed the Tīmūrid state into an empire. The princely former rulers of the Rājpūts were the heads of enormous clans of related individuals, stratified by wealth and power but loyal to the family as a whole. Akbar recognized these clans as potential structures for the organization of rebellion, and acted both to subvert and to suppress them. He won the loyalty of clan-heads by confirming their control over huge areas of land, in return for which they pledged to respect his sovereignty and imperial authority. The *rajas* were then integrated into the ranks of the mansabdari, and some even became imperial disciples. This process transformed the rajas from the heads of clans to imperial clients, their status now granted to them by the emperor rather than by their clan.[16] Yet Akbar realized that he could not entirely assimilate the rajas, and in recognition of their wide ties to the local population they were allowed special rights within their hereditary fiefs that surpassed those granted to other mansabdari.[17] Akbar also granted to many of these new mansabdari-rajas fiefdoms larger than they would otherwise have inherited, but in return claimed the right to select the rajas' heirs from within the clan.

As well as joining the ranks of the mansabdari, the rajas were also one of many classes that controlled the production of agricultural goods from the land. These zamindari classes, as we have seen, could be key allies of the empire. This was especially true of powerful zamindari who together controlled many subordinate landholders

[15] Kappeler, *The Russian Empire*, 36–38.

[16] Norman P. Ziegler, "Some Notes on Rājpūt Loyalties During the Mughal Period," in *The Mughal State 1526–1750*, edited by Muzaffar Alam and Sanjay Subrahmanyan (Delhi: Oxford University Press, 1998), 168–212.

[17] John F. Richards, *The New Cambridge History of India*, vol. 5, *The Mughal Empire* (Cambridge: Cambridge University Press, 1993), 67.

and peasants. These zamindari were allowed to retain a portion of all revenue collected from their lands, the rest being passed on to the state. The emperors' administrators set the annual proceeds, and in bad years some zamindari had trouble paying it, a situation that provoked some resentment. The situation was further aggravated by struggles, in the more peripheral provinces, between zamindari and state-appointed administrators.[18]

This arrangement, flexibly applied to each of the provinces, generally functioned well under Akbar. A system of imperial provincial governors (*faujdari*) operating from state forts could deal with dissatisfaction using local resources but, if not, the imperial army were available. Generally, however, the associative and accommodative structure of the empire and its tolerant ethos maintained the emperor's authority. This was true, at least, until the reign of the Emperor Aurangzeb. Aurangzeb not only created a colonial divide by adopting an Islamic identity for the imperial administration, but also vigorously expanded the empire into regions that were difficult to control—especially eastern Bengal and the Deccan. The result was a series of uprisings, both religious in tone and with the backing of important zamindaris. A number of imperial officials realized the danger, and attempted to maintain the more tolerant policies of Aurangzeb's predecessors. In 1669, the suppression of non-Muslim merchants in Surat by a kâdî-magistrate was halted by local governors, who managed to convince the emperor to rein in this particular persecution. Aurangzeb, however, continued to favor Muslims in his policies, to promote conversion, and to aggravate religious tensions. Resistance to these measures culminated in the first general revolt of the rajas, and later by a moderate party at court who chose as a figurehead Aurangzeb's son. The emperor's successful suppression of these rebellions, and the continuation of his policies, substantially weakened the empire in the late seventeenth century.[19] For the first time, imperial governors—especially of the Hindu-majority states in the Deccan region—had to keep the imperial army mobilized to deal with the day-to-day administration of their provinces.

Religious tolerance had proven to be an important issue in Spain as well, where the *reconquista* had brought large numbers of Muslims and Jews under the control of the Castilian-Aragonese crown. Ferdinand and Isabella had forged alliances with a few disaffected Muslim aristocrats of Granada in the 1480s, largely by promising to allow Islam to be practiced in the state and to respect the claims of the collaborators. By 1501, however, the religious nature of the crown's claims to legitimacy and lobbying by the Church transformed the situation, and Muslims were forced either to convert or to emigrate. Arabic books were burned, and Muslim identity and culture was suppressed.[20] Spanish Jews faced the same choice—convert, emigrate, or die—following a royal decree in 1492.

Ferdinand and Isabella's Habsburg successors embraced this alliance with the Church, which became a principal funding source and recruiting aid for Philip II's campaigns against his rebellious Protestant subjects in the Netherlands. Yet it is important to note that Philip considered the Dutch neither religious dissenters nor colonial subjects, but rather rebels against their legitimate ruler.[21] In fact, Philip treated all of his domains in Europe—Spain, the Netherlands, and parts of Italy—as metropolitan provinces rather than as colonies. Spanish control in North Africa can be deemed colonial, but the tiny Spanish enclaves there were maintained almost entirely through military force, if with little support from the local population. Outside of the Americas, therefore, Spain's only real colony was in the Philippines. There, the Spanish crown had established a miniscule base in 1564, and the colony was both distant enough and weak enough that the appointed governors relied on local collaborators and negotiated for their continued existence with local

---

[18] S. Nural Hasan, "Zamindars Under the Mughals," in Alam and Subrahmanyan, *The Mughal State*, 284–300.
[19] Richards, *The Mughal Empire*, 165, 175–184.

[20] Henry Kamen, *Empire: How Spain Became a World Power 1492–1763* (New York: HarperCollins, 2003), 18–21.
[21] Ibid., 177–180.

leaderships. However, the colony was never self-sustaining, and by the 1570s the burgeoning city of Manila was largely run by the Chinese and Japanese merchants who provisioned it and used it as a base of operations. The Spanish presence was maintained more by Jesuit priests and a smattering of independent traders than by imperial agents.[22]

Ming China, which is generally understood to be lacking a colonial empire, again represented a variation on early modern imperial state management. On their northern border, the re-building of the Great Wall in the sixteenth and seventeenth centuries arguably created the most firmly demarcated political frontier in the early modern world. On the Ming side of this border, the provinces were administered as core regions of the metropole. The same was true of the provinces facing Tibet. Only in regions of the southern provinces of Yunnan, Guangdong, Guangxi, Guizhou, and Sichuan was anything approaching a colonial model adopted. Here, significant ethnically non-Chinese populations co-existed with Chinese communities. Their semi-autonomous chieftains were co-opted whenever possible as "native officials," or *tusi*, and charged with managing most of their communities' day-to-day affairs. Imperial officials were detailed to assist and manage them. Collusion between these two groups sometimes led to corruption and abuses. The tusi system was considered impermanent, as Ming policy was generally directed as the assimilation of these groups, partly by the resettlement of ethnic Chinese populations in their midst.[23]

THEMES IN EARLY MODERN COLONIALISM

By reading through these narratives, it is possible to tease out several themes that highlight the similarities and contrasts in the strategies adopted by early modern empires. At the heart of these strategies were several contradictions that

marked sixteenth- and seventeenth-century colonialism as much as they later marked nineteenth- and twentieth-century versions. In the first place, colonialism was the result of policies mapped out in imperial metropoles such as Muscovy and Lisbon but that had to adapt to a variety local conditions. This helps to explain, for example, the many different relationships between Ottoman Istanbul and its various provinces. Second, early modern empires wavered between trying to bind colonial populations to the state and depicting them as different from metropolitan citizens. In this process, religion and language played the role of categorizing populations that was later dominated by race. The contradiction between trying to convert subjects to the religion of the state—be it Islam or Christianity—and separating them into special categories is a good example of this. In a related process, colonial regimes tried to operate through local collaborators and at the same time made frequent use of violence and force. In some cases, like Russian Siberia, the two processes overlapped heavily.

Throughout this period, across these empires, the ultimate arbiter of colonial policy was the profit motive of the state. New territories potentially provided revenues both in terms of imperial involvement in or tariffs on commerce and in land taxes. Two possible dangers threatened these profits: the collapse of state authority on the one hand and rising costs on the other. Imperial bureaucracies, officers, and garrisons cost money, and emperors and their advisors gradually came to recognize that alliances with local elites and accommodative policies were ways to avoid these costs. Another strategy was to invite the participation of religious institutions, merchants, or metropolitan land-owning classes who could share the cost. There was a danger to this, however, as these groups all had their own objectives and sets of practices. Religious extremism, commercial and agrarian exploitation, and brutality on the part of official and unofficial agents of empire often caused rebellion or resistance, which in turn lowered imperial profits or raised costs.

All of this underlines the fact that these vast empires were only possible with local cooperation,

---

[22]Ibid., 202–236.
[23]F.W. Mote, *Imperial China 900–1800* (Cambridge: Harvard University Press, 1999), 704–705, 717.

and that this cooperation was reliant upon the demonstration of a certain respect for local elites and sometimes peasants. The centrality of imperial-local alliances to the profitability and stability of colonial rule is demonstrated time and again in the historical record. The Russian empire is just one example. The Russian czars chose to confirm the authority of Muslim landowners in Kazan despite the exhortations of the Orthodox Church, and attempted to win Siberian chieftains as allies, a policy that sometimes led to disagreements with Russian adventurers and trappers who wished to exploit them. As we have seen, similar dynamics existed in each of the other early modern empires.

This does not meant that violence as a tool of colonial rule was absent, however. Although dynastic marriage, inheritance, and treaties served to augment imperial possessions, war remained the principal means of territorial acquisition. Yet because of the spiraling costs of gunpowder armies, overwhelming force could usually be employed only briefly. Longer imperial wars sometimes brought empires to their knees. Two examples of this stand out: the Habsburg exertions of the Thirty Years' War and the Mughal Emperor Aurangzeb's suppression of the revolt of the rajas. Both were initially successful, but proved so costly that they essentially bankrupted the state, in the latter case permanently.

Aside from force and negotiation, imperial states could, and sometimes did, encourage settlement of metropolitan or other loyal citizens overseas as a means of controlling distant or rebellious provinces. This was the policy practiced by the Russians in Novgorod, the Habsburg Emperor Ferdinand II in Bohemia, and the Ming emperors in the southern provinces. Often, colonists became assimilated to local norms. Just one example is the almost complete assimilation of the Ottoman janissaries in Tunisia, but there are many more. Assimilating conquered peoples to the culture of the metropole was much more difficult, especially where religion intervened. In most cases, assimilation through conversion, the transfer of language and culture, and official transitions in status remained an underlying process in

early modern empires at least as important as the development of colonial policies that recognized the separateness or different status of some subjects of the empire.

Can all of these accurately be called *colonialism*? The usefulness of this term in explaining these early modern policies and practices is still debatable. Even when a definite definition is established as to what colonialism is—as we have tried to do in this book—its application to specific situations to the early modern context remains problematic. Nevertheless, it is important to recognize that the colonial forms that characterized later empires were not entirely absent from this period, and that there were continuities between Eurasian and North African empires in the fifteenth through seventeenth centuries and later forms of rule in Africa, Asia, and the Americas.

THE ECONOMIC UNDERPINNINGS OF EARLY MODERN INTEGRATION

We have already seen that early modern empires developed as a whole unit, shaped by the interaction between colonial periphery and imperial metropole. Equally, empires formed in the context of increasing global integration, as expanding trading relationships and new sailing technologies transported goods, knowledge, and people rapidly across vast distances. Much of this interaction was unofficial, carried out by merchants, adventurers, refugees, and missionaries. However, the increasingly competitive global environment drove even states separated by great distances to send emissaries to negotiate with each other and in some cases to form official alliances.

Perhaps because financial and commercial data is the best-preserved set of sources for this period, this global interlinking has been understood by most world historians largely as a story of economic integration, as we saw in chapter 1. Beginning around 1380 in some regions, the effects of a rebounding inter-continental trade began to be felt across Eurasia and North and East Africa by the mid-fifteenth century. West Africans, too, came to participate in this system; first along

long-standing trans-Saharan routes, and then by engaging in maritime trade with Europeans along the coast as well. Starting at the end of the fifteenth century, the enormous commercial networks of the Americas were integrated as well. With the exception of Polynesia, by 1500 there can be said to exist a truly global commerce. Perhaps the best-known aspect of this exchange was the network that linked silver from the mines of Peru and Mexico to buyers in China and India via either Europe or the Philippines. Along the way, states and rulers attempted to siphon off some of the profits as taxes, or through direct participation in trading companies. Admittedly, the debate over the significance of global trade to economies in various regions of the world remains unresolved.[24] Nevertheless, after 1500 its importance to local economies, and to state taxes, only grew.

It should be no surprise that imperial governments would be interested in profiting from both local and long-distance trading. The rising cost of military technology and human power, and the multiplication of wars, necessitated that new sources of revenue be found outside of relatively stagnant taxes on cultivated land. This drive for revenues helps to explain, of course, why the Spanish and Portuguese crowns authorized, sponsored, and later tried to monopolize expeditions to find new routes to the trade goods of the east. For the Portuguese, this led them south around the tip of Africa. The Spanish monarchs largely concentrated on routes across the Atlantic, which eventually brought them to the Americas. These narratives are relatively familiar, and are often presented as proof of western European exceptionality in this period. In fact, however, the opposite is true. The same motivations drove empire-building in Russia, for example, where they help to explain the czar's support for the

exploration and conquest of the fur-producing regions of Siberia. Equally, they account partly for the support of the Ming Emperor Chengzu (the Yongle Emperor, 1402–1424) for the vast naval expeditions of his admiral Zheng He. Financial motives can also be found in the Ottoman quest to control the southern Europe-to-Asia route through Egypt, and the Mughal conquest of the excellent Indian Ocean port of Gujarat. Of course economic motivations alone cannot sufficiently account for empire-building, but the competition for a piece of this global trade does help to explain how commercial goals could be wedded to imperial ideologies without too much difficulty.

IMPERIAL INTERACTION AND GRAND ALLIANCES

Economic objectives thus underpinned the development of a worldwide imperial atmosphere in the early modern era. Tied to ideological and political/strategic goals, they led the grand empires into conflict with each other, and with the other large states of the period. Historians have traditionally dealt with these clashes and alliances in different regions—Europe and the Mediterranean, Central Asia, the Indian Ocean, the Americas—independently. In fact, however, they were connected to a surprising degree. These regions were not civilizational fault lines, but rather zones of interaction. Away from imperial cores, identity was often more fluid and societies more pluralistic. People on either side of a border often identified to some degree with those on the other side, especially if the border was recently imposed. This tended to fuel commerce, cultural exchange, and even inter-migration. This was especially true when states were allied or in a period of détente, but even open warfare seldom stopped interaction. Moreover, imperial rulers depended on this interaction and commerce for much of their income, and thus could not discourage it for long.

Despite the mutual interdependency of the great empires and states, there emerged in the early modern period an unprecedented system of diplomacy, coalition-building, and warfare that

[24] For more on this debate and early modern global trade, see Kenneth Pomeranz, *The Great Divergence: China, Europe, and the Making of the Modern World Economy* (Princeton, NJ: Princeton University Press, 2000); Patrick O'Brien, "European Economic Development: The Contribution of the Periphery," *Economic History Review*, New Series, 35 (1982); and Andre Gunder Frank, *ReORIENT: Global Economy in the Asian Age* (Berkeley: University of California Press, 1998).

mobilized the massive armies and navies as well as the growing bureaucracies of the state in what at times approached the levels of world war. A religious undertone existed in these conflicts. Russia, the Habsburg empires of Austria and Spain, and Portugal all claimed leadership of the Christian world at times in order to more effectively challenge their Ottoman or other Muslim opponents. Similarly, the Ottomans, Mughals, and at times Safavî professed to represent the interests of Islam against Christian opponents. Yet, while heartfelt, this crusader militancy was abandoned when convenient. Indeed, the Habsburgs' most passionate opponents were Christians: not only European Protestants but especially their co-religionists the Catholic Kings of France. Similarly, the Ottomans' main rivals in this period were the Muslim (Shî'i) Safavî and, until 1516, the Egyptian Mamlûk state.

Underlying the Christian–Muslim conflict were economic and political goals that included the control of vital maritime trade routes along the Mediterranean and Red seas and overland trade routes in Central Asia. Along these corridors flowed much of the commerce between Asia and Europe/North Africa. In the fifteenth century, these routes were all largely in the hands of Muslims, a reality that was partly responsible for the Iberian states' attempts to find alternate routes to Asia around Africa or across the Atlantic. Yet, as we have seen, Spain and Portugal also chose for ideological, political, and economic reasons to challenge the Muslim states of the North African Maghreb for control of the western Mediterranean.[25] As we have seen, the defenders of several of these states turned to the Ottomans for support. The Sa'âdi rulers of Morocco occupied an intermediate position, attempting to rebuff both sides by playing them off against each other.

This sixteenth-century extension of the Ottomans' influence to the western Mediterranean punctuated a century of westward expansion. By 1517, the Ottomans had defeated their greatest rival of the time—the Mamlûk state of

Egypt—and were expanding from their long-held Balkan Christian provinces into new regions of Europe. In 1526, the Ottomans defeated a Hungarian-Bohemian army at Mohács, ironically ushering in Habsburg rule in Bohemia and the unconquered portions of Hungary. Ottoman support for Adal, and the Portuguese response in support of Ethiopia, completed a broad triangle from Tripoli to Hungary to the Horn of Africa across which the Ottomans, Habsburgs, and Portuguese faced each other was being billed as a holy showdown between Christianity and Islam. The reality, however, was far more complex. Among the Ottomans' allies against Habsburg Austria were the Christian border state of Transylvania, independence-minded Hungarian magnates, and even some Protestant groups. Even more significant were the beginnings of a Franco-Ottoman alliance. The French had fought three long wars against Habsburg encirclement during the reign of Charles V, and by the 1540s were exploring the idea of coordinating their campaigns with the Ottoman armies. In time this relationship would lead the Safavî Sultans and the Habsburgs to attempt an anti-Ottoman counter-encirclement.[26]

Traditional Europe-centered histories of this conflict culminate in the sea battle of Lepanto. For this reason, at least, this battle deserves further attention. One place to start the story of this famed encounter is in the Spanish province of Granada, where a 1568 rebellion among practicing and hidden Muslims quickly drew support from North Africans and Ottomans. Much of the Spanish army was garrisoning the Netherlands, and when the Ottoman navy opened another front in the eastern Mediterranean, Philip II was forced

---

[25] Kamen, *Empire*, 155–156, 182–184.

[26] The evolution of these great alliances is explored in Victor S. Mamatey, *Rise of the Habsburg Empire 1526–1815* (New York: Holt, Rinehart and Winston, 1971), 10–11, 27, 30–35, 44–46. See also David P. Ringrose, *Expansion and Global Interaction, 1200–1700* (New York: Addison Wesley Longman, 2001), chapter 2; and David Nicholas, *The Transformation of Europe 1300–1600* (New York: Bloomsbury Press, 1999), 277–281.

to respond creatively. He did so by engineering an agreement, called the Holy League, with Venice and the Vatican. Together, this alliance of a theocracy, a monarchical empire, and a republic put together a giant fleet in 1571. The bulk of their ships were galleys rather than the newer caravels, as were those of their Ottoman opponents. On 7 October, this fleet surprised the Ottoman galleys, of which 190 were captured.[27]

How significant was this victory? Although European scholars from the nineteenth century onward declared it to have been the turning of the tide in a great and assumedly age-old Christian–Muslim conflict, it was in fact nothing of the sort. The Ottomans rapidly rebuilt their Mediterranean fleet, which within four years was in operation as far west as Tunis in support of an army of janissaries. Their advance into the western Mediterranean was only halted because the Ottomans were forced to face a renewed Safavî threat in the east. Meanwhile, the Holy Alliance crumbled: Venice departed the confederation quite rapidly, and in 1580 a truce was signed between the Ottoman and Spanish crowns.[28] A similar agreement was reached between the Austrian Habsburgs and the Ottomans in 1606, ushering in a 50-year period of détente in eastern Europe, which allowed the Habsburgs to concentrate on repressing Protestantism.

From the perspective of the Safavî Sultans, the Ottoman-Habsburg truce was a disaster that allowed the Ottoman Sultans to recapture the provinces of Iraq, greatly reducing Safavî power. In desperation, in 1559 Shah Abbas I reached out in turn and proposed an anti-Ottoman alliance to both the Russian czars and Catholic kings and queens.[29] The proposed alliances failed to come to fruition for several reasons. Most importantly, although Russia was still smarting from an abortive Ottoman invasion of Astrakhan in 1569,

the new Czar Boris Godunov (1598–1605) had just taken the throne and was concerned with solidifying his authority and expanding Russia's influence in the Baltic region. Nor were either of the Habsburg emperors interested in breaking their truces with the Ottomans. In the end, Shah Abbas only managed to interest the English in an alliance, and that alliance was aimed against the Portuguese, rather than the Ottomans.

Portuguese-Safavî antagonism was based on events in another zone of interaction—the Indian Ocean and western Pacific. This region—stretching along the coast and into the interiors of China and Japan, South-East Asia, India, Persia, the Arabian Peninsula, and East Africa—had formed a coherent commercial system since about the eighth century. Unlike in the Mediterranean, the distances between landmasses in this area were vast, and although there were plenty of naval battles, maritime empire-building was difficult. In this environment, interlocking circuits brought goods long distances through the hands of many middlemen—Swahili, Arab, Gujarati, Malabari, Malay, and Chinese merchants among them.[30] Connections between these groups were often formed on the basis of a shared religion, with Islam, Hinduism, and Buddhism playing prominent roles. Along with religion and goods, humans circulated throughout the region, so that Chinese elites played a major role in Javanese ports, Iranians had a prominent role in the Mughal Empire, and Arab expatriates helped to populate coastal East African cities.

In this zone, as in others, the early fifteenth century was a period of commercial and demographic recovery. Yet, while empires and centralized states were being built and armies were clashing on land, no hegemonic power arose to control maritime trade, despite the presence between 1405 and 1433 of enormous Chinese expeditions led by the famous eunuch admiral

---

[27] J.H. Parry, *The Age of Reconnaissance* (London: Phoenix Press, 2000), 121; and Kamen, *Empire*, 182–186.

[28] Andrew C. Hess, "The Battle of Lepanto and Its Place in Mediterranean History," *Past and Present*, 57 (1972), 53–73.

[29] Sanjay Subrahmanyam, *The Portuguese Empire in Asia, 1500–1700: A Political and Economic History* (Harlow: Longman, 1993), 148.

[30] Janet Abu-Lughod, *Before European Hegemony: The World System A.D. 1250–1350* (New York: Oxford University Press, 1989), parts II and III.

Zheng He.[31] Following a struggle for power in the court that ensued following the death of the Yongle Emperor, these expeditions ended abruptly. A variety of arguments are given for this reversal: the lack of a significant economic return upon investment, the ultimate victory of land-owning aristocrats and scholar-bureaucrats over merchants within the court of the Ming Emperor Xuangong (1426–1435), and the ongoing threat of invasion from the interior of Asia. The termination of official expeditions did not, of course, seriously diminish trade across the Indian Ocean and western Pacific. It did, however, create a maritime power vacuum. In the fifteenth century, merchant ships plying these waters had to worry only about pirates. There were no powerful naval fleets, no great battles.[32] Thus, it was a markedly different type of zone of interaction from the constricted, contested waters of the Mediterranean. All of that changed to some degree with the arrival of the Portuguese.

THE PORTUGUESE *ESTADO DA INDIA*

Was the Portuguese entry into the Indian Ocean and East Asian zones something entirely new and unique in world history, as has been argued by generations of European and North American historians such as J.H. Parry, Theodore K. Rabb, and David Landes? Or was it rather merely a variation on trends already existing among empires and smaller states in the region as argued by Asian historians such as Sanjay Subrahmanyan and K.N. Chaudhuri as well as world historians such as Kenneth Pomeranz and Andre Gunder Frank? The answer lies somewhere in between, since the origins of the Portuguese overseas empire must be located in its local context in Portugal as well as larger trends in imperial interaction, imperialism, and colonialism in the early modern world.

In the first place, the successive Portuguese expeditions that created the Estado da India—the Portuguese Indian Ocean empire—were driven by an entrepreneurial spirit born of the particular Portuguese version of an imperial mission. As we saw in chapter 1, Portuguese imperial ideology bound together a Catholic-monarchical messianism with the sense of a national-religious mission and a search for profits. This ideology appealed to both the royal court and merchants, and their multi-sectoral alliance was emblematic of the transformation of the early modern era among many Eurasian and North African societies. In Portugal, this alliance was expressed in the form of a maritime empire rather than an overland empire, largely because of geography. Perched on the very western edge of Eurasia, Portugal had no overland outlet for expansion, and thus had to look seaward for military adventures: across the Straits of Gibraltar to North Africa, into the Atlantic, and around Cape Bojador to West Africa.

Portugal's location also put it at an extreme commercial disadvantage during the fifteenth-century Eurasian economic recovery. Like other European societies, early modern Portugal increasingly demanded consumer goods from China, South-East Asia, India, and other eastern producers. In order to reach Portugal, however, these goods had to pass through the hands of many middlemen—especially Mediterranean trading powers such as Genoa and Venice. This drove up the cost of the goods, and set Portuguese merchants to dreaming of a route to the riches of the east that would avoid all of these middlemen. An additional motivation lay in the potential for finding a maritime route to the gold fields of West Africa, and in this way outflanking the Moroccans

---

[31] The closest the region came were the voyages of the Chinese Muslim eunuch Zheng He's fleet. Dispatched by the Yongle emperor in 1405, Zheng He's fleet consisted of 300 ships in an expedition unlike anything ever seen before. Its 27,000 sailors, soldiers, and support personnel would have overwhelmed both of the fleets of galleys at Lepanto. The largest ships were 400 feet-long "treasure ships" that towered above the European caravels. By contrast, the Spanish armada that threatened to conquer England in 1588 consisted only of 130 ships, the largest being the 22 fighting galleons of about 140 feet in length. See Kuei-Sheng Chang, "The Maritime Scene in China at the Dawn of Great European Discoveries," *Journal of the American Oriental Society*, 94 (1974), 347–359.

[32] K.N. Chaudhuri, *Trade and Civilisation in the Indian Ocean: An Economic History from the Rise of Islam to 1750* (Cambridge: Cambridge University Press, 1985), 63.

who monopolized this trade. Their dream became realizable in the late fifteenth century, when naval technology finally arrived in Europe that made long-distance voyages across the equator possible; in the form of the square-and-lateen-rigged caravel. Although the caravels were tiny vessels, with a capacity of under 300 tons (in contrast to the 25,000 ton capacity of Zheng He's treasure ships), these caravels nevertheless proved themselves up to the task.

The subsequent building of the Estado da India was not a single grand venture, but an unfolding process in which short-term goals predominated and the state was only one of many actors influencing the development of the empire. Thus, the Portuguese overseas empire was perhaps the most extreme example in this period of merchant power through sectoral alliances with the state and religion. Although this enterprise was officially governed by royally appointed viceroys or governors, the operation of the empire was characterized by ongoing friction between the state and its officials and royal traders, independent merchants and adventurers, and the church.

The realities of geography exacerbated this friction. Vast distances separated Portugal and the royal court at Lisbon from its settler colony in Brazil (first claimed for the crown in 1500), from coastal positions in Africa, and from the string of forts and territories being built across the Indian Ocean. The functioning of the empire required all of these territories to be organizationally and commercially interlinked. Brazil (discussed in chapters 3 and 4) rapidly came to demand not only slave laborers from Africa but also foodstuffs and basic manufactured goods to sustain the plantations, which were so oriented toward the production of sugar and other cash crops that even in this region of agricultural wealth they could not feed themselves. As the empire expanded, ships passed back and forth between Europe, Asia, the Americas, and Africa carrying merchants, sailors, soldiers, officials, settlers, exiles, transported convicts, vagabonds, officials, slaves, and refugees. They brought with them not only commodities such as sugar and silver, but also ideas, technologies, plant and animal species, and

diseases.[33] Such exchanges between the metropole and periphery, and among regions of the periphery, were of course present in the Ottoman, Habsburg, Mughal, and other early modern empires. For the Portuguese maritime empire, however, the great distances and diversity of populations encompassed made control even more difficult. Thus, contrary to popular understanding, the Portuguese empire was distinguished from other empires of this era largely by the weakness of the Portuguese crown abroad, its reliance upon both Portuguese and non-Portuguese collaborators, and hence its rapid decentralization. This trend is demonstrated by the establishment and functioning of the Estado da India in Africa and Asia. Because in these regions there was no massive transfer of Portuguese settlers and government officials, the main inhabitants of the Portuguese forts and positions strung along the oceanic trade routes from 1482 to 1650 were local populations, alongside Portuguese sailors, soldiers, merchants, and of course Christian priests from around the empire. As we will see in chapters 3 and 4, this decentralized model was largely copied by the Spanish and other Europeans in the Americas and Asia in the sixteenth and seventeenth centuries.

The first Portuguese expeditions to sub-Saharan Africa were largely carried out by merchants who hoped to find trade goods—especially malagueta peppers and perhaps gold. In 1469, Dom Afonso V (1432–1481) granted a merchant by the name of Fernão Gomes, a monopoly on trade on the "Guinea"—or west—coast of Africa. His success in locating several sources of West African gold motivated the Crown to re-assume control of the venture, and in 1481 it was not an independent merchant but rather the royal agent Diogo de Azambuja who was allowed by a coastal community in what is now Ghana to build a fort in their territory. The commercial motivation of the expedition was betrayed by the name given to this fortress—São Jorge da Mina, or

---

[33] This is the thesis of A.J.R. Russell-Wood, *The Portuguese Empire, 1415–1808: A World on the Move* (Baltimore: Johns Hopkins University Press, 1998).

"Saint George of the Mine." Yet despite the construction of this and other forts built along the "Gold Coast" (as it came to be labeled), Portuguese authority was severely restricted, and their tenuous hold on these forts—which functioned as both defensive establishments and markets—was only maintained by alliances with the leadership of some small local states for whom the Portuguese presence and trade was advantageous.[34] Together with the local royal commercial administrator, or *factor*, these local chiefly officeholders and merchants largely monopolized shore-to-ship commerce, together excluding when possible both African and European independent traders. This was informal colonialism at its most limited—at no point did the Portuguese control any extensive inland region—although the forts and markets as well as surrounding towns did come under Portuguese authority and law.

Meanwhile, the Portuguese were establishing subsequent positions further along the African coast as expeditions pushed further and further to the south. In 1482, Afonso's successor João II sponsored an expedition whose goal was to find Christian kingdoms in Africa and Asia, but which instead found the growing state of Kongo. An alliance between the two states was quickly formed, and royal diplomats and officials were dispatched alongside priests. However, independent Portuguese adventurers also arrived in the kingdom, whom the Kongolese King was quick to co-opt by appointing them to positions at his court. As a result, Portuguese royal agents were often frustrated in their attempts to gain a commercial advantage by resistance from an alliance of the Kongolese state and its Portuguese employees.[35] Perhaps fortunately for the Portuguese kings, the expansion of the slave trade in this region and local rivalries soon diminished Kongolese royal authority and facilitated the extraction of wealth from the region, especially in the form of slaves.[36]

In 1487–1488, a fleet under Bartholomeu Dias rounded the Cape of Good Hope and gained access to the Indian Ocean. This expedition was followed by another, under Vasco da Gama, which left Portugal in 1497 and arrived in the Indian Ocean the next year. The first large-scale commercial societies da Gama encountered were the Swahili city-states, of which the southernmost outpost was Mozambique. The rulers of these states, however, viewed da Gama with suspicion, and refused to allow him to establish permanent trading positions. In response, in 1502 da Gama bombarded the harbor of the large city-state of Kilwa and forced the ruler, *Shayk* Ibrahim, to pay an annual fee and to acknowledge Portuguese sovereignty. This set the pattern for Portuguese rule in the area, which during this era was largely based on force and did not extend far into the interior. In fact, many of the Portuguese garrisons were withdrawn for much of the sixteenth century, and were only replaced in the 1590s when an ally was found in the ambitious Sultan of Malindi.[37]

As along the east coast of Africa, the Portuguese soon found that Asian states were generally too strong to be conquered, and that the only, limited military advantage they possessed was their ships. Even in maritime technology, however, some Asian states were quick to catch up. By 1508, Gujarati shipwrights were replicating caravel-building techniques, and maritime states like the Sumatran principality of Aceh were arming their vessels with cannon as good as or better than those of the Portuguese.[38] Nevertheless, da Gama was able to score a number of quick victories, and these paved the way for the first viceroys sent out from Portugal—Francisco de Almeida (1505–1509) and Afonso de Albuquerque

---

[34] For more see John Vogt, *Portuguese Rule on the Gold Coast 1469–1682* (Athens: University of Georgia Press, 1979); and Albert Van Dantzig, *Forts and Castles of Ghana* (Accra: Sedco Publishing, 1980).

[35] John Thornton, "Early Kongo-Portuguese Relations: A New Interpretation," *History in Africa*, 8 (1981), 183–204.

[36] The story of the Kongolese state, which we began in chapter 1, is continued in chapter 4 of this volume.

[37] "East Africa: The Coast," in *Africa from the Sixteenth to the Eighteenth Century*.

[38] For more on the debate on this subject, see P.J. Marshall, "Western Arms in Maritime Asia in the Early Phases of Expansion," *Modern Asian Studies*, 14 (1980), 13–28.

(1509–1515)—to build or capture fortified positions, of which the most important were Goa and Cochin in India, Hormuz on the Arabian Peninsula, and the port state of Melaka on the coast of Malaysia.

The building of this empire was a collaborative effort between the Portuguese and some Asian elites who found their presence, their military force, and their willingness to use violence to be useful. Albuquerque's 1510 assault on Goa, for example, was heavily promoted by a Hindu pirate-aristocrat named Timmayya.[39] Timmayya and other mercenaries mustered thousands of men in the service of the Portuguese Crown, and were well rewarded. Timmayya, for example, was given the monopoly on tax collection for Goa, of which he was allowed to extract a percentage for himself.[40]

In choosing allies, the Portuguese had certain preferences. For example, during their struggle against the Mamlûk fleet (until 1517) and later against the Ottomans over control of the pepper and spice trade, Portuguese governors like Albuquerque turned to Hindu elites and especially to Christian converts like those from Malabar. Usually, however, the alliances were merely opportunistic. The Tamil community of Melaka assisted the Portuguese in order to expel their Gujarati rivals. Malabaris often converted to Christianity as a result of their conflict with Muslim neighbors. The Portuguese could not afford to be picky, and their ships were soon full of servants, sailors, and slaves of many nationalities, their forts manned by a multi-national corps of adventurers and mercenaries. The Portuguese-born population of the Estado da India remained small, and the Crown only minimally encouraged emigration.[41]

Meanwhile, the differing visions of Portuguese agents of the crown, merchants, and priests slowly fragmented the empire. The Crown had hoped to maintain a monopoly on trade,

initially through the establishment of a royal-private company with factors in each of the important Asian and African ports. In 1504, Dom Manuel I experimented with allowing private traders to travel to Asia in return for a 28.5% tariff on all goods, but this ended in 1506 with the re-assertion of the royal monopoly.[42] Lopo Soares (1515–1520) was the first governor to encourage the return of private trade, and in subsequent decades Portuguese kings struggled to maintain some authority and level of income by protection rackets and selling long-term "contracts" to Portuguese and Asian traders. Successively, however, they lost control of even the Portuguese merchants, some of whom converted to Islam and became closely integrated into local communities. Meanwhile, attempts to come to an understanding with Muslim states were often undercut by the clergy. Religious issues also disrupted the most profitable wing of the empire, the Portuguese monopoly on transporting Japanese silver to China. In 1587, enraged at Jesuit interference in matters of state, Tokugawa Ieyasu suppressed Christianity in his realm and threatened to expel the Portuguese. Fortunately for the Estado da India, he was too pragmatic to carry out that threat.

However by 1580, despite the (temporary) unification of the Portuguese and Spanish crowns, the Estado da India's control over the pepper and spice trade was in rapid decline. The empire was in retreat; only in Sri Lanka was there any expansion. Riven by internal disagreement, the empire was also under attack by expanding Mughal and Ottoman states and by a resurgent Aceh, which was slowly building its own commercial empire based upon Indonesia.[43] Meanwhile, two other European maritime states—England and the Netherlands—were experimenting in Indian Ocean waters. Dutch and English captains often came to agreements

---

[39] Subrahmanyan, *The Portuguese Empire*, 68.
[40] G.V. Scammell, "Indigenous Assistance in the Establishment of Portuguese Power in Asia in the Sixteenth Century," *Modern Asian Studies*, 14 (1980), 1–11.
[41] Russell-Wood, *The Portuguese Empire, 1415–1808*, 60–62.

[42] The most complete and compelling text on the private-royal struggles for supremacy in the Estado da India remains. Subrahmanyan, *The Portuguese Empire*, 56–61, 67–69, 74, 112–114.
[43] Parry, *The Age of Reconnaissance*, 242.

with local rulers to collaborate in disrupting Portuguese aims.[44]

On the East African coast, an alliance of Swahili rebels with a Muslim ruler from the Arabian Peninsula, supported by English and Dutch ships, expelled the Portuguese from all ports except the most southerly. A similar alliance of Dutch, English, and African polities forced them to abandon most of their West African forts as well. Although Portugal would hang on to minor positions in Macao, Goa, Timor (Indonesia), and a few colonies in West and East Africa until 1975, by 1650 the Estado da India was effectively moribund.

Conclusion

The maritime empires of Spain and Portugal are often depicted as something entirely new, exceptionally European, and utterly unique in world history. In fact, however, they arose out of a vast early modern system of imperial interaction across Eurasia and much of Africa, they interacted in a largely equal manner with Eurasian and African polities, and they practiced styles of colonial rule (and arguably colonialism) similar to those developing in contemporary empires elsewhere.

In Asia and Africa, the Estado da India characterized most the weakness of state control over vast distances and their utilization of a relatively thin veneer of official agents. Unlike most other great empires of Eurasia, whose colonies were contiguous with the metropole, the Estado da India was too thinly stretched and too far away from the metropole to be governed effectively. Thus, the empire's agents came to rely heavily on independent merchants and on cooperation from local rulers and groups. They therefore came to accept many local practices and wielded power only very carefully. In fact, however, this was not exceptional. In the Russian empire of the Romanovs and the Ottoman Empire, as well, the most distant territories were largely self-governing, imperial governors often made use of unofficial

agents, and imperial interference with local culture was kept to a minimum. Thus, Ottoman Moldavia and Russian Siberia were largely seen as sources of revenue for the Crown, a perspective mirrored in the Portuguese Estado da India. At the same time, however, the maintenance of these distant territories allowed the monarch to claim to audiences at home to be pursuing its religious and spiritual civilizing mission.

Other than distance, factors such as population density and security could limit the states' abilities to effect colonial policies. Thus, Habsburg Hungary was able to preserve many of its traditions and political independence because of its position facing the Ottomans, and thus were the Hindu Rājpūts generally able to negotiate religious freedom because of their large populations and their military and economic value to the Mughal emperors. Colonialism was not always so thin a façade, however. Where possible, empires exerted much more pressure and control over their territories. This was true in the inner provinces of the Ottoman and Russian empires and in Habsburg Bohemia after the Thirty Years' War, for example.

Just as the Estado da India was a variation on early modern colonialism, so too were the Spanish and Portuguese empires in the Americas, and later those of other European states. Born of imperialism forged in the context of Eurasia, they developed unique types of colonial rule in the context of the Americas.

Questions

1. Scholars have generally not labeled the actions and policies of the Habsburg, Ottoman, Mughal, Russian, and Ming administration in their peripheries in this period as "colonialism." Do you think it would be correct to apply this label in any of these cases? To what degree did these administrations conform to the definition of colonialism used in this book?

2. It is possible to argue that there existed in the sixteenth and seventeenth centuries a "global imperial competitive context" that promoted imperial expansionism. Would you agree with this assessment? Why or why not? If so, what were its causes?

3. How did the Portuguese Estado da India work? Would you consider it an empire? Why or why not?

---

[44]Ringrose, *Expansion and Global Interaction*, 154–159.

CHAPTER 3

Imperialism: Intersecting Empires in the Americas

The "discovery" of the Americas by Europeans ushered in a new era in the global history of imperialism and colonialism. Spanish and Portuguese conquest and settlement in the "New World" represented an unprecedented episode in imperial expansion because the territories claimed were so vast and because they were ruled from metropolitan centers across thousands of miles of ocean. In addition, as we will see, diseases that accompanied Europeans to the Americas had a devastating effect on American populations, which resulted in massive population loss. As a result, European expansion in the New World involved the unparalleled replacement of indigenous populations by new ones from both Europe and Africa.

That said, many of the imperial policies pursued by Iberians in the Americas echoed policies already established by the early modern Eurasian empires discussed in chapters 1 and 2. Indeed, the Spanish and Portuguese faced many of the same issues in the New World they and their competitors had in the Old—both continued to struggle with the tensions between metropolitan policies and local conditions, between the assimilation or segregation of indigenous peoples, and between the use of collaboration and brute force. Moreover, Iberians brought their experiences and their ideologies with them to the Americas, which included recent experience conquering and colonizing the Canary Islands in the Atlantic as well as strong beliefs about their religious responsibility to aggressively spread Christianity to unbelievers. Finally, Iberians were spurred by the very same motivations in the Americas that had driven all of the early modern Eurasian empires: the desire for profit, the struggle for supremacy, and the push of powerful internal cultural forces.

This chapter explores the foundation and development of these first two European empires in the Americas, and focuses particularly on the ways in which motivations, justifications, and methods brought from the Eurasian context blended with American circumstances, empires, and peoples to produce a new type of imperial rule in the early modern period. In order to tell this story, we need to move back and forth between the imperial metropole and the American territories. We will begin in the Iberian Peninsula, where we explore the ideas and experiences that motivated exploration and conquest. We then move to the Americas, where these pre-existing ideas and experiences were confronted by the realities of diverse lands and peoples. The Iberian colonies and outposts that developed in this context—from their structure to their composition as well as their economic enterprises—were thus the result of the complex interactions between

Empires of the Americas and Early Spanish Settlements, c. 1519

very different peoples, environments, and disease regimes. Moreover, their establishment altered the way Europeans thought about empire and imperial expansion for the next 500 years.

IBERIAN MOTIVATIONS FOR EXPLORATION, TRADE, AND CONQUEST

As we saw in chapters 1 and 2, imperial expansion and the establishment of colonial settlements were common features among the powerful early modern Eurasian states. Indeed, the acquisition of territory and the control of lucrative commodities such as spices and silk were sought by most states as a route to increased power.[1] In the fifteenth century, however, trade in both silk and spices was dominated in the eastern Mediterranean by the Venetians and in the central and western Mediterranean by the Ottomans. For western Europeans hoping to break into the trade in such commodities, this meant that the most convenient and established routes were already jealously guarded by strong maritime powers. If these powers were to be bypassed, new trade routes would have to be found.

For the Iberian states of Portugal and Spain, this search for trade routes (and the profit that promised to accompany them) was an effective motivator for exploration. In the case of Portugal—a relatively small state with limited resources and a rich and powerful Spanish neighbor—the desire for trade and profit outweighed the desire for substantial territorial gains until the last half of the sixteenth century. As we have already seen in chapter 2, this led the Portuguese to establish a series of state-supported networks of trading posts that extended from West Africa to South-East Asia by the early sixteenth century. However, since many of the peoples with whom the Portuguese traded commanded political and economic power in their own right, the Portuguese

tended to focus their efforts on trade rather than conquest.[2] An exception to this rule were the islands of Madeira, which were discovered in the fifteenth century by Portuguese sailors as they were attempting to make the return trip from West Africa by tacking with the winds. In fact the Portuguese had located three island groups: the Azores, the Madeiras, and the Canaries, the latter two of which boasted warm Mediterranean climates suitable for growing tropical and subtropical vegetation. Here the Portuguese saw an opportunity, for they found it was easy to grow one of the trade items they so eagerly sought elsewhere: sugar. Moreover, since the Madeiras were uninhabited, the land was theirs for the taking. With Portuguese financing and management along with unfree labor from Africa, Europe, and the neighboring Canary Islands, by the 1470s Madeira was producing 200 tons of sugar annually for export to European markets.[3] Thus in addition to the trading post model of expansion, the Portuguese also provided an early model of an agricultural plantation society based on slave labor and overseas markets. When transferred west across the Atlantic to the Americas, it would prove to be a powerful model indeed.

Spanish rulers were similarly motivated to seek new trade routes in the fifteenth century by a desire for profit, but they were also closely tied to the desire for territorial expansion and the power such expansion might bring to the state. When Isabella of Castile and Ferdinand of Aragon married in 1469, the unification of their respective territories established the Spanish kingdoms as territorial European forces to contend with in their own right. Isabella's Castile, in particular, was extremely wealthy and powerful, and the Queen herself had enormous resources at her fingertips. Moreover, as we have seen, Castile had taken a leading role in the *reconquista*, a centuries-long

---

[1] Douglas Egerton, Alison Games, Jane Landers, Kris Lane, and Donald Wright, *The Atlantic World: A History, 1400–1888* (Wheeling, IL: Harlan Davidson, 2007), 43.

[2] George Raudzens, *Empires: Europe and Globalization, 1492–1788* (Phoenix Mill: Sutton Publishing, 1999), 24, 28–29.

[3] Egerton et al., *The Atlantic World*, 54. For a fuller explanation of this process in the Canaries and neighboring Atlantic Islands, see Alfred Crosby, *Ecological Imperialism: The Biological Expansion of Europe, 900–1900* (Cambridge: Cambridge University Press, 1986), chapter 4.

struggle to re-conquer the Iberian Peninsula from Muslims who had invaded in the eighth century. Indeed, Isabella and her nobles had only just conquered the last Muslim stronghold of Granada when she agreed to finance Christopher Columbus's first voyage in 1492—a conquest that placed the Iberian Peninsula entirely under Christian rule for the first time since the eighth century. Isabella also strongly supported the final conquest of the Canary Islands, which was completed by Spanish forces between 1492 and 1495.[4] In the context of this drive for territorial expansion and the consolidation of Spanish power, Isabella's decision to provide financial backing for Christopher Columbus's scheme to reach the Indies via the Atlantic seemed to be a logical extension of her desire to secure both new territories and new wealth.[5]

Both the reconquista and the conquest of the Canaries were critical factors in determining the behavior and attitudes of individual Iberian conquerors as well as monarchs when they came across previously unknown lands in the Americas. In 711, Muslims from North Africa advanced into the Iberian Peninsula and established a capital at Cordoba in southern Spain. By the tenth century, Cordoba was the largest city in Europe, and Muslim Spain and Portugal had grown wealthy and prosperous. Christians in Europe, however, did not look kindly on a Muslim stronghold so close to their own bases of power, and in the eleventh century they initiated the first of a series of Crusades to win back the Iberian territories. By the mid-thirteenth century, Christians had won Portugal and large portions of Spain from the Muslims, who retreated to Granada in southern Spain. Over the course of two more centuries, Iberian Christians continued to fight to dislodge the remaining Muslims in the peninsula, and were finally successful with Isabella and Ferdinand's capture of Granada in 1492.[6]

This reconquest of the Iberian Peninsula imbued Spanish territorial expansion with a particular religious fervor.[7] Christians who had fought to retake Spain and Portugal wanted to root out all non-Christian elements from the peninsula either by conversion or expulsion. They also sought to purify Catholic Christianity from corrupting influences either within Christianity or from Islam or Judaism. Indeed, these efforts at purification motivated Isabella and Ferdinand to institute the Spanish Inquisition in 1480, which sought to investigate and eliminate religious sentiments that deviated from strict Catholic doctrine.[8] By the terms of the treaty that marked the surrender of Muslim Granada to Castile and Aragon, Muslims were supposed to maintain their freedom to worship. Yet the tradition of forced conversions in previously re-conquered territories was difficult to stem, and by 1501 Muslims in Granada were given the option to convert or to leave Spain altogether. Jews had suffered a similar fate nine years earlier: by the Alhambra Decree, Isabella and Ferdinand required that all Jews leave Spain immediately on pain of death. Those Jews or Muslims who chose to stay by converting to Christianity were closely monitored by the Spanish Inquisition for apostasy.[9] The reconquista also stimulated the development of a gendered conception of conquest and empire in Iberia in which male "honor" encompassed capturing women from opposing groups and enslaving them. These women played important and often contradictory roles in empire-building in the Iberian region. Some were high-status hostages, while others were treated as lowly slaves. They were seen as exotic foreigners, but assimilated into society over time. Finally, while they were often treated with violence, they also sometimes took on the position of cultural "middlemen"

---

[4] David Weber, *The Spanish Frontier in North America* (New Haven, CT: Yale University Press, 1994), 20.

[5] Raudzens, *Empires*, 46.

[6] Lyle N. McAlister, *Spain and Portugal in the New World, 1492–1700* (Minneapolis: University of Minnesota Press, 1984), 56; and Egerton et al., *The Atlantic World*, 49.

[7] Anthony Pagden, *Lords of All the World: Ideologies of Empire in Spain, Britain, and France, c. 1500–c. 1800* (New Haven, CT: Yale University Press, 1995), 74.

[8] Egerton et al., *The Atlantic World*, 48–49.

[9] For the history of Jews in the Iberian Peninsula, see Jonathan Ray, *The Sephardic Frontier: The Reconquista and the Jewish Community in Medieval Iberia* (Ithaca, NY: Cornell University Press, 2006). For the history of the Inquisition, see Joseph Perez and Janet Lloyd, *The Spanish Inquisition: A History* (New Haven, CT: Yale University Press, 2007).

guiding negotiations and trade between the different sides.[10] Thus by the time Spaniards began interacting with peoples of the Americas, there existed a centuries-long tradition of forced conversion, violent conquest, and spiritual justification that guided Spanish relations with non-Christians.

The long and brutal conquest of the Canary Islands during the fifteenth century also set important precedents that helped guide the attitudes and actions of both Spaniards and Portuguese in the Americas. The Portuguese, having already established lucrative sugar plantations on Madeira by 1470, had been interested in the Canaries both because of their potential for plantation agriculture and because they supported an indigenous population (the Guanche) who might be able to provide the labor for such endeavors. However, Portuguese attempts at conquering the islands were not successful, and the most they were able to do was to capture Guanches to work as slave laborers elsewhere. The Spanish were more successful, although stout Guanche resistance meant that it took a well-equipped army six years (1478–1484) to overcome the largest island and another three years (1492–1495) to conquer the remainder.[11] Once acquired, land in the Canaries was allocated as estates and ranches to leaders of the conquering forces, who then forced the surviving Guanche to work it for them in order to produce cash crops for export to Europe—an important precedent that would be revisited again in the Americas.[12]

By the time Columbus sailed for what he thought would be the Indies in 1492, both the Spanish and the Portuguese had been recently shaped by a religious ideology that justified territorial conquest as well as forced conversion, and by practical experience in conquering new lands and peoples. This preconditioning was to have important ramifications for Spanish interactions with the societies they encountered in the Americas, and also for Portuguese actions in Brazil.

THE FIRST IBERIAN COLONIES IN THE AMERICAS

The modern European "discovery" of the Americas was accidental. Christopher Columbus—an Italian seafarer from Genoa—calculated that he could reach India and other eastern lands by going west across the Atlantic rather than through the Mediterranean or down the coast of Africa and across the Indian Ocean. That this discovery occurred under the Spanish flag was also accidental, for Columbus had tried without success to convince first the Portuguese and then the English of his scheme.[13] Even when Isabella of Spain finally agreed to support Columbus, she gave him only three small ships bought and outfitted with her own private money. Funds for the remainder of the costs had to be raised privately.[14]

Columbus badly underestimated the distance between Europe and Asia, and thus on October 12, 1492, he and his men struck land not in India but in the Caribbean islands. The people they found there—the Taino—were densely settled in island chiefdoms based on agriculture, hunting, fishing, and sea-borne trade. Initially, Columbus and his men hoped to establish trade relations with the Taino based on the Portuguese trading-post model because of the riches and spices Columbus hoped they would possess. At first, the Taino received the Spanish foreigners with warmth, and were enthusiastic about trade opportunities. However, relations between the Spanish and the Taino went sour within a few short months, when it became clear that Taino trade items would not satisfy the Spanish. From first contact, the Spanish had been heartened when they saw that the Taino ornamented their ears and their noses with gold, and they hoped the Taino would produce huge

[10] James F. Brooks, *Captives and Cousins: Kinship and Community in the Southwest Borderlands* (Chapel Hill: University of North Carolina Press, 2002).

[11] Felipe Fernandez-Armesto, *Before Columbus: Exploration and Colonization from the Mediterranean to the Atlantic, 1229–1492* (Philadelphia: University of Pennsylvania Press, 1987), 207–212.

[12] McAlister, *Spain and Portugal in the New World* 63–65; Egerton et al., *The Atlantic World*, 51–54; and Raudzens, *Empires*, 42.

[13] Geoffrey Symcox and Blair Sullivan, *Christopher Columbus and the Enterprise of the Indies* (Boston: Bedford St. Martin's, 2005), 12.

[14] Raudzens, *Empires*, 46.

quantities of the metal for trade. But the Spanish were quickly disappointed in the amount of gold they were able to acquire through peaceful means, and in 1493, Columbus—now reinforced after a second voyage by more than 1,000 new Spanish settlers—set about getting the gold they so desperately sought through violence and force.[15]

This transition from a trading to a conquest model was consistent with a Spanish mindset forged during the reconquista and the subjugation of the Canary Islands. When the Spanish could not get what they wanted from the Taino, they turned instead to territorial acquisition and to appropriating both the land and the people for themselves—justified at least in part by the fact that the Taino were heathens and thus did not deserve the same consideration as Christians. Now, Taino and Taino lands captured by the Spanish were distributed to individual conquerors through a system called the **encomienda**.[16] This system put the labor of the Taino at the disposal of Spanish overlords, who used it greedily in the pursuit of gold.[17] Since the Spanish had already initiated a system like this in the Canaries in order to provide labor for sugar plantations, the biggest departure from this model was the purpose to which the labor was put. In the Caribbean, the Spanish had become a conquest society based primarily on the extraction of precious metals.[18]

The Taino did not passively acquiesce to Spanish designs: indeed, resistance began a few months after the first arrival of the Spaniards, and continued in periodic bursts throughout the decade of the 1490s.[19] The Spanish responded with violence, killing resisters as well as those who aided them and burning towns and crops. In the end, with the help of European diseases (discussed later in this chapter), the Taino found themselves alienated from their own land and even from command over their own labor.[20] Less than two decades after the Spanish arrival in 1492, the Taino population shrank from between a half-million and a million people to only about 60,000. Meanwhile, and in spite of high mortality rates among Europeans, the Spanish settler population had grown to about 10,000 people, nearly all of whom wanted to strike it rich and return wealthy to their homeland.[21]

Despite the growing population in the Caribbean islands, Spanish settlers were not particularly happy there. The supply of available gold in the islands was much smaller than most had hoped, and once its supply dwindled, Spanish settlers had to turn their attention to more mundane methods of making a livelihood such as producing cow hides and growing agricultural crops. Moreover, Spanish settlement in the Caribbean had been marked from the beginning by Spanish–Taino violence as well as internecine fighting between themselves. In fact, Columbus proved so inept at establishing stable rule in the Caribbean that in 1502 Isabella appointed a royal governor, subject now to the Spanish crown, in his place.[22] To make matters worse, the Caribbean islands were not particularly agriculturally productive in the first two decades of the sixteenth century, which made their expense and the trouble of administering them somewhat difficult to justify. Spain had not found another way to Asia, nor had it found the riches or glory its adventurers had so desired. Thus far, the profits of the newly expanded Spanish Empire seemed limited indeed.[23]

Some Spanish colonists, however, still hoped to strike it rich by discovering new places in the Americas that would, this time, deliver the wealth they so desired. The governor of the Caribbean, having heard rumors of fantastic wealth on the mainland of the Americas, sent two expeditions in 1517 and 1518 to search for it. These expeditions were successfully repulsed by indigenous forces

[15] Egerton et al., *The Atlantic World*, 85.

[16] Philip Curtin, *The Rise and Fall of the Plantation Complex: Essays in Atlantic History* (Cambridge: Cambridge University Press, 1998), 68.

[17] James Lockhart and Stuart B. Schwartz, *Early Latin America: A History of Colonial Spanish America and Brazil* (Cambridge: Cambridge University Press, 1983), 68–70.

[18] Egerton et al., *The Atlantic World*, 84.

[19] Ibid., 87.

[20] The story of the Taino is addressed in detail in Irving Rouse, *The Tainos: Rise and Decline of the People Who Greeted Columbus* (New Haven, CT: Yale University Press, 1992).

[21] Raudzens, *Empires*, 51.

[22] Symcox and Sullivan, *Christopher Columbus*, 26.

[23] Raudzens, *Empires*, 52.

on the American mainland, but in 1519 an ambitious settler named Hernando Cortes took it upon himself (without permission) to set out on yet a third expedition. This time, he would find one of the two wealthiest societies ever established in the Americas.

AMERICAN IMPERIALISM

As we have already seen in chapters 1 and 2, empire was hardly only a European phenomenon in the early modern period. Neither was it an exclusive feature of the Old World. Indeed, by 1450 the Americas were home to a variety of expansive, complex societies, from the Iroquois federation and Pueblo culture in North America to the Mexica, Maya, and Inca of Mexico, Central America, and South America, respectively. Could any of these be said to have been indigenous empires? Historians normatively identify two American polities as pre-Columbian empires: the Aztec state ruled by the Mexica people and the vast Andean state of Tawantinsuyu ruled by the Inca and usually identified as the Inca Empire. These two states deserve special consideration here both because they are often identified as empires and because they were among the first mainland societies to encounter the Spanish, and thus bore the brunt of their hunger for precious metals as well as the diseases that accompanied them.

In 1450, the Valley of Mexico boasted the densest population in the Americas, supporting as many as 25 million people.[24] By 1428, the predominant power in the region was the Aztec "triple alliance" based on three cities—Tenochtitlan, Texcoco, and Tlacopan—which commanded a large and growing empire. Tenochtitlan was the largest of these cities and, with a population of about 150,000 inhabitants, can be said to constitute a metropolitan capital.[25] Although the formal

Aztec Empire itself was a relatively recent creation, the tradition of empire-building in Mexico and Central America was not. Between 600 and 900 CE, the Maya of Central America and southern Mexico created a series of competing city-states that were distinctive for their cultural achievements in astronomy, language, and architecture. At the same time, a mysterious people from northern Mexico built a massive city at Teotihuacan (near Mexico City), and from there conquered neighboring societies. After the fall of Teotihuacan in the eighth century, in the tenth century invading peoples from the north—the Toltecs—established a new capital at Tula. Between the tenth century and 1175, when they were vanquished by new invaders, the Toltecs forcibly conquered large portions of central Mexico and made a lasting impact on the region's peoples via their accomplishments in warfare, religion, agriculture, and the arts.[26]

After the fall of the Toltecs in the twelfth century, no central authority dominated the Valley of Mexico. Instead, a variety of linguistic and cultural groups battled one another for dominance. One of these groups was the Mexica (also known as Aztecs), who originally migrated to the region from the north in about 1250. Their rise to power stemmed from humble beginnings, since they commanded neither valuable land nor wealth for about a century after they settled on the shores of Lake Texcoco. In 1325, however, they established themselves on marshy islands in the middle of the lake, and from the security of this position, they gradually gained power. In the 1430s, the Aztecs established an alliance between their capital at Tenochtitlan and the neighboring cities of Texcoco and Tlacopan. By 1504, the Aztecs dominated that alliance and had become the most powerful state in central and southern Mexico. When the Spanish arrived in Tenochtitlan in 1519, the Aztecs controlled a territory of approximately 200,000 square miles.[27]

The Aztec state pursued a self-consciously imperial agenda. The idea was to gain and maintain power over neighboring as well as distant

---

[24] Stuart Schwartz, ed., *Victors and Vanquished: Spanish and Nahua Views of the Conquest of Mexico* (Boston: Bedford St. Martin's, 2000), 14.
[25] Edward E. Calnek, "Aztecs and the Valley of Mexico," in *Expanding Empires: Cultural Interaction and Exchange in World Societies from Ancient to Early Modern Times*, edited by Wendy F. Kasinec and Michael A. Polushin (Wilmington, DE: Scholarly Resources, 2002), 212.

[26] Schwartz, *Victors and Vanquished*, 4.
[27] Calnek, "Aztecs and the Valley of Mexico," 218.

states in order to exact tribute—whether of goods, resources, or people. This tribute, in turn, would increase the power of the state, allowing the accumulation of wealth, prestige, and still more territory. The tribute also played two other important roles. First, it fed the massive city of Tenochtitlan, which after around 1440 was not self-sufficient in foodstuffs. Second, it formed the basis of the wealth of the nobility, who were correspondingly pro-expansion.[28] To these ends, during the fifteenth century the Aztecs transformed from their clan-based origins to a highly stratified, centralized polity based on the values of warfare.[29] Indeed, Aztec boys were raised from birth to be warriors, and military accomplishment was the primary way that manliness was gauged. This culture of aggression was bolstered by a cosmology that depicted the Aztec as having a duty to maintain the balance of the cosmos by sacrificing war captives to sustain the god Huitzilopochtli. It was further supported by a revisionist history of the state, established by the ruler Tlacaélel, that wiped away the Aztec's humble origins and replaced them with a glorious, if manufactured, past.[30] Together, these factors constituted a very real culture of imperialism in the Aztec metropole.

As a result, the fifteenth-century Aztec periodically mustered vast armies, which were then used to pressure other states in the region to recognize the Aztecs as their overlords. If these states acquiesced, the use of violence might be avoided. If they did not, Aztec armies used force to compel submission.[31] The result was the frequent acquisition of new territory and an ever-increasing empire. But the empire was less formal than informal. Conquered territories were not so much ruled as bullied. In early conquests, the Aztec rulers had distributed conquered territory to nobles, but this practice ended quickly, partly because the rulers distrusted the noble class and

did not wish to provide them with territorial power bases. Nor did the state establish a colonial bureaucracy, other than a small group of officials whose job was to collect and store tributary payments. Finally, the conquered societies were not radically reformulated. Instead, local elites were required to provide periodic tributes of people and goods, but were otherwise largely left alone.[32]

Because of or despite this system, the Aztec Empire faced difficulties in maintaining its integrity. Part of this stemmed from the manner in which imperial territory was attained: that is, through threatened or actual military violence. This tended to instill lasting resentments and a constant desire to rebel—an occurrence the Aztecs faced repeatedly. Resentments also multiplied once Aztec rule was established, since the tribute exacted was often crushing, including humans required for sacrifice to Huitzilopotchtli.[33] Interdynastic marriages did occur with some frequency, which may have helped create a sense of imperial unity at an elite level.[34] Yet the fact remains that the only centralized imperial administrative system the Aztecs maintained was the one designed for the collection of tribute. The result was an empire that seemed to be ruled from a powerful center, but in actuality left considerable local autonomy to subordinated states.[35] To make matters more tenuous, at the turn of the sixteenth century the Mexica Empire was under greater stress than normal, as a series of poor harvests and droughts had left vassal states more rebellious than ever, particularly because the Mexica sought to appease their gods through ever-increasing human sacrifices drawn from its empire.[36]

For all its potential fragility, however, the Aztec Empire that Hernando Cortes encountered in 1519 was still yet a strong, powerful state in possession of an excellent army as well as material wealth, the likes of which few Europeans had

[28] J. Rounds, "Lineage, Class and Power in the Aztec State," *American Ethnologist*, 6 (1979), 73–86.
[29] Egerton et al., *The Atlantic World*, 69.
[30] See Charles C. Mann, *1491: New Revelations of the Americas Before Columbus* (New York: Alfred A. Knopf, 2006), 118–119.
[31] Schwartz, *Victors and Vanquished*, 12.

[32] Ross Hassig, *Mexico and the Spanish Conquest* (Norman: University of Oklahoma Press, 2006), 28.
[33] Raudzens, *Empires*, 54–55.
[34] Calnek, "Aztecs and the Valley of Mexico," 216.
[35] Ibid., 219–220.
[36] Egerton et al., *The Atlantic World*, 94.

ever seen. Tenochtitlan, its capital city, was literally alive with trade in staple as well as luxury products, including gold, silver, and precious gems. It was these luxury items—and the dreams of riches and glory that went with them—that inspired Cortes to attempt to conquer the city for himself.

Far to the south, along a narrow strip of land between the Andes mountains and the western shore of South America, another major American empire formed at approximately the same time as the Aztec Empire in central Mexico. As in the Valley of Mexico, both the Andean highlands and the coastal region were populated by a variety of complex societies in the first millennium CE. After about 1000 CE, regional states in either the highlands (Chucuito) or the lowlands (Chimu) controlled increasingly large territories, but no single state was able to impose order on the whole region for long. In part this was because of the tremendous geographical obstacles of the region, especially the harsh mountainous terrain of the Andean highlands themselves. In spite of such obstacles, however, in the early fifteenth century the dynamic highland Inca state—whose inhabitants had arrived on the shores of Lake Titicaca in the mid-thirteenth century—embarked on a campaign of conquest that quickly brought most of the Andean highlands and lowlands under their control. By the end of the century, the Inca Empire stretched more than 2,500 miles from north to south and included more than 10 million people.[37]

The rapid rise, massive size, and incredible wealth of the Inca Empire bore some resemblance to those of the Aztec Empire. So too did motivations for expansion, which required a steady stream of new territories in order to keep new wealth coming into the central state. In the Inca case, however, the motivation to acquire new wealth came from religious beliefs about the sanctity of the goods and property of deceased rulers. Indeed, the Inca treated deceased rulers—who were believed to be descended from the sun—as beings with active roles in the world of the living. Their bodies were preserved through mummification, they were consulted during

decision-making processes, and they accompanied living rulers in celebration parades. Because of their continuing presence, the Inca believed that deceased rulers also continued to own all of their possessions. Living rulers, therefore, had to secure new wealth of their own through conquest.[38]

Despite some chronological and motivational similarities, however, the structure of Inca rule differed considerably from the Aztec. Indeed, whereas the Aztec did not pursue policies of colonization or assimilation, the Inca pursued both. Given the ethnic and linguistic diversity of the peoples living in the various geological zones of the region, most of the peoples conquered by the Inca were not related to them. Rather than allow conquered areas local rule, the Inca sought to assimilate all of its subjects and then to rule them through centralized institutions and administrative districts. To achieve this, the Inca first conducted a large-scale census of each conquered territory. They then co-opted local leaders into the new order, requiring elites from conquered areas to re-settle in Cuzco, both so that their families would not rebel and so that they could learn Inca ways. This was especially done through the institution of *aclla*, or "chosen women," who were taken from among conquered people and placed in temples or royal courts under the direct control of the imperial bureaucracy. There, they served the dual purpose of tying the conquered elite to the state and of subordinating them to the empire's control.[39]

The Inca also sent populations of loyal citizens and priests to live among—and keep an eye on—conquered peoples. There, they were supposed to teach conquered populations how to speak the Incas' Quechua language as well as how to act and look like an Inca. Additionally, the Inca invested significant labor and money in imperial infrastructure such as roads, canals, and storage houses for imperial goods. Much of this labor came from the local population, who paid "tribute" to the state by working for a portion of

---

[37] Ibid., 72.

[38] Ibid.

[39] Irene Silverblatt, "Imperial Dilemmas, the Politics of Kinship, and Inca Reconstructions of History," *Comparative Studies in Society and History*, 30 (1988), 83–102.

the year as tomb guards, honey-gatherers, road laborers, salt miners, cocoa cultivators, weavers, hunters, potters, and farmers for the benefit of the Inca royalty and religious establishment.[40] Partly because of this huge labor resource, by the turn of the sixteenth century the Inca Empire was the strongest state ever created in South America, incorporating massive resources and wealth into a centralized, powerful state that commanded millions of people as well as fantastic wealth.

In 1519, Hernando Cortes marched into Tenochtitlan as a renegade representative of one of the most powerful states in Europe. Thirteen years later, in 1532, Francisco Pizarro—another fortune-seeker—would do the same at Cajamarca in Inca territory. Although neither Cortes nor Pizarro had the official sanction of the Spanish crown beforehand, both hoped to conquer the respective territories and gain sanction by offering their monarch a percentage of the plunder. The state they hoped to represent was greedy, expansive, and sought power in competition with its rivals. Yet so too were the states Cortes and Pizarro confronted. Like the Spanish, the Aztec and Inca empires sought territory, wealth, and power. Like the Spanish, the Aztec and Inca were experienced at using threats and violence to achieve their expansive aims. Like the Spanish, religious motivations played a role in the expansive motivations of both the Aztec and Inca empires. And while the Spanish had a military advantage because of their metal weaponry and horses, both the Aztec and Inca empires had the advantage of numbers and of defending their home territories. Yet by 1530, both American empires had been vanquished and subjected to new Spanish conquerors. How could they have effected these stunning victories over two such powerful states in so short a time?

THE COLUMBIAN EXCHANGE

The most significant answer seems to lie not in some inherent Iberian superiority in empire-building, but rather in invisible exchanges of

microbes that resulted in massive demographic catastrophe among the peoples native to the Americas. Indeed, diseases unknowingly brought to the Americas by European explorers wreaked havoc among every kind of society whether large or small, wiping out entire populations and seriously weakening others. As a result, resistance to European incursions in the Americas was hampered from the very start, while rapid population decline effectively cleared the land for European settlement. Thus, unlike in Asia and Africa where imperial designs among competing states were long hemmed in by strong, stable powers, in the Americas the new colonizers were presented with an opportunity to take advantage of indigenous decline and seize control over huge swathes of territory.

When Christopher Columbus and his men arrived in the West Indies in 1492, they set in motion a process of exchange that had profound effects for the whole world. This exchange—now known for obvious reasons as the **Columbian Exchange**—had cultural and economic aspects, to be sure, but in fact some of the most important exchanges occurred at the microbial level, as diseases and maladies unknown to either side found utterly new hosts. They also occurred at the environmental level, as foodstuffs and animals previously known only in the Americas or in Afroeurasia now began to move freely between the two worlds. After two centuries of such momentous exchanges, both the Old and the New worlds were transformed. For the "old," Afroeurasian world, one important transformation included the addition of valuable new food items into the diets of people as far flung as Ireland, China, and sub-Saharan Africa. For the "new," American world, however, the most important transformation involved the deadly effects of Afroeurasian pathogens among its peoples, which in turn helped pave the way for imperial conquest by Europeans.

What caused the dramatic effects of the Columbian Exchange, and how precisely did it aid in European empire-building in the Americas? Beginning about 12,000 years ago, the land bridge linking the Americas with Afroeurasia across the Bering Strait disappeared as a result of rising sea

---

[40]Catherine J. Julien, "How Inca Decimal Administration Worked," *Ethnohistory*, 35 (1988), 264.

levels. As a result, the peoples of the Americas were almost completely separated from Old World peoples until the Spaniards arrived in 1492. In other words, for 12 millennia the people as well as the plants and animals of the Americas developed in isolation from Afroeurasia according to specific environmental conditions.[41]

Some human developments were similar: for example, agriculture and writing developed in the Americas just as it had done in Afroeurasia, as did the birth of hierarchical societies and patriarchies. In other ways, however, developments in the Americas followed a different course from those of the Old World. For example, plant species such as corn, potatoes, and tobacco were unique to the Americas, and thus American peoples had a different set of choices regarding possible domesticated crops. Just as importantly, not long after humans arrived in the Americas all of the large mammals that existed there became extinct. As a result, when humans in the Americas began to turn to settled agriculture, they did not have the choice to domesticate large mammals such as cattle or horses. Because of this, American societies did not develop innovations like the wheel, which proved unnecessary without large animals to pull carts or push plows. Furthermore, other animals familiar across much of Afroeurasia—including sheep, pigs, chickens, and goats—were nonexistent in the Americas. In fact, the only domesticable animals available to American peoples were the dog, the turkey (in North America), the llama/alpaca and guinea pig (in the Andes region of South America), and the Muscovy duck (in the South American tropics).[42]

The absence of domesticable animals is critical to our story, because in the Old World the domestication of animals such as sheep, chickens, goats, and cattle contributed greatly to the development of serious diseases such as influenza,

smallpox, measles, and pertussis. In fact, many of these serious diseases resulted from microbes that started off in herds of domesticated animals and then made the jump from their animal hosts to human hosts. The jump was made much easier because early Afroeurasian communities that relied on domesticated animals for food and labor tended to live in close proximity to their herds—even keeping them inside their houses for protection or warmth. Over time, a number of these microbial jumps occurred between domesticated animals and humans. In addition, because of the land connections across much of Afroeurasia, these diseases were able to spread to much of the Old World population. While these diseases continued to be serious for the peoples of the Afroeurasia, the human population that survived them over the generations tended to pass on an acquired, partial immunity to their offspring.

Without many domesticable animals and living in enforced separation from Old World peoples, the people of the Americas remained freer from the type of contagious diseases that so often plagued the Old World. Some contagious diseases did exist, to be sure, and included dysentery, pneumonia, and possibly syphilis. But the "crowd" diseases of the Old World did not exist, which meant that American peoples—when exposed to them—had no immunity whatsoever to them. Therefore, when Europeans carrying these diseases inadvertently spread them among American peoples, sickness struck with deadly virulence.

Although historians and demographers continue to debate population estimates in 1492, the most recent estimates tend to range between 40 and 70 million, with approximately 20 to 25 million of those living in the densely populated region of Mexico.[43] To understand the profound advantages the Spanish gained by the spread of their own pathogens, we need only look to events immediately following contact with indigenous peoples. For example, when Christopher Columbus

---

[41] For a full explanation of these processes, see Alfred Crosby, *The Columbian Exchange: Biological and Cultural Consequences of 1492* (Westport, CT: Greenwood Press, 1972); and Jared Diamond, *Guns, Germs, and Steel: The Fate of Human Societies* (New York: W.W. Norton, 2005). Even more forcefully put forward in Mann, *1491*.

[42] Diamond, *Guns, Germs, and Steel*, 213.

[43] This is extensively argued in Mann's *1491*. See also David Lentz, *Imperfect Balance: Landscape Transformations in the Precolumbian Americas* (New York: Columbia University Press, 1983), 5.

landed on the island of Hispaniola in 1492, demographers estimate that about 1 million Taino lived there. Yet within only two decades, only about 60,000 Taino remained.[44] And while some deaths occurred because of conflict, the lion's share resulted from exposure to Old World diseases.

Even more direct evidence comes from Hernando Cortes's conquest of the Aztec city of Tenochtitlan. Certainly, there is little doubt that Cortes's actions in his quest to conquer the great Aztec city relied on violence, cunning, and military advantage. After all, Cortes and his forces had horses, firearms, metal spears, and armor, not to mention a host of indigenous allies who seized the opportunity to oppose their Aztec overlords. Moreover, the initial Aztec response to Cortes and his entourage was unsure and ambivalent—the Aztec Emperor Motecuzoma could not decide whether to welcome or oppose the newcomers, and his eventual decision to allow them into his city allowed the Spaniards to make a bid to control the city and plunder its treasures.[45] Once the Aztec leadership organized sufficiently to fight back, however, they were able to expel the Spanish invaders and drive them back to the coast. When Cortes returned to Tenochtitlan in 1520 to try his luck at conquest again, Aztec resistance was fierce. Whether they could have driven the Spaniards out for good is not known, however, because in that year Tenochtitlan was struck with an outbreak of smallpox, which immobilized and demoralized its population. With no immunities to such a disease, its effects were appalling: men, women, and children screamed with pain from blisters that erupted all over their bodies, and people were so sick that they could not move from their beds, much less minister to others in need. The epidemic was so severe that it may have killed as many as half of Tenochtitlan's people. Indeed, a century after multiple exposures to Old World pathogens, Mexico's population had declined from about 25 million to about 1 million people.[46]

Once Old World diseases were introduced into the Americas, they spread like wildfire. Through trade and migration among American peoples, disease was able to spread to remote areas of both continents in advance of European contact. This was certainly true in the Andean region of South America, where the Inca civilization suffered from a devastating bout of smallpox five years before the Spanish conqueror Francisco Pizarro ever arrived. From an original population of over 10 million in the Inca Empire, the devastation of European diseases was so great that there may have been only 2 million left by the time Pizarro arrived. The Inca ruler himself, Huayna Capac, died during the epidemic, leaving his empire in a state of civil war over his succession.[47] What was true of South America was equally true of North America, and thus the task of staking claim to territory in the Americas was made infinitely easier for Europeans as a result of the inability of indigenous peoples to resist the lethal onslaught of foreign pathogens. Within about one century after the arrival of Columbus in the Caribbean, between 90 and 95% of indigenous Americans had perished before these diseases.

To make matters even more favorable for would-be European conquerors, the Columbian exchange of diseases was highly unequal. New World peoples did not seem to carry any diseases that were lethal to Europeans with the possible, though disputed, exception of syphilis. Yet even syphilis was different than Eurasian crowd diseases, because it could only be transmitted sexually and spread rather slowly, whereas European diseases were transmitted through the air and thus spread more rapidly. In addition, while New World peoples were succumbing en masse to Old World diseases, the spread of New World crops such as corn and potatoes to Afroeurasia actually helped increase Old World populations. Indeed, once American corn and potatoes were transplanted across the ocean, people from Europe to China discovered that their nutritional value and ease of cultivation were superior to many Old World crops. Potatoes, for example, are nearly nutritionally

---

[44] Guns, Germs, and Steel: *The Fates of Human Societies* (New York: W.W. Norton, 1997), 213.
[45] See the documents in Schwartz, *Victors and Vanquished*, 99.
[46] Ibid., 14; and Egerton et al., *The Atlantic World*, 155. Egerton gives the lower figure of 750,000.

---

[47] Egerton et al., *The Atlantic World*, 101.

complete, can be left in the ground for gradual harvesting, and can produce up to four times more food per acre than grains such as wheat and oats. As a result of the use of New World crops such as potatoes and corn, Old World populations increased at precisely the time New World populations were plummeting. Without the highly unequal effects of the Columbian Exchange on Afroeurasia and the Americas, then, the initial European conquest could not have occurred as it did. While there were certainly other factors at play in eventual Spanish conquest—including steel weaponry and the aid, in Mexico, of Aztec enemies—disease played a decisive role.[48] As it happened, the diseases inadvertently introduced by Europeans allowed the conquerors more latitude in claiming unprecedented swathes of land for their own purposes than had yet occurred anywhere else in the world.

IBERIAN EMPIRES IN THE NEW WORLD

The opportunities created in part by such massive demographic decline in the Americas resulted in the establishment of vast Spanish colonies in North, Central, and South America and in the enormous Portuguese colony of Brazil. As we have already seen, the structure of these colonies was deeply informed by the ideologies and experiences that Iberians brought with them. Yet Iberian colonialism in the Americas was not a simple matter of grafting preconceived ideas onto new spaces and peoples. Indeed, regardless of their pre-existing imperial ideas, plans, and experiences, both Spanish and Portuguese styles of colonialism and colonial rule had, like the Eurasian empires of the past, to conform to local conditions.[49] The desire to find and exploit mineral wealth, therefore, meant little if there was no such wealth to be found. In such circumstances, ideas were adapted to conditions on the ground, and it was on this basis that colonial models based on resource extraction, cash crop agriculture, and forced labor were developed to their fullest extent.

Although Spanish and Portuguese colonialism in the Americas were in some ways remarkably similar, differences in local conditions between New Spain (Mexico) and Peru on the one hand and Brazil on the other resulted in the development of two different models of colonial settlement and rule.[50] In New Spain and Peru, the Spanish developed a colonial model based in large part on the extraction of mineral wealth and the use of forced labor—both Indian and African—to accomplish it. In Brazil, where mineral wealth was not discovered until much later in the colony's interior, the Portuguese instead developed a colonial model based on the mass production of sugar through plantation-style agriculture, based also on forced Indian and African labor. Both models were designed to maximize profits for colonists and, secondarily, for the imperial metropole, and both were geared toward participation in global markets. Both models, in addition, increasingly attracted envy as well as emulation by other European states keen to make their own profits from the vast expanses of the Americas.

As we have already seen, Spanish hopes in the New World had centered from the very beginning on trade in gold. Finding no silk, spices, or other light, highly valuable luxury items in the Caribbean islands, Spanish settlers immediately turned their attention to the gold they saw ornamenting the bodies of the indigenous Taino. Although it is certainly true that the supply of gold in the Caribbean islands was far too small to satisfy Spanish ambitions, most of the component parts of the resource-extraction model were developed there and then were exported to the American continent—where Spanish expectations of mineral wealth and local conditions made a far closer match than in the Caribbean.[51]

First, in order to obtain the gold they so desperately wanted, the Spanish required labor. In

---

[48] For more on the Spanish alliances with Aztec enemies, see Raudzens, *Empires*, 58–59.

[49] Lockhart and Schwartz, *Early Latin America*, 59–60.

[50] McAlister provides a helpful comparative analysis of Spanish and Portuguese colonialism in the Americas in *Spain and Portugal in the New World*, 266 ff.

[51] Lockhart and Schwartz, *Early Latin America*, chapter 3.

the Caribbean, most of the existing gold had not been previously mined, which meant that it first needed to be extracted from the rivers and soils of the islands. Since the number of Spanish settlers was small, they needed to find ways to acquire Indian labor to do their mining for them. The encomienda system that developed to fill this need was an attempt by the Spanish to commandeer local labor while leaving the land itself in the hands of indigenous peoples. At its most basic, the encomienda system bestowed upon powerful and wealthy Spanish settlers a group (or groups) of Indians, whose labor was subject to their whims.[52] With this labor, wealthy encomenderos were able to reap the profits of mineral extraction at very little cost to themselves, while inflicting terrible suffering on Caribbean islanders. And although both the gold supply and the supply of Taino laborers themselves died out by the early sixteenth century, by then the encomienda system was developed enough to be exported to new Spanish colonies.

In addition to the encomienda system, the Spanish in the Caribbean also established an urban pattern of settlement that would characterize its colonies on the American mainland. Rather than evenly dispersed settlements of small villages and individual landholdings, the Spanish pattern retained a densely populated, European-style urban nucleus surrounded by hinterlands populated by Indians and periodically marked by a mission station or fortress. Additionally, the typical layout of Spanish colonial cities—with a square at the center, surrounded by a town council building, a church, shops, and residences marked off in a grid-like pattern of streets—was first devised in the Caribbean and then copied in the rest of Spanish America.[53]

Patterns of administration established in the Caribbean also persisted throughout the period of Spanish conquest in the Americas. Most important was the relationship between private enterprise and the state. Caribbean events set a precedent that left most of the risk and financing of exploration and initial conquest up to individual adventurers, with the imposition of royal control following later. For example, on the island of Hispaniola the crown initially allowed Columbus to govern until his inability to maintain order prompted Isabella to name a royal governor in 1502.[54] Additionally, experience in the Caribbean fueled a pattern of expansion into new areas of the Americas by providing a base from which discontented or adventurous individuals could seek out even more profitable areas and peoples to conquer—in the hopes, of course, of receiving royal blessings after the fact.[55] It was just such a "relay" expedition that brought the discontented, glory-seeking Hernando Cortes into contact with the Aztec Empire. The Spanish colony of New Spain, in turn, provided a similar base for others— like Francisco Pizarro—who were in search of new riches in South America.

By the time Cortes made his journey to the Valley of Mexico in 1519, Spanish patterns of labor exploitation, settlement, administration, and expansion had already been developing in the Caribbean for three decades. Although the peoples Cortes encountered in the valley were quite different from the Taino, these basic patterns adapted quite well to the new circumstances. Indeed, both the Aztec and the Inca empires encompassed large, sedentary, highly developed populations ideal for providing vast quantities of labor. Moreover, both New Spain and Peru possessed quantities of precious metals in amounts far in excess of anything the Caribbean colonists could have imagined. As a result, the Caribbean islands—which had initially inspired the Spanish style of colonial rule— quickly became a backwater, while New Spain and then Peru took center stage.[56]

The Spanish conquest of the Aztec and Inca empires in 1519 and 1532, respectively, meant that Spaniards had taken the two wealthiest empires in all of the Americas for themselves. To be sure, men who sought glory and riches would

---

[52] Ibid., 92–96.
[53] Egerton et al., *The Atlantic World*, 105–106; and ibid., 66–67.
[54] Symcox and Sullivan, *Christopher Columbus*, 26.
[55] Lockhart and Schwartz, *Early Latin America*, 78.
[56] Ibid., 92.

seek other, comparable civilizations, but none could equal the natural and human resources of New Spain and Peru. As in the Caribbean, both empires were conquered by adventurers hoping to gain personal wealth and then to apply for royal recognition from the Spanish crown. Cortes, in fact, had not been authorized by the royal governor of Hispaniola to carry out his expedition, and after initial contact with Tenochtitlan he had had to race back to Veracruz to do battle with a force sent to capture him.[57] However, once the size and wealth of both empires had been clearly demonstrated, the conquerors had little difficulty convincing the crown to recognize their actions and to claim the territories for Spain. In fact, this pattern of after-the-fact imperial recognition, dubbed "man-on-the-spotism" by historian Philip Curtin, became a phenomenon of European imperialism right through the twentieth century.

While the Spanish crown did not control the pace of exploration or the speed of conquest, it did assert royal control over American territories in both Mexico and Peru shortly after their subjugation. Already in 1524, the crown had formalized its claims to rule in the Americas through the creation of the Council of the Indies, which was intended to be the supreme legislative and judicial body for all of its territories.[58] The Council, which ruled from Spain, assumed control over the *Casa de Contracion* (House of Trade) in Seville and reserved final authority for all colonial decisions. In 1535, the Council created the viceroyalty of New Spain, based in Mexico City, and in 1544, it created the viceroyalty of Peru, based in Lima.[59] Through the authority of the Council, these two viceroyalties were to exert jurisdiction over all Spanish territories. To complement as well as to check the power of the two viceroys, the Council also created *audiencias*—royal courts of justice and appeal—in both viceregal capitals. As the empire grew over time, audiencias were also established in Guatemala, Guadalajara, Charcas,

Quito, and Panama. Alongside the civil governmental apparatus, the viceregal capitals became the sites of archbishoprics, which then appointed bishops to cities throughout the empire.[60]

The imposition of this institutional structure, however, was not responsible for the distinctive shape of the Spanish Empire in the Americas. Rather, it was an "institutional overlay" that, as other scholars have noted, "represented formal and permanent recognition of what local people had already built upon a local base."[61] Indeed, using their Caribbean experience as a guide, Spanish conquerors in both the Valley of Mexico and Peru continued their highly urban settlement pattern. On the American mainland, however, the Spanish built their first cities not on new ground but right on top of the pre-existing cities of the Aztec and Inca. In Mexico City, for example, Spanish conquerors built their main church atop of the site where the main Aztec temple had been, while their governor's palace stood on the site of the Aztec imperial residence.[62] Likewise, the imperial capitals in both viceroyalties dominated the economic and political life of the Spanish colonies just as the Aztec and Inca capitals had done before them. In important ways, then, the Spanish grafted themselves onto a pre-existing imperial structure that also happened to agree with Spanish predilections for centralized, urban lifestyles.

Spanish objectives also traveled with them from the Caribbean. Primary among these objectives was the search for precious metals. Although that search had had disappointing results in the West Indies, on the mainland it was to bear rich fruit. Initially, conquistadors in both Mexico and Peru obtained their long-sought precious metals through plunder. Both the Aztec and the Inca had great stores of jewels, sculptures, and ornaments made of precious metals and gems, and these the conquerors immediately took for themselves or else sent to the Spanish monarchs to curry royal favor. Once the plunder was complete, Spaniards

---

[57] Egerton et al., *The Atlantic World*, 99.

[58] McAlister, *Spain and Portugal in the New World*, 183.

[59] John Robert Fisher, *The Economic Aspects of Spanish Imperialism in America, 1492–1810* (Liverpool: Liverpool University Press, 1997), 47.

[60] Lockhart and Schwartz, *Early Latin America*, 92. The Casa de Contracion was itself established only in 1503.

[61] Ibid.

[62] Ibid., 89; and Egerton et al., *The Atlantic World*, 104.

in both territories turned to the search for profitable mines. In Mexico, gold mining dominated at first, but the discovery of rich silver mines in Zacatecas in 1547 prompted a shift to silver mining on a massive scale. Two years earlier, in 1545, the discovery of one of the world's richest silver mines at Potosí in the Peruvian highlands led to a similar shift.[63] By 1550, the primary raison d'être for the Spanish Empire in the Americas had become the extraction of precious metals on a scale the world had never before seen.[64]

By the end of the sixteenth century, the structure of Spanish imperial rule in the Americas was well established. Once the riches of the mainland were discovered, Mexico City and Lima quickly became the dominant centers, around which secondary urban networks, ocean ports, and fringe areas developed. Although Spain claimed vast territories in North, Central, and South America, the two regions that promised the greatest profits always received the most attention from the crown and from settlers alike.[65] The dominance of Mexico and Peru, and the primary importance of resource extraction in both, in turn had important effects for the social construction of the Spanish Empire. Indeed, labor systems as well as settlement patterns reflected Spanish priorities, although these were always tempered by local conditions.

As in the Caribbean islands, Spanish desires to make the most of available precious metals could not have been effected without vast amounts of labor. Also like the Caribbean, the Spanish on the mainland expected to command this labor on highly advantageous terms, and to use it however they saw fit. In fact, Spanish conquistadors extended the encomienda system from the Indies to both Mexico and Peru, allocating the labor of indigenous groups to conquerors and wealthy settlers for their personal use.[66] Yet the encomienda system did not work as well on the mainland, especially for resource extraction, partly because the location of the best mines was often far from the biggest encomiendas. Additionally, by 1540 the system itself was under scrutiny by Spaniards who argued that it engendered both abuse and cruelty, and that the need for labor outside encomiendas encouraged settlers to enslave Indians. In 1542, the Spanish crown issued the New Laws, which both outlawed Indian slavery and mitigated the utility of the encomienda system in central areas of the empire.[67]

Instead, the Spanish turned to a system of tribute labor they called the *repartimiento* (Mexico) and the **mita** (Peru).[68] These systems were not Spanish imports, but rather adaptations of existing imperial Aztec and Inca tributary labor arrangements to the new rulers' needs. As we have seen, the densely settled populations of the Aztec and Inca empires were accustomed to tribute requirements in the form of goods as well as labor. Once again, then, pre-existing conditions on the American mainland accorded well with Spanish ideas about labor formed during the Caribbean phase. Under the repartimiento and the mita, the Spanish demanded that indigenous communities provide a set number of adult male laborers for a temporary period—usually several months.[69] These laborers could be assigned to a variety of tasks including mining outfits, building projects, agricultural tasks, and domestic labor. This was not slave labor, because Indian laborers received wages: however, treatment of the laborers was often harsh, and the tasks they were assigned to do—especially mining—were frequently life-threatening.[70]

Had the populations of the mainland Indians remained stable, Spanish labor requirements

---

[63] See the discussion on mining in Fisher, *The Economic Aspects of Spanish Imperialism*, 93 ff.

[64] Raudzens, *Empires*, 66.

[65] Egerton et al., *The Atlantic World*, 110.

[66] For an in-depth exploration of the encomienda system as it was transferred from the Caribbean to Central America, see Lesley Byrd Simpson, *The Encomienda in New Spain* (Berkeley: University of California Press/ACLS Humanities E-Book, 2008).

[67] Egerton et al., *The Atlantic World*, 152–153. However, the encomienda system survived in fringe areas of the Spanish Empire for centuries.

[68] Mark Cocker, *Rivers of Blood, Rivers of Gold: Europe's Conquest of Indigenous Peoples* (New York: Grove/Atlantic, 1998), 108.

[69] Jeffrey Cole explores the mita system in detail in terms of its relationship to the mines in Potosí. See *The Potosí Mita, 1573–1700: Compulsory Indian Labor in the Andes* (Stanford: Stanford University Press, 1985).

[70] Egerton et al., *The Atlantic World*, 154.

under the repartimiento and the mita might have been sustainable. Yet as we have already seen, indigenous populations during the Spanish conquest were anything but stable. Epidemic disease—after initially hitting both Mexico and Peru in the second and third decades of the sixteenth century—continued to ravage indigenous populations in waves. Throughout the sixteenth century, the population of Mexico fell precipitously from its original 25 million to a low of between 750,000 and 1 million by the early seventeenth century. Indigenous populations of Peru also fell rapidly, reaching an all-time low in the early eighteenth century of just over 600,000—down from more than 10 million at the time of contact.[71] In such a context of demographic collapse, Spaniards found it necessary to turn first to wage labor and then—in cases where even regular wages could not produce the needed labor—to slaves brought from Africa. It is important to note that at no time did Spanish settlers intend to do such work themselves: as with other cases of modern colonialism, part of the Spanish imperial model from the reconquista and the conquest of the Canaries right through to the Caribbean and mainland American phase was the necessity for Spaniards to separate themselves from menial labor, which was to be done by conquered groups clearly outside the pale of Spanish civilization.

Spanish priorities in Mexico and Peru also deeply affected settlement patterns, which themselves had long-term consequences for the social composition of Spanish America. Although both areas had been conquered by a handful of ambitious men, a more general Spanish immigration began as soon as it was clear that there were riches to be had. Between 1506 and 1600 alone, approximately 400,000 Spaniards migrated to the American territories.[72] Most of these migrants were young Spanish men, many of them nephews of minor landholders or second or third sons, who hoped to make their fortunes in the Americas and then return to Spain. Spanish women migrants were rare in the early years of conquest, and as a result Spanish

men frequently intermarried with indigenous women. In many cases, Spanish men sought women from indigenous noble classes. Such marriages were sexual as well as strategic unions, because they tended to ally noble families from the pre-contact period to influential settlers.[73] In the meantime, the children of these unions (known in Spanish as **mestizos**) formed an intermediary group between the conquerors and the conquered, who both eased the process of colonial formation through their dual identification and also posed new problems about the assimilation of groups on the margins of the ruling class (discussed more fully in chapter 5). The result was a multi-layered yet starkly hierarchical social world in which a relatively small population of Spaniards—located primarily in urban centers—dominated a much larger fringe population of Indians and, increasingly, Africans. In the middle was a large and growing population of mestizos, who themselves were the product of a settlement pattern created by Spanish imperial priorities.

While the Spanish Empire in the Americas was focused on resource extraction, the Portuguese created a very different—but no less important—imperial model in Brazil. The difference resulted in large part from local conditions, because the peoples of the area were not urbanized or densely settled like the peoples of the Andes or the Valley of Mexico, and furthermore they had little that the Portuguese wanted in terms of trade items except Brazil wood.[74] When a Portuguese mariner accidentally "discovered" Brazil in 1500, then, it was not considered a particularly important find. Initially, in fact, the Portuguese crown leased the rights to trade and settle there to private traders.[75] It is also important to remember that while the American colonies were the focus of Spanish imperial ventures during the sixteenth century, the Portuguese possessed an extensive network of trading posts in Africa and Asia where they were already expending a tremendous amount of

---

[71] Ibid., 155.
[72] Raudzens, *Empires*, 66.

[73] Egerton et al., *The Atlantic World*, 104.
[74] Brazil wood was used as a dye in Europe.
[75] Raudzens, *Empires*, 38.

energy.[76] As a result, the Portuguese were not inclined to think of Brazil as much more than a minor outpost.[77]

Focused efforts to establish formal colonial rule in Brazil, therefore, only occurred later because of competition from international rivals (especially the French) rather than convictions about the value of the territory. Five years after the Portuguese "discovery," French traders began to stake their own claims to Brazilian territory. By 1530, these claims had grown serious enough to prompt the Portuguese crown to send 400 settlers to the area, along with the first royal governor. When a new wave of French settlers arrived in Brazil in 1555, the Portuguese royal governor decided to fight. By 1567, the Portuguese had driven the foreign competition out and had made—with royal blessings and aid—far more strenuous efforts to establish a colonial settlement there. As in Spanish America, then, the Portuguese model of colonial expansion in the Americas began with chance and private initiative, and only later became an enterprise sanctioned by the crown.[78]

As the transformation to royal colony was taking place, Portuguese settlers—by now fairly certain that their American colony was not going to yield riches in silver or gold like those in Spanish America—had begun to turn to agricultural enterprises to make their fortunes.[79] Indeed, Portuguese colonists in Brazil had easy access to large tracts of land, and they sought to produce whatever crops might be exported at a profit. Using their experience from the island of Madeira, they brought sugar cane to Brazil, where it thrived.[80] By the last quarter of the sixteenth century, Brazilian sugar plantations were producing more sugar for the European market than anywhere else in the world.[81]

As in Spanish America, both the labor needs and the settlement pattern of Portuguese Brazil reflected the priorities of the colony. Plantation agriculture, like resource extraction, requires significant and continuous labor. At first, Portuguese settlers—who were already experienced with African slavery—enslaved local Indians for this purpose.[82] Yet it was difficult to maintain an adequate supply of Indian labor because, as in Spanish America, Brazilian Indians were highly susceptible to European diseases. In many places, whole villages were wiped out as epidemics swept through the region, so that even increased slave raids into the Brazilian interior could not keep pace with Indian mortality.[83] Additionally, Brazilian Indians frequently ran away into the forest, further depleting the labor supply. In response to such a labor gap, by 1560 Portuguese settlers in America were increasingly turning to African slaves. By the beginning of the seventeenth century, as other scholars have argued, "the transition to African labor in the plantation zones of coastal Brazil was complete."[84] The result was a tiny Portuguese ruling class (which numbered about 207,000 by 1572) that set itself apart from a much larger enslaved Indian and African laboring force.[85]

Like the Spanish, the settlement patterns of the Portuguese reflected colonial more than metropolitan priorities. Generally speaking, the purpose of colonial settlement in Brazil was profit rather than the recreation of Portuguese society in a new place. Because of this, few Portuguese women settled the area, which meant that Portuguese men frequently chose sexual partners among indigenous groups. Once again, the result was a large and growing mixed-race population that occupied an important middle ground between the conquerors and the conquered.[86]

---

[76] Lockhart and Schwartz, *Early Latin America*, 181.

[77] A.J.R. Russell-Wood's *The Portuguese Empire, 1415–1808: A World on the Move* (Baltimore: Johns Hopkins University Press, 1992 and 1998) does a good job of exploring Brazil in the context of the greater Portuguese empire.

[78] Lockhart and Schwartz, *Early Latin America*, 191.

[79] Gold was in fact discovered in Brazil, but not until 1693 in the highlands. Ibid., 226.

[80] Ibid., 193.

[81] Raudzens, *Empires*, 38.

[82] Peter Winn, *Americas: The Changing Face of Latin America and the Caribbean* (Berkeley: University of California Press, 1992), 70.

[83] Lockhart and Schwartz, *Early Latin America*, 198.

[84] Ibid., 200.

[85] Raudzens, *Empires*, 38.

[86] Lockhart and Schwartz, *Early Latin America*, 235.

The Portuguese imperial model in the Americas, in many ways, turned out to be quite unlike the Portuguese trading-post model we saw in chapter 2. While it had begun in much the same way, foreign competition and then the establishment of sugar plantations had transformed it into a settlement colony based on commercial agriculture. This model was also distinct from the Spanish model, which was based on the extraction of precious metals from two central areas with rich imperial histories of their own. In the main, these differences were the result of varying local conditions rather than design. Indeed, it would be difficult to argue that the Spanish and Portuguese empires that developed in the Americas were the result of coherent imperial policies formed in the metropole and implemented abroad. Rather, they were the result of past experience in the Iberian Peninsula and in the Canary and Madeira islands, religious and economic motivations for expansion, and ideas about conquest and labor on the one hand, and the complex realities of local conditions, resource availability, and human mortality in the Americas on the other.

As it happened, both models of empire—once developed—were to have enormous consequences for the global economy and for the further spread of empire in the Americas and elsewhere. The Spanish had stumbled into a system which sought to take advantage of the mineral resources of an external territory on a scale never before tried and with rich results. The Portuguese, in contrast, had developed a system that expanded the plantation model of the Canaries and Madeiras to an unprecedented and extremely profitable degree. Neither model would have been possible without the demographic collapse of millions of indigenous Americans, and both would inspire imitators who sought to get in on the riches of the Americas for their own purposes.

Initially, the imperial model that was most inspiring to outsiders was the Spanish one, because during the sixteenth century Spanish colonists became some of the wealthiest people in the world. By 1600, Spain commanded the largest supply of precious metals in the world, which attracted the jealous envy of rival states as well as greedy individuals. After 1571, when Spanish forces seized Manila in the Philippine Islands, Spanish ships were able to ship their precious cargoes directly from the Americas to the rich and prized markets of China. Moreover, such massive amounts of silver enriched the monarchs of Spain to such a degree that they were able to fund continual wars against their enemies in Europe.

Such riches encouraged not only envy but also competition. Those European states that felt the brunt of Spanish ambitions funded by New World silver, in particular, hoped to disrupt the flow of Spanish silver and also claim some for themselves. By the seventeenth century, France, the Netherlands, and England had begun to claim American territories for themselves—each hoping to find their own Potosí in order to replicate Spanish success. Yet ironically the model most European newcomers to the Americas would come closest to replicating was not the Spanish but the Portuguese. Although it was not clear at the time, the Spanish had already conquered the areas most convenient for the extraction of precious metals. The lands that were left were far better suited to agriculture, hunting, or timber. In areas conducive to tropical or subtropical agriculture, the Portuguese model of using African slave labor for the purpose of exporting cash crops for a global market—a subject explored in the next chapter—proved especially relevant.

Just a century after Iberians first arrived in the Americas, both continents were utterly transformed: the original inhabitants had been dramatically reduced, outside European forces now claimed huge portions of the available land, and new economic, political, and social arrangements had been introduced that would have profound effects for the entire world. The Americas, indeed, had become a vast laboratory for new forms of long-distance imperial expansion and colonial settlement under the Iberians: in the centuries ahead, the experiment would continue under the aegis of new imperial powers.

Questions

1. Consider the material about Habsburg Spain and Portugal in chapters 1 and 2 in light of the discussion in this chapter. Of all of the Eurasian states and empires, why do you think these Iberian countries were the first to explore the Americas?

2. Do the Aztec (Mexica) and Inca states described earlier fit the definition of "empire" used in this book? Would you consider them to be empires?

3. Explain the relationship between the Columbian Exchange and the fall of the Inca and Aztec states.

4. Compare and contrast the Spanish and Portuguese models of economic colonialism in the Americas. How did they differ? How were they similar?

CHAPTER 4

Colonialism: Competition for Empire and the Rise of the Slave/Plantation Complex

In spite of its abundant colonial wealth, by the first half of the seventeenth century Spain was beginning to lose its dominance in the Americas. Indeed, its very success in the Americas undermined that dominance, for the treasures of Potosí and Zacatecas inspired Spain's European neighbors to search for similar riches in the New World. Moreover, in the sixteenth century Spanish kings used their American wealth to finance long wars against the Dutch, French, and English, in the process incurring among them all a long-lasting desire to crush Spanish power wherever it was vulnerable. This process of competition and antagonism resulted in a variety of efforts by rival European powers both to steal Spanish wealth in the Americas directly and to establish settlements of their own.

While each of Spain's adversaries hoped to find a Mexico or Peru of its own in the Americas, local conditions dictated quite a different reality. Neither the peoples nor the geographies of most of the Americas were conducive to the large-scale extraction of precious metals. As a result, traders and settlers from France, the Netherlands, and England developed a variety of distinctive colonial models suited to local conditions as well as to their unique cultural and political configurations. Yet in the first half of the seventeenth century, Dutch, English, and French colonists each found they could grow lucrative cash crops in their tropical and subtropical settlements, which created broad similarities across the colonies in these regions. While the English in particular focused first on tobacco, by the 1660s the focus was on the most lucrative cash crop of all: sugar. Thanks largely to the aid of Dutch settlers who were familiar with Portuguese sugar plantations in Brazil, English and French tropical colonies—particularly in the Caribbean—were quickly dominated by sugar plantations of their own to feed the apparently insatiable appetites of European consumers. And with sugar came the labor force required to produce it: African slaves. As sugar plantations multiplied in the Americas, so too did the number of slaves. In the process, Europeans created interlinked imperial webs, with strands that crisscrossed the Atlantic between Europe, the Americas, and Africa—each connected in some way by precious cargoes of sugar and slaves.

This chapter explores the competition for colonial settlements that developed in the wake of Spanish colonization of the Americas, beginning with its causes and immediate results as well as

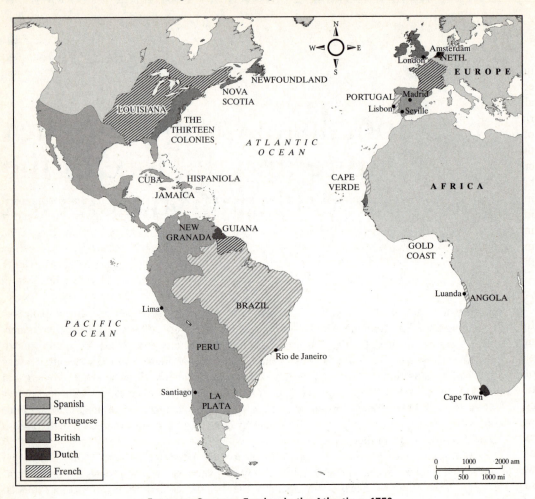

European Overseas Empires in the Atlantic, c. 1750

both its intended and unintended consequences. From there, we move to the rise of cash crop agriculture, with a particular focus on sugar plantations and the development of a slave-based sugar economy in the Atlantic world. Ironically, although European rivals had begun their imperial enterprises in the Americas with the intention of imitating Spain, by 1700 it was already clear that the Portuguese model of combining cash crop production with African slavery had become—for the time being—the dominant imperial model of the modern world. Moreover, in part because of this colonial success, the imitators—especially the English and the French— made great strides in their fervent desire to surpass the wealth and power of imperial Spain.

COMPETITION FOR EMPIRE

In the seventeenth and eighteenth centuries, **mercantilism** was the dominant economic theory guiding most European states. Itself a symptom of the increasing competition in Europe, mercantilism as a set of theories preached that nations competed against each other in the economic as well as the political realm. Although in practice mercantilist theory was interpreted in a variety of ways, one of its most important principles was that each state should be economically self-sufficient. To achieve this, states needed to maintain a favorable balance of trade (where the value of exports exceeds the value of imports).[1] Part and parcel of maintaining self-sufficiency and a favorable balance of trade were rigorous state policies designed to discourage foreign imports through high tariffs and to protect export markets. In addition, mercantilist theory held that the economic health of a state could best be measured by the amounts of precious metals it possessed. In mercantilist theory, then, colonies could help states achieve their economic goals by providing inexpensive sources of raw materials as well as captive markets for exports. Their benefits magnified

considerably if they could also serve as sources of precious metals. In order to provide these benefits, however, trade between states and their colonies required careful regulation to ensure that profits were not diverted to foreigners.[2]

When Spanish conquistadors discovered the rich silver mines of Potosí and Zacatecas in the first half of the sixteenth century, it immediately became apparent to Spain and its neighbors that such access to precious metals gave Spain enormous economic advantages in Europe. Guided by mercantilist policy, Spanish monarchs guarded their American wealth jealously, with the intent of using their annual royal share (one-fifth of the total ore) for the benefit of themselves as well as the state. Foreign ships were not allowed to enter Spanish colonial ports, and all trade with Spanish colonies had to be conducted with special licenses. Locked out of any stake in this massive colonial wealth, Spain's European neighbors understandably looked upon this windfall with envy. To make matters worse, during the last half of the seventeenth century Spain conducted a series of wars against the Netherlands (which was claimed by the Spanish Hapsburgs but began to fight for its independence in 1568), England, and France. These wars were all financed with American silver. Historians now suggest that American silver in fact led Spanish kings to overextend themselves in these long and extremely costly wars, which ironically ultimately undermined Spanish dominance by inducing a continual state of bankruptcy.[3] At the time, however, such a result was not at all clear: in 1588, Philip II mounted a simultaneous attack on the English and the Dutch in what was then "the greatest sea and land offensive in history."[4] Although the offensive ultimately was not successful, Spanish power seemed real enough to those who encountered its wrath.

[1] Muriel Chamberlain, *Formation of the European Empires, 1488–1920* (Edinburgh Gate: Pearson Education Limited, 2000), 33.

[2] Douglas Egerton, Alison Games, Jane G. Landers, Kris Lane, and Donald Wright, *The Atlantic World: A History, 1400–1888* (Wheeling, IL: Harlan Davidson, 2007), 129.
[3] George Raudzens, *Empires: Europe and Globalization, 1492–1788* (Phoenix Mill: Sutton Publishing, 1999), 71; and Egerton et al., *The Atlantic World*, 146.
[4] Raudzens, *Empires*, 72.

Faced with the very real consequences of being on the receiving end of the economic advantages Spain gained from its colonial wealth, it is hardly surprising that rival European states sought some of these advantages for themselves. Yet in the sixteenth century, any overt, organized military challenges to Spanish power in the Americas were out of the question for the English, Dutch, or French. Spain was still the strongest maritime power in the world, and Spanish ships dominated the most valuable Atlantic coastlines in the Americas. Instead, one strategy rival states pursued was outright theft, either by raiding Spanish coastal settlements or by intercepting Spanish ships, loaded with silver, on their way to Spain. In the sixteenth and seventeenth centuries, such theft was authorized and supported by Spain's rivals as a legitimate tool of the state. What Spain saw as blatant piracy, its rivals saw as an acceptable means by which to undermine the power of the Spanish Empire. Even the name of such activities changed to reflect its acceptability: when states lent pirates their support and protection, they were known as corsairs or **privateers**. As corsairs, civilians were granted licenses to plunder any and all Spanish shipping on the seas, supposedly in retaliation for Spanish acts of war on land.[5]

Privateers of several nationalities were active in the Atlantic during the sixteenth and seventeenth centuries, but states tended to sanction especially high levels of piracy during periods of intense conflict with Spain. For this reason, French privateers dominated Atlantic waters in the first half of the sixteenth century, when France was frequently at war with Spain. English privateers then dominated during the last half of the century, when Queen Elizabeth I sought to combat Spanish interference in Europe. In the first half of the seventeenth century, the Dutch superseded both the French and the English during a period of resistance and rebellion against Spanish control over the Netherlands. Generally, privateers focused on Spanish ships that stopped in Cuba on their way from Veracruz or Cartagena to Spain.

Some individuals were highly successful: the English Francis Drake brought so much Spanish treasure back from his raids in the 1570s that Queen Elizabeth knighted him, while the Dutch Piet Heyn's capture of the entire Spanish fleet in 1628 yielded a profit of 8 million pesos.[6] Yet the Spanish learned quickly from privateers, and already by the 1520s treasure ships traveled in convoys for protection. When convoys did not prove adequate, in 1561 the Spanish instituted a system by which treasure ships traveled from Cuba to Spain twice a year in fleets escorted by armed warships.[7] Despite Heyn's success in 1628, privateers found outright capture of Spanish fleets increasingly difficult by the mid-sixteenth century. Because of this, privateers turned also to plundering Spanish coastal settlements and forts in and around the Caribbean, making for a rough, violent, and tenuous life for many Spanish settlers, not to mention for the peoples of the Americas.[8]

Some of the earliest activities of the French, English, and Dutch in the Americas were not, then, based on the desire to establish permanent settler colonies, but rather were designed explicitly to horn in on Spanish imperial wealth. In fact, early colonial outposts established by both the French in Florida and the English in North Carolina were chosen not for their productive worth but because of their convenience as way stations for privateers hoping to prey on Spanish ships and settlements in the Caribbean.[9] Piracy also was behind the seizure, by both French and English citizens, of land in the Caribbean itself: by the mid-seventeenth century the French claimed the western half of Hispaniola, Martinique, and Guadalupe, while the English claimed Barbados, Antigua, St. Kitts, Nevis, and Jamaica. Each new

---

[5] Egerton et al., *The Atlantic World*, 133; and ibid., 73.

[6] For Drake, see John Hampden, *Francis Drake, Privateer: Contemporary Narratives and Documents* (Birmingham: University of Alabama Press, 1972); for Heyn, see Kris E. Lane, *Pillaging the Empire: Piracy in the Americas, 1500–1750* (Armonk, NY: M.E. Sharpe, 1998), 67.
[7] Egerton et al., *The Atlantic World*, 116, 134, 143.
[8] For a good description of this rough world, see Richard Dunn, *Sugar and Slaves* (New York: W.W. Norton & Company, 1972).
[9] These forts were Fort Caroline and Roanoke, respectively.

claim in the Caribbean provided a base for privateering, smuggling, and raiding in an effort to disrupt Spanish profits. These practices remained part of state-sanctioned imperial policy well into the seventeenth century.[10]

NEW EUROPEANS IN THE AMERICAS—ENGLISH, FRENCH, AND DUTCH COLONIAL EFFORTS

In addition to outright theft, some groups of Europeans sought to compete with the Spanish by establishing their own settlements. Their problem, especially until the last half of the seventeenth century, was that they could not establish settlements too close to the centers of Spanish power without inviting an armed response. Even though Spanish power declined over the course of the seventeenth century, Spain continued to control the seas as well as the most important coastal areas in Central and South America as well as the Caribbean.[11] This meant that newcomers were forced to pick colonial settlements from areas where the Spanish had no interest, which for all practical purposes meant North American lands north of Florida.

The extent to which these new settlements represented state policies of imperial expansion—or even state-supported colonialism—varied widely. English settlement, for example, was only loosely tied to the state, and in most cases was initially established by private enterprise. Royal control tended to be extended later, especially in response to territorial threats by competing European powers. Like the English, French efforts at colonization at first relied on private enterprise loosely sanctioned by royal license. However, by the last half of the seventeenth century the French monarchy became increasingly invested in improving the growth and success of its colonial empire through directed state policies. The Dutch, who were far more interested in trade than in colonial settlement, relied on private trading companies to manage their trade and settlement efforts, although these companies were themselves tightly tied to the ruling powers of the state. By 1650, the result of all these colonial efforts produced a wide array of settlements, trading posts, and forts in the Americas and beyond, chosen largely on an ad hoc basis and managed only loosely by metropolitan centers in Europe. Moreover, none of these efforts had located treasures or produced profits sufficient even to come close to Spanish colonial successes in Mexico or Peru.[12]

English attempts to profit from the Americas centered around three areas before 1650: the mid-Atlantic region of Virginia and Maryland, New England, and islands of the Caribbean unoccupied by—or in some cases newly conquered from—the Spanish. In each case, private initiative was crucial, while the crown played a much smaller role. In 1607, the newly formed Virginia Company established a settlement at Jamestown. King James I had provided the settlers a royal charter authorizing settlement, but financing for the effort was organized privately in a joint-stock company owned and controlled by individual investors. And while the Company did periodically report to a Royal Council on Trade in London, its day-to-day management, operations, and activities were left almost entirely in private hands. This investment model was not unique to English operations in the Americas: in fact, a similar joint-stock operation had been initiated by the English East India Company (EIC) in 1601 for the purpose of setting up trading operations in India. The model was decidedly Portuguese, but with some innovations. In the English version, the state granted monopoly trading rights to the EIC, but the company itself was financed entirely by private investors who purchased individual shares. The goal in India, at least until the eighteenth century, had been not conquest but to set up protected trading posts for the purpose of acquiring spices and other exotic goods. The

---

[10] Egerton et al., *The Atlantic World*, 146.
[11] Raudzens, *Empires*, 73.

[12] For a comparative exploration of the early modern European empires in the Americas, see Jack Greene and Philip Morgan, eds., *Atlantic History: A Critical Appraisal* (Oxford: Oxford University Press, 2009).

goals of the Virginia Company were similar: to seek out, like the Spanish had done elsewhere in the Americas, gold and silver mines as well as any other high-value items that could be sold at a profit in Europe.[13] Jamestown was to function as a lucrative trading post in which settlers would maximize available resources and funnel them back to Europe, where investors would grow rich.

The **Company** had chosen Virginia not because its location was ideal, but because it was the most southerly land they could claim without arousing Spanish ire. Yet unlike the EIC, the Virginia Company did not realize its trade objectives in Virginia.[14] Not only were settlers unable to find minerals or other luxury items, but initially they could not even feed themselves.[15] Death rates were staggering: over half the colonists died between 1607 and 1610 from disease and malnutrition. By 1616, only a meager 351 out of the 1,700 migrants who went to Jamestown still survived.[16] To make matters worse, relations with local Indians were poor, characterized by mutual brutality and occasional all-out assaults. In its first years, the survival of the settlement seemed tenuous indeed.[17]

That all changed when Virginia settlers discovered that tobacco—transplanted from Trinidad—not only grew well in the colony, but fetched high prices back in England. In 1617, the first cargo of tobacco made its way from Virginia to England. The profits realized caused a surge in investment capital, and in the six years between 1617 and 1623, 5,000 new settlers arrived every year.[18] These settlers arrived with the intention of either setting up or working on tobacco farms, which meant that the boundaries of settlement continually spread north, west, and south of Jamestown into Indian territory. By 1624, Virginia had grown so large and so profitable that the English monarch began to pay attention. In that year, King James I revoked earlier charters giving the Virginia Company the power to run its political affairs, and in their place he appointed a royal governor. In theory, then, Virginia became a crown colony ruled directly by the king. In practice, however, the colony continued to rule its local affairs without much interference from the king except at the highest governing levels.[19]

This lack of centralized, royal control over Virginia was even more exaggerated in the New England colonies. In 1620, a group led by religious dissidents desiring both profit and a place to freely practice their own brand of Protestantism secured a royal charter to settle American lands. Late in that year, 120 settlers arrived near Cape Cod, and settled themselves in a town they named Plymouth. These settlers benefited from tragedy, because Indian groups local to the area had recently suffered a violent wave of epidemics as a result of contact with European traders. As a result, the coast of what is now Massachusetts seemed only sparsely settled by Indians, and land was open for the taking. Although the settlers who went to New England did hope to profit from their new home, they were significantly different from the Virginia settlers in that whole families tended to migrate together. Moreover, the idea in New England was not to make money in the Americas and then return to England; rather, the goal was to make permanent, prosperous communities abroad.[20]

It quickly became clear to New England settlers, however, that they would not make their riches from trade in furs or luxury goods. Tobacco also did not grow well in the northern climate. As

[13] Raudzens, *Empires*, 97; and Egerton et al., *The Atlantic World*, 175.

[14] James Horn, "Tobacco Colonies: The Shaping of English Society in the Seventeenth Century Chesapeake," in *The Oxford History of the British Empire: The Origins of Empire*, edited by Nicholas Canny (Oxford: Oxford University Press, 1998), 174.

[15] For the precariousness of the Virginia Colony, see Niall Ferguson, *Empire: The Rise and Demise of the British World Order and the Lessons for Global Power* (London: Allen Lane, 2002), 49–52.

[16] Jordan Goodman, *Tobacco in History: The Cultures of Dependence* (London: Routledge, 1993), 134.

[17] J.H. Elliott, *Empires of the Atlantic World: Britain and Spain in America, 1492–1830* (New Haven, CT: Yale University Press, 2006), 15.

[18] Goodman, *Tobacco in History*, 134–135; and Raudzens, *Empires*, 103.

[19] Raudzens, *Empires*, 104.

[20] Elliott, *Empires of the Atlantic World*, 156–157.

a result, colonists set themselves to the task of subsistence agriculture and the exploitation of abundant timber supplies in the region. While colonists did not grow spectacularly wealthy like the Spanish in Mexico, their settlements grew steadily during the first half of the seventeenth century.[21] By 1650, settlers numbered 22,900 in spite of the difficulties of the harsh New England winters, and new groups began their own settlements in Connecticut, Maine, New Hampshire, and Rhode Island.[22]

Yet in spite of the initial royal charters that authorized them to settle in the Americas, these New England settlers initially resisted even the idea of imperial control from London.[23] In 1641, the Massachusetts colony declared itself to be an independent republic; two years later it was joined by Connecticut in what they called the "New England Confederation." New Englanders formed their own local governments as well as taxation structures with little influence from England.[24] However, these declarations of independence occurred at a time when England itself was completely absorbed in a civil war, and could thus do little to impose its will on New Englanders. When the civil war and related turmoil was over in 1660, the New England settlements were forced to accept a royal governor. Yet even then the crown exacted minimal taxes from its subjects, and New England settlers went about their business much as they had done before.

English settlers also established a presence on those islands in the Caribbean not already occupied by the Spanish. Initially these settlements were dominated by corsairs, buccaneers, and traders hoping to steal treasure from Spanish ships and nearby settlers. In the 1620s, however, settlers and entrepreneurs who had seen the wealth created by tobacco production in Virginia began to grow the crop on the islands, which turned a tidy profit. Yet like the Virginia and the New England settlements, these efforts at settlement were not directed by a central authority or institution. Rather, they were initiated and funded by private interests, where the authority and influence of the crown was minimal.

Perhaps it is not surprising that the English crown played such a marginal role in the initial establishment of its North American colonies. After all, England was a comparatively small European state, and was not yet a major player in European politics. The years from 1640 to 1660 were tumultuous because of civil war, and for much of the seventeenth century the English were intensely involved in protecting their island state from the designs of more powerful states such as Spain and France. French efforts, however, were both more centralized and more focused than English efforts. Indeed, although the French monarchy went through a period of weakness between 1610 and 1661 as a result of a succession of minority kings, by the 1630s individuals acting on behalf of the crown attempted to direct colonial efforts far more thoroughly than their English counterparts.[25]

French colonization in the Americas did not, however, begin with strong royal direction. In the first two decades of the seventeenth century, the weakness of the French crown meant that, as in the English case, initial French claims in the Americas were made by private interests acting under royal license.[26] This was the basis of the establishment of French Acadia (now Nova Scotia) in 1605, Quebec in 1608, and St. Kitts in 1623. But the two French settlements in modern-day Canada did not thrive: French Acadia boasted only 500 settlers by mid-century, and Quebec colony was held by several hundred French settlers and missionaries, who were sustained largely by the fur trade. To procure the much coveted furs, French traders relied on Indians, who found it increasingly necessary to expand their hunts into the territories of neighboring Indian groups. As a result, the French in

---

[21] Virginia DeJohn Anderson, "New England in the Seventeenth Century," in Canny, *The Origins of Empire*, 208.
[22] Raudzens, *Empires*, 108.
[23] Anderson, "New England in the Seventeenth Century," 193.
[24] Elliott, *Empires of the Atlantic World*, 147.

[25] Raudzens, *Empires*, 120.
[26] Frederick Quinn, *The French Overseas Empire* (Westport, CT: Praeger Press, 2000), 41.

Quebec found themselves in continual conflict with Indians who were not suppliers in the fur trade. Aside from St. Kitts, where French settlers were beginning to prosper from tobacco plantations beginning in the 1620s, by the 1630s the French presence in the Americas was both miniscule and tenuous.[27]

Under the leadership of Louis XIII's powerful first minister Cardinal Richelieu, who served in that capacity from 1624 to 1642, the French crown initiated a concerted effort to direct and control colonization efforts more effectively. In Quebec, the crown appointed a royal governor for the first time in 1632, and increased its supervision over the major fur-trading company in the region. Colonists were encouraged to settle (although efforts in this area were largely unsuccessful), as were Catholic missionaries. In St. Kitts, the crown increased both its oversight and its financial support of the chartered company that operated the colony, and strongly encouraged new settlers to migrate. In contrast to the North American colonies, the crown's efforts in this regard were far more successful, and the French West Indian colony prospered. By 1650, in addition to St. Kitts the French claimed the islands of Guadalupe (1635), Martinique (1635), Tortuga (1639), and St. Domingue (1641). By 1700, the French West Indies population had grown to 44,000 persons.[28]

The other major European competitors for American wealth were the Dutch, who were motivated both by the desire for profit and by a strong desire to disrupt Spanish colonial efforts. Like the English, their preferred method of establishing colonial ventures was through privately owned joint-stock trading companies. However, the Dutch versions of these companies were tied far more closely to the state, since the same wealthy merchants who invested in them tended also to control Dutch political affairs. As a result, Dutch trading companies were likely both to act in the interests of the state and to seek the highest profits.[29]

Like the Portuguese, the Dutch were more interested in maritime trade than in establishing permanent colonial settlements. However, when the promised profits were large enough or when international conflict over territory looked likely, Dutch traders established not only trading posts but claimed the hinterlands beyond. Such had been the case for the Dutch East India Company (VOC), the first Dutch joint-stock company created for gaining a toe-hold in the Asian spice trade. Founded in 1601, the VOC made its first significant gain in 1605 when it captured a Portuguese fort on the Indonesian island of Amboina. In 1610, the Company made further gains when it received permission from the Japanese to set up a trading post in Hirado. In 1611 the Company built a trading post at Batavia (modern Jakarta) on the island of Java. Yet some VOC officials began to argue that the trading company should go beyond simply trading: instead, the Company could maximize its profits by controlling the spice trade at every level, from growing to exporting. Thus, between 1619 and 1623, the VOC began a process of brutal conquest in Java as well as the crucial spice islands nearby, and by the end of that period it had become not just a trading company but a territorial power as well, with all the necessary rights to wage war as well as to conduct trade.[30]

Inspired by the success of the VOC and inflamed by renewed war with Spain, in 1621 the Dutch founded the West India Company (WIC) to focus on trade, colonization, and war in the Atlantic. The company had two primary missions: to make a profit and to disrupt Spanish imperial concerns whenever and wherever possible. Like the VOC, the WIC was financed by private capital closely linked to the centers of state power and was authorized to raise its own armies, wage war, and conduct foreign policy. In fact, Piet Heyn—the privateer who captured the Spanish

---

[27] Ibid., 45.
[28] Ibid., 56. The date of occupation for St. Domingue was unofficial, as effective occupation was established in about that year but was only formally recognized in 1697.

[29] Raudzens, *Empires*, 83.
[30] For more on the early VOC, see M.C. Ricklefs, *A Modern History of Indonesia Since c. 1200*, 3rd edition (Stanford: Stanford University Press, 2001), chapter 6.

fleet in 1628—was financed and armed by the WIC, whose investors saw a fantastic return in that year.[31]

The trading and colonization efforts of the WIC were focused on a variety of areas in the Atlantic. Even before the formation of the WIC, a Dutch captain had laid claim to the area around modern Manhattan on the Hudson River by leaving one of his crewmen in the area before returning home.[32] Once the WIC was operational, however, the company returned to the area in earnest. They quickly constructed Fort New Amsterdam, and from there conducted a brisk trade in furs as well as fish. Although New Amsterdam remained primarily a trading post, it did attract a small number of settlers who set themselves up as farmers. These settlers, however, were too few in number to adequately resist being overrun by the English, who as we know had established strong colonies in New England and in Virginia. As a result, during an Anglo-Dutch conflict in Europe, in 1664 English ships sailed into Hudson Bay and conquered New Amsterdam. The Dutch settlers of the colony were incorporated into the new English colony, which was renamed New York.

A far more important object of the WIC's attention in the Americas was Brazil, which by the first half of the seventeenth century was already Europe's largest supplier of sugar. In addition to its potential for profitability, another reason the WIC found Brazil so attractive was that taking control of the territory would affect both the reputation and economy of Spain as well as Portugal, since the two monarchies had been united since 1580.[33] Although conquest in Brazil was resisted by the Portuguese, armed WIC fleets managed to take Bahia in 1624 and then Pernambuco in 1630. Now possessed of some of the primary sugar-producing regions in the Americas, the Dutch realized they could increase their profits by gaining access to a regular supply of slaves to feed the labor demands of their Brazilian sugar plantations. Once again focusing on Portuguese

territories, the WIC turned its attention to capturing Portuguese slave trading posts in Africa itself. It took time, but between 1637 and 1642 the WIC managed to wrest control of Portuguese forts in Elmina and Axim, both on Africa's Gold Coast.[34]

In the meantime, the WIC sponsored efforts to expand its American territories by conquering the Caribbean islands of Curacao, Aruba, and Bonaire in 1634. Like many Caribbean islands, Curacao in particular was extremely useful as an entrepot for smugglers and privateers hoping to profit from Spanish treasure. Yet WIC officials also saw an opportunity to spread sugar-cane production from their newly conquered Brazilian territory to their Caribbean outposts, thereby increasing potential profits. Even more importantly, WIC operatives began to spread their newly gained knowledge and technical expertise in sugar-cane production to other Caribbean islands belonging to the British and the French. Once WIC forces captured Elmina and Axim, moreover, company officials were happy to transport African slaves not just to their own territories in Brazil and the Caribbean, but to the territories of the British and the French as well. Although it was not immediately clear, this transfer of technology, slaves, and expertise was to have a rapid and profound effect on the future of empire and colonialism around the world.

By 1650, Dutch, French, and English competition with the Spanish for riches and territory had produced a wide variety of colonial ventures in the Americas. Most of these ventures were financed and sponsored not by policy emanating from centralized state governments, but rather by private interests operating under royal or state sanction. In the cases of the English and the French, royal control was initially quite limited, and—in the case of the English—remained so throughout much of the seventeenth century. In the Dutch case, state control was severely limited given the ability of the WIC to govern itself. Moreover, the locations of French, Dutch, and English colonies and forts were not always ideal,

---

[31] Egerton et al., *The Atlantic World*, 145.
[32] Ibid.
[33] The two monarchies were united from 1580 to 1640.

[34] Egerton et al., *The Atlantic World*, 145; and Raudzens, *Empires*, 87.

and in places such as Virginia, New England, and Canada tended to be chosen more for their distance from Spanish territory than anything else. Finally, the colonial ventures of Spanish competitors attracted settlers in widely varying degrees. In the case of both the French and the Dutch, American colonial efforts failed to attract many permanent settlers even when encouraged. In the case of the English, however, colonization in the Americas eventually attracted large numbers of settlers—albeit of different sorts—in Virginia and New England.

Although none of these colonial ventures had stumbled upon a new Peru or Mexico, by the middle of the seventeenth century they had produced two extremely important results for the future of imperial expansion in the Americas and beyond. First, their efforts to thwart Spanish success in the Americas had largely been successful. Constant conflict with its European neighbors had caused Spain to overextend itself financially, while the ever-present threat of piracy forced Spanish monarchs to spend huge sums to defend its fleet.[35] English, French, and Dutch wars severely reduced Spain's naval power, ending by 1650 the Spanish mastery of the seas. Second, French and English power—with critical Dutch aid—were on their way to displacing Spanish power in the Americas not just militarily but also economically. While the location of their colonies had been determined on the basis of a variety of conditional and contingent circumstances, after 1630 the Dutch WIC nevertheless found itself in command of large sugar-producing regions as well as—after 1638—a regular supply of African slaves. Dutch efforts to extend sugar production in the Caribbean breathed new life into a social and economic system that would transform the Atlantic world.

THE SUGAR REVOLUTION

Neither African slavery nor sugar production was new to Europeans or to the Americas in the mid-seventeenth century. In fact, Portuguese traders had been trafficking in African slaves since 1441, when they made their first raid in West Africa, captured 12 African men, and sold them in Portugal. By the mid-fifteenth century the Portuguese discovered that purchasing West African slaves was safer and more efficient than raiding, and by 1460 they were bringing 500 slaves annually to Portugal and Spain as a result. Once the plantation economies of Sao Tome and the Canary and Madeira islands were well established by the end of the fifteenth century, the Portuguese trade in African slaves grew to several thousand per year.[36] Also as a result of the Atlantic plantation colonies, sugar had been exported to Europe as a luxury item since the last four decades of the fifteenth century. Once in the Americas, Iberians established new plantations in both the West Indies and Brazil to feed the growing European demand for the sweet taste of cane sugar. These plantations expanded the availability of sugar dramatically. However, it was only after the expansion of sugar plantations to the English and French islands of the Caribbean that a true "sugar revolution" occurred.[37] This revolution made many of those involved in sugar production very wealthy indeed, whether through growing the cane itself, supplying the African slaves that made up its primary labor force, or trading in manufactures or foodstuffs necessary for procuring either sugar or slaves. This growing wealth, in turn, caused the northern European powers to become far more interested in—and invested in—their overseas empires than ever before.

As a result of chronic labor shortages discussed in chapter 3, both the Spanish and the Portuguese had already begun to rely on African slave labor in the Americas during the sixteenth century. As early as 1510, Ferdinand of Spain authorized 50 African slaves to be sent from Spain to shore up the gold-mining labor force on the island of Hispaniola. Eight years later, Charles (Ferdinand's successor) issued the first license for importing slaves to the Indies directly

---

[35] Raudzens, *Empires*, 89.

[36] Philip Curtin, *The Rise and Fall of the Plantation Complex*, 2nd edition (Cambridge: Cambridge University Press, 1998), 43.
[37] The phrase is Curtin's. Ibid., chapter 6.

from Africa.[38] After that point, such licenses—known as *asientos*—were granted on a competitive basis to slave traders from a variety of European states. By 1601, slave traders had already transported 150,000 African slaves to the territories of Spanish America.[39] Once in Spanish America, African slaves were used for a variety of tasks such as mining, domestic service, and agricultural labor—including sugar cultivation. Indeed, some settlers recreated the sugar plantation model already established in the Canaries, and began to cultivate sugar on Hispaniola and then along the coast of the Gulf of Mexico.[40] However, sugar production in Spanish America did not become a priority during the sixteenth and seventeenth centuries given the profitable nature of mining and ranching.[41]

The Atlantic slave trade expanded dramatically when Portuguese colonists in Brazil began to grow sugar cane for export on a wide scale in the sixteenth century. As we saw in chapter 3, initial attempts to secure Indian labor were repeatedly frustrated by high mortality rates as well as frequent desertion. By 1560, colonists increasingly turned to African slaves to provide the needed labor, procured by their Portuguese countrymen who operated a variety of trading posts along the west coast of Africa. Indeed, by 1600 approximately 30,000 African slaves labored in Brazil, comprising nearly a third of the population.[42] These numbers continued to rise in the seventeenth century, when approximately 4,000 to 5,000 slaves reached Brazil from Portuguese trading posts every year. By 1800, the colony had received 2.5 million slaves. In fact, more slaves were imported to Brazil than any other location in the Americas.[43] Instead of merely functioning as

a supplementary labor force, Africans and their descendants came to comprise the majority of Brazil's population.

The particular needs of sugar production help explain the need for such vast quantities of labor in Brazil. Sugar cane is a member of the grass family whose thick stem produces a juicy pulp full of sucrose.[44] Once planted, the first crop takes between 15 and 18 months to mature, after which the 10-foot stalks are cut back for harvest. Following the initial harvest, the canes grow back from the same stalks every nine months, allowing each field of cane to produce additional crops at peak production for three or four years.[45] In the Americas, the harvest season for sugar cane lasted about nine months, beginning at the end of July. During that season, sugar cane had to be cut, loaded on carts, and processed nearby, since the sucrose in the cane diminished quickly once cut.[46] Cutting the cane was difficult work because the stalks themselves were heavy and unwieldy, which meant that the cutting and loading of the plant was back-breaking and labor-intensive work. And since sugar cane grows only in tropical and sub-tropical climates, this back-breaking work was always carried out in very hot temperatures.

The labor requirements of sugar production did not stop with the planting and harvesting of the plants, however. Since the canes lost sucrose so quickly after cutting, they had to be processed immediately. This was not a small matter, for sugar processing required specialized machinery, technology, and expertise—all of which was centralized around the location of an on-site sugar mill. At the mill, sugar cane first had to be pressed between powerful rollers to squeeze out the juice from the stalk.[47] After pressing, the syrupy juice from the cane had to be boiled in a succession of large cauldrons until it was clean and purified. Once this was done, the syrup was pressed into

[38] Elliott, *Empires of the Atlantic World*, 99.

[39] Ibid., 100.

[40] Egerton et al., *The Atlantic World*, 202.

[41] Erik Gilbert and Jonathan Reynolds, *Trading Tastes: Commodity and Cultural Exchange to 1750* (Upper Saddle River, NJ: Pearson Prentice Hall, 2006), 94.

[42] James Lockhart and Stuart B. Schwartz, *Early Latin America: A History of Colonial Spanish America and Brazil* (Cambridge: Cambridge University Press, 1983), 202.

[43] Ibid., 216.

[44] Gilbert and Reynolds, *Trading Tastes*, 85.

[45] Lockhart and Schwartz, *Early Latin America*, 205.

[46] Sidney Mintz, *Sweetness and Power: The Place of Sugar in Modern History* (New York: Penguin, 1985), 49–50.

[47] In large mills, these machines were powered by water; in small mills, they were powered by oxen.

cone-shaped molds and set to dry. After several weeks, the molds were taken off and the "sugar loaves" were sent to Europe for refining.[48]

Clearly, every step of the sugar production process, from growing the crop to extracting the sugar, was extremely labor intensive. When Portuguese colonists could not find enough Indian laborers to perform the tasks necessary to produce sugar, they turned to African slaves. Increasingly, African slaves provided the labor for cutting, harvesting, and loading the cane; they also provided the labor for pressing, boiling, and forming the juice into sugar. But because sugar production required so much labor and such specialized equipment, it could only be undertaken by wealthy colonists who had the financial resources both to acquire large tracts of land and slaves and to build and operate a sugar mill to process their own cane. In Brazil, these operations came to be known as *engenhos*—a term that referred to the entire unit of production from the land, mill, and the house to the slaves who worked it.[49]

When the Dutch seized Pernambuco from the Portuguese in 1630, they learned first-hand the complex labor requirements and technologies required for sugar production. As we have already seen, at this time the Dutch also became increasingly interested in establishing themselves as slave traders in West Africa in order to provide a ready supply to their new Brazilian enterprise. In addition, Dutch entrepreneurs who gained experience in Brazil began to apply their experience in running sugar plantations to Dutch possessions in the Caribbean.[50] When the Portuguese regained their independence from Spain in 1640, it became clear that Portugal would henceforth have the leisure to focus its full attention on re-conquering Pernambuco. As a result, many Dutch settlers and traders affiliated with the Dutch WIC sought to transfer their knowledge and skills not only to Dutch Caribbean possessions, but to English and French possessions as well.[51] Their interest was

hardly altruistic. Rather, by 1640 the WIC was realizing high profits not so much from the production and sale of Brazilian sugar itself, but from supplying slaves to Brazil from West Africa, and then from selling processed sugar back in Amsterdam.[52] In other words, it was the maritime commerce in carrying commodities that the WIC wanted. As long as Dutch ships were able to do this, the WIC was not particular about the nationality of those producing the sugar. In fact, Dutch entrepreneurs encouraged their French and English rivals to adopt sugar production in their Caribbean possessions, offering everything from "management expertise, technical proficiency, and even Italian-made machines for milling the cane."[53] In 1640, Dutch entrepreneurs arrived in the English Caribbean island of Barbados with the goal of teaching the English settlers to grow and produce sugar. In doing so, they contributed to a revolution that would transform the Atlantic empires.

Before the Dutch introduced sugar to Barbados, the English settlers there were engaged primarily in the production of tobacco. Indeed, by the mid-seventeenth century tobacco had become something akin to the gold that English settlers in the Americas had been looking for. To be sure, Europeans had known about tobacco since the earliest days of contact, and during the sixteenth century Spanish settlers grew the New World crop along the coast of Venezuela for export—at a high price—to Europe.[54] By the turn of the seventeenth century, wealthy Europeans had already developed a taste for smoking the high-priced plant, and entrepreneurs with an eye toward turning a profit experimented with it in a variety of locations. But when the English settlers at Jamestown produced their first crop of tobacco in 1612, they quickly realized they had found a cash crop that might salvage their disastrous attempt at establishing a colonial presence in Virginia. By 1616, the Virginia colony was exporting 1,250 pounds of tobacco to England; by 1628, exports reached

---

[48] Lockhart and Schwartz, *Early Latin America*, 206.
[49] Ibid.
[50] Curtin, *The Rise and Fall*, 82.
[51] Elliott, *Empires of the Atlantic World*, 106.

[52] Egerton et al., *The Atlantic World*, 190.
[53] Ibid.
[54] Goodman, *Tobacco in History*, 132, 135.

370,000 pounds.[55] Thereafter, the economy of Virginia—now based almost wholly on tobacco production—boomed.

As a result of tobacco's success in Virginia, tobacco production in English territories spread rapidly. Not surprisingly, settlers in neighboring Maryland quickly adopted the crop, and by 1639 the tiny population of just 300 exported 100,000 pounds of tobacco to England. By the time the English began settling the Caribbean islands in the 1620s, they did so with the express purpose of growing tobacco for export. As the founder of St. Kitts said himself, the island was an ideal location for a colony because it provided "a very convenient place for the planting of tobaccos, which ever was a rich commoditie."[56] As a result of tobacco, the English population in St. Kitts and then Barbados expanded rapidly: by 1638, the islands boasted 12,000 and 10,000 settlers, respectively. In that same year, barely two decades after being first settled, the two islands produced 705,000 pounds of tobacco between them.[57]

When Dutch entrepreneurs began to sell their sugar-producing knowledge to English settlers in the Caribbean, it was in the context of an already-thriving cash crop economy based on tobacco. Yet the tobacco economy of the English Caribbean, like its counterpart in Virginia, was a world away from the Brazilian engenhos. Unlike the huge, capital-intensive sugar estates of Brazil, English tobacco culture did not require large tracts of land or complicated technology. Tobacco is fairly simple to grow, requiring only a limited amount of labor (to tend the plants and keep them free of pests) and a barn for curing and drying the leaves. Moreover, a single tobacco plant can yield more than two square meters of leaf, which meant that even a small crop could yield a profit.[58] As a result, although some tobacco farmers held large estates and grew quite rich, many others held minimal lands and produced only small crops annually.

Also unlike Brazilian engenhos, in the first half of the seventeenth century English tobacco farmers did not tend to rely on African slave labor to produce their crops. Instead, they relied primarily on white indentured labor from Europe. This labor was available because of population growth and economic dislocation in the British Isles, which meant that there was a ready supply of impoverished young men and women who sought to relieve their poverty by selling—or indenturing—themselves into servant-hood for a period of four to eight years.[59] Indenture was not exactly a popular choice. The journey to the Americas was long and difficult, mortality rates in both Virginia and the Caribbean continued to be very high in the seventeenth century, and working conditions for indentured servants could be brutal. Rather, indenture seems to have been the last resort for the desperately poor who, in exchange for passage to the Americas and their labor, expected to receive a specified sum of money in addition to their freedom when their contracts expired.[60] Over the course of the seventeenth century, tens of thousands of these indentured laborers made their way to the Caribbean and Virginia—most to work on tobacco farms.

With the introduction of sugar-cane production to the English and French Caribbean in 1640—first to English Barbados and then rapidly to other Caribbean islands—the social and economic structure of the islands experienced a dramatic transformation. Only five years after the introduction of sugar cane to Barbados, 40% of the island was planted in the crop. By the 1670s, Barbados produced more than half of the sugar consumed in England. With sugar came other changes. Because of the capital and technology required in sugar production, smallholders could not hope to grow the new crop as they could with tobacco. As a result, wealthy planters bought up much of the available land, on which they established large estates of 200 acres or more—each serviced by an expensive sugar mill. Small farmers were bought out, and after 1645 many English settlers who could not

---

[55] Ibid., 134–135.
[56] Quoted in ibid., 139.
[57] Ibid.
[58] Ibid., 7.

---

[59] Egerton et al., *The Atlantic World*, 163.
[60] Ibid., 164.

afford large estates on Barbados left the island to settle elsewhere.[61] Meanwhile, the labor demands of sugar soon outstripped the supply of European indentured laborers from England. With Dutch encouragement and using Dutch-supplied slaves, English planters on Barbados increasingly relied on Africans to work their plantations.[62] As more and more land was devoted to sugar, more and more slaves were brought to the island: by the 1680s, 75% of the population in Barbados, or 50,000 people, was made up of African slaves.[63]

As Barbados went, so too did the rest of the Caribbean. By the beginning of the eighteenth century, English, French, Dutch, and Spanish possessions in the Caribbean were all primarily devoted to the production of sugar and, by extension, to the massive importation of African slaves. The European desire for sugar seemed insatiable, as every increase in supply was outstripped by demand. Increased demand for sugar, in turn, drove the demand for slaves. Numbers help to tell the story: in the second quarter of the seventeenth century, about 180,000 Africans were brought to the Americas as slaves. However, in the third quarter of the century—as the sugar revolution was sweeping the Caribbean—that number rose to 370,000. Even though the Atlantic slave trade long predated the Caribbean sugar revolution, more than 90% of Africans sold into slavery in the Americas arrived after 1650.[64] Furthermore, of the approximately 11 million Africans who survived the trip from Africa to the Americas, 80% of them were sold in the sugar-producing colonies of Brazil and the Caribbean.[65]

SUGAR, SLAVERY, AND TRANSATLANTIC SOCIETIES

It is hardly overstating the case to say that the sugar revolution had profound effects on much of

the world, from the Atlantic world of Europe, the Americas, and Africa to China, India, and beyond. Imperialism and colonialism facilitated both the general and the regional effects of the sugar revolution, while at the same time the sugar revolution helped to shape the direction of imperialism and colonialism in new ways. Indeed, by the end of the eighteenth century—when the sugar/slave system reached its peak—the webs of those northern European empire-builders who had once sought to imitate the Spanish had grown ever stronger, and now included strands that connected the world's peoples in ever closer relationships.

Obviously, any economic system that depends on the forced labor of millions is bound to impact the region of their origin in important ways. This was certainly true of West and West-Central Africa, where most slaves sold into American slavery originated. Indeed, during the eighteenth century through the first half of the nineteenth century, historians believe that the Atlantic slave trade may have been "the defining institution for West and West Central Africans, the slavers and the enslaved alike."[66] At the same time, it is important to keep in mind that the effects of the slave trade were highly complex, and as a result were not uniform across time or space. For one thing, areas with a consistent supply of slaves shifted over time: the availability of slaves increased dramatically, for example, in areas experiencing warfare between rival African states. In such areas, victorious states frequently sold both combatants and civilians of the opposing side into slavery. However, once the wars were over, the availability of slaves tended to diminish. Furthermore, the extent to which inland African societies felt the impacts of the trade also varied by time and place.[67] As the trade increased in volume in the eighteenth century, slave raiders reached further and further inland to procure the slaves they needed. In one area at the end of the eighteenth century, slaves were being

[61] Curtin, *The Rise and Fall*, 83.
[62] For a thorough treatment of the link between sugar and slavery, see Richard Sheridan, *Sugar and Slavery: An Economic History of the West Indies, 1623–1775* (Baltimore: Johns Hopkins University Press, 1974).
[63] Curtin, *The Rise and Fall*, 83.
[64] Egerton et al., *The Atlantic World*, 191.
[65] Ibid., 187.

[66] Ibid., 242–243.
[67] An excellent discussion of this may be found in John Thornton, *Africa and Africans in the Formation of the Atlantic World, 1400–1680*, 2nd edition (New York: Cambridge University Press, 1998).

brought to the Atlantic coast from as many as 1,000 miles inland.[68]

For all of these reasons, it is difficult to generalize about the effects of the Atlantic slave trade on West and West-Central African peoples. In spite of this lack of uniformity, one thing seems certain: the Atlantic slave trade, wherever it occurred, spurred significant social, cultural, economic, and political changes. Exactly how these changes were manifested varied greatly. In some areas of West Africa, it seems that the numbers of people sold into the slave trade slowed population growth, while in others—particularly between 1730 and 1850—population seems to have been significantly reduced.[69] Also, even though the Atlantic slave trade was not as dominated by male slaves as historians had previously thought, it does seem that the preference for male slaves in the Americas and the preference to retain females in coastal Africa led to a sexual imbalance in some African societies. This may have had important implications for marriage and sexual relations as well as for the division of labor in many African societies. Finally, the increasing dominance of the Atlantic slave trade in West African societies seems to have increased the number of slaves held by West Africans themselves.[70]

Politically, the slave trade may have led to a number of transformations in various parts of Africa. Generally, its effect was to break down large states by promoting war and internal political competition among elites. For example, the slave trade has been implicated in the destruction of the Jolof Confederation in Senegambia and the Kongo Kingdom in West-Central Africa.[71] The most extreme example may have been in the region around Kongo, where political break-up was so severe as to produce anarchical and destructive cults like the Jaga that were entirely bent on destruction since there was little expectation of not being enslaved in the near future. In other regions, states acted as "vampires," enslaving their own and neighboring populations rather than encouraging productive growth.

However, this situation did not uniformly lead to political fragmentation. In some parts of Africa, especially the West African regions that came to be known as the Gold and Slave coasts, large states emerged in this period. The most notable of these were Asante and Dahomey. The former, especially, has been labeled an *empire*. Is this label accurate? In this region, as elsewhere, the slave trade had caused competition between elite, wealthy groups in the coastal polities who sought to increase their wealth by forming powerful alliances that could control the slave trade with Europeans.[72] This sometimes led to situations in which European–African alliances were pitted against each other in both commercial and military struggles that mirrored larger Atlantic struggles. In the seventeenth century, for example, the Dutch recruited African allies to fight long-standing Portuguese–African alliances. In the interior, similarly, large states jockeyed to control profitable trade routes first in gold, kola nuts, and cloth and then in slaves. Asante emerged the victor in its area in this process over the course of the eighteenth century. Politically centered upon a confederation of five allied states all speaking closely related (Akan) languages, by

---

[68] Egerton et al., *The Atlantic World*, 248.

[69] For an excellent demographic analysis, see Patrick Manning, "The Slave Trade: The Formal Demography of a Global System," in *The Atlantic Slave Trade: Effects on Economies, Societies, and Peoples in Africa, the Americas, and Europe*, edited by Joseph Inikori and Stanley Engerman (Durham, NC: Duke University Press, 1992); and Egerton et al., *The Atlantic World*, 241.

[70] The institution of slavery was common in West Africa long before European contact. However, West African slavery tended to be regarded as one among many forms of dependency within West African societies, and slaves mainly functioned as domestic workers alongside other servile workers. Owning slaves was often regarded as a mark of status, and thus when greater numbers of slaves became available as a result of Atlantic networks, their numbers in West African societies grew. For a full exploration of slavery in African societies, see Paul Lovejoy, *Transformations in Slavery: A History of Slavery in Africa* (Cambridge: Cambridge University Press, 1983).

[71] Boubacar Barry, *Senegambia and the Atlantic Slave Trade* (Cambridge: Cambridge University Press, 1998), 44, 80, 86; and John Thornton, *The Kingdom of Kongo: Civil War and Transition, 1641–1718* (Madison: University of Wisconsin Press, 1983).

[72] Egerton et al., *The Atlantic World*, 242, 245.

the early nineteenth century this metropole had come to dominate both the coastal trading towns of the south and large, non-Akan-speaking states in the north.[73] They built this into a vast commercial enterprise. The northern territories were loosely ruled as tributary states, with the main tribute coming in the form of humans who were then transported to the coastal towns for sale as slaves. In these coastal towns, the Asante government maintained trade representatives. However, their control over the peripheries of this commercial network was probably too diffuse to be easily defined as an *empire*, despite their ability to maintain their commercial ascendancy through force when necessary.

Millions of ordinary Africans found their lives affected by the slave trade in a variety of ways. For those who procured slaves, functioned as middlemen between slave raiders and European traders, or who controlled the slave trade in their region, the Atlantic slave trade could be both lucrative and a means to greater power.[74] Some groups, fearful that they would be swallowed up by slave raiders, allied themselves with powerful states in order to protect themselves. In general, however, the social and economic impact of the slave trade was enormously negative. Productivity fell as entire communities were forced to relocate to remote, inaccessible areas where raiders would find abduction very difficult such as caves, marshes, and mountaintops.[75] Many others armed themselves, built fortified towns, and did their best to survive under the circumstances. At the same time, the uncertainty of living in a situation where kidnapping and war were ever-present weakened family relationships and cultural institutions. Few who lived in the increasingly large orbit of the Atlantic slave trade were untouched by its existence.

This was especially true, of course, for those millions of individuals who were captured and sold into slavery. Whether they were captured in war, sold as a result of debt or crimes, or captured by entrepreneurs who preyed on vulnerable villages, the conditions of the Atlantic slave trade were brutal. After making it to the Atlantic coast as prisoners, survivors of the often-difficult journey from their homes often had to wait on board slave ships for weeks or even months before reaching full capacity and sailing for the Americas. Once on their way, captured slaves endured harsh conditions during the infamous Middle Passage across the Atlantic. Cramped space, unsanitary conditions, problems with the purity of food and water, and the frequent brutality of slavers led to a mortality rate of between 12 and 15% of slaves during the height of the slave trade.[76] What this meant is that approximately 1 to 1.5 million people died as a result of sickness, dehydration, and deprivation during the Middle Passage. Moreover, if slaves survived the trip across the Atlantic, the great majority of them could expect lives of extremely difficult labor in hot, tropical climates, where they would be subject to a variety of brutalities and where their bodily needs for rest, caloric intake, and medicine would be largely ignored.

The effects of the Atlantic slave trade went beyond the issue of whether or not one found oneself on the wrong end of the trade, important though it was. In fact, there was more to the Atlantic slave trade than the trade in slaves. Africans required payment for every slave sold, and this meant that the centuries of the Atlantic slave trade saw the importation of a wide variety of goods into West African trading networks. Contrary to received wisdom about the slave trade, Africans did not accept worthless, cheaply made items in return for slaves.[77] West Africans had been part of sophisticated trading networks with inland and North Africa for many centuries, and traders there were neither naïve nor easily dominated. In order to obtain slaves, Europeans

---

[73] John K. Fynn, *Asante and Its Neighbours 1700–1807* (Evanston, IL: Northwestern University Press, 1971); and Ivor Wilks, *Forests of Gold: Essays on the Akan and the Kingdom of Asante* (Athens: University of Ohio Press, 1993).
[74] David Northrup, *Africa's Discovery of Europe, 1450–1850* (New York: Oxford University Press, 2002), 98.
[75] See Sylviane Diouf, ed., *Fighting the Slave Trade: West African Strategies* (Athens: Ohio University Press, 2003).

[76] Egerton et al., *The Atlantic World*, 199.
[77] Northrup, *Africa's Discovery of Europe*, 81.

found that they had to carry a variety of trade goods from all over the world. Primary among these were cottons and other cloths from India and Europe, iron bars and metal products, firearms, liquor, and tobacco. While the impact of these imports on African societies has been disputed, in general historians believe that Africans incorporated and adapted these new products into their existing cultural and political practices, which in turn produced changes. Imported cloth, tobacco, and liquor, for example, all functioned as status symbols alongside other African-produced commodities, while imported iron and metal was put to use in functional ways by local artisans. Imported firearms were once believed to have been a major factor in encouraging further slave-raiding and internal warfare in West Africa, but historians now dispute this, arguing instead that firearms functioned mainly as status symbols or as a means of self-protection from wild animals and other humans. In any case, it is clear that Africans sought a wide variety of goods in return for African slaves and it seems, as David Northrup argues, they "got what they wanted, at prices they were willing to pay, and believed themselves better off for the exchanges."[78]

The scale of the Atlantic slave trade obviously drew Africans and Europeans into closer social and economic relationships than ever before. As we know, Portuguese traders had been engaging in the slave trade since the fifteenth century. When sugar took hold in Brazil, they found a lucrative market for ever greater numbers of slaves. Then, when Dutch traders conquered northern Brazil, they realized they could make extraordinary profits by taking a share of the slave trading business in Africa in order to supply the plantations of Pernambuco. Thus, when the Caribbean islands began to be drawn in by the sugar revolution, European entrepreneurs from a variety of states were quick to see the potential for huge profits by providing African slaves to meet the insatiable demand for the labor required by sugar plantations. So too did all of the European states

who sponsored colonies in the Caribbean. Indeed, as a result of the sugar revolution, the Dutch, French, and English states each grew increasingly interested in their colonies and colonial ventures across the Atlantic, and sought to maximize their share of the profits.

Part of these efforts involved attempts to control the slave trade by granting monopolies to government-sanctioned joint-stock companies, much like the EIC and VOC. Direct colonization of large African territories was generally out of the question: coastal West African states tended to be too strong for European powers to dominate, and in any case the disease regime of tropical Africa worked against Europeans. Even had Europeans been able to impose their will on substantial portions of West Africa, European mortality due to yellow fever, sleeping sickness, and other maladies was extremely high—making it very difficult to hold a position once taken. As a result, Europeans wishing to trade in West Africa found it necessary to seek the permission of local rulers before setting up trading posts. As we have already seen, they also found it necessary to trade in items that Africans were willing to buy.

These relationships could not be said to be colonial. Even inside the small communities that surrounded European forts and trading posts, local rulers held sway. In fact, Europeans entered many of these African states as land renters and subordinates rather than rulers. Nevertheless, it occurred in the context of imperial economic competition. The idea behind monopoly slave trading companies was not colonization but rather control, and in the second and third quarters of the seventeenth century the Dutch, English, and French governments established such companies as a way of ensuring that their own ships supplied slaves to their own colonies. In the process, the governments would make a tidy profit. In reality, however, such schemes did not work. Slave trading was far too profitable a business to keep smugglers out, and by the end of the seventeenth century smugglers had so overrun the trade that all three governments let the company charters expire.[79]

---

[78] Ibid., 98.

[79] Curtin, *The Rise and Fall*, 131–132.

Moreover, while West and West-Central Africa was not directly colonized on a large scale by European powers until the era of the Atlantic slave trade was over, the region was nevertheless affected deeply by imperial ties. Most importantly, the Atlantic slave trade first swelled to large proportions as a result of imperial needs and concerns; namely, to solve chronic labor shortages in the American colonies. Moreover, by the seventeenth and eighteenth centuries, mercantilist policies dictating that each state should exclusively provision its own colonies led to a massive increase in slaves sought by competing Europeans.[80] Thus, the existence of empire itself was in large part responsible for the size and scale of the Atlantic slave trade. This, in turn, guided European interest in African trade, and led European governments to expend considerable resources in order to protect that trade. When it was clear that trade monopolies were impossible to enforce, European states nevertheless established fortified trading posts, staffed with small garrisons, in order both to defend the trade of their countrymen from other Europeans and to ensure that their countrymen remained in the good graces of local African rulers.[81] Additionally, the trade goods that Africans demanded in return for slaves came not just from Europe but from colonial outposts from the Americas to Asia. For example, beginning in the eighteenth century much of the high-quality cotton cloth demanded by Africans was obtained in India through the networks of quasi-imperial joint-stock companies like the East India Company.[82] The tobacco Africans sought came from European colonies, particularly Virginia and Maryland, while rum was produced in the New England colonies from the very Caribbean sugar that stimulated demand for slaves in the first place. Thus, the Atlantic slave trade was a critical part of a network that was spurred and dominated by the demands of an American imperial system increasingly based on sugar.

The effects of this system on the Americas were as profound as they were in Africa. In the main sugar-producing areas of the Caribbean and Brazil, the need for constant influxes of African labor defined the social structure. Indeed, wherever sugar dominated, so too did slave populations: by the late seventeenth century, Africans dramatically outnumbered Europeans in every sugar-producing area. The result was a small, elite, white land-owning class supported by massive populations of African slaves. Areas that had once been densely populated by Indians, such as Brazil, now bore only traces of earlier inhabitants. Much the same could be said for the natural environment in such areas. Sugar plantations tended to be large: on Barbados, for example, 200 acres was a typical size.[83] As more planters sought to make their fortunes from the lucrative sugar market, more land was cleared for the crop. Land prices accelerated rapidly, and because of its value nearly all available land was devoted to sugar production. By the turn of the eighteenth century, natural environments in the main sugar-producing areas of the Americas looked fundamentally different than they had before the advent of sugar.

One result of the growing dominance of sugar plantations in the Caribbean islands was their near-complete reliance on multi-angular trade networks for food, manufactures, and slaves. Conditions for slaves in the Caribbean islands were extremely difficult, which meant that natural reproduction was severely hindered and mortality was high. Because of this, sugar plantations required fresh supplies of slaves in order to maintain the strength of their labor forces. Moreover, since land in the Caribbean was devoted primarily to its most lucrative crop, the islands were unable to feed themselves. Instead, they relied on food imports from the North American mainland. Forests were in short supply on the islands as well, which meant that timber used for building and fueling the sugar mills also had to be imported from the plentiful forests of North America. Moreover, since Caribbean tobacco farms had

---

[80] Vincent Bakpetu Thompson, *The Making of the African Diaspora in the Americas, 1441–1900* (New York: Longman, 1987), 43.
[81] Egerton et al., *The Atlantic World*, 196.
[82] Northrup, *Africa's Discovery of Europe*, 81.

[83] Curtin, *The Rise and Fall*, 83.

been almost completely replaced by sugar plantations, tobacco users in the Caribbean henceforth had to rely on imports from the Chesapeake region of North America. Finally, all manufactured items such as textiles, barrels, and firearms had to be imported either from Europe or, by the late eighteenth century, by the New England colonies.[84]

This dependence, of course, meant that the success of the Caribbean sugar economies also became closely tied to the success of economies in mainland North American colonies and European states. New Englanders grew rich from provisioning the Caribbean islands with food, livestock, and timber. In return for these provisions, traders exported molasses—a by-product of sugar production—from the Caribbean to New England. Once in New England, the molasses was fermented and processed into rum, where it was then sold by traders to the British navy, to lubricate the North American fur trade, and to West Africans in return for slaves.[85] New England companies also profited from the sugar/slave economy by providing insurance for slave ships bound for the Caribbean.[86] The North American Chesapeake colonies were also directly connected to the slave trade, not only because Chesapeake tobacco became an important trade commodity in West Africa, but also because colonists increasingly traded their tobacco for slaves in an effort to establish plantation economies in mid-Atlantic North America. In turn, settlers in North America profited from the sugar/slave economy, and used their earnings to import more European goods. Indeed, as one historian has argued, by the last half of the eighteenth century the "surpluses derived from Caribbean trade appear to have paid for almost a quarter of the increased imports that North Americans bought from Britain."[87]

Neither sugar plantations nor the Atlantic slave trade could have been so profitable for so many people without a huge and growing worldwide market for sugar. This market grew fastest in Europe, but extended to all of the American colonies as well as European trading posts in Asia. In spite of the success of Brazilian sugar production after the late sixteenth century, by the mid-seventeenth century sugar was still a rarity on European tables. Due to its limited production, sugar was expensive, and was a high-priced luxury that only the wealthy could afford. As a result, sugar was purchased in relatively small quantities, like a spice, and was used sparingly.[88] After the explosion of sugar production that occurred in Barbados and other Caribbean islands after 1640, however, the price of sugar steadily declined over the next century and a half. As the price declined, ever more Europeans and Euro-Americans were able to buy it—which they did with astonishing enthusiasm. Significantly, their appetite for sugar was enhanced by a variety of new imperial products that made their way into European diets in the last half of the seventeenth century, including coffee, tea, and chocolate. Indeed, each of these exotic drinks—all of which were brought to Europe through semi-private imperial trading companies like the EIC—was consumed with increasing zeal by the fashionable set in London, Paris, and Amsterdam by the third quarter of the century. And significantly, these fashionable Europeans favored these products far more when they were sweetened with sugar. As the price of both sugar and exotic hot drinks declined over the course of the seventeenth and eighteenth centuries, far more Europeans bought and then became hooked on them, driving up demand and stimulating further production.[89] In 1800, approximately 245,000 tons of sugar reached the world market, and consumption in Britain alone had increased about 2,500% since 1650.[90]

Important as consumption patterns were, Europeans were connected to the sugar/slave system in other ways as well. Indeed, in return for

---

[84] Ibid., 141–142. See also Dunn, *Sugar and Slaves*.
[85] Curtin, *The Rise and Fall*, 142.
[86] Egerton et al., *The Atlantic World*, 202.
[87] David Richardson, "The Slave Trade, Sugar, and British Economic Growth, 1748–1776," in *British Capitalism and Caribbean Slavery: The Legacy of Eric Williams*, edited by Barbara Solow and Stanley Engerman (Cambridge: Cambridge University Press, 1987), 130.

[88] Mintz, *Sweetness and Power*, 83.
[89] Gilbert and Reynolds, *Trading Tastes*, 97; and ibid., chapter 3.
[90] Mintz, *Sweetness and Power*, 73.

sugar imports as well as to lubricate the wheels of the Atlantic slave trade, Europeans traded a wide variety of manufactured goods including, most importantly, textiles, iron bars, and firearms both to the Americas and to West Africa. Many of the cotton textiles traded to both areas came first to Europe from India, after which they were resold in the Atlantic market. Other cloths designed specifically for West African tastes were manufactured in the Low Countries, England, and eastern Europe.[91] Manufactured metals also did a brisk business in West Africa, where by the eighteenth century iron bars were one of the leading items in the Atlantic trade. Copper and brass were similarly crucial in that century. David Northrup suggests that exports of copper and brass rose from about 325 tons a year in the first decade of the century to nearly 2,900 tons a year in the last decade.[92] In addition, Europeans sold ever-increasing numbers of firearms to West Africans after 1650. During the last half of the eighteenth century alone, when the trade in firearms had greatly accelerated, Africans bought over 20 million guns from European traders. The impact of such trade certainly increased the volume of European exports. In Britain, for example, the demand for manufactured goods just from the Caribbean islands alone likely "increased total exports from Britain by almost £1.75 million per annum between the late 1740's and the early 1770's."[93]

In fact, the supply of European manufactured goods in the Atlantic trades was so great that some historians have suggested a link between European industrialization and the sugar/slave system. Indeed, in his 1944 *Capitalism and Slavery,* Eric Williams famously argued that the profits made in the Atlantic slave trade helped provide the financing for the Industrial Revolution, which in turn allowed Britain to dominate world trade. As Williams saw it, the Atlantic trades in sugar and slaves created new markets for British products while at the same time creating new industries in Britain from the import of slave-produced raw materials. In addition, the Atlantic trades also stimulated British shipping and shipbuilding and led to the growth of important British seaports, which thrived on the exports and imports made possible by sugar and slaves. Finally, Williams argued that the enormous profits of the sugar/slave system gave rise to the expansion of banking in Britain by enormously rich West Indian planters, who in turn financed the new plants and factories built to keep up with increased international trade.[94]

Few historians today would accept Williams's arguments without qualification, but after more than a half-century of historical debate and research it seems clear that some of his arguments linking the sugar/slave system and the development of British industry were correct. British exports of manufactured items doubled in value between 1669 and 1774, but the share of those exports going to Europe "fell from 82 percent to 42 percent, while the share going to America and Africa rose from 12 percent to 43 percent."[95] Moreover, all of the leading British growth industries in the last half of the eighteenth century— including iron, copper, brass, cotton and linen textiles, and woolens—came increasingly to depend on African and American markets as a result of the Atlantic trades, which in turn accelerated British industrial output in that period.[96] And, some historians have argued that the cotton textile industry in Britain (which was, after all, the first to industrialize) could not have been so quick to experiment with innovation if new markets in Africa and the Americas had not encouraged demand and competition.[97] Still others, while taking issue with the idea that the Atlantic trades generated massive profits, have nevertheless argued

---

[91] Northrup, *Africa's Discovery of Europe*, 83.
[92] Ibid., 85.
[93] Richardson, "The Slave Trade," 131.

[94] Eric Williams, *Capitalism and Slavery* (New York: Perigee Books, 1944), 98.
[95] Barbara Solow and Stanley Engerman, "British Capitalism and Caribbean Slavery: The Legacy of Eric Williams: An Introduction," in Solow and Engerman, *British Capitalism and Caribbean Slavery*, 10.
[96] Richardson, "The Slave Trade," 105.
[97] See, for example, Joseph Inikori, "Slavery and the Revolution in Cotton Textile Production in England," in Inikori and Engerman, *The Atlantic Slave Trade*.

that even modest profits from colonies in this period might have given Britain enough of an edge to jump-start industrialization.[98] In any case, it seems clear that the sugar/slave system so central to the developing British Empire in this period may have been enough to spur the beginnings of British industrialization—a process that itself would have major consequences for imperialism in the nineteenth century.

The complex web of trade networks created by the Atlantic trades deeply shaped developing imperial and colonial relationships in the Atlantic world and beyond. At the start of the seventeenth century, Spain was the dominant colonial power in the Americas, and all of its northern European rivals sought to create similar empires for themselves. The reality, as we have seen, was far different, and resulted instead in a variety of ad hoc colonial settlements that were—more often than not—managed with only limited oversight from the metropolitan centers. This lack of oversight began to change when colonists discovered cash crops. Indeed, 12 years after the colonists in Virginia began to grow tobacco at record profits, as we know, King James abolished the governing function of the Virginia Company and established it as a royal colony. Once the Dutch helped introduce sugar to the islands of the Caribbean after 1640, however, both the French and the English governments sought far greater participation in the governance in—and protection of—their now incredibly profitable islands. In accordance with mercantilist principles, both the English and French governments sought to maximize their profits from the colonial trades by regulating trade. In 1660, the English government formalized existing regulations in the Navigation Act, which legislated that all trade with English colonies had to be carried in English ships.[99] Furthermore, the colonies were forbidden from shipping their most important products—including

sugar and tobacco—to anywhere but England or other English colonies. To further regulate trade, the Staple Act of 1663 forbade the colonies from importing goods not of English origin unless they were shipped through England first. Beginning in 1670, the French too legislated that foreigners could not trade in French colonial ports, and that the colonies could not conduct trade with any foreign states.[100] In addition to maximizing profits, such legislation was designed to stymie the efforts of rival states from edging in on colonial profits. In return, metropolitan governments used their navies to protect their precious colonies from the military advances of rival states. The result was increased competition between all of the European states involved in colonial ventures in the Americas.

This increased competition frequently manifested itself in the form of war: from the mid-seventeenth through the mid-eighteenth century, wars with colonial dimensions erupted regularly between the English and the Dutch (1652–1654, 1664–1667, 1672–1674), the English and the French (1689–1697, 1740–1748, 1756–1763), and the English and the Spanish (1701–1713, 1739–1741). Although these wars were frequently complex and sometimes hinged on other issues in addition to imperial competition, each state tried to use the wars as a means of wresting colonial territory from their rivals, or as a way to promote their own trade interests in the Atlantic. This meant that colonial territory sometimes flipped between metropolitan powers during or after wars. Indeed, the islands of Trinidad, Tortuga, and Providence experienced this kind of flip-flopping in the eighteenth century. Wars also gave foreign militaries excuses for invading the colonies of their enemies, and then using the conquered territories as pawns in peace negotiations. By the eighteenth century, all of the European players involved in colonizing the Americas viewed colonial possessions as essential to foreign policy, and viewed threats to their colonies as threats to the state.

The astonishing part of this story is that those North American territories that had not so long

---

[98] Kenneth Pomeranz, *The Great Divergence: China, Europe, and the Making of the Modern World Economy* (Princeton, NJ: Princeton University Press, 2000), 206–207.

[99] After the 1707 Union of England and Scotland, this act included Scotland as well.

[100] Chamberlain, *Formation of the European Empires*, 34.

before seemed peripheral to British and French state interests had become—in the space of just over a century—major areas of strategic concern. That this was so was due not to the discovery of precious metals, as it had been for the Spanish. Rather, these one-time Spanish rivals had found a new kind of wealth in the form of sugar and slaves. The results of reaping this wealth had enormous consequences for peoples and economies all over the world. And those who found themselves in the best position to exploit this new system were also the same powers who came to lead the system.

Questions

1. What was mercantilism? How did it affect the development of European colonies in the Americas?

2. Empires are often built in periods of intense competition in which states have to respond to threats from each other. How and why did the development of a Spanish empire in the Americas jump-start the Dutch, English, and French Atlantic empires?

3. In general, what were the roles of the English, French, and Dutch states in establishing and maintaining the colonies discussed in this chapter? What were the roles of private individuals and groups? Compare and contrast where appropriate.

4. Describe the significance and results of the "sugar revolution" for African, American, and European societies in this period.

5. Based on the description in this chapter, would you characterize the Asante state as an empire? Why or why not?

6. Empires are often discussed as being "networks." How did the empires covered in this chapter function as transatlantic and even global networks? How and by what ties and links were the metropoles and the various periphery regions connected?

CHAPTER 5

Empire: Empire, Identity, and the Making of New Societies in the Atlantic World

In October 1789, a small group of *gens de couleur* (free people of color) presented the French National Assembly with a list of grievances. The French Revolution had begun in the spring of that year, and the Assembly was preoccupied with matters of liberty and equality, citizenship and slavery. These gens de couleur hoped to remind the newly formed Assembly that there were individuals who considered themselves French citizens but who were being cruelly oppressed in the French Empire. The individuals in question, they argued, were free people of color of mixed French and African descent like themselves, who lived and labored in the French Caribbean. They argued that although they were "born citizens and free, they live as foreigners in their *own fatherland*. Set apart in the most degrading fashion, they find themselves enslaved even in their liberty." To remedy the situation, the assembled gens de couleur entreated the National Assembly representatives to "gloriously complete your work, by ensuring the *liberty of French citizens* in both hemispheres."[1] Additional grievances soon arrived from West Africa, where French-speaking African and Afro-French *habitants* (citizens) of several small coastal towns demanded new economic and political rights.[2]

Clearly, the grievances of the gens de couleur and the habitants demonstrate that in the eighteenth century there were individuals who considered themselves French citizens even though they had neither grown up in France nor had undisputed French ancestry. Their grievances also make it clear that their claims to citizenship were not uncontested, because French settlers in the Caribbean and merchants in West Africa routinely sought to deny them the rights and status normally afforded to Europeans. Yet despite such treatment, these communities identified themselves as free French citizens with the right to openly petition the French National Assembly. What interests us here is that the very existence of the gens de couleur in the French Caribbean and the habitants in West Africa was a direct result of an imperial system based on slavery and sugar production. Under such a system, some slaves in the French Caribbean managed to secure their freedom, while sexual relations between slave owners and slaves had inevitably produced

---

[1] Laurent Dubois and John D. Garrigus, *Slave Revolution in the Caribbean, 1789–1804: A Brief History with Documents* (Boston: Bedford St. Martin's, 2006), 68–69, emphasis added.

[2] Jean-Pierre Biondi, *Saint-Louis du Sénégal: Mémoires d'un métissage* (Paris: Editions Denöel, 1987), 7, 72–73.

mixed-race populations, some of whom were manumitted. At the same time, even Africans and inhabitants of the Americas without French ancestry began to identify as French. In the Caribbean, the result was an increasing population of gens de couleur, who found themselves on the margins of slave society, neither equal with European settlers nor enslaved. The identities they formed, then, were based on a mixture of identification with European society as well as with the oppression of dark-skinned peoples. In short, theirs were identities uniquely borne of imperial circumstances.

As the earlier examples indicate, the effects of early modern imperial ventures went far beyond the exploitation of new resources, trade in new commodities, and increased international rivalries between competing states. By bringing new people to new places, creating new power structures, introducing new methods of trade and interaction between peoples, and mixing disparate cultures together, imperialism and colonialism in the early modern period created new peoples and societies in many places around the world. Some regions, like the Americas, were fundamentally transformed in almost every way, and the societies that emerged there became unique mixtures of cultural, political, and religious blending. Other areas, like the Indonesian islands, coastal West Africa, and India, did not initially experience such fundamental or widespread changes, but were nevertheless deeply affected by new imperial and colonial relationships. In fact, life for many of the people who lived in places touched by imperialism and colonialism in the early modern period—including Europe itself—was very different than it had been before.

One of the most fundamental and pervasive transformations brought about by imperial and colonial relationships was in terms of *identity*, or how people thought about themselves and their relationship to others in the world. Although identities are not quantifiable in the same way as, say, commodity production, the creation of new identities as a result of imperialism and colonialism is nevertheless crucial to understanding the shape of the modern world. Indeed, the new economic

and political relations brought about by imperialism and colonialism led to completely new mixtures of people, settlement patterns, approaches to law, and cultures based on blends of disparate religions, languages, music, clothing, and foods. In some cases, the new circumstances created by colonialism caused individuals to formulate overtly imperial identities that emphasized the connections between European settlers and the people in the mother countries from whence they came. In other cases, the creation of new social and cultural groups—like the aforementioned gens de couleur—led to the formation of identities quite distinct from any that had existed before. By the eighteenth century, a multiplicity of complementary as well as competing identities had emerged in all of the existing colonies and colonial outposts. These developments influenced the course of history just as surely as trade, greed, or warfare, for they led not only to new cultural forms but to new alliances, oppressions and, eventually, the creation of wholly new states.

This chapter begins with an explanation of identity and the role of identity formation in history, and then moves on to explore the specific social, material, and legal conditions that fostered the creation of new identities within the Spanish, Portuguese, British, French, and Dutch colonial empires. Thereafter, the chapter uses case studies and specific examples to demonstrate some of the processes by which new identities were formed and expressed in this period.

THE ROLE OF IDENTITY IN HISTORY

Identity is a complex and multi-faceted historical phenomenon, since it operates at both individual and group levels. At the individual level, each person tends to identify himself or herself as a member of a particular family, ethnic group, gender, profession, religion, state, and so on. It goes without saying, therefore, that individual identities can be as varied as the number of existing individuals. At the group level, however, multiple individuals come to share a sense of commonality based on one or more of the aforementioned features. Individual and group identities combine when people associate with one another or act together to forward common agendas based on their political, religious, ethnic, or gender affinities.

The process of identity formation is further complicated by several factors. First, individuals might well identify with more than one social group, location, or culture depending on the context. For example, an individual can identify as a woman, a former slave, an Akan-speaker from West Africa, a Christian, a farmer, and a political radical all at the same time. At some times, her occupational identity might be more important to her than her religious or ethnic identity, and vice versa: likewise, she may or may not choose to associate herself with others who share aspects of her identity. Moreover, certain aspects of her identity—such as her religious and political identities—might exist in contradiction to one another, even if she identifies with both. Second, identities are neither static nor stable. Rather, they are constantly being formed and re-formed through day-to-day engagement with social and material conditions.[3] As a result, identities shift and change over time. If the aforementioned woman had won her freedom on the French island of St. Domingue around the turn of the nineteenth century, for example, her identity might have gradually shifted from being an Akan from West Africa to being a citizen of the new black nation of Haiti. Third, identity formation at both the individual and group levels often occurs in the context of deeply unequal social relations. This frequently means that people—especially those with low social or economic status—are not entirely free to choose their own identities. Instead, some people are forced to act within the parameters of certain identities assigned to them from the outside because of factors such as poverty, occupation, skin color, ethnicity, or gender.[4] For example, during the

period of French colonization of St. Domingue, the former slave mentioned earlier would almost certainly have been "assigned" an identity as a racially inferior human by the French, even if such an identity did not accord with her own sense of self. In turn, identities "assigned" by outsiders can encourage otherwise disparate individuals to come together as a unified group, often for the purpose of insisting on better treatment. Fourth and finally, identity is felt and expressed in both the hearts and minds of humans and in the physical, material world through the use of specific words, symbols, dress, foods, actions, and interactions. If the freed slave on St. Domingue had wanted to signal her identity as a revolutionary, for example, she could have done so both by her words and actions and by donning the revolutionary cockade of the French Revolution. Thus, identities are constantly being shaped, performed, and reinforced in both the mental and the physical worlds.[5]

In spite of its complexity as a concept, historians study identity and identity formation because it is so crucial to understanding past events. Without identity, neither individuals nor groups could meaningfully differentiate between themselves. Hence, without identity there would be no loyalty, no patriotism, no collective action, and no sense of where one fits into the larger social and cultural context. In the context of early modern imperialism and colonialism, identity was especially important because massive movements and dislocations of people threw individuals and groups together in new ways and in new places, which had profound consequences for the ways people thought about both themselves and others. For example, without the sugar plantations of the Portuguese colony of Brazil, Indians, Africans, and Europeans would not have lived together in such close proximity in that location. Because they did,

---

[3] Antoinette Burton, *At the Heart of the Empire: Indians and the Colonial Encounter in Late-Victorian Britain* (Berkeley: University of California Press, 1998), 15, 20; and Kathleen Wilson, *The Island Race: Englishness, Empire and Gender in the Eighteenth Century* (London: Routledge, 2003), 3.
[4] For an excellent example of the way these unequal relations played out in the United States, see Matthew Guterl, *The Color of Race in America: 1900–1940* (Cambridge: Harvard University Press, 2002).

[5] Wilson's chapter on T.C. Phillips is particularly evocative in this regard. See "The Black Widow: Gender, Race and Performance in England and Jamaica," in *The Island Race*. See also Heather Streets, *Martial Races: The Military, Race, and Masculinity in British Imperial Culture, 1857–1914* (Manchester: Manchester University Press, 2004), chapter 6.

each group was forced to adapt to the presence of the others and to re-think their identities in relation to the others. The result was a wholly new set of identities than had existed in the past: identities that were neither Portuguese, Indian, nor African but an eclectic mixture of all three, shaped both by material conditions and by social and economic circumstances. In addition, new commodities, trade patterns, and global interactions brought about through networks of empire similarly altered the ways both individuals and groups related to the intellectual and physical worlds. As we have already seen, the introduction of sugar and other imperial commodities into European diets altered European culture in myriad ways. Eventually, the consumption of such products, as in the case of British tea drinking, became a fundamental part of national identities. Over time, the new identities that resulted from imperial and colonial relations in the early modern period led to new alliances, political affiliations, social relations, cultural fusions, and—eventually—new nations altogether.

NEW SOCIETIES, NEW PEOPLES IN THE AMERICAS

One of the most important causes behind the formation of new identities during the early modern period was the movement of such large numbers of people to the European colonies and colonial outposts. Migrants were both voluntary and forced, and represented a variety of classes, occupations, and gender distributions depending on conditions in the home countries as well as in the colonies. In general, during the early modern period far more people from both Europe and Africa migrated to the American colonies than to colonies and outposts in other parts of the world (aside from a few small exceptions like the Cape of Good Hope in southern Africa). As a result, the formation of new identities, societies, and peoples stemming from interactions between new people and new places was especially pronounced in the Americas. At the same time, even the presence of relatively few new migrants could lead to new cultural fusions and new ways of understanding social relations, as was the case in West Africa, India, and Indonesia before 1800.

In the Americas, both European and African migrants faced new climates, environments, and peoples. In addition, groups native to the Americas experienced not only occupation by foreigners but also demographic collapse and the resulting dislocation associated with it. As a result, cultural transformation was a fact of life for many inhabitants in the Americas during the early modern period.[6] That said, the degree to which groups in the Americas formed new societies depended on the groups involved, the location of the colony, the numbers and sexual distribution of incoming migrants, and the particular institutions of colonial culture and policy. Because of these and other factors, the new societies that developed in Spanish, Portuguese, British, and French America were in some ways similar and in other ways quite distinct.

In the Spanish Americas, cultural transformation was predicated partly on the size and location of the European population, the sexual ratio of immigrants from Spain, and the nature of Spanish institutions and policies themselves. Between 1500 and 1800, about 700,000 Spaniards migrated to the Americas.[7] Although the numbers were hardly insignificant, the areas claimed by the Spanish were enormous, and by far the vast majority of Spanish migrants settled in the urban areas of Mexico and Peru. What this meant was that large populations of Spaniards lived in urban centers, while the countryside and marginal areas remained dominated by Indian populations. Moreover, the uneven application of the Spanish presence in outlying areas was accentuated by the fact that Spanish settlers sought to govern peoples outside the reach of the major urban centers through indigenous political and social structures.[8]

Although this strategy allowed for a certain amount of autonomy, it did not mean that Indians in peripheral areas were protected from the impact of Spanish rule. As we have already seen,

---

[6] Douglas R. Egerton, Alison Games, Jane Landers, Kris Lane, and Donald Wright, *The Atlantic World: A History, 1400–1800* (Wheeling, IL: Harlan Davidson, 2007), 258.
[7] John Kicza, *Resilient Cultures: America's Native Peoples Confront European Colonization, 1500–1800* (Upper Saddle River, NJ: Prentice Hall, 2003), 175.
[8] Ibid., 69.

indigenous populations suffered greatly from epidemic disease in the first century of Spanish rule, and as a result social relations were deeply disrupted. In addition, the Spanish did remove the elements of indigenous administration they found most threatening to their rule, including the highest ruling elites, the military organization, and indigenous priests. Thus, although many aspects of pre-conquest life remained, the highest structures were all replaced by Spanish institutions.[9] The Spanish also aggressively sought—as much as possible—to convert Indians to Catholicism, which brought further change to such regions.[10] For example, Catholicism had extensive effects on the role of women in society. On the one hand, Catholicism forbade female priests, thus eliminating traditions of women as oracular prophetesses, shamans, and priests. Catholic and Spanish law also restricted women's sexuality and penalized their promiscuity.[11] Spanish material and linguistic culture also penetrated to peripheral areas, bringing changes to Indian cuisine, dress, art, and language. In spite of all these changes, however, in many of these outlying areas ethnic and local identities and traditions persisted.

In the urban areas of Mexico and Peru, the pace of social and cultural transformation was far more intense. This was partly due to the numbers of Spanish settlers, since they tended to concentrate in these regions. In addition, Indians from a variety of ethnicities flocked to urban centers in search of work, which allowed different peoples to come into sustained contact on an unprecedented scale.[12] Even more important was the growth of large mixed-race populations in these areas. The reason for this was, in large part, a function of Spanish emigration patterns. Until the eighteenth century (when larger numbers of Spanish women began to emigrate to the Americas), Spanish settlers were comprised largely of men who hoped to

make their fortunes and then return to Spain. This meant, of course, that there were few Spanish women in the colonies to choose as sexual or marriage partners. In the absence of Spanish women, Spanish men commonly took Indian women as their wives. Among the Spanish elite, this practice was believed to have strategic as well as sexual value, for Spanish men sought to cement alliances to traditional indigenous ruling houses through their choice of spouse. By choosing wives from among the indigenous elite, Spanish men hoped to both consolidate their rule and reinforce their own legitimacy.[13] In addition to these high-status alliances, many Spanish men sought more casual sexual relationships with Indian women from a variety of classes and occupations, and with African slave and free women as well.

The logical product of these relationships was a large mixed-race population in Spanish America. And while Spanish policy generally encouraged such relationships, the children of these unions were not considered equal. Rather, the Spanish recognized a bewildering variety of mixed-race gradations depending on how much European, Indian, and African blood ran through an individual's veins. The general rule was that an individual's status was commensurate with the amount of European blood he or she could claim: the more European, the higher the status. The Spanish fascination with these hierarchical gradations was reflected in the multiple terms they used to designate people of different *castas*, or mixed-race castes: for example, *mestizo* referred to one Spanish and one Indian parent, *cholo* referred to one mestizo and one Indian parent, and *zambo* referred to one Indian and one African parent. By the end of the colonial period, castas outnumbered Spaniards all over Spanish America, comprising 21% and 29% of the population in Mexico and Peru, respectively, to the corresponding Spanish percentages of 18 and 12.[14]

In Spanish America, mixed-race people tended to be raised with an awareness of Spanish

---

[9]Ibid., 81.

[10]J.H. Elliott, *Empires of the Atlantic World: Britain and Spain in America, 1492–1830* (New Haven, CT: Yale University Press, 2006), 245.

[11]Pamela McVay, *Envisioning Women in World History: 1500–Present*, vol. II (New York: McGraw-Hill, 2009), 82–84.

[12]Kicza, *Resilient Cultures*, 78.

[13]Egerton et al., *The Atlantic World*, 264.

[14]James Lockhart and Stuart B. Schwartz, *Early Latin America: A History of Colonial Spanish America and Brazil* (Cambridge: Cambridge University Press, 1983), 342.

culture, and many identified with Spanish customs, language, and law. Particularly in the urban areas where they were concentrated, Spanish mestizos and cholos tended to occupy a variety of respectable occupational positions, while zambos and other individuals of African descent occupied lower positions in society.[15] It must be emphasized, however, that the casta classification system appeared more rigid than it really was: for example, mestizos frequently passed as Spaniards, while cholos often gained status as mestizos. During the eighteenth century, when the Spanish crown was in need of revenue, certificates of pure Spanish parentage could also be purchased from the crown by anyone with the money to pay.[16] Spanish law also contributed to the fluidity of the castas. Beginning in the sixteenth century, the Spanish developed a plural system of law in the Americas that recognized the separate status of the castas from Spaniards. Under this system, neither Spaniards nor castas were subject to all of the same laws. As a result, at some times it was more convenient for an individual to claim mestizo status at one time (if, for example, they were trying to avoid being taken before the Spanish Inquisition) and as a Spaniard at another. This blurring of casta lines was common in colonial Spanish America.[17]

Alongside Spanish, Indian, and mixed-race populations was a relatively large population of free blacks in Spanish America. In the three centuries from Spanish conquest to 1886, approximately 1.5 million African slaves were transported to the Spanish Americas.[18] Many of these slaves were able to become free because of Spanish law regarding slavery. As we saw in chapter 3, Spain had a long tradition of slavery within its own borders long before the American conquests. This tradition was based on Roman law, which stipulated that—although legal—slavery was contrary to human

nature. Because of this, Roman law favored manumission and, especially, self-purchase, and also imposed restrictions over slave owners in terms of treatment of slaves.[19] Although Spanish slavery was far from benign, the prior existence of this legal culture allowed many African slaves in Spanish America to purchase their freedom, which in turn led to the creation of a new social group. In Spanish America, then, the size and nature of Spanish immigration coupled with colonial policies and institutions encouraged the development of a wide variety of new social and cultural groups, whose very existence ensured identity transformations in those societies.

Portuguese Brazil shared many characteristics with Spanish America—including similar migration patterns, the development of a large mixed-race population, similar laws regarding slaves, and a finely tuned recognition of ethnic background—but due to the dominance of slavery in its economy, the resulting society was quite different. Beginning with the settlement of Brazil in the last half of the sixteenth century until 1800, about 523,000 Portuguese settlers emigrated to the colony. As in the Spanish case, these numbers were not insignificant but were small in relation to the territory occupied. Also like the Spanish case, until the eighteenth century (when larger numbers of Portuguese women began to emigrate) most Portuguese settlers were male fortune-seekers. Because of this sexual imbalance in migration patterns, Portuguese men chose sexual partners from local populations.

Yet the available local populations in Brazil were not predominantly Indian as they were in the Spanish Americas. Brazil had been less densely settled by indigenous peoples than many parts of the Spanish Americas to begin with, and the local populations that did exist were decimated by disease or else moved into the forests to avoid Portuguese domination. Indeed, by the late colonial period Indians made up only about 4.5% of the Brazilian population, compared to around 60% in much of Spanish America.[20] This situation, as we have already seen, led the Portuguese—who

[15] Kicza, *Resilient Cultures*, 80.

[16] Egerton et al., *The Atlantic World*, 286.

[17] Lauren Benton, *Law and Colonial Cultures: Legal Regimes in World History, 1400–1900* (Cambridge: Cambridge University Press, 2002), 83–86.

[18] Sue Peabody and Keila Grinberg, *Slavery, Freedom, and the Law in the Atlantic World: A Brief History with Documents* (Boston: Bedford St. Martin's, 2007), 15.

[19] Ibid., 16.

[20] Lockhart and Schwartz, *Early Latin America*, 401.

began to establish a booming plantation sugar economy in the late sixteenth century—to seek an alternative labor force in Africa. Between 1550 and 1800, about 2.5 million African slaves were brought to Brazil, which meant that the African population far outstripped the Portuguese population early in the colony's history.[21] As a result of these circumstances, Portuguese men tended to choose sexual partners from among the African population who had been brought to the colony.

Alongside the small Portuguese and large African populations, then, there developed in Brazil a large population of mixed-race people. As in Spanish America, these mixed-race persons were legally and socially classified on a hierarchical scale, depending on the amount of European, African, or Indian blood an individual supposedly carried. As in Spanish America, these groups had many names: among them, *mulato* denoted mixed European and African parentage, *caboclo* denoted mixed European and Indian heritage, and *cafuzo* denoted mixed African and Indian heritage. By the late eighteenth century, nearly 66% of the Brazilian population was mulato or black, known collectively as *pardos*, while only 30% was identified as Portuguese.[22]

In part because of the Portuguese legal tradition regarding slavery, by the late colonial period nearly 30% of the mulato and black population in Brazil was free. As in the Spanish case, Portuguese slave law developed from the Roman tradition that favored human liberty.[23] Thus, when slaves had the money to purchase their freedom or when slave owners wished to free certain slaves (such as their sexual partners or their own children born to slave women), there were no legal barriers to stand in the way. This free black and mulato population was paralleled by large numbers of runaway slaves in the colony, who came together in the forests and created their own communities outside of Portuguese control.

Finally, even slaves in Brazil were classified into different groups based on social and economic hierarchies. Because of the brutal nature of slavery in the colony as well as the tropical climate, African slaves brought to Brazil tended to have very short life spans. This meant that the Portuguese required a constant supply of new slaves to take the place of the old. However, new slaves direct from Africa were considered dangerous, uncivilized, and untrustworthy, since their old lives a world away tended to be fresh in their minds. In contrast, once Africans acculturated to Portuguese and to life in Brazil—when they became known as *ladinos*—they were seen as more dependable and held higher status.[24] Slaves born in Brazil, known as *crioulos*, stood even higher on the slave hierarchy, while mulato slaves were seen as the most intelligent and skillful of all the slave groups. Thus, as had happened under different circumstances in Spanish America, nearly three centuries of migration and colonization to Brazil had led to the existence of completely new social groups, each one of which began to develop distinctive identities in light of social and material circumstances.

Although the West Indian sugar islands were claimed by a variety of competing powers—including Spain, Britain, and France—their near-complete dependence on African slavery, their geographic proximity, and their similar social structures allow them to be more fruitfully discussed as a group rather than separately. It is certainly the case that the West Indian colonies differed quite dramatically from other British, French, and Spanish continental colonies. In fact, a brief study of conditions in the West Indies helps to demonstrate that imperial identity formation can have as much to do with the circumstances of migration and economic conditions as it does with the particular characteristics of colonizing groups.

One might expect the West Indian colonies to have developed similar social structures to Portuguese Brazil, given their common economic base in plantation sugar production and slavery. Yet there were several variations in the West Indian cases that had important ramifications for the development of new social groups in those

---

[21] Ibid., 216.
[22] Ibid., 401.
[23] Peabody and Grinberg, *Slavery, Freedom, and the Law*, 21.

[24] Lockhart and Schwartz, *Early Latin America*, 217.

colonies. First, even large West Indian islands like Spanish Cuba were much smaller than Brazil, which meant that the European settler populations also tended to be much smaller. For example, in 1790 the European population on the most important French sugar island of St. Domingue (modern Haiti) was about 40,000 in comparison to Brazil's 1.5 million. This meant, among other things, that the mixed-race populations that developed in the West Indies were proportionately smaller than in Brazil. European populations in the West Indies also tended to be extremely transient as a result of high mortality rates due to tropical illnesses such as malaria, yellow fever, and dysentery, which necessitated a constant infusion of new Europeans just to maintain the population. Also, European landowners in the West Indies frequently absented themselves from their properties for much of the year, leaving the management of plantations in the hands of overseers.

Moreover, in comparison to Brazil, African slave populations in the West Indies were proportionately much larger: on the French sugar islands of Martinique and Guadeloupe, African slaves made up 90% of the population by the eighteenth century.[25] In St. Domingue in the same period, 500,000 slaves dwarfed the 40,000 Europeans on the island. In one sense, however, the Brazilian situation closely resembled that of the West Indies in that the brutal conditions of West Indian slavery were so severe that constant cargoes of new African slaves were necessary to maintain the population. Indeed, slightly more slaves ended up being transported to the West Indian islands than to Brazil during the period of the Atlantic slave trade—percentages that made up 40% and 38% of all African slaves, respectively. Finally, except on the Spanish islands where the legal tradition favored manumission, the number of free blacks in the West Indies was proportionately much smaller than in Brazil. For example, the free black population on St. Domingue—where French law was far less amenable to manumission—was only about 30,000 strong by the end of the eighteenth century. All of these features of the West Indian

islands—from small European and free black populations to enormous African populations continually being infused with fresh, highly rebellious slaves direct from Africa—resulted in a variety of highly contentious social groups who developed distinct identities based on racial exclusion, violence, and the struggle for power.

The British North American colonies, excepting the West Indian sugar islands, developed quite a different social structure than the Spanish or Portuguese colonies—differences that were critical for identity formation. For one thing, unlike Spanish and Portuguese colonists, British colonists had little toleration for sexual unions that produced mixed-race children. Such unions did occur, but when they did British colonists were generally unwilling to accept mixed-race persons among them. British fathers of mixed-race children were much less apt to recognize their mixed-race children—whether with Indian or African women—or to live with or marry non-European women.[26] The reasons for this tendency seem to have been both cultural and practical. In terms of culture, the English may have been predisposed to fear mixing with indigenous populations from their earliest colonial ventures with the Irish. Beginning in earnest in the sixteenth century, just after England's turn to Anglican Protestantism, English monarchs sponsored colonial settlements in Catholic Ireland. There, the ruling mentality dictated that mixing with the native inhabitants of Ireland would cause English settlers to degenerate into backwardness and heresy. This mentality seemed to be firmly established among some of the first colonizers to the Americas in the seventeenth century, and may have shaped English interactions with indigenous Americans.[27]

More practically, the English aversion to cultural mixing was relatively easy to maintain because the sexual imbalance between British

[25] Dubois and Garrigus, *Slave Revolution in the Caribbean*, 12.

[26] Egerton et al., *The Atlantic World*, 265.

[27] Elliott, *Empires of the Atlantic World*, 235; see also Nicholas Canny, "The Marginal Kingdom: Ireland as a Problem in the First British Empire," in *Strangers Within the Realm: Cultural Margins of the First British Empire*, edited by Bernard Bailyn and Philip Morgan (Chapel Hill: University of North Carolina Press, 1991).

men and women was not as pronounced as it was in either the Spanish or Portuguese colonies. In the New England colonies, whole families tended to migrate together, which made sexual liaisons with indigenous women less necessary. In addition, these families represented a wide variety of occupational and class backgrounds, with the result that British colonists in New England were able to rebuild aspects of their old societies more thoroughly than colonists who moved to areas with a distinct sexual or class imbalance. Moreover, the relatively healthy climate in the New England colonies allowed mortality rates to remain fairly low, which allowed for consistent natural reproduction and population growth. And while interaction with local Indian populations was substantial, it was also marked by increasing hostility and warfare as it became clear to nearby Indian groups that their territories were subject to continual infringement. By the eighteenth century, Indian groups native to the New England region found themselves on the margins of an ever-widening British sphere of influence.[28]

The British colonial experience in the mid-Atlantic and southern colonies was governed by a different set of circumstances, which in turn shaped regional identities in those areas. As in the West Indies, by the eighteenth century the coastal areas of this region had adopted plantation-style, slave-based agriculture. Early English settlers had continually pushed Indians native to the area west through fierce conflict, which meant that the indigenous population had all but vanished from this fertile region by then. Instead, the area was dominated by a small class of elite, European landholders, supplemented by a large population of middling to poor whites. This white population was descended, in part, from the large number of English indentured servants who had—prior to the introduction of African slaves—migrated to work the coastal plantations of their social superiors. Once plantation owners shifted to slave labor, the black population of the coastal region quickly rivaled, and then exceeded, the white population. Yet although the slave trade continued in this

region into the nineteenth century, the absolute numbers of slaves who were transported to the area was far smaller than in either the West Indies or Brazil. Indeed, the slave trade to the British North American colonies represented only about 5% of all slave traffic in the early modern period. As a result, the populations of European and African descent in this region were more balanced than in the West Indies or Brazil. Moreover, British law in the slaveholding colonies neither favored manumission nor permitted free black or mixed-race persons to function easily in society.[29] So although communities of free blacks in these colonies existed, it was more difficult for them to thrive than it was in Spanish or Portuguese America.

Away from the coastal regions, British colonial life in the mid-Atlantic and southern colonies was dominated not by slave-based plantation agriculture but by smallholding families—many of them descended from indentured laborers, others new migrants from areas such as Scotland and Ulster—who continually pushed the frontiers of British America westward.[30] Hostility with native Indian groups dated from the earliest years of the Virginia colony in the seventeenth century, and continued—along with periods of interaction and cooperation—through the eighteenth. As in the New England colonies, Indian groups in the mid-Atlantic and southern colonies continually found their territories limited by European encroachment. Many sought to fight the Europeans, but a combination of epidemic disease and warfare also led many other groups to flee further westward to avoid contact with the Europeans.

Taken as a whole, by the eighteenth century the population in the British colonies was growing quickly, both through natural reproduction and continued European and African migration.

[28] Egerton et al., *The Atlantic World*, 268.

[29] Laws regarding slaves and slavery varied from British colony to British colony, with South Carolina having the most severe legal code. Yet legal obstructions in all slaveholding colonies were more restrictive than in Spanish or Portuguese America. See Philip Morgan, "British Encounters with Africans and African-Americans, circa 1600–1780," in Bailyn and Morgan, *Strangers Within the Realm*, 176. See also Peabody and Grinberg, *Slavery, Freedom, and the Law*, 10.

[30] See Maldwyn Jones, "The Scotch-Irish in British America," in Bailyn and Morgan, *Strangers Within the Realm*.

Indeed, by the middle of the century about 2 million British settlers live along the eastern seaboard, from the New England colonies in the north to Georgia in the south. When compared to the number of Spanish, Portuguese, or French migrants to the Americas, these numbers are especially significant. And although there were important differences between the New England colonies and the southern colonies, this critical mass of colonists—coupled with the fact that many more British women migrated to the Americas—was to have profound effects for the formation of new identities in British North America.

The French colonial possessions in North America presented yet another variation in colonial structure. Unlike the British colonies in continental North America, very few French colonists were attracted to French claims in the vast territory of Canada. Given the cold climate and the attendant difficulties of establishing large agricultural communities in much of the region, the primary purpose of French activity there was to participate in the fur trade. While some French traders trapped fur-bearing animals themselves, most furs were obtained through an alliance with the Huron and later other Indian groups, who obtained the furs from far-flung areas and brought them to French settlements for barter. Unlike the settlers in British New England, nearly all of the French settlers in Canada were men who hoped to do well in the fur trade and return home. Some French colonists set themselves up as farmers in the St. Lawrence River Valley, but their numbers were tiny: in the 1630s, French colonists in Canada numbered less than 1,000. Fifty years later, their numbers had increased to about 10,000, but only 1,100 of those were women.[31] By 1760, when French Canada was lost to the British as a war prize, French settlers numbered about 70,000: a miniscule population compared to their British competitors from the south.[32]

Because there were so few French women in Canada, unions with Indian women were both tol-erated and encouraged. As in Spanish America, these unions were believed to have strategic value as well: since French traders relied so heavily on Indian fur trappers for their survival, marriage to local women with ties to such tribes was considered advantageous. Yet although French ideas and culture must have had some impact on the children of these mixed-race unions, a distinct identity developed only slowly among this group because they tended to be raised as Indians within their mothers' communities. Available evidence indicates that such individuals—unless they converted to Christianity—were accepted as full members of Indian society, and thus a sense of their separateness from both Europeans and Indians was slower to develop than elsewhere. Nevertheless, over time a distinct mixed-race (*métis*) identity developed in French Canada. Once the colony was transferred to British control, the original French settler population also maintained its distinct identity in opposition to an influx of British settlers. In the meantime, a variety of Indian tribal communities continued to interact with both groups of European settlers.

NEW SOCIETIES, NEW PEOPLES IN AFRICA AND ASIA

In contrast to European colonies in the Americas, European outposts and colonies in Asia were structured quite differently, with critical effects for identity formation. Indeed, in the East Indies (modern Indonesia) and India, European interests focused on trade more than on conquest or settlement until the eighteenth century. Trading companies such as the Dutch East India Company and the English East India Company sought to establish fortified trading posts in each of these regions in order to carry out lucrative trades in spices, fabrics, and other exotic goods. Conquest on a large scale was impractical: local states and rulers were far too powerful to allow their sovereignty to be swept aside and, unlike in the Americas, the disease regime did not work against local inhabitants. As a result, European colonial outposts in these areas were administered by small numbers of European men with the

---

[31] Kicza, *Resilient Cultures*, 114.
[32] Frederick Quinn, *The French Overseas Empire* (Westport, CT: Praeger, 2000), 68.

aid of local collaborators. In the early modern period, most people living in the Indonesian islands or the Indian sub-continent would never have come into direct contact with a European.

That is not to say, however, that transcultural contact did not shape the identities of either Europeans or local inhabitants. This was especially true in Asian coastal towns and their littorals that became the focus of intercontinental trade in this period and in the Indian Ocean islands that attracted settlers and merchants. In South Asian localities such as Ceylon, Melaka, and Malabar, European sailors, priests, and merchants intermingled from an early date with not only South and South-East Asians but also Arab and Chinese merchants and settlers to create a highly diverse and mixed society. Because the Dutch frequently captured these positions from the Portuguese in the seventeenth century, a layering effect took place. In the absence of European women, Dutch officials and soldiers often took wives from among the mixed Portuguese–Asian populations.[33] Identity was equally complex in the French colony of Mauritius, where not only Asians and Europeans but also enslaved Africans became layered in a complex mix of religions (Hinduism, Islam, Catholicism), assigned racial identities, and occupational classes in the eighteenth century.[34]

By the eighteenth century, the respective European trading companies operating in India and the Indonesian islands began to assume territorial power as well. This process involved conquest of vulnerable areas, usually achieved with locally raised armies, and placed increasing swathes of territory under European rule. Because of the dearth of European women, both Dutch and English men took local women as concubines, and inevitably produced a growing group of mixed-race offspring. In the Dutch East Indies, this process was encouraged until the nineteenth century, whereas it remained an unofficial practice

in British India. These mixed-race populations served as cultural bridges between the European and Asian worlds, and became part of a process of exchange in which new commodities, foods, linguistic expressions, dress, music, and other cultural forms moved between cultures. These exchanges, although initially on a more limited scale than those that took place in the Americas, nevertheless encouraged both Europeans and non-Europeans to adopt new practices, commodities, and beliefs into their own cultures.

The situation in and around the European positions in sub-Saharan Africa exhibited both similarities and differences to the experience elsewhere in this period. The differences were partly the result of an increasingly hardened European racism toward Africans, perhaps exacerbated by the Atlantic slave trade. Nevertheless, here as elsewhere inter-racial sexual liaisons and marriages had an important place in the creation of new identities and in the bridging of cultural differences. In the Senegambian trading city of Gorée, for example, African women who formed relationships with Portuguese merchants and officers in the sixteenth century and their descendants formed a powerful class known as *signares*, who came to control a large portion of both local and international trade by making use of their relationships to both Europeans and powerful African families.[35] When the region passed into the French sphere, these signares joined the habitant class of Euro-Africans and French-educated Africans who rapidly became the traders and professional classes of Gorée and other French-speaking West African towns.

Nor were the African and Asian maritime populations distinct from each other, but rather during this period the Portuguese and later other European trading empires increasingly mixed them up. The Cape of Good Hope region in Africa is a case in point. Here by the mid-seventeenth century, Dutch settlers interacted not only with the indigenous population—numerically declining due to the introduction of Eurasian diseases—but

---

[33] Dennis B. McGilvray, "Dutch Burghers and Portuguese Mechanics: Eurasian Ethnicity in Sri Lanka," *Comparative Studies in Society and History*, 24 (1982), 235–263.

[34] See, for example, Megan Vaughan, "Slavery and Colonial Identity in Eighteenth-Century Mauritius," *Transactions of the Royal Historical Society*, Sixth Series, 8 (1998), 189–214.

[35] Jean Delcourt, *Gorée: Six siècles d'histoire* (Dakar: Editions Clairafrique, 1984).

also imported Asians as slaves and indentured servants. In Kaapstad (today's Cape Town), the result was a highly mixed society. However, society here rapidly became hierarchical, partly because the Dutch settlers rapidly came to include women and partly because of embedded racialist notions.

Clearly, colonial settlement was not uniform in the early modern era. The structure of colonial societies was dramatically shaped by migration patterns, the gender balance among migrants, policies and laws regarding mixed-race unions and slavery, variations among indigenous cultures, economic factors, and the cultural predispositions of colonists themselves. Many colonial societies shared certain features as a result of commonalities in one or more of the aforementioned areas. At the same time, colonial societies in this period were also unique in many ways, based on specific conditions and circumstances. These societies usually featured more hierarchical and rigid categorizations by race and ethnicity than the imperial peripheries described in chapters 1 and 2, but usually not so much as those of later periods. Often there were forces pulling them in both directions. Metropolitan ideologies of racialism and gender discrimination competed with the sense of a mission to "civilize" and domesticate Americans, Asians, and Africans and sometimes admiration for them. In all cases, these were modified by realities on the ground such as settlers' demographics, the diffuseness of imperial power, and the strengths and attitudes of local populations. One thing all colonies did share was that each colonial venture produced new social groups and even new peoples altogether. As part of this process, these new groups and peoples began to form new identities, and though these identities would shift and change over time, they would nevertheless have enormous consequences for the history of the world.

THE PROCESS OF IDENTITY FORMATION

Scholars working in a variety of disciplines have spent a lot of time and ink trying to describe the process of identity formation in colonial contexts.

At what point did colonial peoples begin to think of themselves as distinct from their home countries? What processes made this happen? Of course, the answers to these questions are extremely complex and are different from group to group. Yet it is nevertheless clear that many of the new groups formed in the context of empire did, over time, develop a variety of distinct identities as a result of the unique circumstances, new environments, and marriage/sexual patterns just discussed. These identities, in turn, helped to shape the course of history. This section uses the two concepts of *creolization* and *acculturation* to explore some of the processes by which groups formed new identities in colonial contexts. Rather than catalog every early modern colonial society as we have done in the first part of the chapter, however, here we focus on specific examples that—while unique in many ways—are meant to be suggestive of larger phenomena.

Creolization

The words *creole* and *creolization* have been used in a variety of ways over time and in different places. **Creole** has generally been understood to mean either a person of European or African descent who was born in the Americas or a type of language that developed as a result of mixing two or more languages together. **Creolization**, in contrast, is most often understood as a creative and dynamic process by which individuals and groups in new places come to form new, hybrid identities as well as hybrid cultural expressions of those identities. In other words, it is a process of adaptation, adoption, and interchange. Over time, the process of creolization produces groups whose cultural and social identities differ recognizably from those in the societies they left behind. In this section, we explore the process of creolization among two very different groups: the Spanish in New Spain (Mexico) and African slaves in the Caribbean.

Although the term *criollo*, or creole, was first used in the middle of the sixteenth century to describe African slaves born in the Americas, by the end of the century Spanish writers were beginning to apply the term to Spaniards who had been born in the American colonies. Used to describe Europeans, it was not meant to be a flattering term. Rather, Spaniards like Fray Bernardino de Sahagun argued that "Those who, very like Indians, are born there, resemble Spaniards in appearance, but not in their nature and qualities."[36] And while many Spanish writers were highly critical of creoles in New Spain—believing, among other things, that they had degenerated into uncivilized beings—they nevertheless were correct in their observation that Spaniards born in America were not exactly like Spaniards born in Spain.

Yet until the second half of the eighteenth century, creoles born in New Spain largely refused the label. They considered themselves Spanish, called themselves Spanish, identified with Spanish customs and history, spoke the Spanish language, and tried to stay abreast of Spanish fashions and tastes. Thus, they were deeply offended at the insinuation that they were somehow not as good as "true" Spaniards.[37] In spite of such indignation, however, it could hardly be denied—especially over the course of generations of settlement in New Spain—that there were differences between the creoles and those who had been born in Spain (called *peninsulars*). For one thing, individuals born in New Spain had no direct connection with Spain itself. They could, and did, imbibe Spanish customs, habits, and memories through their parents, grandparents, friends, associates, and new immigrants, but their own realities lay in the landscape and environment of the Americas rather than in Europe. And this reality, as we know, was unique. In New Spain, creoles were born into a world in which Spaniards were a minority, and in which Spanish-style urban enclaves existed alongside large and diverse indigenous populations. Moreover, the role of sex in New Spain had fundamentally changed the social landscape. Creole society in New Spain could not be easily or conveniently divided between "Spanish" and "indigenous" because in so many families there were mixtures of the two. As a result of such mixing, creoles

learned not only about Spanish culture but also about Indian cultures. The role of indigenous women was critical in this process, for even though many of those who married or bore the children of Spaniards learned Spanish and converted to Catholicism, they nevertheless imparted to their children memories of their languages, foods, religious customs, and art.[38]

To be sure, the dominant culture in New Spain was recognizably Spanish: the lingua franca was Spanish, Catholic churches dotted towns and countryside alike, the architecture recalled Spanish influences, and styles of dress were distinctly European. At the same time, creole culture also incorporated aspects of the Indian cultures to which it was so closely connected. New words found their way into the language, new styles of art were adopted, Spanish and Indian cuisines merged, and folktales stemmed from both Spanish and Indian origins. By the eighteenth century— once it was clear that indigenous peoples in New Spain were no longer a threat to Spanish rule— creoles even began to take pride in the pre-conquest history of the Aztecs, pointing to their ferocity as a testament to the prowess of the creole descendants who had conquered the area. By 1700, Spanish creoles had also created a political and economic system that was far less dependent on Spain than ever before. New Spain had grown wealthy from its abundant silver, its agricultural resources, and its textile production, and—as a result of contraband trade—creole elites operated a society that proclaimed its undying allegiance to Spanish authority even as it acted increasingly on its own behalf.[39]

The growing sense of creole identity in New Spain based on the new circumstances and environment of the Americas was also fed by the negative treatment creoles received at the hands of peninsulars. Indeed, peninsulars regularly scorned creole culture, arguing that creoles had

---

[36] Elliott, *Empires of the Atlantic World*, 234, 236.
[37] Ibid., 238.

[38] Isabel P.B. Feo Rodrigues demonstrates the critical importance of sex and sexual relations to the process of creolization in "Islands of Sexuality: Theories and Histories of Creolization in Cape Verde," *International Journal of African Historical Studies*, 36:1 (1993), 83–103.
[39] Elliott, *Empires of the Atlantic World*, 229, 242.

been irreparably marred by their close connection to Indians, and that they were thus inferior to "real" Spaniards. Part of the reason for this scorn was self-interested and practical: by the eighteenth century in particular, competition for administrative and judicial appointments in New Spain was intense, and creoles and peninsulars regularly competed for the limited positions available. By tarring creoles with the brush of inferiority, then, peninsulars hoped they could convince Spanish authorities to give them the best appointments. In fact, colonial reforms during the eighteenth century (discussed in greater depth in chapter 7) did aim to place peninsulars in nearly all of the highest colonial positions—a move that was deeply unpopular with creoles.[40] And while creoles and peninsulars were never wholly separate—intermarriage regularly blurred the lines between them—the loudly proclaimed sense of superiority of many peninsulars over creole culture encouraged creoles to think of themselves as a distinct group with a distinct identity.

Although the experience of Spanish creoles in New Spain was unique in many ways from other European creoles in the Americas, certain aspects would have seemed familiar to Portuguese creoles in Brazil, British creoles in New England, or French creoles in St. Domingue. First, the mere fact of being born outside Europe into a world with different social, political, and economic realities than the home country lent itself to the formation of identities based at least in part on these new circumstances. Over time, successive generations grew increasingly invested in these new realities even as they tried to maintain connections with their European past. The result was often a hybrid sense of group identity—at once connected to Europe and yet shaped recognizably by new institutions, social groupings, or economic conditions. Second, even among groups who identified very strongly with the home country—like New England colonists in the eighteenth century—scorn from those born in Europe often encouraged a separate sense of identity. Thus, colonists frequently found themselves rebuffed as coarse and

degenerate by the very people whom they identified as their country people. When this occurred, European creoles tended to form defensive identities that continued to privilege their European heritage while emphasizing what was noteworthy and distinct about their own culture. In time, some groups of European creoles came to realize that their new identities as separate groups were so well developed that they no longer wished to think of themselves as European, and sought independence from their home countries.

In contrast to European creolization, the process of creolization for Africans in the Caribbean—or anywhere in the Americas, for that matter—was far different. Where many Europeans had choices about where to go and what livelihood to choose, Africans had none. African migration was forced rather than voluntary, of course, which meant that the individuals involved emphatically did not want to move to a new land. African slaves also had no control over their geographical destinations or over their labor once they arrived in the Americas. Also unlike Europeans, Africans were not allowed to bring their physical culture with them—clothing, furniture, artwork, and wealth all had to be left behind. Once in the Americas, African slaves could not write or receive letters from their families and loved ones back home, and thus could not stay abreast of events or fashions in the communities of their origin.

If the aforementioned features of slave migration were not difficult enough, once on the slave ships Africans generally found themselves culturally and linguistically isolated from their fellow passengers. Because slave ships tended to include individuals of diverse ethnic and linguistic background, slaves immediately "entered a world where they had no kinfolk, no old friends, and no fellow villagers. Some might pass years without speaking to a single person who knew their mother tongue."[41] In some areas where slave concentrations were particularly high, such as St. Domingue or Cuba, slaves with common ethnic or linguistic

---

[40]Lockhart and Schwartz, *Early Latin America*, 346–352.

[41]David Northrup, *Africa's Discovery of Europe, 1450–1850* (New York: Oxford University Press, 2002), 122; and Nanette de Jong, "An Anatomy of Creolization: Curacao and the Antillean Waltz," *Latin American Music Review* (2003), 234.

backgrounds did exist in high enough concentrations that individuals from the same ethnic group might find one another. However, most plantations in the Caribbean were characterized by their ethnic variety rather than their ethnic similarity. In addition, it was very difficult for slaves to maintain any kind of social stability once on Caribbean plantations because mortality rates were extremely high. Back-breaking labor, insufficient rest and food, and hot, tropical climates made the lives of many Caribbean slaves extremely short: in Jamaica in the eighteenth century, so many slaves had to be replaced due to mortality that more than three-quarters of the slave population was African born at any one time.[42] And while slaves direct from Africa brought fresh cultural influences and memories to slave communities, they continued to hail from a wide variety of ethnicities and linguistic groups and thus contributed to the already-existing African heterogeneity on the islands.

The circumstances of African migration to the Caribbean, then, meant that most slaves not only had to adapt to new environments and new peoples, but that they had to do so in the harshest of conditions and without people from their own homelands to provide social and cultural stability. As a result, African cultural contributions in the Americas cannot easily be characterized as "survivals" of the cultures of their specific homelands so much as "hybridizations" of many African cultures.[43] Just to be able to communicate, slaves found it necessary to make rapid adaptations. In some islands, slaves communicated by using colonial languages such as English, French, and Spanish. In places where particular African ethnicities dominated—as in eighteenth-century St. Domingue, where many slaves came from the Congo region—slaves learned African languages different from their own in order to communicate. More frequently, however, slaves from a variety of ethnicities combined parts of colonial languages and various parts of African languages to come up with a new "pidgin,"

or creole, language altogether. Such languages developed in Jamaica, Guyana, Aruba, St. Lucia, and many other Caribbean locations. Commonly, creole languages used the vocabulary of the dominant colonial language with a grammatical structure that reflected diverse African languages.[44]

The adaptation, borrowing, and regional specificity of creole languages were also reflected in other aspects of African creolization in the Caribbean—particularly in terms of music, dance, cuisine, and agricultural practices. Since slaves found themselves in the midst of people from so many different backgrounds and ethnicities, new rhythms and dances developed, each incorporating a variety of African colonial sounds, instruments, beats, and movements with aspects of colonial music. Over time, these rhythms developed into clearly identifiable musical traditions. Indeed, many twentieth-century Caribbean musical styles—such as Reggae, salsa, merengue, and calypso—have their roots in this period of creolization. Moreover, although slaves were not able to bring agricultural implements with them to the Caribbean, they did bring considerable experience as farmers as well as tastes that had developed in their home countries. In the Caribbean, slaves used this knowledge along with available foods to form highly specific regional cuisines that reflected local ingredients, colonial tastes, and a variety of African influences. Additionally, many of the most important domesticated plants in the Caribbean came from Africa, including two kinds of millet, bananas, yams, and akee—a fruit that has become one of Jamaica's national dishes.[45]

Unlike Spanish creoles who commanded considerable power in New Spain, African slaves in the Caribbean occupied the lowest social position in society. Because of this, slaves were faced not only with creatively adapting to a multitude of African cultures in their midst, but with the necessity of conforming—at least outwardly—to the customs and culture of the colonial power. For example, slaves were generally required to give up

---

[42] Egerton et al., *The Atlantic World*, 269–270.
[43] This point is extensively argued in John Thornton, *Africa and Africans in the Making of the Atlantic World, 1400–1800* (Cambridge: Cambridge University Press, 1992).

[44] Morgan, "British Encounters with Africans and African-Americans," 204.
[45] Ibid., 209.

their African names and to take European names given to them by their owners. More critically, slaves were often forbidden to practice African religions, and in many places were encouraged to become Christians. In response, many Caribbean slaves adopted the outward signs of conversion while continuing to worship in their own way secretly. Sometimes, as in the case of the Voudun religion of St. Domingue, slaves combined aspects of Catholicism—particularly the veneration of saints—with a combination of West African beliefs and practices to form a new form of religion altogether.

As a result of the particular structure of African slave migration to the Caribbean, a wide variety of regional identities grew out of the necessities of adaptation to both European and other African cultures. Although there were broad similarities between many of these identities, there were also important differences depending on the dominant European culture, local environmental conditions, and the African ethnicities involved. The biggest constant linking all of these new slave cultures together was the fact of their oppression by European colonial masters. Yet while this oppression made it quite easy for slaves to identify themselves in opposition to Europeans, it did not conversely make it easy for slaves to form more universal identities or to take collective action. Slave resistance and even rebellion was widespread across the Caribbean, but coordinated efforts even across the same island were difficult because of regulations regarding slave movements and the certainty of swift and brutal punishment.

Compared to the process of creolization among Spanish creoles in New Spain, creolization among African slaves in the Caribbean was a far more traumatic and difficult process. Moreover, creolization among Caribbean slaves resulted in a wider variety of hybrid cultures, both because of the lack of ethnic uniformity among Africans and because of the diversity of places they landed. Nevertheless, as in New Spain the process of creolization resulted in the creation of a variety of new identities, all of which were the product of the new circumstances brought about by imperial relationships in the Americas.

Acculturation

Although the process of creolization always involved acculturation, acculturation did not always result in creolization. Creolization, as we know, refers to a specific process by which foreigners adapt to new environments and form new identities in their new homes. Acculturation, on the other hand, is a far more general term that can apply to any people and reference any aspect of cultural adaptation. Simply put, **acculturation** refers to modifications in culture, beliefs, or values as a result of borrowing from or adapting to other cultures. Although twenty-first-century American culture publicly values acculturation, historically it was not a universally positive phenomenon: at times it could have beneficial effects, at others it was a relatively neutral process, while at still other times it was the result of radical disruption and social dislocation. In the context of early modern colonialism, nearly every group experienced varying degrees of acculturation as a result of interactions with new groups, ideas, and commodities. This process of borrowing and adaptation, in turn, had important effects on identity formation.

Examples of acculturation in colonial contexts are plentiful because cultural borrowing and adaptation in some form was nearly universal. We have already explored linguistic changes among African creoles in the West Indies, but linguistic changes occurred among nearly every group that came into contact with new groups. From the earliest period of colonization right through the early modern period, indigenous peoples and European conquerors and settlers found it necessary to communicate clearly with one another. To facilitate this communication, both indigenous peoples and Europeans formed intermediate, pidgin languages in much the same way that African creoles did. As a result, new words, expressions, and place names entered the lexicons of people all over the Americas and in colonial outposts elsewhere. In fact, in some cases these linguistic adaptations have endured to the present. Among Micmac speakers in modern Canada, words originally borrowed from Basque explorers and traders in the sixteenth century still exist, including, for example, the words for "shirt" (*atlai*) and "king" (*elege*).[46] Similarly, Mexican Spanish integrated hundreds of indigenous Nahuatl words, including well-known terms such as *tomato* and *chocolate*.[47]

Diets also changed markedly as a result of colonial contact and trade. Faced with new environments and climates, European settlers often found it necessary to adapt to local cuisines simply in order to survive. All American schoolchildren learn that the settlers of New England fared much better once local Indians introduced them to maize, but this is just the tip of the iceberg. The transfer of food items from culture to culture accelerated at a remarkable rate during the early modern period, as trade and contact between distant places expanded rapidly. Tomatoes, corn, potatoes, tobacco, and chocolate—all products of the Americas—were introduced to Europe, Asia, and Africa, while foods like apples and meat-animals like chicken, pig, cow, and goat were brought to the Americas by colonists and then adopted into the cuisines of indigenous groups. While it may be difficult to imagine Italian food without tomatoes or Mexican food without chicken, it is nevertheless the case that these items were the products of adaptation.

Similarly, the introduction of mass produced sugar—itself a quintessentially colonial product—to people and places around the world led to significant dietary changes in multiple locations. Particularly when accompanied by other exotic products such as coffee (from the Near East), tea (from China), or chocolate (from Central and South America), sugar frequently became associated with culturally distinct dietary practices. For example, British people in Britain and the Americas came to associate drinking sweetened tea as a mark of Britishness; the Dutch felt similarly about drinking hot, sweet chocolate, as did the French about sweetened coffee. Such was the pace of dietary adaptation in areas affected by colonialism and colonial trade that by the seventeenth century traders on the West African coast of Upper Guinea were able to eat "citrus fruits, poultry,

and pigs from Portugal; pineapples, chiles, and peanuts from South America; and bananas, mangoes, and paddy rice from South Asia."[48]

Religion was another area in which significant acculturation occurred in colonial contexts. This was especially true with regard to Christianity in Spanish and Portuguese America, because missions and evangelism among indigenous people were especially strong in those locations. By the eighteenth century, Christianity had gained wide acceptance among many indigenous groups of Spanish America. In part, this was because many ethnic groups in Spanish America were willing to incorporate the gods of conquerors into their own pantheon. In part it was because of the efforts of missionary priests, who set out to teach indigenous peoples about what they believed was the "true" and only religion. Yet the nature of indigenous conversion allowed for the incorporation of a variety of indigenous beliefs and practices into this new Christianity. Indeed, religious instruction for the majority tended to focus on the basics of Catholicism: priests would offer instruction on the sacraments as well as the most important rituals but were only able to offer extended religious education to the sons of elites. In rural areas, this lack of sustained education was especially acute, since a priest might only visit isolated villages once or twice a year. In addition to this somewhat incomplete transfer of Catholicism, certain aspects of Catholic worship—such as veneration of the saints—fit very well with indigenous beliefs. Many ethnic groups in Spanish America already believed in a group of specialized individuals with supernatural abilities, and thus were able to adopt the Spanish form without producing a fundamental change in worldview. The result was a syncretic form of Christianity that focused on community identification with individual saints. At various times during the year, communities arranged for religious festivals in which an image of a revered saint would be paraded around the village, allowing each individual to renew their local identification with a particular deity.[49]

---

[46] Edward G. Gray and Norman Fiering, *The Language Encounter in the Americas, 1492–1800* (New York: Berghahn Books, 2000), 31.

[47] Kicza, *Resilient Cultures*, 91.

[48] George Brooks quoted in Egerton et al., *The Atlantic World*, 262.

[49] Kicza, *Resilient Cultures*, 86–90.

Acculturation was not just a one-way street. Europeans borrowed in multiple ways from indigenous cultures beyond language and diet. This was particularly true in areas where Europeans made up a small majority of the population, or in areas where European communities were threatened by powerful indigenous groups. For example, in West African trading posts, British outposts in India, or French trading towns in modern Canada, Europeans comprised a tiny minority within or alongside powerful states. As a result, Europeans found it both necessary and prudent to learn indigenous languages, to practice skilled diplomacy, and to conform to indigenous customs. In the highly competitive atmosphere of West African trade, Europeans from a variety of states vied to shower local rulers with gifts and to conform to expected social standards in the hopes of winning local favor. In the British outposts of India, European representatives of the East India Company found it expedient in the seventeenth and eighteenth centuries to adopt elements of Indian wardrobe, diet, and housing. So distinctive were these men that, when they returned to Britain (frequently as wealthy men), they were referred to disparagingly as *nabobs*, from the Urdu term *nawab*, or Muslim nobility.[50]

Even in places where Europeans were not a tiny minority, the existence of threatening states on the borders of European settlements frequently required adaptation to indigenous ways. By the eighteenth century, for example, English, French, and Spanish settlers engaged in elaborate treaty ceremonies with Indian groups across eastern North America. These ceremonies followed Indian, not European, protocol, and included formal pronouncements, feasting, gift-giving, singing, and dancing. While Europeans might well have wished to avoid such ceremonies, in certain locations their power was not secure without ensuring alliances or peace with Indian groups on their own terms. Modes of warfare in the Americas also reflected European adaptation to Indian ways, particularly in border regions: for example, European soldiers frequently adopted leather leggings and modeled Indian techniques of moving through the forests.[51]

Acculturation could occur even in places where local inhabitants had no contact, or only limited contact, with other groups. This was certainly the case where food items were concerned, since borrowing and adaptation could occur between far-distant cultures. This was also the case with certain items of material culture. In the interior regions of North America, for example, Indian groups who had very limited contact with Europeans nevertheless incorporated a wide variety of European goods—including metal pots, weapons, cloth, and tools—into their daily lives.[52] These items frequently brought change to Indian lives by making warfare more deadly, work more efficient, and cooking easier, but they did not commonly involve massive changes in social structure, ideology, or beliefs.

On the other hand, acculturation sometimes entailed far more complete and traumatic adaptations. This was especially true for the indigenous peoples of the Americas who bore the brunt of initial contact with Europeans. As we saw in chapter 3, these groups first suffered appalling death rates as a result of the introduction of Old World diseases. In addition, conflict with Europeans over territory often led to warfare, which reduced Indian numbers even further. As a means of survival, Indian groups in North, Central, and South America sometimes sought to move away from lands occupied by Europeans. This movement, however, brought fleeing Indians into contact with other, previously settled, Indian groups. In some cases, the remnants of Indian groups seeking new homes sought incorporation into stronger groups: such was the case with the Tuscarora of North Carolina, who in the eighteenth century were so decimated by conflict with Europeans as well as other Indians that they fled north and petitioned the Iroquois to absorb them.[53] In other cases, several different groups of Indians who had been similarly decimated banded together to become new people.

---

[50] An excellent account of the phenomenon of the nabob is Percival Spear, *The Nabobs: A Study of the Social Life of the English in Eighteenth-Century India* (Oxford: Oxford University Press, 1998).

[51] Egerton et al., *The Atlantic World*, 297, 300.
[52] Kicza, *Resilient Cultures*, 145.
[53] Ibid., 140.

The Catawba of western North Carolina were one such people, who faced the monumental challenges of blending a variety of languages, customs, and traditions to form a new identity.[54]

Obviously, neither creolization nor acculturation should be regarded as necessarily easy or positive. For many people affected by colonialism—particularly indigenous Americans and African slaves—the two processes were profoundly difficult and painful. At the same time, it is clear that the processes of creolization and acculturation were crucial to the formation of new social groups, new cuisines, new musical rhythms, new methods of interaction and—perhaps above all—new identities.

Indeed, colonialism in the Americas and elsewhere quickened the global scope and scale of intercultural interaction, adaptation, and borrowing to an unprecedented degree. The result was a multitude of local and regional cultures that incorporated new elements while also retaining aspects of the home cultures.

It should be clear, however, that inter-cultural borrowing and adaptation did not mean that colonial societies valued social equality. Rather, even as colonial societies were maturing into distinct (and, in the case of Spanish and Portuguese America, mixed-race) cultures during the eighteenth century, Europeans sought ever harder to draw distinctions between themselves on the one hand and indigenous and African peoples on the other. Prior to the eighteenth century, Europeans tended to regard these distinctions in terms of levels of civilization or religion—arguing, for example, that Nahua Indians were inferior because they were not Christian. During the eighteenth century, these distinctions were increasingly made not on the basis of civilization or religion but on "race." The most important feature of "race" was that it was identifiable, according to Europeans, by skin color. Although race was conceived slightly differently by each colonial society and varied depending on whether or not African slavery formed an important part of the economy, in the eighteenth century Europeans in all of the colonies and outposts began to use race as a marker of difference between themselves and their colonial

subjects. This trend was clearly visible in terms of the law, as many colonial societies began to impose ever more restrictions on racial mixing, on professions open to non-Europeans, and on freedom of movement among non-Europeans. In the French colonies, a law of 1779 even forbade African and mixed-race people from dressing or wearing their hair in the manner of Europeans.[55]

Thus, even though people in the colonies had developed a variety of new identities, these identities were hardly harmonious. Rather, colonial identities—both within and between colonies—were often in competition with or in outright opposition to one another. Indeed, European creoles developed a sense of themselves as different from those born in Europe (and nursed their wounded egos at being scorned by their former compatriots) even as many of them scorned and brutalized African slaves, indigenous Americans, or lower-class Europeans. Notwithstanding ironies such as these, it is nevertheless the case that colonialism had given rise to new identities as a result of new circumstances, new kinds of exchange, the formation of new social groups, and a breathtaking variety of cultural adaptations and adoptions. The importance of these new peoples and identities on the history of empire was profound, for in the period between 1770 and 1820 these identities would become crucial in a series of revolutions that literally rocked the world: but that is the story of chapter 7.

Questions

1. Based on the information presented in this chapter, which factors influenced the different models by which identities were formed in various parts of the Americas and coastal Asia and Africa in this period?
2. What are the distinctions between the processes of creolization and acculturation? How are they related?
3. Scholars often argue that identity is "socially constructed"—that is to say that race, gender, class, and other markers are not absolutes but vary in their importance and the way they are understood across different societies and times. Do you agree or disagree? Use the information in this chapter as evidence for your position.

---

[54] Egerton et al., *The Atlantic World*, 272.

[55] Peabody and Grinberg, *Slavery, Freedom, and the Law*, 7.

CHAPTER 6

Imperialism and Colonialism: Asian Land Empires in a Global Age

In most comparative or global studies of empires and imperialism, the story becomes riveted to the Atlantic world during the sixteenth and seventeenth centuries. The story of the construction, and later fragmentation, of American empires by European metropoles is so dramatic that it seems to drown out events elsewhere. This single-minded concentration of attention on the Atlantic in this period has focused our attention on the great "progressive" revolutions that are enshrined at the heart of what it means to be European or American—the Enlightenment, the rise of parliament in Britain, the French Revolution, the American Revolution. By contrast, western historians have traditionally represented the experiences of the Ottoman, Chinese (Manchu or Qing), and Mughal empires in this period almost exclusively through stories of decline, and thus as hardly worthy of study. These states are depicted as rapidly falling into economic and techno-logical obsolescence in the face of western industrial domination. Of the Asian empires, only Russia under the Romanovs is somewhat included as part of the story of the rise of the west in this period—perpetually poised both geographically and technologically between European progress and Asiatic decline.

The rise of "world history" as a field of study has exploded this narrow focus, as many world historians have argued that Asia—and especially China and India—remained global eco-nomic powerhouses until well into the nineteenth century.[1] Even they, however, admit that the Atlantic empires were massively significant in the construction of the modern world, not least because industrialization of Britain (and later the world) appears to have been made possible at least partly through the harnessing of American natural resources and African labor to

---

[1] The recent transformation of historians' perspectives on modern Asian history is well demonstrated by the career of one of the fathers of world history, William McNeill. In his seminal textbook *The Rise of the West: A History of the Human Community* (Chicago: Chicago University Press, 1963), McNeill dramatically contrasts western European progress and Asian decline in this period, with Russia under Peter the Great facing both ways. However McNeill, to his credit, has continually revised this argument, and in his recent work has focused more on the similarities and shared experiences than differences among European and Asian states in the seventeenth, eighteenth, and early nineteenth centuries. See, for example, the book he co-wrote with J.R. McNeill, *The Human Web: A Bird's-Eye View of World History* (New York: W.W. Norton, 2003).

European—and especially British—economies.[2] The relative advantages that this transformation gives to western Europe seem, in this context, to help explain the eighteenth-century fragmentation of Mughal India, the slow inward collapse of the Qing Dynasty in China and Central Asia, the retreat and eventual dismemberment of the Ottoman empires, and even the Russian Revolution and the demise of the last Tsars.

This chapter seeks to understand these four vast Asian empires somewhat more comprehensively within the global history of imperialism.[3] Recent studies based on deeper readings of data and documents suggest that Asian empires dealt with a series of global and local challenges during this period with varying success. As world historians have noted, many of these challenges were the result of the shifting global economies. Asian empires both profited from and were threatened by these changes. It seems likely that right up until the nineteenth century, Asia (and especially China and India) continued to be an important engine for the global economy, first consuming vast amounts of American silver and later releasing it back into the global economy. As producers of manufactured goods destined for intercontinental trade, the factories of Shanghai and Calcutta were overtaken in importance in the early nineteenth century by those of northern England. Meanwhile, Central Asia and the Indian Ocean remained significant marketplaces for both

goods and ideas. At the same time, however, imperial governments in Asia struggled to control both foreign and domestic merchants in this period, to restrict dangerous imports and sensitive exports, and eventually to cope with the low prices of Britain's industrial goods.

The Asian empires also faced both new and continuing difficulties ruling vast multi-ethnic populations; both in creating internal cohesion and in maintaining their grip on very different groups of people. In some cases they did so with extraordinary success, conducting experiments and developing models of colonial rule that would be copied by the western Europeans who observed them during this period. Often, however, these internal challenges were reinforced by changes in the global situation to create dramatic empire-wide crises. Such global trends included the ramifications of the Industrial Revolution in Britain, the worldwide growth in the power of the mercantile class, dramatic increases in population, and the global diffusion of nationalist ideologies.

In this chapter, we focus on the stories of the Mughal, Manchu (in China and Central Asia), Russian, and Ottoman empires in the period 1650–1850 by looking at their strategies in constructing and maintaining their rule over their metropoles and their colonial territories and subjects. It is their fates as empires—not as people—with which we are chiefly concerned. In the first section, we briefly survey the status of the empires in the seventeenth century. We identify both continuities and changes from earlier periods. In the second section we focus on the challenges to their stability and cohesion that subsequently emerged. Three types of shared and interrelated challenges stand out. First, and arguably most importantly, were challenges to imperial authority and power by both rogue imperial agents and local authorities across the empire. Their acts of defiance were inspired in part by the second challenge: a changing and increasingly competitive global context. Over the course of the 200 years covered in this chapter, new trading opportunities driven in part by increasing trade with Europe and its American colonies stimulated the ambitions of both commercial elites and those who controlled land and

---

[2] A founding contribution to this argument was Eric Williams, *Capitalism and Slavery* (New York: Perigree Books, 1944), 98. One of the more recent proponents of this thesis is Kenneth Pomeranz. See Pomeranz, *The Great Divergence: China, Europe, and the Making of the Modern World Economy* (Princeton, NJ: Princeton University Press, 2000), 3–4, 19–23, 55, 125, 161, 185, 264. This thesis is not without opponents: see, for example, Patrick O'Brien, "European Economic Development: The Contribution of the Periphery," *Economic History Review*, New Series, 35 (1982).

[3] We call these empires Asian since they had Asian metropoles. This is something of a simplification, but a necessary one. We recognize that Romanov Russia held significant European (and later North American) territories and that Peter I moved his capital to St. Petersburg, arguably in Europe. We also recognize that the Ottomans occupied or had imperial relationships with territories and populations in both Europe and Africa during this period.

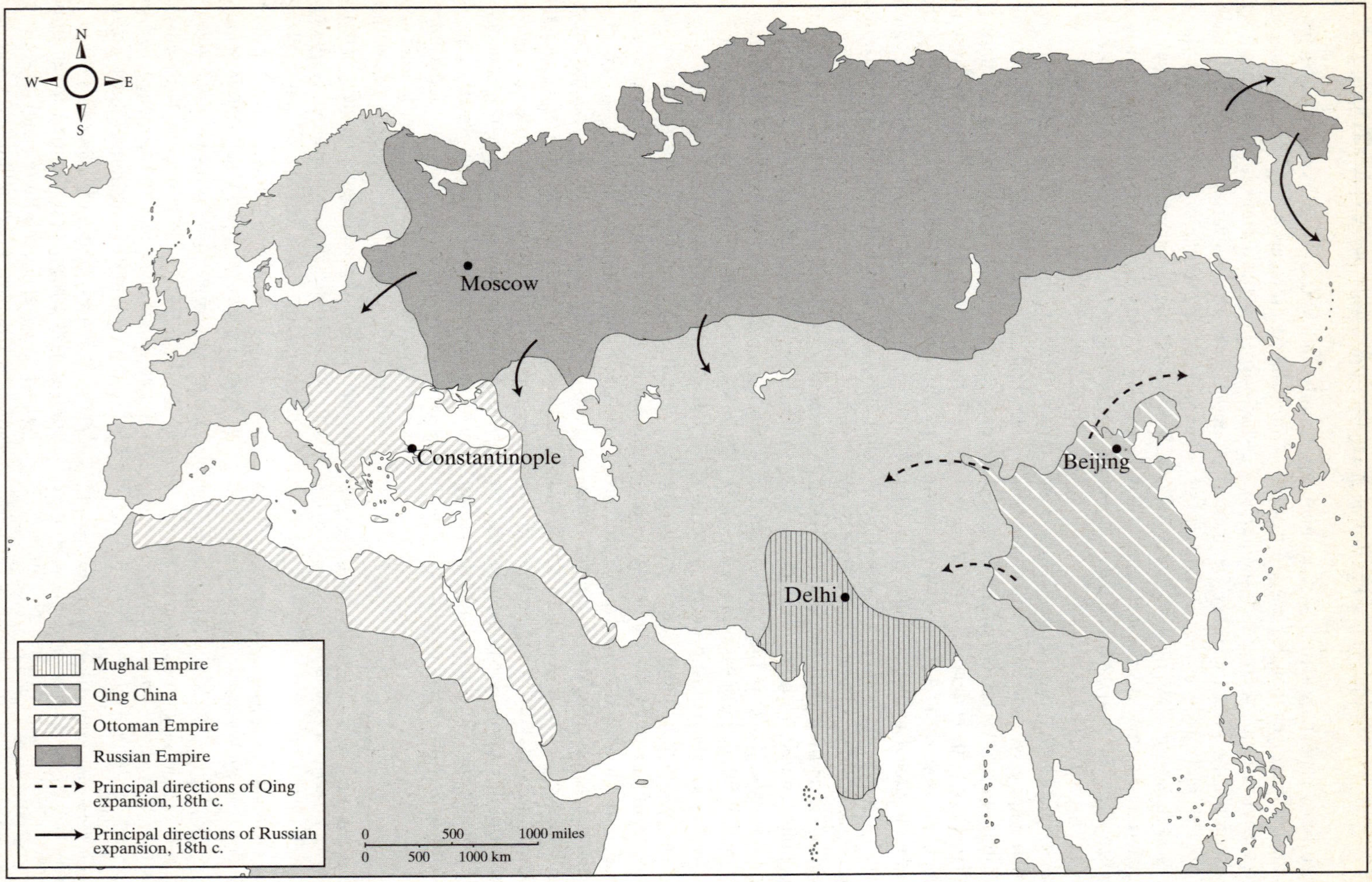
N
W
E
S
Moscow
Constantinople
Beijing
Delhi
Mughal Empire
Qing China
Ottoman Empire
Russian Empire
Principal directions of Qing expansion, 18th c.
Principal directions of Russian expansion, 18th c.
0 500 1000 miles
0 500 1000 km

Asian Empires, c. 1700

labor in the four Asian empires. Similarly, the loyalties of imperial agents and colonial subjects alike were tested by the empires' competitions for territory and influence in Central Asia. Finally, these four empires struggled with the age-old imperial problem of balancing the competing needs of metropolitan sectors (merchants, landowners, soldiers, and clergy) that profited from exploiting colonial subjects and the need to extend certain rights and protections to the subjects in order to win their loyalty and cooperation.

The leaderships of the empires reacted to these challenges in a variety of ways, and in the third section of this chapter we explore the great varieties of strategies and policies they employed. Some of their approaches showed remarkable flexibility, while others were rather rigid, and the results were diverse. We survey these results in the fourth section, and argue that they cannot simply be interpreted as "Asiatic failures." The Russian Empire is the most dramatic contradictory example. From a low point in the early seventeenth century, under the Romanov family Russia expanded hundreds of miles to the west and thousands of miles to the east and south, until by 1850 it encompassed more than 22 million square kilometers and 150 million people. Not all Asian dynasties were so successful at maintaining their hold over far-flung territories. The Ottoman Empire shrank rather dramatically in the eighteenth century, due to both defections by their own governors and defeats by rival powers. Despite internal and external problems, however, the Ottoman state arguably remained a moderately important global player. Thus, scholars continue to be divided as to whether its eventual demise in 1917 can be attributed at least more properly to the exigencies of the First World War or to long-term imperial failures. Results for the Qing rulers of China and much of Central Asia were equally mixed. While successfully holding together a region whose population probably topped 400 million people by 1850, the Qing emperors were nevertheless ineffectual at combating significant internal unrest and challenges from outside by the first decades of the nineteenth century. Perhaps the most unambivalent imperial disintegration was that of the Mughal

(Tīmūrid) emperors, whose empire was already fragmenting by the time the British East India Company (EIC) began to supplant them as hegemons of South Asia in the late eighteenth century. Despite this collapse, however, the institutions they created largely survived to be inherited by Queen Victoria of Britain when she became Empress of India in 1858.

CONTINUITY AND CHANGE FROM THE MID-SEVENTEENTH CENTURY

The emperors who ruled most of Asia in the mid-seventeenth century all claimed their authority partly as the heirs to earlier rulers, and often ruled over areas that had been integrated into imperial states for centuries by utilizing long-standing institutions. At the same time, however, the period from 1600 to 1650 was a time of significant transformation both globally and in each of the four empires discussed in this chapter.

In two of the Asian empires—Russia and China—the early seventeenth century brought with it the handing over of the imperial throne to a new dynasty. In China, the Ming emperors were replaced by a group of former vassals from Central Asia in 1644. The new emperors came from among the decentralized Jurchen—or Manchu—peoples, whom they had begun to organize into a single state on the edge of Ming China from about the 1580s. Gradually, these Manchu leaders added Mongols and other neighbors into the militarized state, and in 1637 they forced the Korean king to recognize them as overlords. Adopting Chinese styles of bureaucracy and government, they named themselves the Qing Dynasty, a rival to Ming China to the east. Their expansion was facilitated in part by the weakness of Ming rule in the early seventeenth century, as plague, poor harvests, and corruption severely diminished the authority and legitimacy of the central regime. The result was an explosion of bandit movements and rebels that threatened even the Ming capital. In fact the Manchu rulers entered China in 1644 as "saviors," allying themselves with the Ming general Wu Sangui against rebels who had sacked Beijing and who had forced the last Ming emperor to commit suicide.[4] Together, the Qing forces (made up of Manchu troops, their Mongol vassals, and their Korean tributaries) along with Wu Sangui's forces defeated the rebels at the Battle of Shanhaiguan. Rather than restoring Ming rule, however, the Qing used the opportunity to establish their own control over most of China. Under this new dynasty, China was just part of a vast and multi-ethnic empire. Because of its wealth and size, however, it could not simply fit in as a conquered territory, but instead was transformed into the imperial metropole, albeit one whose inhabitants were subject to the rule of an occupying class. Beijing remained the seat of governance for the Qing, as it had been for the Ming before them, and the new rulers kept in place many of the bureaucratic and economic institutions through which their predecessors had ruled. However, they also imposed a new ruling class—thousands of Central Asian warriors organized into military "banners," or regiments.

Nor did Qing expansion end with the conquest of China. In the late seventeenth century, and especially during the rule of the Kangxi Emperor (1661–1722), the Qing Empire spread westward into Central Asia until it came up against the Russian Empire, which was expanding eastward into Siberia. By the mid-eighteenth century, Russian strength had effectively halted the Qing expansion. The Yongzheng Emperor (1723–1735) and the Qianlong Emperor (1735–1796) for a while tried to sidestep Russian Siberia by diverting their efforts into the Tarim Basin of Central Asia, but Qing expansion was effectively halted by 1800 and soon after began to recede as Russian influence in the region grew.

The Russian Tsars who had halted Qing westward expansion were members of the Romanov Dynasty, who like the Qing had seized power in the early seventeenth century. Following the death of Tsar Feodor Ivanovich, last ruler of the Rurik Dynasty in 1598, poor harvests and political turmoil had paved the way for invasion by Russia's rivals to the west, the Polish–Lithuanian Commonwealth and the Kingdom of Sweden. This period, known to Russians as the *Time of Troubles*, was ended in 1613 only by the election of the wealthy noble Mikhail Romanov as Tsar (1613–1645). Romanov could claim to be related to earlier dynasties, and his family was powerful in Moscow politics, but more importantly he was a skilled and ruthless politician. Under his rule, the tide of events reversed. Poland–Lithuania and Sweden were temporarily bought off, and order was restored to the realm. His successors Alexis I (1641–1676) and especially Peter (Pyotr) I (1682–1725) built on this stability to defeat Russia's rivals and to claim enormous territories to the west including the Ukraine, much of Poland, and a number of provinces on the Baltic Sea. In 1809, Finland was added as well. Meanwhile, the Romanov Tsars were also pushing both eastward toward the Pacific and southward, where they captured several provinces from the Ottoman Empire. This expansion into Central and East Asia reached a climax during the reign of the foreign-born Tsarina Catherine II (1762–1796), under whose control Russia added millions of Muslim and Siberian subjects and even planted small colonies on the Pacific Coast of North America.[5]

The Ottoman rulers experienced no such dynastic transition as Russia and China in the seventeenth century. However, beneath the continuity of the dynasty, important political transformations did take place.[6] Perhaps the most significant of these was the demise of the *timar* land system. The practice of rewarding important soldier-nobles (*sipâhîs*) for their service by giving them control over revenue-earning lands (the timar) and

---

[4] Useful general histories of the Qing Dynasty include Jonathan Spence, *The Search for Modern China* (New York: W.W. Norton, 1990); and *The Cambridge History of China*, vols. 9, 10, and 11 (Cambridge: Cambridge University Press), 1978, 1980, and 2003, variously edited by John K. Fairbank and William J. Peterson.

[5] Among the most accessible general histories of Russia in this period are Chester S.L. Dunning, *Russia's First Civil War: The Time of Troubles and the Founding of the Romanov Dynasty* (University Park: Pennsylvania State University Press, 2001); and Nicholas V. Riasanovsky and Mark Steinberg, *A History of Russia* (New York: Oxford University Press, 2004).

[6] Important general histories of the Ottoman Empire in this period include classics such as Marshall Hodgson, *The Venture of Islam* (Chicago: The University of Chicago Press, 1977), as well as newer texts such as Jason Goodwin, *Lords of the Horizons: A History of the Ottoman Empire* (New York: Henry Holt, 1998).

tenant-farmers had been at the foundation of the Ottoman success in expansion and system of governance for centuries. But with the state no longer rapidly expanding after about 1600, there was no new land to reward sipâhîs. Nor was there a great need for the armored cavalry they provided in the new age of professional firearm-equipped armies. Meanwhile the timar system had failed economically because the tenant-farmers had no inducement to make improvements to land that they themselves did not own. Thus under the reign of Mehmed III (1596–1603), large numbers of sipâhîs were dismissed and their land transferred away from them.

Mehmed's actions followed his victory against a coalition of enemies at the 1596 Battle of Haçova, in which the sipâhîs performed particularly poorly, and victory was salvaged only by the disciplined fire of janissary musketeers. However, Haçova was one of the last Ottoman victories in their see-saw struggle against the Russians, Persians, and Habsburgs. By the late seventeenth century, the tide had turned against the Ottoman Sultans. In Europe, the Habsburgs defeated a final Ottoman sortie against Vienna in 1683, and then drove them back by 1699 out of Hungary. In 1718, Sultan Ahmed III (1703–1730) was forced to cede much of Serbia and Wallachia as well. Ahmed was also driven out of Azerbaijan by the Persian forces of Nāder Shāh Afshār. Perhaps even more damagingly, in the late eighteenth century Russian forces drove the Ottoman Sultans from most of their Central Asian territories. Finally, the vital province of Egypt asserted its autonomy (if not technically its independence) in the early nineteenth century under the former janissary general Muhammad Ali Pasha.

While retreating from outlying territories, however, the Ottoman Sultans of the eighteenth and nineteenth centuries by and large managed to defend the heartland of their multi-ethnic empire. The same cannot be said of the Tīmūrid Mughal dynasty. In the early seventeenth century, to be sure, emperors such as Shah Jahan (1628–1658) and Aurangzeb (1658–1707) had continued the expansion of their predecessors. However, the push southward into the Deccan region of South

Asia under Aurangzeb proved enormously expensive and eventually counter-productive. While bringing southern Indian princes like the Marathas temporarily under Mughal rule, Aurangzeb severely depleted the state's finances, caused turmoil in the *mansabdar* class, and eventually stimulated large-scale opposition that severely weakened the emperors' abilities to enforce their writ over large areas. A series of challengers began to replace them in various regions, including Sikh rulers in the north, Hindu Marathas in the south, Persian nobles allied with Nāder Shāh Afshār and Afghani warlords in the west, and finally the EIC in the east. By the late eighteenth century, the Company had become the de facto sovereign over large regions of the empire, and the Mughal Empire was largely defunct.

Many of the themes of Eurasian empires of previous centuries were repeated in these four states. The legitimacy of the state was promulgated through both religious and secular rituals that ideologically linked the emperors' health and position to the prosperity of the empire as a whole. Similarly, in each case the emperors built on the styles and methods of ruling multi-ethnic societies used by the dynasties and rulers who came before them without adopting many fundamental changes.

Moreover, although they were centrally ruled and depended upon cultures of imperialism that glorified the ruling class, their monarchs relied upon the cooperation of various sectors of the population, but especially elite land-owning classes. These classes, whether mansabdars, sipâhîs, Manchu mandarins, or Russian nobles could usually be relied upon to turn out in times of war and generally to support their emperor. To a certain degree, this model of sectoral alliance was typical of land-based empires. It differed quite a bit, however, from the types of alliances necessary to construct oceanic empires. In the Portuguese, Spanish, and later European empires, merchant and banking classes wielded disordinate power as a sector. Missionaries, too, played a much larger role. However, the distinction should not be carried too far. As we will see, later, merchants and bankers as well as religious officials were employed to various degrees by the Asian land empires in this period, and land-owning aristocratic and gentry classes were vital soldiers and investors in the European empires in the Atlantic and Indian oceans as well.

Another important distinction to note is that with the possible exception of Russian Siberia, settlers and officials from these four empires never outnumbered the local inhabitants of the colonial peripheries that they ruled. The Siberians appear to have been as susceptible to diseases carried by settlers as the North Americans just across the Bering Straits, but the same was not true elsewhere. Thus like in most of maritime Asia and coastal Africa, but unlike in large regions of the Americas, acculturation and assimilation were slow processes and the metropolitan settlers and officials were almost as likely to adopt some cultural forms from their hosts as the other way around.

OPPORTUNITIES AND CHALLENGES

While the experiences of the large Asian empires differed widely between 1650 and 1850, they were linked together by a shifting global situation that included demographic, economic, and social transformations that transcended borders. These changes were experienced in unique, but not incomparable, ways by the peoples and leaders of the four empires.

One of the most significant of these transformations was the enormous increase in population levels around the world after about 1550. This global population boom was partly a result of the importation of new foodstuffs from the Americas, maize corn from meso-America increased calorie yields per acre over many other grains in Europe, Asia, and Africa, while potatoes allowed for the cultivation of previously marginal sandy land.[7] Other factors behind the boom may have been the result of sociological changes or the relative political stability of Eurasia in this period. Several of

the more populous regions of Asia, especially China, northern India, and the Ottoman heartland, were especially affected.

Arguably, however, the growth in populations began to outpace the growth in food production in many areas by the mid-seventeenth century. This imbalance may have put a strain on imperial stability in several ways. In the first place, the currency demands of growing populations may have increased Asian states' reliance on American silver, and thus on European trading companies.[8] However, even this new source of silver may have been insufficient for the needs of the burgeoning populations of Asia. Together, food and currency shortages may in some cases have led to falling standards of living, which in turn may have helped spur late eighteenth-century rebellions in Russia and the Ottoman Empire, and early nineteenth-century unrest in China.[9] Combined with the ideological resentment of some colonial subjects, such material suffering was a potent motivation for revolt, as in the Greek uprisings against Ottoman rule in the 1770s.

Conversely, however, the period between 1650 and 1850 witnessed an enormous growth of international trade that created the opposite problem for many empires; the creation of wealthy new elites whose prosperity was not tied to the fortunes of the emperor. Trade in this period burgeoned in ports around Asia that fed the maritime trade with Europe, Africa, and the Americas. It also increased in Central Asia as the expansion of Russia and the Qing Empire created stability in that zone.[10] The result was the emergence of commercial, trading classes in each of these four empires. These merchants represented something of a problem for the empires. Unlike the Qing "banner troops," the Mughal mansabdari, or the Ottoman sipâhîs and janissaries, they did not owe

---

[7] Alfred Crosby, *The Columbian Exchange: Biological and Cultural Consequences of 1492* (Westport, CT: Greenwood Press, 1972), 165–207; and Jack A. Goldstone, *Revolutions and Rebellions in the Early Modern World* (Berkeley: University of California Press, 1991).

[8] Andre Gunder Frank explores this connection in *ReORIENT: Global Economy in the Asian Age* (Berkeley: University of California Press, 1998), although he admits to a lack of data.
[9] William H. McNeill, "The Ottoman Empire in World History," in *The Ottoman State and Its Place in World History*, edited by Kemal H. Karpat (Leiden: Brill, 1974), 44.
[10] James D. Tracy, "Studies in Eighteenth Century Mughal and Ottoman Trade," *Journal of the Economic and Social History of the Orient*, 37 (1994), 197–201.

their position to the imperial government but rather to their connections to their trading partners both locally and elsewhere in the world. As a result, they often resented attempts by distant emperors to tax them, and instead invested in local government and long-distance trade. Their role in unraveling empire in this period can be seen most dramatically in the demise of the Mughal Empire. While Mughal emperors continued to concentrate their attention on satisfying the needs of their land-owning mansabdars, they missed the threat growing in their port cities of South Asia, where wealthy merchants were creating alliances with regional opponents like the Marathas as well as extra-continental challengers like the EIC.

Aside from Russia, the rulers of the great Asian empires were unable to build extensive alliances with the rising wealthy transnational merchant classes partly because they were preoccupied by their overwhelmingly important sectoral alliances with agricultural producers. In Qing China, for example, the government's economic objectives were first and foremost to encourage greater agricultural production so as to meet the needs of the growing population. As a result, Qing economic policy was structured to support family farms and to intensify land use rather than to support the needs of merchants, especially in terms of keeping laborers on land rather than making them available as factory workers.[11] While logical, given the difficulty of feeding China's massive population, these policies also meant that the Qing also missed out on a great deal of tax revenues that were desperately needed for imperial projects.

In the Ottoman Empire, by contrast, the economic shift was marked by the replacement of the sipâhîs as local power-brokers in the imperial provinces by a multi-faceted group known as the "notables," or **ayans**. This group included local pro-Ottoman elites, merchants from among colonial subject populations, and Ottoman officials who put down roots locally. In many cases, the power of these ayans was stimulated by their growing economic wealth as merchants involved in regional or inter-continental commerce. While the ayans were often not outwardly rebellious, they were also only selectively loyal to the Sultans. When they were unhappy, they sometimes held funds back from the central state and instead supported movements for local autonomy. In the eighteenth century, this process weakened Ottoman rule in the Balkans and Lebanon.[12] By the nineteenth century, ayans even sometimes were able to control parts of the empire with relative impunity, as occurred with important pastoral families in the steppeland provinces and with ayans in Lebanon and Kurdish regions. Yet few ayans were openly rebellious, and most preferred to try to shape the state to their own needs. Some of the most powerful and autonomous, for example, were also active promoters of economic and political reforms in the central government. Their biggest opponents in this were the permanent janissary soldier-class, who in the seventeenth and eighteenth centuries became defenders of the older order on which their own power rested.[13] The janissaries especially opposed the creation of the type of professional bureaucracy necessary to the successful running of a modern empire because such a class would threaten their own hold on power. The struggle between ayan reformers and janissary conservatives, in the end, was more damaging to the empire than the actions of either class alone.

Russia is unique among the four great Asian empires in that economic elites did not successfully build local challenges to imperial authority in this period. In part this may be a result of the fact that their economic needs were largely being met by the ongoing expansion eastward in this period. Like the British crown, the Romanovs were able during this period to harness the commercial aspiration of merchants to the expansion

---

[11] See Madeleine Zelin, "The Structure of the Chinese Economy during the Qing Period: Some Thoughts on the 150th Anniversary of the Opium War," in *Perspectives on Modern China*, edited by Kenneth Lieberthal et al. (New York: M.E. Sharpe, 1991), 31–67.

[12] Kemal H. Karpat, "The Stages of Ottoman History: A Structural Comparative Approach," in Karpat, *The Ottoman State*, 92–93; and Donald Quataert, *The Ottoman Empire, 1700–1922* (Cambridge: Cambridge University Press, 2000), 46–48.

[13] Andrew C. Hess, "Comment," in Karpat, *The Ottoman State*, 92–93; and Quataert, *The Ottoman Empire*, 49–50.

of the empire, and vice versa. The Romanovs' conceptualization of sectoral alliance was generally to cluster the army, merchants, and religious authorities under the autocratic hand of the czar. In this they largely succeeded, partly because they continued to meet the aspirations of these groups in newly conquered territories, and partly because any insubordination was crushed with overwhelming force. Within this system, the Romanovs were able to control merchants by granting or withholding licenses to trade for furs and other valuable goods in the imperial periphery, and through the institution of the *gosti*, state merchants who depended on the Tsars as patrons.

Outside of Russia, the rise of commercial elites was a potentially dangerous trend for the large land-based empires of Asia. For example, historian of India Christopher Bayly argues that the failure of the Mughal state can be attributed to the fact that "wealthy and prideful men found less and less reason to support the myth of empire to the disadvantage of their own real local interests."[14] The emerging global mercantile class often found little in common with the rulers of the large, agrarian land empires in which they lived. Especially problematic were merchants who were also colonial subjects. These individuals were doubly alienated from the metropolitan government by their class and their ethnicity or religion. With their money and connections, they could and did become the focus of anti-imperial rebellions, especially in times of drought, falling standards of living, or other crises.

Each empire faced slightly different problems in working with subject populations. The expanding Russian empire, for example, had to deal with the integration of huge numbers of non-Russians: Cossacks, Poles, Siberian peoples, Kazakhs, Finns, Estonians, Georgians, Armenians, Uzbeks, and Lithuanians. By 1795, only about 53% of the empire's population was Russian, and by 1834 that proportion was down to less than half. To varying degrees, these groups enjoyed a sense of a national identity prior to conquest that they strove

to maintain, and that sometimes formed the core ideologies of rebellions. For example, in 1794 and again in 1830, a large proportion of the ethnic Polish population joined in revolts that had nationalist overtones. By the mid-nineteenth century, nationalist movements in Poland, Finland, Estonia, Georgia, and Armenia threatened the state.[15] In addition to such national affiliations, religion was an important rallying cry for anti-imperial resistance. The Russian Tsars were eastern Orthodox rulers over a vastly multi-denominational empire. By 1850, they had acquired large populations of Catholics and Jews in the west, animists such as the Bashkirs to the south, and Muslims in the south and east. In some instances, religion was a rallying cry for unity in resisting Russian rule, as with the Muslim uprisings among the Kazakhs in the 1790s and in the Caucasus in the 1820s.[16] But the need for national or religious affiliation to bind rebels together should not be overstated. Often, anti-Russian or anti-Romanov insurrections were alliances of opportunity among impoverished peasants and herders, as with Pugachev's Rebellion of 1773–1774, which tied together Russian peasants with Cossacks, Bashkirs, and Kazakhs.[17]

The Manchu rulers of the Qing Dynasty also faced the difficulty of tying multiple ethnic groups together. Perhaps the most difficult relationship was with the ethnic Han Chinese population. While the new emperors were careful not to mistreat the Chinese bureaucrats and peasant farmers upon whom they relied, a number of cultural flashpoints did appear. One of these was the treatment of women. Like many imperial conquerors, the Manchu believed that they had acquired authority over Chinese women as the spoils of victory. Thus during the conquest, a number of rapes and abductions occurred. When women and their husbands or fathers began to demand compensation or child support as had

---

[14] Christopher Bayly, *Imperial Meridian: The British Empire and the World, 1780–1830* (London: Longman, 1989), 34.

[15] Andreas Kappeler, *The Russian Empire*, translated by Alfred Clayton (Harlow: Longman Press, 2001), 216–220.

[16] Robert D. Crews, *For Prophet and Tsar: Islam and Empire in Russia and Central Asia* (Cambridge: Harvard University Press, 2006), 4.

[17] Michael Khodarkovsky, *Russia's Steppe Frontier: The Making of a Colonial Empire, 1500–1800* (Bloomington: Indiana University Press, 2002), 172–174.

been available under the Ming emperors, the Manchu rulers passed edicts forbidding them from doing so. The result was a certain amount of outrage in some circles. At the same time, however, the Manchu adopted a veneer of particularly conservative Confucian attitudes in order to appear as "Chinese" as possible. Their interpretation of these values led them to further reduce the rights of women, although in this case there was no outraged response.

Anti-Qing rebels in the southern provinces as early as the 1640s tried to portray themselves as the defenders of the Chinese against foreign rulers, although in fact this strategy was not very successful in the early decades of the dynasty. Because the Qing emperors were careful to portray themselves as defenders of Confucianist values and not to maltreat important local classes, "Chinese" resistance to Manchu rule built very slowly and would only mature at the beginning of the twentieth century in the Boxer Rebellion. In part, the choice of peasants not to actively support anti-Qing movements in the seventeenth and eighteenth centuries was the happy outcome of the emperors' continued support for and protection of peasant agricultural producers. Only in the nineteenth century did decreasing standards of living led to the emergence of new resistance ideologies. The two most dramatic were the Taiping Rebellion of 1850–1864, which was based on a charismatic mix of Christian and Confucian ideals, and the Dungan Revolt of 1862–1877 that was built around Muslim, pastoral identities.[18]

In the Ottoman Empire, perhaps the most serious challenge by colonial subjects is also among the least well known: the emergence of the ultra-conservative Wahhabi sect in late eighteenth-century Arabia by Muhammad 'Abd al-Wahhab.[19] The Wahhabi were merely one of many "cleansing" movements to emerge out of Arabia over the centuries aimed at returning to a purer Islam that rejected the embellishments of emperors like the Ottomans. However, it gained strength as the Ottomans were defeated by Christian powers in a series of conflicts, and especially with France's invasion of Egypt in 1798. 'Abd al-Wahhab argued that the Ottomans had lost the favor of God. By 1802, Wahhab's followers had occupied Mecca, and only major campaigns in the second decade of the nineteenth century restored a veneer of Ottoman rule over much of Arabia.

Meanwhile, in the north and west of the empire, nationalist movements among Christian subjects in the nineteenth century were significant, not least because their leaders could appeal to western European powers and to Russia for support.[20] This threat deepened with the Treaty of Küçük Kayanarca, forced on the Ottomans by Russia in 1774. The treaty gave Russia the right to build an Orthodox Church in Istanbul and accepted the Tsars as "protectors" of the Orthodox community. Similar concessions to Britain and France soon followed, the former assuming protection over Catholic and Nestorian Christians, the latter over Jews and Protestants in the empire. These groups constituted a large proportion of the mercantile class of the empire, and their subsequent revolts, although couched in the language of nation and religion, often were partly in pursuit of pragmatic economic goals. However, it must be remembered that many non-Muslims remained either habitually or opportunistically loyal to the state, which offered them many advantages. In fact, non-Muslim women often chose to prosecute their husbands in cases of divorce or to claim their inheritance rights in the Ottoman Muslim courts using Sharî'a laws, which guaranteed them more property and parental rights than those of their own communities.[21] Similarly, some of the Sultans' most steadfast financiers were Christians and Jews.

Opposition to Mughal rule in South and Central Asia also often represented the conjunction

---

[18] For more on the cosmology and ideology constructed by the leaders of the Taiping Rebellion, see Jonathan D. Spence, *God's Chinese Son* (New York: Norton, 1996).

[19] Quataert, *The Ottoman Empire*, 50–57; and Caroline Finkel, *Osman's Dream: The Story of the Ottoman Empire 1300–1923* (London: John Murray, 2006), 411–413.

[20] Philip Curtin, *The World and the West* (New York: Cambridge University Press, 2002), 180–181.

[21] Pamela McVay, *Envisioning Women in World History: 1500–Present*, vol. II (New York: McGraw-Hill, 2009), 59.

of the economic aspirations of merchants and political elites with the dissatisfaction of the mass of colonial subjects in a region. The ideologies through which their resistance to imperial rule was expressed were often religious. Thus, for example, a series of late eighteenth-century rebellions in the Punjab took on a flavor of Sikh nationalism, while those in the Deccan and especially among the Marathas sometimes appeared as Hindu religious movements. This has sometimes led to interpretations of the decline of the Mughal Empire that focus on the supposed religious intolerance of the late Mughal rulers. Admittedly, religious sentiment did play a role in an era in which some Mughal rulers, like Aurangzeb, intermittently persecuted non-Muslims. Nevertheless, to understand these revolts as religious movements is to seriously underestimate the significance of the political and economic aspirations of their leaders, especially those who were closely tied into the global economy.[22]

In fact, the Mughals faced a more debilitating internal challenge during this period: internal unrest among the mansabdari class similar to that faced by the Ottomans with their sipâhîs. As with the Ottomans, the empire had been built through the exertions of these militarized, land-owning elite. So long as new lands became available through expansion, these classes could be rewarded for their services in exchange for loyalty. As the empire began to shrink, however, it became more difficult for emperors to reward these classes with new lands and honors. We have already seen, earlier, how this contributed to the decline of the sipâhîs in favor of the ayan class under the seventeenth-century Ottoman emperors. The problem was even more pressing for their contemporaries, the Mughal emperor Aurangzeb and his successors. In his constant wars of expansion in the Deccan, Aurangzeb created alliances with large numbers of local warlords and other elites by appointing them as mansabdars. These new nobles then demanded land for themselves. But because Aurangzeb was unable to win significant territories, he was unable to reward them properly. As a result, the size of the average landholding of mansabdars under Aurangzeb declined year after year, and therefore so did their average income. As this process continued under his successors Bahadur I (1707–1712) and Farrukhsiyar (1713–1719), the relationship between the Mughal emperors and the sector on which they most relied to maintain the empire became poisoned.[23]

Even while dealing with internal issues brought about partly by a changing global economy, the Asian empires also had to protect their borders from rivals. The most threatening of these were not (in most cases) western European maritime empires, but rather other Asian powers. Central Asia during the seventeenth, eighteenth, and nineteenth centuries was the site of rivalry and intermittent warfare along enormous and shifting boundary lines. The two fiercest competitors in the late seventeenth and early eighteenth centuries were Russia and the Qing emperors, who repeatedly clashed in Siberia, Mongolia, and the Amur region. For a period between 1650 and about 1800, the Manchu held the upper hand, aided by Central Asian groups such as the Kalmyks who felt threatened by Russian imperialism.[24] In the early nineteenth century, however, Qing expansion was effectively brought to a halt and even reversed by Russian forces. This victory marked the Russian ascendance in Central Asia. To the west, the contest between the Tsars and the Ottoman Sultans had swung the way of Russia decades earlier. By 1774, Russia had acquired a great deal of the Ottoman's Central Asian territory and controlled a larger Muslim population than did the Sultans, although they were halted in

---

[22] For a clear synthesis of the origins of these revolts, see Barbara D. Metcalf and Thomas R. Metcalf, *A Concise History of India* (Cambridge: Cambridge University Press, 2002), 23–25, 29–33.

[23] An important article on this process is J.F. Richards, "The Imperial Crisis in the Deccan," *Journal of Asian Studies*, 35 (1976), 237–256.

[24] George V. Lantzeff and Richard A. Pierce, *Eastward to Empire: Exploration and Conquest on the Russian Open Frontier, to 1750* (Montreal: McGill-Queen's University Press, 1973), 182. See also Khodarkovsky, *Russia's Steppe Frontier*, 142.

the southern Caucasus. Only the Mughal empire was insulated from this competition of empires, although their own Central Asian territories were slowly eaten away in the eighteenth century by Afghani and Persian forces. The trend was even more dramatic in their South Asian territories, where western Europeans were able to make the most significant territorial inroads. While bits of India were snapped up by Portugal and France, it was the EIC that profited the most, acquiring so much territory that it slowly became more of a para-governmental organization than a trading company. As we will discuss in chapter 8, the EIC became a territorial government first in the Mughal provinces of Bengal, Bihar, and Orissa in 1765 by treaty with the Mughal emperor Shah Alam II, and they gradually assumed control of other provinces of the crumbling empire over the next hundred years. Elsewhere, western European inroads into the sovereignty of the Asian empires were more limited: as "protectors" of non-Muslim populations in the Ottoman Empire, or by unequal treaties forced at gunpoint upon the Qing that established Guangzhou and other ports as trading entrepots outside of imperial administration in the mid-nineteenth century.

IMPERIAL STRATEGIES AND COLONIAL MODES OF RULE

Between the seventeenth and nineteenth centuries, the Romanov, Qing, Ottoman, and Mughal rulers pursued a variety of strategies aimed at maintaining the stability of their empires, whether in territorial expansion or decline. As in previous eras, these strategies ranged from buying or inveigling the loyalty of colonial subjects to imposing brute force meant to quash their resistance or opposition. In some cases, imperial governments experimented with inducing colonial populations to assimilate or otherwise trying to bridge the gap between themselves and their diverse subjects. In other situations, conversely, they created special rules aimed at maintaining or increasing the distance between metropolitan citizens and the ruling class on the one hand and colonial subjects on the other. Often, a variety of strategies were

employed simultaneously. In this, the Asian empires were similar to the European empires of the same period. Arguably, however, a distinction can be made between them. In the four Asian empires, centralized control was generally more effectively established and responses to challenges more often emanated from central authorities. This meant that the responses were often more coordinated but less rapid than in the oceanic European empires, where distance and the more extensive power of men-on-the-spot meant that reactions to challenges were more often localized. Again, this distinction should not be carried too far, as in each case there were important exceptions.

Historians have proposed a variety of models through which to view the policies of the Asian empires during these two centuries. The most widely embraced has been to portray it as a period of struggle between reformers and conservatives. Usually, in this view, reformers are seen as those who most try to emulate the expanding European empires (especially Britain). Conservatives, on the other hand, are seen as resisting these changes. This dichotomy is not as useful for our purposes as a more complex view, in which we see emperors and their officials as putting forward a wide variety of strategies, some intensely innovative and other less so, to deal with the challenges of ruling vast land empires in an increasingly globalized age.

The Russian Empire's attempts to grapple with its multi-cultural and multi-denominational population are an interesting case in point. The Romanovs are perhaps best known as autocrats who centralized imperial authority and power in their own hands, and certainly they were not loathe to use forts and soldiers to impose their will on newly conquered territories. Nevertheless, their policies toward their colonial subjects were in fact frequently quite flexible and responded well to local conditions. Romanov "creeping colonialism" both in the Ukraine and Central Asia often began with treaties by which Russia extended "protection" to Cossack or other rulers against neighboring nomadic groups. The Russians also gave presents and otherwise sponsored the nobility of these groups. Inevitably, the rulers would balk at accepting some Russian demand, but by that time members of the nobility would have been well and truly bought, and willing to support Russia against their own leaders. Any continuing organized resistance could, if necessary, be quashed by military invasion or the expropriation of land or cattle. The rulers could then be deposed or left as powerless titular figures. This strategy could be adapted to almost any situation. In Poland, a huge proportion of the nobility were simply absorbed into the Russian *boyar*, or noble, class.[25] In Kazakhstan, the Kazakh Khans were replaced by a class of wealthy landowners sponsored by the Russians.[26] The Romanovs' flexibility could even encompass the virtual autonomy of Finland, which the Tsars correctly recognized was virtually impossible to rule effectively as foreigners without granting the nobility a degree of self-rule. These accommodations to local elites were much wider than in most later imperial systems.

Under Catherine II and her successors, the state also allied itself with a wide range of religious elites. All subjects were compelled to belong to religious or confessional groups, whether Muslim, Christian, or Jewish. The Russian government then patronized the clergy of these groups, building mosques, madrasas, seminaries, and churches and recognizing their religious and sometimes legal authority.[27] The degree to which this policy was implemented varied, however. Jews, for example, found their rights most restricted and experienced significant oppression, although this was partly a result of local rather than imperial laws.[28]

A third policy of the Romanov Tsars was to encourage migration and resettlement within the empire. The greatest of these movements, probably, was the settlement of Russian peasants from the increasingly densely populated metropole into the more sparsely populated lands of Siberia and Central Asia. Between 1550 and 1850, probably

6 to 7 million Russians and Ukrainians made this move.[29]

The responsiveness of the Romanovs to local conditions was balanced by a willingness to use force to cut off or put down rebellions. For example, some of the massive migration of the eighteenth and nineteenth centuries can be attributed to draconian policies aimed at dispersing potentially rebellious groups. Even more dramatic, perhaps, was the rapid response of Tsar Nicholas I (1825–1855) to nationalist movements in Poland, which he put down through immense violence and repression.[30]

Like the Romanovs, the Manchu administrators of the Qing Dynasty also had to deal with the problem of ruling an expanding multi-ethnic empire. Prior to the conquest of China, the Manchu emperors had mainly governed related pastoral groups such as the Mongol, Duar, and Oroqen. These pastoralists were rapidly assimilated into the Manchu political-military system of "banners," or clan-based regiments. After the invasion of China, the Manchu continued to assimilate new Central Asian populations in this way, governing culturally similar peoples through informal, negotiated alliances with the local hereditary authorities.[31] Korea was similarly allowed to remain largely autonomous following its 1637 conquest by the Manchu so long as it paid tribute to the Qing emperors and provided troops for campaigns in China. The entire empire was bound together by the adoption of Ming-style bureaucratic efficiency, with captured or recruited Chinese officials serving alongside the Manchu military elite.

Both the assimilation of Central Asian pastoralists and the tributary status of Korea were relatively successful policies for the Manchu, but neither could provide a model for the problem of

---

[25] Kappeler, *The Russian Empire*, 82.

[26] Khodarkovsky, *Russia's Steppe Frontier*, 149–183.

[27] Crews, *For Prophet and Tsar*, 8–9.

[28] Kappeler, *The Russian Empire*, 90–92.

[29] David Moon, "Peasant Migration and the Settlement of Russia's Frontiers, 1550–1897," *Historical Journal*, 40 (1997), 859–893.

[30] Kappeler, *The Russian Empire*, 216–218, 247–278.

[31] For a survey of research on the Qing Dynasty in Central Asia, see Eveyln S. Rawski, "Reenvisioning the Qing: The Significance of the Qing Period in Chinese History," *Journal of Asian Studies*, 55 (1996), 829–850. See also Peter C. Perdue, *China Marches West: The Qing Conquest of Central Eurasia* (Cambridge: Belknap Press, 2005).

how to rule the vastness of populous, urban China that faced the Qing following their 1644 victory at Shanhaiguan. Like other pastoral empire-builders who had found themselves dominating a larger agrarian and urban population, the Qing had to decide whether to adapt themselves to the culture of the far more populous Chinese or to remain alien rulers. Their solution was to maintain themselves as an alien ruling class. Soon after establishing their court in Beijing, the Qing monarchs enforced segregation between militarized garrisons of Manchu, Mongols, and other Central Asians on the one hand and the Han Chinese population on the other. They also expelled Chinese inhabitants from the area surrounding the Forbidden City—the imperial palace in Beijing—and replaced them with loyal Manchu banner troops. In the countryside of northern and central China, the Central Asian conquerors were established as a segregated ruling class when Prince Regent Dorgon (1643–1650) put important Manchu families in charge of vast estates.[32]

At the same time, however, the Qing conquerors recognized that they depended heavily on the cooperation of Chinese administrators, of whom the most important was the brilliant former Ming administrator Hong Chengchou. Having thrown his support behind the Qing, Chengchou helped to rebuild the civil service of China, and the larger empire. He also negotiated alliances between the Manchu and several autonomous Chinese generals in the south that helped to end resistance there. Nor was Chengchou alone in reaching an accommodation with the new rulers. The Qing victory over the last of the Ming forces in these provinces was also facilitated by alliances between the Manchu and non-Chinese chieftains in the southern frontier provinces of Yunnan, Guizhou, and Sichuan. As a result, the chieftains of these groups became important long-term partners in the Qing administration of South-West China.[33]

However, the Qing emperors rightly perceived that the greatest threat to their rule of China was not resistance by the remnants of the Ming nobility, but rather the potential for rebellion by China's hundreds of millions of peasants. The growing population of China under Qing rule stretched food production to its very limits, and drought, high taxes, or other disruptions could bring on crises quite rapidly. Therefore, the foundational policies of the Qing rulers were to support agricultural producers. On the one hand, the Qing strove to protect peasants against taxes by local landlords, usurious loans, and other impediments to their productivity. On the other hand, they carefully held back from intervening in production itself, thus giving the farmers relatively free reign to profit from their own hard work. By contrast, however, the Qing intervened heavily in international trade, and as a result discouraged the development of a large, powerful merchant class.[34] Both of these policies would have major repercussions for China in the nineteenth century, but until 1800 at least the Qing emperors managed to successfully stimulate food production so as to feed their growing population and maintain a reasonably high standard of living.

The Mughal emperors also relied heavily on their control over food-producers for both income and stability. Yet their ability to effectively manage and profit from peasant production was limited by the needs of their principal imperial agents, the mansabdars. During the early period of Mughal expansion, the Tīmūrid Dynasty had successfully bought the loyalty of local elites by co-opting them into this militarized, land-owning "noble" class. In his attempted conquest of the Deccan in the seventeenth century, Emperor Aurangzeb continued and expanded this strategy. His wars, however, were fought at the very limits of the empire and largely bankrupted the state. After a series of setbacks, Aurangzeb attempted to buy the loyalty of some of his opponents by

---

[32] See, for example, Rawski, "Reenvisioning the Qing," 832; and F.W. Mote, *Imperial China 900–1800* (Cambridge: Harvard University Press, 1999), 829–858.

[33] John E. Herman, "Empire in the Southwest: Early Qing Reforms to the Native Chieftain System," *Journal of Asian Studies*, 56 (1997), 47–74.

[34] A very useful comparative study of Chinese and British economic policy in this period is Peer Vries, *Via Peking Back to Manchester: Britain, the Industrial Revolution, and China* (Leiden: CNWS, 2003).

offering them positions as mansabdars. Many accepted his offer, but nevertheless the Mughals failed to add much new territory to the empire. As a result, Aurangzeb was unable to find sufficient lands to offer to the new allies, and could only pay them off by taking some territory from existing members of the mansabdari class. A consequence of this policy was to effectively bankrupt many mansabdars, some of whom became openly rebellious. At the same time, Aurangzeb also alienated many Hindu and Sikh mansabdars by appearing to favor Muslims in civil services, by building controversial mosques, and by taxing Hindus more heavily than Muslims.[35] The result at the edges of empire was the rise of anti-Mughal coalitions such as the Marathas, whose leadership were often drawn from Hindu former mansabdars. Even in older parts of the empire, some regional governors and Hindu mansabdars asserted their autonomy as the prestige of the emperors crumbled.

To the west, the Ottoman emperors similarly faced the prospect of imperial disintegration, although they dealt with it somewhat more effectively. The Sultans' principal problems in the eighteenth and early nineteenth centuries lay in dealing with growing fissures in their society. These were reflected not only in the bickering between the reformist ayans and the conservative janissaries, but also in the rise of nationalist movements among ethnic and religious minorities. The challenge for the Ottoman emperors was to find a way to reassert their own legitimacy and authority over these groups in order not to go the way of the Mughal Tīmūrid Dynasty, and their policies reflect this effort. In the late eighteenth century, for example, the emperors passed a series of laws stipulating the dress of different ethnic and religious groups and classes within the empire in an attempt to re-establish their authority as the arbiters of rank and status in the empire.[36] Soon after, the energetic Sultan Selim III (1789–1807) instituted a series of reforms

aimed at sapping the power of the janissaries and stopping the empire's decline. Sometimes known as the *New Order*, Selim's efforts were primarily military but also included new laws governing economic and fiscal policy. Although Selim was assassinated in 1807 by janissaries, his successor Mahmud II (1808–1839) restarted the reforms.[37] Subsequently known as the *Tanzimat*, these policies were aimed at re-establishing the state as the patron of all Ottomans. Mahmud hoped to rebuild his subjects' loyalty to the throne partly by guaranteeing rights of citizenship to all inhabitants of the empire including Christians and Jews. The laws he passed also expanded the bureaucracy, reformed the military, and built new infrastructure in an attempt to re-impose the power of the state. Some of these reforms were successful, but others were resisted by various interest groups such as religious authorities, janissaries, ayans, and the nationalist leaders.[38] As a result, the Ottoman emperors of the nineteenth century were only partly successful in convincing their non-Turkish-speaking subjects to remain loyal to the Ottoman Empire and nation. Yet they held on to many of their provinces until fragmented by the events of the First World War, a story that is told in chapter 14 of this volume.

QUESTIONING IMPERIAL DECLINE

By 1850, the technological and industrial gap between the foremost industrialized empires of the world (especially Britain) and most of the great land empires of Asia had become quite marked. Whatever their economic and social conditions, as empires the Ottoman, Mughal, and Manchu states

---

[35] However, he continued to patronize some Hindu temples. Metcalf and Metcalf, *A Concise History of India*, 21–22.
[36] Quataert, *The Ottoman Empire*, 44.

[37] Mahmud was, in fact, the successor to Mustafa IV (1807–1808), who was briefly put on the throne by janissaries following the murder of Selim III, before being himself assassinated.
[38] For differing views, see Quataert, *The Ottoman Empire*, 62–65; Hourani, "The Ottoman Background of the Modern Middle East," the third Carreras Arab lecture of the University of Essex, November 25, 1969; Nawaf A. Salam, "The Emergence of Citizenship in Islamdom," *Arab Law Quarterly*, 12 (1997), 125–147; and Bernard Lewis, *What Went Wrong? The Clash Between Islam and Modernity in the Middle East* (New York: Harper, 2003), 82–116.

were in great peril if not outright decline by the mid-nineteenth century. Meanwhile, Britain was building the world's first industrialized overseas empire, soon to be emulated by other western European powers, the United States, and Japan.

Traditionally, historians have trumpeted this divergence as a clear example of the triumph of "western" culture and economies, describing Britain and other "western" nations as being vibrant, egalitarian, and innovative while seeing the large Asian empires as being stagnant, despotic, and conservative, with Russia somewhere in between.[39] In this changing world, their logic seems to suggest, it was almost inevitable that the Asian empires would collapse or at least become heavily dependent upon their ascending European competitors. A number of more recent analyses, while taking issue with the inevitability of the divergence, have also framed the histories of the Ottoman, Mughal, Manchu, and to a lesser degree Russian empires in terms of their abilities to respond to changing patterns of global commerce and increasing European productivity.

The global, economic story of this period is an important one to tell in the context of imperial change in this period, but it does not stand alone. Rather, global economic change is significant to us because of the way it impacted the relationships between imperial dynasties and the societies over which they ruled, both metropolitan citizens and subject populations. For the vast Asian empires of 1650–1850, changing global conditions were not simply a major threat in and of themselves, but rather because they helped to shift the internal dynamic between ruler and ruled. Rising population levels, the growth of inter-connected commercial elites worldwide, the invention and diffusion of nationalist or religious ideologies, the availability of technology, and the flow of cash and resources all affected the abilities of the Tīmūrids, Qing, Ottoman, and Romanov dynasties to rule their subjects. Perhaps most importantly, the differences in technology and power available to the metropole and its peripheries in each case were

much less marked during this period than those of the European overseas empires, especially in the Americas. Each dynasty reacted to these challenges through a variety of strategies, some of which were successful, others not. The result was not a single "Asiatic" trend but rather a great deal of diversity in the situation of the four Asian empires by about 1850.

The Tīmūrid rulers of the Mughal Empire adjusted least well in the eighteenth century. The critical years were probably 1719–1720, during which four emperors reigned for ridiculously short periods. But the empire had already been crumbling during the rule of Farrukhsiyar. Under his reign, regional governors largely ruled their provinces as autonomous domains, while external enemies such as Afghans, Marathas, and the EIC made huge inroads into Mughal territory. The Tīmūrids' main failing in this era was their inability to either satisfy the mansabdari class on which they relied or replace them with another power elite, such as merchant-notables. Frustrated by their falling incomes, the mansabdars failed to support the empire in critical moments. At the fringes of the empire, they even switched their allegiance to coalitions led by the rising merchant classes of South Asian cities such as the Marathas. This trend was merely exacerbated by the fights over succession that broke out in the early eighteenth century at the imperial center. Furrukhsiyar himself had to fight two financially ruinous succession wars before he could cement his claim. Upon his death after ruling for only six years, the flurry of short-lived emperors who succeeded him exercised decreasing authority over a shrinking empire. Their collapse was of enormous significance—where once the Mughal had plowed the taxes they collected back into the local economy, after about 1720 a great deal of that money poured out of the region. Much of it ended up in the coffers of British merchants and administrators who invested it in their own domestic development.[40]

[39] See, for example, David Landes, *The Wealth and Poverty of Nations* (New York: W.W. Norton, 1998).

[40] For useful histories of this transition, see Metcalf and Metcalf, *A Concise History of India*, 21–22; and C.A. Bayly, *The Raj: India and the British 1600–1947* (New York: Abbeville Press, 1994).

Comparisons between the Ottoman and Mughal empires are common for this period, and certainly some similarities existed. Like the Tīmūrids, the Ottoman Sultans faced the challenges of dealing with a declining land-owning militarized class on whom their power had previously largely relied—sipâhîs—as well as with an emerging commercial class, the ayans. They also had to deal with extensive outside interference in their affairs, especially in the eighteenth century, as Russian and western European powers sponsored potentially rebellious religious and ethnic communities. However, the governments of Sultans Selim III and Mahmud II were more effective than their Tīmūrid colleagues in reversing the fragmentation of their empire. Their principal strategies were to build a stronger imperial bureaucracy and army and to bind religious and ethnic minorities closer to the throne by promulgating policies of assimilation rather than segregation. These policies could potentially have transformed the far-flung empire into a nation-state with a single, dominant Ottoman identity. By 1850, they even seemed to some degree to have succeeded.[41] The state had reasserted its power over many previously semi-autonomous regions, military and diplomatic moves had halted both Russian inroads and the loss of rebellious European provinces, and infrastructure and commerce had improved. Beneath the surface, however, competing ideological formations still simmered. Balkan Christian nationalism, pushed by the commercial aspirations of Christian merchants and pulled by the sponsorship of outside powers, was especially divisive. Meanwhile, the conservatism of the janissary corps, always a threat to reformist Sultans, prevented the government from going far enough toward meeting their needs. Yet while these problems remained significant, the core of the empire was in many ways more robust in 1850 than it had been for two centuries. However, as we will see in future chapters the important exception to this was in the realm of finance, where European banks in the nineteenth century were beginning to make big inroads into the Ottoman public as well as private financial affairs.

While the Ottoman and Mughal emperors struggled from the mid-seventeenth century to halt territorial fragmentation and retreat, Russia under the Romanovs spent much of this period expanding. This process, however, created its own set of problems. Rather than having to deal with disgruntled militarized classes with declining incomes, the Romanovs were primarily concerned with the difficulties of administering vast new and diverse subject populations. While willing to use force when necessary, the eighteenth- and early nineteenth-century Tsars largely found it more productive to work through "confessionals"—religious elites—as well as secular nobles and notables willing to act as allies. Under Catherine II, this strategy was remarkably successful, and accounts for the empire's abilities to rule a diverse set of subjects: from Polish agriculturalists to Central Asian pastoralists and even Siberian hunters. The migration of Russians and Ukrainians as settlers into the vast eastern territories also helped to stabilize the imperial periphery.

At the center, meanwhile, the Romanovs held on to power tightly, tying the Russian merchant class closely to themselves by jealously guarding the rights to the fur trade and watching carefully over the aspirations of the nobility. As a result, Russia in 1850 seemed a powerful and successful empire. In hindsight, there were certain cracks beneath the surface—the low standard of living for many peasants, simmering dissatisfaction among the nobility and officer class, and the growth of nationalist consciousness in Georgia, Armenia, Poland, and Finland.[42] In general, however, the Romanovs seemed at the time to have the resources and ability to deal with these problems and to quash rebellions if they emerged through their strong imperial army and dominant state bureaucracy.

Like imperial Russia, the empire of the Manchu spent much of the period 1650–1850 expanding first into China and then into the vastness of Central Asia. They were thus largely

[41] See Quataert, *The Ottoman Empire*, 63–67; and Hodgson, *The Venture of Islam*, 176–248.

[42] Kappeler, *The Russian Empire*, 216–280.

able to effectively reward their own version of the Tīmūrids mansabdars and the Ottoman sipâhîs: the Manchu and Mongol banner troops. This expansion ended around 1760 under the Qianlong Emperor, who, having split the nomadic populations of Central Asia with Russia, must have justifiably felt that he had eliminated the biggest external threat to his empire. Thus, as historian Peter C. Perdue points out, he hardly felt it necessary to treat diplomatically with the British envoy, Lord Macartney, whose entreaties to trade he rejected.[43] He was in fact telling the truth when he declared to Macartney that there were few things that his empire did not "possess … in prolific abundance." It was only by selling opium, largely grown in their new Indian provinces, that the EIC managed to break into the Chinese market in a significant way. As EIC opium flooded into southern China in the early nineteenth century, the Qing emperors began to realize the threat it represented not only to the productivity and safety of their population, but also to the economic well-being of the state. Their attempts to halt the sale of opium set up a conflict between Britain and the Manchu Empire that culminated in the Opium Wars fought in southern China during 1839–1842 and 1856–1862.[44]

The Opium Wars revealed several latent problems of Qing rule. First, the banner troops were still configured as cavalry armies—perfect for facing nomadic Central Asians but useless against the industrialized fleet and army of the British Empire. Local Chinese troops, meanwhile, had been neglected purposefully so as to keep them from potentially forming the core of a rebel force. Neither of these forces could stave off a humiliating series of defeats for the Qing in the First Opium War. The Daoguong Emperor (1820–1850) was forced to sign the Treaty of Nanjing, which threatened both the legitimacy and the authority of China's Manchu rulers.[45] Their treaty opened the taps to EIC opium

even wider, increasing the drain of cash from China and contributing to the impoverishment of the rapidly increasing peasant population. This economic reversal finally cancelled out the Qing emperors' policies of protecting the livelihoods of agriculturalists. The resulting rural poverty was partly responsible for the Taiping rebellion, which broke out in central China in 1850. By 1860 the Chinese provinces of the empire were in disarray, and in many regions local warlords and foreigners diverted taxes from the central government and ruled with impunity.

It is possible to explain these results for all four empires in a variety of ways, and certainly one—the Mughal Empire—is in terms of imperial success and failure. Each regime walked a tightrope between alienating their colonial subjects and assimilating them fully. In doing so, they had to balance the needs of powerful commercial, religious, and especially militarized land-owning elites in the metropole and in the colony. Their strategies, moreover, had to constantly change to respond to shifting conditions within the empire and globally. The most effective policies were also often the most costly. In collecting taxes to pay for them, however, the emperors had to balance the needs of the state with the livelihoods of landowners, peasant-producers, or merchants. Too many taxes could easily cause their subjects to find common cause in national, ethnic, or religious affiliation. Any such crack was especially fatal in this period, as empires and chartered companies emanating from Europe were looking for ways to break into Asian markets without the restrictions placed on them by imperial governments. By 1850, the success of Asian empires in walking this tightrope varied. The Tīmūrids had utterly failed, and the authority of the Qing was receding in China, but the Romanovs and Ottomans had both devised solutions that worked in the short term, at least. In the wake of the Industrial Revolution that began in Britain in the late eighteenth century, the remaining Asian empires would be increasingly challenged—along with much of the rest of the world—by European states whose wealth, reach, and will to expand were approaching new horizons.

[43] Perdue, *China Marches West*, 550–551.
[44] For a socio-political narrative of opium and state policy in this period, see Timothy Brook and Bob Tadashi Wakabayashi, eds., *Opium Regimes: China, Britain, and Japan, 1839–1952* (Berkeley: University of California Press, 2000).
[45] Vries, *Via Peking Back to Manchester*, 32.

Questions

1. Describe the challenges faced by the Tīmūrid (Mughal), Manchu (Chinese and Central Asian), Russian, and Ottoman empires in the period 1650–1850. To what degree were these challenges unique to the period, and to what degree are they reflective of the types of challenges earlier empires faced as discussed in chapters 1–5?

2. Compare and contrast the strategies the empires discussed in this chapter employed to overcome the challenges that faced them in this period. To what degree did each succeed, and how do you explain this variance?

3. To what degree is it correct to suggest that the empires discussed in this chapter functioned fundamentally differently from European-based overseas empires in the same period? To what degree is this dichotomy a false one? Use evidence from this chapter and chapters 3–5 to defend your answer.

CHAPTER 7

Empire: Revolutions in the Atlantic World

Between 1763 and 1825, France, Britain, and Spain lost huge portions of their American empires. In some cases, these losses were the result of territorial concessions to one another in the aftermath of war. In other cases, they occurred as a result of revolutions initiated by colonial subjects themselves: first in British North America, then in French St. Domingue, and finally in Spanish and Portuguese America. The end result was that, by 1825, territorial divisions in the Americas had been radically reconfigured. By then, the Americas were no longer predominantly colonial lands controlled by overseas powers. Instead, most American territory (with the important exceptions of British Canada and many Caribbean Islands) was organized into a series of independent states, free from allegiance to any imperial metropole. Indeed, some of the new American states were on their way to becoming imperial metropoles themselves.

How are we to interpret these dramatic territorial and political reconfigurations that occurred in the Americas in the late eighteenth and early nineteenth centuries? Was it, as has been suggested by some scholars, the beginning of an imperial "interlude" in which the power of empires in the Atlantic zone retreated for a time, and if so why? A variety of explanations have been advanced, but we will set out to establish in this chapter that these transformations were unequivocally the result of both *imperial* challenges and *colonial* tensions. In the first place, the sundering of political ties between European metropoles and their American possessions was clearly the result of conflict between imperial metropoles and colonial subjects, as in all cases the rebels sought to re-order imperial relationships. Thus, it is possible to look at the rebellions in St. Domingue, British North America, and Spanish America as anti-colonial wars of liberation. To some degree, we will make that argument in this chapter by connecting it to chapter 5, in which we discussed the formation of new identities in the American colonies.

However, the emphasis in this chapter is on our second contention: that imperial competition was the critical context for the monumental shifts that occurred in the Americas in ways that both prefigured and continued to play a role in affairs throughout the revolutionary period. We begin by arguing that the wars of empire fought between the British, French, and Spanish in this period—particularly the Seven Years' War—were critical for creating the conditions for later revolutions in the Americas. Further, we argue that continuing wars—especially the French Revolutionary and

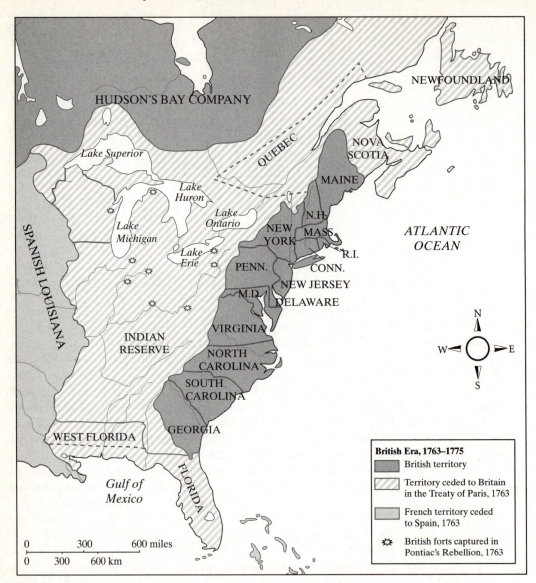

British Era, 1763–1775

☐ British territory

▨ Territory ceded to Britain in the Treaty of Paris, 1763

▨ French territory ceded to Spain, 1763

✺ British forts captured in Pontiac's Rebellion, 1763

Territorial Exchanges in the Americas Resulting from the Seven Years' War, 1756–1763

Napoleonic wars, which themselves had blatantly imperial dimensions—helped determine the timing and success of revolutions in the Americas, and contributed in important ways to the strength or weakness of all the newly independent states. Thus, we argue that the period of the "Atlantic Revolutions" should be understood not just as a series of conflicts *within* the European empires of the Americas, but also as a result of violent and costly imperial competition *between* the European powers themselves. In the end, the European powers extended themselves so far for the sake of imperial competition that they inadvertently provided the opportunity for their own colonial subjects to throw off their rule altogether.

By emphasizing the importance of war, we do not mean to deny the roles played by ideology and identity in the revolutionary struggles that rocked the Americas. As we saw in chapter 5, colonial societies in the Americas had developed distinct identities as a result of the circumstances of empire. Although most colonial subjects of European ancestry did not initially desire political independence in the mid-eighteenth century, the circumstances of their relationships both with the metropole and with their new homelands nevertheless encouraged colonial subjects to perceive themselves differently from their European counterparts. At the same time, colonists in the Americas—especially in British America—were influenced by the same Enlightenment ideals of liberty, equality, and rationality that were simultaneously circulating through much of Europe during the eighteenth century. These ideals, in turn, frequently provided the rationale that justified calls for imperial reform in this period. Yet we argue that, even more than ideology, it was war and its consequences that exacerbated colonial discontent to the point of rebellion. Additionally, we argue that war played a crucial role in determining the timing—as well as the success—of the revolutionary movements that literally redrew the map of the Americas.

This chapter begins with the Seven Years' War, for it was this imperial war that both encouraged discontent in British North America to boil over into open rebellion and determined the French response to the American Revolution a few years

later. We then move to the American Revolution itself, for this conflict led to the first imperial rupture in the Americas. Its success, in turn, triggered responses in France, St. Domingue, and Spanish America. From there we explore the French Revolutionary Wars brought on by the heady fervor of revolutionary ideals. Our focus, however, is not on the effects of the French wars in Europe, but rather on the Caribbean sugar-growing island of St. Domingue. There, a massive slave rebellion—prompted both by revolutionary ideals and opportunities provided by international war—turned into a struggle for independence that would span more than a decade. Following the French Revolutionary Wars, we turn to the Napoleonic Wars that followed closely on their heels, for it was these wars that created the conditions for the Spanish American colonies to finally declare their independence from Spain. In order to put together a complete picture of the Atlantic as the environment for these events, we also briefly look the way in which events in European-occupied South Africa in the same period had similar overtones to those across the Atlantic. Finally, we bring this information together to assess the legacies of three centuries of imperial competition between the European powers in the Americas, and the effects of such competition on the maintenance of a stable imperial system.

As a side note, it is intriguing—and perhaps important—that this political reconfiguration in the Atlantic world happened over approximately the same period as the Qing, Ottoman, and Mughal empires experienced some serious difficulties in managing some of their own colonial possessions (chapter 6). Is there some kind of connection? The timing is not exact, and the situations all appear to have been different. Nevertheless, this is a question that it may be worth scholars' asking in the future.

THE SEVEN YEARS' WAR AND ITS CONSEQUENCES

On December 11, 1753, a 21-year-old Virginian colonist named George Washington rode into the French Fort LeBoeuf in the Ohio country. Washington had been sent by the lieutenant governor of Virginia to carry a letter to the fort's commander, Captain Jacques Legardeur. The letter expressed concern over recent French activity in the Ohio Valley—particularly over the construction of a series of forts on the Ohio River. It asserted that the lands on the river were "known to be the property of the Crown of Great Britain," and informed the French commander that he was required to depart from the region forthwith. The French reply, which Washington carried back with him to Virginia, was terse. Legardeur observed that he was there on the orders of his superiors, and furthermore that his own king's title to the land was "incontestable." He would stay right where he was.[1]

Anglo-French tensions over rights to the Ohio Valley had been brewing for decades before Washington set out on his mission. The French, who already claimed territories to the north in Canada and to the south in the Mississippi Valley, wished to create a network of fortified trading posts to connect their North American territories. They also—with the active help and approval of the Iroquois Indians who populated the area—sought to prevent British colonists from expanding their claims westward and from interrupting communications between French North American possessions. Moreover, since no one yet knew if a Northwest Passage to the Pacific Ocean actually existed, the French wanted to make sure the British did not find it before they did.[2] The British colonists, for their part, did not want to be hindered in their search for good land by either French or Indian claims, and continually came into conflict with both groups over boundary disputes. Back in London, the British government was concerned mainly to prevent its old enemy from gaining the upper hand in North America.

In May 1756, these tensions boiled over into open conflict when the British government formally declared war on France. The Seven Years' War (1756–1763), which was fought simultaneously in North America, Europe, and India, was one of the most important wars of empire in the modern period.[3] The reasons why this can be considered an example of an imperial war are many. First, the conflagration itself started in the Americas, and was fought on both sides with a conscious strategy of defending imperial territories. Second, the eventual British victory over the French destroyed French imperial claims in North America and left Britain the undisputed power in the northern portion of North America. Third, reform measures meant to rationalize and consolidate imperial rule by both the British and Spanish governments after the war exacerbated tensions between both metropoles and their colonies. In the British case, these measures led to revolution and the loss of 13 of its American colonies. Finally, the success of the British in the Seven Years' War encouraged both the French and the Spanish to lend their support to the American rebels in the 1780s, whose eventual victory would have been nearly impossible without such powerful allies.

Initially, the war went badly wrong for the British. Between 1755 (before the formal declaration of war) and 1757, the French inflicted a series of humiliating defeats on British forces. But when William Pitt became prime minister of Britain in 1757, he resolved to turn the war around. His strategy revolved around focusing British war efforts on North America, even though there were active theaters in Europe and India at the same time. To do this, he gave the British navy the resources to establish British naval supremacy in the Atlantic, which allowed British ships to disrupt enemy trade, to harass enemy territory, and to provide reinforcements for its land campaigns. He also committed, by the end of the war, upwards of 30,000 British regular soldiers—in 32 regiments—to the North American campaign.[4]

The payoff was spectacular. In 1759, British forces conquered Quebec, and then in 1760—

---

[1] Fred Anderson, *Crucible of War: The Seven Years' War and the Fate of Empire in British North America, 1754–1766* (New York: Alfred A. Knopf, 2000), 44–45. Anderson provides a detailed and analytic exploration of the entire war from start to finish.

[2] J.H. Elliott, *Empires of the Atlantic World: Britain and Spain in America, 1492–1830* (New Haven, CT: Yale University Press, 2006), 292.

[3] Matt Schumann provides a transatlantic view of the importance of the war in *The Seven Years War: A Transatlantic History* (London: Routledge, 2008).

[4] Anderson, *Crucible of War*, chapter 21; and Elliott, *Empires of the Atlantic World*, 294, 298.

with the fall of Montreal—they completed the conquest of Canada. British forces also captured the French West Indian sugar islands of Martinique and Guadalupe. Meanwhile, the Spanish government regarded British successes against the French with increasing alarm. Fearing that they were next to be pushed out of North America, in 1761 the Spanish government (whose monarch, since 1700, had been a member of the same Bourbon ruling family as the French monarch) allied itself with France.[5] The next year the British government declared war on Spain, and British troops promptly invaded and conquered the Spanish ports of Havana (Cuba) and Manila (the Philippines). By 1763, continued British successes prompted both France and Spain to sue for peace.

The resulting Treaty of Paris (1763) revealed a stunning British victory. While the British returned the French sugar islands of Martinique and Guadalupe, they kept Canada—thus removing the French entirely from the Ohio Valley. Britain also added to its North American territories by taking Florida from Spain in exchange for the return of Havana and Manila. As a concession for losing Florida, the French ceded the vast Louisiana territory to Spain. The result was the total destruction of French power in continental North America. Britain emerged ascendant, and now faced only Spain as an imperial rival in the Americas.[6] Elsewhere, they also strengthened their positions in India, a storyline that we will pick up on other chapters.

Yet the British had only achieved victory at huge cost to themselves. The war had placed an enormous financial burden on both the government and British taxpayers. Indeed, during the war British taxpayers paid 26 shillings a head to help pay for the upkeep of British troops—a nearly intolerable strain for many.[7] And while British colonists in North America paid far less in taxes for

the war (a mere 1 shilling), such a tax rate represented a steep increase over previous years. Moreover, colonists saw far more combat than their fellow taxpayers across the Atlantic. In New England, for example, almost all adult men saw combat at some time during the war. Meanwhile, in spite of increased taxes the British government had run up a massive war debt, which comprised almost half of the government's entire peacetime budget.[8]

Britain's post-war problems did not end there. In addition to the vast sums the government had spent on the war itself, it now faced the even greater financial burden of administering and defending its much increased territories, two of which—Quebec and Florida—had significant non-English, Roman Catholic populations. Moreover, now that the French were out of the way on British America's western frontier, there was no one to stand between British colonists and the Indians who populated the area.[9] As a result, the British government anticipated much-increased costs for defending expansion-minded colonists from attack as they moved into Indian territory. In fact, in 1765 the army estimates alone for defending North America were £400,000. Given that total tax revenues from the North American colonies were only £80,000 for the same year, it is small wonder that in the immediate post-war environment the British government determined to undertake a program of reform designed to boost revenues from its American colonies.[10]

Britain was not alone in its financial difficulties after the war. The Spanish government, too, had grown deeply concerned over the costs of imperial defense and the inefficiencies of its tax collection system in the Americas. Although Spain had not gained any new territories during the war—and in fact lost Florida to the British—the Spanish government worried about the possibility of future British aggression in the Americas.

---

[5] Since 1700, the ruling Spanish monarch was a member of the same ruling family—the Bourbons—as the French monarch, and this family relation sometimes encouraged Franco-Spanish cooperation.

[6] Anderson, *Crucible of War*, 505–506; and Elliott, *Empires of the Atlantic World*, 295.

[7] Elliott, *Empires of the Atlantic World*, 298.

[8] Douglas Egerton, Alison Games, Jane Landers, Kris Lane, and Donald Wright, *The Atlantic World: A History, 1400–1888* (Wheeling, IL: Harlan Davidson, 2007), 329, 335.

[9] Robert Middlekauff, *The Glorious Cause: The American Revolution, 1763–1789*, 2nd edition (Oxford: Oxford University Press, 2005), 58.

[10] Elliott, *Empires of the Atlantic World*, 306.

As a result, imperial defense took on a new importance. Yet armed defense was expensive, as the British well knew, and would require more efficient tax collection in the Americas if it were to be affordable. By the mid-eighteenth century, however, colonists in Spanish America had become experts in tax evasion and smuggling in order to circumvent the restrictive mercantilist trade policies of the Spanish metropole. In addition, Spanish-speaking creoles had gained considerable power in the institutions of colonial government such as the Audiencias, which meant that they were in a better position than ever to look after their own economic interests.[11] In real terms, both developments translated into sustained revenue loss for the Spanish crown. To reverse the situation, in the aftermath of the Seven Years' War the Spanish government embarked on a course of bold reforms designed to increase imperial revenues and, in the process, provide the necessary funds to safeguard the empire from British aggression.

Rather than apply reforms to all of Spanish America at once, however, the Spanish government decided to begin with the island of Cuba. Cuba was perfect as a laboratory for the new reforms both because of its small size and because established traditions and legacies had recently been disrupted as a result of British capture during the war.[12] There, the Spanish minister worked in conjunction with the elite of the island to iron out a compromise. In essence, the economic aspect of the solution they agreed to was a substantial increase in taxes—along with more efficient collection—in exchange for liberalizing some of the trade restrictions that barred Spanish colonists from trading directly with one another.[13] The reforms also included changes to the civil administration of the empire by the creation of intendancies, or provincial administrators who possessed sweeping powers over the territories under their control. These posts, staffed only by Spaniards, were meant to ensure

greater metropolitan control over colonial affairs. To emphasize this metropolitan control, the reforms also stipulated that posts in the Audiencias would henceforth be staffed overwhelmingly by men from peninsular Spain. Once reforms in Cuba were underway, Spanish ministers turned to other areas of the empire. In 1765, the reforms were applied to New Spain, and in the next few decades to the rest of Spanish America as well.

Although these Bourbon reforms—named for the Spanish dynasty under which they were instituted—were unpopular and at times stirred up violent rebellion, they did not prompt revolution. In part, this resulted from the consistency and coherence of the reforms themselves, and their systematic application to the whole empire over a period of several decades. In addition, the administration at the heart of the empire in Spain remained consistent throughout this period, and even where there was disagreement between ministers all nonetheless agreed on the need for serious, systemic reform if Spain were to maintain its empire.[14] Perhaps even more importantly, the Spanish crown had a long tradition of interference in, and involvement with, ruling its American colonies. Indeed, Spanish colonists had plentiful experience with colonial initiatives emanating from Spain. Thus, while colonists were certainly unhappy about the nature of some of the Bourbon reforms, the precedent of overseas interference in their affairs had deep roots. Even so, by the turn of the nineteenth century, the Bourbon reforms were a mixed success. On the one hand, they had increased both trade and revenue in many parts of the Spanish Empire at a critical time. On the other hand, they exacerbated social and political tensions that caused many creoles to look upon peninsular Spaniards—and the Spanish crown—with increased, and potentially explosive, resentment.[15]

In contrast to the mixed results of the Bourbon reforms, British reform efforts in North America proved disastrous. In the aftermath of the Seven Years' War, the British government, not

---

[11] Ibid., 302.
[12] James Lockhart and Stuart B. Schwartz, *Early Latin America: A History of Colonial Spanish America and Brazil* (Cambridge: Cambridge University Press, 1983), 352.
[13] Elliott, *Empires of the Atlantic World*, 304.

[14] Ibid., 306.
[15] Jay Kinsbruner, *Independence in Spanish America: Civil Wars, Revolutions, and Underdevelopment*, 2nd edition (Albuquerque: University of New Mexico Press, 2000), 22–23.

surprisingly, believed it was vital for North American colonists to shoulder more of the burden of their own administration. In order to accomplish these aims, British ministers felt it necessary both to limit future costs of defense as well as to increase efficiencies in tax collection to help pay for existing defense needs.[16] Yet the succession of British ministries that sought to rationalize costs and increase revenues had not reckoned with the resistance they would face from American colonists. In contrast to Spanish America, North American colonists had grown used to running their own affairs without continuous and direct interference from the crown. As we saw in chapter 3, interest in the British North American colonies had been somewhat late in coming, and the British government had largely been content with decentralized colonial rule up through the eighteenth century. Indeed, although each colony had a royal governor appointed by the king, colonial assemblies levied the taxes that paid those salaries and thus maintained considerable political leverage. Thus when the British government—by the eighteenth century dominated by parliament and the king's ministers—sought to assert greater control over the colonies, it came into direct conflict with colonists' own ideas about themselves, the world they had built in the Americas, and the nature of their relationship with Britain.[17]

Of immediate concern to the British was the curtailment of military expenditures in North America. Yet the removal of the French had left the British to face a variety of potentially hostile Indian tribes and confederations along the entire western frontier. Indeed, many Indian groups—particularly those in the Ohio Valley region—were unhappy with the British victory in the Seven Years' War, and were not inclined to accept British dominance. In the spring of 1763, the Ottawa chief Pontiac—who had allied himself with the French during the war—formed a coalition with the Delaware, Seneca, Huron, and Chippewa

Indians and rose up in revolt against the British. The conflict, known as Pontiac's Rebellion, was a bloody and expensive affair that took three years to put down. It also convinced British ministers that the western frontier would likely remain a source of constant conflict between settlers and Indians and that this, in turn, would entail a continuing drain on British finances.[18]

In an effort to placate Indian hostility, in late 1763 the British Secretary of State for the South (Lord Halifax) set out the boundaries of British North America, beyond which Britons could not settle. By the terms of Halifax's Proclamation Line, all lands to the west would be set aside as Indian territory, while all lands to the east would remain under British sovereignty. To ensure that both colonists and Indians conformed to the borders set out by the British government—and to reduce the likelihood that war would erupt from conflicting claims—the line was to be defended and patrolled by British regular soldiers, whose expenses would be paid by the colonists themselves. In creating the Proclamation Line, then, Halifax hoped he had reached a permanent, and relatively inexpensive, solution to the problem of conflict along the frontier.[19]

Rather than perceive this as a sensible gesture, however, British colonists in North America reacted to news of the Proclamation Line with outrage. They viewed Halifax's solution as unfairly curtailing their right to stake out new claims in territories to the west. Indeed, they perceived the proclamation as heavy-handed interference that furthermore would impose a substantial, permanent, and expensive standing army on colonial soil. Their response was outright defiance: by the mid-1770s, about 50,000 settlers had moved west of the Proclamation Line. In fact, so many defied the boundary that British regular soldiers largely gave up trying to stop them.[20]

British efforts to boost revenues by the more efficient collection of customs duties met with even greater resistance. In 1764, Lord of the

---

[16] Middlekauff, *The Glorious Cause*, 62.

[17] Stephen Conway, *War, State, and Society in Mid-Eighteenth Century Britain and Ireland* (Oxford: Oxford University Press, 2006), 246.

[18] Anderson, *Crucible of War*, 634.

[19] Elliott, *Empires of the Atlantic World*, 305.

[20] Lester D. Langley, *The Americas in the Age of Revolution, 1750–1850* (New Haven, CT: Yale University Press, 1996), 21.

Treasury and Chancellor of the Exchequer George Grenville instituted changes designed to enforce the collection of taxes on imports via the American Revenue (Sugar) Act. This act strengthened the presence of the British navy in American ports, and encouraged the vigorous collection of taxes on items such as molasses, sugar, coffee, and certain wines. Colonists were incensed. In part this was because colonial merchants had a long tradition of evading royal taxes through working deals with customs agents, and thus the new act had the potential of cutting into their bottom line. More fundamental, however, was the fact that Grenville had imposed these taxes via the British Parliament, in which the colonies had no representatives and no voice. To colonists, then, the act reeked of tyranny.

Events in 1765 further exacerbated these concerns. In that year Grenville ushered the passage of the Stamp Act through parliament, which imposed a tax on all legal documents, newspapers, playing cards, and pamphlets. Given the lively print culture and the tendency of colonists to confirm agreements with legal documents, the Stamp Act would have had an impact on the vast majority of colonists. The response, therefore, was furious. Rioting erupted in Boston, and 9 of the 13 colonies viewed the act as such a threat that, in October 1765, they gathered together in a Congress in order to discuss common grievances and avenues for redress. Despite the many differences that divided the peoples of the 13 North American colonies, representatives of the congress agreed that, as British citizens, they should not be subjected to taxation by a parliament in which they had no legal representation.[21] To reinforce the point, they coordinated a non-importation movement in which colonists would refuse to purchase British manufactured goods.

By then, the central disagreement between the colonists and the British Parliament was clear. Parliament believed it had sole sovereign authority over the North American colonies, which gave it the legal right to legislate, tax, and make policy for them. For parliament, this sovereignty made

colonial consent unnecessary. British colonists, on the other hand, insisted they could not be taxed, legislated, or governed without their own consent through some kind of parliamentary representation.[22] British colonists furthermore believed their demands reflected the right of all British citizens to demand accountability from authorities at all levels. In part, their position was based on the English Revolutionary Settlement of 1688–89, which had settled a civil war in England by dispensing with the tyranny of the later Stuart kings and guaranteeing Britons legal and political security with a Bill of Rights. In addition, many colonial leaders of this period had been schooled in Enlightenment ideals that viewed the function of government in terms of the protection of life, liberty, and property. When combined with a colonial past of relative autonomy along with British ideas of natural rights, these Enlightenment ideas provided colonists with a powerful language with which to reject any government action perceived as autocratic or tyrannical.[23]

Despite these fundamental disagreements over the nature of the imperial relationship, most colonists did not envision a permanent separation with Britain until as late as 1775. Until that time, many hoped their protests would spur parliamentary reforms designed to heal the deteriorating transatlantic relationship. Indeed, in spite of rising tensions colonial leaders continued to identify strongly with British cultural, social, and legal traditions, and many maintained connections with the imperial center through personal connections, consumption patterns, or by engaging in the lively transatlantic print culture.[24] Yet in the decade between 1765 and 1775, a succession of British ministries encouraged so much suspicion, ill will, and resistance with their inconsistent policies that they managed to unite the 13 colonies against the British government in spite of colonists' continuing belief in the noble heritage of British traditions.

Realizing that the Stamp Act was virtually impossible to enforce given the extent of colonial

---

[21] Elliott, *Empires of the Atlantic World*, 313, 315.

[22] Middlekauff, *The Glorious Cause*, 128–129.

[23] Elliott, *Empires of the Atlantic World*, 333.

[24] Linda Colley, *Britons: Forging the Nation, 1707–1837* (New Haven, CT: Yale University Press, 1992), 134.

resistance, parliament rescinded the duties only a year later in 1766. If that might have eased metropolitan–colonial tensions, they were raised once again with the immediate passage of the Declaratory Act, which essentially affirmed the sovereignty of parliament by insisting on the right "to bind the colonies in all cases whatsoever."[25] The very next year, Chancellor of the Exchequer Charles Townshend—who replaced Grenville after his dismissal in 1765—introduced a new bill that placed import duties on a variety of goods entering into American ports, including glass, paint, lead, and tea. Its primary purpose was similar to the purpose of the failed Stamp Act: to increase revenues from the colonies in order to defray their expense. Once again, however, colonists reacted with hostility to taxation imposed by parliament without the consent of colonial assemblies. The fundamental issue over the imperial relationship—and parliament's right to dictate that relationship—had not changed. For the next three years, until 1770, colonists resumed their nonimportation protests with ever greater cooperation and communication between the colonies. Faced with such resistance and a consequent inability to raise revenues from the new taxes, parliament repealed all of the duties except one: the remaining tax on tea would symbolize parliament's continuing right to levy taxes without colonial consent.

Despite the repeal of the Townshend Acts, tensions between parliament and the colonists continued to rise. There were a number of reasons for this, but only some of them had to do with economic and material concerns. Perhaps more importantly, through the years of boycotts and trade disagreements many colonists had come to identify themselves as a group apart from the metropolitan British, and vice versa. This may have influenced the ways in which colonists and British imperial representatives acted toward each other in moments of tension.[26] One such moment

occurred on March 5, 1770, when British regular soldiers in Boston fired on an unruly crowd and killed five civilians. Similarly, in December 1773 another group of Boston colonists ruined £10,000 worth of East India Company tea by throwing it overboard into Boston Harbor. In retaliation, the government of Lord North responded in 1774 with the Coercive (Intolerable) Acts that closed Boston Harbor to commercial activity and rescinded many of the powers of the Massachusetts colonial assembly.[27] By this time, however, colonists had grown used to sharing information and offering mutual support through correspondence societies and nonimportation networks. Thus, when the British government sought to punish the Massachusetts colony, other colonists—under the leadership of Virginians—regarded the punishment as a collective threat.

During the summer of 1774, delegates from all of the colonies met in the First Continental Congress to discuss strategies for redress, and to voice a unified expression of colonial rights and a determination to continue meeting. After the Congress, colonial assemblies increasingly took matters into their own hands, while royal governors—with no way of enforcing their supremacy—could only sit back and watch. By the time the second Congress met in May 1775, British and colonial troops had already skirmished in the Massachusetts towns of Lexington and Concord. By then, colonists were determined that separation from Britain was the only answer, and colony after colony declared independence. On the other side of the Atlantic, the British government acknowledged that its 13 American colonies were in a state of open rebellion. Realizing that the colonies needed a unified legal standing with which to declare themselves a republic, in the spring and summer of 1776 the Congress issued a formal Declaration of Independence.[28] By the terms of this document, which was signed by representatives of all 13 colonies, the North American colonies were "absolved from all allegiance to the British crown, and that all political connection

---

[25] Quoted in Middlekauff, *The Glorious Cause*, 144; and Elliott, *Empires of the Atlantic World*, 317.

[26] See, for example, T.H. Breen, " 'Baubles of Britain': The American and Consumer Revolutions of the Eighteenth Century," *Past and Present*, 119 (1988), 73–104.

[27] Langley, *The Americas in the Age of Revolution*, 31.

[28] Elliott, *Empires of the Atlantic World*, 348.

between them and the State of Great Britain, is and ought to be totally dissolved."[29]

More than any other single factor, the Seven Years' War had created the conditions under which revolution had become possible. Indeed, the enormous expense of the war prompted the British government to insist on more efficient—and more thorough—revenue collections as well as to restrict colonial settlement to the west. In the process, these efforts triggered a crisis in imperial relations by clearly highlighting divergent opinions about where sovereignty over colonial governance lay. For the British government, sovereignty clearly lay in parliament. From the perspective of the colonists, however, sovereignty could not lie in an institution in which their own assemblies had no representation. This issue, which had been latent before the war, became a focal point in colonial relations after its conclusion. In addition to underscoring colonial tensions about the nature of sovereignty, the Seven Years' War also eliminated one of the threats that had historically drawn Britons and colonists together: the French. With the French presence eliminated, the necessity of maintaining armed British soldiers on the frontier seemed, to the colonists, repressive rather than protective. Finally, the experience of fighting the war allowed colonists the opportunity to experience a greater sense of common cause with each other than ever before. When this reinvigorated sense of common cause was turned against the British after the war and justified with a language of natural rights, it became a powerful tool of separation.

THE WAR OF AMERICAN INDEPENDENCE AND ITS LEGACIES

By all accounts, the colonists who severed their ties with Britain ought to have lost the war that ensued. The British army, though not without its own problems, was a disciplined and well-trained force—especially when compared with the untrained and ill-equipped soldiers who initially enlisted in what became the Continental army. The British also had

the most powerful navy in the world in 1775, and with it they controlled the American coast. The colonists, on the other hand, had only merchant vessels and no formal navy. Moreover, the British government possessed the finances of an established state and experience in carrying out overseas wars, while the colonists had a brand-new Congress with little experience conducting governmental business of any kind. To make matters even more difficult for the colonists, tens of thousands of colonists remained openly or covertly loyal to the crown. Finally, in 1775 the fledgling state had no allies to whom they could turn for military aid.

And yet the American colonists did not lose the war. Contrary to initial expectations on both sides of the Atlantic, by September 3, 1783, Great Britain was forced to formally recognize the independence and sovereignty of the United States of America in the second Treaty of Paris. The British lost the war for a variety of reasons, some of which included poor—or at least unimaginative—leadership at the ministerial level, incompetency or complacency by the generals charged with carrying out the war, and divisions in parliament and the British public about the justice of the war itself.[30] Most important, however, was the fact that the colonists were eventually able to recruit powerful allies in France and Spain to aid them in their struggle—allies who had both the means and the motivation to tip the scales in favor of the colonists. In the end, then, it was their military assistance that allowed the Americans to emerge victorious in 1783. Thus, the Enlightenment ideals of liberty, equality, and the pursuit of happiness so loudly espoused by the Americans were able to reverberate around the Atlantic world only as a result of the test of imperial competition and war.

The first year of the war was a difficult one for the Americans. The fledgling Continental Congress had chosen the Virginian George Washington to lead the new nation's forces, and although he proved an able leader, his poorly equipped and hastily trained army suffered serious setbacks in 1776.[31] Between August and

---

[29] The Declaration of Independence, closing paragraph.

[30] Middlekauff, *The Glorious Cause*, 344–345.

[31] David McCullough tells this story in an accessible way in his *1776* (New York: Simon & Schuster, 2005).

October of that year, American forces were repeatedly defeated or forced to retreat in New York and New Jersey. Not until Washington crossed the Delaware River and captured Trenton, New Jersey, in December did his Continental army manage a clear victory over British forces.[32]

Congress knew its best hope lay in establishing powerful allies to aid its cause. The most likely target was the power who had recently lost the most to Britain and had the greatest desire for revenge: France. In fact, France had offered its unofficial support and encouragement to the Americans since 1775. French ministers understandably took pleasure from Britain's difficulty, and extended the hand of friendship to the enemy of their own long-standing enemy. But overt financial and military support was another matter altogether.[33] In 1776 and 1777, a swift British victory seemed entirely possible, and the French were loath to invest in a losing proposition after having suffered such massive losses in the Seven Years' War. Even the charming and well-liked Benjamin Franklin was initially unsuccessful at brokering an alliance with the French when Congress sent him to Paris for precisely that reason in December 1776. In order to convince the French to back the Americans with more than just friendship, the Continental army had to prove that it might be able to hold its own against the British.

This proof finally began to materialize in October 1777. On the 17th of that month, American forces captured the British army under General Burgoyne at Saratoga, New York, forcing his surrender. The French were suitably impressed. By February 1778, France and the United States entered into a formal defensive alliance, thus giving the United States the support it needed to defeat the British. The British reaction to the Franco–American alliance was to declare war on France. Suddenly, the war had transformed from an internal colonial conflict to an expensive international war in which both sides were far more evenly matched. To complicate matters even further for the British, in 1779 Spain—still smarting

from the loss of its territories in Florida—also entered the war on the side of the Americans.[34] The astonishing victories won by the British from the French and the Spanish during the Seven Years' War had now come home to roost with a vengeance.

By 1780, French support in particular began paying off for the Americans. In that year a large French force arrived in the United States under the Comte de Rochambeau, which guaranteed highly trained reinforcements against British regular and Hessian mercenary troops. Even more importantly, the French were critical players in forcing the British to surrender at Yorktown, Virginia, on October 19, 1781. With American forces surrounding him on land, the British General Cornwallis had planned to flee the town via the sea. However, a French naval force in the Chesapeake Bay blocked Cornwallis's exit, making his escape impossible. Although the war continued into 1782, the surrender at Yorktown ensured an eventual American victory.[35] In November 1782, the British signed the Articles of Peace, and on September 3, 1783, both the British and the Americans signed the Treaty of Paris that officially ended the war.

By the terms of the Treaty, Britain recognized the independence of the United States, which now was to encompass all territories from the Great Lakes in the north to Florida in the south, and from the Atlantic Ocean in the east to the Mississippi River in the west. In addition, Britain gave Florida back to Spain.[36] For their part, the Americans acknowledged British sovereignty over Canada, and agreed to repay outstanding debts to Britain. The French (and to a lesser extent the Spanish) had avenged themselves from past defeats at the hands of the British. For their financial investment, they had humbled Britain and helped divest it of a huge portion of its American empire.

French support in particular had proven critical to the success of the American Revolution. In

---

[32] Middlekauff, *The Glorious Cause*, 363–366.
[33] Ibid., 406.

[34] See ibid., chapter 17.
[35] Ibid., 590.
[36] Max Savelle, *Empires to Nations: Expansion in America, 1713–1824* (Minneapolis: University of Minnesota Press, 1974), 226.

very real terms, the Revolution was won not in the political theater or because of lofty Enlightenment ideologies, but rather as a result of wars both past and present. Just as the occurrence of the American Revolution had been contingent on the conflicts that erupted between the British state and colonists at the end of the Seven Years' War, so too was the success of the Americans contingent upon lingering French and Spanish hostility from that conflict. In other words, it was war more than any other factor that shaped both the timing and the success of the American Revolution by providing the conditions for it to begin in the first place and by determining who would join who as allies.

The American Revolution had obvious consequences for imperialism in the Atlantic world, since the independence of the United States vastly decreased the size of Britain's colonial holdings in the Americas. Yet the consequences of the Revolution for imperialism went far beyond the obvious. For Britain, the loss of the American colonies encouraged a gradual shift in imperial energies away from the Americas and toward Asia—including, especially, India.[37] For Spain, although it had not been an important player in determining the outcome of the war, its participation on the side of the Americans nevertheless had important financial and political consequences for its own American empire. For France, the consequences of the Revolution were critically important in two senses: first, because the financial costs of the war had drained the French treasury and contributed to political instability in France itself and, second, because the ideals of the American Revolutionaries inspired French Enlightenment thinkers to believe that they, too, could initiate their own revolution against tyranny.

These empire-spanning ramifications deserve some further consideration. Let us begin with Spain. The decision of Spain's Charles III to enter the war on the side of the Americans was both clear and curious. Over the course of the eighteenth century, it had become apparent that Spain's status as a major European power depended on its ability to maintain a strong hold on its American empire.

Spain itself was extremely poor, and revenues from the Americas were critical to the survival of the Spanish government. It was for this reason that the Spanish crown embarked upon the Bourbon reforms, which—as we have already seen—were designed to sharply increase colonial revenues and to centralize colonial administration.

In the context of Spanish efforts to retain great power status through fiscal and political reforms in the last half of the eighteenth century, the decision to enter the American Revolutionary War on the side of the Americans makes sense. In the event of an American victory, Spain had the opportunity to contribute to the weakening of one of its primary rivals in the Americas and also to regain its lost territories in Florida. Yet the timing of the war was also dangerous. Even without the extra expense of war, the Bourbon reforms placed tremendous financial strain on various communities in Spanish America. Moreover, once Spain entered the war increased revenue flows became that much more important to the financial health of the crown, which in turn increased the urgency of the reforms. As it turned out, the decision to make an enemy of Britain cost Spain and Spanish America dearly. Indeed, once Spain declared war the British lost no time in blockading Spanish American ports, which in turn paralyzed trade at a critical time.[38] These economic difficulties were compounded by the fact that the rapid institution of the Bourbon reforms in Peru and New Granada spurred two massive (and expensive) rebellions in 1780 and 1781, respectively.[39] Although both rebellions were eventually suppressed, they highlighted the fact that when colonial reform efforts met with urgent financial needs in the colonial metropole and serious economic disruption, especially when caused by war, the results could be volatile.

While the motivations for Spanish entry into the war seem relatively clear—even if they in fact backfired—Spanish support of a colonial rebellion nevertheless placed the Spanish government

---

[37] This shift toward Asia will be discussed in chapter 8.

[38] Elliott, *Empires of the Atlantic World*, 355, 372.

[39] The rebellion in Peru was led by Juan Candor Condorcanqui, who called himself Tupac Amaru after the last Inca king, while the rebellion in New Granada was called the Comuneros Rebellion.

in a curious position. In essence, the highly centralized and authoritarian Spanish government lent its open support to a rebellion designed to eliminate metropolitan control over colonial affairs at precisely the same time it was attempting to reassert its control over its own colonies. Fortunately for the Spanish, Enlightenment ideologies in Spanish America did not tend to challenge the authority of either the church or the crown in the eighteenth century, and thus American cries for liberty from a tyrannical monarch echoed only dimly in the Spanish colonies.[40] In addition, print culture was more limited in Spanish America than in its northern counterpart, so that participation in an active print culture was curtailed outside of the major metropolitan areas. Nevertheless, the implications of a successful American Revolution were not lost on Spanish ministers. They feared that the precedent of imperial rupture, once initiated, would inevitably be taken to heart by Spanish American creoles.[41]

The American Revolution also had long-term consequences for what was left of the French Empire in the Americas. As we have already seen, the decision of the French king to aid the Americans in their revolution was taken in large part in retaliation for French losses during the Seven Years' War. Yet despite the critical nature of French aid to the success of the Revolution, the decision to contribute so much to the war turned out to be deadly to the French monarchy. Even before the American Revolution, the finances of the French government were in disarray. The multiple and expensive wars of the French kings in the seventeenth and eighteenth centuries—not to mention the lavish expenses of the French court—put the French government in massive debt by the early 1770s. As a result, France could ill afford the 1 million French livres—the equivalent of about a quarter of the total French debt—the government contributed to the American war. Indeed, French aid to the Americans exacerbated a financial crisis that, by 1789, forced the French

King Louis XVI (1754–1793) to call on the French representatives of the people in order to stave off utter and complete bankruptcy. This calling of the Estates General, in turn, was the first step in a revolution that would eventually abolish the French monarchy and lead to years of turmoil in France, Europe, and the Atlantic world.[42]

In addition to impoverishing the French crown, the American Revolution encouraged the French Revolution in another way as well. For decades, France—and especially Paris—had been at the center of the Enlightenment intellectual movement. Thinkers and writers such as Voltaire (1694–1778) and Jean-Jacques Rousseau (1712–1778) had spurred widespread discussion of ideas such as religious tolerance, the establishment of rational societies through reason and merit, the institution of political liberty, and equality before the law. In Paris and around the Atlantic world, such ideas fueled radical reinterpretations of ideal governments based on democratic consent and freedom from the barriers of class and birth. When American colonists achieved a revolution based on these ideals, enthusiasts of Enlightenment ideals in France could point to the first instance in which such ideals had successfully been put into practice. Thus, when Louis XVI called the Estates General in 1789, many representatives of the Third Estate—the common people—had far more in mind than resolving the immediate economic crisis.[43]

THE FRENCH REVOLUTIONARY WARS AND THE FRENCH CARIBBEAN

As it turned out, the French Revolution was far more revolutionary than its American counterpart. Whereas the American Revolution did indeed establish independence and a republican form of government, in social terms both its aims and its outcomes were somewhat conservative.

---

[40] Jaime E. Rodriguez, *The Independence of Spanish America* (Cambridge: Cambridge University Press, 1998), 36–37.
[41] Elliott, *Empires of the Atlantic World*, 367.

[42] For a detailed look at the events that led to revolution, see William Doyle, *Origins of the French Revolution*, 2nd edition (Oxford: Oxford University Press, 1988).
[43] Georges Lefebvre, Elizabeth Moss Evanson, and Paul Beik, *The French Revolution: From Its Origins to 1793*, 2nd edition (London: Routledge, 2001), 82–85.

American revolutionaries never sought to overturn the social order, based as it was on the dominance of white men of property. Moreover, American revolutionaries sought to preserve much of their European culture and customs, as well as the British system of law. In contrast, French revolutionaries—particularly during the most radical years of the Revolution between 1793 and 1794—sought not only political reform but the eradication of the entire social order. From the abolition of class distinctions, to the insistence of equality for all men, to the declaration of a republic and the execution of King Louis XVI on January 21, 1793, French revolutionaries went much further than the Americans in their efforts to remake society.

However, as French revolutionary fervor grew so too did the potential for conflict with neighboring European leaders who deeply feared the implications of revolutionary ideas for their own people. In fact, beginning in 1792 France plunged into war first with Austria and Prussia and then, in 1793, with Spain, Portugal, and Great Britain. These wars persisted for a decade. Although a brief peace was reached in 1802, the wars broke out again under the new French leader Napoleon Bonaparte (1769–1821) and only finally ended with his defeat at the Battle of Waterloo in June 1815.[44] When combined with revolutionary ideologies, these 23 years of war had enormous consequences not just for the countries of Europe, but for countries and colonies half a world away across the Atlantic in the Caribbean and in Spanish and Portuguese America. Once again, the combination of revolutionary ideologies and war provided opportunities for colonial subjects to act, while the chaos of shifting alliances helped determine the fate of all the Atlantic empires.

When the Estates General met for the first time in May 1789, more than the metropole was abuzz with the anticipation of reform. Indeed, although Louis XVI had called the Estates General in order to deal with the fiscal crisis of the French state, many French citizens had far grander visions that included economic, social, and political reform. Among these citizens were those who lived—or had vested interests—in the French Atlantic colonies. In particular, wealthy white planters from the French sugar islands of St. Domingue, Martinique, and Guadeloupe had grievances against French trade regulations that restricted them from selling sugar and buying slaves on the open market. Hearing that the Estates General would be called, then, white planters from the largest and most productive island of St. Domingue elected representatives to take their concerns to Paris, where their demands for trade liberalization could be heard by all.[45]

As we saw in chapter 4, although St. Domingue was socially, politically, and economically dominated by white planters, slaves made up nearly 90% of the population. Thus, while the island supported 500,000 slaves, only 30,000 whites and about 25,000 free people of color lived on the island. Moreover, the slave regime on St. Domingue—as in the rest of the Caribbean—was extremely brutal.[46] Slave mortality was high, which meant the constant replenishing of slave numbers with fresh bodies from Africa. By the start of the French Revolution, in fact, two-thirds of all slaves on St. Domingue had been born in Africa.[47]

And in 1789, it was not only the wealthy white planters who had been paying attention to developments in Paris. As early as July 1789, slaves in the French Caribbean began to grow restive at rumors that the king of France had ended slavery. On St. Domingue, free people of color also looked hopefully to Paris for reform,

---

[44]For a narrative account of the French Revolutionary Wars, see Gregory Fremont-Barnes, *The French Revolutionary Wars* (Oxford: Osprey, 2001).

[45]Laurent Dubois, *Avengers of the New World: The Story of the Haitian Revolution* (Cambridge: Harvard University Press, 2004), 71–72; and Laurent Dubois and John D. Garrigus, *Slave Revolution in the Caribbean* (Boston: Bedford St. Martin's, 2006), 16.

[46]C.L.R. James evokes the brutalities of the slave regime in the West Indies particularly well. See C.L.R. James, *The Black Jacobins: Toussaint L'Ouverture and the San Domingo Revolution*, 2nd edition (New York: Vintage Books, 1989), chapter 1.

[47]Dubois and Garrigus, *Slave Revolution in the Caribbean*, 13.

since whites on the island refused to allow them access to political or social power despite the wealth of many of their number. In addition, the large group of poor whites on St. Domingue also desired reforms that would allow them greater opportunities for social and economic advancement. Indeed, at the start of the French Revolution four groups with competing interests—wealthy whites, poor whites, free people of color, and slaves—viewed events in France through the prism of their own interests and grievances, and sought to turn them to their advantage.[48]

All four groups gained a much clearer sense of how the Revolution might affect their island world when the National Assembly in Paris approved the Declaration of the Rights of Man on August 26, 1789. The Declaration, which was meant to provide the foundation for a new French constitution, proclaimed that "men are born free and remain free and equal in rights," and that all men had the right to "liberty, property, security, and resistance to oppression."[49] White planters from St. Domingue and other sugar islands were alarmed at the radical potential of such a declaration for their slave societies, and sought immediately to use their influence to prevent it from being applied in the Caribbean. St. Domingue's free people of color, on the other hand, were delighted, and began pressing the National Assembly to apply the principles of the Declaration to the colonies. Meanwhile, the island's poor whites—jealous of the economic success of many free people of color—loudly demanded that discriminatory laws based on race be strictly maintained. By the spring of 1791, the National Assembly had made its choice: on May 15, constituents voted to give full French citizenship to all free men of color who had property and who were descended from two free parents.[50]

The result in St. Domingue was civil war: over the next nine months, fighting broke out between groups of poor whites and free people of color.

While poor whites, free people of color, and wealthy whites were fighting to preserve their own interests, slaves in St. Domingue's northern province seized the opportunity provided by the instability in the colony to revolt. On the night of August 22, 1791, approximately 1,000 slaves rose up in a well-coordinated uprising that destroyed 200 sugar plantations and over 1,000 coffee estates. This was not a revolt with limited aims. Rather, the slaves sought to overturn the very economic and social structures of the society in which they toiled. Perhaps theirs were not generally "revolutionary" ideals recognizable as those of Enlightenment France, but nevertheless theirs was a struggle for liberty and equality of labor, and of the choice not to labor if they did not wish it. Their demands ranged from reforms of the slave system—such as extra days working for themselves or abolition of the whip—to the ejection of all whites from the island and an end to slavery altogether. Because this was a popular message, as the slaves gained ground they also gained new recruits. In just a few short weeks, their ranks swelled to 10,000 or 20,000, and they organized themselves into an increasingly powerful army.[51]

By the autumn of 1791, St. Domingue was in chaos. Although the French Legislative (formerly National) Assembly twice sent commissioners and troops to restore order in the colony, fighting continued unabated. Over the next two years, the Revolution in France also accelerated: in 1792, the Legislative Assembly declared war on Austria, proclaimed France a republic, and tried Louis XVI for treason. Finally, on January 21, 1793, the king was executed by vote of the Assembly. The execution of the king had dramatic effects on St. Domingue, because it led to war with both Spain and Britain. With the entry of these two countries into the war against France, the turmoil caused by the French Revolution became a general European war. At that point, the largest and most profitable French sugar

[48] For the development of the conflict between these competing groups, see ibid., chapter 3. Carolyn Fick talks about the ripeness of St. Domingue for Revolution in "The French Revolution in San Domingue: Triumph or Failure," in *A Turbulent Time: The French Revolution and the Greater Caribbean*, edited by Barry Gaspar and David Geggus (Bloomington: Indiana University Press, 1997).

[49] Articles I and II from the Declaration of the Rights of Man and the Citizen.

[50] Dubois and Garrigus, *Slave Revolution in the Caribbean*, 19–22.

[51] Dubois, *Avengers of the New World*, 98–113.

island became fair game in a war with international stakes.[52]

The slaves who had rebelled in 1791 were hardly a disorganized rabble. In part, this was due to the fact that many of the slaves who took part in the insurrection had military experience, since many had fought in the ferocious civil wars of Central Africa in the eighteenth century. In addition, its leaders were skilled, able, and ruthless. Indeed, they tended to hail from the most skilled positions in plantation society, and included a large number of slave drivers who had long experience in organizing people. Some leaders were also free people of color who had experience owning or leasing their own land and organizing their own labor. Toussaint L'Ouverture, who became the rebellion's most important leader between 1793 and 1802, was such a man.[53] Having been born a slave, L'Ouverture had attained his freedom and, prior to the rebellion, was the owner of a coffee plantation that used rented slave labor for its workforce.[54]

Although rebel slaves successfully repulsed repeated French attacks in 1791 and 1792, they realized that the long-term survival of the insurrection required aid, especially in terms of money and weapons. For that reason, slave leaders had been in regular contact with the Spanish, whose colony of St. Domingo shared the island with St. Domingue. For their part, some Spanish leaders on the island had been happy to help any movement that might hurt French profits. However, in 1791 and 1792 Spanish aid had to remain unofficial since Spain had no official quarrel with France. All that changed in 1793, when Spain went to war with France over the assassination of Louis XVI. Now, in a sustained attempt to thwart the French in St. Domingue, Spanish leaders in St. Domingo increased their material aid, began commissioning the leaders of the revolt—including L'Ouverture—as officers,

and granted both land and freedom to soldiers who would fight against the French. At this stage, Spanish aid was a critical factor in the continuing success of the revolt.[55]

In the meantime, the entry of the British into the war against France in the same year also influenced the strength of the slave rebellion. This occurred in two ways. First, once the war was official the British navy immediately began to interfere with French ships trying to reach the Caribbean colonies, thus disrupting the provisioning of the French colonists in St. Domingue. Second, at the invitation of French colonists who feared that revolutionary ideas were threatening the survival of slavery, British troops invaded western and southern St. Domingue in September 1793.[56] This did not, however, weaken the rebellion in the way French colonists had hoped. Instead, the French commissioners who had been charged with restoring order to St. Domingue in 1792 now acted desperately to stave off counter-revolutionary French colonists, British invaders, and Spanish-aided rebels. To do this, they began offering both freedom and amnesty to any rebel groups who would fight against the enemies of the French Revolution. When this tactic proved a relative success, the commissioners extended their offer of liberty to soldiers' families. Finally, during the British invasion, they offered emancipation in all the provinces of St. Domingue in exchange for armed support.[57]

By the time the French National Convention (formerly the Legislative Assembly) received word of the practical abolition of slavery in St. Domingue, the Revolution had entered its most radical phase. Conservatives and moderates had been purged from their offices, and the Convention was more inclined than ever to be sympathetic to the plight of slaves. Thus, by a vote on February 4, 1794, the Convention ratified the decision already made in St. Domingue and extended it to all French colonies. The new constitution that came into effect in 1795,

---

[52] Dubois and Garrigus, *Slave Revolution in the Caribbean*, 26.
[53] Toussaint L'Ouverture's given surname was Breda, but he took the name L'Ouverture—which means *the opening*—during the rebellion.
[54] Dubois, *Avengers of the New World*, 171.

[55] Langley, *The Americas in the Age of Revolution*, 116; and Dubois and Garrigus, *Slave Revolution in the Caribbean*, 27
[56] Langley, *The Americas in the Age of Revolution*, 118.
[57] Dubois, *Avengers of the New World*, 154–159.

moreover, specifically abolished slavery and guaranteed that henceforth all colonial subjects would be subject to the same laws as the French.[58]

When Toussaint L'Ouverture learned that the French National Convention had abolished slavery, he promptly resigned his Spanish commission to side with the French. Now, instead of using Spanish aid to defeat French colonists hostile to emancipation, he used French aid both to defeat counter-revolutionary French forces and to beat back Spanish as well as British advances. As a result of his skill and leadership, L'Ouverture was repeatedly promoted and, by 1797, had become the highest-ranking officer on the island. By 1798, he had won back much of the island for the French and began to set his sights on Spanish St. Domingo.[59] In spite of his work for the French, however, L'Ouverture was no stooge. Rather, he took whatever opportunities arose during the chaos of war to ensure that St. Domingue did not revert to slavery. As an extension of this policy, by 1797 L'Ouverture increasingly took political control into his own hands by negotiating policy with both the British (with whom the French were at war) and the Americans (who were engaged in an undeclared war against France from 1798 to 1800). These negotiations, made possible by the fact that the governments of both countries saw French disadvantage in L'Ouverture's advantage, allowed St. Domingue to trade with British Jamaica and the United States. In effect, L'Ouverture made certain that St. Domingue would not be left without a way to obtain arms or provisions should French support for emancipation disappear.[60]

As it turned out, L'Ouverture's precautions were prescient. In 1799, a coup d'etat brought Napoleon Bonaparte to power in France—and with him a far more conservative agenda than the revolutionaries who had abolished slavery in 1794. In fact, Napoleon's new constitution sought to re-establish slavery in French colonial territories. The idea was to revitalize the French economy via the plantation system in the West Indies, and to

support it with agricultural resources from the newly re-acquired Louisiana territory.[61] Yet Napoleon's efforts to reverse the situation in St. Domingue ended in failure. Even when French troops arrived there in 1802 and took L'Ouverture back to France—where he died in prison the next year—brutal efforts to disarm former slaves merely resulted in a new uprising.[62] Aided by arms and provisions supplied by the United States, by 1803 Jean-Jacques Dessalines, L'Ouverture's top officer, had united many of the rebels under his authority even as French forces were decimated through combat and disease. In 1804, Dessalines declared the Republic of Haiti an independent nation (thus leading us to call this series of uprisings *the Haitian Revolution*).[63] Faced with the loss of France's most important sugar island, Napoleon gave up his dream of a renewed sugar empire and sold his recently reacquired Louisiana territory to the surprised administration of Thomas Jefferson in the United States.[64]

Clearly, revolutionary ideologies played a critical role in touching off the violent conflicts that wracked St. Domingue for 15 years. Indeed, these ideologies—themselves inspired by the success of the Americans in their revolution—provided a language by which French citizens and subjects in both the metropole and the empire re-evaluated their social and political positions on the basis of ideas such as liberty and equality. The effects of such a language had obvious implications for slave societies. In the context of St. Domingue's divided and fraught social structure—in which competing groups nursed serious grievances against a variety of authorities—such ideas were bound to be explosive.

Yet as important as ideologies were in the Haitian Revolution, it was the opportunities offered by war that determined its shape and eventual outcome. As in the American Revolution, war

---

[58] Dubois and Garrigus, *Slave Revolution in the Caribbean*, 29.
[59] Dubois, *Avengers of the New World*, 236–237.
[60] Ibid., 224–225.

[61] Dubois and Garrigus, *Slave Revolution in the Caribbean*, 33.
[62] Dubois, *Avengers of the New World*, 293.
[63] James, *The Black Jacobins*, 370.
[64] Paul Lachance, "Repercussions of the Haitian Revolution in Louisiana," in *The Impact of the Haitian Revolution in the Atlantic World*, edited by David Geggus (Columbia: University of South Carolina Press, 2001), 210.

shaped the nature of available alliances for the rebels on St. Domingue: indeed, aid and assistance provided at one time or another by Spain, France, Britain, and the United States was critical to the success of those who fought to maintain their freedom on the island. In addition, the chaos that resulted from the rapidly shifting circumstances of war allowed the leaders of the Haitian rebellion to skillfully play one power off the other and to change sides when necessary. In the absence of war and the assistance of various allies, it seems far less likely that the rebels could have staved off French efforts to re-establish authority indefinitely. Even so, Haitian emancipation and eventual independence came at a tremendous cost: several hundred thousand people on the island are estimated to have died in the conflict, in addition to more than 100,000 French and British soldiers. Moreover, settlements and farms all over the colony were destroyed, making recovery a long and difficult process. Nevertheless, international war had helped create the conditions for the founding of the first black republic in the Americas in 1804, altering once again the shape of empire in the Atlantic world and adding to the legacy of successful revolution that others could point to in their own struggles.

THE NAPOLEONIC WARS AND THE SPANISH AND PORTUGUESE AMERICAS

Just as war created the conditions for an independent Haiti, so too did it create the conditions for—and shape the outcome of—independence in the Spanish and Portuguese Americas. Here again ideology played a role in the particular ways that some creole leaders responded to events in the metropole, but ideology alone cannot explain the transition to independence of nearly every Spanish colony and Brazil by 1825. To understand such a dramatic shift, we must turn to the international context of the French Revolutionary Wars and, especially, the Napoleonic Wars that followed close on their heels.[65]

As we have already seen, during the last half of the eighteenth century Spanish creoles nursed substantial grievances with regard to their relationship to the imperial metropole. The Bourbon reforms, which sought greater centralization and higher taxes, caused real economic hardship and also discontented many creoles who had become used to positions of power in the administration of the colonies. Yet despite these grievances, few creoles suggested that independence from Spain was the answer to their problems in this period— even in the wake of the American, French, and Haitian revolutions. In part this was because the long tradition of Spanish intervention and involvement in colonial affairs made it easier for colonials to accept reforms from the imperial center. In addition, as jarring as the reforms had been, they were applied with consistency by resolute representatives of the Spanish Crown across Spanish America. Perhaps even more important, however, was the fact that creole demands for greater autonomy were always complicated by fears of being overwhelmed by mixed-race, Indian, and African majorities in many Spanish colonies. Indeed, the tense multi-racial composition of Spanish American colonies had the effect of muting radicalism among creoles who believed their own privileged position in society depended on Spanish support. While a few creole intellectuals—among them the future revolutionary leader Simon Bolívar—were inspired by the revolutionary events of the late eighteenth century, many more viewed the idea of colonial independence as a double-edged sword. Thus, while a few saw developments like the Haitian Revolution as a positive step, others regarded it with horror as they realized the potential for their own societies to be turned upside down.[66]

At the end of the eighteenth century, however, war initiated unplanned changes that derailed the Bourbon agenda of centralization and control. Although the Spanish had sided with the British against the French in the early years of the French Revolution, in 1796 the Spanish crown reversed course and allied itself with France

---

[65]Lockhart and Schwartz, *Early Latin America*, 412.

[66]Ibid., 409–410.

against Britain. War against Britain turned out to be an unmitigated disaster for Spain, because the British once again used their powerful navy to disrupt trade between Spain and its American colonies. So severe was this disruption that Spain was forced to open its ports on both sides of the Atlantic to neutral powers such as the United States.[67] In the absence of access to Spanish shipping, meanwhile, Spanish American merchants grew increasingly commercially independent of Spain.[68] Decreases in revenues from American trade were exacerbated by the increased costs of war, which in turn placed serious strains on Spanish finances. By 1798, the crown was forced to sell off church property in Spain to generate more revenue, and in 1804 it extended this policy to its colonies. This decision had profound consequences, because the church—with its extensive American properties—had been crucial for its role in extending credit to colonists in need of loans. Denuded of substantial portions of its properties and wealth after 1804, however, the church was no longer able to perform its function as creditor, and many colonists found themselves in dire economic trouble as a result.[69]

If war with Britain had not made sustained contact and efficient commercial relations with the imperial metropole difficult enough, Spanish colonists found themselves in an even more dire situation when Napoleon invaded and conquered Spain itself in 1808. In Spain, Napoleon forced the abdication of the existing king, Carlos IV, and replaced him with his brother Joseph. Meanwhile, Carlos's heir Ferdinand VII was forced to remain as Napoleon's "guest" in France until 1814. With their king deposed and a pretender on the throne, Spanish colonists were suddenly confronted with the fact that there was no longer a legitimate authority in Spain to rule the empire. This implosion of authority at the center of the empire left a vacuum in which Spanish American elites—both creole and peninsular—found themselves thrown back ever more on their own devices. The situation was that

much more startling because, unlike their earlier counterparts in British America, Spanish Americans did not have a well-developed tradition of popular political participation, colonial assemblies, or inter-colonial coordination.[70] When royal authority disappeared, then, it became clear that the men with the most leadership experience tended to hail from the military and colonial militia. As a result, in much of Spanish America such men quickly began to take control of their varied local situations. By 1810, elites in Argentina, Chile, Venezuela, and New Granada had formed military juntas for the purpose of providing leadership in the absence of royal authority.[71]

Although elites in nearly every Spanish territory claimed to have taken power in the name of the legitimate Spanish king, in some areas the implosion of royal authority allowed liberal radicals the opportunity to openly pursue their agenda of independence from Spain. Thus in Caracas, Venezuela, the young revolutionary idealist Simon Bolívar convinced enough of the creole elite of the values of liberty that the colony declared itself a free and independent nation in 1811. In other areas, such as New Spain, mixed-race and Indian peoples sought to capitalize on Spanish weakness by creating a mass movement that would bring about greater social equality in the state. Thus in 1810, under the leadership of a parish priest named Miguel Hidalgo, thousands of mixed-race and Indian peasants rose up in general rebellion. Although creoles in New Spain had originally believed Hidalgo's revolt would strengthen their claims for greater autonomy within the Spanish imperial system, the violence of the peasants and their program of social reform soon caused creoles to band together with peninsulars to crush it.[72] Meanwhile, the declaration of independence in Venezuela plunged the territory into civil war, and by 1812—just one year after its creation—the new republic was dead. In Venezuela as in much of the rest of Spanish America, demands for autonomy and independence continued to be tempered by

[67] Elliott, *Empires of the Atlantic World*, 372–373.
[68] Lockhart and Schwartz, *Early Latin America*, 413.
[69] Elliott, *Empires of the Atlantic World*, 373.

[70] Ibid., 375.
[71] Lockhart and Schwartz, *Early Latin America*, 416.
[72] Rodriguez, *The Independence of Spanish America*, 160–164.

elite fears of social revolution from below.[73] Many believed that the price of independence might be the loss of their own privileged place in Spanish American society. At the same time, for all practical purposes colonists in Spanish America ruled themselves between 1808 and 1814, and they grew increasingly used to exercising their powers of self-rule.

This was not lost on the Spanish Cortes, the national assembly that, from 1810, ruled in place of the king in the British-protected city of Cadiz. Fearing a permanent rupture between the colonies and Spain, in that year the Cortes invited Spanish American representatives to Cadiz in order to take part in restructuring the Spanish government. Although there was much the Cortes did not understand about colonial—especially creole—grievances, the new constitution issued in 1812 did attempt to address some of them. By the terms of the new constitution, Spain and the Americas were to be transformed into a single nation-state, in which the Americas would no longer be subordinate but would be an extension of Spain itself. Henceforth, the Americas were to be divided into 20 provinces, each with representative elected bodies. Moreover, all Spaniards were to be considered equal in the new nation-state, and there were to be no property or literacy requirements for the franchise. In the Americas, Indians—but not slaves—were also to be eligible to vote as Spaniards, and freedom of the press was to be uniform.[74] In practical terms, this meant that 93% of Mexico City's adult males were suddenly placed on the voting register in 1813. People in towns and cities, spurred by an inspired popular press, quickly grew politicized as they realized they were about to have a voice in elected government.[75]

Although the new arrangements were far from perfect, the constitution of 1812 did at least envision unprecedented political change in order to keep the colonies in the imperial fold. However, a turn of events in 1814 made the new constitution obsolete. In May of that year, King Ferdinand

VII was restored to the throne. This, of course, is what the leaders of the Spanish American juntas and coalitions had been saying they wanted since 1808, and indeed Ferdinand's restoration could have been handled in such a way as to encourage the colonies to reconcile themselves with metropolitan interests. But Ferdinand and his court were completely out of touch with the situation in the Americas, and with the extent to which his subjects were unwilling to relinquish control over local affairs without serious concessions. Almost immediately after resuming control, Ferdinand abolished the constitution of 1812 and—rather than compromise with the colonies—sent Spanish troops to restore the authority of the crown in the Americas.[76]

Initially, Spanish efforts to restore order in the Americas met with considerable success. By 1816, royalist forces had prevailed in Chile, New Spain, Venezuela, and New Granada. A year later, the only movement still seeking autonomy that had not been defeated was in Buenos Aires, Argentina.[77] Yet royal oppression and violence encouraged those most desperate for change to persist. Advocates of independence, in particular, were able to convince many of their compatriots to support separation from the crown once and for all. Indeed, by 1817 the goal of total separation from Spain had become, for the first time, general throughout most of Spanish America.[78]

Armed with the will to fight and aided by Spanish ineptness, a huge geography, and limited British aid, Spanish Americans turned the tide of fortune in their favor after 1817. In the south, the Argentine general José de San Martín's army of the Andes achieved success in liberating Chile in 1818, and Peru in 1821. In the north, Simon Bolívar—the Venezuelan liberal general who had helped engineer the first republic of Venezuela in 1811—succeeded in liberating New Granada by 1819, and then Venezuela itself in 1821. Further to

---

[73] Elliott, *Empires of the Atlantic World*, 381.
[74] Rodriguez, *The Independence of Spanish America*, 91–92; and ibid., 384, 386.
[75] Elliott, *Empires of the Atlantic World*, 386.

[76] Rodriguez, *The Independence of Spanish America*, 106.
[77] Lockhart and Schwartz, *Early Latin America*, 416; and Elliott, *Empires of the Atlantic World*, 389.
[78] Rodriguez, *The Independence of Spanish America*, 240; and Lockhart and Schwartz, *Early Latin America*, 417.

the north, Mexico too became independent in 1821 after the conservative general Agustin de Iturbide allied with more radical rebels against Spanish authority, declaring Mexico a Catholic constitutional monarchy. In the same year, St. Domingo—the first Spanish colony in the Americas—also gained its independence. After Mexico declared its independence, the Central American colonies gained their independence almost by default. Finally, with the liberation of Bolivia in 1825, Spain's three-century dominion over most of South America came to an end. Thus just one-quarter of the way through the nineteenth century, Spain's once-grand American empire had been reduced to just two surviving colonies: Cuba and Puerto Rico.[79]

The Napoleonic invasion of the Iberian peninsula had also led to the independence of Brazil from Portugal, but in quite a different way. As in late eighteenth-century Spanish America, Brazilian subjects—creole, mulatto, and African—had nursed grievances with regard to the relationship between the metropole and the colony. A few had been inspired by the ideals of the American and French revolutions, and had launched unsuccessful revolts in protest of tax collection, racism, or the lack of free trade.[80] Yet it was not until the invasion of Portugal by Napoleon that the relationship between Portugal and Brazil underwent substantive change. In 1807, tired of putting up with Portuguese aid to his British enemies, Napoleon sent an army through Spain to conquer Portugal. However, by the time the French army arrived in Lisbon, the Portuguese King Joao VI and his entire court had fled—under a British naval escort—to the Brazilian capital of Rio de Janeiro. Thus, unlike the Spanish American colonies after Napoleon's conquest of Spain the next year, Brazilians were not faced with a power and sovereignty vacuum after the fall of Portugal.

Instead, the source of legitimate royal authority had now moved inside the colony itself.[81] Indeed, Brazil in this period was ruled as a kingdom equal in status to Portugal itself, and benefited from the introduction of royal institutions such as schools, a military academy, and financial institutions.

The Portuguese king and court remained in Brazil until 1820, when a liberal revolt in Portugal led the Portuguese to demand that the king return to his rightful place in Lisbon. Leaving his son Pedro to rule as regent, King Joao returned to Portugal. The new Portuguese parliament was not satisfied, however, and quickly rescinded Brazil's status as an equal kingdom and demanded that Pedro return to Portugal as well. At the urging of Brazilian colonists who had grown used to being governed from within their own borders, Pedro declined to return to Portugal. Instead, in 1822 Brazil declared itself independent from Portugal, with Pedro as king. The transfer of power, while not entirely amicable, had at least been relatively peaceful.

In Spanish America—in contrast to Brazil—independence had to be won through prolonged violence. There, war had created the conditions first for serious instability and economic hardship, and then—after 1808—for a crisis in legitimate authority that encouraged already discontented subjects to take matters into their own hands. Yet unlike the American or the Haitian Revolution, the timing of Spanish America's independence struggles were not conducive to playing the great European powers off one another. Indeed, although intercontinental wars had provided the opportunity for Spanish American wars of independence, by the time those struggles were fully underway Europe was once more at peace. As a result of the peace, Spanish Americans were not able to secure substantial military aid from powerful alliances like the Americans had done with the French during their own revolution. The best Spanish American forces could hope for was encouragement by U.S. and Haitian representatives, as well as occasional military support by the British navy.

---

[79] For a nuanced account of Spanish independence, see Rodriguez, *The Independence of Spanish America*, chapters 4 and 5.

[80] These revolts included the Minas Gerais revolt of 1788–1789 and the Bahian plot of 1798. Lockhart and Schwartz, *Early Latin America*, 411.

---

[81] Ibid., 413–414.

This lack of aid, in turn, prolonged the conflicts with Spain, which in turn left far greater destruction of lives and property in their wake.[82] In addition, whereas international warfare had proven to be an economic boon to the newly independent United States because of increased demand for natural resources, peace had the opposite effect on the economies of the newly independent Latin American states. Instead, after independence most of the new states faced decreased economic demand, stiff competition from an increasingly confident United States, and economic pressure from British interests.[83]

Finally, both the nature of Spanish American society and the character of the various independence struggles left a legacy of strong military participation in the governments of the newly independent states. Men with military experience had filled the power vacuum created by the implosion of Spanish imperial power, and years of prolonged warfare enhanced the power of centralized military caudillos once independence was won. Such a legacy cast a long shadow over the new states of Colombia, Peru, Bolivia, and Venezuela—a legacy that contributed to instability in many of the new states for much of the rest of the nineteenth century. For Spanish America, international war had indeed provided the opportunity for independence to occur, but its cessation in 1815 also created the conditions for those independence struggles to be long, violent, and bloody.

ATLANTIC REBELLIONS AND GLOBAL WARS IN SOUTHERN AFRICA

During the late eighteenth and early nineteenth centuries, the situation in the European settlements and colonies in Africa was to some degree different from that of the Americas. This was largely due to local conditions. In those parts of Africa where settlements had been established, European penetration tended to be limited in both cultural and territorial terms, as we have seen in chapter 5. While a class of Africans and Euro-Africans developed in some parts of coastal West Africa who engaged Enlightenment ideals of liberty, participated in the Atlantic economy, and at times protested the actions of some European administrators, large-scale formal colonial rule and large numbers of settlers generally did not exist for them to contest.[84]

At the very tip of southern Africa, however, the situation was different. Over the course of 150 years beginning in the mid-seventeenth century, significant numbers of Dutch and some French Protestant settlers built up a large community at the Cape of Good Hope. Their settlement was promoted by their location on a key trade route between the Atlantic and Indian ocean world, by the congenial Mediterranean-style climate, and by the fact that much of the local population in the region succumbed quite rapidly to diseases brought by the immigrants.

The situation of this southern African settlement zone was similar enough to the Americas to deserve some attention during this period. As in many of the American colonies, the class and racial categorization of society here was complex with officials of the Dutch East India Company (VOC) at the top, European settlers beneath them as a farming and professional class, and African and imported Asian servants, laborers, and slaves at the bottom. There was also a growing mixed-race group who fit into several class categories. The presence of slavery was also an important similarity, and as in the Americas many of the enslaved were forced immigrants—in this case brought by the Dutch from their colonies in Malaysia.

Two events in southern Africa deserve special attention in this chapter. The first was the British occupation of the Cape, which actually occurred twice. The first, briefer British occupation occurred in 1795, following the defeat of the Netherlands by revolutionary French forces. The

---

[82] Rodriguez, *The Independence of Spanish America*, 244; and Elliott, *Empires of the Atlantic World*, 392.
[83] Rodriguez, *The Independence of Spanish America*, 245.

[84] See, for example, James R. Sanders, "The Political Development of the Fante in the Eighteenth and Nineteenth Centuries: A Study of a West African Merchant Society," unpublished dissertation, Northwestern University, 1980.

British, in response, occupied the Cape to keep the French from gaining it. It was returned in 1803, but then seized more permanently in 1806 to keep it out of the hands of Napoleon, who had again occupied the Netherlands. In both cases, the underlying issue was control of the important Atlantic-to-Indian ocean trade routes and thus command of the resources flowing to Europe from Asia. Arguably, it was these resources that helped Britain and its allies to win the long war against Napoleon.[85]

The second event that deserves our attention was a slave uprising that took place in 1808 at the Cape. This was only one of many rebellions among slaves, indentured servants, and other low-status peoples in the region, but it was significant in several ways. South African historian Nigel Worden, who has worked at length on this subject, points out that the leaders of the uprising were three slaves from Cape Town who had met in the port city a number of Atlantic revolutionaries. These included two Irish soldiers who had apparently told them that there was no slavery in Europe as well as other sailors and transients who told them about revolutions in France and rebellions in the Americas. They were also reacting to the abolition of the import slave trade into the colony by the new British rulers after 1806 and the military defeat of their Dutch owners by British forces. However, despite criminalizing the slave trade, the British did nothing to emancipate the slaves already in the region. Thus, these three slave leaders attempted to replicate the revolution in St. Domingue themselves. What is perhaps most interesting is that, as in St. Domingue, the leaders did not try to organize a mass escape or an orgy of destruction, but instead tried to overthrow their oppressors and create a brand-new society with themselves on top. It seems likely that this decision was inspired by the revolutions in Europe and the Americas. In the end, the 1808 uprising failed. The combination of a united front of Dutch-speaking settlers and British military force shut the rebels down in a way that had not been possible in much of the Americas. Nevertheless, the way in which it happened and the goals of its leaders suggest a common connection to events on the other side of the Atlantic.[86]

Conclusion

In the 62 years between the end of the Seven Years' War and Bolivian independence, the map of the Americas was dramatically redrawn. European overseas imperial projects in the Americas, which had begun at the turn of the sixteenth century and had proceeded to claim the entire Caribbean and most of the North, Central, and South American landmasses, were entirely changed by the early nineteenth century. Spanish territories had been reduced from gigantic proportions to two Caribbean islands, British claims had shrunk to Canada and a few West Indian territories, French territories were now limited to a few small sugar islands, and Portuguese territories were completely eliminated. In most cases, colonists descended from Europeans—and in the case of Haiti, Africans—forcibly threw off metropolitan rule in this period in favor of self-rule.

This dramatic shift in the composition of the European empires in the Americas was a result of many factors. As we saw in chapters 3 to 5, most of the imperial powers struggled with the difficulties of maintaining adequate control over their colonies throughout the early modern period. All experimented with centralization, decentralization, administrative innovation, labor practices, and trade regulation in order to achieve a balance between metropolitan profit and continued colonial growth. Their methods included brutal practices of slavery, harsh labor regimes, and the encouragement of cash crop agriculture—which, in addition to epidemic disease, completely transformed American populations and landscapes. All of the imperial

---

[85] For more on South African period, see the superior general text edited by Christopher Saunders, *Readers Digest Illustrated History of South Africa* (New York: Reader's Digest, 1994).

[86] Nigel Worden has lectured extensively on this event. One brief summary of his argument is available online at http://www.iziko. org.za/education/pastprogs/2008/slavery2008/Iziko_1808_Worden. pdf.

powers also struggled with problems of culture and identity as colonial circumstances led both metropolitan and colonial subjects to view themselves in opposition to one another. And, as colonial societies grew and matured, perceptions of unfair treatment and cultural disdain from metropolitan peoples caused increasing colonial discontent. When combined with eighteenth-century Enlightenment ideals about liberty, equality, and good government, such discontent found eloquent justification and articulation.

Yet the transition to independence of most European colonies in the Americas cannot be explained solely by the difficulties of constructing overseas empires or of diverging identities. It is possible, of course, that such problems and tensions would have someday led to independence in all of the American territories. The point here, however, has been that—despite a certain level of colonial discontent—independence was not an ambition of *any* of the European colonial leaders until the last three decades of the eighteenth century. Thus, historical circumstances rather than ideological forces were critical in determining the timing of the revolutions that led to American independence. In particular, wars fought between the major imperial powers in the eighteenth century—culminating in the Seven Years' War—created the conditions both for the eruption of the American Revolution and for the alliances that would ultimately help it to succeed. In turn, both the American Revolution and British successes in the Seven Years' War contributed to the timing and alliance systems of later revolutions and wars, including the French and Haitian revolutions, the French Revolutionary and Napoleonic wars, the Spanish American wars of independence, and Portuguese independence. In most cases, wars of empire highlighted problems of colonial discontent while also providing opportunities for colonial subjects to exploit metropolitan weaknesses and to play rival imperial powers off one another for their own gain. Moreover, the interlinked nature of each of these conflicts helps to explain both their rapid succession in this period and their broadly similar consequences in terms of permanent imperial rupture. Indeed, just as war between European competitors for empire had helped carve out the various American empires, it had just as surely torn them apart.

Questions

1. How did competition among imperial powers help to create the setting for rebellions in the Atlantic world in the late eighteenth and early nineteenth centuries? What was the role of economic issues in stirring up resentment among settlers in the colonies? How were the two intertwined?

2. How did competition among imperial powers contribute to the *success* of the St. Domingue (Haitian) and American revolutions and the rebellions in Spanish Latin America?

3. It is sometimes argued that the metropolitan imperial governments' interests and colonial settlers' interests are often at odds in empires with large settler populations. Is there evidence of that occurring in this period? Why do you think that might be?

4. What were the impacts of the American Revolution for the Spanish, French, and British empires?

5. Compare and contrast the slave revolution in St. Domingue to the 1808 uprising in the Cape Colony. What seems to have been the objective of the rebels in each case? How is each linked to the French Revolution? How was each resolved? What were the similarities and differences between them?

CHAPTER 8

Imperialism: The Industrial Revolution and the Era of Informal Imperialism

The transition of most American territories to independence in the early nineteenth century marked the end of three centuries of unprecedented imperial conquest by European powers. Most of the Americas were no longer viable as sites of colonial settlement and exploitation, while those that were left—including the Caribbean sugar colonies—became increasingly less profitable in the first decades of the century. Yet the desire to trade, to find sources of raw materials, and to dominate lucrative markets remained. To satisfy those desires, those European states that were still able had to look either for new places to extend their rule or for new ways to impose their economic will in distant lands.

In the post-revolutionary period, one European state above all others was most prepared to seek new colonies and new markets: Britain. In part, this was a result of the relative weakness of Britain's main rivals in the early nineteenth century. Indeed, Spain emerged from its Atlantic wars weakened and indebted, while in France the twin traumas of war and revolution resulted in a succession of internal upheavals that frequently distracted the state from colonial ventures. The Napoleonic conflict had influenced Britain to adopt a global strategy of building a navy that could chase the French and their allies out of South Africa, the Caribbean, and the Mediterranean, and to some degree this orientation remained after the war. To be sure, there were other victors in this conflict, but Russia was involved in its mainland empire (see chapter 6) and Prussia in building a German nation-state. That left Britain virtually alone as a power able to extend its military might around the globe between 1812 and 1880. Equally important, however, was Britain's greatly increased economic strength as a result of the new technologies of the Industrial Revolution. Britain was the first state in the world to industrialize, and by 1830 new methods of transport—particularly railroads and steamships—were revolutionizing access to remote regions of the world. British textile factories demanded large supplies of cotton from overseas regions, while finished British goods demanded overseas markets. By 1880, industrialization had also transformed weaponry and communications, which meant that in addition to being able to go farther and faster than ever before, Britons could now coerce their rivals, defend their interests, and convey critical information over long distances. In this period, British wealth, technology, and

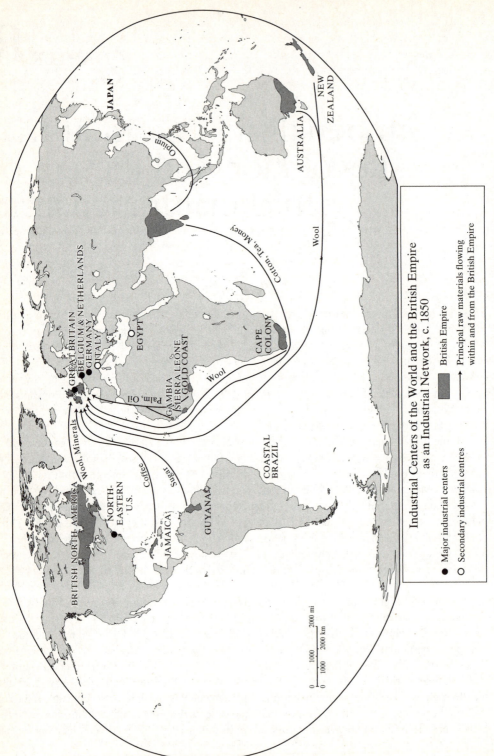

Industrial Centers of the World and the British Empire
as an Industrial Network, c. 1850

● Major industrial centers

○ Secondary industrial centres

British Empire

→ Principal raw materials flowing
within and from the British Empire

Industrial Centers of the World and the British Empire as an Industrial Network, c. 1850

desire for markets were powerful forces in extending British influence across the globe. Although Britain was not without rivals, its dominance as the world's greatest power was not seriously challenged until the last two decades of the nineteenth century.

Historians have long acknowledged British dominance in world affairs in the middle decades of the nineteenth century. Yet they have also argued that the principles of free trade rather than imperial expansion characterized this period. As a result, this era has tended to be viewed as one of relative inactivity in terms of imperial expansion. Sandwiched between the dramatic imperial transformations of the Atlantic revolutions and the period of massive imperial expansion between 1885 and 1914, these decades have often been depicted as the calm between two imperial storms. According to this school of thought, British economic dominance was so complete in this period that the extension of empire was unnecessary—if the British could go where they liked and trade where they pleased without serious rivals, imperial expansion was not needed.

Yet is it accurate to argue that this period was characterized by imperial *inactivity*? Contradicting this interpretation is evidence that even when European states did not pursue active policies of imperial expansion, such expansion nevertheless frequently occurred. Thus, the British completed their territorial expansion on the sub-continent of India and also conquered significant portions of South-East Asia and South Africa in precisely these decades. The French, despite internal difficulties, also expanded their formal empire to include Algeria and Indochina, while the Dutch consolidated their control over Java and its surrounding islands. In addition, British colonists in Canada, Australia, and New Zealand had continental (or island-wide) ambitions for colonial settlement, and in the process forcibly enlarged the British Empire. In the newly created United States, Europeans and their descendants expanded westward all the way to the Pacific Ocean, confiscating indigenous lands as they did so. Finally, alongside these significant

efforts to expand formal empires, European powers—especially the British but also the French—used their wealth and technologies to control and dominate a variety of states throughout the world including Latin America, the Ottoman Empire, and China. Indeed, using methods of *informal imperialism*, European powers sought to impose their economic and political will on these areas without having to resort to the expense of formal colonial conquest.

This chapter charts the enormous amount of imperial activity in the middle decades of the nineteenth century, and argues for its critical importance in the later explosion in formal imperial expansion after 1885. We begin by outlining the debate over the character of the period generally, and then move on to its most important story: the impact of the Industrial Revolution on the ability of Europeans—especially the British—to gain an unprecedented edge over a wide variety of states in this period. Industrial technologies such as the steamship, breech-loading rifle, and telegraph were crucial tools for enhancing the coercive power of European states. Europeans found rival states far more willing to concede demands for trade when those demands were backed by gunboats and repeating rifles. We then move to the phenomenon of informal imperialism, in two ways. First, we discuss it as a type of *culture of imperialism* within Europe. Second, we explain it as a process by which Europeans—again especially the British—exerted significant control over other states without resorting to formal conquest during this middle decades of the nineteenth century. It is in these areas of influence, coercion, market dominance, and preferential concessions that the full extent of European influence can be seen in this period. Finally, we discuss the formal imperial expansion of Britain, France, the Netherlands, and the United States in this period of supposed imperial inactivity. This expansion demonstrates not only that imperialism was alive and well, but also that the huge burst of formal expansion in the late nineteenth century had strong precedents in this earlier, less openly antagonistic, period.

INFORMAL EMPIRE—ANTI-IMPERIALIST OR IMPERIALIST?

This last statement is a significant one, because it defies the orthodox interpretation of western European, U.S., and colonial settler cultures in the middle decades of the nineteenth century as being largely anti-imperial. This has especially been the received view of this period for the British Empire, which has received the bulk of the attention of scholars of imperialism for this period since even before Charles R. Fay apparently coined the phrase *informal empire* in 1934.[1] Before the 1950s, most scholars studying British attitudes toward the empire have depicted them as having alternating periods of imperialist and anti-imperialist sentiments. Following the American Revolution, they argued, British enthusiasm for empire began to sour, and this accelerated in the mid-nineteenth century until it just about disappeared. Underpinning this decline was a switch from empire as an economic tool to *free trade*, in which the British largely came to believe that the global capitalist economy could run best without costly imperial interference. As evidence, they pointed to parliamentary debates and official memoranda in which officials contemplated retreating from far-flung colonies or refused to commit funds to new conquests and to literature and other sources that betrayed a certain weariness with empire-building in Britain.

In 1953, however, two historians named John Gallagher and Ronald Robinson challenged this view. They pointed out that even as these debates were occurring and literature was being published, Britain was engaged in massive expansion in Canada, Australia, India, and elsewhere. Although they focus on policy, rather than sentiment, Gallagher and Robinson suggest that there was no anti-imperial interlude in the mid-nineteenth century, but rather a consistent and continual press for empire.[2] In fact, they argued,

free trade and capitalism were not inconsistent with imperialism, but merely led to a different kind of empire—one that featured gunboats and missionary-merchants more than permanent colonial armies and governing officials, but an empire nevertheless.

This new type of empire featured some formal expansion, but more often British economic objectives in this period were realized as a result of temporary shows of force or the threat of force and interference in the affairs of foreign governments in ways that clearly impeded their sovereignty but did not formally acquire it. Because of this, many scholars have argued that this type of economic expansion represented a distinctive form of domination called *informal empire*.[3] The idea that economic relationships could be considered imperial is still controversial: some scholars argue that the term *informal imperialism* is too vague, or that it assumes too much intent on the part of the dominant state. Others believe that the term encourages the belief that all unequal economic relationships are somehow "imperial."[4]

Notwithstanding these objections, focusing solely on formal imperial expansion provides only a partial view of the extent and importance of European influence around the world in this period.[5] Instead, formal empire co-existed with informal empire, which Jurgen Osterhammel has defined as existing when more powerful states achieve economic advantages for themselves over less powerful states via unequal treaties and legal concessions, as well as by heavy-handed political

---

[1] Charles R. Fay, *Imperial Economy and Its Place in the Formation of Economic Doctrine, 1600–1932* (Oxford: Clarendon, 1934).

[2] John Gallagher and Ronald Robinson, "The Imperialism of Free Trade," *Economic History Review*, New Series, 6 (1953), 1–15.

[3] The first to forward this idea were John Gallagher and Ronald Robinson, in "The Imperialism of Free Trade," *Economic History Review*, Second Series, VI (1953).

[4] One of the most vocal critics of the idea of informal imperialism was D.C.M. Platt, "The Imperialism of Free Trade: Some Reservations," *Economic History Review*, Second Series, XXI (1968); and "Further Objections to an 'Imperialism of Free Trade,' 1830–1860," *Economic History Review*, Second Series, XXVI (1973).

[5] This is, in fact, the main argument in Bernard Semmel, *The Rise of Free Trade Imperialism: Classical Political Economy, the Empire of Free Trade, and Imperialism, 1750–1850* (Cambridge: Cambridge University Press, 2004).

and military interference.[6] Osterhammel further argues that informal empire—as opposed merely to economic dependency—was characterized by a variety of observable features, which could include a legal structure that privileged foreigners, a free trade system imposed by external forces, and the use of intervention either through force or through institutions such as imperial consuls.[7] Using this definition as a guide, one can argue that European—especially British—influence in Latin America, the Ottoman Empire, and China represented a form of imperialism that was clearly related to (if not the same as) formal political control.

INDUSTRY AND EMPIRE

Informal imperialism as defined by Osterhammel could only occur because of shifts in technology and economic production that began in Britain in the eighteenth century, which in turn began to have serious implications around the world in the nineteenth century. Until this period, the ability of Europeans to enforce their will in most of Asia and Africa was limited at best. Unlike indigenous American populations, whose ability to resist had been seriously compromised by epidemic disease, populations in South, South-East, and East Asia as well as in North and sub-Saharan Africa did not suffer similar fates. Instead, the disease regime in those locations tended to work against Europeans, who frequently succumbed to diseases such as malaria, cholera, yellow fever, and dengue fever well into the nineteenth century.[8] Without the advantage of a favorable disease regime, during the early modern period Europeans in Asia and Africa found that they

were simply one more group competing for trading rights and resources in distant lands. Although Europeans had well-equipped ships and knowledge of many of the world's oceans, until the mid-nineteenth century their infantry weapons did not give them a clear technological advantage over potential rivals. As a result, Europeans found it necessary to carefully cultivate alliances with a variety of Asian and African states in order to gain or maintain access to trading posts, territory, or trade goods. With the exception of the British acquisition of Bengal in 1757, until the nineteenth century Europeans were in no position to impose large-scale territorial control in most of Africa or Asia.[9]

In the nineteenth century, however, the relatively tenuous position of Europeans in these regions began to change as a result of the Industrial Revolution.[10] The Industrial Revolution began in Britain in the late eighteenth century, when a series of technological innovations allowed the mechanization of key industries.[11] Among the earliest and most important of these occurred in the textile industry, including the development of Samuel Crompton's spinning mule (1779) and Edward Cartwright's power loom (1785), both of which dramatically increased cotton textile production. Although both the mule and the loom were originally powered by water, by the last decade of the eighteenth century they had been harnessed to James Watt's modified steam engine,

---

[6] Jürgen Osterhammel, "Britain and China," in *The Oxford History of the British Empire*, vol. III, *The Nineteenth Century*, edited by Andrew Porter (Oxford: Oxford University Press, 1999), 148–149.

[7] Ibid., 149.

[8] For a detailed exploration of the effects on Europeans of the disease regime in the tropical world, see Philip Curtin, *Death by Migration: Europe's Encounter with the Tropical World in the Nineteenth Century* (Cambridge: Cambridge University Press, 1989).

[9] Philip Curtin, *The World and the West: The European Challenge and the Overseas Response in the Age of Empire* (Cambridge: Cambridge University Press, 1992), 3.

[10] Daniel Headrick, *The Tentacles of Progress: Technology Transfer in the Age of Imperialism, 1850–1940* (Oxford: Oxford University Press, 1988), 5. For changes in Europeans' attitude toward non-Europeans as a result of the Industrial Revolution, see Michael Adas, *Machines as the Measure of Men: Science, Technology, and Ideologies of Western Dominance* (Ithaca, NY: Cornell University Press, 1990).

[11] One historiographical school, beginning with Eric Williams's *Capitalism and Slavery* (Chapel Hill: University of North Carolina Press, 1944), has long argued that Britain's Industrial Revolution was indebted to the profits made from the sugar islands in the West Indies during the seventeenth and eighteenth centuries. See chapter 4 for this argument.

which was developed in 1765.[12] By the turn of the century, a young boy operating two steam-driven power looms could produce 15 times the cloth of the fastest hand weaver. By 1830, more than half a million Britons worked in the textile industry, many of them in large factories powered by massive steam engines.[13] As a result, the production of finished, inexpensive cotton cloth exploded. The sale of this cloth (among other manufactured items) in both domestic and international markets provided a strong stimulus to British trade around the world.

The use of steam power was crucial to the growth of other industries as well. These included iron production, for which steam provided power for the bellows and rolling mills used in iron smelting and refining. By the end of the eighteenth century, large quantities of inexpensive iron helped fuel the production of industrial machinery, ships, buildings, and bridges.[14] In the early nineteenth century, steam and iron began to be used together in the development of mechanized transportation. In 1815, George Stephenson developed the first steam-powered iron locomotive. Between 1830 and 1870, Britons had already laid about 13,000 miles of railroad, enabling both people and goods to move around the country much faster than ever before. In addition, by 1830 steam engines were successfully adapted to water transport, which allowed ships to travel against the winds and up fast-flowing or previously un-navigable rivers. By the 1830s, the use of steamships had reduced the length of the trip between Britain and India to about a month, down from the five to eight months in the fastest sailing ships of the eighteenth century.[15]

Although many of these technological innovations occurred first in Britain, other areas—especially in the neighboring European continent and the United States—soon began to industrialize as well. By the 1820s, Belgium, parts of France, and parts of the northeastern United States developed regions that focused on the production of coal, iron, or textiles. In the 1840s, German regions also began to produce large amounts of coal and iron. By the middle of the nineteenth century, France, Germany, and the United States had laid thousands of miles of railroad, and had adopted mechanized water transportation as well.[16]

Between 1830 and 1875, technological innovations in western Europe and the United States continued at a dizzying rate. In 1856, the Briton Henry Bessemer developed a blast furnace capable of producing large quantities of inexpensive steel, and in subsequent decades the strong, resilient alloy began to replace iron in tools, buildings, and machines. Like iron before it, steel became one of the primary building blocks of industrialization in the latter half of the nineteenth century. Innovations revolutionized the field of communications as well. In 1838, for example, the American Samuel Morse demonstrated that electromagnetic signals could be transmitted by wire, which then led to the creation of telegraph lines around the United States and many parts of the world by the 1860s. By 1868, an overland telegraphic message could reach from Britain to its colonial territories in India in as little as five days, whereas only a decade earlier news between the two would have taken a month or more via ship.[17]

As the speed of production, transport, and communications increased, technological innovations

---

[12] For an economically technical overview of the Industrial Revolution in Britain, see Donald McCloskey, "The Industrial Revolution 1780–1860: A Survey," in *The Economics of the Industrial Revolution*, edited by Joel Mokyr (Rowman & Littlefield, 1985).

[13] Jerry Bentley and Herbert Ziegler, *Traditions and Encounters: A Global Perspective on the Past*, 4th edition (New York: McGraw-Hill, 2008), 818.

[14] For an overview of the impact of iron in the Industrial Revolution, see Chris Evans, "The Industrial Revolution in Iron in the British Isles," in *The Industrial Revolution in Iron: the Impact of British Coal Technology in Nineteenth Century Europe*, edited by Chris Evans and Goran Ryden (London: Ashgate, 2005).

[15] Headrick, *The Tentacles of Progress*, 20.

[16] For more on the industrialization of other European states, see Peter Stearns, *The Industrial Revolution in World History*, 3rd edition (Boulder, CO: Westview Press, 2007), chapter 3.

[17] Daniel Headrick, *The Invisible Weapon: Telecommunications and International Politics, 1851–1945* (Oxford: Oxford University Press, 1991), 20. In ideal conditions, telegraphic transmissions could travel overland between Britain and India in as little as 24 hours, whereas problems in the line could delay transmission for weeks; Heather Streets, *Martial Races: The Military, Race, and Masculinity in British Imperial Culture, 1857–1914* (Manchester: Manchester University Press, 2004), 30. Prior to 1841, travel to India via ship took approximately two months.

also increased the efficiency of weaponry. During the 1860s, Europeans and Americans developed new weapons that improved both the speed and accuracy of infantry firepower. Until that time, Europeans had equipped their armies with flint-lock muzzle-loading muskets, which could be quite effective when used with well-trained units. Yet Europeans had also traded and sold these muskets to a variety of states in the early modern period, which meant that some African and Asian states employed similar weapons. Others, like the Ottomans and some South-East Asian states, manufactured effective muskets of their own. As a result, Europeans could not always rely on superior infantry firepower. The introduction of breech-loading rifles in the 1860s, however, altered this relative equality in weapons technology.[18] Breech-loading rifles allowed European soldiers to fire six times a minute—a significant improvement over flintlocks, which could only be fired once a minute. In addition, breech-loading rifles were up to eight times more accurate than flintlocks. Now, European armies had a distinct advantage over foreign armies in the non-European world.

By the middle decades of the nineteenth century, the global implications of the Industrial Revolution were becoming clear. Europeans and Americans, led by the British, now had a dramatically increased capacity for mass-producing inexpensive manufactured items, especially textiles. Such large-scale production demanded markets, which entrepreneurs now sought all over the world. With the ability to travel farther and faster via railroads and steamships, few markets seemed too remote to enterprising industrialists. In places where inadequate transportation discouraged penetration into the interior of Africa or continental Asia, steamships could penetrate upriver or railroad networks could be built. To facilitate the transfer of both people and goods in India's interior, for example, by 1870 British companies had laid 5,000 miles of track on the sub-continent.[19]

Mass production in industrializing regions also demanded mass quantities of raw materials, such as cotton for textiles and timber for construction and railways. Moreover, increasing urban populations demanded adequate supplies of meat and grain. To meet these needs, most industrializing nations—with the exception of the United States—had to rely on extra-territorial sources of supply. With the new, faster modes of transport brought about by rail and steam, these sources could be truly global in scope. Indeed, among the many items Britons imported by mid-century were raw cotton from the American South, beef from Argentina, palm oil from West Africa, and tea from China.

All of this is to say that the states that industrialized between 1780 and 1870 had powerful motives for seeking sustained interactions with a wide variety of states and regions all over the world. The mechanization of key industries, the rapid burst of building, and the creation of vast transport networks all demanded raw materials that had to be supplied by foreign sources. In addition, the production of manufactured goods in such volume demanded markets in which they could be sold. While domestic markets were important, they were far too small to consume the quantities of finished goods produced by mechanized industries. As a result, entrepreneurs had to seek profitable markets abroad, anywhere they could find them. By the middle decades of the nineteenth century, industrial means of transport via rail and steamship meant they could go very far indeed in their search.[20]

The possession of industrial transport, communications, and weaponry also allowed Europeans to conduct their negotiations for materials and markets from a position of power.[21] Even when target populations did not wish to sell raw materials or buy finished goods on the terms Europeans proposed, industrial transport and weaponry made resistance difficult: now, Europeans had the means

---

[18] Curtin, *The World and the West*, 27–28.
[19] Robert Kubicek, "British Expansion, Empire, and Technological Change," in Porter, *The Nineteenth Century*, 251.

[20] For more on the restructuring of the world economy as a result of the Industrial Revolution, see Stearns, *The Industrial Revolution in World History*, 81–85.
[21] Kubicek, "British Expansion, Empire, and Technological Change," 248.

to back up their negotiations with the potent threat of force. This *gunboat diplomacy*, as it came to be known, increasingly characterized the ways industrialized states approached economic and political relationships with non-industrialized states in the nineteenth century. Indeed, the technological advantages gained during the Industrial Revolution allowed Europeans to pursue their will far more effectively than in the past.[22] As we shall see, in some instances this ability was expressed in the formal conquest of new territories, while in others informal networks more than sufficed. Both types of cases, however, testified to a global shift in the balance of power toward those nations that industrialized first.

CULTURES OF INFORMAL IMPERIALISM

As a result of its leading role in the Industrial Revolution, the mid-nineteenth century was a time of unprecedented British dominance in global affairs. No state could match its technological power until the last quarter of the century, and its would-be rivals on the continent were often preoccupied with domestic issues for much of this period. This British dominance was reflected in a new economic policy that reversed all the old maxims of protectionist mercantilism in favor of the ideals of **free trade**. This set of policies called for the dropping of tariffs and taxes that restricted the free flow of goods and, later, capital (or money) among countries. In other words, the British government now believed that corporations should be able to buy, sell, and invest wherever they chose and that economic success should be based on which companies could offer the best prices for their goods. It was a decision that made sense for an industrialized society that could produce goods more cheaply than their competitors overseas. As the pre-eminent economic power in

the world, Britons quite literally could afford to promote trade without any of the protective restrictions of the past.[23]

Although this idea of free trade had its roots in the Enlightenment—perhaps best expressed by Adam Smith's *An Enquiry into the Nature and Causes of the Wealth of Nations*—it did not gain wide public purchase until the 1820s, when the international conditions favored it, at least to British eyes. The idea was that state intervention in the economy—via tariffs, protected markets, or trade restrictions—was inefficient and economically disadvantageous.[24] Instead, believers in free trade argued that when individuals consumed and labored in their own interests in a market free of artificial interventions, markets would regulate themselves to the most efficient levels possible. In the new atmosphere of British economic dominance in the early decades of the nineteenth century, reform-minded public crusaders and state officials alike were increasingly determined to dismantle the protectionist policies of British foreign trade in favor of allowing markets to regulate themselves.[25] Thus, between the 1820s and 1840, Britain abandoned its Corn Laws (designed to protect British agriculture from less expensive foreign imports). Outside Britain, trading monopolies in the colonies—notably the East India Company monopoly of the China trade—were also abandoned in this period.

Free trade also made itself felt in the reversal of Britain's role from a major slave transporting and consuming society to a leading abolitionist power. By the second decade of the nineteenth century, not only had Britain banned its citizens from participating in the Atlantic slave trade, but parliament had authorized seizing ships of other powers carrying slaves. By 1834–1835, slaveowning was banned throughout the British Empire. Arguments in favor of abolitionism were

---

[22] There is a growing historiography that addresses the shift in power toward Europe—and especially Britain—as a result of the Industrial Revolution in comparative perspective. See, for starters, Kenneth Pomeranz, *The Great Divergence: China, Europe, and the Making of the Modern World Economy* (Princeton, NJ: Princeton University Press, 2001).

[23] C.A. Bayly, *Imperial Meridian: The British Empire and the World, 1780–1830* (London: Longman, 1989), 237.

[24] For Smith's arguments in full, see the reprint entitled *Wealth of Nations*, 3rd edition (Amherst, NY: Prometheus Books, 1991).

[25] John Patrick Tuer Bury, *The New Cambridge Modern History* (Cambridge: Cambridge University Press, 1960), 342.

based partly in support for free trade (and free labor) as a more efficient system than slavery. Yet perhaps more importantly, abolition was a cultural expression of two shifts within British society. First, it signaled the rise of a new elite—the factory owners and financiers of the Industrial Revolution—who used it to attack the power of the old aristocratic slave-owning classes with whom they were competing. They did so not only in political and economic terms, but also in moral terms. This was expressed by the rise of evangelical societies within the Christian sects to which these new wealthy and middle-class families tended to belong—the Quakers, Methodists, and Baptists, for example. Such sects preached that free trade and free labor were not only more efficient but more moral than slavery.[26] A second important shift was the movement of working-class Britons to oppose slavery and the slave trade. By early in the nineteenth century, British public opinion had quite firmly shifted against slavery and toward a sense of a British duty to end it.[27]

Both of these shifts reflect a transition toward a new cultural idea of "Britishness" that was wrapped up in the promotion of "middle-class" values. Simply put, the rise of the industrial classes and the unparalleled power of Britain fed the nationalist idea that Britain was the height of "civilization." This encompassed a number of ideas. One of these was the elevation of middle-class views of British domesticity, especially the idea of the stable family headed by a free labor-working father with democratic political rights, supported by a subordinate mother who ran the household at home, and containing disciplined children. This was promoted as the perfect family.[28] Similarity, they developed ideals of a British "morality" based on free male labor, female child-rearing, and a sense of propriety. Those families who conformed earned "British" rights like democratic participation, and even those who could not were to be given aid of some sort as a "humanitarian" duty.

These ideals were embraced by the middle class as proof of their domestic superiority over the old nobility. They were aspired to by the lower classes as evidence of their own worth. Finally, they came to be exported overseas through several mechanisms. The first was abolition. A second was missionary activity, by which not only the new Christianity and humanitarian aid but also middle-class values could be brought to the far corners of the empire and beyond. Through missionaries from Britain (and later France and the United States), not only Jesus but also a whole cultural package could be exported abroad. This included "free trade," for the missionaries brought with them their belief in the redemptive power of the domestic family and the laboring father possessing a waged job, an entrepreneurial activity, or a small farm. Thus, missionaries quickly became involved in commerce and in re-engineering societies to fit their own vision of a moral society.[29] Nor were these ideas only expressed in religious terms. In the British Empire and to an even greater degree the French Empire, the revolution had left a secular republic and the idea of the civilizing power of industrial technology. Thus, infrastructure like roads and railroads, and exporting British or French culture became a powerful additional stimulus to and justification for investment and interference abroad in this period.

In this way, ideas that might seem to be anti-imperial in theory—abolition, humanitarianism,

[26] See Roger Anstey, "The Pattern of British Abolitionism in the Eighteenth and Nineteenth Centuries," in *Anti–slavery, Religion, and Reform: Essays in Memory of Roger Anstey*, edited by Christine Bolt and Seymour Drescher (Folkstone: W.Dawson, 1980). Also by the same author "Religion and British Slave Emancipation," in *The Abolition of the Atlantic Slave Trade*, edited by David Eltis and James Walvin (Madison: University of Wisconsin Press, 1981).

[27] Seymour Drescher, "Whose Abolition? Popular Pressure and the Ending of the British Slave Trade," *Past and Present*, 143 (1994), 136–166.

[28] For examples of how this operated, see Catherine Hall, *Civilising Subjects: Metropole and Colony in the English Imagination, 1830–1867* (Chicago: University of Chicago Press, 2002).

[29] Brian Stanley, "'Commerce and Christianity': Providence Theory, the Missionary Movement, and the Imperialism of Free Trade, 1842–1860," *Historical Journal*, 26 (1983), 71–94.

morality—could in fact support imperial activity. Gunboat diplomacy in China or Latin America, for example, could be portrayed not as imposing the will of the more powerful but as shepherding backward societies into the civilized world. Missionaries could aid European companies in taking over the economies of Algeria or Indonesia as a means to help raise them into the brotherhood of men. Finally, the occupation of parts of East Africa could win popular support in Britain as a means of ending the slave trade there. Beneath it all was the combining of free trade, humanitarianism, and abolition in what could arguably be described as a unified culture of imperialism. While certainly not every member of society embraced this urge, or understood it in the same way, nevertheless it became a dominant cultural ideal in the mid-nineteenth century.

INFORMAL IMPERIALISM IN ACTION

Overseas, this culture of imperialism operated in several ways, but with economic factors usually at the fore. Having pulled down trade barriers in Britain and its colonies, British merchants and state representatives also sought to remove similar barriers imposed by other states. The motives for this were urgent: Britons required steady supplies of raw materials at the best possible prices to feed their growing industries, and they wanted unfettered markets in which to sell their vast quantities of finished products.[30] Thus, securing "free trade" agreements with all states and regions that attracted British economic interests became a top priority for merchants and government officials alike. However, since one of the primary goals of British activity abroad was to secure economic markets, formal conquest was often considered unnecessary. In fact, many British statesmen believed that conquest was downright undesirable, provided British economic goals could be achieved without it. Hence the development of informal empire.

The earliest proponents of the concept of informal imperialism and informal empire focused on its impact on European influence in Latin America.[31] When nearly all the states of Latin America broke free from Spanish control during the second and third decades of the nineteenth century, British statesmen and merchants looked hungrily to the new states as vast potential markets for British goods. As we have already seen, the Spanish tightly restricted trade with Latin America, and sought to preserve its lucrative exports and markets for itself. With independence, however, Britons envisioned huge new markets for their finished manufactured items. Indeed, the desire to wrest Latin America from the grip of Spanish economic control had formed part of the rationale behind Britain's tacit—and sometimes open—support of Latin American revolutionaries. In 1824, Britons were optimistic that their efforts had paid off: according to British cabinet minister George Canning, Britons could rejoice that "Spanish America is free; and if we do not mismanage our affairs sadly, *she is English.*"[32]

As Spanish control disappeared, British diplomats rushed in to capture the markets of Latin America by signing commercial treaties with the elite creole leaders of a wide variety of states.[33] Subsequently, British goods and investments poured into Latin America. As early as the 1820s, 13% of British exports—three quarters of them textiles—went to Latin America.[34] In the two decades between 1840 and 1860, the value of British exports tripled from £5 million to £14 million, and these numbers only continued to rise until the beginning of the twentieth century. British imports from Latin America also increased rapidly over the course of the century,

---

[30] Semmel, *The Rise of Free Trade Imperialism*, 218.

[31] Gallagher and Robinson, "The Imperialism of Free Trade," 1953.

[32] Quoted in Peter Winn, "British Informal Empire in Uruguay in the Nineteenth Century," *Past and Present*, 73 (November 1976), 102. Italics added.

[33] Robert D. Aguirre, *Informal Empire: Mexico and Central America in Victorian Culture* (Minneapolis: University of Minnesota Press, 2005), xx.

[34] Alan Knight, "Britain and Latin America," in Porter, *The Nineteenth Century*, 127.

and strong British markets for raw materials encouraged the newly independent states to specialize in single products—such as wool, cattle, and timber—for export. Along with exports and imports, British investment in Latin America rose steadily—from £81 million in 1860 to £1,181 million in 1913—throughout the nineteenth century, particularly in Argentina, Brazil, and Mexico. Argentina, in fact, took as much British investment as its actual colonies in Australia and South Africa.[35] While the form of these investments began as shares in government bonds, after 1860 they increasingly took shape as direct investments in railroads, public utilities, insurance companies, and banking.[36] In practical terms, as was the case in Uruguay by 1880, this meant that in some places nearly all infrastructure and large-scale commercial enterprise were controlled by Britons. As the British minister to Uruguay claimed in 1881, "All the industrial enterprises in this country which are of any importance are in English hands. Railways, Tramways, Banks, Docks and … Gas and Water supplies, have been established by English capital, and are managed by Englishmen."[37]

Control over the transportation and financial infrastructures in countries such as Uruguay, Argentina, Brazil, and Mexico placed Britons—both diplomats and businessmen—in positions of power. Control of the railways, for example, meant that British companies could fix freight charges at very high rates without regard for competition. High freight charges, in turn, ensured that farmers and entrepreneurs who produced inexpensive raw materials or manufactured goods for the domestic market were unable to afford to ship their goods via rail. As a result, internal domestic markets remained small, local, and undeveloped, and were unable to compete with inexpensive British manufactured items shipped from abroad. At the same time, those who produced lucrative items that would sell well on the international market were able to afford the high

freight charges. Thus, control over the railways helped to stimulate the production of raw materials destined for the international market dominated by Britons, and simultaneously helped to stifle domestic markets that might compete with British imports.[38]

In addition to intensive involvement in the economies of many Latin American states, the British government also proved willing to intervene directly in political matters. This was especially true in the first few decades after Latin American independence, particularly between 1820 and 1850. For example, when Brazil and Argentina came to blows over rights to the territory of the Banda Oriental in the 1820s, the British government used its authority and power to essentially create an entirely new state in the disputed area: Uruguay. In 1833, a dispute between Britain and Argentina over the ownership of the Falkland Islands led the British government to use the Royal Navy to take the islands by force.[39] In 1845, Britain joined with France to blockade the Argentine port of Buenos Aires as part of a larger (unsuccessful) effort to defeat the anti-European forces of Juan Manuel de Rosas. The reasons were clear: to protect British economic interests and investments in the country. As a Foreign Office memorandum put it in 1842, "inasmuch as the commercial interests of Great Britain are so mixed up with her Political strength, … it becomes necessary to support the one in order to maintain the other."[40] In 1859, the British government used the Royal Navy once again, this time to intimidate the Mexican government to pay the outstanding interest on its debts to British investors.[41] Moreover, in the decades following Britain's abolition of the slave trade in 1807, the British frequently used the Royal Navy to interfere with slave ships destined for Brazil. With the largest and most powerful navy in the

---

[35] Ibid., 135.
[36] Ibid.
[37] Quoted in Winn, "British Informal Empire," 112.

[38] Ibid., 118.
[39] Sharon Korman, *The Right of Conquest: The Acquisition of Territory by Force in International Law and Practice* (Oxford: Oxford University Press, 1996), 105.
[40] Quoted in Winn, "British Informal Empire," 106; and Knight, "Britain and Latin America," 130.
[41] Aguirre, *Informal Empire*, xix.

world, there was little the Brazilian government could do to stop them. Clearly, then, there were numerous occasions on which the British intervened in the affairs of Latin American countries that would have been intolerable between two equally sovereign states. Although these interventions were justified in terms of maintaining "free" trade, the naked use of force in this period frequently demonstrated that Anglo-Latin American trade was far more "free" for Britons than it was for Latin Americans.

After 1860, there were fewer occasions on which the British found it necessary to intervene so violently in Latin American affairs. This was not because Latin America ceased to be economically important to Britain: on the contrary, as we know, British trade with and investment in the region grew steadily over the course of the nineteenth century. Instead, British influence had been so successful among the elite ruling classes of Latin America that there was little need to use force to gain their cooperation in this period. In Latin America, British economic influence was often accompanied by British cultural influence, in which Latin American elites absorbed British values and games along with the dictums of free trade. As a result, by 1860 many Latin American leaders had grown to accept the need for British-style "free trade," especially because collaboration with Britons was often quite lucrative for the ruling classes.[42]

Moreover, even if Britons had been inclined to intervene directly in Latin American affairs after 1860, by then it was increasingly clear that the United States viewed Latin America as a region of special strategic concern. In 1823, the U.S. government had issued the Monroe Doctrine as an explicit statement of its antagonism toward any European power that pursued an active policy of colonization in Latin America or the Caribbean. Outwardly anti-imperialist, this policy in fact helped to establish something of an informal empire for the United States itself. Although the doctrine had few teeth at first, by the 1840s the British government had come to accept that

military intervention in Latin America would be taken as an act of aggression against the United States.[43] As a result, such intervention was increasingly discarded as a viable option. Instead, Britain remained committed to securing trade agreements and investment projects on terms that would serve its economic interests. In doing so, it created a series of relationships that constituted more than simple dependency: rather, these relationships frequently limited the power of Latin American leaders to act independently and in the interests of their own countries.[44] By the last two decades of the century, this problem was compounded by increasing competition from other newly industrialized states—including France, Germany, and the United States itself—who sought similar economic influence in the region. Thus, the informal imperialism pioneered by the British in the middle decades of the nineteenth century did not disappear after 1880, but instead was extended to include more Euro-American competitors for Latin American markets.[45]

Although historians focused first on Latin America as the quintessential example of informal imperialism, an even stronger case can be made for its practice in the Ottoman Empire and China. Indeed, European influence in both areas relied far more on explicit arrangements such as treaties, legal concessions, and consular systems. Such official structures were necessary because both empires—in spite of increasing internal weakness as well as external pressures—were populous and extensive, and had well-developed markets, imperial institutions, and state traditions. As a result, even in their weakened state they were better equipped to resist European attempts to manipulate their economies and their political

---

[42] Knight, "Britain and Latin America," 134.

[43] Frederick Stirton Weaver, *Latin America in the World Economy: Mercantile Colonialism to Global Capitalism* (Boulder, CO: Westview Press, 2000), 45.
[44] Tony Smith, *The Pattern of Imperialism: The United States, Great Britain, and the Late-Industrializing World Since 1815* (Cambridge: Cambridge University Press Archive, 1981), 23–24.
[45] Knight, "Britain and Latin America," 142–144. For the German competition, see Ian L.D. Forbes, "German Informal Imperialism in South America Before 1914," *Economic History Review*, New Series, 31:3 (August 1978).

institutions than the newly created Latin American states. Furthermore, Europeans had a legacy of relations with both the Ottoman Empire and Qing China that preceded their new-found power as industrial states. In these relationships, Europeans had had to play by the rules set down by strong empires, and had been compelled to operate through state channels in order to be heard. As the power dynamic shifted toward Europeans during the Industrial Revolution, negotiations with both states continued to be conducted through official channels and through legal concessions rather than through ad hoc arrangements with like-minded elites.

From a European perspective, both empires were worth sustained efforts to win such concessions. The Ottoman Empire, with its vast Mediterranean territories in Europe, West Asia, and North Africa, occupied a critical strategic area, promised vast potential markets for European industrial goods, and controlled valuable exports in silks, cereals, opium, and raw cotton. China, while of less concern for its strategic value, nevertheless controlled the finest exports in silk, tea, and porcelain in the world. Moreover, with a population of over 400 million in the mid-nineteenth century, China presented dream-like possibilities as an insatiable market for European textiles and other manufactures.[46]

As in Latin America, the British played a leading role in the extension of European influence in both the Ottoman and Chinese empires during this period. Given the stakes involved, however, other states also vigorously sought to receive a share of the potential rewards. Foremost among these was France, whose government continued to compete with British influence even in the midst of its own crises at home. In addition, by the end of the century Russia, Germany, Japan, and the United States also sought to gain influence in one or the other empire. In spite of these competing interests—which became more significant by the end of the century—neither the Ottoman

nor the Chinese empires were made to submit to formal imperial rule by a foreign power. In the first place, conquest of either empire would have been extremely difficult given the size and structure of both, and thus any attempt to do so would have required huge sums of money as well as a lengthy, expensive period of pacification. Second, the most powerful industrial states involved—especially Britain—were prepared to use every means at their disposal to keep such an event from happening. The British government, in short, neither wanted to conquer either empire for itself, nor did it wish any other power to do so. Rather, British strategy was to prop up both imperial structures sufficiently to allow them to persist, while all the time profiting handsomely from an enforced official policy of "free" trade.

British interest in the Ottoman Empire stemmed from its mid-nineteenth-century foreign policy that, among other things, sought to establish "paramountcy" in the Mediterranean. Using its recently acquired industrial power, successive British governments sought to keep the Mediterranean safe for international commerce and, at the same time, to thwart French and Russian interests in the region.[47] By the early nineteenth century, the safety and integrity of the Ottoman Empire—and thus the security of the Mediterranean—had become a grave concern to the British government, for internal pressures threatened to collapse it from within. Attempts by the Ottoman Sultans at reform met with fierce resistance by entrenched interests within the empire, and various conquered provinces seized upon the disarray in order to assert greater autonomy.[48] Such was the case with the Ottoman general Muhammad Ali who, in 1805, seized control of Egypt and began to rule it as an autonomous region. In fact, Ali became so autonomous that he began threatening other Ottoman territories. When he invaded and conquered Syria in 1831, it quickly became clear that Ottoman forces were no match for him. Faced with such a potent threat, Sultan Mahmud II

[46] Timothy Parsons, *The British Imperial Century, 1815–1914: A World History Perspective* (Lanham, MD: Rowman & Littlefield, 1999), 92.

[47] Bayly, *Imperial Meridian*, 104.
[48] Donald Quataert, *The Ottoman Empire, 1700–1922* (Cambridge: Cambridge University Press, 2005), 55.

turned to the British for help.[49] Britain, with its strong desire to maintain Mediterranean security, had no desire to see the Ottoman Empire dismantled. As a result, the British government consented to use its forces to drive Muhammad Ali out of Syria. The cost to the Ottomans, however, was steep: from that point, the British viewed themselves as Ottoman "tutors" who would keep the empire intact while leading it to modernity.[50]

One aspect of the new era included, predictably, the insistence that the Ottoman Sultans open the empire to free trade. Historically, Europeans had maintained a long tradition of trade with the Ottoman Empire. In the early modern period, this trade was lucrative enough that Ottoman Sultans had allowed foreigners special privileges in established trading posts within the empire.[51] Within these trading posts, Ottomans left matters of law, religion, and discipline up to the foreign representatives who controlled them. Foreign traders at these posts then operated through Ottoman intermediaries—often Jews or Christians—to obtain items for export. In effect, these concessions allowed foreigners extraterritorial rights within established areas, and minimized foreign interaction with Muslim populations. By the first decades of the nineteenth century, however, it was becoming clear to increasingly embattled Ottoman emperors that foreign trade was placing undue strain on the Ottoman economy. Inexpensive manufactured items, especially from Britain, threatened to flood the market and undermine Ottoman handicraft industries. In response, in the 1820s the Ottoman government sought to bolster the empire's economy by restricting foreign trade. Their strategies included limiting exports to foreign traders, placing high tariffs on imports, controlling the movements of foreign merchants, and establishing state monopolies on key commodities.[52]

In light of Britain's desire to open the world to free trade in this period, it is not surprising that Ottoman restrictive measures were considered particularly unacceptable to both the British government and British merchants. Thus, when the Sultan asked for British assistance in ridding Syria of its Egyptian invaders, British aid came with the condition that these protectionist measures be dismantled.[53] The Sultan had little choice but to agree: in 1838, he signed the Convention of Balta Liman, which abolished state monopolies and fixed foreign import tariffs at only 3%. Henceforth, foreign traders—led by the British—had virtually free reign in Ottoman territories, which now had one of the most liberal trade policies in the world.[54] In addition, foreigners continued to manipulate the historic trade concessions (called **capitulations**) that granted them extraterritoriality and placed them outside the bounds of Ottoman law.[55] To increase their influence even further, European traders took to the practice of granting citizenship to their Jewish and Christian trading partners, which effectively placed them above Ottoman law as well.[56]

With the abolition of state monopolies, Ottoman Sultans lost an effective means of raising money to finance government institutions and projects. Yet given the unrest within the empire, the looming specter of foreign intervention, and then the expense of the Crimean War in 1854–1856, money—for modernizing the army, for improvements to infrastructure—was crucial.[57] In the absence of state monopolies, then, Ottoman Sultans increasingly borrowed from foreign sources—especially Britain and France. Britain issued its first major loan to the Ottoman government in 1854: over the next two decades, 13 more

[49] Parsons, *The British Imperial Century*, 107–108.
[50] Ibid., 108.
[51] Halil Inalcik, Suraiya Faroqhi, Donald Quataert, Bruce McGowan, and Sevket Pamuk, eds., *An Economic and Social History of the Ottoman Empire* (Cambridge: Cambridge University Press, 1997), 728–729.
[52] Parsons, *The British Imperial Century*, 108–109.

[53] Inalcik et al., *An Economic and Social History of the Ottoman Empire*, 764.
[54] Ibid., 826.
[55] Martin Lynn, "British Policy, Trade, and Informal Empire in the Mid-Nineteenth Century," in Porter, *The Nineteenth Century*, 112.
[56] This practice also had the effect of accentuating already-latent tensions between non-Muslims and Muslims in the Ottoman Empire.
[57] Roger Owen, *The Middle East in the World Economy, 1800–1914*, 2nd edition (London: I.B. Tauris, 1993), 100.

followed.[58] France likewise became deeply involved in Ottoman lending, frequently in conjunction with Britain. Indeed, by the end of the nineteenth century French investors held 50% of the Ottoman debt.[59] Both Britain and France became so involved in Ottoman financial solvency that, in 1854, they jointly created the Ottoman Bank (later called the Imperial Ottoman Bank) in order to issue Ottoman currency.[60] In the early 1870s, the Ottoman government was so hopelessly indebted to foreign banks that it was forced to take further loans just to make payments on the interest. By the middle of the decade, it could not even manage the interest, and in 1876 it stopped almost all cash payments on its loans entirely.[61] Although the government tried to declare formal bankruptcy in 1879, its creditors were unwilling to accept this position. Instead, in 1881 Britain and France joined together to manage the finances of the empire through the Ottoman Public Debt Commission.[62] Through this commission—which was in operation until 1914—foreigners took control of tribute from Ottoman territories as well as all taxes and tariffs on key items such as tobacco, silk, and salt in order to repay the Ottoman Empire's creditors in Britain and France. In the process, the Ottoman government was deprived of nearly a quarter of its total annual revenues, further weakening the empire's sovereignty.[63]

Despite the intense involvement of European powers in the internal economic and political affairs of the Ottoman Empire, neither Britain nor France wished to see it dismantled entirely.[64] From their perspective, the security of the Mediterranean as well their investments would best be protected by maintaining the integrity of the empire rather than letting it be demolished. Indeed, the integrity of the empire was so important to the British government that it was prepared to go to war to defend it against those powers that would tear it apart.[65] Foremost among the latter was Russia, who long desired access to a warm water port on the Mediterranean, and hoped to exploit Ottoman weakness to obtain one. In 1854, the Russians invaded Ottoman provinces in Romania on the pretext of protecting Orthodox Christians. Britain and France, fearing the consequences of a Russian victory, joined forces against the Russians, and fought for two years to keep the Russians from tearing apart the empire. Although the Crimean War was poorly fought and even more poorly managed on all sides, by 1856 the Anglo-French forces had secured a marginal victory, thus staving off the Russian threat for the time being.[66]

The informal imperial relationships pursued by both Britain and France in Ottoman territories were pursued with equal vigor by both powers in Egypt. Although Egypt was nominally part of the Ottoman Empire, in the early nineteenth century Muhammad Ali had transformed it, de facto, into an autonomous province. To cement this autonomy, Ali and his successors embarked upon an ambitious modernization campaign to bring western-style infrastructure and military reforms to the region. This included, among other things, concessions to a British company to build railways as well as concessions to a French company to build what would become, at its completion in 1869, the Suez Canal.[67] By mid-century, this campaign was increasingly financed with foreign—especially British and French—loans borrowed on Egyptian cotton futures. Egypt's Nile River Valley had proven a fertile region for the production of cotton, and when the American Civil War

---

[58] Lynn, "British Policy, Trade, and Informal Empire," 112.
[59] L. Bruce Fulton, "France and the End of the Ottoman Empire," in *The Great Powers and the End of the Ottoman Empire*, edited by Marian Kent (London: Routledge, 1996), 141.
[60] Owen, *The Middle East in the World Economy*, 103.
[61] Ibid., 108.
[62] Ibid., 191.
[63] Parsons, *The British Imperial Century*, 111.
[64] Quataert, *The Ottoman Empire*, 56.

[65] Andrew Lambert, *The Crimean War: British Grand Strategy, 1853–56* (Manchester: Manchester University Press, 1991), xx–xxi.
[66] For a detailed account of the causes and events of the Crimean War, see Trevor Royle, *Crimea: The Great Crimean War, 1854–56* (London: Palgrave Macmillan, 2004).
[67] For an account of the arrangements surrounding the concessions to build the Suez, see Rondo E. Cameron and Mark Casson, *France and the Economic Development of Europe, 1800–1914: Evolution of Modern Business, 1800–1945* (London: Routledge, 2000), 472.

caused the worldwide cotton supply to decrease, the price of Egyptian cotton rose dramatically. However, when American cotton returned to the market after the war's end in 1865, the resulting drop in cotton prices threw the Egyptian government into a vicious cycle of debt. Shortly afterward, British interest in Egypt spiked as the newly completed Suez Canal turned out to be the quickest and most important route between Britain and India.[68] Thereafter, the British government regarded the protection of Suez as a core part of its overall foreign policy. Thus, when the nearly bankrupt Egyptian government offered to sell its 44% share in the Canal, the British snapped it up immediately.[69] Now, one of the world's most important waterways was owned and run completely by foreigners. Yet the sale could not even begin to stem the tide of Egypt's financial ruin. In 1876, Egypt went bankrupt along with the rest of the Ottoman Empire and, like the Ottoman Sultans, Egypt's leaders were forced to surrender control of its financial affairs to Europeans.[70] Only a few years later, in 1882, the British government dispensed with the pretense of Egyptian sovereignty and occupied the country in order to ensure the security of the Suez Canal.

Clearly, even though European powers did not formally dismember and conquer the Ottoman Empire—with the exception of Egypt in 1882—it is difficult to understand the nature of Euro–Ottoman relations without reference to informal imperialism. By the middle of the nineteenth century, Ottoman sovereignty was severely impaired. Foreigners claimed extra-territorial rights that held them above the law, "free" trade was imposed by these same foreigners by coercion, Ottoman Sultans no longer controlled the empire's finances and debt, and outsiders even fought Ottoman battles for them. Thus, while the Ottoman Empire still appeared to exist as a sovereign entity on paper, over the course of the nineteenth century the ability of its government to

determine the future of the empire was increasingly subordinated to the will of foreigners from the newly industrialized west.

A similar situation occurred in China. As we saw in chapter 3, for centuries Europeans had longed to tap into the vast markets of China in order to obtain silk, tea, and porcelain. Yet through the early modern period, with the exception of American silver, the Chinese had little need of European goods or products. Even by the early nineteenth century, the Chinese remained resolutely unenthusiastic about European manufactured items, and thus maintained a highly favorable balance of trade with the west.[71] European commercial frustrations in China were accentuated by the Qing Empire's trade policies and attitude toward foreigners. The Qing disdained the influence of westerners—whom they called *barbarians*—and sought to rigidly control their movements and livelihoods in China. All European traders, therefore, were confined to trading houses in the southern city of Canton. They had no rights, and were not allowed to broker trade deals on their own. Instead, they had to rely on Chinese middlemen, called *Hongs*, to acquire Chinese trade goods. In addition, European merchants were not allowed to interact with the general Chinese population in Canton, and they were forbidden to learn Chinese. With foreigners limited to such a small area, Chinese officials were able to keep an eye on their transactions as well as their potential for negatively influencing Chinese citizens. Moreover, since foreign trade was not crucial to the Chinese economy, Chinese officials levied heavy tariffs and other fees on both imports and exports.[72]

While these policies were extremely irksome to Europeans—especially those, like the British, who had begun to tout the benefits of free trade— in the early decades of the nineteenth century there was little to be done about it. Even though the Qing Empire had been weakened during the

---

[68] Ironically, the British had strongly protested the building of the canal because they did not want competition from the French over transport routes in the country. Ibid., 474–475.
[69] Parsons, *The British Imperial Century*, 112.
[70] Lynn, "Policy, Trade, and Informal Empire," 113.

[71] To understand the Chinese perspective on foreign trade before 1850, see R. Bin Wong, *China Transformed: Historical Change and the Limits of European Experience* (Ithaca, NY: Cornell University Press, 1997), 142–149.
[72] Parsons, *The British Imperial Century*, 93.

eighteenth century as a result of internal tensions and population pressure, it was still far too large and strong a state to challenge outright. In any case, few Europeans with interests in China considered conquest as a viable option throughout most of the nineteenth century: such an undertaking would have been extremely difficult, liable to failure, and prohibitively expensive. What Europeans wanted most of all was not territory but trade, and thus their goal was to seek free access to Chinese markets rather than territorial rule.

Although the Chinese remained resistant to the charms of most European manufactured items, in the late eighteenth century British merchants succeeded in finding a product that Chinese consumers would buy: opium. This opium was produced in India and was traded, along with ivory, cotton, and sandalwood, under a monopoly held by the British East India Company (EIC). Once the opium and other Indian products were sold in China, the EIC used the profits to purchase Chinese tea, silk, and porcelain for the British market. Although opium was illegal to buy or sell in China and thus had to be smuggled into the state, its profits made it worth the risks. By 1828, the EIC profits from the opium trade alone paid for the entire British investment in Chinese tea in that year.[73] So profitable was this trade, in fact, that the Chinese international balance of trade shifted from a $26 million surplus in the 1810s to a nearly $40 million deficit in the 1830s.[74]

The profitability of opium was not lost on British advocates of free trade. In 1833, they successfully lobbied to break the EIC's monopoly, after which a variety of private companies began trading in the drug. Thereafter, the already-booming opium trade grew even faster: 35,445 chests of opium weighing 150 pounds each were imported into China by 1835, compared to 9,708 in 1820. Lin Zexu, the Chinese official charged in 1838 with investigating the harmful effects of such widespread opium use in China, estimated

that Chinese users smoked over 100 million taels worth of opium that year, while the entire Chinese government expenditures for the year totaled only 40 million taels.[75] Faced with such a serious problem, in 1839 the Chinese government decided to crack down. In March of that year, Lin Zexu went to Canton and promptly arrested dealers and their accomplices, executed addicts, and destroyed over 20,000 crates of opium.[76] He then closed Canton to all foreign traders so they could not resume their illegal trade in the future.

British merchants in China and their supporters in Britain were outraged. Preferring to ignore the illegality of the opium trade in China, these Britons urged the British government to retaliate against the Chinese in defense of the principles of free trade. Armed with steamships, superior weaponry, and British-led Indian troops, between 1839 and 1842 the British Royal Navy inflicted defeat after defeat on Chinese ports and cities. At one point, the newly built iron-clad steamship *Nemesis* single-handedly defeated an opposing force of 15 Chinese junks.[77] When British steamships finally blockaded the Grand Canal—China's most important inland waterway—the Chinese government sued for peace.[78]

Recognizing British military superiority over Chinese imperial defenses, both Britons and Chinese realized that Sino–British relations would never be the same. Indeed, the Treaty of Nanjing that marked the end of the First Opium War in China also marked the beginning of British informal imperialism in that country. Although Britons could not obtain everything they wanted from the Chinese, the resulting settlement permanently abandoned the strict trade regulations of the past. In addition to a large indemnity to pay for British damages (including the loss of opium stores), four new trading ports were opened to foreign trade,[79] import tariffs were

---

[73] Hunt Janin, *The India-China Opium Trade in the Nineteenth Century* (Jefferson, NC: McFarland, 1999), 39.
[74] Parsons, *The British Imperial Century*, 98.

[75] Frank Sanello, *The Opium Wars: The Addiction of One Empire and the Corruption of Another* (Naperville, IL: Sourcebooks, Inc., 2004), 38.
[76] Ibid., 55.
[77] Adas, *Machines as the Measure of Men*, 186.
[78] Parsons, *The British Imperial Century*, 98.
[79] These were Shanghai, Ningpo, Foochow, and Amoy.

set at 5%, and the island of Hong Kong was ceded to Britain.[80] As in the Ottoman Empire, British citizens were also granted extra-territoriality, which meant that they were no longer subject to Chinese law. Fourteen years later, tensions between the Qing government and foreign traders erupted—on a very thin pretext—into a second war. This time, however, British and French interests in China joined together to defend European trade. By the time the Arrow War was over in 1860, Europeans had forced even further concessions from the Chinese. Thereafter, 10 new ports were opened to foreign trade, and all westerners were allowed to move around freely within China.[81] So one-sided were these treaties that, cumulatively, they became known in China as the Unequal Treaties. The Chinese discovered that Europeans—confident now in their military ability to impose their will—were prepared to enforce their newly won free trade arrangements through violence.[82]

The treaties were only the beginning. In the 1860s, the British created an institutional apparatus to support their economic and political activities in the treaty ports and beyond. In the economic sphere, in 1863 Sir Robert Hart created the Chinese Imperial Maritime Customs (IMC) department.[83] Although the IMC was actually a branch of the Chinese government and its chief was responsible to the emperor, it was both headed and mainly staffed by highly paid Britons.[84] Its chief purpose was to ensure the proper assessment and collection of customs duties on foreign trade in coastal Chinese cities, which it did extremely efficiently. It also greased the wheels of trade by improving harbors and shipping lanes and by disseminating commercial information. The IMC did not exert financial control over the Chinese government, but rather upheld both the principle and the practice of free trade in China in two ways: by making sure the Chinese government did not impose illegal tariffs and by providing logistical support to foreign traders.[85] For most of the nineteenth century, however, those who gained most from this institution were those who had the largest interest in the China trade: the British. The IMC also provided critical support for the ailing Qing Dynasty, for by the end of the century its collections provided the government with one-fifth of its total annual revenues.[86]

The economic presence of the IMC was complemented by a political arm: the British consular system. The function of the consuls was to ensure that the Chinese and the British upheld both the spirit and the law of the treaty system. In 1869, the British Foreign Office decided that a consul should be appointed to every city in which the IMC had a commissioner. Given that the IMC operated in approximately 40 cities, the British consular network—and its supervision of affairs in coastal cities—grew to be one of the biggest in the world.[87] Meanwhile, the treaty ports themselves grew into what Jürgen Osterhammel calls *micro-colonies*.[88] Within these micro-colonies, foreigners created small, self-governing islands of sociability and commercial activity.[89] They were supported by diplomatic consular intermediaries as well as the judicious treaty enforcement provided by the IMC. They were able to move around freely within China without being subject to laws other than their own, and they were able to trade on terms that were clearly beneficial to themselves. Moreover, investments—in railroads, shipping, and other industries—flowed into China from Britain, extending British influence from the treaty ports further inland.

Yet as in the Ottoman Empire, the British did not favor the extension of these micro-colonies into widespread formal imperial control. Having gotten

---

[80] Parsons, *The British Imperial Century*, 98–99. For a detailed explanation of commercial and political aspects of the Treaty, see John King Fairbank, *Trade and Diplomacy on the China Coast: The Opening of the Treaty Ports, 1842–54* (Stanford: Stanford University Press, 1969), chapters 8 and 9.

[81] Osterhammel, "Britain and China," 146.

[82] Ibid., 154.

[83] Lynn, "British Policy, Trade, and Informal Empire," 111.

[84] Osterhammel, "Britain and China," 156.

[85] Ibid., 157.

[86] Parsons, *The British Imperial Century*, 100.

[87] Osterhammel, "Britain and China," 155–156.

[88] Ibid., 149.

[89] For more on the character of British settlements in the treaty ports, see Robert Bickers, *Britain in China: Community Culture in Colonialism, 1900–1949* (Manchester: Manchester University Press, 1999), chapter 3.

what they wanted in terms of trade, they were content to help maintain the Qing government and to defend it against internal enemies as long as it remained open to British guidance.[90] This situation only began to change after 1880 when, as in Latin America, competition from other European states as well as the United States and Japan grew ever more fierce. The result was an increase in formal expressions of foreign control in China—especially in clearly demarcated "spheres of influence," in which competing nations carved out their own slice of China. Although these spheres of influence never became formal colonies, they increasingly blurred the line between informal and formal imperial control.

While the British led the way in informal imperial influence during the middle decades of the nineteenth century, they were by no means alone. Other industrial powers also pursued similar arrangements in a wide variety of locations around the world in this period. Indeed, French, Russian, and American interests sought concessions in China in this period, and by the end of the century so too did the Germans and the Japanese. In 1853, a United States naval fleet commanded by Commodore Matthew Perry famously—and quite literally—used "gunboat diplomacy" to persuade Japan to open its ports to American ships and American trade. In the Near East and North Africa in the mid-nineteenth century, the French maintained huge financial investments in Ottoman Turkey [it is Ottoman Turkey], Egypt, Tunisia, and Morocco. In the Ottoman Empire and Egypt, as we have seen, the French were part of the European commissions that assumed control over those regions' finances in 1876. Even before that, during the 1860s, the French, British, and Italians had already taken charge of Tunisia's chaotic and nearly bankrupt financial system. In Morocco, the French established preferential trading privileges 40 years prior to the imposition of direct French rule in 1904.[91] French and British interests also competed

in Thailand for informal influence during the nineteenth century. Indeed, those states that could command the military and technological might to do so sought to emulate Britain and secure as many preferential, advantageous arrangements with non-industrial states as possible. By the last half of the nineteenth century, these efforts had resulted in increasing competition between all of the great powers: a situation that laid the foundations for the overt scramble for empire that characterized the period between 1885 and 1914.

As these accounts of European influence in Latin America, the Ottoman Empire, and China indicate, there was clearly more to the history of imperialism in the nineteenth century than those places that could be colored red on imperial maps. While informal imperial influence sometimes did not achieve the goals of its European advocates—unequal agreements could not, for example, make Latin American peasants wealthy consumers, nor could they adequately penetrate China's huge internal markets[92]—such influence nevertheless had important effects on European relations with the rest of the world. This was particularly true of Britain which, as the leading industrial and economic power, established highly unequal economic and political relationships with a variety of client-states in this period. These relationships entailed something more than dependency: rather, through treaties, consuls, and violence, they frequently interfered with matters of sovereignty. Thus, while the client-states discussed earlier might not have formally "belonged" to any formal empire in this period, neither were they fully able to determine their own futures. Because of this, they must be considered not simply in terms of the dictates of "free trade," but in the context of imperialism as well.

FORMAL EXPANSION IN THE ERA OF INFORMAL IMPERIALISM

As we have seen, European influence in Latin America, the Ottoman Empire, China, and elsewhere was often intrusive even though Europeans

---

[90] Osterhammel, "Britain and China," 157.

[91] Robert Aldrich, *Greater France: A History of French Overseas Expansion* (London: Palgrave Macmillan, 1996), 29, 31.

[92] Osterhammel, "Britain and China," 161.

did not claim these areas as formal colonies. Because of this, and because the principles of free trade were frequently advocated more loudly than those of imperial conquest, historians once tended to view this period as a time of relative imperial inactivity. This perspective, however, was faulty in two ways: first, because it did not regard informal influence as a phenomenon closely related to imperialism and, second, because it failed to adequately acknowledge the extent to which formal imperial conquest continued alongside informal imperialism. Yet between 1820 and 1880, European empires annexed, conquered, or otherwise won control of huge territories in Asia, Africa, the Pacific, and continental North America. This process, although it included new areas, was hardly new. Rather, formal imperial conquest in the middle decades of the nineteenth century shared important continuities with past conquest in the Americas and elsewhere, including persistent issues regarding competition between rival European states, the need to secure vulnerable borders once conquest occurred, and the aggressive expansion of settler societies. In addition, this period also shared important continuities with the later period of **High Imperialism**, in which industrial powers suddenly and antagonistically grabbed as many formal colonies as possible. Indeed, it was in this preceding period when the foundations for such explosive rivalry were laid, for industrial powers—especially Britain—had already begun to use their technological might to carve out significant portions of Asia and Africa. When other states caught up with, and then surpassed, Britain by the end of the nineteenth century, they all sought to reap the rewards of empire for themselves. Armed with steamships, railroads, telegraphs, and repeating rifles, these powers increasingly came into conflict with one another over trading rights and the use of natural resources—and the race for the extension of formal rule was on. This process, which is discussed in chapter 10, only really took off in the 1880s. Its precedents, however, were already firmly set by the expansion of formal imperialism in the mid-nineteenth century. This section briefly outlines the nature and direction of this earlier expansion to underscore its range and scope.

Given Britain's leading role in the informal imperialism of the nineteenth century, it should be of little surprise that the island nation led its rivals in formal territorial conquest in this period as well. In addition to its formidable influence in Latin America, the Ottoman Empire, and China, Britain added hundreds of thousands of miles to its formal empire in the early and mid-nineteenth century. These territories were diverse, ranging from India, Burma (later renamed Myanmar), Ceylon (Sri Lanka), and Malaya to South Africa, Australia, New Zealand, and Canada: they included tropical, temperate, and even sub-arctic regions, and they ranged from strategic outposts to settlement colonies.

In 1800, by far the most important British overseas possessions were in India. Although British interests had assumed territorial control of Bengal in 1757, the move was not made directly by the British government but by the EIC—the trading company that had maintained monopoly rights to trade in India since 1600. Prior to 1757, the company's original territorial claims had been limited to fortified trading posts in Madras (later renamed Chennai), Bombay (Mumbai), and Calcutta (Kolkata). However, in that year a dispute with a Mughal vassal in Bengal led to a battle in which the Company's forces emerged victorious.[93] In recognition of this victory, the Mughal Emperor Shah Alaam II (1759–1806) granted the Company the right to administer the taxes and finances of Bengal in 1759. As it turned out, the Company soon discovered that the profit from collecting taxes in the rich agricultural region of Bengal was even more lucrative than profits from trade. This fact was not lost on the British Parliament, which passed a series of acts between 1778 and 1793 that placed the EIC under its supervision and control, and which arranged for a portion of the profits to go directly to the British government

---

[93] This was the Battle of Plassey, led on the British side by Robert Clive. For a thorough treatment of the early EIC see K.N. Chaudhuri, *The Trading World of Asia and the English East India Company, 1660–1760* (Cambridge: Cambridge University Press, 2006).

in London.[94] As part of these arrangements, the Company was held responsible to a Board of Control based in London, whose chairperson held a position in the British cabinet. As a result, the British government ruled India by proxy through the Company.[95]

With such rich profits to be made from land taxes, the EIC had every incentive to increase its territories. Moreover, as a territorial power the EIC had constantly to be on guard from incursions or threats made by rival Indian or European powers. Indeed, expansion often occurred as a result of attempts to secure internal peace within India or as a way of keeping vulnerable territory out of the hands of competitors.[96] Thus, during the last two decades of the eighteenth century, the EIC used its territorial position in Bengal—and its growing Indian-based military force—to consolidate its rule on the sub-continent. As a result of these campaigns, by 1800 the EIC had already emerged as the largest single territorial power in India.[97] However, the EIC did not stop there: instead, for the next 60 years the EIC expanded its territories to include almost the whole of the Indian sub-continent. This growth was caused not so much by an official policy of forward movement emanating from London, but rather by a combination of opportunity, preventative measures, the liberal interpretation of orders by "men on the spot," and the perception of self-defense.[98] Thus, Ceylon was added in 1816 when it was permanently taken from the Dutch at the end of the Napoleonic Wars; much of southern India was added in 1818 as a result of a series of wars against the Maratha state; the province of Sindh was annexed in 1843 as a result of fears over Russian expansion in Central Asia; the Punjab was conquered in 1849 because of both its threat as a military competitor and its strategic value as a buffer to Russian expansion; the north-central province of Awadh was annexed in 1856 over a technicality regarding the succession of its ruler; and portions of Burma were annexed in 1862 as a result of anti-British activity.

British rule in much of north-central India was seriously challenged in 1857 when both the Bengal army and the peasants in the region rose in rebellion against the Company. Labeled *the Mutiny* by the British, this uprising had a number of disparate causes, only some of which were dissatisfaction with EIC rule. The British crown's response was indicative of the government's commitment to its ever-increasing territorial claims on the sub-continent: once the rebellion was bloodily suppressed in 1858, the Company was dismantled and India was placed under the direct rule of the British crown. Henceforth, India would no longer be ruled by proxy, but directly. Thus in the era of "informal empire" and "free trade," Britain had managed to acquire the largest, most lucrative colony in its history.[99]

Perhaps not surprisingly, growing British interests in India increased the strategic, economic, and political importance of other areas in Asia to the re-emerging imperial powers of Europe and the nascent expansionist states of the United States and Japan. This was especially true of South-East Asia, whose mainland and islands occupied a critical region between India and the lucrative markets of China. Of particular importance was access to the Straits of Malacca, a narrow body of water between the Malay Peninsula and the island of Sumatra, through which all ships traveling between the South China Sea and the Indian Ocean had to pass. Moreover, both the Dutch and the Spanish already had long-term interests in the Indonesian archipelago and the Philippines, respectively, and the British were anxious to secure their own footholds in the area.[100] By 1786, they

---

[94] Mia Carter and Barbara Harlow, *Archives of Empire: From the East India Company to the Suez Canal* (Durham, NC: Duke University Press, 2003), 14.

[95] Claude Markovits, Nisha George, and Maggy Hendry, *A History of Modern India, 1480–1950* (London: Anthem Press, 2002), 238–239.

[96] Bayly, *Imperial Meridian*, 106.

[97] John Keay details these late eighteenth-century campaigns in *India: A History* (New York: Grove Press, 2001), chapter 16.

[98] There were times, such as between 1828 and 1836, that the government in London expressly did not favor expansion, even though expansion continued to occur.

[99] The 1857 Rebellion will be explored more fully in chapter 9.

[100] A.J. Stockwell, "British Expansion and Rule in South-East Asia," in Porter, *The Nineteenth Century*, 371.

succeeded in this effort by assuming control over the port of Penang on the west coast of the Malay Peninsula. Two decades later during the Napoleonic Wars, British interests in the region were heightened when the Dutch king in exile asked the British to occupy all Dutch overseas territories in order to keep them from the French. In 1811, therefore, British forces occupied the territories of the Dutch East India Company (VOC) in Java and Sumatra. Although these territories were returned to the Dutch in 1816, the experience had convinced the British of the need to temper Dutch influence in the region.[101] As a result, in 1819 Sir Stamford Raffles arranged a treaty with local rulers that ceded the island of Singapore—located at the heart of the Straits—to the British. In 1824, an Anglo-Dutch treaty led to the British acquisition of the port of Malacca, and two years later the British amalgamated Penang, Malacca, and Singapore as the Straits Settlements, to be administered under the authority of the EIC in Bengal.[102] Singapore was quickly recognized for its enormous strategic as well as economic value, and thereafter British interests in the region grew rapidly. By 1874, when the British began to insist on the installation of residents in all of the autonomous states on the Malay Peninsula, the foundations for the transfer of the whole region to formal imperial rule were already well in place.

The security of India was also partially behind formal British expansion in South Africa during the nineteenth century. We have seen in chapter 7 how the Cape Colony, on the southern tip of the African continent, was established in the seventeenth century by the Dutch, who used it as a way station between Europe and its possessions in the Indonesian archipelago. As in Java, during the Napoleonic Wars the British occupied Cape Town in order to keep it from the French.[103] Unlike in Java, the British never returned this

colony to its former owners, preferring instead to keep it for themselves because of its strategic value along the sea routes from Europe to Asia. Although the first 5,000 British settlers did not arrive until 1820, already by 1811 British forces had begun the process of forcibly removing Africans from the most fertile lands in the region.[104] From that point forward, conflicts with neighboring African states as well as the 20,000 original Dutch settlers—who did not take kindly to British rule—drove European territorial expansion in South Africa for the rest of century. Thus, problems with the Zulu state led the British to establish a second colony in Natal in 1843. Meanwhile, between 1834 and 1840 about 15,000 Dutch Afrikaners left British territory to set up independent settlements further inland. As a result of this outward movement of both English-speaking and Dutch-speaking settlers, the territory under European control doubled between the 1830s and the 1850s.[105] Thus, even though the most significant British expansion in South Africa took place after 1873, as in South-East Asia the foundations for such expansion had been laid much earlier in the nineteenth century.

Formal British expansion also occurred in North America during the middle decades of the nineteenth century. Following American independence in 1783, British North America was comprised of Upper Canada (later renamed Ontario), Lower Canada (Quebec), New Brunswick, and Nova Scotia. In the early decades of the nineteenth century, tensions between French and British settlers as well as tensions between colonial settlers and the British government exploded, between 1837 and 1838, into armed rebellion in both Lower and Upper Canada.[106] Faced with demands for greater autonomy, and wary of provoking Canadian settlers into intransigent rebellion, the British government conceded to experiment with

---

[101] Ibid., 374.

[102] Barbara Watson Andaya, *A History of Malaysia* (Honolulu: University of Hawaii Press, 2001), 126. In 1867, the administration of the Straits Settlements was shifted to the Colonial Office.

[103] Christopher Saunders and Iain R. Smith, "Southern Africa, 1795–1910," in Porter, *The Nineteenth Century*, 597.

[104] Leonard Thompson, *A History of South Africa*, 3rd edition (New Haven, CT: Yale Nota Bene, 2001), 54–55.

[105] Saunders and Smith, "Southern Africa," 601, 603.

[106] For a detailed account of these rebellions in Lower Canada, where they were more severe, see Allan Greer, *The Patriots and the People: The Rebellion of 1837 in Rural Lower Canada* (Toronto: University of Toronto Press, 1993).

a new type of colonial rule: responsible government.[107] By the terms of arrangements made between 1840 and 1841, both Upper and Lower Canada were amalgamated into the United Province of Canada, Canadian settlers assumed authority over internal affairs (including the ability to set taxes and tariffs), and the powers of the British governor-general were reduced.[108] Britain, for its part, retained authority over matters relating to external affairs. These arrangements were extended in 1867, when the British North America Act joined the United Province of Canada with New Brunswick and Nova Scotia to create the Dominion of Canada. Under the Act, Canada became a self-governing colony with the British monarch as its head, while external affairs continued to be overseen by the British government. The transition to responsible government, however, was significant far beyond Canada. Indeed, once the model was tested in Canada, it was quickly applied to a variety of other colonies in which British settlers predominated. Thus the Canadian model created, in effect, an alternative between direct rule and informal imperialism that structured not only British rule in the "white" settler colonies, but would one day provide inspiration even for non-European colonies wishing to retain some form of attachment with Britain.[109]

The extension of Canada from the Atlantic to the Pacific coasts over the course of the nineteenth century demonstrated the ways in which formal territorial expansion in this period could result from the aggressively expansionist tendencies of European settlers. Between 1826 and 1837 alone, 300,000 British immigrants arrived in Canada, while another 600,000 arrived between 1840 and 1857.[110] By 1871, 3,689,000 colonists made their home in Canada—a dramatic increase from the 430,000 who lived there in 1814. Population pressure, in turn, spurred land hunger, which encouraged the desire for further territorial expansion. Thus, in 1870 the dominion added the province of Manitoba to its territories, and in 1871 the Pacific coast province of British Columbia also joined the confederation. By that time, plans for a trans-Canadian railway were well under way. In the three decades following its completion in 1885, most of the rest of the territories that make up modern Canada were incorporated into the dominion. As was the case in most of the "white" settler colonies in this period, territorial expansion in Canada was made far easier by the plummeting population of native peoples: between 1814 and 1911, the native population decreased from 200,000 to about 100,000 as a result of disease and alcoholism.[111] As a result of this decline, few could contest the expropriation of land that accompanied Canadian expansion and transformed it into a continent-wide territory in less than a century.

On the other side of the world, the nineteenth century also saw the expansion of formal British territorial claims in both Australia and New Zealand. Although both had been claimed by the British explorer Captain James Cook in the 1770s, their distant location delayed immediate settlement.[112] However, by the end of the eighteenth century that very distance recommended the use of Australia as a penal colony for the many criminals that ran afoul of the British judicial system. As a result, criminals began to be transported to the tiny British colony at New South Wales in 1787. The idea quickly caught on, and for the next 30 years thousands of criminals followed. In 1803, enough criminals were being transported to justify the opening of a new penal colony on Van Diemen's Island (Tasmania).

---

[107] For a full exploration, see Phillip A. Buckner, *The Transition to Responsible Government: British Policy in British North America, 1815–1860* (Westport, CT: Greenwood Press, 1985).

[108] Edward Porritt, *Evolution of the Dominion of Canada: Its Government and Its Politics* (New York: World Book Company, originally from the University of Michigan, 1918), 248.

[109] In 1931, the "white" dominions were incorporated into the British Commonwealth of Nations. However, after decolonization many former British colonies also opted for incorporation into the Commonwealth.

[110] Ged Martin, "Canada from 1815," in Porter, *The Nineteenth Century*, 535.

[111] Ibid., 533.

[112] Donald Denoon, Philippa Mein Smith, and Marivic Wyndham, *A History of Australia, New Zealand, and the Pacific* (Oxford: Wiley-Blackwell, 2000), 87.

In 1824, yet another colony was opened at Moreton Bay.[113]

Between the 1830s and the 1850s, however, free immigration to Australia increased dramatically as Britons began to appreciate the commercial possibilities of sheep farming and gold mining. In fact, free immigration increased so rapidly that the transportation system was gradually eliminated between 1840 and 1868. As in Canada, the European population in Australia surged in the mid-nineteenth century, its population growing from a mere 15,000 in 1815 to 1 million in 1861. Also like Canada, Australia's Aboriginal population halved in the same period, falling from 500,000 in 1815 to about 250,000 in 1861.[114] This was no coincidence: European populations inflicted terrible abuse on Aboriginal populations even as they displaced them from the lands they relied upon for sustenance. In the eyes of the land-hungry settlers, however, nomadic Aborigines did not have a legitimate claim to the land, which left it open for the taking.[115] This attitude was encouraged by colonial policy, for during the nineteenth century both newly arrived colonists and criminals who had served their time were eligible for large land grants without regard to Aboriginal communities. By the 1860s, the construction of railways increased the reach of settlers as new lines opened the vast interior of the continent. As a result, by the end of the nineteenth century Britons claimed the entirety of the Australian continent, and had divided it into six distinct colonies. Given the domination of all the colonies by British settlers, responsible government on the Canadian model was extended to all of them beginning in the 1850s.[116]

Further to the south and east than Australia, New Zealand was only formally annexed by the British in 1840. Although sailors and missionaries had been visiting the island for 50 years prior to annexation, it was only when the French began to demonstrate serious interest in the north island that the British decided to act.[117] To cement their claim to the islands, in 1840 the British signed a treaty with some of the indigenous Maori tribes. This Treaty of Waitangi sanctioned British overlordship and the right to settle in return for British protection of Maori land. The terms of the treaty, however, were not well observed, and Maori dissatisfaction with the British resulted in a series of wars in the 1860s and 1870s. These wars, which resulted in a decisive Maori defeat, were used to justify huge land confiscations from the Maori population, and in turn allowed British colonists to claim ever more territory across both islands.[118] As in Australia and Canada, this process was spurred by a dramatic increase in European immigration: from a mere 2,000 in 1840, by 1896 the European population had grown to 701,000. Also like Australia and Canada, the rising European population was mirrored by a plummeting Maori population, which descended from a high of 70,000 to 90,000 in 1840 to a low of 42,000 in 1896.[119] Having moved from a minority to a majority population in only half a century, the New Zealand Europeans also followed the other "white" settler colonies in the transition to responsible government.

Although Britain added by far the most extensive territories to its formal empire in the middle decades of the nineteenth century, it was hardly alone. The United States, which itself had severed its colonial relationship with Britain, also busied itself with an imperial expansion of its own in this period. Indeed, what became known in the 1840s as "manifest destiny"—the idea that the United States was destined to reach from the Atlantic to the Pacific across the North American continent—nevertheless involved similar processes of violent displacement and territorial expansion as those

---

[113] For a history of Australia as a penal colony, see Robert Hughes, *The Fatal Shore: A History of the Transportation of Convicts to Australia, 1787–1868* (London: Knopf, 1987).

[114] Donald Denoon and Marivic Wyndham, "Australia and the Western Pacific," in Porter, *The Nineteenth Century*, 548.

[115] Ibid., 563.

[116] Ibid., 555.

[117] Raewyn Dalziel, "Southern Islands: New Zealand and Polynesia," in Porter, *The Nineteenth Century*, 573, 577.

[118] Tom Brooking, *The History of New Zealand* (Westport, CT: Greenwood Press, 2004), 59.

[119] Dalziel, "Southern Islands," 581–582.

employed by European settlers elsewhere.[120] Over the course of the nineteenth century, the territories claimed by the United States ballooned to include the 1803 Louisiana Purchase from the French, the 1819 cession of Florida from the Spanish, the 1845 winning of Texas from Mexico, the 1846 addition of the Oregon territory, the 1848 Mexican Cession, and the 1853 Gadsden Purchase from Mexico. As in Canada, Australia, and New Zealand, the extension of actual control over these vast areas involved the naked use of force to subdue existing populations, the imposition of a completely new form of government, and the near-total replacement of indigenous peoples by settlers. Thus, while Americans may have seen their nation's expansion—as Thomas Jefferson put it—as "an empire of liberty," for indigenous peoples there was little to differentiate between an empire built by Americans from an empire built by Britons.[121]

The French, too—despite internal difficulties—added significant territories to their formal empire during the "era of informal imperialism." In fact, it was in this period that the conquest of the two most important French colonies—Algeria and Indochina—was begun. The conquest of Algeria was a long process, but it commenced in 1830 when French troops occupied Algiers in retaliation for a perceived insult to the French consul by the Ottoman bey.[122] In reality, the invasion was engineered by Charles X of France as a way of distracting the French people from his extremely unpopular government.[123] Although the attempt at distraction failed—Charles was dethroned that very year—the French investment in Algeria did not. For the next four decades, French control was extended to the Algerian interior by a succession of

brutal military administrations. By 1879, the French had pacified most of the interior, and had forcibly removed the original population from the most fertile lands along the coastal strip. In place of these displaced inhabitants came European settlers (including French but also Spanish, Maltese, and Italians), who were granted rights to the best land in the region.[124] As a result of this policy, the European population surged, increasing from a mere 37,000 in 1841 to 279,000 in 1871.[125] Even by the middle of the nineteenth century, Algeria had come to be considered a crucial part of the French colonial empire: so crucial, in fact, that in 1848 its territories were incorporated into the structure of France itself as official departments.[126]

Indochina was neither close to France nor did it become a settler colony. Nevertheless, during the middle decades of the nineteenth century the French were persistent in their efforts to add the region to their formal empire.[127] The impetus in this case was great power rivalry: when the British gained the island of Hong Kong in 1842 at the end of the Opium War, French merchants and statesmen began to clamor for an Asian toe-hold that would allow access to the lucrative markets of China. For this reason, the French began to focus on Indochina, where there had been a French missionary presence since the eighteenth century. This turned out to be a difficult task, as the area that comprises modern Vietnam had been unified at the start of the nineteenth century under the Nguyen emperors at Hue. This internal cohesion allowed a concerted response even against French steamships, and thus two separate attempts to gain territory in northern Indochina—in 1856 and 1858—resulted in French failure.

[120] Mark S. Joy, *American Expansionism, 1783–1860: A Manifest Destiny?* (London: Pearson Longman, 2003), 87.
[121] Ibid., 17.
[122] The incident occurred as a result of the bey asking the French consul about when the French were going to pay their significant debts to the merchants of Algiers. The consul's response was so arrogant that the bey swatted him on the arm six times with a fly whisk, and told him to leave his presence. Aldrich, *Greater France*, 25.
[123] Ibid., 26.

[124] Frederick Quinn, *The French Overseas Empire* (Westport, CT: Praeger, 2000), 125. Many of these French settlers came from the French provinces of Alsace and Lorraine in 1871, which were lost to Germany during the Franco-Prussian War. Thousands of French men and women decided to emigrate rather than remain under German rule.
[125] Aldrich, *Greater France*, 28.
[126] Patricia Lorcin, *Imperial Identities: Stereotyping, Prejudice, and Race in Colonial Algeria* (London: I.B. Tauris, 1999), 7. The territories that became departments were Algiers, Oran, and Constantine.
[127] Aldrich, *Greater France*, 73.

However, after the second failed attempt the French retreated to the southern city of Saigon. In 1859, they succeeded in occupying the city, and three years later they successfully negotiated a treaty with the Nguyen that ceded Saigon, the three southern provinces of Cochinchina, and the island of Poulo Condore.[128] Having established this base, the French continued to establish their position in South-East Asia against both neighboring and Great Power threats. Thus, fearing British designs on the region, in 1863 the French established a protectorate over Cambodia in order to reserve it for themselves.[129] By the end of the nineteenth century, the French had established formal colonial rule over the provinces of Annam, Tonkin, and Laos as well. Thus for the French as for the British, the massive expansion of the last two decades of the nineteenth century was preceded by significant formal expansion in the previous decades.[130]

Even a small imperial power like the Netherlands expanded the boundaries of its formal empire during the "era of informal empire." Although the VOC had established a presence in the Indonesian islands in 1602, by 1800—when the Dutch government abolished the VOC and assumed direct control of its territories—Dutch sovereignty was limited only to the north coast of Java and some of the spice islands to the east.[131] When the British assumed control of Java during the Napoleonic Wars, however, they managed to conquer the powerful kingdom of Yogyakarta in Java's interior, which added significantly to Dutch territories when the British returned them in 1816.[132] The Dutch administrators who succeeded the British then embarked on similar programs of conquest and domination, which in 1825 resulted in a massive war of resistance by several Javanese states. When the Dutch emerged victorious in 1830 after five years of warfare, they assumed a far greater sovereign role in Javanese affairs than ever before.[133] After 1840, they also began to assert greater control over many of the outer Indonesian islands, and by the early twentieth century they had established control over most of what is now modern Indonesia. Thus in the Dutch East Indies as elsewhere, the consolidation of imperial rule in the late nineteenth and early twentieth centuries was preceded by an earlier period of formal expansion in the mid-nineteenth century.

Conclusion

Far from being a period of calm between two imperial storms, the period between 1820 and 1880 was one of enormous significance for the extension of European imperial power throughout the world. For the first time in history, European states possessed decisive technologies that allowed them the ability to subdue non-industrial regions in nearly every part of the globe. In particular, Britain's industrial economy allowed it to command huge export and import markets, while its steam-powered Royal Navy enabled it to extend its will even to hostile areas. Indeed, Britain's clear economic and technological dominance in this period meant that it experienced little competition from rivals as its merchants and advisors influenced the economic, political, and social worlds of societies as far afield as Latin America, the Ottoman Empire, and China. As a result, there was often little need to engage in the expense and difficulty of formal imperial conquest when it was clear that informal means were equally effective in carrying out British objectives. Yet as we have argued, the absence of formal control did not equal the absence of an imperial impulse. Thus, not only did a unique culture of imperialism emerge in Britain and to a lesser degree other industrialized society, but it is also clear that British—and later other European and American—interference in a variety of states in this period significantly impaired their sovereignty.

[128] Quinn, *The French Overseas Empire*, 139.
[129] Aldrich, *Greater France*, 79
[130] Ibid., 87.
[131] M.C. Ricklefs, *A History of Modern Indonesia Since c. 1200*, 3rd edition (Stanford: Stanford University Press, 2001), 146.
[132] Ibid., 149.
[133] Ibid., 155.

Moreover, even though informal imperialism was a significant feature of the mid-nineteenth century, European and American states continued to add territories to their formal empires in Africa, Asia, the Pacific, and the Americas at a rapid pace. As we have seen, the most important colonial territories of both Britain and France—India, Algeria, and Indochina—were all conquered (or nearly conquered) in this period. In addition, nearly every state with pretensions to Great Power status in this period was beginning to explore colonial possibilities as a way of competing with Britain and its distant rival, France. Therefore, if the explosion in formal imperial conquest after 1885 appears as an abrupt change of course, perhaps it appears less so when placed in the context of the intense imperial activity that occurred in the middle decades of the nineteenth century.

Questions

1. Consider the example of the British Empire and metropole in the period discussed in this chapter in light of the definitions used in this book. Could this be described as a period of imperialism? Was the British Empire of this period an empire? Why would you use these terms, or why not?

2. Describe the cultures of imperialism that dominated Britain and to a lesser degree France and the United States in this period. How might these cultures have resulted partly from the technological and productivity changes of the Industrial Revolution? How might they have created policies and practices of informal empire?

3. Explain the ways in which informal empire impaired the sovereignty and operations of the state in Latin America, China, and the Ottoman Empire during the period discussed in this chapter.

CHAPTER 9

Colonialism: Change, Response, and Resistance in the Colonies

*With hearts filled with the deepest gratitude, and impressed with the
utmost reverence, we, the undersigned native inhabitants of Calcutta
and its vicinity, beg to … offer personally our humble but warmest
acknowledgements for the invaluable protection which your
Lordship's government has recently afforded to the lives of the Hindoo
female part of your subjects, and for your humane and successful
efforts in rescuing us for ever, from the gross stigma hitherto attached
to our character as wilful [sic] murderers of females*[1]

*It is well known to all, that in this age the people of Hindostan, both
Hindoos and Mohammedans, are being ruined under the tyranny
and oppression of the infidel and treacherous English. It is therefore
the bounden duty of all the wealthy people of India … to stake their
lives and property for the well-being of the public.*[2]

*Pangeran Dipanagara said calmly:
"if you are afraid to oppose the
Dutch, from now on
once and for all become (my) enemy!"*[3]

*settlement on the land, and the development of the mineral and
other resources of the country, have been in a great degree
prohibited by the hostility of the blacks, which still continues with
undiminished spirit.*[4]

---

[1] Petition delivered to governor-general of India Lord William Bentinck, on behalf of Raja Ram Mohan Roy and others on January 16, 1830, regarding the abolition of *sati* (widow immolation). Quoted from Barbara Harlow and Mia Carter, *Archives of Empire*, vol. I, *From the East India Company to the Suez Canal* (Durham, NC: Duke University Press, 2003), 370.

[2] Manifesto of the King of Awadh, as printed in the Delhi Gazette on September 29, 1857, urging wealthy Indians to rebel against British rule. Quoted from ibid., 429.

[3] Verse 18 from the *Babad Dipanagara*, the epic story told about the Java War against the Dutch from 1825 to 1830. From Peter Carey, "The *Babad Dipanagara* in Java," in *The Indonesia Reader: History, Culture, Politics*, edited by Tineke Hellwig and Eric Tagliacozzo (Durham, NC: Duke University Press, 2009), 121.

[4] Report from the Queenslander newspaper, February 15, 1879, in Queensland, Australia. Quoted in Henry Reynolds, *The Other Side of the Frontier: Aboriginal Resistance to the European Invasion of Australia*, 3rd edition (Sydney: University of New South Wales Press, 2006), 115.

As these quotations suggest, the populations of the new colonies brought into the overseas empires in the wake of the Industrial Revolution were not merely passive recipients and objects of colonial rule. Rather, expansion prompted a variety of responses from colonized peoples, from accommodation to resistance and outright aggression. Having already explored the causes, nature, and scope of nineteenth-century imperial expansion, therefore, we now focus our attention on what this expansion might have meant for the people who lived through it. How, in other words, did the imposition of colonial rule in this period impact the lives of the people who actually experienced it? The multiple and complex answers to this question highlight the ways in which the massive global forces related to imperial expansion had real, tangible consequences for individuals at all levels of society. Indeed, we argue that the social, political, and economic changes wrought by colonial rule were deep and widespread in this period, and that the legacy of these changes were critical in shaping colonial experiences in the ensuing period of High Imperialism. In some ways, the colonialism of the short nineteenth century discussed in this chapter can be seen as a series of experiments in colonial rule for industrial empire. Thus, many of the ideas and types of experiences raised in this chapter are discussed again in chapters 11 and 13, although others were discarded by the later dates covered in those chapters.

Although colonialism prompted significant changes both for colonized peoples and colonial rulers, the nature and extent of these changes varied widely. As we already know, colonial rule during the middle decades of the nineteenth century hardly represented a monolithic system. First, a variety of states were involved in colonial enterprises in this period, and each differed in terms of colonial structure, policy, and ideology. Second, imperial powers with multiple colonies often pursued differing policies and practices even amongst their own colonial possessions, depending on local conditions as well as the economic or strategic purposes each colony was supposed to serve. Third, the peoples and environments of the various colonies differed widely, which meant that colonial powers were faced with a variety of responses and challenges in every location they sought to claim. Clearly, then, colonialism was experienced in multiple ways according to location, ruling power, mode of governance, and the identities and life experiences of the colonial subjects. As a result of this astonishing variety, it would be impossible to discuss the realities of colonial life in any singular way. Instead, the goal of this chapter is to explore some of the features of colonial life that recurred over and over in spite of differences in location, imperial power, mode of governance, or colonial social configuration. These features, we argue, recurred not because colonial systems were all the same, but because the imposition of colonial rule necessarily shifted both the internal and external dynamics of power in any given location—shifts that, in turn, nearly always elicited responses among colonized and colonizing populations. Therefore, even while the nature of such shifts and responses varied, it is nevertheless still possible to explore them from a global, holistic perspective.

This chapter begins by grounding our discussion of commonalities in colonial experiences in a discussion of the multiple types of colonial rule that co-existed in this period. We believe that comparisons and connections are most useful when they are made with an awareness of historical complexities and differences. The chapter then continues by discussing some of the features of colonial rule that tended to recur in multiple locations even in spite of the varied and complex nature of colonial governing systems. Specifically, we explore the recurrent themes of political change, violence, economic change, and social transformations as a result of new ideas about difference, education, and law. Finally, we discuss some of the means and strategies by which local populations resisted colonial rule in this period. Although we point to a wide variety of examples throughout all of the sections, each also devotes detailed attention to India. The reasons for this are fourfold: first, by continually returning to a single case study, we hope to provide a level of continuity and detail in the midst of such a wide-ranging and global discussion. Second, although imperial powers claimed many colonies in the middle decades of the nineteenth century, none were comparable in size or importance to India. We already know that India was the premier colony of the premier imperial power in the world at this time. Even more importantly for our purposes, the majority of colonized people in the world were Indian: even in 1914 (*after* the Scramble for Africa in the late nineteenth century dramatically increased global colonial claims), 6 out of every 10 people ruled by westerners hailed from India.[5] Third, India is an ideal case study because its colonial history spanned so many of the modes of government under discussion here, including a shift from proxy rule to crown rule, the inclusion of areas of both direct and indirect rule, and sustained (albeit limited) interactions between colonial settlers and colonized subjects. Finally, because the British experience in ruling India was so important, their policies and practices there were widely observed and—both in other contemporaneous colonies and in later periods—widely mimicked in colonies elsewhere. Thus, our goal in consistently returning to India is not to imply that India's experience was representative, but to explore more fully the wide range of social, political, and economic impacts colonial rule could engender in a single, and very important, location within our global discussion.

MODES OF GOVERNANCE

The colonies in existence during the middle decades of the nineteenth century were a hodgepodge of administrative styles. As we have seen, many were acquired as a result of war or settlement after war, some were expanded opportunistically by eager settlers or administrators, some were taken for strategic purposes, and some were meant to serve economic purposes. Moreover, the process of imperial expansion usually occurred over time, often in direct response to events on the ground. And, since even the largest empires were constantly short of money, most colonies were administered in the most cost-effective way possible. It has even been said that Britain, at least, acquired its empire in this period not by plan but rather through "a fit of absent-mindedness." As we saw in the last chapter, this description is not entirely correct. Nevertheless, during this period colonial rule was often designed on an ad hoc basis, after the process of conquest was well underway or even completed. What this meant was that most colonial powers did not have a *grand plan* for colonial expansion, or even a coherent system for administering them.[6] In Britain, for example, the administration of its multiple colonies was overseen by no fewer than three ministries in the nineteenth century: the India Office, the Colonial Office, and the Foreign Office.

This lack of coherence at the metropolitan centers was echoed in the colonies. As a result, a variety of modes of governance came to characterize colonial rule in this period. Broadly speaking, they can be grouped together under four major administrative styles: direct rule, indirect rule, responsible government, and proxy rule. Direct rule refers to those colonies in which imperial powers claimed full sovereignty over a given territory. In these cases, pre-existing powers were swept aside in favor of imperial administrations sent from metropolitan centers. In addition, direct rule usually involved the imposition of metropolitan legal, political, and social structures on colonial territories. Examples of direct rule in this period were numerous, and included the British "crown colonies" of the West Indies, Burma, the Straits Settlements and, after 1858, India.[7] Dutch territory on most of Java was directly ruled after 1830, as were the French territories of Cochinchina, Tonkin, and Algeria. Although direct rule allowed (at least in theory) for the maximum amount of control by the imperial power, it also had a major disadvantage: cost. Indeed, direct rule required significant

---

[5] Scott Cook, *Colonial Encounters in the Age of High Imperialism* (London: Longman, 1997), chapter 6.

[6] Jürgen Osterhammel, *Colonialism* (Princeton, NJ: Markus Weiner, 2005), 51.

[7] Crown colonies indicated that colonial rule was carried out by a royally appointed governor and his administration.

investment by colonial powers, especially in terms of salaries for administrators, establishing and maintaining a colonial bureaucracy, and defense.

Because of these disadvantages, imperial powers in a variety of locations came to rely on a host of arrangements that have come to be understood as *indirect rule*—that is, areas in which colonial powers claimed sovereignty but left existing structures more or less intact, and then imposed their own authority over those structures. In such cases, colonial "advisors" or "residents" made policy in conjunction with indigenous authorities according, at least in part, to established customs. At the same time, colonial powers reserved matters of foreign policy, international relations, and internal security for themselves.

The idea behind indirect rule was to maintain stability and to keep costs low: some historians, in fact, refer to this style of rule as *colonialism on the cheap*. In general, this strategy was useful and successful enough that by the early twentieth century indirect rule would come to dominate colonialism globally, as we will see in chapter 13. Yet indirect rule often involved a higher level of interference in existing structures than the definition implies. In some cases, for example, existing authorities were hostile to imperial rule, or were otherwise considered inappropriate governing partners. In these instances, colonial powers did not hesitate to handpick their preferred "traditional" rulers, or to depose those they did not like. Moreover, indirectly ruled colonies were subject to new regimes of taxation and economic integration that often produced massive change among both urban and rural populations. Examples of indirect rule in the middle decades of the nineteenth century included the 40 large and hundreds of small Princely States of British India that were left to govern their own internal affairs with the help of a British resident; areas of the Dutch East Indies, especially on the outer islands; and parts of British Malaya.[8] A variant of indirect rule was

the "protectorate," in which colonial powers did not claim full sovereignty but nevertheless established control over external affairs. In this period, colonial states established protectorates over Annam, Cambodia, and Laos (France) as well as Egypt (Britain).[9]

Another broad category of colonial governance emerged in the mid-nineteenth century with the establishment of responsible government in the settlement colonies of British North America, Australia, and New Zealand.[10] In each of these colonies, large settler populations came to dominate and then outnumber indigenous populations as a result of both disease and warfare. In addition, these settler populations—who tended to see themselves as equals with other Britons—began their lives in the colonies with far greater participation in internal affairs than did their counterparts in non-settler colonies. For example, each maintained colonial legislatures, and therefore had some input on the direction of colonial policy. Over time, especially as the colonies attracted increasing numbers of immigrants, settlers in these colonies began to demand increasing internal autonomy from the imperial metropole. Thus, beginning in Canada in the 1840s, the British government began to relinquish control over internal affairs in the settler colonies, reserving control only over foreign affairs for themselves. By the time colonists in Australia and New Zealand had grown numerous enough for self-government, the transition to responsible government for European-dominated colonies had come to be seen almost as a matter of course.

A final category of colonial governance was that of rule by proxy via chartered companies. As we know, this mode of governance was common in the early modern period, and was practiced by the British, French, and Dutch in a variety of locations around the world. By the nineteenth century, most chartered companies—including, most recently, the Dutch East India Company in 1800—had been

---

[8] For a thorough treatment of indirect rule as practiced by Britain in India, see Michael Fisher, *Indirect Rule in India: Residents and the Residency System, 1764–1858* (Oxford: Oxford University Press, 1994).

[9] Osterhammel, *Colonialism*, 42.

[10] A classic source on this issue is Arthur Berriedale Keith, *Responsible Government in the Dominions* (Oxford: Clarendon Press, 1912).

dismantled in favor of other colonial arrangements. An important exception to this was the British East India Company (EIC), which continued to rule most of India until the Sepoy Rebellion of 1857. When the rebellion was finally crushed in 1858, Indian colonial rule was transferred to the British crown. Yet corporate interests sometimes in this period still briefly occupied or managed large areas in lieu of the crown, as the British South Africa Company did before the British government assumed formal control of Rhodesia in southern Africa in the early twentieth century.

Southern Africa, in fact, was during the nineteenth century an agglomeration of different styles of colonial rule separated by independent states. The European settlers of the Cape Colony slowly gained internal self-rule on a model not dissimilar if more limited to that of Australia and Canada, especially through the creation of a local parliament in 1853. Meanwhile, British governors slowly extended their control over densely populated African communities to the east whose labor was desired by settlers. The administration of these areas alternated between direct rule (by "magistrates" and military men) and indirect rule through chiefs. Meanwhile, in the interior numerous African and Dutch-speaking Afrikaner communities continued to exist in independent states. With the "discovery" of diamond deposits in the 1870s, British and European corporations began to stake out claims or try to influence and control local government as well. This type of "confusion" was not restricted to southern Africa, either. At the edges of many overseas colonies of this period, and even in the middle of British India, a hodgepodge of political colonial arrangements existed for much of this period.

Because colonial modes of government differed so widely, so too did experiences of colonialism. In some areas under indirect rule, for example, the obvious legal, political, and social effects of colonialism were limited to areas near the centers of power, and contact with colonizers themselves were infrequent. In such places, colonial subjects tended to feel the economic effects of colonialism most strongly, as the impact of taxation and integration into the global economy disrupted labor practices and settlement patterns.

In areas under direct rule, in contrast, the imposition of a wholly new political power with its attendant legal and political structures often encouraged a more intense and widespread encounter with colonialism. In such places, rulers and ruled confronted one another, cooperated with each other, and adapted—willingly or not—to new ideas, policies, and environments. Even outside the centers of power, colonized people under direct rule found themselves subject to new laws, new power relations, new ideologies, and sharply changed economic realities. Settler colonies produced yet another set of colonial experiences. In these areas, colonial rule had the potential to fundamentally transform nearly all aspects of society as a result of violent competition for land and resources, the imposition of new legal, political, and economic structures, and the migration of wholly new populations. Thus, when exploring connections and comparisons in the ways people experienced colonial rule in the middle decades of the nineteenth century, it is important to understand the effects differing modes of governance might have had on those experiences.

COMMON THEMES IN NINETEENTH-CENTURY COLONIALISM

While keeping this diversity in mind, we now turn to some of the themes and features that tended to be common to experiences of colonialism even across colonial modes of government, region, or ruling power. Indeed, nearly all colonial regimes involved the forcible imposition of foreign power structures, the incorporation of local economies into global economic networks, the introduction of new social relationships, and responses that ranged from adaptation to resistance. Whether ruled directly or indirectly, with settlers or without, colonial rule prompted change at many levels of society, from elite authorities to peasants. Thus, while the nature of such change varied over time and space, we argue that there were enough commonalities in both the causes and the direction of these changes to warrant their exploration from a global perspective. Moreover, because the lessons learned by the imperial powers were put into use during the New Imperialism and High Imperialism of the late nineteenth and twentieth centuries, it is important to discuss this period when trying to understand later developments.

Political Change

The most obvious commonality between colonial experiences everywhere in this period was political transformation. In every case, colonial rule involved the complete or partial replacement of existing authority structures with foreign authorities or hand-picked local authorities. With direct rule, earlier structures and leaders were entirely displaced, and colonial powers imported their own bureaucracies and staff to manage the highest colonial offices. In settler societies, the imposition of new authorities was accompanied by waves of foreigners intent on establishing themselves on the land—a process that further dislocated existing social and political arrangements. Even under indirect rule, where existing structures were not entirely replaced, foreign residents and their entourages clearly usurped the sovereignty of existing authorities, and held the trump card of military interference if their guidance and advice were ignored.

Such shifts in power clearly meant a loss in status and authority for existing leaders and rulers as well as their staffs and families. Yet the effects of political change were not limited to elites. Rather, the replacement of existing leaders often entailed radical changes in networks of communication and negotiation that disrupted long-established patterns for entire peoples. In Australia, for example, the imposition of settler authority established Europeans as the only legitimate arbiter of grievances and disputes. In practice, this meant that Aboriginal groups who were used to fighting and negotiating with one another as autonomous units were no longer able to determine inter-group power relations without reference to settler authorities. In addition, the existence of colonial authority—whether direct or indirect—could have major political implications for surrounding indigenous groups not yet under colonial control. In Dutch Java and the British Straits Settlements, for example, colonial rulers frequently used established toe-holds of power to coerce or intimidate neighboring states to accept either indirect rule or colonial overlordship.[11]

In still other locations, shifts in political power to colonial authorities could mean a sudden loss of access to accepted hierarchies of authority, or a loss of ability to negotiate in culturally specific ways. For example, landlords in Bengal had long had the ability to negotiate with Mughal authorities when natural disasters made it impossible to pay land taxes on time. When the British assumed control of the province in the late eighteenth century, however, landlords lost this ability and, in many instances, their land as well.[12] The annexation of the state of Awadh, also in India, is another case in point. Until 1856, the EIC had ruled the external affairs of Awadh indirectly. In that year, however, the Company deposed the King of Awadh and annexed the region on the pretext that the king did not have a legitimate heir. In place of the king, the Company placed a British chief commissioner who introduced new laws concerning the ownership of land, which dispossessed many of the influential landlords who traditionally were at the head of society. Peasants, who had long relationships with their landlords, were no longer able to negotiate with them over tax rates. Moreover, under direct British rule these tax rates increased markedly, causing widespread suffering among the peasantry. As a result, the shift in political authority in Awadh alienated not only the ruling and landlord class of the state, but caused deep consternation among the peasantry, who in turn loudly protested the deposition of their king.[13] Clearly then, the imposition of foreign political rule in areas of direct, indirect,

---

[11] A.J. Stockwell, "British Expansion and Rule in Southeast Asia," in *The Oxford History of the British Empire*, vol. III, *The Nineteenth Century*, edited by Andrew Porter (Oxford: Oxford University Press, 1999), 383. For the British, this process was most important beginning in the 1870s.

[12] For a detailed exploration of early British rule in Bengal, see P.J. Marshall, *Bengal: The British Bridgehead: Eastern India, 1740–1828*, 2nd edition (Cambridge: Cambridge University Press, 2006), chapters 4 and 5.

[13] Rudrangshu Mukherjee explores all of these issues, which helped lead to the outbreak of rebellion in the area in 1857, in his *Awadh in Revolt, 1857–1858: A Study of Popular Resistance* (Delhi: Oxford University Press, 1984), chapter 2.

and settler rule could initiate profound changes that reverberated far beyond the limited circle of elites.

The Use of Violence

Perhaps not surprisingly, the imposition of new political powers nearly always involved the use of violence or, at the very least, its threat.[14] Established authorities did not usually give up their power and status easily, and colonized populations were frequently unwilling to cooperate willingly with new laws, tax codes, or restrictions on the use of land. As a result, the imposition of colonial rule usually involved not only violent conflict during the first phase of conquest, but the continued use of violence in order to maintain control. In fact, one of the central problems of colonial rule from the colonizers' point of view was how to gain and maintain a monopoly on the use of violence. For colonized peoples, this often translated into a long series of bloody encounters with the colonial state.

Although the use of violence during conquest was nearly ubiquitous, its timing varied according to local conditions as well as metropolitan imperatives. In some cases, such as Java and India, Europeans were initially intent on trade rather than conquest, and violent conflict was purposefully kept to a minimum. It was only much later in the eighteenth and nineteenth centuries that the Dutch and British trading companies attempted territorial expansion—and it was at that point that large-scale violence erupted. In other areas, including Cochinchina, Tonkin, and Algeria, the first attempts by the state (in these cases, France) to impose colonial rule had to be established by the use of violent force from the very start. The settlement colonies and territories of New Zealand, Australia, Canada, and the western United States offer yet another model, as violent force by the colonial state in these areas flared most strongly after European settler populations began to compete with indigenous populations for control of land. In still other places— such as the indirectly ruled Princely States of India, parts of British Malaya, and the French protectorate

of Cambodia—conquest was won largely by the threat of violence, and its use was reserved for occasions of disobedience or intransigence.

Once conquest was complete—which could take years or even decades, as in the case of Algeria—colonial states found they could only maintain control with the continued use of violence. Rebellion, resistance, and unrest were constant problems as colonial states sought to impose their will on subject, and often very dissatisfied, populations. As a result, military and police forces were ubiquitous features in colonial life. Some of these forces were brought from the metropolitan centers. The British army, for example, maintained garrisons in nearly all of its many colonies in the middle decades of the nineteenth century. Where army garrisons were weak, moreover, the British navy provided critical support in areas of crisis. The French also used their own military forces to subdue their colonies: indeed, Algeria was ruled by a French military government until 1870.

Yet colonial claims were far too vast, and European armed forces far too small, to provide an adequate defense against rebellion and unrest in the colonies. For this reason, colonial authorities had little choice but to buttress metropolitan forces with forces drawn from local populations. In settler societies such as Canada, New Zealand, Australia, and the western United States, settlers themselves were often eager to protect their claims with the use of violence. In these areas, in addition to large-scale military conflict (especially in New Zealand and the United States), violence and brutality often occurred on much smaller scales as individuals and groups competed fiercely over claims to land. Since the goal of settlers was usually the complete removal of indigenous populations from the best available lands, small-scale violence and brutality—including kidnappings, rape, massacres, and opportunistic murders—were common features of frontier life.[15]

---

[14] For a study of colonial wars, see J.A. de Moor and H.L. Wesseling, *Imperialism and War: Essays on Colonial Wars in Asia and Africa* (Leiden: Brill Press, 1997).

[15] For the Australian frontier, see Reynolds, *The Other Side of the Frontier*; for the American West, see Robert Utley, *The Indian Frontier, 1846–1890* (Albuquerque: University of New Mexico Press, 2003); for New Zealand, see Richard Hill, "The Policing of Colonial New Zealand: From Informal to Formal Control, 1840–1907," in *Policing the Empire: Government, Authority, and Control, 1830–1940*, edited by David M. Anderson and David Killingray (Manchester: Manchester University Press, 1991).

In areas without large European settler populations, however, the demands of defending territory and maintaining internal order resulted in the enlistment of large numbers of colonized men into colonial armies and police forces. When this occurred, colonial powers transferred the burdens of battle and colonial warfare onto colonial populations themselves, in the process exacerbating divisions between colonial populations and leaving a legacy of heightened internal violence. In French Indochina, for example, the use of violence by military forces was supplemented by a large indigenous police force. This force, in turn, was feared and hated by most Vietnamese subjects because of its reputation for brutality. In the Dutch East Indies, meanwhile, the Dutch population was so small that control could only be maintained by creating locally raised mercenary armies to defend their claims.[16] Those who did enlist provided the labor for the subjugation not only of Java in the mid-nineteenth century, but for the conquest of the outer islands in later decades.

Nowhere did the use of indigenous military forces—or the use of violence to maintain order more generally—reach the scale of British India.[17] In part, this was a result of the vast territories the EIC conquered, as well as the relative size of the Indian and European populations on the sub-continent. Indeed, the Indian sub-continent comprises more than 3 million square kilometers, and by 1830 the EIC ruled 150 million people. Over the course of the next four decades, moreover, new conquests and annexations increased the populations under British control to about 250 million. In contrast to the large and diverse population on the Indian sub-continent, the British population was miniscule: in 1813, there were fewer than 45,000 Europeans (not all of them British) on the sub-continent, including military personnel.[18] Even by the end of our period, in 1882, only 80,000 Britons made India their home. Thus, unlike Canada, Australia, New Zealand, Algeria, and even South Africa, India was never a settler colony. Instead, like Indochina, the Straits Settlements, and the Dutch East Indies, the European population remained a tiny minority, outnumbered by a much larger indigenous population. Moreover, Indians were hardly docile subjects: every extension of Company territory had to be won through violent conquest, and every region so conquered had to be monitored constantly for rebellion.

Given the size of the British population in India and the turbulent nature of Indian society, EIC leaders understood from the outset that without men to conquer additional territories, defend existing claims, and secure internal order, it could never survive. Thus, in the century between 1757 and 1856, the Company built a vast military force in India.[19] By 1856, its combined Indian troops from its three regional armies numbered 280,000 men. In contrast, the combined European contingent comprised only about 40,000 men.[20] Midway through the nineteenth century, then, the Indian army had become the largest all-volunteer mercenary army in the world and a powerful strategic tool for British dominance, which the Company—and then the British crown—used to maintain order both in India and in other British colonies.[21]

---

[16] Bouda Etemad, *Possessing the World: Taking the Measurements of Colonization from the 18th to the 20th Century* (Oxford: Bergahn Books, 2007), 39–42. The French also used indigenous troops in Indochina, but not significantly until the 1880s. For an account of the composition of the Dutch East Indies army, see Jaap de Moor, "The Recruitment of Indonesian Soldiers for the Dutch Colonial Army, 1700–1950," in *Guardians of Empire: The Armed Forces of the Colonial Powers, c. 1700–1964*, edited by David Killingray and David Omissi (Manchester: Manchester University Press, 2000).

[17] For more on the use of the military in British India, see Heather Streets, *Martial Races: The Military, Race, and Masculinity in British Imperial Culture, 1857–1914* (Manchester: Manchester University Press, 2004).

[18] D.A. Washbrook, "India, 1818–1860: The Two Faces of Colonialism," in Porter, *The Nineteenth Century*, 413.

[19] Douglas Peers, *Between Mars and Mammon: Colonial Armies and the Garrison State in India, 1819–1835* (London: I.B. Tauris, 1995), 74.

[20] For the strength of European forces, see T.A. Heathcote, "The Army of British India," in *The Oxford Illustrated History of the British Army*, edited by David Chandler (Oxford: Oxford University Press, 1994), 381; for antagonisms between Crown and Company troops, see Peter Stanley, *White Mutiny: British Military Culture in India* (New York: New York University Press, 1998), chapter 1. The three regional armies, or *presidencies*, as they were called, were in Bengal, Madras, and Bombay.

[21] Strength quoted from Stanley, *White Mutiny*, 9.

Indian men joined the Company armies in Madras (later renamed Chennai), Bombay (Mumbai), and Bengal for a variety of reasons. First, the British tended to recruit from populations, like the Rajputs of northern India, who came from long traditions of pre-colonial military service, and who perceived military service as both a respectable and honorable means of employment.[22] In the Bengal army—the largest of the three regional armies—Company commanders recruited especially diligently from among the highest castes of Indians. According to Company tradition, high-caste Brahmans and Rajputs shared affinities with Europeans as a result of their refined tastes, relatively tall stature, and their tradition of leadership. Second, the salaries offered by the Company were respectable and steady, which provided a strong financial motive for many soldiers to "eat the salt" of the European foreigners, as it was commonly put. Third, military service in the Company frequently offered added benefits—in the form of special pay or land grants—for those willing to serve in foreign stations, and for those with long service, good conduct, or conspicuous acts of bravery in battle.[23] Indeed, although local conditions varied between colonies and colonial powers, the practices employed by the Indian army—targeted recruiting among special populations, steady pay, and exclusive privileges—were frequently employed in other areas where large indigenous forces were required for the maintenance of colonial rule. Recruits for these forces rarely thought of themselves as sharing a common national bond with other colonial subjects in any case, and colonial authorities frequently went to great lengths to ensure they were amply rewarded for their services.

Yet in India and elsewhere, the existence of these forces greatly escalated the use of violence against local populations. Over the course of the first half of the nineteenth century, for example, hundreds of thousands of Indians found themselves faced with the naked use of violence by Indian army soldiers. Some of these people were soldiers who fought on the losing side in wars against the EIC: as such, after conquest they frequently found themselves without jobs, and were forced instead onto the land as peasants or into some other profession. Moreover, once the Company conquered a territory, its leaders used the army to secure internal peace by disarming the peasantry and suppressing banditry. Many farmers, therefore, found themselves surrendering the weapons they had always used to protect themselves to Indian soldiers, often at gunpoint. And once the tax rates had been assessed for a given region, EIC officials often used the military to force payment from recalcitrant peasants.[24] For these people, then, life under colonial rule seemed to be heavily buttressed by the ever-present threat and use of physical force by Company troops. In India as elsewhere in this period, violence was never very far from the surface of colonial life.

However violent force was organized or employed, it is worth remembering that its use lay at the heart of all colonial administrations in this period. Few states relinquished their authority to outsiders by choice, and even after conquest it was usually necessary to use violent force to quell unrest and maintain order. Even in times of relative peace, the presence of large standing armies, police forces, militias, or armed civilians kept the threat of violence just under the surface of colonial rule. Moreover, the initial use of violence in conquest and "pacification"—alongside the continuing presence of armed forces—often meant that personal and state violence became a persistent feature of colonial rule for individuals at all levels of society.

---

[22] Douglas Peers, "Sepoys, Soldiers, and the Lash: Race, Caste and Army Discipline in India, 1820–50," *Journal of Imperial and Commonwealth History* 23:2 (1995), 218. See also Dirk Kolff, *Naukar, Rajputs, and Sepoy: The Ethnohistory of the Military Labor Market in Hindustan, 1450–1850* (Cambridge: Cambridge University Press, 1990).
[23] For the issue of land grants, see Seema Alavi, "The Company Army and Rural Society: The Invalid Thanah 1788–1830," *Modern Asian Studies* 27:1 (1993). Soldiers who committed acts of bravery received both recognition in the form of the Indian Order of Merit (est. 1837) and increased pay according to rank and the number of acts committed. Even one recognized act of bravery brought with it a one-third increase in pay and pension. See also Alavi's *The Sepoys and the Company: Tradition and Transition in Northern India, 1770–1830* (Delhi: Oxford University Press, 1995).

[24] Washbrook, "India, 1818–1860," 404–406.

Economic Changes

In addition to the political transformations and the experience of violence common to most colonies in the middle decades of the nineteenth century, economic changes also deeply affected colonial subjects in this period. While the intensity of these changes naturally varied by location, they occurred alike in colonies under direct, indirect, and settler rule. The reasons for this near-universal character of economic change resulted from the dual effects of colonial tax collection and increasing integration into global (and increasingly industrialized) markets, both of which were intimately related. Indeed, although tax collection was common to many areas of the world prior to colonial rule, European colonial administrations tended to be more insistent about the regularity with which taxes were collected, without regard to their subjects' ability to pay.[25] Colonial authorities also established monopolies over certain popular necessities such as salt (India and Indochina), as well as drugs such as alcohol (Indochina) and opium (India and Indochina), and required that purchasers pay taxes on each. Even more important, European colonial administrations nearly everywhere insisted that colonial subjects pay taxes in cash rather than in kind. In other words, not only was there little flexibility in colonial systems of tax collection, but colonial subjects also had to translate their revenues from crops or services into cash. In general, this meant one of two things: colonial subjects either had to sell their labor to people who would pay them in cash, or they had to grow crops that would sell in a cash market.

In India, the effects of tax collection in cash proved devastating to millions of colonial subjects. In 1757, when the Company acquired the rights from the Mughal emperor to collect the land taxes from Bengal, its leaders realized the vast potential for wealth such rights could have. Bengal was a fertile, wealthy territory, and its taxable wealth alone exceeded the EIC's previous profits from trade. Yet with the advent of

Company rule, Mughal regulations that kept peasants' tax burdens from climbing too high were disrupted. As a result, both tax collectors and landlords working under the auspices of the EIC resorted to massive corruption and extortion, causing peasant tax burdens to rise drastically. After a huge famine in 1770 and several unsuccessful measures to stem the negative effects of excessive taxation, in 1793 the British Parliament stepped in to institute what became known as the Permanent Settlement. As part of the Settlement, land taxes were fixed in perpetuity in order to ensure that peasants endured a reasonable tax burden.[26] At the same time, however, the Settlement insisted on cash payments and made no allowances for times of economic crisis or natural disasters, and thus provided for the confiscation and sale of any properties for which tenants and landlords could not pay. Thus, the Permanent Settlement unintentionally created a market for land in Bengal that had never existed before, and resulted in a major shift in the landlord class from the landed elite to Indian civil servants, merchants, and others who had learned to use the British court system to their advantage. This shift in landownership, in turn, led many new landlords to insist that their tenants grow crops that would yield the highest profits—in other words, cash crops that could be sold on international markets rather than food crops for subsistence and regional markets. Thus, in spite of Parliament's attempts to alleviate the worst effects of extortion on the peasant population of Bengal, economic transformations as a result of EIC policies on taxation were profound.

Moreover, as the Company added new territories to its Indian empire outside of Bengal, officials were under no obligation to extend the Permanent Settlement and its fixed tax rates. Rather, Company policy in new territories was expressed in what became known as the *ryotwari* system, under which individual peasants (*ryots*) were taxed directly by the government instead of

---

[25] Osterhammel, *Colonialism*, 72.

[26] For the debate leading up to the Permanent Settlement, see Ranajit Guha, *A Rule of Property for Bengal: An Essay on the Idea of Permanent Settlement* (Hyderabad: Orient Longman, 1982). For the outcomes of the Permanent Settlement, see Marshall, *Bengal*.

through a middleman/landlord, as in Bengal. Under this system, land was taxed not according to actual revenues produced by crops, but according to estimates of soil productivity. Thus, the better the land, the higher the tax assessment. Assessments were extremely high (often one-third of the revenues produced by crops), could be increased from year to year, and were required to be paid in cash without exception.[27] The results of the ryotwari system were several. First, the demands of such high assessments caused many peasants to go into arrears and lose their land. Second, peasants increasingly chose to raise cash crops in order to pay their taxes with specie, which frequently meant, as in Bengal, the neglect of critical food crops. Finally, assessments based on land quality led desperate peasants to move from productive lands with high assessments to marginal lands with lower assessments.[28] This, however, had the effect of placing individual peasant families at greater risk of famine when times got tough, as they did during a major depression that occurred between 1820 and 1850. Clearly, economic policies related to taxation alone could be enough not only to cause widespread suffering among colonial populations, but to redistribute the land to new owners as well as encourage the growth of crops deemed most desirable by the colonial state.

Indeed, the issue of raising cash crops to pay taxes was directly related to the other major impetus behind economic change under colonial rule in this period: increasing integration into ever larger global markets. Even in areas where colonized subjects had limited contact with colonizers, the processes involved in global economic integration could prompt massive change and social dislocation within colonial communities. As we have already seen, by the middle decades of the nineteenth century industrial technology made it easier and cheaper to move products around the world, which in turn meant that the markets for cash crops were far larger than ever before. By the nineteenth century, Euro-Americans had developed strong affinities for a variety of tropical and semi-tropical products, including not only sugar, tobacco, and indigo, but also coffee, tea, chocolate, opium, and spices. Given these conditions, colonial authorities and those affiliated with the colonial state encouraged colonial subjects to grow cash crops that could easily be sold on international markets for relatively high prices. Colonial states, in turn, could ensure a profit from such crops either by purchasing them at fixed levels from peasants and then selling them at a profit, or—as under the ryotwari system—by direct taxation on the peasantry. However it was done, the end result was an increase in the taxable income of the colonial state and, frequently, the economic exploitation of colonial subjects.

An infamous example of the wide-ranging economic effects of colonial cash-cropping was the Cultivation System practiced on Dutch Java from 1830 to 1870. Under this system, the Dutch government of the East Indies used its authority to force Javanese peasants to grow cash crops—especially coffee, sugar, and indigo—at low fixed prices, which the government then sold at high prices on the international market.[29] Government officials assigned each village a particular cash crop, and villagers were expected to devote a maximum of one-fifth of total village land to its cultivation. In addition, villagers were expected to provide 66 days of *corvée* (unpaid) labor per year in the production of these crops. From the perspective of the Dutch East Indies government, the Cultivation System was a spectacular success: the value of exports from Java increased from 11 million guilders in 1830 to 125 million in 1870, while government revenues jumped from 19 million guilders in 1830 to 124 million in 1870.[30] Nor was the lesson lost on colonial planners—the obvious "success" of policies like this one would make taxation a cornerstone of colonialism in

---

[27] For a detailed development of the ryotwari system, see Burton Stein's biography of the man credited with its creation, *Thomas Munro: The Origins of the Colonial State and His Vision of Empire* (Delhi: Oxford University Press, 1989).

[28] Washbrook, "India, 1818–1860," 419.

[29] Cornelis Fasseur, *The Politics of Colonial Exploitation: Java, the Dutch, and the Cultivation System*, 2nd edition (Ithaca, NY: Cornell Studies on Southeast Asia, 1994), 27.

[30] Pierre van der Eng, "Cultivation System," in *Oxford Encyclopedia of the Modern World*, edited by Peter Stearns (New York: Oxford University Press, 2008), 391.

later periods. But from the perspective of Javanese peasants, the results were far less positive. For one thing, Dutch officials tended to increase land tax assessments on lands that produced cash crops, which meant that any profits peasants made from the crops tended to be negated by increased tax dues. In addition, raising cash crops sometimes caused serious hunger and suffering, since land that could have been devoted to food production (particularly rice) now had to be diverted to cash crop production. Some crops, particularly indigo, also exhausted the soil, which further reduced the ability of the land to provide either food or cash crops.[31] Peasants felt the burdens of cash crop production even more strongly in cases where the cropland was located far from home, which resulted in reduced ability to oversee subsistence crops. Finally, when entire villages were forced to grow one particular cash crop, global fluctuations in price and demand could have devastating effects for village communities. In fact, the system was so destructive to the peasantry that the Dutch government abandoned it in the 1870s. By then, however, one thing was certain: through the economic policies of the colonial government, nearly every village and peasant in Java had felt the impact of being brought into a globalized cash economy even if they had never met a Dutch person.[32]

Economic changes associated with increasing integration into global markets were not always related to the need for colonial subjects to raise cash for taxation. In some cases, incorporation into a European empire also meant the destruction of pre-existing economies based on craft production. The classic example of this occurred in India under the EIC. Prior to Company rule, India had been widely known as the *workshop of the early modern world* for its inexpensive yet high-quality production of lightweight cotton textiles.[33] Yet the connection with Britain via Company rule allowed the British Parliament—influenced by manufacturers intent on capturing Indian markets—to impose tariffs on Indian

cotton goods while providing an open door to British goods in India. Over time, the penetration of factory-produced British goods into Indian markets, coupled with the exclusion of Indian goods from British markets, undermined the viability of India's textile-producing areas. The collapse of these industries, in turn, contributed to a 30-year depression between 1820 and 1850, and resulted in the loss of livelihood on a massive scale. Consequently, thousands of Indians affected by these changes left towns and urban centers to return to the land. Ironically, then, India became more agrarian and rural in the first half of the nineteenth century than ever before.[34]

Economic changes caused by the growth of global markets and the rise of cash economies also resulted in mass movements of people within and between colonies, which themselves had strong economic—not to mention social and political—implications for those living under colonial rule. These mass movements occurred both among colonizers and colonized peoples. Among colonizers, the search for profit via cash crops or natural resources resulted in worldwide population shifts from Europe to the colonies, and in the case of the United States, to the American west. Among the most powerful economic incentives for such movement in this period was gold: discoveries of the ore in California (1848), British Columbia (1850), and Australia (1851) in the mid-nineteenth century prompted mass migration, the construction of boom towns, and the creation of large, permanent European settlements. These migrations, in turn, put increased pressure on indigenous lands, created the conditions for heightened colonial conflict, and often succeeded in driving indigenous peoples from their lands. Apart from gold rushes, tens of thousands of Europeans moved out into the colonies in order to establish themselves on farms and plantations devoted to crops that would sell well on the international market. Indeed, in the century between

---

[31]Fasseur, *The Politics of Colonial Exploitation*, 44.
[32]Ibid., 34.
[33]Washbrook, "India, 1818–1860," 397.

[34]Ibid., 403. For a broad exploration of economic change in India during this period, see K.N. Chaudhuri, *The Economic Development of India, 1814–1858: A Selection of Contemporary Writings* (Cambridge: Cambridge University Press, 1971).

1815 and 1914, 22.6 million Britons alone left their homes and migrated overseas, both to the colonies and to the United States.[35] In French Algeria, hundreds of thousands of European colonists moved onto land originally owned by indigenous Algerians, as well as onto previously unfarmed swampland that had been drained by massive French engineering projects. The result for millions of colonized subjects was massive dispossession from the land and, in Canada, New Zealand, Australia, and the United States, the creation of special reserves—nearly always on marginal land—for settlement. Nor were such reservations merely a feature of this period. Their obvious utility would be noted by colonial planners in the twentieth century who would recreate them in some of the more settler-dominated colonies of the New Imperialism such as Kenya and South Africa (see chapter 13).[36] Once transferred to these reserves, people in each location discovered that the lands were both too small and too marginal for everyone living on them to subsist. Consequently, in order to survive, millions of men and women found it necessary to go to work for the settlers as menial laborers and servants.

Indeed, colonized subjects moved frequently as a result of economic forces. As we have already seen, sometimes colonized peoples were forced to move off their lands as a result of European immigration, and this type of movement certainly caused social and economic dislocation. But there were other types of movement as well. In some cases, the need to work for cash prompted colonized subjects to move to locations within colonies that provided access to cash-paying jobs. This could include both seasonal and permanent migration to cash crop plantations or urban areas where European companies or residences were likely to be found. In other cases,

global demands for labor in a variety of colonial contexts prompted huge population shifts from one colony to another. Once slavery was abolished in the British Empire in 1833, colonies that had relied on slave labor experienced an acute shortage of labor. In these instances, cash-poor colonial subjects or poverty-stricken individuals from non-colonial areas sold their labor as indentured servants. The numbers were enormous: between 1841 (when the system was initiated) and 1910 (when it waned), about 150,000 indentured servants from India, China, Africa, and the Pacific were shipped to colonies around the world every year—a total of over 10 million in all.[37] While these migrations focused mainly on the sugar-growing colonies that had once depended on slave labor—particularly the Caribbean colonies and Mauritius—after 1860, they included locations in South Africa, Australia, and South-East Asia. These population shifts not only siphoned off many desperately poor and therefore potentially rebellious colonial subjects to new locations, but also fundamentally reshaped the structure and composition of colonial societies at their destination sites.

Even in the absence of direct contact between colonizers and colonized peoples, the economic transformations set in motion by colonial rule in this period literally affected millions of colonial subjects and colonists from a variety of locations, occupations, and social classes. Whether through new taxation regimes, the transition to cash economies, integration into global markets, or mass movements in population as a result of economic pressures, economic change began to transform even the most local levels of colonial life in this period.

Social Transformations

In addition to political change and the use of violence in nearly every colonial society in this period, colonial rule usually entailed significant social transformations as well. Perhaps not surprisingly, the shape of these transformations was

---

[35] Marjory Harper, "British Migration and the Peopling of the Empire," in Porter, *The Nineteenth Century*, 75.
[36] There are no easily accessible comparative works discussing these reservations in global perspective. However, South African and U.S. systems of "reservations" are discussed in comparative analyses in several articles published by the journal *Safundi* and, interestingly, in the eleventh- and twelfth-grade history curriculum in South Africa.

[37] David Northrup, "Migration from Africa, Asia, and the South Pacific," in Porter, *The Nineteenth Century*, 88.

even more varied than the economic changes discussed earlier, given the individuality of humans and the variety of peoples involved in colonial locations in this period. Yet even amongst this variety, certain themes and issues stand out. For example, the particular ideas about difference Europeans and Euro-Americans brought with them to the colonies in this period were broadly similar, which in turn had comparable social consequences in many regions of the world. In addition, colonialism always involved new encounters between peoples, including not only encounters between colonizers and colonized but also new relationships between colonized groups. Finally, the introduction of European systems of education and law resulted in new social configurations in a variety of colonies around the world.

Scholars disagree about the extent to which Europeans arrived in the colonies with preconceived ideas about difference.[38] Yet as we have seen in previous chapters, it seems clear that Europeans already had a long tradition of regarding indigenous peoples in the Americas and in Africa as inferior. In the early modern period, much of this sense of European superiority was derived from the belief that non-Christians were less civilized than Christians. In the wake of the Industrial Revolution, however, many Europeans came to believe that their ability to command industrial technology was evidence that there was something inherently more "advanced" about Europeans and their descendents. As a result, Europeans increasingly viewed those who did not have comparable technologies as less developed as well as less intelligent.[39] By the early decades of the nineteenth century, these views were supplemented by new theories that located race as the main source of difference between peoples.[40] As early as 1815, European scientists were already deeply engaged in theorizing that physical differences—especially skin color—between groups of people denoted other kinds of differences, particularly relating to intelligence and ability.[41] Over the next six decades, scientists, naturalists, and explorers used these ideas to classify the world's peoples on a hierarchical scale, from the least to the most racially developed.[42] Although these theories were not unified and were sometimes contradictory in this period, in general they joined ideas about physical difference with ideas about technical superiority, so that the further a group was from Europeans in terms of technology and appearance, the further down it was placed on the hierarchy of the "races." As we will see in later chapters, these theories of human development and "scientific" racism would solidify and go on to underpin the vast expansion of colonies in Africa, South-East Asia, and the Pacific by the last decades of the nineteenth century.

Given these intellectual trends, it seems likely that Europeans who traveled to the colonies in the middle decades of the nineteenth century brought some definite ideas with them about European superiority. In addition, the main colonizing powers each had their own culturally specific ideas about superiority: Britons celebrated their long tradition of stability and the rule of law; the French celebrated the legacy of the French Revolution for the causes of liberty, equality, and brotherhood; the Dutch celebrated their liberalism and stability; and the Americans celebrated their ideas about freedom that had been enshrined in the revolution. Against these idealistic visions

---

[38] There is a large historiography about when and where ideas about difference—and particularly race—formed among Europeans. Edward Said, for example, famously argued in *Orientalism* that Europeans had already constructed ideas about difference between themselves and Orientals long before the nineteenth century. Others, however, have argued that ideas of difference were formed as a result of particular experiences such as the slave trade or colonial rule.

[39] Michael Adas, *Machines as the Measure of Men: Science, Technology, and Ideologies of Western Dominance* (Ithaca, NY: Cornell University Press, 1990), chapter 3.

[40] In fact, Roxanne Wheeler argues that the transition to a focus on skin color had already occurred by the end of the eighteenth century. See *The Complexion of Race: Categories of Difference in Eighteenth Century British Culture* (Philadelphia: University of Pennsylvania Press, 2000), 9.

[41] Martin S. Staum, *Labeling People: French Scholars on Society, Race, and Empire, 1815–1848* (Montreal: McGill-Queen's University Press, 2003); Waltrad Ernst and Bernard Harris, *Race, Science, and Medicine, 1700–1960* (London: Routledge, 1999), 5.

[42] Robert Miles, "Apropos the Idea of 'Race' ... Again," in *Theories of Race and Racism: A Reader*, edited by John Solomos et al. (London: Routledge, 2000), 125.

of their own cultures and capabilities, Europeans increasingly disparaged the qualities of colonial subjects in the language of race that was so fashionable in European society.

That said, however, it also seems likely that the experience of colonialism shaped Euro-American ideas about difference as well. Indeed, the practical necessities of justifying colonial conquest and then maintaining order—often by violence—encouraged Europeans to emphasize differences between themselves and those they ruled. By insisting on differences, colonizers were better able to maintain boundaries between themselves and those they colonized. Thus, whether in India, Vietnam, Australia, North America, South Africa, the Indonesian islands, or Malaya, colonizers increasingly referred to colonial subjects as inherently lazy, deceitful, dirty, backward, corrupt, in need of "uplifting," or depraved, depending on the context. Even the colonial critic P.L.F. Philastre wrote positively in the early 1870s of the French presence in Indochina, arguing that it was necessary "to raise up the Annamite people from the state of moral degradation into which they have fallen."[43] Ideas and practices relating to gender also influenced European beliefs about the racial inferiority of colonized peoples: in Algeria, for example, the Islamic practice of veiling women and keeping them secluded reinforced ideas about the inherent nature of Algerian backwardness, while in India the practice of *sati* (widow immolation) encouraged Europeans to think of Indians as barbaric and without morals.[44] Men as eminent as G.W.F. Hegel commented on the practice of sati, concluding in his 1822 *Philosophy of History* that "the morality which is involved in respect for human life, is not found among the Hindoos."[45]

These attitudes did more than simply shape European ideas about colonized people. Rather, they were also critical for shaping relations between colonizers and colonized and for informing the social geographies that characterized colonial societies. European beliefs in their own superiority shaped the ways they interacted with colonized peoples, from elites to peasants—interactions that frequently translated into condescension, dismissiveness, and even verbal or physical abuse. In cases where colonial subjects rebelled or questioned European authority, colonizers used the language of race as justification for severe retribution. During the Sepoy Rebellion of 1857 in India, for example, Britons regularly called rebellious soldiers *niggers*, and some even sanctioned the annihilation of all the "races" involved in the rebellion.[46] Racial ideologies also justified the exclusion of colonial subjects from positions of political power, particularly when such power could be extended over Europeans. Thus, in the Indian army colonial subjects could never outrank even the most junior British officer, while Indian civil officials were limited to the lower ranks of service. Settler societies were even more exclusive: in Australia, the United States, and South Africa, colonized subjects were allowed virtually no political role in this period. Meanwhile, in Dutch Java—where mixed-race unions were common—high colonial positions were almost always reserved for "pure" Europeans.[47]

Even social geographies in the colonies were influenced by European ideas about difference. For example, in many colonies Europeans segregated themselves away from colonial subjects in special neighborhoods, each built with reference to European styles. In Batavia, for example, the Dutch built an exclusive community replete with churches, houses, and a town hall according to Dutch architectural styles, and even installed canals through the main thoroughfares to remind them of home. Saigon, as well, featured French-style buildings for colonists, while Indian cities

---

[43] Quoted in Frederick Quinn, *The French Overseas Empire* (Westport, CT: Praeger Press, 2002), 143.

[44] For Algeria, see Julia Clancy-Smith, "Islam, Gender, and Identities in the Making of French Algeria, 1830–1962," in *Domesticating the Empire: Race, Gender, and Family Life in French and Dutch Colonialism*, edited by Julia Clancy-Smith and Frances Gouda (Charlottesville: University of Virginia Press, 1998); for the case of sati in India, see Lata Mani, *Contentious Traditions: The Debate on Sati in India* (Berkeley: University of California Press, 1998).

[45] Reprinted in Harlow and Carter, *From the East India Company to the Suez Canal*, 375.

[46] Streets, *Martial Races*, 72.

[47] Jean Gelman Taylor, *The Social World of Batavia: Europeans and Eurasians in Colonial Indonesia*, 2nd edition (Madison: University of Wisconsin Press, 2009), 115–118.

like Calcutta (later renamed Kolkata) featured segregated (and often walled) British neighborhoods replete with European plants in the gardens.[48] In settler societies, colonists took residential segregation to the extreme by removing colonial subjects to reservations and keeping the land for themselves, as they did in Algeria, Australia, South Africa, the western United States, and New Zealand.

Residential segregation, not surprisingly, extended to social segregation as well, as Europeans isolated themselves by participating in exclusive leisure activities and attending European-only clubs. This pattern was particularly noticeable in British colonies. In nineteenth-century British India, for example, the "club" became the center of social life for all Britons, where men went to drink and talk business and women went to socialize. Britons insisted that clubs were European preserves—havens of Britishness in the midst of foreign soil—and thus refused membership to all Indians. Having denied Indians membership on the basis of race, however, they also denied them the ability to carry on the necessary social networking for working their way up in the colonial hierarchy. In this way, ideas about race—which justified the exclusion of Indians from British neighborhoods and clubs in the first place—also made it impossible for Indians to participate fully in the political and social worlds of the colonial regime, thus increasing antagonisms between colonizers and at least some groups of colonized subjects.[49]

However much Europeans tried to insist on racial exclusiveness and the maintenance of clear boundaries, social encounters between colonizers and colonized nevertheless occurred with great frequency—contact that, in turn, shaped social and political relations in fundamental ways. Critical among these encounters were the sexual relationships that occurred in every

colony between foreign colonizers and colonized subjects—especially between European men and colonized women.[50] These relationships were widely viewed by nearly every colonial administration of this period, including settler societies, to be inevitable. As a result, nearly every colony provided some kind of allowance for them. In some cases, this meant that colonial authorities looked the other way when colonized women were kidnapped and raped—a feature not uncommon to life on the Australian outback, for example.[51] In other cases, as in India, the Company (and then the Crown) provided European soldiers' barracks with nearby access to brothels so that soldiers did not resort to homosexuality.[52] In Java, by contrast, the Dutch encouraged colonial officials at all levels to take Javanese concubines for the duration of their posts.[53] It is important to note that this type of sexual license, while a feature of colonialism for much of the nineteenth century, would become far less acceptable to metropolitan public opinion as racism hardened colonialism in the twentieth century.

Historians have argued about whether these sexual relationships were a positive or negative force in relationships between colonizers and colonized subjects.[54] While there is little doubt that some relationships of genuine affection occurred in colonial situations, more often these relationships were based on ideologies of social and racial inequality that frequently worked to the detriment of colonized women. In India, for

---

[48] The British went even further in creating a home-like, segregated environment in the hill stations in the Himalayan mountains. See Dane Kennedy, *The Magic Mountains: Hill Stations and the British Raj* (Berkeley: University of California Press, 1996).

[49] For more on British clubs in India, see Mrinalini Sinha, "Britishness, Clubbability, and the Colonial Public Sphere," in *Bodies in Contact: Rethinking Colonial Encounters in World History*, edited by Tony Ballantyne and Antoinette Burton (Durham, NC: Duke University Press, 2005).

---

[50] Sexual relationships between European women and colonized men did occur, but they were considered highly scandalous.

[51] Reynolds, *The Other Side of the Frontier*, 174–175.

[52] Kenneth Ballhatchet, *Race, Sex, and Class Under the Raj: Imperial Attitudes and Policies and Their Critics, 1793–1905* (London: Palgrave Macmillan, 1980).

[53] Ann Stoler, *Carnal Knowledge and Imperial Power: Race and the Intimate in Colonial Rule* (Berkeley: University of California Press, 2002).

[54] The most explosive example of this is the debate between Ronald Hyam and M.T. Berger over Hyam's book, entitled *Empire and Sexuality: The British Experience* (Manchester: Manchester University Press, 1990), which argued that sex between colonizers and colonized peoples was a positive force for cultural understanding. Berger refuted such claims in his "Imperialism and Sexual Exploitation: A Review Article," and Hyam responded in "A Reply," both in the *Journal of Imperial and Commonwealth History* 17 (1988).

example, neither Indian mistresses nor mixed-race children were acknowledged by the state, which meant that they were not able to share any of the benefits of Britishness. In Australia, people of mixed races found that they were neither welcome in their own communities nor in the European settler community, and frequently found themselves living in poverty and isolation. Even in Java, where mixed sexual relations were encouraged, **concubinage** was favored over legal marriage. Fathers of mixed-race children had the option of recognizing their children, but they were not obligated to do so.[55] Moreover, when a Dutch colonist left the East Indies, he was perfectly within his rights to leave his concubine and children without any provision for the future. Thus, even while sexual relationships formed part of the colonial experience in almost every colony, the inequalities inherent in such relationships tended to reinforce notions of European superiority and increase the alienation of colonized people rather than ameliorate them, even as they created new communities of mixed-race children.

Regular social encounters between colonizers and colonized also occurred in the most private domestic spaces of colonial life. In almost every colony, including settler colonies, Europeans depended on colonized subjects to perform the everyday tasks of cooking, cleaning, washing, and child care. Thus, even in segregated neighborhoods, in clubs, or on plantations, some colonized subjects became integral parts of the personal spaces, domestic lives, and social institutions that colonizers sought to keep private. Relationships between colonizers and colonized were frequently tense and conflicted in these spaces, since colonized subjects gained critical access to colonizers' homes, food, treasures, and children. In the process, these relationships allowed colonized subjects everywhere to learn about the weaknesses, secrets, and fears of their colonial overlords.[56]

In addition to the new social encounters that occurred as a result of colonial rule, in many places colonialism resulted in entirely new social configurations. One of the most important of these new configurations was the development of new classes of European-educated colonial subjects—a process that began in this period and became ever more important toward the end of the nineteenth century. In almost every colony except settler societies, Europeans were unable to rule without the help of colonized subjects. In indirectly ruled colonies, this was obvious: in such areas, European residents and advisors clearly relied on colonized subjects to perform most administrative work, from tax collection to maintaining order. But even in directly ruled colonies where colonizers imported an entire ruling bureaucracy, the tasks of administration were too large—and European communities too small—to rely on European labor alone. Even in 1925, for example, only 5,000 French administrators in Indochina ruled a population of approximately 30 million.[57] Indeed, efficient colonial administration required more than just the maintenance of standing armies and police forces to keep order. If colonizers hoped to consistently extract maximum taxes from populations as well as keep tabs on developments in urban areas and distant provinces, they also had to establish a variety of administrative offices where minor officials could survey local areas and records could be created, filed, and copied for the centers of administration. In the major colonial centers, demand for clerks and minor officials was particularly intense for record-keeping, tax collection, copying official and semi-official correspondence, and assisting European administrators. Especially in densely

---

[55] For an exploration of sexual relationships in Dutch colonial Java, albeit for a slightly later time, see Frances Gouda's chapter on "Gender, Race, and Sexuality: Citizenship and Colonial Culture in the Dutch East Indies," in her *Dutch Culture Overseas: Colonial Practice in the Netherlands Indies, 1900–1942* (London: Equinox Publishing, 2008).

[56] For an exploration of the tensions and dynamics involved in domestic relationships, see Rosemary George, "Homes in the Empire, Empires in the Home," Cultural Critique (1994), 26. Stoler suggestively explores these relationships, albeit for a later period, in chapter 7 of *Carnal Knowledge and Imperial Power*.

[57] Ronald J. Cima, ed., *Vietnam: A Country Study* (Washington, DC: GPO for the Library of Congress, 1987).

populated colonies such as India, Indochina, and the Dutch East Indies, these needs required the labor of thousands. In India, for example, the need for English-educated Indians was so intense that, in 1857, the EIC opened the first English-based universities. Thirty years later, after the transition to Crown rule and just after the end of our period, more than 60,000 Indians had entered such universities.[58]

The creation of these European-educated groups had enormous implications for social relations within the colonies, both in the short and the long terms. In fact, their existence gave rise to entirely new social configurations that were not a part of "traditional" ruling elites. Although the numbers of people who received European educations were always small in proportion to total colonial populations, their particular experience of colonial rule had profound implications for the future. First, these men—and, by extension, their families—became uniquely positioned arbiters between Europeans and colonial subjects. Through their European educations, they became intimately familiar with European culture, methods, and ideologies. As colonial subjects themselves, however, they also remained rooted in their own local and regional cultures, and served as vital translators—albeit from their own class perspective—of colonial life. Moreover, they also became agents of change within their own societies as well. One well-known example was the English-educated Indian Raja Ram Mohan Roy. As a Hindu and Indian, Roy believed in the beauty of his religion. At the same time, through his contact with Britons and British education, he also came to accept a variety of British criticisms regarding contemporary Hinduism. His response, in the early decades of the nineteenth century, was reform. According to Roy, if contemporary Hinduism could be reformed to a more "pure" state based on early teachings and writings, such efforts—including the abolition of sati and child marriage—would not only revitalize the religion but might also moderate

British views about the debased nature of Indian society.[59] Roy's views were welcomed by many other educated Indians in the first half of the nineteenth century, who joined forces with him to lobby for such reforms. As a result of their efforts, educated Indians were crucial in abolishing sati (1829) throughout British India. Such reforms helped to transform Indian social life in important ways, as they not only brought changes to contemporary Hindu practices but also galvanized other social groups in India to articulate strong defenses against reforms inspired by British ideas.[60]

The introduction of European-style education was not the only feature of colonial life that led to new social configurations. Except in areas under indirect rule, where colonizers sometimes maintained one legal system for themselves and another for colonial subjects, Europeans imposed their own legal systems and legal ideas on colonial populations. The decisions of these courts, in turn, could fundamentally reshape social geographies as well as relations between competing social groups.[61] For example, one of the most fundamental aspects of European legal thought was the belief in the sanctity of private property, even when such ideas were interpreted differently in colonial societies. As a result, those who knew how to utilize European court systems had a strong advantage to winning disputes over property ownership and use. We have already seen how Indians allied with the EIC were able to take advantage of the British court system to win the lands of landlords who defaulted on their taxes. Land transfers as a result of legal decisions were particularly common in settler societies, since settlers and colonial authorities used the force of European law to literally write indigenous peoples off the land.

The imposition of European law could also result in more subtle—but no less important—social transformations. Indeed, legal decisions

---

[58] Washbrook, "India, 1818–1860," 417; and Robin Moore, "Imperial India, 1858–1914," in Porter, *The Nineteenth Century*, 431.

[59] Judith Brown, *Modern India: The Origins of an Asian Democracy* (Oxford: Oxford University Press, 1985), 77–78.
[60] Washbrook, "India, 1818–1860," 397.
[61] It should be kept in mind, however, that this process was uneven and messy, as pointed out by Lauren Benton in *Law and Colonial Cultures: Legal Regimes in World History, 1400–1900* (Cambridge: Cambridge University Press, 2002).

handed down by European courts had the tendency to create hard boundaries between otherwise fluid social situations, which in turn created precedents for future decisions along similarly fixed lines. One example of the consequences of such legal decisions occurred with regard to the Indian caste system. Prior to Company rule, ideas about caste in Indian society varied widely according to location, *varna* (caste division), and *jati* (lineage or occupational group). Moreover, although the caste system was hierarchical, it seems that the boundaries between both varnas and jati were relatively fluid and changeable over time. As outsiders, however, Britons viewed the caste system as an ancient and fixed expression of Indian culture, with firm boundaries and rigid distinctions. They were guided in this interpretation by those Indians upon whom they most relied for translating Indian culture—high caste, literate, Brahman men. Not coincidentally, those Indians of the highest castes had the most to gain from maintaining firm boundaries between the varnas, and also practiced a more strict form of Hinduism than those of lower castes. And since it was high-caste Hindus who had the ear of Company administrators, it was their ideas about caste that most strongly shaped British ideas. In turn, the effects of these ideas were felt in real ways by real people through the newly introduced court system, where EIC judges turned out opinions and set precedents regarding a wide variety of caste relations.[62] In accordance with high-caste prescriptions, then, EIC judges used their ideas about the firm boundaries between caste groups in ways that restructured property ownership, marriage, inheritance, and public worship.[63] Over time, Indian social practices with respect to caste were redrawn according to the legal interpretations of British judges.

Although the social transformations that accompanied colonial rule varied widely by location, mode of governance, and ruling power, it is nevertheless clear that social change was widespread and significant nearly everywhere. European ideas about difference were crucial in the creation of many of these changes, but so too were social encounters between new groups of people. In some areas, moreover, social change was so significant that it led to the creation of new social configurations, themselves spurred by the introduction of colonial systems of education and law.

RESISTANCE TO THE IMPOSITION AND EFFECTS OF COLONIAL RULE

Given the myriad social, political, and economic changes typical of so many colonial situations—as well as the violence frequently used in their institution—it is perhaps not surprising that resistance was one of the most ubiquitous features of colonial life all over the world. Resistance could take many forms: it could be active or passive, violent or nonviolent, coordinated or uncoordinated. The most pervasive type of resistance—as well as the most difficult to prevent—was the millions of individual acts of defiance colonized subjects employed in order to retain dignity in the face of humiliation or subjugation. Laborers who were physically or verbally abused at the hands of colonizers or their allies, for example, might deliberately slow their speed of work or engage in acts of sabotage.[64] Women who became pregnant through forced concubinage might consume herbs or medicines to induce abortion. Men forced into servitude, military service, or intolerable working conditions might desert. Peasants faced with crushing tax burdens might engage in illegal squatting to avoid taxes, while laborers, servants, and clerks might line their pockets by stealing from their masters. Colonial subjects of all classes and occupations could also respond to disparaging treatment through anti-colonial songs and stories, subversive folktales, or by spreading unflattering rumors.[65]

---

[62] This is one of the central arguments in Susan Bayly, *Caste, Society, and Politics in India from the Eighteenth Century to the Modern Age* (Cambridge: Cambridge University Press, 1999).
[63] Washbrook, "India, 1818–1860," 415.

[64] James C. Scott, *Weapons of the Weak: Everyday Forms of Peasant Resistance* (New Haven, CT: Yale University Press, 1987), 33.
[65] James C. Scott, *Domination and the Arts of Resistance: Hidden Transcripts* (New Haven, CT: Yale University Press, 1990), chapter 6.

Although it is impossible to know with precision how often these kinds of resistance occurred, historical research indicates it was extremely widespread in colonial societies. Moreover, because the techniques of such resistance did not encourage open confrontation, it was often—somewhat ironically—far more successful than armed rebellion in achieving its goals. Tax evaders and squatters, for example, seriously cut into the revenue of colonial states, while laborers who deliberately slowed their work reduced the profitability of their masters' enterprises.[66] Perhaps more importantly, individuals who resisted their domination regained a small amount of control over both their lives and their dignity.

Yet not all resistance employed such clandestine strategies. Invasion, conquest, and change as a result of colonial rule also sparked open confrontation and violent responses regardless of mode of governance. In some cases, open defiance from existing stakeholders began prior to invasion: in 1848, for example, the Vietnamese Emperor Tu Duc, who harbored an abiding dislike of Catholicism, tried to rid his kingdom of French missionaries even before the French government attempted to capture the area for itself. Moreover, when the French did send an armed contingent to Annam in 1856—accompanied by a threatening letter addressed to the emperor—Tu Duc insulted the French emissary by sending the letter back unopened.[67] Such initial defiance could also be violent, as it was in Algeria. There, the Ottoman dey responded to the initial show of French military force in 1827 by destroying French trading posts. Once the French retaliated by invading the state in 1830, open Algerian resistance to French rule continued until 1870, and was only put down with the application of brutal military force.[68] On Africa's Gold Coast, the Asante Confederation responded to British interference with four separate military confrontations between 1823 and 1874.

In other cases, initial interactions between Europeans and indigenous peoples were relatively friendly until Europeans' full intentions became clear. In New Zealand, European settlers persuaded Maori leaders to tolerate their presence, and in 1840 the two groups even entered into a major treaty of understanding that delineated the fair division of land between them.[69] Only when it became overwhelmingly clear that Europeans were not honoring the terms of these treaties did some Maori groups raise arms against them in a series of wars between 1845 and 1872.[70] In Java, the small Dutch presence had been just one among many competing mini-states in the region during the seventeenth and eighteenth centuries. This meant that Dutch officials were not free to simply impose their will on neighboring states without the judicious use of diplomacy. As a result, until the nineteenth century local states did not view the Dutch as conquerors set on sovereign control of the island. When it became clear that the Dutch did indeed intend to wrest sovereignty from local states in the early decades of the nineteenth century, several Javanese kingdoms banded together under Prince Diponegoro in a major—albeit ultimately unsuccessful—war to crush Dutch power from 1825 to 1830.[71] In Australia, the initial reception of settlers by Aboriginal groups varied widely from peaceful to violent, but violence increased markedly once it became clear that settlers were determined to claim exclusive title to the land.[72] In the western United States, meanwhile, resistance by the Lakota tribe to encroachment by the United States on their lands in the Black Hills finally resulted in the Great Sioux War of 1876–1877.[73]

---

[66] Scott, *Weapons of the Weak*, 31.
[67] Robert Aldrich, *Greater France: A History of French Expansion Overseas* (London: Palgrave, 1996), 76.
[68] Ibid., 26–27.

[69] This was the Treaty of Waitangi.
[70] Donald Denoon, Philippa Mein-Smith, and Marivic Wyndham, *A History of Australia, New Zealand, and the Pacific* (Oxford: Blackwell, 2000), 130–132.
[71] Jean Gelman Taylor, *Indonesia* (New Haven, CT: Yale University Press, 2003), 232–234.
[72] Reynolds, *The Other Side of the Frontier*, chapter 3; and Ann McGrath, ed., *Contested Ground: Australian Aborigines Under the British Crown* (Crows Nest NSW: Allen & Unwin, 1995), 15, 19.
[73] For an Indian perspective on this war, see Jerome Greene, *Lakota and Cheyenne: Indian Views of the Great Sioux War, 1876–1877* (Norman: University of Oklahoma Press, 2000).

Sometimes resistance occurred when the changes wrought by colonial rule pushed colonized subjects to desperation. In these cases, violent rebellion might occur after months, years, or even decades of discontent, and then be sparked by a single event. In Jamaica's 1865 Morant Bay Rebellion, for example, the arrest of a black man accused of trespassing ignited years of frustration and maltreatment into a wave of violence and murder directed against British colonists.[74] Yet perhaps the most famous example of simmering discontent exploding into rebellion occurred during the Indian Rebellion of 1857. Ironically, the spark that lit this rebellion occurred within the army built to secure British rule in India. In 1856, soldiers in the Bengal army became aware that the cartridges for the new Enfield muzzle-loading rifles being issued to the East India Company Army were greased with the fat of pork and beef. For Hindus, eating or touching beef to the lips meant a loss of caste, and for Muslims, the ingestion of pork was repugnant to the faith. Thus, it seemed to many that the British were deliberately and openly trying to make both Hindu and Muslim soldiers lose their religion, because army drill required that the soldier bite off one end of the cartridge before loading the rifles. Upon investigation, Company administrators discovered that tallow or lard had in fact been used to lubricate the cartridges, and it was suspected that animal fat from pigs or cows had inadvertently been included in the mixture.[75] Although the British military administration moved quickly to correct the blunder by allowing the cartridge to be torn with the hands, the damage had already been done.[76] Many regiments refused the cartridges, and when 85 men from the 3rd Native Cavalry in Mirath

(Meerut) were publicly degraded and imprisoned for refusing orders to use them, the next day—May 10, 1857—the whole regiment mutinied in protest and killed their British commanders.[77]

After this first mutiny, regiment after regiment in the Bengal army followed suit, until 61 of the 74 regiments of Bengal infantry rebelled, as well as all of the regiments of the Bengal light cavalry. Over the summer of 1857, most of north-central India became lost to British control. In the province of Awadh, as well as in other areas nearby in Uttar Pradesh, civil rebellions stemming from economic suffering accompanied the military rebellion and changed its tenor to an all-out popular revolt that enveloped all classes of the population.[78]

In fact, the Indian Rebellion (originally called the Sepoy Mutiny) was a response not just to one event but rather the combination of transformations that colonialism entailed in this period. For example, many Indian soldiers who joined were partly motivated by anger at the increasing racist terminology and treatment exerted by their European officers. They were spurred on and joined by nonsoldiers whose participation was partly a religious protest against the actions of Baptists and other Christian missionaries in a predominantly Muslim and Hindu area. Another main point of contention was the replacement of the king of Awadh, discussed earlier in this chapter. The king's replacement was part of a series of "reforms" that would

---

[74] For a detailed account of the rebellion at Morant Bay and its consequences, see Thomas Holt, *The Problem of Freedom: Race, Labor, and Politics in Jamaica and Britain, 1832–1938* (Baltimore: Johns Hopkins University Press, 1991), chapter 8.

[75] Surendra Nath Sen, *Eighteen Fifty-Seven* (Delhi: Publications Division, 1957), 42.

[76] T.A. Heathcote, *The Indian Army: The Garrison of British Imperial India, 1822–1922* (London: David and Charles, 1974), 86.

[77] The general rebellion discussed here refers only to the Bengal army. The Bombay and Madras armies, with very little exception, remained quiet during the rebellion—a fact that was widely used after the Uprising to support the continuance of the three-army system. The reasons they did not rise with the Bengal army have been hotly debated, but it is generally agreed that distance between the armies discouraged communication, and that the particular conditions in the Bengal army of mass disaffection and religious grievances did not exist in either the Madras or Bombay armies.

[78] An early attempt to locate the rebellion as a large-scale peasant revolt in addition to a military mutiny was described in S.B. Chaudhuri's *Civil Rebellion in the Indian Mutinies, 1857–1859* (Calcutta: World Press Private, 1957). Eric Stokes later took up the subject in *The Peasant Armed: The Indian Revolt of 1857* (Oxford: Clarendon, 1986), as did Mukherjee in *Awadh in Revolt* and Ranajit Guha in *Elementary Aspects of Peasant Insurgency in Colonial India* (Delhi: Oxford University Press, 1983).

have seized any princely state whose rulers did not have a direct heir or were deemed "incompetent," and would then have placed them under direct company rule. Since many soldiers were from Awadh, this act helped to provoke them to join the rebellion. Finally, the rebels were joined by some peasants who found labor on plantations under British rule or British taxes too onerous for them and hoped for something better, although their role was not nearly as important as that of the army.

Only in the autumn of 1857 did British counter-rebellion measures begin to have serious impact on the progress of the revolt. By the middle of November, British-led forces had retaken both Delhi and Lucknow, and by the middle of 1858 most Britons were confident of eventual victory.[79] The price, however, had been extremely high in Indian lives, as British and allied forces had used appalling violence against both soldiers and civilians in order to suppress the rebellion.[80] Moreover, the EIC had been completely discredited, and in 1859 the British crown assumed direct control over the colony.

The Indian Rebellion was only the largest and most violent rebellion to occur in the middle decades of the nineteenth century. In almost every location, some colonial subjects grew so desperate or dissatisfied with colonial rule that they resorted to open, armed resistance. In many instances, such resistance remained local, as individuals or small groups sought to rid themselves of a particularly onerous oppressor, or else sought redress for being wronged, humiliated, or impoverished. In other instances, however, armed resistance was severe enough to pose a real threat to the continuation of colonial rule—as it was in India in 1857 or in Java between 1825 and 1830. In some places, including French Indochina and Algeria, resistance never disappeared entirely, and continued to flare throughout this period. When viewed in conjunction with the nonviolent, individual resistance that occurred on a daily basis in every colony, it is clear that resistance was a pervasive feature of colonial experiences across spatial and national boundaries.

Conclusion

Although it is impossible here to address what colonial rule might have meant for each of the millions of individuals who lived during this period, it is possible to say that the experience of colonialism was rarely, if ever, neutral. Whether living under direct, indirect, or settler rule, colonial subjects were faced with significant—sometimes momentous—change. Such change, indeed, could be extreme, and could include loss of life during conquest, pacification, or rebellion; loss of political power; and loss of property or livelihood. Change could also include new or increased impoverishment due to colonial tax regimes and incorporation into the global economy, adjustment to new legal structures, migration, or the introduction of new social arrangements. Experiences of colonialism were frequently turbulent, difficult and, in many areas, negative—which helps to explain high levels of resistance from colony to colony. At the same time, colonial rule also sometimes worked to the benefit of colonial subjects who allied themselves to colonizers through military, police, or administrative service, or who found ways to profit from colonial economic arrangements. Despite significant differences between local colonial realities, then, the forced imposition of power, the near-ubiquitous use of violence, and broadly comparable economic and social pressures produced enough similar results to make colonial experiences in this period recognizable across the boundaries of space, type, or ruling power.

Moreover, each of the features of colonial experience discussed earlier continued in importance—and were expanded upon—in the

---

[79] Surendra Sen provides an in-depth narrative of the events of the rebellion in his *Eighteen Fifty-Seven*; as does Christopher Hibbert, albeit more apologetically, in *The Great Mutiny: India 1857* (New York: Viking, 1978). P.J.O. Taylor has produced the useful *What Really Happened During the Mutiny: A Day-by-Day Account of the Major Events of 1857–59 in India* (Delhi: Oxford University Press, 1997).

[80] Streets, *Martial Races*, 65–67.

period of High Imperialism that began at the end of the nineteenth century. Indeed, the modes of government, military organizations, economic systems, and social ideas (particularly regarding difference and race) developed in this period continued to inform metropolitan and colonial authorities in the late nineteenth and twentieth centuries. Perhaps even more importantly, the new social configurations that had their start in the middle decades of the nineteenth century—especially the rise of a European-educated elite—would become ever more important in the later period, as would the plentiful models of resistance and rebellion to colonial rule.

Questions

1. As we saw in the previous chapter, this period is often described as one of "informal empire." Does the information presented in this chapter suggest that this description is incorrect or correct? Why and how?

2. What did colonialism "mean" in India during this period? In what ways did life change for much of the population? How did they "experience" colonialism?

3. In what ways was the Indian Rebellion of 1857 a response to some of the common colonial experiences of this period as discussed in the second section of this chapter?

CHAPTER **10**

Imperialism: The New Imperialism and the Scramble for Colonies

In 1902, the liberal English economist John Hobson wrote that Britain had over the preceding three decades undertaken a **New Imperialism** that straddled the globe. He based this assessment on "concrete facts," and argued that "European nations, Great Britain being first and foremost, [have] annexed or otherwise asserted political sway over vast portions of Africa and Asia, and over numerous islands in the Pacific and elsewhere."[1] A firm supporter of the "little England" policy that was at heart a rejection of empire, he expressed alarm that "[w]ithin fifteen years some three and three-quarter millions of square miles were added to the British Empire." Hobson was only the first of many contemporary scholars, politicians, and critical thinkers to recognize a new, global era of imperialism emerging sometime between 1870 and 1880. Today, most historians continue to accept this decade as a benchmark in the history of imperialism, and indeed of the world.

Yet the idea that Britain, Europe, and the whole world entered a new era of imperialism in the last decades of the nineteenth century is entirely open to question. As we saw in chapter 8, over the century following the independence of 13 North American colonies in the 1770s, Britain had dramatically increased the size of its empire once again. The remaining North American colonies had tripled their dimensions and been unified into the territory of Canada. Two new, enormous colonies had come into existence in Australia and New Zealand, and were slowly filling up with Britons. On the tip of Africa, the tiny Napoleonic war prize of Cape Town had been built into a substantial territorial possession through the subjugation of both earlier waves of Dutch settlers and the indigenous population. Perhaps most importantly, India, one of the wealthiest and most populous regions of the world, had gradually been brought under Crown authority.

Nor was Britain the only empire-builder of that period. The 13 seceded colonies, unified as the United States of America, had spent much of the century between 1770 and 1870 slowly annexing the vast area to their west, eventually sweeping across the prairies and forests of middle America to the Pacific Ocean, and even capturing a portion of the territory of Mexico. Mirroring this, the great Russian state had continued its march eastward and to the south from its West Asian metropole. The steppes of Central Asia and the vast forests and tundra of Siberia had

---

[1] John A. Hobson, *Imperialism: A Study* (London, 1902), part I, chapter 1.

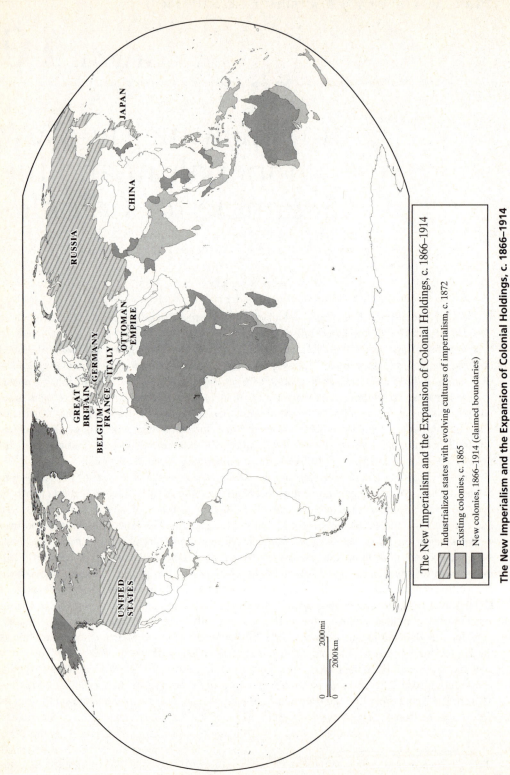

The New Imperialism and the Expansion of Colonial Holdings, c. 1866–1914

Industrialized states with evolving cultures of imperialism, c. 1872

Existing colonies, c. 1865

New colonies, 1866–1914 (claimed boundaries)

The New Imperialism and the Expansion of Colonial Holdings, c. 1866–1914

both succumbed to its armies, priests, trappers, and administrators.

By and large, this early to mid-nineteenth-century process of territorial acquisition had not been overly competitive. Aside from sustained but usually low-level Anglo–Russian rivalry at the border of the Russian and Ottoman empires, and a brief period of Anglo–American antagonism over the Pacific north-west of North America, the three great expansionist powers maintained tensely cordial relations. Starting in the 1880s and extending well into the twentieth century, however, not only did Anglo–Russian–American rivalries intensify, but these three states were also joined by a host of new and re-emerging imperial competitors. Each of these sought to control and even formally acquire new overseas territories. The main theatres of this renewed imperialist thrust were Africa and South-East Asia, but the renewed struggle for power and influence extended to the Ottoman Empire, Latin America, East and Central Asia, and the Pacific Ocean as well. The principal competitors, aside from Britain, the United States, and Russia, were Germany, France, the Belgian monarchy, and more latterly Italy. Japan had the dubious honor being both the object of imperialist interest in the first stages of the New Imperialism and a competitor in later stages. Together, these states came to be known in the late nineteenth century as the world's "great powers."

Despite the obvious continuities with the preceding century, this New Imperialism arguably did represent something new in terms of an expanded *capacity* and *will* to acquire new formal colonies as well as spheres of influence. The Russian, American, and British expansions of the century from 1770 to 1870 had largely represented triumphs over sparsely populated groups, many of them hardly recovered from diseases brought by the invaders: this was certainly the case in the Cape Colony of southern Africa, Australia, much of North America, and Siberia. India was the largest (and most important) exception. During much of this period, imperialist powers had truly lacked the ability, as we have seen, to dominate or defeat Asian and African societies. By the late nineteenth century, however, this changed for a brief period as the technology gap, and especially the weapons gap, between industrial and non-industrialized states briefly expanded. But the New Imperialism was not, overall, merely the result of the industrial powers' capacity for conquest. It was also the result of a new will to dominate others, representative of fierce cultures of imperialism that were emerging in industrialized and industrializing societies.

In this chapter we introduce the New Imperialism, a concept that encompasses the next four chapters. We center this introductory chapter for this period around two questions. The first is "what was the New Imperialism?" In this chapter, we define the New Imperialism as both a period and a process. As a period, the New Imperialism describes an era of inter-continental formal empire-building that began in the last quarter of the nineteenth century and was largely completed by the beginning of the First World War in 1914. As a process, the New Imperialism involved not only the construction of the structures of these formal empires, but also the creation of new cultures of imperialism among citizens of the metropole and of new forms of colonialism that were implemented in the imperial periphery. We consider both of these issues in the first section. The second question we ask in this chapter is "why did the New Imperialism happen?" We investigate this issue through a running debate among scholars and observers who variously point to economic, demographic, cultural, geo-political, and social transformations in both the imperial metropoles and the independent regions of Africa and Asia as causative to this process. Finally, we attempt to show how these different factors worked together and against each other through three case studies covering north-eastern Africa, Burma (now officially named Myanmar), and the Caribbean island of Haiti.

WHAT WAS THE NEW IMPERIALISM?

The most obvious materialization of the New Imperialism was the rapid acquisition of formal colonies in Africa, Asia, and the Pacific by both existing and new imperial powers based in Europe, North America, and Japan. In the three decades beginning around 1874, the principal industrialized or industrializing imperial powers—Britain, France, Japan, Germany, Belgium, Russia, and the United States—claimed more than 9 million square miles of territory with barely any reference to the wishes of its existing population. This figure is even more amazing because it does not include the eastward drive of Russia across the Asian continent, or the westward drive of the United States across North America—both of which were largely completed in this period.

Perhaps the most astonishing element of this formal imperial expansion was the division and conquest of almost all of Africa—the so-called *scramble for Africa*. Prior to the 1870s, the sections of this vast continent controlled by outside powers were limited to small enclaves. Although technically the Ottoman Empire still had sovereign rights in some parts of North Africa, in fact its power had lapsed. One former province, Algeria, was claimed by France, but French troops could only truly control the coastal region. French authority in the Senegal River Valley of West Africa, briefly asserted at the beginning of the century, was in fact also receding. At the southern end of the continent, Britain held the Cape Colony and the diminutive province of Natal. These colonial possessions were neighbored by two small "republics" ruled by Afrikaners—descendents of Dutch servants of the Dutch East India Company (VOC), their Malaysian servants, French refugees, and some African women—which despite being obvious products of imperialism cannot correctly be considered part of any overseas empire. On the west coast, small French, Dutch, and British positions still existed around some of the slave castles built in the sixteenth and seventeenth centuries, but the real authority of their governors often ended at cannon range. The oldest European colonies in existence were the Portuguese possessions of Angola and Mozambique, although these at times struggled to stay in existence. Thus, formal European imperialism in Africa was in recession in the late nineteenth century, and no new imperial push was in sight. In fact, in 1865 a

British Parliamentary Committee recommended withdrawing from West Africa entirely in light of anti-imperial popular opinion and a lack of economic motivation. Nor did any other European governments seem to want the costs associated with an African empire.

By 1914, this situation was entirely reversed. In the intervening half-century, almost all of Africa had been claimed as colonies or protectorates by European powers—only Ethiopia in the east and Liberia in the west maintained their sovereign status. Although many Africans still denied and even fought against colonial domination, the often violent process of "pacifying" local populations was well under way. In this scramble for African territory, France and Britain had been the greatest winners. France had added almost the entirety of West Africa and much of North Africa in a broad swathe from Senegal and the Ivory Coast across the Sahara to Algeria and Morocco and into the interior of Central Africa. France also claimed the huge island of Madagascar. New additions to the British Empire included not only the most populous region of West Africa (Nigeria, with 15 million inhabitants), but also the length of the Nile River from Egypt upriver to the Sudan and Uganda, as well as neighboring British East Africa. From South Africa, the British Empire now extended deep into the interior, into a vast zone named Rhodesia after Cecil Rhodes, the mining magnate and imperialist who had led its conquest. The young states of Germany and Italy had contented themselves with cherry-picking. Libya was claimed, although only slowly conquered, as the cornerstone of a new Italian Mediterranean empire, and Italian interests were secured on the horn of Africa, although an Italian invasion of Ethiopia had ended disastrously in 1896. Germany's acquisitions were strategically positioned to put pressure on Britain: Togoland neighbored British Gold Coast, German East Africa was contiguous to British East Africa, German South-West Africa bordered South Africa, and German Cameroon abutted British Nigeria. Finally, much of the interior of Central Africa, which was at one point the personal possession of the King of

Belgium, passed the hands of the government of that tiny state in 1908.

The states of mainland South-East Asia, previously too powerful to be threatened by any outside power other than China, also came under imperial assault in the last quarter of the nineteenth century. Here, British expansion from India reached out to Burma, Malaya, and even into Central Asia in competition with Russia. France confined itself principally to the vast region of Indochina (modern Vietnam, Cambodia, and Laos), which it managed to acquire only through the mobilization of huge military and economic resources. Japan, the object of U.S. imperial attention at the beginning of the period, was a major imperialist competitor by its end. The industrializing Meiji regime built itself an overseas empire haltingly at first, but then more confidently. By 1910, Japan had acquired Taiwan, Korea, and the Bonin and Kurile Islands. Further to the east, in the Pacific, Japanese interests overlapped with British, German, and American aspirations as small and large islands were gobbled up. The largest prize, the Philippine Islands, were won from Spain by the United States in a turn-of-the-century war.

Outside of the formal empires, competition between industrial empires for influence over independent states was fierce. Britain's pre-eminence in commercial and political links to China and the Ottoman Empire were increasingly challenged around the turn of the century by the United States, France, Germany, Russia, and Japan. Latin America was a competitive field as well for Britain and the United States. By the 1890s, imperial fleets from all of the large industrialized navies were touring the world's ports in a show of force, while in the capitals of dozens of small states imperial diplomats struggled for influence and position.

Behind this worldwide struggle was a transformed global political and economic environment. Gone was Britain's mid-nineteenth-century industrial advantage and naval monopoly (discussed in chapter 8), replaced by greater parity among a number of states that had successfully industrialized. With it went the mid-century tranquility of Europe,

swept away by the political unification of two new states in the 1870s: Germany and Italy. The emergence of two strong European powers where before there had existed merely collections of small principalities threatened the security of their neighbors. A unified Germany, especially, was a threat to France, Russia, and the remains of the Habsburg Empire based in Austria. The resulting instability of the once stable European balance of power and the struggle for commercial advantage overseas led to diplomatic jockeying and the threat of outright war in Europe at several points during the period of expansion, and each new colonial conquest by one state fueled expansionism among its rivals. In the new atmosphere of economic competition, cultures of imperialism developed, stimulated by fears of economic recession and stoked by populist politicians. The new language of these imperialist ideologies was nationalist and racialist, often backed by distortions of the new sciences of evolution and anthropology and by evangelical religion. All of these drove a will to expand—the sense of an imperial mission—that despite local variations was shared among the populations of the industrialized and industrializing metropoles.

The cultures of imperialism of the great powers were furthered by the growing technological gap between industrialized and non-industrialized societies. This disparity had been slowly opening over much of the nineteenth century, but by the 1880s Japanese, U.S., and western European populations were fully aware of their technological advantages. This in turn fed a mounting sensibility that technology equaled civilization, and that technologically advanced societies had the right and the responsibility to "civilize" those societies that had fallen behind. As historian Michael Adas has observed, it led them to evaluate and rank people and societies on the basis of the machines they possessed.[2] The subsequent seizure of African land and

---

[2] Michael Adas, *Machines as the Measure of Men: Science, Technology, and Ideologies of Western Dominance* (Ithaca, NY: Cornell University Press, 1990).

resources, for example, was frequently justified by arguments that Africans lacked the machines to exploit them. Similarly, Asia was depicted as a continent of stagnant societies just waiting for European (or Japanese) vigor to renew it. This mechanistic ideology had a very real economic component as well: for industrial societies, the new colonies represented sources of raw materials for their factories and markets for their goods.

Technology not only contributed to the motives for imperial expansion; it also provided the means by which it could occur. The late nineteenth-century weapons gap was a case in point. In European armies, as in Japan and the United States, the smooth-bored, ball-firing muzzle-loading musket was increasingly replaced in the 1860s by rifled, breech-loading weapons that fired cartridges. These new weapons were more accurate and could be fired much more rapidly. Augmented by new artillery and magazine-equipped machine guns such as the maxim, these rifles transformed warfare. The increasing tensions of the period also led to national conscription and militia service that increased the size of European, American, and Japanese armies, although professionals still did much of the bloody work overseas. At sea, the industrial powers gained an overwhelming military advantage with the development of iron-clad steamships that could sail up rivers and that were virtually impervious to older weapons. Even before the New Imperialism really began, these ships won signal victories for Britain against China and Burma, and the appearance of U.S. steam warships shocked Japan out of its complacency.[3]

Steamships, too, were part of the communications revolution that enabled metropoles to remain in contact with distant, densely populated colonies. Regular steamship routes ran across every ocean by the 1850s, and were especially vital to the maintenance of the British Empire. British imperial needs also drove the building of the Suez Canal, which opened in Egypt in 1869. Despite initial flaws, in the long run this new route revolutionized communications between Britain and its eastern empire, and thus became a focus of the imperial struggle. Another important communications tool was the telegraph. In the 1860s, Britain laid telegraphs across India for the first time, and by 1870 this "jewel" of a colony was connected by Britain by a network of telegraph cables that paralleled the steamship routes. Eventually, the radio would replace the telegraph, but only after the New Imperialism reached its apex.

Despite these innovations, much of the tropical band of Asia, Africa, and the Americas were protected by endemic diseases to which North Americans and Europeans had little resistance and of which malaria was the greatest killer. However, these diseases were to some degree tamed by nineteenth-century medical innovations. The development of cheaply produced quinine (originally distilled from the bark of the cinchona tree in the 1820s) gave Europeans at least a fighting chance against the malaria plasmodium in Africa, as it did for U.S. armies in the Philippines and Japanese forces in the Pacific.

Not all historians accept, however, that the technological advantages of the imperialist powers in the late nineteenth century constituted a *new* gap between colonizers and colonized. They point out that military advantages had been vital to earlier imperial conquests, as the gunpowder revolution of the fifteenth through seventeenth century demonstrates. Moreover, many of the major technological innovations described earlier were the products of long series of incremental changes rather than a single act of invention, and some—like the steamship and quinine—were available long before 1880. Technology, therefore, represents not only one of the novelties of the New Imperialism but also a link to earlier periods.

Another key link between the early and mid-nineteenth-century period of British informal imperialism and the New Imperialism was the

[3] Two important and immensely readable sources on technology and imperialism are Daniel R. Headrick, "The Tools of Imperialism: Technology and the Expansion of European Colonial Empires in the Nineteenth Century," *Journal of Modern History*, 51 (1979), 231–263; and Robert Kubicek, "Empire and Technological Change," in *The Oxford History of the British Empire*, vol. III, *The Nineteenth Century*, edited by Andrew Porter, (Oxford: Oxford University Press, 1999), 247–269.

British relationship with India. As discussed in previous chapters, the gradual occupation of India by the British East India Company (EIC), and after 1857 by the Crown, presented British administrators, royals, merchants, and soldiers for the first time with the challenge of ruling dense, ethnically and culturally diverse populations without the aid of large numbers of settlers. It also exposed them to the solutions to this problem developed by their imperial predecessors, the Mughals. Mughal colonial techniques, and those pioneered or further developed by the British in India, were adapted in the late nineteenth century first for new British colonies of exploitation and later by other European powers ruling empires in Africa and Asia for the first time. Thus it was above all in India, in the mid-nineteenth century, that the strategies of the New Imperialism were learned.

WHY DID THE NEW IMPERIALISM HAPPEN?

While some scholars argue that this scramble for new colonies and overseas empires represents a truly revolutionary transformation in global relationships, others see it as merely an intensification of trends already existing in earlier decades of the nineteenth century. Yet whether amplification or revolution, the processes of the New Imperialism were central to the reshaping of the global economy and to international politics and left no cultures or societies unaffected. It is for this reason that the task of explaining the origins, or causes, of the New Imperialism has occupied numerous scholars since John Hobson at the turn of the twentieth century. It is possible to divide the many theories as to why the New Imperialism happened thematically into geo-political, economic, cultural, and social explanations. It is also possible to divide theories by location: they variously find the causes of the New Imperialism within the metropole, in the relationship between the industrialized nations, or at the imperial periphery. In this chapter, we argue for a more holistic approach. In the first place, no single causative factor is sufficient to explain this set of events. More importantly, it is impossible to try to locate the origins of the New

Imperialism solely in any one region, polity, or set of polities. Instead, the answer must be found by investigating on a global scale.

The international scale of the New Imperialism was evident even to many who witnessed it first-hand. Thus, even contemporary scholars observed that the various national cultures of imperialism were emerging from within a wider matrix—the relationship between the great powers. They observed that the industrial economies, sophisticated armies, and diplomatic savvy of these states were drawing them in the late nineteenth century into a competitive cycle that culminated in the taking of colonies and the struggle for influence overseas. Yet while almost all who wrote about the New Imperialism agreed that this process was taking place, they could come to no consensus as to why it was occurring, thus beginning a debate that continues today.

Economists and economic historians tend to see competition between industrial economies running short on materials, markets, and places to invest money at the heart of this conflict. For much of the nineteenth century, industrial Britain had fed its factories with raw materials from every continent and British firms had considered the entire world one vast market for its processed goods. By the last quarter of the century, however, British industry was competing with a host of emerging industrial economies—especially Germany, Belgium, France, the United States, and later Russia and Japan. The result was a series of market gluts that were key factors in economic setbacks such as the depression of 1874, which affected both factories and agriculture in Europe and the United States.

The competition for markets extended around the world. British merchant firms operating in Asia, Latin America, and Africa for example began to have to compete more and more with rival firms from Europe and—in East Asia and Latin America especially—the United States. This increasing commercial competition in many cases immediately preceded formal colonialism, and thus suggested a link between them.

For Hobson, looking at late nineteenth-century Britain, the connection was obvious. Hobson argued that the decades-long depression that began in 1874 was caused by the saturation of the domestic market for industrial products. Britain simply could not consume the processed goods it was producing. As a result, Hobson argued, British companies began to invest overseas at a faster and faster pace. Increasingly, however, they found rival firms selling industrial products in every location, and this drove down prices and, consequently, profits. The factory owners and investors' strategy, in response, was to put pressure on the government to conquer these "markets" by military force, and then to have their government grant them a monopoly through protectionist policies that excluded French, American, and German firms.[4] Similar processes were at work in their rivals' states as well.

Hobson's theories were picked up by socialist thinkers of the early twentieth century, especially Rosa Luxemburg and Vladimir Ilyich Lenin. Luxemburg saw imperialism as simply another phase in the struggle by capitalist society to oppress the working class.[5] The power of capitalists (wealthy investors) and industrialists, she argued, could only survive if capitalism continued to expand. It was this force that drove imperialism. Lenin's work complimented this idea. For Lenin, imperial expansion was merely the "last phase" of capitalism. Running out of places to invest their money within Europe, Lenin argued, national groups of investors divided the world up among themselves, and then used state governments to enforce their will.[6] In Lenin's interpretation, as in those of Luxemburg and Hobson, governments were merely tools of the upper economic classes.

Because the connections between the needs of industrial economies and the policies of imperialism seem so evident, economic theories of the origins of the New Imperialism continue to resonate. Two of the most important theorists to pursue this theme in recent years are Anthony Hopkins and Peter Cain, who focus especially on a very wealthy class of financiers, whom they titled the gentlemanly capitalists. They argued that this class guided the expansion of the British Empire from within a 1-square mile financial district in London known as the City. Cain and Hopkins have studied the connections between policy-makers and these financiers extensively, and the level of detail they are able to present makes their work especially convincing.[7] Some of their critics, however, have put a twist on this debate by suggesting that some of the financial motivation for imperialism came from the periphery rather than the metropole. Settlers, for example, may have played a key role, as may have small trading firms that had been set up by Europeans and Americans in Asia and Africa. Similarly, a few economists have focused on the ability of non-European agents to play British, French, American, and other firms against each other and thus drive prices down. Their evidence suggests that a "global" economic perspective on the New Imperialism is long past due.

However, most scholars writing today reject the idea—espoused by Lenin, Luxemburg, and other "Marxist" historians—that economic motives alone can sufficiently explain the emergence of late nineteenth-century cultures of imperialism. A large group, for example, now point to popular opinion and culture as important factors alongside material economic concerns. Hobson himself had acknowledged this factor, if only by suggesting that the wealthy classes used popular nationalism to promote imperialism by convincing the people of Britain to blame the unfair policies of rival nations for the economic depression that began in 1873. In order to appease the people, politicians thus had to follow the policies of imperialism promoted by the wealthy. Later theorists have also suggested that, by focusing popular anger on rival states, ruling elites and the wealthy may also have diverted that anger from themselves. In this way, nationalism allied with imperialism was an important tool for defusing

---

[4] Hobson, *Imperialism*.

[5] Rosa Luxemburg, *The Accumulation of Capital* (London: Routledge and Kegan Paul, 1951). First published in German in 1913.

[6] Vladimir Ilyich Lenin, *Imperialism: The Highest Phase of Capitalism* (New York: International Publishers, 1939). First published 1916.

[7] Peter Cain and Tony Hopkins, *British Imperialism 1688–2000*, 2nd edition (New York: Longman, 2001).

the threat of socialists who were trying to bring down the wealthy classes. In Germany, for example, the monarchist Chancellor Otto von Bismarck used popular imperialist policies to pursue his conservative aims. Faced with a large opposition to his policies made up of liberals and socialists, he used the promise of building an overseas empire to split the pro-empire liberals from the anti-empire socialists. He was then able to drive the socialists underground without any complaint from the liberals, which ironically left the liberals without any potential allies. In the end, therefore, the promise of empire helped to ensure the triumph of conservative monarchism in the new Germany. This kind of process, by which powerful groups use imperialism to defend their privileges, is sometimes called *social imperialism.*

Not everyone, however, accepts this view of imperialism as a planned project of elite classes. One of the most influential recent historians of the New Imperialism, D.K. Fieldhouse, has argued instead that nationalism and imperialism were largely unguided mass hysterias and were not controlled by wealthy elites.[8] He suggests, instead, that nationalism emerged because of a number of circulating trends of the era. One was the emergence of racism couched in pseudo-Darwinian terms. Popular writers of the middle and late nineteenth century throughout Europe wrote of the idea that "superior" societies could reasonably conquer or even commit genocide against "inferior" societies, and argued that the very fact that imperial conquest was possible legitimized it as a policy. This acceptance of conquest, and even genocide, as a natural process is reflected in the words of the English philosopher Herbert Spencer in 1850, "the forces which are working out the great scheme of perfect happiness, taking no account of incidental suffering, exterminate such sections of mankind as stand in their way."[9] While his racism was sometimes used to describe rival neighbors (such as the

British depiction of the Germans as brutes or the German depiction of the French as feeble and effeminate), it was more commonly applied to Asians, Africans, and other non-European populations. These groups were variously described as child-like, feminine (and thus weak), savage, or insane. As we have seen earlier, the great differences in technology between industrialized and non-industrialized societies made this task easier, not only by enabling colonial conquests but also by providing another justification for conquering "less-developed" societies.

The other side of this doctrine of national superiority was the development of "civilizing missions" in which, as in fifteenth-century Spain and sixteenth-century Russia, religion became a key prop for imperialism. As we saw in chapter 8, Evangelical Protestants in Britain and the United States, and to some degree in continental Europe, had begun to form domestic missionary societies as early as the late eighteenth century. These were soon active in India and, by the middle of the nineteenth century, Protestant missionary societies were operating on every continent. Catholic missions such as those of the *peres blancs* joined them in the 1880s. These religious groups both reflected and reinforced the notion of a religious mission to "civilize" among the populations of industrial societies. Fused to secular ideas of the civilizing power of commerce and technology and to popular nationalism, they formed a powerful cultural force within imperial societies.[10] We will see in the next few chapters how these ideas spread across the empire (chapter 12) and shaped colonialism in the colonies (chapters 11 and 13).

While jingoistic nationalism and the sense of a civilizing mission were undoubtedly cultural forces of great significance, they merely reinforced the competition between the industrialized great powers, whose governments acted both in defense of their economic and strategic interests and in the spirit of national status and pride. In this process, Britain was forced to react to rivals such

---

[8] D.K. Fieldhouse, *The Colonial Empires* (London: Weidenfeld, 1965).
[9] Herbert Spencer, *Social Statistics* (London: Watts, 1850), 416.

[10] Cf. Alice Conklin, *A Mission to Civilize: The Republican Idea of Empire in France and West Africa, 1895–1930* (Stanford: Stanford University Press, 1997).

as Russia, Germany, and France that threatened their intensely globalized economy. Particularly of concern were the fragile tendrils that connected them to India and onward to China. The British economy depended intensely on the China–India trade, and therefore Britain carefully protected not only the frontiers of their Indian empire but also the geographic chokepoints in the western (Morocco and Spain) and eastern (Egypt) Mediterranean, especially after the building of the Suez Canal connecting the Mediterranean to the Red Sea and hence the Indian Ocean. German and French interference in Morocco thus drew a British response, as did German, French, and Italian threats to the upper Nile River. Similarly, the establishment of a German colony in South-West Africa forced Britain to increase its attention to the Cape Colony in southern Africa, the most vulnerable point along the long southern route to India. In this way, British empire-building can be viewed as simply an attempt to defend its economy from its great power competitors.

In fact, however, the situation was even more complex. Britain's empire-building was at least partly a response to threats from societies in Africa and Asia as well as the other industrial powers. In the 1960s, Ronald Robinson and John Gallagher argued that for Britain, much of the impetus for the New Imperialism came from changing conditions in the periphery. In *Africa and the Victorians: The Climax of Imperialism in the Dark Continent*, the two historians focused not on increasing rivalry with France and Germany but on the emergence of nationalist groups in Africa that threatened both the profitability of British overseas corporations and, more importantly, the security of the empire. Of special concern to them was the rise of an indigenous "constitutionalist" movement in Egypt, which gained power in the late 1870s at the expense of Khedive (monarch) Isma'il Pasha, an ally of the British. This movement enjoyed broad-based support in Egypt from liberal reformers, Muslim conservatives, anti-European landlords, and disgruntled army officers—all of whom had reasons to resent British influence. They also perceived a threat from the autonomous European settlers in southern Africa—especially

Dutch-speaking white settlers, or Afrikaners— whose close ties to Germany appeared especially menacing to Britain and who clashed with English-speaking colonists of the Cape Province. These challenges from societies in southern Africa and Egypt weighed heavily upon the imperial government because of their importance to British national security, but Robinson and Gallagher have also pointed out many other instances of African populations and leaders who increasingly opposed, contested, or tried to win a portion of the profits of British informal imperialism.[11] In many cases, these movements merely highlighted the weakness of the allies on whom Britain's vast informal empire relied: the princes and shahs who owed their wealth to British trade, but who were threatened by popular unrest combined with the intrigues of Britain's rivals.

Published in 1961, Robinson and Gallagher's book challenged historians' presumptions that the populations of the imperial periphery were not merely blank slates upon whom empires played out their games, and that their lands were not merely the playing field. Instead, the two scholars suggested that they were participants in the turmoil that drove the New Imperialism. Other important participants were expatriate citizens of the industrialized states: missionaries, merchants, settlers, military men, and travelers from the metropole who had settled and worked on the edges of empire. In the 1970s, Fieldhouse began to concentrate on these individuals as agents of imperialism. Calling them *men-on-the-spot*, he argued that in many cases they were the true empire-builders. Like Robinson and Gallagher, Fieldhouse had extensively searched the British archives for evidence of how colonies had been established. In many cases, he found that conquest and annexation had not been explicitly ordered by imperial governments. Instead, men-on-the-spot—European, U.S., or Japanese citizens or official agents of these governments

---

[11] Ronald Robinson and John Gallagher with Alice Denny, *Africa and the Victorians: The Climax of Imperialism in the Dark Continent* (New York: St. Martin's Press, 1961).

acting without order—had taken the initiative themselves. Often, they were reacting to either some decision by indigenous rulers or by members of the local population that cut into their profits, or to interference by rival companies or from another industrialized state. Their reaction was to use force to solve the issue. In many cases, their superior technology allowed these groups and individuals to establish de facto control over a region, which was only subsequently legitimized by the home government.[12]

Together, these many theories make evident the global nature of the New Imperialism. Imperial expansion was driven by changing conditions at the edges of empire, by technological and cultural shifts in the industrialized metropoles, and by competition among the great powers. Thus, any attempt to write a complete history of the New Imperialism must recognize that events and trends in these three sets of zones continually affected each other. In economic terms, we can see that throughout this period, the friction between industrialized states was inflated by competition for overseas markets and sources of raw material. On the other side of the equation, being on the receiving end of this competitive market empowered African, Asian, Latin American, and Pacific merchants and rulers to pursue their own political and economic goals. This in turn frustrated European, U.S., and Japanese merchants and governmental representatives on the spot, who subsequently became agents of imperialism, mobilizing their advanced military technology and sense of superiority to carve out new colonies even without orders. The populations of the metropoles saw these ventures as economically profitable and proof of their national superiority, and usually celebrated them enthusiastically. This, in turn, encouraged politicians to endorse them. This combination of factors was recognized by figures such as French Prime Minister Jules Ferry, who defined them in an 1884 speech before the Chamber of Deputies as being "connected to three sets of ideas: economic ideas; the most

far-reaching ideas of civilization; and ideas of a political and patriotic sort."[13] Together, they made for a very global, self-perpetuating process that ran on long after it was economically profitable. In the end, even the great Sahara desert was the scene of a race between Britain and France, while nearly landlocked Germany acquired islands in the Pacific for which they had no real use.

The processes that drove the New Imperialism can be illustrated by turning to a particular perspective: that of Whitehall, the administrative heart of the British Empire and the center of what Robinson and Gallagher have called the *official mind*. In the 1880s, officials of the Colonial Office and Foreign Office found themselves besieged on all sides. British merchants, and the investors in their companies, were howling about falling profits as U.S. clipper ships infringed on the opium trade, U.S. banks began to cut into British banking profits in China, and U.S. industry ramped up its competitiveness in Latin American markets. In Africa, French and subsequently German annexation of territory closed off important potential markets. Meanwhile, European rivals including not only France and Germany but also Russia and Italy threatened the vital routes to the east through the Mediterranean and around the Cape. Russia was especially a threat, as the czars solidified their positions on the edges of India. The same routes were also threatened by nationalist movements in Egypt and South Africa, while an industrializing Japan eyed economically profitable positions in East Asia long dominated by British shipping. Domestically, meanwhile, pro-empire opinion was being stoked by reports from missionaries abroad, by children's books and church hymnals expressing the duty to "civilize," and by newspapers frantically reporting the advance of imperial competitors. Is it any wonder that the policy-makers sitting in the government offices in Whitehall reversed their course of "free

---

[12]D.K. Fieldhouse, *Economics and Empire* (London: Wiedenfield and Nicolson, 1973).

[13]Jules Ferry, "Speech Before the French Chamber of Deputies, March 28, 1884," in, *Discours et Opinions de Jules Ferry*, edited by Paul Robiquet (Paris: Armand Colin & Cie., 1897), v.1.5, 199–200.

trade" and "informal empire" and began to endorse the acquisition of colonies? Meanwhile, similar if unique calculations were being made within the governments of Japan, the United States, France, Germany, and other imperial metropoles.

In the rest of this chapter, we will zoom in to look at how a variety of different factors and events in many regions worked together to produce new colonies and "protectorates" in four places: the South-East Asian state of Burma, the interior of north-eastern Africa, the Caribbean island nation of Haiti, and the East Asian peninsular state of Korea. In each case, occupation was a result of a convergence of factors local, imperial, and global in scope.

THE ANNEXATION OF BURMA, 1885

The story of the British annexation of Burma illustrates the changing global environment of the 1880s. Over the course of the nineteenth century, British authorities in London and Delhi had come to consider Burma part of their sphere of influence. Situated on the eastern frontier of the South Asian sub-continent, Burma's kings had been resolute opponents as well as important trading partner to Mughal India in the seventeenth and eighteenth centuries. Their nineteenth-century heirs resented the attempts of the British administrators of India to reign them in, and clashes between the EIC and Burmese forces twice culminated in war: in 1824–1826 and again in 1852. In both cases, British-led EIC forces had a marked technological superiority and British steamships and cannon ensured victory in key battles. The results deprived Burma of several key provinces and facilitated British economic infiltration into the region.

Yet while both wars expanded the British Empire, they were met with some displeasure from a British public and cabinet hostile to increased imperial responsibilities. This was especially true in the case of the Second Burmese War (1852), which had been prompted by the arrest of two British merchant captains. Rather than consulting with Whitehall, British Indian administrators and naval commanders on the spot had launched an immediate and very successful invasion. Back in London, however, the still disapproving cabinet, responding in part to domestic public pressure, censured the officer in charge and tried to limit the territorial gains of the war. In 1867, and again in 1879, factions in Britain and in the British Burmese settlement of Rangoon tried to rally the country to conquer the bulk of Burma, but the cabinet and Whitehall continued to resist such pressures, instead being content to extract certain economic concessions on the Burmese King Mindon in the interests of "free trade." By the early 1880s, however, the situation was reversed and in November 1885 a British Indian force invaded and conquered Burma with the full backing of the Crown and cabinet. What had changed in the intervening years to shift the British government's stance on the annexation of Burma?

There are generally two explanations given for the 1885 invasion of Burma. The first centers upon global strategic issues: especially the priority of defending British India against expansionist French activity to the east. Admittedly, France was fighting a bitter war of aggression against Chinese forces in South-East Asia and looked likely to establish a permanent base just to the east of Burma. Yet this commitment had in fact reduced, rather than expanded, the likelihood of French intervention in Burma because it restricted available resources, and throughout 1885 the French vehemently denied having any interests in the area. Thus, historians are left debating whether the newly elected prime minister of Britain, the Conservative Marquess of Salisbury (Robert Arthur Talbot Gascoyne-Cecil), was unconvinced by their denials or merely disregarded them because he had other reasons to want to invade Burma.

Proponents of the latter argument suggest that Salisbury's principal motivation was the greed of his backers in the business community. They suggest that the fear of French intervention drummed up in the press and invoked in speeches by Salisbury was merely a tool of commercial interests, and especially gentlemanly capitalists, who used it to win popular support for an invasion that served their interests alone. This interpretation focuses on the increasing frustration of

British business in the face of new Burmese policies that levied taxes on imports and nationalized industries in which British corporations were involved. Certainly, the timing of the November invasion, almost immediately after these policies were implemented, suggests a connection, but were British business interests in Burma so powerful that they could actually translate into an invasion of Burma?

In order to examine this issue, we must look also at the actions of the Burmese monarchy. The event that sparked the long fuse of the 1885 invasion was the enthroning of a new Burmese king, Thibaw, in 1879. Because Burmese rulers practiced polygamy, they tended to have many sons, and thus the struggle for succession was often quite lively. This was true in 1879, when the violence that accompanied the crowning of King Thibaw disrupted commerce and as a result prompted some Britons in Rangoon to call for an invasion. Partly because the British army was already engaged in campaigns against potent foes in Afghanistan and southern Africa (the Zulu state), the official response was merely to withdraw the British representative in the Burmese capital of Mandalay.[14]

Having seized the throne, however, Thibaw was faced with a dire economic problem. In order to resist both internal revolt and future British invasions, the Burmese state needed to acquire modern weapons and industry. However, its treasury was in no condition to afford these developments, as it had lost several key rice-producing provinces in the two earlier wars with the EIC and had subsequently been forced to sign treaties that favored British corporations logging and mining in Burma. As a result, the state was obliged to import (and pay for) food and at the same time to sell Burmese resources—especially teak and rubies—for little or no profit.

Thibaw's response was farsighted. First, he expanded irrigation projects in the remaining provinces in order to increase food production. Second, in order to pay for this new infrastructure and for defensive modernization, his government

raised tariffs on imports and sought to recapture the teak and ruby industry from British-based companies. Finally, in 1883 his government sent a mission to Paris to negotiate a trade agreement with the French government of Jules Ferry, who also agreed secretly to provide Burma with arms in case of a British invasion.

So long as the military provisions of this 1883 agreement remained secret, British officials could continue to consider Burma safely in their sphere. The interests of British merchants and investors based in London, Delhi, and Rangoon, on the other hand, were seriously threatened by Thibaw's reforms. This was especially true of the Bombay Burmah Trading Corporation (BBTC), a partnership that was heavily invested in the teak industry. In early 1883, Thibaw's government launched an investigation of the BBTC, which it accused of failing to pay royalties to the Burmese state. As it became increasingly clear that they would be found guilty and forced to pay a large fine, the BBTC began to look for ways to manufacture a diplomatic incident that would provoke an invasion. In July, their agents uncovered evidence of the secret Franco–Burmese protocol, and passed it on to Lord Randolph Churchill, Salisbury's Secretary of State for India. Meanwhile, the Burmese government announced in August that the company would be forced to pay fines and back payments of more than £100,000. Led by the BBTC, the merchant community of Rangoon, aided by bankers interested in the Burmese ruby trade, turned to business associates back in Britain to add their voices to their calls for an invasion. The resulting lobbying by chambers of commerce in London and other major cities was effective for several reasons. One was the close relationship between these gentlemanly capitalists and members of the cabinet. Another arose from the instability of the Salisbury administration, which hoped that a quick victory would gain them space to solidify their hold on government. Both of these factors fed the conviction among Conservative party leaders that in this era of intensifying nationalism, imperialism was one of the most popular planks in their platform. Their plans for Burma were aided by the British

[14]A.J. Stockwell, "British Expansion and Rule in South-East Asia," in Porter, *The Nineteenth Century*, 389.

government's ability, in early 1885, to force the French to back down from their promises to the Burmese through diplomatic means. Thus, the decision was made to issue an ultimatum to Thibaw, demanding independent arbitration of the BBTC claims. The refusal of the Burmese government to agree to this extraordinary measure resulted in the invasion of early November 1885.

The 1885 conquest of Burma was the culmination of a long history of British military superiority and commercial interests in the region, and is related closely to Britain's desperate need to hold India. However, it must also be seen in the context of Burmese attempts to maintain their independence by modernizing and by playing Britain and France off against each other. That these efforts did not succeed was partly a result of agitation by Rangoon merchants and other men-on-the-spot, and partly due to political factors in Britain aided by the temporary lack of major British wars elsewhere.

THE STRUGGLE FOR THE UPPER NILE VALLEY: THE RACE FOR FASHODA FROM BRITISH, FRENCH, AND AFRICAN PERSPECTIVES, 1896–1899

One of the most celebrated episodes in the New Imperialism was the famous race for Fashoda—a sparsely settled township in what is today southern Sudan. Fashoda's principal importance to France and Britain was its strategic location astride the White Nile, and hence its potential as a base for controlling the Nile flood and thus threaten or conversely strengthen British control of Egypt.[15] Thus beginning in the late 1880s, this town and the surrounding region became the focus of attention by pro-empire lobbies in France, Britain, and to a lesser degree Italy. Even aloof Germany and distant Russia could not ignore its importance. Yet it was local conditions and the

actions of African governments and power-brokers that most shaped the race to control it in the late 1890s.

In imperial terms, the race for Fashoda brings together several stories more usually treated as discrete episodes. The most obvious is the British relationship with Egypt and their joint attempts to control the Sudan. In the event, however, the Italian effort to conquer Ethiopia, British interests in Uganda, and a French push into the interior from West-Central Africa also played a role.

The most obvious reason for a confrontation at Fashoda was the geo-political rivalry between the European great powers. Egypt's strategic importance to the British Empire, following the construction of the Suez Canal, was exceeded only by India. Its economic importance as a node of commerce was matched by the income generated by its government's extensive debts to British bankers. The interest on this debt, a result largely of Egyptian attempts to modernize, assumed massive proportions in the late nineteenth century and forced the Egyptian Khedive Isma'il to sell his 44% share in the Suez Canal to the British Crown in 1875. By depriving him of a proportion of the profits on the canal's operation, this only brought the Egyptian throne more under the control of bankers from whom Ismail had to borrow larger and larger sums of money. By 1879, British and other European bankers were so influential in Egyptian politics that they were able to depose the Khedive in favor of a more easily controlled ruler, his son Tewfik. Tewfik, however, was in turn forced off the throne by anti-British nationalists led by Colonel Urabi Pasha in 1882. In response, a British fleet bombarded the city of Alexandria and landed an armed force that re-installed Tewfik on the throne. The result was a system of *dual control* in which the British government and, to a lesser degree, a committee representing European bankers from many states manipulated Egyptian policy. By the early 1890s, the British administrator, the Earl of Cromer, acted essentially as prime minister of Egypt.

Egypt in British hands ensured that the eastern Mediterranean and Red Sea remained open to British shipping. Yet Britain's interference was

---

[15] The Nile River is fed by two major tributaries—the Blue Nile that begins in Ethiopia and the White Nile that flows from what is today Uganda.

unpopular and their hold fragile. More than any-thing, Whitehall feared that an enemy could dam the Nile somewhere along its enormous length and thus starve Egypt. Thus, they began to take an interest in upriver regions and states such as Buganda, Ethiopia, and the Sudan. In response, however, so did France, Germany, and Italy. In each of these regions, local rulers tried to play European powers against each other. The Kabaka (king) Mutesa II of Buganda was an able player, manipulating Catholic and Protestant missionar-ies and their supporting governments against each other. In the Sudan, as well, Britain found itself unable to impose its will against an array of oppo-nents led by the Mahdi Muhammad Ahmad, a Muslim revivalist who claimed to have been anointed to lead the faithful against evil in the form of British and Egyptian occupational forces. Muhammad Ahmad's greatest achievement was his ability to unite a large proportion of the ethni-cally and linguistically disparate inhabitants of the Sudan. This he did both by deftly appealing to local anger at the material demands of the Anglo-Egyptian rulers and by utilizing messages of reli-gious purity and righteousness that appealed to both orthodox and Sufi strains of Islam prevalent in the region.

Yet perhaps the biggest threat to British and other European hegemony in the region was that put forth by the state of Ethiopia (Abyssinia). On March 1, 1896, Ethiopian Emperor Menelik suc-cessfully defeated an invading Italian army at the Battle of Adua. This victory had far-reaching implications for the strategic disposition in north-eastern Africa. Italy's advance into Ethiopia had been accepted by Britain, in part because the Italians had in turn agreed to accept the upper Nile River as remaining within the British sphere of influence. The Ethiopians, by contrast, claimed this region for themselves. Moreover, they were in the process of developing close ties with France and its ally Russia; in fact Russian-made artillery and French rifles had significantly contributed to Menelik's victory at Adua. The Russian alliance with France, formally signed in 1894, already threatened British control over the eastern Mediterranean. The Ethiopian victory at Adua and

the threat of a Russo–Franco–Ethiopian alliance more than anything prompted Prime Minister Salisbury's government (re-elected in June 1895 after three years of Liberal party administration) to act to occupy the upper Nile Valley in force.[16]

The British had a lot of catching up to do. France had already launched a string of expedi-tions from its holdings in western Africa to claim Fashoda in 1893. In May of that year, the patriotic *Comité de l'Afrique française*, a pressure group with close ties to several parliamentarians, had sponsored an expedition meant to antagonize the British in retribution for being frozen out of Egypt by Britain a decade earlier. This first expe-dition was launched from western Africa, but failed due to the inexperience of its leaders. A year later, a second expedition set out from the same region under the command of the experi-enced adventurer Victor Liotard, but was diverted into the new Central African colony of Ubangi. A more serious expedition set out from Ubangi in late 1895 led by Jean-Baptiste Marchand, a major in the Marines.[17] Marchand began this difficult endeavor very cautiously, however, and moved only slowly toward the Nile.

While both Salisbury and his predecessor, the Earl of Rosebery, had made a fuss over the Liotard and Marchand expeditions, the British parliament and public weren't inclined to support a British push into Central Africa before 1896. For one thing, there was little potential for economic gain in the region, and the costs of the expeditions and of ruling the region were thought to be considerable. Nor could much enthusiasm be whipped up for a civilizing mission, although both Rosebery and Salisbury tried. Before briefly becoming the prime minister, Rosebery had served as foreign secretary and in that capacity had made a case for the annex-ation of the neighboring state of Buganda on the grounds of spreading Christianity and discouraging

---

[16] Robinson and Gallagher, *Africa and the Victorians*, is still the paramount strategic analysis of the situation leading to the Fashoda incident.

[17] Darrell Bates, *The Fashoda Incident of 1989* (Oxford: Oxford University Press, 1984), 3–5, 8, 17–19.

slavers in the area. His arguments won little traction, however, until the crisis provoked by Adua in 1896. The unexpectedly real threat of a hostile Franco–Ethiopian alliance controlling the upper Nile pushed Britain over the edge, and politicians and newspapers began to spout jingoistic rhetoric. Suddenly, the press was full of calls for civilization to be advanced in the Sudan and of speculation as to the potential economic rewards to be reaped by the first state to claim Fashoda. Both of these themes were picked up by missionist evangelical societies and church pastors, and became the topics of public lectures around Britain. Pushed along by popular sentiment, Parliament thus voted to fund a series of projects, including a railway to what was now being called Uganda from the east coast.

Salisbury's response was to authorize an armed invasion of Sudan by an Anglo-Egyptian army. This force mustered in 1898, and marched southward into Sudan under Lord Horatio Herbert Kitchener. In September 1898, Kitchener defeated the Mahdi's army (now under the command of Khalifa Abdullahi ibn Muhammad al-Ta'ashi) at Omdurman near modern Khartoum. The way was now open to Fashoda. Upon arrival, however, Kitchener found Marchand's small French expedition already installed. Yet, although he was first, Marchand's expedition was unable to claim the territory in the face of Kitchener's superior forces, and he soon withdrew.

The race for Fashoda brought France and Britain closer to war than they had been for more than a half-century. Its capture firmly cemented European imperialism in the Sudan, and secured for Britain control of the Nile. It also helped to accelerate competitive imperial culture in both metropoles by stirring up sentiment against each other. The principal causes of the crisis are generally acknowledged to be strategic concerns, with economic hopes and cultural nationalism playing supporting roles. Yet viewing the race as purely a contest between two European rivals misses the picture. In the upper Nile Valley, Emperor Menelik of Ethiopia, the Mahdi, and Kabaka Mutesa of Uganda were important players alongside Italy, France, and Britain, and the defense of Egypt with its canal was Britain's paramount goal.

JAPANESE POLICY FORMATION AND THE INVASION OF KOREA, 1874–1910

The Japanese occupation of Korea in 1910 serves as an example of the way that the wider struggle for supremacy among the imperial powers could be shaped by very local factors and histories. The regional context for the rise of Japanese overseas imperialism was the increasing interference in East Asian affairs by European powers and the United States around the middle of the nineteenth century. Many Japanese aristocrats (*daimyo*) were especially concerned by Britain's humbling of Qing Dynasty China in the Opium Wars of 1834–1843 and 1856–1860. These wars ended in a series of treaties that reduced China to a semi-dependent state and also led to an increased British and U.S. naval presence in the region. In 1852 and 1854, the Japanese Tokugawa Shogun Yoshinobu was similarly forced to sign an uneven treaty upon terms dictated by U.S. President Millard Fillmore. This humiliation undermined his authority, and the scene was set for an 1867 rebellion by dissatisfied daimyo, especially from the regions of Choshu and Satsuma. While technically restoring the figurehead Meiji emperor, the victorious daimyo actually seized power themselves as an oligarchy, or committee of powerful families, and by 1869 their revolution was complete.

One overriding concern of the new Meiji oligarchs was to avoid becoming a victim of imperialism like China. Therefore, they undertook to create modern industry and a modern military in self-defense. Several of the daimyo involved had already been modernizing their provincial forces for several decades, and these units now became the core of a centralized modern army. Under the direction of the Meiji state, a modern armaments industry and navy also began to take shape.

At the same time, Meiji administrators selectively adapted some aspects of European and U.S. political systems, and Meiji scholars began to interpret and discuss many of the core ideologies of imperialism.[18] Guided by these thinkers, the new rulers of Japan consciously sponsored a popular nationalism that both articulated the Meiji oligarch's wariness of western imperialism and supported modernization. Because Japan was comparatively late to industrialize, and because its islands lacked sufficient raw materials, the Meiji government realized the strategic value of neighboring mainland Asia and surrounding islands. However, Britain, Russia, the United States, and other imperial powers were increasingly impinging upon these regions, and the oligarchs identified their actions as threatening national interests. As a result, as early as 1873 some Meiji officials began to agitate to annex Korea, using the refusal of the Korean monarch to recognize the Meiji government as a justification. These proponents of invasion, however, were defeated by a "peace" party who felt that Japan was not yet ready for this endeavor.[19]

By the late 1890s, the Japanese government and especially the military were more confident. In 1894, long pent-up tensions between Japan and China exploded. Public support for a war was high, and the Meiji leadership wanted to test their new weapons. In the event, Japan's military advantage was complete. Not only were Chinese forces expelled from Korea and the Liaotung Peninsula, but Japan annexed the island of Taiwan and the Liaotung province as well, although western powers forced them to return the latter territory. With China chastised, Russia became the great threat to Japanese economic and security goals in Korea. Having reached the Pacific Ocean some years before, the Russians were intent on securing their naval and economic power in the region. But this threat too was turned back by Japan's victory in the 1904–1905 Russo-Japanese War, clearing the way for a Japanese "protectorate" over Korea. Over the next five years, Korean institutions were subverted and weakened,

and in 1910 Japan formally annexed Korea as a colony.[20]

This long process of Japanese interference in occupation of Korea was largely driven by the security concerns of a state undergoing defensive modernization. For the Japanese, an independent Korea was less a threat than a Korea under Chinese or, especially, Russian domination. The economic needs of Japanese industry were also a concern. Korea was a source of much needed raw materials and possibly a major market for Japanese goods. In this case, though, it was less private enterprise, the state economic planners that most valued an occupied Korea; since for much of this period, Japanese banks didn't have the capital to invest in the peninsula in any case. Meiji state planners were constantly frustrated by what they saw as disorganization and lack of infrastructure in Korea that limited its usefulness as a producer of strategic raw materials. By occupying the region, they hoped to impose a more efficient system of economic dependency.

Justifying and promoting these actions was the development of a Japanese imperial ideology that was both singular and shared characteristics with European and U.S. cultures of imperialism. The abortive 1873 plan to invade had been partly prompted by the militaristic jingoism of the samurai class. Following the quashing of the samurai, however, nationalist writers tended rather to view overseas imperialism as a necessary component of defensive modernization and the only way to avoid becoming a dependent of western empires. This idea was haphazardly advocated by Japanese adventurers and businesspeople in Korea. By the early twentieth century, a more sophisticated ideology had emerged. On the one hand, Japanese writers spoke of their cultural affinity with the Koreans, and depicted the Japanese empire as a way of redeeming all of Asia from the dual threats of "decay" and of western imperialism. On the other hand, Japanese nationalism promoted a nationalist

---

[18] Philip Curtin, *The World and the West: The European Challenge and the Overseas Response in the Age of Empire* (Cambridge: Cambridge University Press, 2002), 156–172.
[19] Marlene Mayo, "The Korea Crisis of 1873 and Early Meiji Foreign Policy," *Journal of Asian Studies*, 31 (1972), 798.

[20] Ramon H. Myers and Mark R. Peattie, *The Japanese Colonial Empire, 1895–1945* (Princeton, NJ: Princeton University Press, 1984), 14–17.

sense of racial superiority and a right to rule. This combination of civilizing duty and entitlement not only built popular support for the aspirations of Meiji military leaders and administrators, but also exemplifies the very real fragility of Japan's independence from foreign domination.

PUBLIC OPINION IN THE UNITED STATES AND THE INVASION OF HAITI, 1915

The United States' intervention in Haiti in 1915 must be understood both in its immediate context and in a much longer history of the region. As we have seen in previous chapters, Haitian slaves allied with free people of color to achieve their freedom and the independence of St. Domingue in a bloody revolution that began in 1791. However, they were given little time to organize their new state, and were forced to repel successive invasions by Britain, France, and Spain in less than a decade after their independence.

Popular opinion in the young United States was at first ambivalent toward their fellow revolutionaries. On the one hand, the Haitians marched under the banner of liberty and the repulse of European control of the Americas. On the other hand, the specter of a black slave revolution haunted the slave-owning classes of North America. Thus, the U.S. government had refused to recognize or authorize trade with its sister-state until 1865, when the processes unleashed by the U.S. Civil War forced an end to legalized slavery at home. The commencement of diplomatic relations at the end of that war ushered in a period of new U.S. investment—and informal empire—in the island, but North American firms quickly found themselves competing with German and French corporations in almost every sector: buying Haitian sugar, controlling the Haitian national bank, operating Haiti's railroads, and selling manufactured goods to Haitians. The desire of U.S. business to drive out French and German competition exacerbated the increasingly bellicose foreign policy of turn-of-the-century presidents, and in the years leading up to 1900 U.S. forces were dispatched temporarily to Haiti on eight separate occasions, although they were always quickly withdrawn. In 1904, President Theodore Roosevelt promulgated the "Roosevelt Corollary" to the 80-year-old Monroe Doctrine, proclaiming the right to intervene in the affairs of American states in support of U.S. strategic interests and the economic interests of American financiers. This belligerence, coupled with the ability to dispatch and maintain naval and marine forces in the region, supported the ability of U.S.-based corporations to become the dominant sellers and investors in the Haitian economy by the outbreak of the First World War. Military power could be employed to threaten or replace antagonistic regimes with ones friendly to U.S. investment, to embargo the island, or to support rebel movements. Its employment helped a U.S. company win a contract to build a new Haitian railway in 1908, and in 1910 North American stockholders finally gained full control of the Haitian national bank.

Inevitably, U.S. intervention during this period of informal empire contributed to the political upheaval and economic upheaval that periodically marked Haitian society in the nineteenth and twentieth centuries. It was a series of chaotic episodes of this nature that eventually prompted U.S. President Woodrow Wilson to begin a formal and long-term occupation of the island in 1915. The downward spiral began in 1911. A violent coup in that year was followed rapidly by the deaths in office of two consecutive presidents, and to a further coup by the insurgent Oreste Zamor in 1914. In an attempt to stabilize his administration, Zamor approached Wilson for assistance, but while his request was still being considered Zamor was overthrown by a third coup that brought Joseph Davilmar Théodore to power on November 7, 1914. Théodore was unable to satisfy either the rural peasants who were his main supporters or the small urban elite, and he resigned on February 22, 1915. He was succeeded by a former ally, Jean Vilbrun Guillaume Sam. Sam was similarly unsuccessful in calming the situation, and in frustration ordered the execution of 167 of his opponents on July 27, 1915. In revenge, their families sought him out and literally dismembered him.

The resulting situation in Haiti presented an opportunity for the United States to intervene in the name of *civilization*. Although President

Wilson was a reluctant imperialist who had initially sought to avoid overseas military adventures, he was also an idealist with a "vision of a liberal international order based on capitalist economic development, free trade, and the rule of law."[21] For Wilson, the occupation of Haiti was a duty. Haitians, he believed, would profit from the stability brought by intervention. That the invasion would also aid U.S. economic interests could not be denied, but stimulating the economic integration of Haiti into the capitalist sphere of the United States would, Wilson believed, be to everyone's benefit. Combined with an implicit racism that denied the ability of peoples of African descent to rule themselves in a "civilized" manner, these ideas justified the invasion.

According to historian Mary Renda, popular opinion in the United States generally aligned itself behind Wilson largely because of the paternalistic notion that intervention would save Haitians from themselves. The occupying force would bring roads, telephones, and other infrastructure to the Haitians. In this way, the United States would be a father to Haiti, whose inhabitants were clearly depicted in newspaper articles, cartoons, and the popular press either as children or young girls, or conversely as a violent mob that had to be calmed down by a stern fatherly figure. Promoting this vision were investors and businesspeople, some of whom acted as the main sources of intelligence to White House policymakers. Their principal concern was the large and profitable Haitian debt to U.S. banks, on which Haiti now threatened to default. In order to build support from the military, they manufactured or played up rumors of possible involvement by the local German business community in the overthrow of Sam. In this, the second year of the First World War, Wilson was especially concerned in keeping the conflict from spreading to the Americas. Haiti was dangerously close to the just-opened Panama Canal, a key strategic asset for the U.S. navy. In stoking these concerns, however, the business community was being insincere. Although competition between German and U.S. investors in Haiti over the previous few years had been fierce, the German business community was small and isolated by the war from military support. Thus, they were merely a convenient specter for proponents of the invasion, who played on the public's and White House fears as well as their race-tinted notions of a civilizing mission. They primed the pump, however, and Wilson ordered an invasion just one day after Sam's execution, on July 28, 1915. The United States would continue to occupy Haiti until August 1934.

Conclusion

These four examples illustrate the complexities of the New Imperialism. Emerging from within industrializing societies, imperialism represented the intertwining of political, economic, social, and cultural factors. It also represented the rising tensions between these societies, which were increasingly competing with each other for global markets and raw materials. Finally, the New Imperialism was shaped by the actions of states and peoples around the globe whose struggle to make a place for themselves in a changing world was often seen as a challenge to the industrial great powers. Thus, every incident in the expansion of the imperial powers of the late nineteenth and twentieth centuries was a combination of global and local factors. This was equally true of their simultaneous attempts to impose colonial orders over their newly conquered colonies.

Questions

1. What was "new" about the New Imperialism, and what was not?
2. What are the major positions taken by scholars as to why the New Imperialism happened? Do you find any of them to be especially convincing or unconvincing, and why?
3. In what way were the processes described in the upper Nile Valley, Korea, and Haiti in this period representative of the New Imperialism?

---

[21] Mary A. Renda, *Taking Haiti: Military Occupation and the Culture of U.S. Imperialism 1915–1914* (Chapel Hill: University of North Carolina Press, 2001), 113.

CHAPTER 11

Colonialism: Colonial Subjects and the Pacification of Colonies in the Era of the New Imperialism

The New Imperialism resulted in the emergence of enormous formal empires that tied together distant parts of the world. Its ideologies and technological transformations shaped the modern world. Its conquests resulted in the formation of colonies in localities across much of Asia, the Pacific, and Africa. Like the New Imperialism, the colonial experience of the late nineteenth and early twentieth centuries also took place around the world and affected billions of people. And like the New Imperialism, it helped shape the world as it is today.

This chapter is primarily concerned with the onset of colonialism in the colonies created in the era of the New Imperialism. The colonialism of this period (1874–1914) was characterized by both transitions from and continuities to earlier forms of colonialism founded in early modern Eurasia and North Africa (discussed in chapter 2), in the American colonies of the same period (chapter 5), in the colonies of settlement of the early and mid-nineteenth century, and especially in India (chapters 8 and 9). While not yet as standardized as it would be after the First World War, the form of colonialism predominantly practiced during the early years of the New Imperialism was often more invasive and extensive than in earlier periods. Thus, the period discussed in this chapter was one in which the great modern empires of Europe, Japan, and the United States slowly felt their way toward the strategies that would allow them to control their colonies and affect the lives of their colonial subjects far more than had ever been possible. As a result, the colonial administrations of the early years of the New Imperialism exhibited a wide variety of experimental techniques that would in later years become somewhat more refined. Even in the beginning, however, colonialism remained concerned with exerting control and claiming sovereignty over populations who were seen as being different from (and usually inferior to) those of the metropole.

The purpose of this chapter is to explore ways in which we can understand the experimental colonial policies and practices of this transitional period as occurring in "zones of interaction." Our chief concern in doing so is to move beyond simple narratives that focus on the one-sided imposition of imperial power. Instead, we try to look at the interactions between imperial agents and subjects as a complex, messy process. This is only one of many possible approaches to this period, but it is an important topic to discuss here. Moreover, it is not a topic upon which we will expand in later chapters.

In order to try to get this lesson across, we have chosen to use a unique structure in this chapter. The first section of this chapter comprises two standard narratives of the British annexation of the Gold Coast and the French occupation of the states of Vietnam, Cambodia, and Laos. We then move on to introduce two important ways of thinking about these narratives. Thus, the second section discusses methods and mechanisms of colonial occupation from the perspective of those agents of the imperial powers charged with establishing the new colonies. In the third and fourth sections, we switch views and look at this new colonialism from the perspective of the people living in the colonies and discuss the ways in which they acted to try to shape it to their needs. We do this by exploring the actions of these groups and individuals, actions that have most often been described by scholars as either *collaboration* or *resistance*. In chapters 13 and 15, we will expand on this further by exploring a wide range of activities and actions of colonial subjects beyond this crude dichotomy. Finally, the chapter closes with another look at the stories of the Gold Coast and Indochina but this time with these complex perspectives and issues added.

THE PACIFICATION OF VIETNAM AND THE GOLD COAST

Contemporary writers often use the word *conquest* to refer to the process by which free states became colonies and independent peoples became colonial subjects. This term reflects the abhorrence most of us have with the violence and autocracy of the New Imperialism. By contrast, during the late nineteenth century, proponents of colonialism often used the term **pacification**, which reflected their beliefs that colonialism was the process of taming both wilderness and savage populations in order to make them amenable to development. Neither term truly suffices to describe the complex processes by which colonies were created, as illustrated by the

processes by which the Vietnamese provinces of the Gold Coast and French Indochina were created as colonies.

Gold Coast is a seventeenth-century English name for a stretch of coastline in West Africa that corresponds roughly to the coastline of the modern state of Ghana. In the era of the Atlantic slave trade (1480–1820), the coastline had been the site of extensive intercontinental trade, exporting first pepper, then gold, and finally enslaved humans and importing in return cloth and other finished products. Merchant companies and state-sponsored monopolies from Portugal, Castile, the Netherlands, Denmark, Sweden, France, Britain, and even German states established forts and factories along the coast, although none ever exerted control far beyond their outposts.[1] As the Atlantic slave trade was slowly quenched, however, transcontinental trade declined and one after another the European companies withdrew until, in 1871, only the English (now British) were left.

In the late eighteenth and nineteenth centuries the real powerhouse in the region was not a European state, but rather an African one. The Asante state, which arose from the region's interior, had begun to emerge around 1700 and by the mid-nineteenth century was something of an empire in its own right: a multi-cultural state that at its core was a confederation built around family relationships but that was also intensely multi-cultural and exerted authority over distant provinces both far into the interior and at the coast.[2] After a successful campaign in 1807, Asante forces had extended a loose authority over many of the small city-states of the coast. Although accepted by some locals, Asante rule was resented by others and rebellions intermittently flared up. Opponents of Asante hegemony resisted their rule by organizing local alliances. Probably the most important of these was the Fante Confederation, a federation

---

[1] Two excellent texts on this period are Albert van Dantzig, *Forts and Castles of Ghana* (Accra: Sedco Publishing, 1980); and Ray A. Kea, *Settlements, Trade, and Polities in the Seventeenth-Century Gold Coast* (Baltimore: Johns Hopkins University Press, 1982).

[2] See chapter 4.

of several coastal states, which along with a number of allied states slowly drew the British into their insurrection against Asante during the 1850s and 1860s. In the early 1870s, this confrontation came to a head as several missionaries were captured by Asante expeditions that also infringed upon British commercial ventures. In Britain, the emerging imperial lobby (including many missionaries) supported sending forces to the region to turn back the "heathen" Asante and to promote commerce and Christianity. They succeeded in 1873, and over the next year an allied British coastal army engaged and defeated several Asante forces and ultimately asserted British control over the southern interior and coast.[3] Despite the fact that neither the Fante nor any of the other small coastal states had legally ceded their sovereign powers to Britain, the Crown organized them into the British Colony and Protectorate on July 24, 1874—one of the first victims of the New Imperialism. The continued presence of the powerful Asante state to the north kept most of the local rulers from protesting this assumption of de facto control by the British, and because of their continued reliance on British military force they allowed local self-rule institutions like the Fante Confederation to fade away. In fact, however, even the Colonial Office continued to regard the Colony itself as only a small coastal stretch and much of the rest of the region including allied local states were described as a Protectorate, thus leaving them technically (de jure) still in possession of their sovereignty.

Thus immediately after 1874, real British authority was weak and even their claims to sovereignty in the Colony were little substantiated. Yet colonial authorities were able to gain true control of the region over the next two decades through a variety of processes. Colonial administrators imposed laws across the Protectorate that allowed them to dominate and regulate functions previously left to local communities, including policing roads, taxing commerce, and trying locals for transgressing a number of new laws

passed by the administration. One of these laws was a prohibition against slavery. Although initially the law was only loosely enforced, it eventually became a useful tool for deposing local rulers who were perceived to be acting against British or missionary interests by accusing them of owning slaves.

Gradually, British law came to supersede local legal systems.[4] The authority of the colonial officials was largely enforced by legal and political means, but military force was still available to the governor and his administrators in times of need. Two further campaigns against Asante in 1896 and 1899–1901 led to its dismemberment and occupation, and gradually the British expanded to the north of Asante as well. One of the most important tools in bringing these new regions under colonial control was expulsion. Rulers who opposed colonialism or otherwise angered the British were exiled. The most important of these exiles was *Asantehene* (king) Prempeh I of Asante, sent to the Seychelles Islands in 1896.

At the same time, the new colonial administrators began to build the infrastructure necessary to control the new colony—roads, police stations, and telegraph lines. Britain also negotiated periodically with its colonial neighbors—the Germans in Togoland and the French in the Ivory Coast and Upper Volta—to gain recognition for their annexations and to set mutually agreeable boundaries. Through these and a variety of other methods, Britain slowly came to control the entire former Asante state and all of its tributaries.

The extension of French control over Indochina was a similarly gradual process. In the early nineteenth century, French and other European missionaries and merchants had begun to gain influence in the region during a period in which Chinese influence was in decline and the powerful kings of Vietnam were suffering from internal disunity. Taking advantage of this situation, Catholic missionaries repeatedly put pressure

---

[3] F.K. Buah, *A History of Ghana* (London: Macmillan, 1995), 85. First published 1980.

[4] See Trevor R. Getz, "Re-evaluating the 'Colonization' of Akyem Abuakwa: Amoako Atta, the Basel Mission, and the Gold Coast Courts, 1867–1887," *Ghana Studies*, 6 (2003), 163–180.

on the French government to intervene in the region, although they were largely ignored by the Republican government of the French Second Republic (1848–1852). It was only following Napoleon III's seizure of power in France in 1852 that missionaries combined with French companies to lobby their government to annex several provinces of Vietnam, largely by invoking nationalistic fears of British interest in the region.

Thus between 1858 and 1882, the French military annexed the southern, lowland provinces of the Vietnamese state (known to the French as Cochinchina) and attempted to extend their control northward into the Tonkin provinces. In the mountainous uplands and cities of the north, however, they faced significant resistance from royal troops backed at times by China and by informal armies of peasants. Finally, in 1883, a succession crisis in Vietnam enabled French diplomats to force the Treaty of Hue on the new king, creating a French protectorate over Tonkin. When some Vietnamese officials questioned the legitimacy of the agreement, the French rounded up a number of them and forced them to sign the agreement as well in 1884. China's Qing Emperor, however, refused to accept this agreement, and only the defeat of his forces in the Franco-Chinese War of 1884–1885 forced him to ratify it.

Technically, the new agreements gave the French authorities only very limited authority in the provinces of northern and central Vietnam. However, resistance by Vietnamese peasants gave some aggressive French colonial army officers the justification they needed to seize additional power. In 1887, the French implemented a policy that led to the creation of the Indochinese Union (colonial French Indochina), in which Annam (the northernmost region of Vietnam) remained a "protected" royal province under the Vietnamese king, Cochinchina remained a colony, and Tonkin became a semi-independent province controlled by an indigenous high commissioner.[5] The Union

also included Cambodia, whose ruler, King Norodom, actually exerted no authority within his own country after having been forced to flee by rebels and Siamese forces. Norodom, in exile, was convinced by the French to sign a treaty of "protection" as his only hope of regaining his throne. In reality, the treaty merely became an excuse for the French conquest of his state.

Although the legal status of each of these provinces of the Indochinese Union was different, French rule over them quickly became standardized as French officials seized control of the local administration. In Tonkin, for example, the authority of the Vietnamese high commissioner was entirely, if unofficially, superseded by that of his French advisor. By wielding the power to replace local officials at will, this "advisor" in reality became just as powerful as the French governor of Cochin. In Annam and Cambodia as well, French officials and representatives gradually collected military and civil power in their own hands. This process was aided by the willingness of the European states—and after 1887 China as well—to accept French claims to sovereignty over the region. Thus although the creation of the Indochinese Union was not ratified by any Vietnamese or Cambodian bodies, it nevertheless was the step that decisively created Indochina as an official French colony by transferring internationally recognized legal authority in the region to France. In 1893, Laos was added to the Union following its cession to France by Siam. Laotians were not consulted in this exchange either. By the mid-1890s, all of these provinces—whether conquered outright or slowly absorbed by treaty or even just by the gradual exercise of more and more power—had in effect become French colonies.

IMPOSING COLONIAL AUTHORITY AND SOVEREIGNTY

The two examples aforementioned are rather typical historical narratives of the processes by which colonial authority was imposed in regions around the world during the late nineteenth and early twentieth centuries. Of course the creation of each colony was a unique process, heavily influenced

---

[5] Thê Anh Nguyên, "The Vietnamese Monarchy Under French Colonial Rule 1884–1895," *Modern Asian Studies*, 19 (1985), 147–162.

by local factors. Nevertheless, there were a number of common factors and experiences shared by populations coming under the control of empires in this period. This is partly the result of a great contradiction within the imperial system of this period. On the one hand, the societies of the expansionist industrial empires of the age–Japan, the United States, and the dominant European powers—were filled with nationalist sentiment and saw each other as competitors. Yet on the other hand, they cooperated to an unprecedented extent in conquering and dividing up enormous landmasses around the world. How did this situation come about?

To find an answer to this question, we have to look closely at the tightrope walked by these governments in this period. Because they were all to some degree parliamentary democracies (often constitutional monarchies) with a multi-party political structure, their political leaders had to respond to pressure from both funders and the electorate. A majority of both not only approved aggressive and expansionist policies, but actually often demanded them. Jingoistic newspapers kept track of every new territory claimed by rivals, and political lobbies supportive of colonialism urged their governments to block them. Businesses looking for trade monopolies provided much of the financial backing for these lobbies. Together, these groups were too powerful to ignore, and politicians within the great powers opposed colonialism only at their own risk. Yet imperialism also had enormous costs. Armed conquest was an expensive endeavor that could quickly drain the states' coffers. This in turn could lead to a reduction in funds available for popular social programs, and thus threaten the government's popularity. Moreover, the balance of power between the great powers was so precarious that warfare between them in the colonies might easily lead to a great conflict at home. Many diplomats and politicians (although not all) hoped to avoid this, both because of its vast cost and for idealistic reasons, and thus drew back from total support for confrontational imperialism.

In order to meet the colonial aspirations of the metropolitan citizenry without going broke or unleashing a world war, therefore, the governments of the industrialized empires developed a system that could allow claims of sovereignty over territories outside of Europe to be established and ratified by means of diplomacy. Employed informally at first, the process was first codified by an agreement signed at the 1884–1885 Berlin Conference.[6] The Conference, and others that followed, were attended by representatives of the major imperial governments and some corporate and "humanitarian" representatives but were closed to representatives from the societies whose independence was being negotiated away.

The agreement signed at the Berlin Conference by the great powers contained three provisions for colonizing Africa:

1. Any of the signatories could extend a claim over an African region so long as it could produce a treaty signed with an African ruler acknowledging its authority.
2. Rival claims by more than one government would be negotiated in a diplomatic context.
3. And once these claims were resolved and were followed by effective occupation, they would be recognized by all signatories to the agreement.

In short, this deal meant that a metropole could gain international recognition of its sovereignty over a new colony without any input from the colony's population: whether Africans, Asians, or Caribbean or Pacific Islanders. The great Ghanaian historian A. Adu Boahen explains how the process typically worked:

> The Scramble was carried on in three stages. The first stage was the conclusion of a treaty between an African ruler and a European imperial power under which the former was usually accorded protection and undertook not to enter into any treaty relation with another European power, while the latter was granted certain exclusive trading and other rights.... The second stage was the signing of bilateral treaties between the imperial powers usually based on the earlier treaties

---

[6] The political history of this process in a purely European context is well explained in Thomas Pakenham, *The Scramble for Africa: 1876–1912* (New York: Avon Books, 1991).

of protection which defined their spheres of interest and delimited their boundaries. . . . It should be emphasized that these European bilateral treaties were concluded without any consultations whatsoever with the African states. The third and final stage was that of the European conquest and occupation of their spheres.[7]

In this way, the empires of the New Imperialism claimed and recognized each others' rights to rule territories not just in Africa but in many parts of the world. Yet just because Britain, France, Japan, or other empires could claim international recognition of their sovereignty over their new colonies did not guarantee that the inhabitants of those colonies would recognize that sovereignty and accept the colonizer's rule. Establishing this internal control was the longest and most convoluted part of the process. It was also often exceedingly violent. Yet ironically Europeans labeled it *pacification.*

How did colonial powers impose control over a territory they had claimed? As in earlier periods, force was one of the chief tools modern colonizers used from the very beginning of the process. The first imperial agents—the much-celebrated explorers of the age—always armed their expeditions. In New Guinea and Central Africa, as elsewhere, these "heroes" murdered to obtain food, to scare local populations, or to force rulers to sign treaties.[8] Usually, these first expeditions were relatively small, and the havoc they wrought was relatively localized. Rather quickly, however, the process of pacification swelled into long, drawn-out campaigns often involving tens of thousands of soldiers and causing enormous casualties. The 1911 Italian expedition to Libya, for example, initially consisted of 20,000 soldiers but swelled to more than 100,000 when resistance proved especially fierce. The Italian invasion was predicted to last less than a year, but in fact it only officially ended 20 years later with the surrender

of major resistance leaders in 1931. In mainland Asia, the Japanese occupation forces that numbered roughly 100,000 in the 1920s had swollen to well over a million by 1940. It is hard to count the number of civilian and military deaths caused by the Japanese campaigns, but probably over 300,000 individuals died in the occupation of the Chinese city of Nanjing alone.

In general, imperial governments preferred to wage short, cheap wars. Large armies overseas could not be sustained either in terms of imperial finances or manpower realities. Soldiers from the metropole (or even brought in from other colonies) cost a great deal of money to maintain and arm. Thus, the most efficient and largest empires quickly abandoned the continual mobilization of massed armies of soldiers from the metropole as a means of colonial administration. They did so through two strategies. The first was to move from a military administration based on actual force to a civilian administration based largely on the threat of force as quickly as possible (discussed further in chapter 13). The second strategy was to replace expensive metropolitan soldiers with cheaper locally recruited troops and police.

Local cooperation was desirable as well in other processes of colonialism, such as the assertion of imperial control of the judicial functions of the state. The role of the law in imposing colonialism should not be underestimated. By claiming the right to try locals, the conquerors asserted their political authority. Perhaps more importantly, law is wrapped up in culture and controlling judicial authority allowed the colonizers to exercise authority over local culture. For example, colonial judiciaries could attempt to abolish institutions of land-owning, divorce, or apprenticeship and replace them with arrangements of their own choosing. However, local populations often resisted the wholesale imposition of law by the colonizers, making its imposition a costly, turmoil-inducing, and often impossible project.[9]

---

[7] A. Adu Boahen, *African Perspectives on Colonialism* (Baltimore: Johns Hopkins University Press, 1990), 33–34. First published 1987.

[8] See especially Sven Lindqvist, *Exterminate all the Brutes* (New York: New Press, 1996).

---

[9] Lauren Benton, *Law and Colonial Cultures: Legal Regimes in World History, 1400–1900* (Cambridge: Cambridge University Press, 2002), 2.

The result was usually a hybrid legal system, in which some elements of pre-existing local laws and even the legal authority of some local judicial figures (chiefs, religious leaders, intellectuals, or formal justices) were retained, but subordinated somehow to the laws of the metropole. In South Africa, for example, colonial magistrates not only claimed the exclusive right to try their African subjects for murder and other major crimes, and to imprison them if they were found guilty, but also accepted that chiefs would try their community members for civil crimes such as adultery, and that the chiefs would have the right to fine or punish them if found guilty. By providing a revenue stream for the chiefs, this system also strengthened the bonds between them and the colonial administration.

Alongside the law, imperial governments often believed that their authority could be extended through the creation of infrastructure. French administrators in West Africa believed, for example, that roads and railroads were as important routes to pacification as were police stations and armies. Ernest Roume, governor of French West Africa from 1902 to 1907, expressed this partly in economic terms, writing that "in West Africa, outside of a very limited number of coastal zones, true economic activity cannot even be conceived without railroads." For Roume, railroads were one route to turning independent African subsistence farmers into dependent wage workers. But as historian Alice Conklin has noted, Roume and his contemporaries saw infrastructure as the key to the moral as well as the economic development of the colonies, which would profoundly "improve" the nature of colonized cultures as well as facilitate French rule. Thus in 1902, he wrote that railroads and commercialization of labor were useful "not only as instruments of administration and of material progress, but also a tool of social progress and truly a work of humanity."[10] Thus, he believed, Africans could become loyal, happy subjects of

the empire, and force would no longer be necessary to rule them.

Roume's plans relied on the gradual increase in France's African subjects' acceptance of French rule. While optimistic, perhaps, his writing reflects a growing awareness of the dependence of colonial authorities from the very beginning on local allies. In almost every colony, colonial rule relied heavily on the cooperation of indigenous and transient individuals and populations. The cooperation of these groups is often troubling to us in this post-colonial age. Why did these groups participate in such alliances? Wasn't their collaboration a betrayal of their people? We tend to cast individuals and groups who lived in the colonies during this period in the roles of the celebrated resistance heroes and the dastardly collaborators, but is this accurate? To even begin to answer this question, we have to shift our view on history away from our contemporary perspective and toward theirs.

PROBLEMATIZING COLLABORATION

In the previous chapter, we mostly explored the New Imperialism from a global perspective. We also zoomed in to explore it from a local perspective: that of the Colonial Office and Foreign Office administrators in Whitehall, London. But the New Imperialism looked very different when viewed from the Asantehene Prempeh I's palace in Kumasi, the capital of Asante, or from a mountain village in Tonkin. In the past, historians have suggested that the viewpoints of these communities were more localized and provincial than the global view of Whitehall's officials. Subsequent research has suggested that this picture of non-Europeans as incurious or ignorant of global conditions is inaccurate. Rather, the global worldviews of the Asantehene's court or of Tonkin farmers were produced both by different information and by different viewpoints. These were in turn shaped by their own personalities, by their environments, and by their understanding of their relationships to the cultural and physical world.

For these individuals, the coming of colonialism was important not only as an abstract transfer

---

[10] Alice Conklin, *A Mission to Civilize: The Republican Idea of Empire in France and West Africa, 1895–1930* (Stanford: Stanford University Press, 1997), 53.

of sovereignty, but because it affected in very real ways their lives and those of their friends, neighbors, and countrypeople. But, as we saw in earlier periods, the way in which each individual was affected by colonialism was different, both because their status and livelihood was unique to them and because colonialism's impact varied across and even within societies. A prince or chief who became a subordinate might, for example, find his power and authority drastically changed but his privileged lifestyle less so. A woman who produced goods for a local market might suddenly find her business ruined by cheap imported goods, even though she personally might have little contact with colonizers. A subsistence farmer living far away from colonial capitals might find his life little affected at all, while his neighbor becomes conscripted into the army leaving his family bereft of his support.

Looking at colonialism from the perspective of the colonized can help us understand that colonialism "happened" in many ways. One of the most troubling issues in the establishment of the colonies of the New Imperialism is that it could not have succeeded without the participation of locals. Despite the military advantage of industrialized societies, colonial rule was an enormous drain on the treasury and simply could not be enforced solely by standing armies of Europeans or Americans (the Japanese made a more sustained effort to do so). As we saw in chapters 2, 4, and 9, imperial governments in earlier periods sometimes actively assisted the migration of settlers to newly acquired territories in order to assist in controlling them. However, in the period of the New Imperialism many of the new colonies were in tropical regions that neither attracted nor were healthy for Europeans. Moreover, even when settlers were located in the colonies, their presence often only increased local resistance. Thus from the earliest days of the New Imperialism, colonial subjects were recruited to do much of the work of pacification. Many were brought from other, already-established colonies—Indian troops conquered most of East Africa for Britain, for example, while soldiers from the Caribbean formed large contingents in British West Africa. King Leopold of Belgium recruited men from all over Africa (and Europe) to serve in the police and army forces that kept the Congo oppressed. Nevertheless, colonial administrators rapidly switched to recruiting locals as constables and enlisted soldiers as soon as they were able. These military men were soon joined by other recruited collaborators—chiefs or mandarins who ran whole districts, tax collectors, clerks, and interpreters in the colonial courts.

The term *collaborator* is not an entirely useful one. As a label hung around the necks of individuals, it obscures rather than reveals the complexity of the choices facing colonial subjects. It is important to remember that colonialism was not the only element that figured in the daily lives of people around the world, nor was working within its realities the worst solution they could consider to their own struggles to eat, to survive, and to thrive. An equally important point, perhaps, is that colonialism had blundered into societies with rich tapestries of political, social, and economic conflict and alliance in every region in which it appeared. Rather than being blank slates upon which colonialism could be written, communities in Asia, Africa, and the Pacific were dynamic and changing. States fought against each other, branches of royal families fought for control, businesses sought to exclude each other. In these pre-existing networks and systems, groups who were out of power sometimes saw the invaders as potential allies in regaining it, while those who wielded power sometimes saw colonialism as a way to retain it. From their perspectives, they were using colonialism against their rivals, rather than being used by it. Thus, their goal was not to help establish colonial rule, but rather to improve their own position. Perhaps the most famous example was Emir Hussein of Mecca, who assisted the British in conquering the Arabian Peninsula in the hopes of ruling it as a united Arab kingdom. Less famously, after the king of Kaajor, in West Africa, tried to sack his foremost general, Demba War Sall, the general allied with the French to overthrow him in 1881. Sall was rewarded when the French installed his nephew as "king" of the new protectorate.

Certainly, looking closely at the ambitions and situations of local players helps to clarify the actions of individuals who signed treaties of protection in the first phase of the partition of Africa. It seems inconceivable that a ruler or leadership of a region, state, or peoples would voluntarily transfer sovereignty to Europeans. So why were such treaties signed? There are a number of possible answers. In the first place, most African signatories interpreted the proffered treaties as creating potentially useful and equal alliances with European rulers. They hoped to facilitate trade, to gain possession of weapons and other technologies, and to strengthen their own positions as rulers. In some cases, they hoped that they would also be receiving some assistance against both their own local rivals and other European powers. What they did not usually see was that they were giving up their sovereignty. Often, in fact, the treaties did not say anything about such a capitulation, but were fraudulently interpreted in this way back in Europe. In other cases, explorers and officials played on the illiteracy of African signatories, or produced two copies in two different languages—only the one going home saying anything about the cession of sovereignty. This was a trick played by the French on the *Brak* (king) of Waalo in Senegal. It was also used by the arch-imperialist Cecil Rhodes, who used trusted local missionaries to convince Lobengula, the ruler of Matabeleland in southern Africa, to sign an 1888 treaty granting him mineral rights to the territory. Lobengula signed this so-called Rudd Concession believing that it only gave Rhodes the right to introduce 10 mining inspectors into his territory. In fact, not only was that provision omitted from the paper copy but in addition stated that Rhodes's company could essentially rule the territory as necessary. By 1890, Rhodes's paramilitary forces had conquered much of the territory for the company and, subsequently, British rule.

In other cases, Africans were willing to sign these treaties precisely because they didn't have the right to do so. Nobles or rulers disputing a piece of land might sign a treaty accepting British or French protection over it because signing the treaty legitimized their claim over that of their rivals. The explorers Henry Morton Stanley (representing the King of Belgium) and Pierre de Brazza (representing France) both returned to Europe with treaties signed by minor chiefs who claimed to control the same huge region of central Kongo. Alternately, unpopular or embattled rulers might sign a treaty even when they really exercised little control over the state. Nor was such a practice confined to Africa: we have already seen that it was the strategy of King Norodom of Cambodia, who signed the treaty in 1886 establishing French "protection" while in exile from his state.

In most cases, the signing of treaties represented an attempt by local rulers to improve their own position, but it's important to note that many were also imposed at gunpoint. This was true in Hawaii, where King Kalakaua only accepted a "constitution" ratifying American influence in 1887 after a U.S. warship anchored beside his capital and a militia paid by U.S. planters took to the streets. In the town of Anécho in West Africa, German soldiers simply kidnapped the elders in 1884 and forced them to agree to a treaty prepared beforehand.[11]

Nevertheless, it is indisputable that some Africans, Asians, and Pacific Islanders chose not just to accommodate colonialism but actually to fight alongside or to support European, Japanese, and U.S. forces engaged in campaigns of conquest and pacification. What motivated them to fight for the imperial invaders? Part of the answer lies in the desire for personal gain. In Senegambia, the largest contingents of the French forces were made up of African mercenaries, ex-slaves, and out-of-power noblemen who all gained either money or prestige from their participation. In their conquest of the Zulu kingdom, British generals were assisted by levies from neighboring states formerly subjugated to or raided by Zulu generals. Perhaps it is most important, however,

---

[11] Dennis Laumann, "A Historiography of German Togoland, or the Rise and Fall of a 'Model Colony,'" *History in Africa*, 30 (2003), 195–211.

to place colonialism in local perspective. For many people, the threat of imperial rule by a far-away power paled in comparison to their ongoing rivalries with neighbors. They did not see the struggle in terms of racial conflict—unlike in the industrialized imperial metropoles, where racialism and nationalism were increasingly important, most peoples outside of Europe did not predominantly think in terms of race consciousness or race unity.[12] Thus, they did not always see a conflict in joining with imperial armies in the conquest of a neighboring state.

What all of this evidence suggests is that whereas the rivalries among the imperial powers were temporarily restrained during this period in order to facilitate their various conquests, internal cleavages in African, Pacific, and many Asian societies were exacerbated by the stress of the New Imperialism. These divisions aided in the establishment of colonialism by impairing the ability of populations in these regions to present unified resistance. Fragmentation in African, Asian, and Pacific Islander societies on the eve of conquest took many forms. One type of division was that between rival states. Equally important, however, was segmentation and division within societies. This could be very particular—individuals could simply have a personal grievance with their own government. Alternately, it could be more widespread—as in the case of religious or class divisions. Many early allies of colonial administrations thus fit one of two very different categories: they were from poor and low status groups or they were from important but out-of-power groups. In both cases, they had little stake in the existing system of government and were hoping to raise their status under the new, colonial regime.

One variant on this process was the development of groups commonly known as *modernizers*. This term became popular among scholars in the 1950s when it was still believed that being modern was synonymous with becoming western. These scholars applied the label *modernizer* to

non-Europeans who came to believe that their society could be best served by becoming like those of Europe. In the late nineteenth century, many such individuals and groups emerged around the world. They were generally western-educated and had often traveled to Europe. Many of them argued that their societies could only protect themselves from imperial aggression by reforming as industrialized and organized along the lines of European nation-states. Historian Philip Curtin has labeled this position "defensive modernization."[13]

At the same time, however, these reformers or modernizers were often engaged in philosophical or open conflict with the authorities in their own society who were more conservative and were opposed to the cultural change they demanded. Thus, sometimes, modernizers chose to support the colonial state as a way to advance their social agendas. It was partly for this reason that *The African Times*, a newspaper whose readers were mostly West African modernizers, supported the 1873–1874 British campaign against Asante. Yet only a year earlier, many of these same individuals had been involved in trying to form an independent state on the coast modeled on Britain.[14] As this example shows, modernizers can neither be easily classified as *collaborators* nor *resisters*. A further example is the case of the international network of Islamic modernizers, who strove to meld Islamic precepts and practices with industrial organization and new technologies. In late nineteenth-century Egypt, Islamic modernization was very much the organizing ideology of nationalists who were seeking strategies to create a state capable of standing up to Europeans. In East African coastal cities like Zanzibar, however, modernizers educated in dual Islamic and British systems tended to be proponents of expanded British intervention.

Both the rise of modernizers and the general fragmentation of African, Asian, and Pacific

---

[12] Jürgen Osterhammel, *Colonialism: A Theoretical Overview* (Princeton, NJ: Markus Wiener, 1997), 45.

[13] Philip Curtin, *The World and the West: The European Challenge and the Overseas Response in the Age of Empire* (Cambridge: Cambridge University Press, 2002).
[14] The last existing print copy of *The African Times* is held at the British Newspaper Library in Colindale, but a digital version is now available at http://diva.sfsu.edu.

Island societies in this period were partly a result of global trends. Colonialism profited from the economic disturbances in these regions caused by being drawn into the global industrialized economy. Equally important were the cultural strains created by the introduction of new ideas such as Protestant and Catholic Christianity and industrialized societies' notions of science. These new ideas disrupted the established social and cultural orders, and forced rulers and elites to struggle to manage and balance factions who embraced and rejected them. One illustrative example can be found in the changing policies of the rulers of the centralized East African kingdom of Buganda. In the mid-nineteenth century, as the region slowly became connected to the Atlantic and Indian Ocean economies, this state experienced an influx of Catholic, Protestant, and Muslim traders and missionaries. Each of these groups soon began to win local converts. The Bugandan kings not only strove to play these factions off against each other, but also used them as a tool to reduce the power of their rivals among the chiefly class. In doing so, they sought not only to gain the knowledge of the various missionaries and the wealth of the traders, but to control the process by which their state became integrated into the wider world. They used the foreign priests and missionaries as ambassadors to the British, French, and Egyptian governments as well as sources of information about the wider world. Eventually, however, the last Bugandan king, Mwanga, lost control of the process. Muslim, Protestant, Catholic, and "traditionalist" forces squared off in violent episodes. Finally, Sudanese troops of the EIC intervened on behalf of the Protestant faction, bringing Buganda into the British Empire in 1893. It was this invasion that ended Bugandan independence, but only because this once unified society had been fractured by the cultural and economic stresses of late nineteenth-century globalization.[15]

---

[15] M.S. Kiwanuka, *Semakula, a History of Buganda: From the Foundation of the Kingdom to 1900* (New York: Africana Press, 1972).

PROBLEMATIZING RESISTANCE

In the last section, we saw that the term **collaboration** obscures more than it reveals about the actions of people in the newly forming colonies. The term **resistance** is similarly problematic, although for different reasons. In popular culture today, we tend to depict resistance to colonial imposition in terms of armed warriors bravely fighting invaders in guerilla campaigns and pitched battles. To be sure, military resistance to the process of occupation and pacification did occur—as it had from the earliest times of colonial conquest. Yet focusing solely on this image of armed confrontation not only obscures the difficulty and complexity of resistance by local populations, but also hides the wide range of techniques and strategies they employed.

In order to begin to perceive resistance in a more nuanced way, we have to recognize two key realities of most colonial occupations of this period. The first is that ongoing massive military resistance was usually unsuccessful because of the weapons gap between industrialized and non-industrialized societies. This is not to say that military resistance didn't occur—it often did. As we have seen, Africans, Asians, and Pacific Islanders fought major defensive campaigns in this period, often mobilizing enormous armies or guerilla forces for long periods of time. Sometimes, as for the Maoris of New Zealand, relatively small forces could tie up large occupying armies. Over time, however, the technological superiority and military organization of industrialized imperial armies usually won out. Moreover, the success of the Treaty of Berlin and other agreements meant that while imperial powers could often set African or Asian states against each other, after the mid-1880s Africans and Asians had less ability to really manipulate great power rivalries (despite a few notable exceptions). Thus, societies defending themselves against encroaching colonialism usually fought alone.

A great deal has been written about organized military resistance to conquest, often called *primary resistance*. It is the best-known type of resistance, although ironically it often had little effect in stemming the tide of colonialism. Thus after the first decade of the twentieth century, relatively few major colonial military campaigns were required.

Just because organized military resistance faded for a while following the victories of imperial armies, however, does not mean that colonized populations had come to meekly accept the realities of colonial rule. While organized violent struggle against conquering armies diminished, other forms of resistance emerged. In part this had to do with the changing nature of colonialism. Formal armed resistance was usually organized by monarchs and other powerful men and women. Often, many of the laboring classes cared little about the struggle, since one government was to them much like another.[16] After the armies of the state were defeated, however, colonial administrations became the new rulers. They began to govern, which meant that they taxed the population, sometimes seized their land, and in many ways tried to control and limit their actions. Peasants, herders, and farmers, many of whom may not have cared much about the abstract change of government from an old state to a new empire, did resent the imposition of these regulations and taxes. However, their lifestyles and social organization usually did not lend themselves to organized armed resistance to these facets of colonial rule. Thus, they were less likely to fight the kinds of massive wars that characterized primary resistance and that are easy to see in the historical record. Instead, they tended to engage in less-organized and less-visible strategies of resistance aimed at opposing some particularly onerous colonial tax or escaping being forced to labor on colonial roads or railroads. James C. Scott has labeled these strategies *weapons of the weak*, and writes that it is important:

> to understand what we might call everyday forms of peasant resistance—the prosaic but constant struggle between peasantry and those who seek to extract labor, food, taxes, rents and interest from them. Most forms of

this struggle stop well short of outright collective defiance. Here I have in mind the ordinary weapons of relatively powerless groups: foot dragging, dissimulation, desertion, false compliance, pilfering, feigned ignorance, slander, arson, sabotage, and so on.[17]

This is not to say that violent, organized resistance movements completely disappeared following colonial conquest in the period of the New Imperialism, although in most cases they became more rare and episodic than might be assumed at first. Rather, moving toward an understanding of resistance as more than just pitched battles helps us to perceive that in this early period of the New Imperialism resistance didn't just disappear when the pitched battles ended. Rather, it continued on but in less visible, more subtle forms, often organized at a very local level. A story told by Robert Delavignette, a French colonial officer in French West Africa, illustrates this point:

> When I was head of a subdivision on the Upper Volta, I went on tour in the first months of my stay, and landed unexpectedly in a distant village, little visited. The chief gave me a good reception. I came back there two years later, at the end of my tour, and had a still better reception. The chief, however, did not seem to be the same man. I had before me an old man, while it was a young man who had received me the first time, and I recognized him, standing behind the old man. I asked the two of them why the chieftainship of the village had passed from the one to the other without my being told of it. The old man said to me: "He whom you see behind me was in front of me" and he explained, "It is I who am the chief, today as the other time, and in front of this man, as behind him. But two years ago we did not know you, and he showed himself in my place."[18]

---

[16] An excellent example of this from South-East Asia is Michael Adas, "From Avoidance to Confrontation: Peasant Protest in Precolonial and Colonial Southeast Asia," in *Colonialism and Culture*, edited by Nicholas B. Dirks (Ann Arbor: The University of Michigan Press, 1992), 89–126.

[17] James Campbell Scott, *Weapons of the Weak: Everyday Forms of Peasant Resistance* (New Haven, CT: Yale University Press, 1985), xvi.

[18] Wilfred Cartey and Martin Kilson, *The Africa Reader: Colonial Africa* (New York: Vintage Books, 1970), 78.

Misleading a new colonial officer was a type of resistance, in that it hid the real authority of the community from him. When historians look closely at the historical record, they find evidence of such types of resistance everywhere. Stored goods disappear at inopportune moments. Children misdirect convoys going into the brush. Worker productivity rates fall off sharply after a new tax is imposed. Families hide their children from the census-takers. All of these acts make the process of ruling the colony much more difficult.

These types of resistance were far more common than armed rebellion, and recognizing them makes it even harder to put people into simple categories of *resister* and *collaborator*. Often, in fact, resistance and collaboration were practiced by a single individual: the clerk who also stole, the chief who misdirected, the disgruntled worker who slowed down her labor. These individuals tried to profit from some facets of colonialism, resisted some, and sought to avoid still others.

Indeed, avoidance was one of the most important strategies practiced by colonial subjects. In most cases, avoidance simply meant not being around when workers or soldiers were conscripted, or taxes were collected. But avoidance also could include massive emigrations, as occurred in northern Senegal. In 1884, the French Governor of Senegal outlawed the sale or purchase of slaves in the region. This, along with other impositions, motivated as many as 40,000 people to leave the region and move beyond the limits of French rule into the interior. This migration was remarkably similar to the Great Trek of slave-owning white settlers away from the Cape Colony of South Africa following the British abolition of slavery there in 1834–1835.

Most exit strategies, however, were less dramatic. In many cases, individuals or families fed up with colonial rule just slipped across the border into independent regions. Even after colonialism claimed vast areas, some groups would move among the colonies, seeking the least oppressive regime.

RE-EVALUATING THE PACIFICATION OF THE GOLD COAST AND INDOCHINA

We began this chapter with rather conventional narratives of the conquest of Indochina in South-East Asia and the Gold Coast in West Africa that focused on the processes of conquest and pacification largely from the perspective of the colonial authorities. But these traditional narratives failed to answer important questions. Most significantly, they did not explain the actions of local populations and the roles they played in the process. This information is important not only for colonial but also for imperial history, because without it we cannot understand the ways in which Britain and France (and elsewhere the United States, Germany, Japan, and other powers) parlayed weak positions and trade agreements into colonial rule.

The establishment of the Gold Coast Colony is a case in point. We saw in the earlier narrative that in 1873, at the beginning of the campaign against Asante, Britain could claim legal sovereignty only over a few coastal ports. Even these were mostly "rented" from coastal communities, although in reality rent had not been paid in almost every case for several decades at least. Yet just over a year later, Britain would formally declare a colony over much of the coast and have spread its influence and "protection" deep into the interior. Exactly why and how this happened is not clear, however, in the narrative with which we began this chapter, which viewed the process largely from the perspective of British, but not local, actors.

For the British, the objective of the war against Asante was largely to secure their own economic and strategic position in the region and to carry out their "civilizing" duty. For the inhabitants of the coast, by contrast, the British were merely allies recruited to help in their struggle to liberate themselves from Asante. Among the most important proponents of British intervention in this struggle were a large, loosely knit group of African and Euro-African modernizers mostly based in the coastal cities. Many were professionals such as lawyers and doctors, although most were merchants. These men (and a few women) had access to British officials, spoke their language, and dressed in a similar fashion. In the early 1860s and 1870s, they constructed a campaign to get the British involved in their struggle against Asante. They met with British officials and citizens and regaled them with stories of Asante savageness and barbarity. They published these stories in newspapers or wrote them down in their correspondence. Their goals were not only nationalistic (in support of the small states from which they came) but also commercial: as merchants and investors, they hoped that British rule would bring roads and railroads and other means of expanding their trade.[19] These modernizers also in many cases had become Christians, and recruited the missionaries who preached and taught in their churches to support their campaign to get Britain to commit to a war with Asante.

It was an Asante attempt to renew their control of the coastal towns in 1867–1868 that sparked the creation of the Fante Confederation. As a military alliance, the Confederation was not something new: a number of small states that identified themselves as Fante had previously fought together against Asante incursions. But as it became clear that Britain was not yet ready to militarily intervene in their support, the Confederation slowly came to be led by a group of modernizers who tried to build it into an independent, sovereign state. This group collaboratively wrote a constitution modeled on that of the North German Confederation and began to build an independent state that they hoped would one day rival those of Europe. A similar attempt to build a western-style state was begun in the city of Accra as well. But the Confederation collapsed when, in 1873, the British Crown finally committed itself to the war against Asante.

What caused the collapse of the Confederation? In part, disagreements and competition for power among its principal leaders tore it apart. More significantly, however, local chiefly officeholders and the bulk of the population saw Britain rather than the Confederation as their best hope against renewed Asante rule. The 1873–1874 war hadn't ended in the conquest of Asante, but merely its retreat from the coast, and only Britain appeared to have the military power to keep it from coming back. Thus at the conclusion of the war, most of the chiefs of the allied states made the decision to abandon the Confederation and sign protectorate treaties with the British. By these agreements, they surrendered some of their sovereignty, giving colonial courts limited jurisdiction. After 1874, even the rulers of the larger interior states submitted themselves to British law when required to do so. They did so largely because the Asante threat had not yet disappeared. In some cases, the British were able to use these agreements to replace recalcitrant chiefs with those more amenable to their rule. These new rulers were even more willing to accept British authority. Thus, slowly, the acceptance of British law and British authority spread despite the fact that, as late as 1888, the colonial chief magistrate recognized that British sovereignty *legally* extended no further than the original coastal forts.[20]

Slowly, the secular authorities in southern Ghana were transformed from paramount chiefs holding office based on elections and on their relationships to important families into the paid accomplices of the British. Their loss of the right to try cases and impose fines, along with the abolition of slavery, impoverished them, and they began to rely solely on the colonial administration for funding. This process did not happen without resistance: chiefs sometimes refused to agree to

---

[19] Evidence of this can be found in newspapers such as *The African Times*. Two books dealing with the nineteenth-century Gold Coast modernizers are Roger Gocking, *Facing Two Ways: Ghana's Coastal Communities Under Colonial Rule* (Lanham: University Press of America, 1999); and David Kimble, *A Political History of Ghana: The Rise of Gold Coast Nationalism 1850–1928* (Oxford: Oxford University Press, 1963).

[20] Trevor R. Getz, "The Case for Africans: The Role of Slaves and Masters in Emancipation on the Gold Coast, 1874–1900," *Slavery and Abolition*, 21 (2000), 128–145. Also Roger Gocking, "British Justice and the Native Tribunals of the Southern Gold Coast Colony," *Journal of African History*, 34 (1993), 93–113.

or enforce new laws, merchants sometimes protested market regulations, and groups of young men even attacked the houses of chiefs who cooperated too much. However, the ongoing Asante threat coupled with the increasing presence of a colonial constabulary and military willing to use force helped the administration quell these upheavals. In recognition of the key role played by chiefs, administrators recognized their authority in some matters and shaped colonial laws to suit them, often at the expense of the modernizers. Increasingly, these "educated" men turned in petitions to the governor or crown when unhappy. Yet these petitions, while acts of resistance, also acknowledged the reality of a British sovereignty imposed without conquest or abdication.

The inhabitants of the new colony, along with constables recruited from other parts of West Africa, were available for two further invasions of Asante. The first, in 1896, resulted in the expulsion of the ruling family into exile in the Seychelles Islands, an act intended to behead the state. But Asante resistance was rekindled by Yaa Asantewaa, an important woman who was Queen Mother of one of the central Asante provinces, after the British governor had demanded that the Asante leadership give him the Golden Stool, the throne of Asante. With her grandson in exile, Yaa Asantewaa organized a guerilla campaign, and only a bloody invasion by a large army sufficed to put the rebellion down.

In traditional narratives such as that which begins this chapter, resistance seems to disappear following the defeat of Yaa Asantewaa's rebellion. In fact, however, it was merely transformed. In the early twentieth century, for example, colonial records reveal a series of what are euphemistically labeled *disturbances* following the implementation of new laws and taxes in the colony. These included quite large groups of people parading, demonstrating, and sometimes acting violently.[21] Most of these disturbances were directed at

collaborating chiefs, and they succeeded in severely shaking the governor and his staff. In fact, British rule continued to be contested at every level—by African intellectuals who protested to parliament, by rural farmers who refused to turn out to build roads, and by religious and chiefly officeholders threatening rebellion. Putting out these wildfires occupied much of the time of Britain's imperial "pacifiers" (soldiers and officials), but they were also aided by local help—especially chiefly officeholders recruited and paid to be subordinate administrators of territories their predecessors had once ruled independently.

Yet while clearly demonstrating popular opposition to colonialism, these actions failed to truly challenge the colonial state's hegemony in this period because the demonstrators lacked leadership that could unite them. Those chiefs who had not been exiled had by 1914 become largely co-opted as paid representatives of the colonial state. Meanwhile, the modernizers' ambitions and lifestyles were too different from those of much of the population to allow them to serve as leaders. Thus, resistance most often remained either spontaneous or the act of individuals or small groups.

Understanding the motives and aspirations of chiefs, modernizers, and others in the Gold Coast helps us to understand the process by which it became a British colony. The same is true in Indochina, where a retelling of the French occupation from a local perspective might begin with the decline of the Vietnamese Nguyễn dynasty, which had almost unified the entire region under the rule of King Nguyễn Phúc Ánh at the beginning of the nineteenth century. This monarch brought under his rule not just the provinces of Vietnam, but at least nominally Laos and Cambodia as well. His successors, however, were challenged both by neighboring regional powers—the Chinese Qing emperors and the kings of Siam—and by disgruntled elites and peasants in Laos and Cambodia.

Even in Vietnam, the Nguyễn kings were weaker than they seemed. Forced to continually negotiate rivalries among regional power blocks, they were never truly able to centralize power in their own hands. By mid-century, class struggles between peasants and landlords and religious

---

[21] Anshan Li, "Asafo and Destoolment in Colonial Southern Ghana, 1900–1953," *International Journal of African Historical Studies*, 28 (1995), 327–357.

divisions between Buddhists and the growing Christian community also weakened the state.[22] These divisions made it difficult for kings like Nguyễn Phúc Thì to respond effectively to increasing French intervention. When Napoleon III's armies pushed into the southern provinces, they frequently encountered more resistance from locally organized groups than from royal troops. As a result of this disorganization, the French rather rapidly conquered these provinces, which they renamed Cochinchina, between 1858 and 1862.

As the Vietnamese state retreated, the new colonial authorities began to impose French rule. This meant, in part, sponsoring French companies and missionaries in their respective projects to build plantations and spread Christianity. Many peasants found the projects, and French taxes, unpalatable and resisted both individually and in guerilla groups. Locally organized armed resistance continued effectively for two decades, limiting the ability of the French to expand their influence into northern Vietnam and Cambodia.

The principal cause for the persistence of the guerilla bands was the intensification of plantation agriculture, which kept peasants on the edge of starvation, thus driving them into what the French called *banditry*. These guerilla groups were poorly armed, and in the absence of secular leadership were often led by religious men—monks or "sorcerers"—claiming spiritual powers.[23] They were joined in the 1880s by a dissident Chinese group known as the Black Flags, who had fled to northern Vietnam from China following the collapse of the Taiping Rebellion. In China, they had largely opposed the Qing Dynasty, but in Vietnam they focused their attacks on European shipping and interests. The Black Flags soon gained local volunteers as well, driven both by anger at the colonial state and by poverty and desperation. It was their actions that precipitated the 1884–1885

Sino-French War between France on the one hand and the Black Flags, Vietnam, and Chinese forces on the other hand. Once again, the weakness of the Vietnamese state and French technological supremacy allowed them to defeat their opponents in pitched battles. But these victories, while putting the royalist forces of the Vietnamese kings to flight, left the Black Flags and other rebels at large.

This situation, in which the power of the throne was increasingly weakened while other armed forces were on the rise, was exacerbated by infighting and the deaths of several successive Vietnamese monarchs in 1883 and 1884. It was amidst this tumult that a young and untried king accepted French "protection" on June 6, 1884, in the hopes of protecting himself from rebel forces. Although technically he agreed only to turn over control of the armed force and foreign policy, we have seen that in effect this treaty led to the dismemberment of royal authority.

A similar process explains King Norodom's actions in Cambodia, where in the 1860s real power was divided between Vietnamese and Siamese occupying forces. As France gradually took over the Vietnamese claim, the Cambodian kings tried to re-establish their rule, but they were opposed by both Vietnam and the French colonial administration. The effective opposition to both was increasingly led by monks or organized around ethnicity, as in the case of some minorities, leaving King Norodom without any real legitimacy. Thus, he was forced to agree to a French protectorate as his only hope of reclaiming control over his country. Subsequent French campaigns and diplomacy in Cambodia, and later Laos, largely succeeded in expelling Siamese influence from the region, leaving France the only major power in the region.

While the kings of Indochina were forced by internal division to accept French protection by 1887, however, popular resistance at a grassroots level continued even after the formation of the so-called Indochinese Union. Some of this took the form of avoidance or foot-dragging, but violent resistance continued as well, often in the form of Vietnamese–Chinese and Vietnamese–Cambodian combined units, including the remnants of the

---

[22] J. Chesneaux, "Stages in the Development of the Vietnam National Movement 1862–1940," *Past and Present*, 7 (1955), 63–75.
[23] R.B. Smith, "The Development of Opposition to French Rule in Southern Vietnam 1880–1940," *Past and Present*, 54 (1972), 94–129.

Black Flags. French officials considered two strategies to fight these insurgents. One was to reinforce French forces with European soldiers. The other was to increase the number of Indochinese soldiers. This mirrored a larger debate in which the colonial administration argued whether to bring in large numbers of French officials to run the day-to-day affairs of the colony, or to rely more on the existing mandarin (scholar-bureaucrat) class.[24] Eventually, they decided on the latter policy in both cases.

The new colonial military that the French built to run the Indochinese Union was drawn from Catholic converts and other low-status members of society who saw service in the army as a way to increase their personal status and reverse their powerlessness. These soldiers were often vicious to those who had once exercised authority over them. This was especially true in rural areas where the new recruits often carried out vendettas against civilians from other religious or ethnic groups. This brutality, however, merely provoked increased resistance from the Buddhist majority. In the Vietnamese provinces, such resistance was increasingly prevalent not only among peasants resisting French labor laws and the plantation regime, but also among mandarins who professed loyalty to the king. Their ranks were swelled when the French began to replace older mandarins with new appointments chosen more for their loyalty to the colonial regime than for their skill.

Finally, in the early 1890s the French realized the failure of their initial strategy. Rather than defeating the resistance, the brutality of their largely Catholic colonial militia had merely helped to unite peasants and mandarins under the flag of Buddhism. Thus, the administration began to limit the ill-treatment of peasants, and offered some positions in the colonial administration to senior mandarins. They also proposed certain concessions to rural communities that showed their loyalty to the colonial state. These efforts

failed to quell resistance in the mountains of the north and the marshes of the south, but did gradually win over some village leaders and mandarins who had professed loyalty to the old kings of Vietnam. Gradually, most of the mandarin class were co-opted or comfortably retired.

However, even in this period the administration continued to be plagued by peasant guerillas. Senior military leaders searched for a solution and eventually hit upon supporting ethnic minorities. They hoped to pit these groups against resistance forces that were dominated by ethnic Vietnamese leaders. This "policy of races" worked to some degree, and foreshadowed the policies of divide-and-conquer that would dominate twentieth-century colonialism. Yet despite now being fragmented, armed resistance continued into the early twentieth century, and arguably the pacification of Indochina was never completed. Nevertheless, by the late 1890s resistance was confined to small rural groups often led by monks. First the kings, then the mandarins had given up their legitimacy to lead the resistance movements, and so it continued only on a local and less-organized basis.

Conclusion

The experiences of the Gold Coast and Vietnam give us insight into the functioning of colonialism during the process of conquest and pacification. In many ways, these processes shared many features with earlier periods of colonial conquest, and differed from those by which colonial rule was later maintained. During the process of conquest, metropolitan governments were more willing to provide for the expense and humanpower of massive armies. Thus, violence was more prevalent and experimentation was more accepted than in later periods. Perhaps most of all, most African, Asian, and Pacific Island societies were initially badly prepared to resist colonialism. Imperial armies found it relatively easy in most cases to defeat centralized states in large-scale campaigns. This show of force, along with the assumption by colonial administrations of state

---

[24] J. Kim Munholland, "'Collaboration Strategy' and the French Pacification of Tonkin, 1885–1897," *Historical Journal*, 24 (1981), 629–650.

treasuries and legal authority, convinced kings and chiefs to accept and in some cases to cooperate closely with the state. Those religious and secular authorities who opposed these changes often led resistance movements, but found their authority undercut by administrators and police as well as missionaries and their converts. Meanwhile, local modernizers and scholars often found themselves out of step with the majority of the population and were unable to build mass support for anti-colonial resistance.

Thus during the imposition of colonialism during the New Imperialism, situations were created in which there was a decline in organized resistance following the military or diplomatic collapse of the pre-colonial states and their armies. Yet opposition to colonialism did not disappear in this period, but rather took new forms. Armed groups of rebels, communities, and individuals also continued to resist, often through less-violent and more-subtle means. In order to control this situation, colonial administrations could use force, but this option was usually prohibitively expensive. The administrator who had to call for help too often was not likely to advance quickly in the ranks of the colonial bureaucracy. Wherever possible, therefore, administrators began more and more to lean on local allies who were willing to accommodate and even assist them in various ways. While this strategy had been pioneered in an earlier period, it became far more widespread after the massive expansion of colonial rule that characterized the period of the New Imperialism. To see these local allies simply as *collaborators*, however, is to miss the complexity of colonial subjects' struggles to survive and thrive in a turbulent period.

Questions

1. Read the first and second telling of the conquest and occupation of Vietnam in this chapter. What are the differences between these two accounts? Similarly, what are the differences between the two retellings of the British occupation of the Gold Coast? Which accounts do you prefer, and why? What lessons do you draw from this exercise?

2. A few popular histories of this colonial era divide colonial subjects into "collaborators" and "resisters." Do you feel that this division is a helpful one? Why or why not?

3. Based on evidence presented in this chapter, for what reasons did some Africans, Asians, and Pacific Islanders facilitate or fight alongside the European, Japanese, and U.S. conquerors in this period?

4. What types of resistance did the populations of African, Asian, and Pacific Islanders offer to the imperial invaders of this period? Why do you think historians have in the past focused on military resistance rather than what James C. Scott has called "weapons of the weak"?

5. Re-read the section on resistance to colonial rule in chapter 9. What kinds of continuities and differences do you see between these two periods?

CHAPTER 12

Empire: The Sinews of the New Imperialism

As in previous periods, imperial metropolitan centers of the late nineteenth and twentieth centuries did not exist in isolation from their colonies. Rather, the metropole and colonies were connected by an infinite variety of connections that made the boundaries between "center" and **periphery** very blurred indeed. One way of imagining these connections is to think of them as "sinews"—in other words, as figurative cords linking, and supporting, both metropoles and their colonies simultaneously. Such imagery can help reinforce one of the primary points of this book, which is that empire (and hence imperialism and colonialism) was always a two-way street. In other words, colonies were not simply acted upon by metropoles: instead, both metropoles and colonies shaped, and were shaped by, one another. Empires, then, were not made up of a series of unidirectional actions from the center to the periphery or vice versa, but rather comprised entire systems that were linked together physically, ideologically, socially, and culturally.[1]

Even in the early modern era, we saw that there were multiple sinews that connected the imperial centers with their colonies (see especially chapters 4 and 5). Similarly, the informal empires of the nineteenth century—especially the British Empire—were built on networks of sinews even where formal colonialism did not exist. Trade, capital flows, migration, ideas—all of these linked empires together wherever they existed in the early modern world. During the age of the New Imperialism, however, these links became even more numerous and more intense. Indeed, many of the same technologies that made imperial expansion easier in the late nineteenth century—railways, steamboats, telegraphs, and so on—also made it easier for metropoles and colonies to maintain continuous connections. Trade goods, money, ideas, and people all traveled between metropoles and colonies much more quickly, and much more frequently, than they had in the eighteenth century. As a result, the sinews of empire established during the era of the New Imperialism grew far more extensive than in earlier periods.

The most obvious of these sinews of empire were physical links—people and material—but others were mental—intellectual and ideological. Indeed the two elements were intertwined. For example, trade goods such as tea, rubber, textiles, and gold were material items that bound imperial centers and their colonies through patterns of production and consumption, but that also

---

[1]For the notion of imperialism as a social formation, see Mrinalini Sinha, *Colonial Masculinity: The "Manly Englishman" and the "Effeminate Bengali" in the Late Nineteenth Century* (Manchester: Manchester University Press, 1992), 2. For the links between metropoles and colonies, see Antoinette Burton, "Rules of Thumb: British History and 'Imperial Culture' in Nineteenth- and Twentieth-Century Britain," *Women's History Review*, 3:4 (1994).

shaped peoples' ideas about what it meant to be "civilized." Conversely, although ideas about race, gender, or class did not have a specific material form, they nevertheless traveled throughout imperial systems and had considerable power to shape physical relationships between people in metropoles and in colonies.

This chapter will explore a few of the many and varied sinews that bound empires together in the age of the New Imperialism, including commodities, migration, missionism, violence and war, and ideas about gender, sexuality, and race. Throughout, its purpose will be to demonstrate not only that metropoles and colonies were connected by these sinews, but also to show that it is impossible to understand either locality in the absence of their imperial context. In other words, it is not enough to simply document the ways that migration, militaries, or ideas connected distant locations within imperial systems: rather, it is also necessary to explore the ways in which these imperial connections transformed and fused metropolitan and colonial cultures. In terms of the structure of the book, it also helps us to bridge as well as to move beyond the descriptions of metropolitan cultures of imperialism (chapter 10) and the conquest and "pacification" of colonies (chapter 11) in this period by giving us a sense of how these processes were linked. Finally, it also helps us to set the stage for the age of High Imperialism described in the next three chapters.

However, before we can explore some of the many connections shared across empires in this period, it is important for us to acknowledge that although they were all connected by commodities, war, migration, and ideas, there was nevertheless great variation both within and between imperial systems. There were also differences in the ways sinews connected systems over time. Our point is not to argue that all imperial systems were the same, nor that colonies and metropoles felt the effects of imperial connections in identical ways. Instead, we argue that in spite of local, national, and imperial differences, the sinews of empire shaped metropolitan centers as well as colonies in important ways, and helped to create imperial systems in which the boundaries between metropole and colony could not easily be discerned.

COMMODITIES

It is easy to imagine the sinews of empire in terms of material goods. Products as varied as gold, cotton, coffee, tea, lumber, animal skins, textiles, guns, opium, cacao, rubber, and palm oil filled the hulls of steamships plying the waters between imperial centers and their colonies and back again, connecting points of production with points of consumption. Typically in this period, colonies exported raw materials and tropical products to imperial centers, usually on terms and at prices fixed either by the imperial state or by business interests in the metropoles. Some colonies were so suited to producing particular products that they became mono-crop economies. In such systems, a high proportion of colonial farmers shifted to producing one particular agricultural product in demand by the imperial center—such as cotton in Mozambique, groundnuts in Senegal, or cacao in the Gold Coast—and then were forced to sell them at prices fixed by the imperial state. As we have seen, these farmers included indigenous peasants and plantation-owning settlers as well as migrant workers from impoverished portions of the colony or from neighboring colonies. While mono-crop economies could bring in a decent living for colonial farmers when times were good, they also left them extremely vulnerable in the event of economic downturns, decreases in demand, and competition from other parts of the world.[2] Metropoles, on the other hand, exported their own manufactured goods to their colonies—at advantageous prices—and tended to set up high tariffs to protect themselves from competition with the manufactured items of other states. This situation contrasted with the "free trade" ethos of the mid-nineteenth century, but is in many ways analogous to the mercantilism of early modern Atlantic empires.

---

[2]For a general overview of metropolitan–colonial economic relationships, as well as the debate over the nature of these relationships, see David Fieldhouse, *The West and the Third World. Trade, Colonialism, Dependence and Development* (London: Blackwell, 1999).

Clearly, the economic relationships that emerged through the exchange of commodities between metropoles and colonies were highly unequal. Yet there is no doubt that, unequal or not, these relationships also bound imperial centers to their colonies, and vice versa, in concrete and important ways. Most obviously, these commodity exchanges connected empires through commodity flows back and forth across the oceans. Perhaps more importantly, the production and consumption of imperial commodities transformed the lives of peoples in both colonies and metropoles.

A focus on just one commodity, albeit in two different contexts, can demonstrate the power of material goods to transform both metropolitan and colonial cultures. Consider the case of rubber. Rubber exists both as a wild vine and as a tree, and by the last half of the nineteenth century it had long been prized for the sticky, flexible, waterproof substance both plants yielded when tapped. The real significance of rubber, however, only became clear in the 1880s when it was discovered that rubber could be transformed into pneumatic tires, hoses, and insulation for telegraph, telephone, and electric wires.[3] Thereafter, the industrialized nations of Europe and North America developed a nearly insatiable demand for rubber.

The rubber vine was native to Madagascar, but was also common to the densely forested areas of equatorial Africa. Rubber *vines* are extremely long, and grow up from the ground into the high limbs of trees, in the process winding their way through branches and into neighboring trees. The rubber *tree*, in contrast, was native to Brazil, but in 1876 a Briton sponsored by the British government smuggled Brazilian seeds and cultivated them at the tropical herbarium in Kew Gardens, London. The next year, the British exported seeds to Ceylon (modern Sri Lanka) and Singapore with the intention of setting up large-scale plantations. By the early decades of the twentieth century, many of the imperial powers—including the British, French, and Dutch—had established vast rubber plantations to feed the huge industrial demand for tires, hoses, and gaskets.

Before these rubber tree plantations were able to produce rubber in quantities large enough to meet international demand, however, much of it had to be met by exploiting the wild rubber vines of equatorial Africa. One person who was poised to exploit this opportunity to its fullest was King Leopold II of Belgium, whose personal colony in the Congo was covered with wild rubber. Leopold had obtained this colony through diplomatic maneuvering and outright lies, particularly at the Berlin conference (November 1884 to February 1885) where European powers discussed the partitioning of the African continent (see chapter 10). Through promises that he would bring free trade and "civilization" to his realms, Leopold was able to extract from the major European powers an area more than 80 times the size of his own country. Yet the Belgian government, not having been party to the negotiations and ambivalent about becoming an imperial power, refused to claim the colony as its own. As a compromise, it authorized Leopold to become the sole governing authority for what became known as the Congo Free State on May 29, 1885.[4]

By the 1890s, demand had caused the international price of rubber to rise dramatically, which suited Leopold perfectly. His goal in ruling the Congo Free State was simple: profit, both for himself personally and for the enrichment of his Belgian cities. Yet Leopold knew that the days of wild rubber were numbered, and would someday be surpassed by cultivated rubber tree plantations. As a result, he was in a hurry to extract as much rubber from the Congo as quickly as possible.[5]

To accomplish his goal, Leopold allowed private companies to establish monopoly control of huge territories in the Congo forests. The price they paid for near-total control over the rubber and other resources they found was exactly half of all profits earned, payable directly to Leopold's personal government in Belgium. In addition,

---

[3] Michael Edward Stanfield, *Red Rubber, Bleeding Trees: Violence, Slavery and Empire in Northwest Amazonia, 1850–1933* (Albuquerque: University of New Mexico Press, 1998), 20–21.

[4] Scott Cook, "The Heart of Imperial Darkness: King Leopold's Congo," in *Colonial Encounters in the Age of High Imperialism* (New York: Harper Collins, 1996), 42–43.

[5] Adam Hochschild, *King Leopold's Ghost* (Boston and New York: Houghton Mifflin, 1998), 159–160.

Leopold directly controlled enormous tracts of land for the same purpose—in these areas, all of the profits went directly to Leopold.[6]

The urgency with which rubber was needed, coupled with monopoly control and almost no regulations about how resources were to be extracted, left the system open to horrible abuses. Collecting rubber from wild vines was a painstaking and dangerous process. To obtain rubber, vines had to be cut with a knife, and then a bucket or dish had to be hung to catch the sap. And, although rubber could be tapped from vines at ground level, once tapped dry laborers had to resort to climbing high into the trees to tap a different part of the vine. Even then, entire vines were quickly tapped dry or killed outright, and laborers had to go further and further into the forest to find untapped vines.

Under such conditions, it was difficult to find laborers willing to tap wild rubber vines in the necessary numbers. In response to this labor shortage, both the state and the concession companies established policies of forced labor and of rubber quotas for individuals and villages. In effect, state and company officials—with the help of the *Force Publique*, the Congo Free State's military force—rounded up populations and forced them to collect a specified amount of rubber per capita. Resistance prompted retaliatory violence: villages that refused to collect rubber were burned to the ground, while their members were subject to corporal punishment or murder. Resistance was also met by hostage-taking: men who refused to collect rubber were frequently "convinced" to change their minds when their wives were held as hostages until rubber quotas were met. Those who did not meet their quotas were similarly subject to harsh punishment. Both whippings and amputations—usually of hands and feet—were routine punishments for failing to collect enough rubber.[7]

The result of such a brutal system of rubber collection was massive population loss, not to mention deep psychological trauma, among the peoples of the Congo. Many people died as a direct result of overwork, through being taken

hostage, or by becoming victims to reprisals by state and company officials and subject to whippings, amputations, and murder. Even more people died because the rubber quotas meant that people were unable to tend to the crops that fed them, which resulted in malnutrition, decreased resistance to disease, and starvation. Still others fled, trying to escape the tyranny of the rubber companies. Some died as a result of privation during their flight; others crossed the borders of the Congo Free State into other colonies.[8]

Although the exact numbers of Congolese who died during Leopold's personal reign is unknown, contemporary accounts as well as census records taken in later years indicate that the population may have fallen by as much as 50% to 60%.[9] Such a drop would have meant that the population would have been reduced by somewhere around 10 million people—and all for a system that sought to profit from a commodity that could be sold on the international market.[10] So horrible were the abuses of the Congo Free State that an international movement—aided by information provided by missionaries—developed in the early twentieth century with the sole purpose of removing Leopold from his position as ruler. The movement was eventually successful: by 1908, independent and undeniable confirmations of the brutalities practiced in the colony forced the Belgian government to take Leopold's place as ruler of the Congo Free State.[11]

Meanwhile, back in Belgium, Leopold amassed an enormous fortune from his personal colony. Although no one knows the exact figures, it is likely that he made slightly over a billion dollars in contemporary U.S. currency. With that money, Leopold remodeled palaces, built hotels, monuments, and museums, and undertook huge renovations in both Brussels and Ostend that beautified the cities, established parks, widened streets, and created sophisticated public spaces.

---

[8] Ibid., chapter 15.
[9] Cook, "The Heart of Imperial Darkness," 63.
[10] Hochschild, *King Leopold's Ghost*, 233.
[11] It should be added that even though abuses abated somewhat under the rule of the Belgian government, they did not entirely disappear.

---

[6] Cook, "The Heart of Imperial Darkness," 51–52.
[7] Hochschild, *King Leopold's Ghost*, chapter 10.

The result of all this demonstrates how the sinews of empire—in this case, the commodity of rubber—both *connected* metropoles and colonies and *transformed* each, although in differing ways. During Leopold's personal rule, vast quantities of rubber flowed from the Congo Free State to Belgium, and then from Belgium to the industrial nations of the west. But rubber did more than connect the huge African colony to its tiny European metropolitan center. In Belgium, it translated into money, where it enriched Leopold personally. And even though the Belgian people did not claim the colony as their own until 1908, nevertheless the money from the exploitation of rubber enriched their lives in countless ways through the new beauty of their cities and the employment offered by such vast public works. Meanwhile, the effects of rubber exploitation on the Congolese people was nothing less than catastrophic: while Leopold and the Belgian people enjoyed the fruits of rubber's profits, Congolese people worked under horrifying conditions to produce the commodity itself. In the process, millions of people lost their freedom, their homes, and their lives.

Rubber was also a crucial commodity linking the French metropole with its colony in Indochina. In this case, however, the rubber produced was not from the wild vines found in equatorial Africa, but from cultivated trees grown on huge plantations—the very plantations Leopold had feared would make wild rubber obsolete. The first rubber trees arrived in French Indochina in 1897, but it took several decades to establish productive plantations. Between 1909 and 1918, profits finally started adding up. Thereafter, profits and production rates jumped dramatically through the 1920s and 1930s. From a mere 160 tons of rubber exported between 1909 and 1913, rubber exports grew to 59,450 tons by 1938. By the 1930s, rubber was Indochina's most important export to France.[12]

To encourage the establishment of rubber plantations in Indochina, French companies were granted huge tracts of land over which they were allowed to maintain virtual monopolies over wages, conditions, and prices. Powerful companies controlled the vast majority of all rubber production in Indochina; in fact, only 27 companies owned more than two-thirds of all of the land planted in rubber. The area involved was enormous. By 1927 alone, over 313,000 acres were devoted to rubber, and that number grew consistently through the 1930s.[13]

While Indochinese rubber plantations were lucrative ventures for the French companies involved, they carried enormous environmental and human costs. In terms of the environment, the establishment of rubber plantations meant the eradication of forests in order to make way for row upon row of rubber trees. The human costs were even higher. Rubber plantations require enormous amounts of labor in order to clear the land and to plant, tend, and tap the tens of thousands of trees required to produce adequate rubber supplies. To acquire the needed labor, rubber companies sent recruiters to poor areas in Indochina's cities and villages and even to neighboring colonies and states. Recruiters enticed potential workers by promising free transportation to the plantations as well as free transportation home when contracts were completed. They also offered decent pay, good living conditions, steady work, and plenty of food. Once workers were transported far from their homes to the plantations, however, they frequently discovered that their pay was reduced by innumerable charges and fines, that their living conditions were dismal, that the work was backbreaking and tedious, and that the discipline was harsh and even brutal. Resistance was met with physical punishment and with pay stoppages. Beatings were sometimes fatal. Indeed, out in the forests, far from most towns or cities, plantation managers could rule their domains almost at whim. As one former rubber worker recounted, "whoever cursed the workers well would be quick to get a raise. Whoever beat workers with true cruelty would get a raise especially fast."[14]

[12] Robert Aldrich, *Greater France: A History of French Overseas Expansion* (Houndmills: Palgrave, 1996), 190.

[13] Ibid.

[14] Tran Tu Binh, *The Red Earth: A Vietnamese Memoir of Life on a Colonial Rubber Plantation* (Athens, OH: Ohio University Center for International Studies, 1985), 24.

In the meantime, the French companies who owned the rubber plantations realized magnificent profits. In France itself, the population benefited from the labors of Indochinese workers whether they knew it or not, through the enjoyment of bicycles with rubber tires, rubber gaskets, insulated wiring, and a host of other consumer products produced with the help of rubber or that used rubber in their construction. Thus, as in the Congo, the production of rubber both connected France to its colony in Indochina and transformed life at both ends of the connection. Just as we saw in the Congo, however, these transformations could hardly have been more different: whereas the French could enjoy the multiple uses of rubber without even thinking about where it came from, such enjoyment came at a high price for the Indochinese workers who produced it.

Rubber is merely one example of the many commodities that bound empires together during this period. Many of the commodities that best express national identities in Europe and abroad were products that developed in the imperial context. As we saw in chapter 5, an imperial culture gradually developed in Britain and the British Empire that shared a love of tea grown in India and sweetened by sugar from the Caribbean. In France, the perfume and culinary industries depended on oil expressed from peanuts grown by West African peasants. In Germany, an evolving diamond industry relied on stones found in German South-West Africa. The flow, of course, was reciprocal. French colonial officials and other agents of empire introduced bread to South-East Asia, Americans brought canned meats to Hawaii and the Philippines, and in Africa an evolving urban educated class aspired to wearing suits and ties. In each case, commodities both connected and transformed distant societies and cultures.

MIGRATION

Like commodities, people themselves created important links between metropoles and colonies in the nineteenth and early twentieth centuries, and their frequent and continuous movement back and forth between them constantly blurred the line between metropolitan and colonial cultures. Of course as we have seen, the transmigration of peoples within and between empires had been a feature of earlier empires, yet never at the levels of this period. Indeed, the movement of people around the world in pursuit of the opportunities and demands of colonialism was one of the most important features of the age of the New Imperialism. People moved from every metropolitan center to every colony in this period, although some empires and some colonies attracted far more emigrants than others. Not all settlers came from the imperial metropole—some colonies attracted a multi-national mix of Europeans and non-Europeans. These migrants moved for various reasons: some moved to find a better life than they had before, others moved to join families who had gone before them, while still others planned to work or do business in colonial locations and then return to their places of origin. Millions of people also continued to move—through indentured labor systems—between tropical colonial locations in response to labor demands in the Indian Ocean, the Caribbean, and Latin America. Finally, although their numbers were small, some colonized peoples moved—either temporarily or permanently—from colonial locations to imperial centers. The sheer quantity of these movements could not fail to transform both metropolitan and colonial locations. This process of transformation, in turn, created cultures of empire that were neither solely metropolitan nor solely colonial, but instead were products of the interactions between the two.

By the last three decades of the nineteenth century, the same technologies that facilitated commodity transport—especially steamships and railroads—also made it ever easier for people to move from place to place. Moreover, technologies like the telegraph and the expansion of print media made it easier for people in a wide variety of locations to have access to news and opportunities in far-distant places. Throughout the age of the New Imperialism, citizens and subjects of imperial powers took advantage of the ease of communication and transportation and started new lives abroad.

The great majority of these migrants—nearly 10 million between 1853 and 1920 alone—left from the British Isles.[15] This was due to several factors: first, the sheer size of the British Empire; second, the nature of its colonies in North America and the Pacific; and third, economic and population pressures from within Britain itself. While a significant minority of these emigrants (over 4 million) actually went to the former colony of the United States, nearly all of the rest went to what became known as the "white settler" colonies of British North America (over 2 million), Australia and New Zealand (nearly 2 million), and South Africa (671,000).[16]

Without denying the distinctiveness of each of the white settler colonies, they all nevertheless to varying degrees shared several features that encouraged the development of broadly similar hybrid cultures. For one thing, British North America, New Zealand, the Cape Colony of southern Africa, and Australia—like the United States—had all once been home to large populations of indigenous peoples. These populations, however, had been ravaged by European diseases and by deliberate policies of either annihilation or marginalization. As a result, settlers in these colonies believed that land was theirs for the taking. To some degree, this ethos was shared even in regions where the local population remained large, like the Natal Colony of southern Africa. This belief, in turn, led to an expansive attitude toward the environment in general—an attitude that encouraged excessive exploitation of environmental resources for economic benefit, including extensive logging, hunting, and the use of marginal lands for raising stock. Additionally, settlers tended to develop identities that were a fusion of British cultural practices and norms—such as tea drinking and domestic femininity—with specific ideas about the virtues of whiteness

and "sturdy manhood" (discussed in greater depth in chapter 13).[17] Thus while settler cultures were distinctly different from the metropolitan culture, it was not always easy to define the boundaries between them. Moreover, constant migration to the settler colonies from Britain as well as return migration from the colonies—some 40% of British emigrants returned to the metropole—continued to inform and transform the societies and cultures at both ends.[18]

Portions of the French overseas empire also attracted large numbers of settlers. North Africa, especially Algeria, was both near to France and suited to European lifestyles and disease immunities. Algeria would eventually become home to more than a million Europeans: not only French but also large populations of Sicilians, Maltese, Sardinians, and Italians. Smaller settler communities emerged in South-East Asia and elsewhere in the empire. Significant numbers of Portuguese, Dutch, and German citizens also relocated to colonial possessions, although these numbers remained comparatively small.

Imperial relationships also encouraged major migrations among tropical colonial locations, especially between British imperial possessions. However, the imperial state sought far greater control over these migrants than they did those going to the temperate white settler colonies, partly out of fear of angering the local population and partly because most of these migrants were colonial subjects rather than metropolitan citizens. As we saw in chapter 9, the initial impetus for tropical migrations was the urgent need for labor after slavery was abolished in the British Empire in 1833. Later in the nineteenth century, the establishment of new cash crops and new colonies also stimulated a strong demand for labor. In response to these demands, imperial officials supervised a system of indentured labor that resulted in the migration of nearly 1.5 million Indians, Africans, Chinese, and

---

[15] P.J. Cain, "Economics and Empire: The Metropolitan Context," in *The Oxford History of the British Empire*, vol. III, *The Nineteenth Century*, edited by Andrew Porter (Oxford: Oxford University Press, 1999), 47.

[16] Only a total of 674,000 settlers went to colonies such as India, Kenya, Jamaica, Nigeria, and the Gold Coast in this period. Ibid.

[17] Catherine Hall, "Of Gender and Empire: Reflections on the Nineteenth Century," in *Gender and Empire*, edited by Philippa Levine (Oxford: Oxford University Press, 2004), 70.

[18] Cain, "Economics and Empire," 46.

Pacific Islanders to other tropical colonies between 1834 and 1920. In these destination colonies—which included Mauritius, Malaya, British Guiana, Trinidad, Jamaica, East Africa, and Australia, among others—laborers produced cash crops such as sugar, cotton, coffee, and rubber, or worked as miners for a variety of ores. By far the largest number of migrants came from India (1.2 million), where "push" factors (especially poverty) created a ready and consistent supply of people hoping for better lives.[19] Lebanese and Syrian subjects of the French overseas empire similarly dispersed across France's tropical colonies.

The conditions of migration were far more onerous for tropical migrants than they were for white settlers going to the temperate colonies. First, while the British government provided financial assistance to many white emigrants seeking new lives in the colonies, for colonial subjects from tropical colonies this assistance came with strings attached. The most important of these strings was that passage abroad was paid for in labor: most contracts stipulated five years of labor in return for the passage out and optional return passage. Second, even though travel and work conditions for indentured workers were supposed to be regulated, many abuses occurred. Provisions for sanitary measures and medical care were frequently substandard on the ships, and work conditions once workers arrived were extremely difficult. Still, more than a million people chose to leave their homes for the tropical colonies, and they did so—both men and women, unmarried and married—for many of the same reasons as white settlers: to create for themselves a better life through new opportunities and economic gain.[20] Many of these workers hoped, like white settlers, to return someday to their original homes. Many, in fact, did finish their contracts and go home. Many others, however, stayed on. In some colonies, communities of settlers who

decided to stay in their adopted homes came to outnumber Europeans as well as all other migrant groups. By the early twentieth century, for example, there were more Indians in Natal than there were Europeans, and in Trinidad they formed fully one-third of the population.[21] Such populations, wherever they appeared, transformed the cultures of their new homes through the introduction of new traditions, stories, systems of social organization, and foods. Moreover, they themselves were transformed by the cultures around them as they adopted selected traditions, beliefs, and foods from other migrant and indigenous groups. Just like the white settlers, then, tropical migrants developed fusion cultures in which sharp cultural boundaries could not easily be drawn. Furthermore, these fusion cultures were dependent on imperial structures for their origins and for their maintenance.

A much smaller number of colonial subjects during the age of the New Imperialism traveled from the colonies to live in, or to visit, imperial metropoles. Some came as sailors, merchants, or servants, others came to participate in the several imperial exhibitions put on in metropolitan centers, and still others came to study or simply to travel and observe. Yet although their numbers were small compared to the number of migrants moving out of Britain or to other tropical colonies, they were nevertheless an important link in the connections built by migration between metropoles and their colonies.[22] For those who later returned to the colonies, their observations about life and culture in the imperial metropole provided a wholly new, and sometimes quite critical, perspective on the supposedly "superior" ruling power. Some were shocked, for example, to see widespread poverty in European cities such as London, while others were astonished by lower-class manners or by the ways European women dressed. These observations, in turn, helped

[19] David Northrup, "Migration from Africa, Asia, and the South Pacific," in Porter, *The Nineteenth Century*, 89–90.
[20] Ibid., 95.

[21] Ibid., 96.
[22] Antoinette Burton, *At the Heart of the Empire: Indians and the Colonial Encounter in Late-Victorian Britain* (Berkeley: University of California Press, 1998). This is one of the main contentions of the book.

colonized people form opinions about their colonial rulers.[23]

Colonized peoples in imperial metropoles also found that encounters with metropolitan subjects allowed them to see themselves through the eyes of the colonizers, with often disconcerting results. Many were astonished by the extent to which markers of difference, such as clothing or dark skin color, attracted public attention. Some discovered through such encounters popular attitudes toward race, as well as a marked tendency to assume that all colonized people were uneducated, unintelligent, or "savage" in some way. The looking glass could also be turned the other way, however: as a result of personal encounters with people from the colonies, metropolitan citizens were forced to try and reconcile their preconceived beliefs about race and cultural superiority with what they saw before them. As a result, colonized subjects at the "heart of the empire" helped to shape the ways metropolitan subjects perceived imperialism and colonialism while also shaping the ways other colonial subjects thought about the metropole.

The massive and varied migrations that occurred between and within metropoles and colonies in this period constituted one of the critical connections linking imperial systems. Whether these movements were to temperate or tropical locations, or whether they were from the colonies to the metropoles or vice versa, they created enduring links between distant places even as they transformed cultures and landscapes at their destinations.

MISSIONISM

Missionaries, although also migrants, were nevertheless distinct from other people who moved back and forth within and between empires in this period. First, regardless of denomination their goals were clear: to convert non-Christians to their own version of Christianity, to provide ongoing support to nascent Christian communities, and to promote a particular Christian worldview. Second, missionaries went to both temperate and tropical locations, and tended to live among the people they hoped to convert rather than in segregated communities and enclaves. Third, missionaries had an impact on both colonial and metropolitan cultures out of all proportion to their numbers through their activities, policies, and writings.

Religious groups had been important agents of colonialism in some early modern empires, although others had been broadly tolerant or even encouraged religious diversity. During the mid-nineteenth century, evangelical European and U.S. Christians had become increasingly active overseas. In the subsequent age of the New Imperialism, thousands of missionaries representing nearly every Christian denomination, both sexes, and hailing from every imperial metropole worked in foreign mission stations. In 1900 alone, British Protestant Christian missionaries attached to overseas stations numbered 10,000.[24] Catholic missionaries—especially from France and Iberia—also continued to be active in this period. As with other migrants, ease of transportation and communication made it possible for ever greater numbers of people to travel to distant locations. Missionaries took ample advantage of these opportunities, and established centralized, funded mission stations in nearly every part of the world.

Although the ultimate goal of missionaries was always spiritual conversion, most believed their targets also needed to convert to western modes of dress, behavior, consumption, and family patterns. Thus, along with churches and religious instruction, missionaries frequently established hospitals, schools, and orphanages, which were designed to inculcate western concepts about sexuality, sanitation, and morality. Missionaries were

---

[23] Burton, *At the Heart of the Empire*, 168–169; and Lloyd Braithwaite, *Colonial West Indian Students in Britain* (Kingston, Jamaica: University Press of the West Indies, 2001). For a fictional treatment of the subject, see Bernard Dadie, *An African in Paris* (Chicago: University of Illinois Press, 1994). Originally published 1959.

[24] Andrew Porter, "Religion, Missionary Enthusiasm, and Empire," in *The Nineteenth Century*, 222. This number does not include continental European and American Protestant missionaries overseas.

often highly critical of indigenous cultures, and they sought to intervene in the most intimate aspects of indigenous life—from what to wear, what to cook, and who to have sex with and when—in their "civilizing" project. Yet they were just as often critical of imperial authorities— especially when imperial policy was not in line with their goals or what they believed to be the best interests of indigenous people.[25] In the Congo Free State, for example, it was missionaries who first exposed the truth about the brutal rubber regime even in the face of persecution by the state. In southern Africa and Australia, missionaries even went so far as to arm some indigenous inhabitants against settlers who were seizing their land or massacring them. Similarly, in some cases colonial administrators regarded missionaries as potentially unsettling influences either because they inspired revolts or because they provoked the representatives of indigenous religions. When imperial policies did mesh with missionary goals, however, missionaries worked hand in hand with colonial administrations to effect even those policies that were clearly distasteful to indigenous populations. In most cases, missionaries acted out of a deep sense of Christian righteousness as well as western superiority.

The relationship between missionaries and the establishment of formal colonies was complex but important. In some cases, as in Hawaii and many parts of sub-Saharan Africa, mission stations were precursors to imperial intervention. In such areas, missionaries were active for years or even decades prior to conquest, and their activities helped (favorably or unfavorably) predispose certain segments of indigenous populations to an increased European presence. In other cases, as in Indochina, persecution or attacks against active mission stations provided the pretext for formal conquest. In still other cases, as in British India, missionaries followed in the wake of conquest, and undertook an important part of the legwork in efforts to "civilize" indigenous people. Finally, it

is important to note that local societies and leaderships often accepted missionaries for reasons of their own, as in the Central African state of Buganda, where the king, or Kabaka, hoped to use them to strengthen his own position in relation to that of both Muslim religious authorities and chiefly officeholders.[26] Missionary efforts at conversion were highly successful in some places, as in much of Polynesia. In other areas, like India, conversion was relatively rare. Whether missionaries won the conversion of souls or not, though, their efforts had deep effects on many societies— some with tragic results, and others with complicated and unexpected results.

The example of Victoria, Australia, demonstrates the disruptive potential of missionary work, even when missionaries believed they were doing the right thing. In the last half of the nineteenth century, missionaries established stations in the province in order to protect and "raise up" the Aboriginal population, which had indeed suffered severely at the hands of white settlers.[27] Beginning in about 1860, missions offered work, dormitories for families and individuals, schools, and medical care. By the 1870s, missionaries in Victoria felt that they had made progress: significant numbers of people living on the station had converted to Christianity, men and women were marrying in the Christian way and living in nuclear families, and children were being sent to school. The assimilation of children to Christianity and "civilization" were particular sources of pride, since mission education made a strong impression on their developing minds.

Conflict began to occur, however, when mission-educated Aborigines wished to move off the station—usually in order to find work—with their school-aged children. Missionaries objected to the removal of children primarily because they feared that removal would undo progress toward

---

[25] Hall, "Of Gender and Empire," 64.

[26] Philip Curtin, *The World and the West: The European Challenge and the Overseas Response in the Age of Empire* (Cambridge: Cambridge University Press, 2002), 111–128.
[27] Patricia Grimshaw, "Faith, Missionary Life, and the Family," in Levine, *Gender and Empire*, 273.

Christianization and assimilation. Aborigines were adamant about their right (and their desire) to take their children with them, however, and there was little missionaries could do to stop them. That changed in 1886, when the legislature in Victoria passed an act that legalized the separation of Aboriginal children from parents as long as doing so was in the "best interests" of the children. In the wake of the act, missionaries colluded with the government to remove Aboriginal children from their parents, even if their parents were mission-educated Christians. Missionaries believed that in spite of the desperate pleas of parents who wished to remain with their children, the end result of raising children in a controlled, Christian environment justified the means of separating them from their families. In doing so, missionaries contributed to a process that both helped to weaken Aboriginal society and traumatized parents and children alike until well into the twentieth century.[28]

While the Aborigines in Victoria illustrate the consequences of western missionaries' sense of cultural and spiritual superiority, the example of the Luhya people in (present-day) Western Province, Kenya, demonstrates the sometimes unexpected results of missionary activities.[29] In 1919, the Quaker-based Friends Africa Mission (FAM) set up an orphanage and school for girls that was designed to remake them into models of Christian, westernized domesticity. The FAM was run almost exclusively by women, and the orphanage and school was cordoned off from the rest of society so that the children under its charge could be educated in isolation from the "corrupting" influences of their home villages. The overriding goal of the orphanage and school, of course, was to convert the girls to Christianity. In the meantime, however, the school curriculum was designed to teach girls to be good wives and mothers so that they could bring a new generation to the Christian faith. To accomplish this, the girls were taught skills such as reading, writing, sewing, and cooking, and how to manage money.[30]

The results of these endeavors, however, were not exactly what the Quaker missionaries intended. Rather than transfer their skills to their own homes, many of the girls sought to use them instead to become more independent: some, for example, used their skills to manipulate their choices in marriage partners, while others decided to take jobs and forego marriage altogether. Moreover, even though the intentions of the Quaker missionaries had been to "improve" Luhya society through Christianization and westernization, over time they unintentionally helped to create an educated, Christian elite who—if they married at all—only married mission-educated men, had access to the best jobs, and looked down on their uneducated, non-Christian compatriots. Thus, while the FAM undoubtedly helped to transform Luhya society in the age of the New Imperialism, the direction of those transformations was not simply unilateral. Rather, like other colonized peoples, Luhya girls embraced some of the teachings of the missionaries even while they resisted others. In the process, they created an elite culture based on a fusion of metropolitan and colonial cultural influences.

In addition to their role in transforming colonial societies, missionaries also played an important role in shaping the ways metropolitan peoples viewed the lands and the peoples of the empire. Perhaps the great individual catalyst for this transformation was David Livingstone, the doctor/geographer/missionary who set out to bring Christianity to the interior of Africa in the mid-nineteenth century. Accounts of his journeys—and especially of Henry Morton Stanley's much-publicized search for him ("Dr. Livingstone, I presume?")—dramatically increased European interest in tropical foreign missions. Church congregations raised money, often a little at a time, to send missionaries to foreign lands. In return, they received numerous letters and reports describing both the customs and habits of

---

[28] Ibid., 276–278.
[29] The Luhya are a Bantu-speaking cultural-linguistic group in western Kenya.

[30] Samuel Thomas, "Transforming the Gospel of Domesticity: Luhya Girls and the Friends Africa Mission, 1917–1926," *African Studies Review*, 43:2 (2000).

colonized peoples and the colonial landscape, which would be read out in church or in study groups. These letters, in turn, were critical in stimulating interest in imperial ventures among ordinary Europeans.[31] Missionaries themselves knew how important such written accounts were, if only to keep the money flowing and the missions going. As the General Secretary of the Church Missionary Society put it in 1928, "we at home are responsible for keeping the home fire burning, and it is upon the continual supply of information and news that the prayers' backing depends."[32] Indeed, descriptions of colonized peoples' personal habits, homes, or environment—often, of course, shaped by missionaries' strong sense of what was "right" or "wrong"—helped to structure metropolitan beliefs about empire and imperialism. They also helped to shape metropolitan citizen's notions of their own identity. Late nineteenth-century "Britishness," for example, encompassed a wide variety of claimed characteristics, of which a sense of an evangelical mission was just one. In the end, then, the connections missionaries provided between metropolitan society and the colonies were multi-directional: while they undoubtedly shaped a wide variety of colonial societies, they were also responsible for helping to shape metropolitan interest in, and ideas about, the wider world.

WAR AND MILITARY POWER

As we saw in chapters 9 and 11, all imperial systems in the age of the New Imperialism required institutionalized physical force—armies and police forces—in order to maintain them. Colonies were very often initially obtained and then later expanded through the use of military force: British India, French Indochina, the Dutch East Indies, and the U.S. Philippines are just a few examples that fit this model. Even after conquest, persistent resistance against occupation, economic exploitation, and subjugation in most colonies meant that ruling powers had to rely on military or police forces—and frequently both—in order to stay in power.[33]

Military institutions and the use of military violence were thus important sinews that connected imperial centers to their colonies and vice versa. Moreover, like the other sinews discussed in this chapter, the creation and deployment of military forces in the imperial context also profoundly transformed both centers and colonies in dramatic, although uneven, ways.

It is possible to interrogate the ways in which military institutions connected imperial systems in ways that blurred easy divides between metropolitan and colonial contexts. First, and most obviously, military institutions require people—frequently many thousands of people—who can be trained and mobilized to fight on behalf of the leaders who pay them. In colonial armies, that manpower provided by metropolitan citizens was heavily augmented by colonial subjects. The reason was simple: it was too expensive to maintain entire armies of European soldiers in distant locations. Moreover, some imperial nations (Britain, for example) simply were not able to recruit enough European soldiers to staff their colonial armies. Additionally, most colonial territories were far too vast to be controlled by armies from Europe even if it had been affordable or desirable to do so. And finally, most imperial powers deliberately employed significant numbers of colonized men in their armies in order to cultivate loyalty among certain groups, to employ men

---

[31] Susan Thorne, "The Conversion of England and the Conversion of the World Inseparable: Missionary Imperialism and the Language of Class in Early Industrial England," in *Tensions of Empire: Colonial Cultures in a Bourgeois World*, edited by Frederick Cooper and Ann Stoler (Berkeley: University of California Press, 1997), 7. See also Susan Thorne, *Congregational Missions and the Making of An Imperial Culture in 19th Century England* (Stanford: Stanford University Press, 1999).

[32] Nakanyike Musisi, "The Politics of Perception or Perception as Politics? Colonial and Missionary Representations of Baganda Women, 1900–1945," in *Women in African Colonial Histories*, edited by Jean Allman, Susan Geiger, and Nakanyike Musisi (Bloomington: Indiana University Press, 2002), 97.

[33] For a general discussion of militaries and warfare in the context of imperialism, see J.A. de Moor and H.L. Wesseling, *Imperialism and War: Essays on Colonial Wars in Asia and Africa* (Leiden: E.J. Brill, 1988).

who might otherwise resist colonial rule, and to divide colonized populations against one another.

One of the connections initiated by colonial military institutions, then, was the fact that the men who constituted the European contingents and officer classes of colonial armies were continually moving back and forth between the imperial center and the colonies—frequently, in fact, to multiple colonies.[34] Men moved from Europe to the colonies when they were shipped out for service, and then moved back to the metropoles as they were discharged or invalided. Some moved between colonies as imperial crises emerged, and others were shipped home before being shipped out again for a tour of duty in another colony.

Officers had even greater mobility than enlisted men. Nearly all of the imperial powers in the age of the New Imperialism reserved the positions of commissioned officers to Europeans alone, although colonized men did frequently serve as non-commissioned officers. Because European commissioned officers were in demand, they moved back and forth—and between—colonies much more frequently than regular soldiers. In addition, officers were usually of a much higher class than enlisted men, and could afford the passage home more easily. They were also awarded official home leaves, which made such journeys possible. Finally, many European officers were career officers, which meant that they served for many years and thus had many opportunities to move back and forth between the imperial center and the colonies.

One result of all this movement was that officers and enlisted men alike became important figures both in establishing encounters with colonized people and in transmitting some of what they learned from these encounters—whether positive or negative—back to imperial centers. This was not an isolated phenomenon. Officers in particular had strong motivations to publicize their version of military exploits in the colonies. Especially after the tremendous expansion of the popular press that occurred in most metropolitan centers after the

last quarter of the nineteenth century, officers deliberately used print media to tell tales about their own heroism in battles and colonial military campaigns. Some officers had an even deeper agenda: to convince the public of the value of imperialism and colonial expansion, and to assure them that the use of the military for such endeavors was justified.[35]

The cultural transformations wrought by increasing public knowledge about colonial military affairs were sometimes profound. In the nineteenth-century French Empire, colonial government was typically handed over to the military: Algeria, for example, was entirely under military rule from 1830 to 1870; as was French West Africa into the early twentieth century. In addition, military men were crucial to the conquest of Indochina, Morocco, Madagascar, and the territories of French West Africa, among others. Many of these officers shared a tradition not only of military exploration and conquest, but of scientific curiosity. Given their advantageous positions at the frontiers of European geographical knowledge, they became especially instrumental at helping to create anthropological knowledge about the colonized peoples they encountered. In some cases, officers wrote their own scholarly works, while in others they provided the fieldwork that was then used by French scholars. Such a partnership, indeed, was responsible for the creation of the widespread belief—both in Algeria and in France—that Algerians consisted of two separate "races": the Arab and the Kabyle.[36] This division, in turn, was a critical factor in dictating colonial policy toward both groups during the entire period of French rule in Algeria, especially since it stipulated that Arabs were far inferior to Kabyles.

---

[34] The same was often true of civilian colonial officials as well.

[35] Patricia Lorcin discusses this tendency with regard to French officers in *Imperial Identities: Stereotyping, Prejudice, and Race in Colonial Algeria* (London: I.B. Tauris, 1999), chapters 5 and 6. For the British army, see Heather Streets, *Martial Races: The Military, Race, and Masculinity in British Imperial Culture, 1857–1914* (Manchester: Manchester University Press, 2004), chapter 4.

[36] Lorcin, *Imperial Identities*, 118, 122–123.

In Britain, metropolitan cultural transformations as a result of the military–imperial connection were even more profound. In part, this was because the British Empire maintained much larger colonial armies than any other imperial power. This was especially true of India, Britain's most important imperial possession, where after 1858 the imperial government maintained an army of more than 100,000 Indians complemented by a permanent British garrison of 70,000.[37] Moreover, during the age of the New Imperialism, an influential cadre of British administrators and military officers in India believed that the Russian Empire was intent on undermining British rule in India through its mountainous northwest frontier. Viewed in the context of frosty diplomatic relations with France and increasingly cool relations with Germany, many British officers believed it to be their duty to rouse public interest in preserving the Empire before it was too late.[38]

As in France, then, British officers with experience in the empire—and particularly in India—took advantage of the recently expanded popular press to justify imperial military action and to encourage people to become interested in imperial exploits. They contributed both openly and anonymously to newspapers and journals, they wrote memoirs designed to play up the glories of imperial war, they penned novels and children's books, and they gave public speeches. With scientists and social theorists, they warned of the dire consequences of allowing oneself to become physically unfit, of the dangers posed by sexually transmitted diseases, and of neglecting to do one's duty to one's country by enlisting in some form of military service.

Partly as a result of their tireless work at publicizing the empire—especially where the military was concerned—British officers contributed to a growing militarization of British popular culture in the late nineteenth century. Stories of military heroism and derring-do became increasingly popular among wide sections of the British public in this period, and news of imperial military victories could provoke spontaneous, riotous celebrations in the metropole. A notorious example of this type of celebration occurred in London on May 18, 1900, when Britons received news that the siege of Mafeking had been broken during the South African War. Once the news spread, ordinary citizens went out to the streets, shouting, waving flags, and singing patriotic songs. This type of bellicose, pro-military, hero-worshipping—also known as *jingoism*—became increasingly more common in this period, thanks at least in part to the efforts of military officers themselves.[39]

Military actions and events could also have serious effects on the politics and governments of the metropole, both in Britain and in France. In Britain, for example, news of brutalities inflicted on Afghan soldiers during the Second Afghan War (1878–1880) were so damaging to the ruling Conservative party in Britain that Liberals were able to sweep them out of power in April 1879. The story of General Charles Gordon strikes a similar note. In 1884, the renowned general marched to Khartoum in the Sudan in order to evacuate Egyptian forces (allied with the British) who were being threatened by Sudanese rebels. Instead, Khartoum was besieged, and a relief force sent to aid Gordon arrived too late: in January 1885, Sudanese forces broke the siege, killing Gordon and his fellow defenders. In Britain, the public blamed the government run by the Liberal William Gladstone, and its outraged sentiment led to the collapse of the government in favor of the Conservatives. Much later, in France in 1958, military setbacks during the Franco-Algerian War led the French president to beg the Second World War hero and former French leader

---

[37] For the structure of the Indian army under British rule, see David Omissi, *The Sepoy and the Raj* (London: Palgrave Macmillan, 1994).

[38] Streets, *Martial Races*, chapter 3.

[39] See, for essays on jingoism and popular imperialism, John Mackenzie, *Imperialism and Popular Culture* (Manchester: Manchester University Press, 1986); and John Mackenzie, ed., *Popular Imperialism and the Military* (Manchester: Manchester University Press, 1992). This theme is important for understanding the origins of the First World War as well, as is discussed in chapters 12 and 14.

Charles de Gaulle to come back to power as prime minister in order to resolve the conflict.

The effects of imperial militaries were even more profound in the colonies. Not least, of course, was the fact that these militaries frequently engaged in battles, conquest, and pacification measures that occurred on colonial soil. In fact, imperial military forces engaged in acts of brutality both against their adversaries and against civilians. When colonial forces prevailed against adversaries, it was not uncommon for them to impose slaughter on a vast scale—at the Battle of Omdurman (September 2, 1898), for example, British forces killed 10,000 men and lost only 48. Imperial armies sometimes engaged in the slaughter of civilians as well. When "pacifying" resistant groups in sub-Saharan African colonial possessions, for example, British-led forces sometimes burned entire villages and killed all the livestock in retaliation. This racialist dehumanization of the enemy, with its increasing acceptance of violence against civilians, would also come to have deep repercussions in the metropoles.

Some scholars have even gone so far as to suggest that colonial slaughters were the precursor and root of the Holocaust and racialist genocide in twentieth-century Europe.[40] This connection, which is discussed in greater depth in chapter 13, is based on the idea that the late nineteenth- and early twentieth-century dehumanizing of colonial subjects in colonial literature, official reports, and speeches as "savages" or "animals" who have no title to land or rights was a precursor to similar portrayals of European Jews, Romany (Gypsies), and ethnic minorities in later periods. The connection is most frequently made in the case of Germany, whose Emperor Wilhelm II famously sent troops to put down the 1900 Boxer Rebellion in China with the order to "exterminate the brutes."[41]

Wilhelm's statement is more representative of colonial brutality than exceptionally German. In fact, all of the imperial powers seemed willing to use force at times against civilian populations as well as combatants. Yet, as we will discuss further in chapter 14, historians have been particularly interested in the German treatment of colonial subjects in their African colonies in part because they seem to foreshadow the violence that accompanied German expansion in Europe during the Second World War. One major example was the oppression of Nama and Herero populations that followed a 1903/1904 uprising in German South-West Africa. In the advanced stages of this conflict, General Lothar von Trotha issued an extermination order to his troops commanding them to seal the Herero population into a desert area and fire at anyone who sought to escape. In effect, he therefore sought to exterminate the Herero either by starvation and dehydration or by rifle and artillery. Although the exact death toll and circumstances of this process are still debated, there is little doubt that Troth desired to exterminate the troublesome Herero or that many German and European supporters of colonialism, having fed on a diet of imperial ideology, had little problem with this.[42] This is just one example of the ways in which organized, government-sanctioned violence seems to have transformed European metropolitan society.

The creation, maintenance, and use of imperial armies also transformed colonized cultures in important and enduring respects. Since most imperial powers had to rely on colonized populations to make up the bulk of their imperial armies, problems relating to troop loyalty and reliability were among the colonizers' most important concerns. One solution colonizers resorted to in a variety of colonial locations was the policy of recruiting only from colonized groups deemed to be best suited for military service. By the end of the nineteenth century, the groups that were identified as fitting this description were usually talked about as having particular, inherent,

---

[40] Two important texts that make the connection between colonial brutality and the Holocaust are Hannah Arendt, *The Origins of Totalitarianism* (New York: Meridian Books, 1958); and Sven Lindqvist, *Exterminate All the Brutes* (New York: The New Press, 1996). Originally published in Swedish in 1992.

[41] Henning Melber, "How to Come to Terms with the Past: Revisiting the German Colonial Genocide in Namibia," *Africa Spectrum*, 40 (2005), 139–148.

[42] See Tilman Dedering, "The German-Herero War of 1904: Revisionism of Genocide or Imaginary Historiography?" *Journal of South African Studies*, 19 (1993), 80–88.

"racial" qualities that made them excellent but trustworthy soldiers. In reality, however, those groups said to possess these "martial race" qualities had usually proven themselves to be reliable allies of the colonial powers in the past, and only later acquired the "racial" justifications for preferential recruiting.[43]

British India offers the most wide-ranging and effective case study of martial race recruiting, because the policy completely transformed its massive indigenous army after 1858. Prior to that date, the indigenous component of the British Indian army had been composed of a variety of groups, but none were more important than high-caste Brahmins who dominated the Bengal army—the strongest and largest of the three regionally based forces in British India. In 1857, however, widespread discontent in the Bengal army resulted in the mutiny of 69 out of 74 regiments and a concurrent peasant rebellion. Most of north-central India was out of British control between the spring of 1857 and early 1858. The British did regain control of the area after brutal reprisals and with the help of indigenous groups who did not rebel, but most of the old Bengal army had to be completely reconstructed.

Not surprisingly, the British were reluctant to engage soldiers who had come from the same backgrounds as those soldiers who so recently rebelled. Instead, they gravitated toward those groups who had allied themselves with the British against the mutineers including, most importantly, Sikhs from the Punjab region and Gurkhas from Nepal. Both groups had been marginal to the British Indian army before 1857, but now—when loyal soldiers were so urgently needed—they were hailed as ideal soldiers. Over the course of the rest of the century, preferential recruiting from these and other "martial" groups continued unabated: although they composed less than 10% of the British Indian army in 1856, by 1893 their share was 44%, by 1904 it was 57%, and by 1914 it was 75%.[44]

Over time, the rationale used to justify this preferential recruiting made increasing reference to supposed inherent racial qualities that made these populations such ideal soldiers. These characteristics included physical qualities such as height and light skin color (in the case of Sikhs) or else historical adaptation to environmental extremes such as mountainous terrain and cold weather (in the case of Gurkhas). They also included mental or emotional capabilities such as an instinctual love of fighting and inherent skills adapted to weapon use. In reality, however, neither the Sikhs nor the Gurkhas were distinct "races" even in the nineteenth-century sense of denoting homogenous ethnicities. Sikhism, in fact, is a religion—anyone can convert, and the British Indian army frequently required new recruits to do so. The Gurkha identity seems to have been largely a British creation: in Nepal, none of the indigenous groups defined themselves as such, and Gurkha regiments were frequently made up of several very different Nepalese ethnicities.[45]

The Dutch also practiced preferential recruiting in the East Indies. Essentially, the Dutch had the same problem in the islands of what is now Indonesia as the British had had in India: how to find enough indigenous soldiers to fill the colonial army without running the risk of having the army turned against the colonial state. The most populous island in the Dutch East Indies was Java, which was also the island on which the Dutch had the greatest presence and exerted the greatest control. Yet the Dutch did not trust the Javanese, because they believed—rightly—that the Javanese had the most to gain from rebelling against Dutch rule. Therefore, even as the Dutch continued for practical reasons to enlist Javanese soldiers into the army, they also searched elsewhere for soldiers who displayed the one quality they wanted above all else: loyalty.[46]

Over the course of the eighteenth and early nineteenth centuries, the Dutch experimented with a variety of groups—some even from as far afield as Africa. Then, from the 1830s on, they

---

[43] This is discussed further in the context of the First and Second World Wars in chapter 14.

[44] Omissi, *The Sepoy and the Raj*, 5, 19.

[45] Streets, *Martial Races*, chapter 6.

[46] Jaap de Moor, "The Recruitment of Indonesian Soldiers for the Dutch Colonial Army, c. 1700–1950," in *Guardians of Empire: The Armed Forces of the Colonial Powers, 1700–1914*, edited by David Killingray and David Omissi (Manchester: Manchester University Press, 1999).

worked very hard to recruit men from the island of Ambon, who were reputed (falsely) to have been extraordinarily loyal to the Dutch in the seventeenth century and also had the added attraction of being Christian. Until the 1870s, however, the Dutch had little luck convincing Ambonese men to enlist. Indeed, only after the Dutch created an entire mythology around the past loyalty of the Ambonese and also significantly raised enlistment bounties did men begin to join in significant numbers.[47] Once they did, the Dutch justified their preferential recruiting policy not just in terms of loyalty, but in terms of Ambonese fighting abilities. Even as late as 1935, Dutch officers indicated their continuing belief that the Ambonese had demonstrably superior martial skills than the Javanese.

Even though policies of preferential or martial race recruiting were usually based on a good deal of mythology and wishful thinking, they nevertheless had powerful effects in their respective colonial contexts. Most obviously, preferential recruiting divided colonized populations by labeling certain groups as *martial* and other groups as *non-martial*. Such labeling also had material repercussions, since colonial governments frequently treated supposedly martial groups much more favorably than supposedly non-martial groups. Moreover, those groups outside the magic circle of martial races were prone to be perceived as the opposites of martial groups: where martial races were loyal, non-martial groups were disloyal; where martial races were strong and hardworking, non-martial groups were physically weak and lazy. Thus even mild criticisms of colonial rule, when made by non-martial groups, were liable to be interpreted by colonial states as disloyal attempts to undermine the very fabric of imperial rule.[48]

Clearly, then, the connections linking military institutions and colonial warfare between and among empires in the age of the New Imperialism

not only bound empires more closely together but effected major transformations in both metropoles and colonies. These transformations simply cannot be understood in isolation: rather, they must be seen as part of wider colonial structures that cannot be located only in the "centers" or only in the colonial "peripheries."

GENDER, SEXUALITY, AND RACE

Metropolitan and periphery understandings of gender, sexuality, and race—like commodities, people, and militaries—were constructed and maintained together in an imperial context. However, this shared cultural and ideological development was not always acknowledged by scholars. Just as most scholarship produced before the 1980s sought to understand the origins of the New Imperialism in concrete political and economic rather than intellectual or ideological terms, so too the political economy of empire was studied almost to the exclusion of social and cultural ties. In the last few decades, however, scholars have begun to understand that imperial systems around the world were maintained and legitimized, at least in part, through the use of language and policies based on ideas and beliefs. These ideas and beliefs included convictions about the appropriate behaviors and sexualities of both men and women, and were frequently used to mark distinctions between colonizing and indigenous cultures. They were also frequently inseparable from beliefs and attitudes about racial differences, and were often used to shore up notions about the inherent inequality of colonized peoples. Together, these changing notions helped to shape cultures of imperialism in the metropole, and to create an imperialist worldview that sought to rigidly define the place of every citizen and subject of the empire largely on the basis of their gender and their race.

Colonial encounters between rulers and ruled—varied though they were—molded ideas about gender and race relationships in ways that deeply affected culture in the colonies as well as in imperial metropoles. These changes were not uniform in all colonies, or even within the various

---

[47] Even then, they were only ever a minority in the army. Ibid.
[48] To understand the ways one colonized group was feminized as a result of criticizing imperial policy, see Sinha, *Colonial Masculinity*.

empires. Rather, they were shaped by the local context: existing indigenous cultures, the presence or absence of natural resources, the presence or absence of colonial settlers, the degree of incorporation into the global economy, access to land, and many other factors. Nevertheless, ideas about the (appropriate or inappropriate) nature of these relationships linked metropoles and colonies together even as they altered them.

Imperial perspectives of gender, sexuality, and race were central to colonial endeavors around the world, because they provided legitimation for preserving distinctions between rulers and the ruled, and because they helped colonizers categorize—and hence divide—indigenous peoples into distinct and knowable groups. They were applied informally on a day-to-day basis, and were also used to justify and develop policies that regulated the lives of colonial subjects. While the precise worldview of the colonizers varied across both time and space, the need to clearly mark the boundaries between colonizer and colonized by mobilizing the language and practices of race and gender difference was widely shared across many imperial systems.

Nearly every imperial system, for example, sought to justify the unequal distribution of power between rulers and ruled—and even the existence of colonies themselves—by concerning itself with the sexual behaviors, appetites, and attitudes of colonized men and women. One recurring theme in French Indochina, British India, the Dutch East Indies, and British South Africa—to name only a few—was the idea that white women were in constant danger from the voracious and perverse sexual appetites of colonized men. The fear of rape, and the need to protect white women from it, hence came to justify the strict separation between colonizers and colonized as well as the careful control of both colonized men and white women. As a result, white women often found their lives in colonies paradoxically quite comfortable (due to servants, privilege, and leisure time) as well as quite restricted. Colonized men, for their part, were routinely excluded from positions in which they might have even a remote chance of exercising power over white women.

They also found themselves at risk of severe punishment if they transgressed the boundary between themselves and colonizing women. Perhaps not surprisingly, rhetoric about the need to control colonized men and to protect white women grew more intense in times of high colonial tension.[49]

One example of the ways in which gender could be employed to maintain distinctions between rulers and ruled was the 1883–1884 Ilbert Bill controversy in British India. The bill itself had been designed to concede a very small amount of power to Indian civil servants by allowing Indian judges jurisdiction over some European cases. However, Britons in India vehemently opposed even the slightest suggestion that Indians might be able to pronounce judgment over Europeans, and openly attacked the bill on the grounds that it threatened the safety of white women. Although the bill itself said nothing about women, opponents argued that it opened the door for Indian civil servants—whose ultimate fantasy, they asserted, was the possession of a white woman—to use their new power to take sexual advantage of British women. Moreover, opponents claimed that Indian men could not be expected to treat British women with decency because, they claimed, they treated their own women so poorly. In the end, opposition to the bill among the British community in India was so strong that the administration had to drop it. Indian men had been kept firmly in a subordinate role through rhetorical claims about the gendered consequences of conceding power to colonized men.[50]

The gendering of colonial subjects took place in a context of "scientific" racism, which emerged as a powerful force in the late nineteenth-century industrial societies. These societies did not invent

---

[49] For the ways colonized men were controlled by imperial perspectives on race and sexuality, see the essays in Julia Clancy-Smith and Frances Gouda, eds., *Domesticating the Empire: Race, Gender, and Family Life in French and Dutch Colonialism* (Charlottesville and London: University Press of Virginia, 1998); and Fiona Paisley, "Race Hysteria: Darwin 1938," in *Bodies in Contact: Rethinking Colonial Encounters in World History*, edited by Tony Ballantyne and Antoinette Burton (Durham and London: Duke University Press, 2005).
[50] Sinha, *Colonial Masculinity*, chapter 1.

the notion that there were different "races" or "nations," but it *was* within them that a new notion of race emerged based on the idea that the world could be divided into distinct biological and social groups with different attributes and abilities.[51] A few early models of this type had been developed in the seventeenth century, but probably the first widely read racial hierarchy was that written by Johan Friedrich Blumenbach around 1790. Blumenbach was a protégé of Carolus Linnaeus, an early hero of science who had since the 1730s developed schemes for categorizing plant and animal species. Like his mentor, Blumenbach set to work categorizing the natural world—in his case dividing humans into the "variants" of Negro, Mongolian, Malay, American Indian, and Caucasian. This was also a pursuit of the great father of the French academy, Georges Cuvier, who wrote for example that the "negroid" races "have always remained in a state of total barbarism."[52] Cuvier greatly influenced the seminal British geologist Charles Lyell, who studied the great catastrophes that shaped the past, and who believed that like mountains and rivers, species could erode and disappear. Lyell's book accompanied the father of evolutionary biology, Charles Darwin, on his voyage around the world. Darwin, of course, wrote that species and individuals competed, and that while some throve others did not, and considered the possibility that "the less intellectual races [are] exterminated."[53] From such ideas was modern racism born.

In this environment of increasingly codified racism, anxieties about racial mixing—or miscegenation—also echoed widely across imperial systems in the last half of the nineteenth century. Here again beliefs about gender, race, and sexuality played critical roles in maintaining the separation between rulers and ruled. Most imperial systems were predicated on the belief that colonizing men needed sex in order to be satisfied.

The problem, however, was a shortage of colonizing women in many colonial societies—even those that encouraged settler families. As a result, colonizing men frequently established sexual relations with indigenous women through prostitution, concubinage, or, less commonly, marriage.[54] Such relationships were rarely based on true partnership: even when colonized women entered into them of their own choice (abundant evidence from a variety of locales suggests that the use of force and manipulation was common), they enjoyed few rights or privileges and could be discarded at will. Moreover, these sexual relationships produced a whole set of new problems. Chief among these was how to maintain distinctions between colonizers and colonized given the existence of such intimate relationships. Even more problematic was how to classify and treat the mixed-race children that resulted from these relationships. Inter-racial relationships went right to the heart of the imperial situation. Empire is predicated on the differences between metropolitan citizen and colonial subject, but this inequality can only be maintained so long as people of different status were kept separate from each other. The intersection of race and sexuality was particularly dangerous to the colonial order, both because it suggested that the rigid categories of ruler and ruled could be crossed and because it created physical representatives of this breach in the form of children who could claim multiple heritages.[55]

In the East Indies, Dutch efforts to confront these issues illustrate both the centrality of sex management to imperial projects and the ways state policies about the regulation of sex and race could change over time. Prior to the twentieth century, the Dutch East India Company (VOC) sharply restricted the emigration of Dutch women

[51] Ann L. Stoler, "Making Empire Respectable: The Politics of Race and Sexual Morality in 20th-Century Colonial Cultures," *American Ethnologist*, 16 (1989), 634–660.

[52] William Coleman, *Georges Cuvier, Zoologist* (Cambridge: Harvard University Press, 1964), 143–165.

[53] These connections are made by Lindqvist in *Exterminate All the Brutes*, 97–100.

[54] In British India, the supposed "need" of British men for sex led the British army to establish brothels for its enlisted men. See Kenneth Ballhatchet, *Race, Sex, and Class Under the Raj: Imperial Attitudes and Policies and Their Critics* (London: Weidenfield and Nicolson, 1980); more recently, see Philippa Levine, *Prostitution, Race, and Politics: Policing Venereal Disease in the British Empire* (New York: Routledge, 2003).

[55] For an excellent treatment of this theme, see Ann Laura Stoler, *Carnal Knowledge and Imperial Power: Race and the Intimate in Colonial Rule* (Berkeley and Los Angeles: University of California Press, 2002).

to the East Indies. The VOC reasoned that Dutch men would be more likely to remain in the East Indies if they established long-term relationships with indigenous women. Moreover, indigenous women were less expensive to maintain than European women, and could be expected to perform domestic labor in addition to their sexual functions. For these reasons, the VOC advocated that Dutch men keep concubines—women who shared all the duties of wives without the legal protections and entitlements of marriage. By the 1880s, concubinage was the most common domestic arrangement for European men in the Indies, a situation that produced tens of thousands of mixed-race children. Yet by the turn of the twentieth century, the existence of this large mixed-race population had begun to worry the VOC and the Dutch state, because it threatened to blur the divide between the colonizers and the colonized. To which group did these children belong? Were they Dutch or Indonesian? Would they support Dutch rule, or would they try to subvert it? As evidence of these increasing concerns, Dutch officials increasingly began to argue that Indonesian concubines had neither the skills nor the morals to raise their mixed-race children to be adults worthy of Dutch citizenship. As a result, in the early twentieth century the state reversed earlier policy by seeking to ban the practice of concubinage and to encourage instead the emigration of Dutch women to the Indies. These women, the state now believed, would provide a civilizing influence on Dutch men, and would have the cultural and racial skills to raise their children to be proper Dutch citizens. For European men who could not afford Dutch wives, the state now encouraged prostitution as a means of side-stepping long-term, family-style liaisons with indigenous women. In both the pre- and post-twentieth-century East Indies, state concerns with the sexuality and sexual behaviors of both men and women, colonizers and colonized, highlight the central importance of sex management—and the race and gender relationships such management depended upon—to the imperial state.[56]

In virtually every colonial encounter, the gendered worldviews of the colonizing powers helped to shape colonial practice, law, and culture. As with other colonial projects, however, the way such ideas were translated into policy depended upon the response of colonized peoples, and thus their effect was neither uniform nor predictable.

The case of nineteenth-century Hawaii illustrates the ways colonial ideas about gender could interact with indigenous gender ideas in unexpected ways. Prior to contact with westerners in the eighteenth century, Hawaiian culture had imposed sexual separation between men and women, and mandated that women follow certain eating taboos. In other respects, however, Hawaiian women played important social, economic, political, and spiritual roles, and maintained a large degree of personal autonomy. As western—especially American—influence increased in Hawaii during the nineteenth century, Hawaiian women were criticized as being sexually immoral, were consistently written out of American-dominated politics, and were increasingly defined as legally subordinate to Hawaiian and American men. Thus, as a result of American intervention into Hawaiian society, Hawaiian women's legal and social position deteriorated. Yet these same interventions also led to an improvement in Hawaiian women's position as landholders in the last half of the nineteenth century. This unexpected improvement was the result of the Great Mahele of 1848, when the Hawaiian government—under duress by American interests—divided Hawaiian land into saleable pieces. The overall result for Hawaiians in general was massive dispossession from the land. For Hawaiian women, however, the results were much more ambiguous, because the number of women who inherited land in the post-Great Mahele period dramatically increased. In part, this was a result of indigenous choices and beliefs about women as effective guardians of Hawaiian land. The net effect was the preservation of Hawaiian women's economic and social importance even as their legal status diminished as a result of discriminatory American policies.[57]

---

[56]Ibid., chapters 2 and 4.

[57]Jocelyn Linnekin, *Sacred Queens and Women of Consequence: Rank, Gender, and Colonialism in the Hawaiian Islands* (Ann Arbor: University of Michigan Press, 1990).

Further cases illustrating the interaction of colonial and indigenous gender ideas abound in colonial Africa. In Northern Ghana, for example, the implementation of the British judicial system brought about a deterioration in indigenous women's legal status. In particular, colonial rule sought to introduce and enforce the notion that wives were the property of their husbands—a notion that, although foreign to Ghanaian gender ideas, allowed men to claim increasing legal control of their wives.[58] In colonial Tanganyika, European authorities instituted policies—such as taxation and the conversion of cattle sales to cash—that increasingly defined Maasai men as heads of households and allowed them privileged access to the political domain. Maasai women, who had long played vital economic and social roles within their communities, were thus increasingly marginalized by colonial policies that clearly favored men as political and economic actors.[59] At the same time, African women were not merely passive victims of a patriarchal partnership between colonizers and indigenous males. Rather, African women in many colonial states manipulated colonial court systems for their own benefit, ventured into independent economic enterprises, and moved into new occupations—as teachers or midwives—opened up to them by the colonial encounter.[60]

Colonial administrators and other agents of imperialism over time came to accept that they could not merely stamp their imprint upon local gender and race relations, but would instead have to negotiate with local authorities or, in other cases, see locals subvert colonial projects to their own ends. What imperial agents did not anticipate was that the disruptive effects of the colonial encounter on understandings of gender would influence metropolitan culture as well. In Britain, for example, imperialism informed the gender and racial identities of both women and men, and often provided the context within which claims about appropriate social roles were made. A case in point was the British feminist movement, which developed and grew in the last half of the nineteenth century—and thus coincided with the massive expansion of the British Empire. British feminists advocated equal legal rights with British men, but they justified their claims to equality by arguing for the need to represent and civilize colonized—especially Indian—women. Indeed, feminists argued that the oppressed and degraded condition of Indian women necessitated their own political participation so they could effectively utilize their superior moral authority to "uplift" their Indian "sisters." In this context, British feminists' sense of themselves as women depended heavily on their perception of gender and racial relations in the wider imperial world.[61]

The relationship between gender, race, and imperialism was extremely complex. It was not uniform across space or time, and its precise form varied widely according to local conditions, the colonial culture being imposed, and the specific issues involved. What is clear, however, is that ideas—whether about race or gender—were central to imperial projects around the world, and that they had real, observable effects in the material world both by connecting metropoles with colonies and, through these connections, by transforming both.

Conclusion

Whether through material sinews such as material goods and people, or through less-tangible sinews such as ideas about gender, race, sexuality, or religion, colonies and metropoles were linked in complex ways to one another throughout the period of the New Imperialism. These links both bound empires together and fundamentally transformed all of the cultures, peoples, and societies that comprised them. Thus, the history of people

[58] Sean Hawkins, " 'The Woman in Question': Marriage and Identity in the Colonial Courts of Northern Ghana, 1907–1954," in Jean Allman et al., *Women in African Colonial Histories*.

[59] D. Hodgson, " 'Once Intrepid Warriors': Modernity and the Production of Maasai Masculinities," *Ethnology*, 38:2 (1999), 121–150.

[60] See the essays in Allman et al., *Women in African Colonial Histories*.

[61] Antoinette Burton, *Burdens of History: British Feminists, Indian Women, and Imperial Culture, 1865–1915* (Chapel Hill: University of North Carolina Press, 1994).

and places that were part of imperial systems in this period—whether metropolitan or colonial—cannot be adequately understood in isolation from one another, or from the colonial practices and ideologies that linked them.

Questions

1. Missionism, migration, and trade were features of empires in earlier periods of time discussed in this book. What sets the era of the New Imperialism apart from early modern empires and empires of the mid-nineteenth century?

2. Why do you think scholars have sometimes used the metaphor of "sinews" to explain the ties connecting various parts of empires in this period?

3. How did military experiences in this period affect both imperial metropoles and colonies? Why do you think the effects upon each were different?

4. How did ideas about gender and race combine to legitimize colonial efforts in this period? How did they tend to affect life for colonial subjects as described in this chapter?

Imperialism and Colonialism: Imperial Projects and Colonial Petitions in the High Imperial Era

In the early twentieth century, much of the world's population lived as colonial subjects of great empires. Many resided in territories that had been brought under imperial rule prior to the late nineteenth century—the vast territories of British India, Canada, and Australasia, for example, and the fringes of the Russian Empire. In addition, most of Africa, South-East Asia, and the Pacific Islands as well as parts of East Asia had been added during the expansionist phase of the New Imperialism. As we shall see in chapter 14, the First World War furthered this process by partitioning the former Ottoman Empire and apportioning its territories to European states. Unable to become full citizens of the empires that occupied their homelands, the inhabitants of these territories almost universally remained colonial "subjects," possessing few rights and subject to often violent forms of control by imperial agents and settlers.

This chapter explores the relationships between colonial subjects, colonizers, and other imperial citizens in the overseas colonies that were acquired through the New Imperialism as well as those retained from earlier periods. The period covered, 1890–1945, skips the first years of the New Imperialism and focuses on the rise of High Imperialism. This chronology recognizes that the 1870s and 1880s were periods of experimentation in terms of the styles and methods of colonial rule employed by colonizers, whereas colonialism became far more codified and intensive in its interference in the everyday lives of colonial subjects over subsequent decades. This latter set of experiences is sometimes labeled High Imperialism, but note that the processes described by this term, overlapped chronologically with those labeled New Imperialism and High Imperial eras overlapped.

Ultimately the goal of this chapter is to try to understand the experiences of colonial subjects. Nevertheless, we begin by looking at the colonies through the eyes of citizens of the imperial metropoles, who in the late nineteenth century were trying to order the world to fit their particular worldviews. In the first section of this chapter, we explore those worldviews by connecting the evolving ideologies that drove the New Imperialism (described in chapter 10) and the flows of empire that intensified in this period (described in chapter 12) to the viewpoints of colonizers who arrived as administrators, settlers, missionaries, or even just travelers in the imperial periphery. In the second section, we look at the ways in which these worldviews were translated into projects by which agents of the metropole tried to reshape the colonies to fit their needs.

As we have begun to see in the last few chapters, the power of these colonizers and imperial agents in the late nineteenth and early twentieth centuries was unprecedented. Nevertheless, as in previous eras of empires the inhabitants of the colonized regions did not suddenly become passive subjects on whom the colonizers could imprint their models. Despite inequalities of power, wealth, and status, even these empires were shaped by colonized as well as colonizers. In the third section, we explore the ways in which colonial subjects resisted, modified, amended, and tried to appropriate colonial projects to their own needs. In the fourth section, we show how their actions forced administrators and other imperial agents to search for at least some local allies in order to achieve their own goals. This process produced a situation in which some local subjects of the empire could negotiate, accommodate, and petition to change laws and policies that affected them. However, their ability to do so should not be overstressed, since only a relative few could exercise it with any effectiveness.

THE COLONIZERS' MODEL OF THE WORLD

In looking intensively at late nineteenth- and early twentieth-century colonial experiences, we recognize that this period represented a maturation of colonial practices that had been developed over centuries. In many ways, colonial administrators and other citizens of the metropole faced similar problems in ruling the colonies of the New Imperialism as the representatives of earlier empires such as the Mughals, the Habsburgs, the Spanish in the Americas, or the British in nineteenth-century India. Like the officials and colonizers of these states, they had to develop strategies to rule large, distinctive populations in distant and widely spread regions. They had to figure out how to develop and manage land and segments of the local population and how to defend borders and prevent or overcome insurrection, all

in order to keep the colony stable and if at all possible profitable. Their strategies for doing so required that they mobilize multiple sectors of metropolitan society and that they build alliances with certain local groups and individuals or immigrants from other parts of the empire.

The great modern empires learned many of their colonial strategies from these earlier empires. It is well known, for example, that many of the techniques practiced by British administrators in early twentieth-century Africa were learned from British officials who had used them in India during the nineteenth century. What is not as well known is that many of these strategies were originally adapted from earlier Mughal models of administration there. Similarly, French administrators throughout the empire often applied strategies developed in the mid-nineteenth century in Algeria, which were in turn partly developed from pre-existing policies of Ottoman rulers in North Africa.[1]

Yet as we have seen in the last few chapters, while many of the challenges of colonial rule in the last decades of the nineteenth century and the first decades of the twentieth century were not new, the contexts in which they existed were. Industrialization meant that new technologies of control and violence could be employed in the colonies, and that economic infiltration was often more complete than in earlier periods. At the same time, the ideological framework of colonialism for the first time had to be matched to liberal, parliamentary forms of government and was equally constrained by the emergence of racist ideologies that referenced science. As a result, the colonialism of this period more than any previous period portrayed colonial subjects as alien and inferior to the population of the metropole.

---

[1] There is not a well-developed body of data or scholarship on these types of connections, partly because of Eurocentric blinkers, but they can be seen easily in the papers of administrators like Lord Frederick John Lugard. As an administrator in India, Lugard became an expert in the practices adapted by the British Raj from Mughal rule, and he subsequently brought these strategies to Uganda and then to Nigeria. The obvious source for this is his *The Dual Mandate in British Tropical Africa* (Edinburgh: W. Blackwood and Sons, 1922). But also useful are his reports to the British East India Company and his published instructions to political officers in Nigeria.

How did this happen? As we saw in the last chapter, in the imperial imagination of the late nineteenth and early twentieth centuries, the colonies and their inhabitants came to be represented as the very opposite of the metropole and its citizens. Whereas the industrialized metropole was depicted as rational, progressing, and masculine, the colonies were often depicted as spiritual, stagnant, and feminine. This imagination of difference had important policy implications. For example, in the early years of the New Imperialism (as in the preceding period) colonial governors considered ways of transforming their African, Asian, and Pacific subjects into French, British, German, or other citizens. By the 1910s, however, these early experiments in assimilating colonial populations were being replaced by a much firmer and more permanent dividing line between metropolitan *citizens* and colonial *subjects*. They were also being replaced by projects that categorized and sub-divided subject population along rather rigid lines, and attempted to reshape each divided group to the colonizer's physical needs and intellectual worldviews. To a greater degree than ever before, therefore, the colonial cultures of the High Imperial era assigned different roles and allowed different privileges to every segment of the population based on their perceived race, ethnicity, class, gender, and other categories of status.

This systematization of colonialism was a reflection of metropolitan cultures of scientific racism developed in the wake of Charles Darwin's pioneering work on evolution and inter-species competition (see chapter 12). This is not to indict Darwin for the racial categorization that became central to colonialism. Rather, Darwin's work was adopted and sometimes distorted by societies passionately inflamed by competitive nationalism and by the prospects of scientific technology. Evolutionary theory and science were tools for defining and solving problems. Patriots forging a nation, for example, could also utilize the propaganda of race to make Bretons, Parisians, and Languedocians all feel like Frenchmen. They could use it to compare their nation to others by assigning national traits: for example, contrasting the French notion of *civilisation* (civilization) to the supposed Hunnish brutality of the Germans. They could also use it to justify colonialism. Similarly, through the lens of scientific racism, the deaths of millions in the Pacific or the Americas due to disease could be seen as a natural expression of the survival of the fittest races and the degeneration and extinction of the least fit. Similarly, this ideology could be used to justify the forceful occupation of territory by "superior" peoples, and their subjugation of indigenous populations. Nor was scientific racism merely a justification for colonialism: it could also be used to propagandize support for it. After all, a competitive nation had to constantly prove that it was not degenerating, but rather increasing in strength. One way of doing so was to expand into new territory. Yet another was to expand the population of the "race" or nation, which of course also drove the need to claim more territory.

Racism also manifested itself in the colonies through the science of eugenics, which was based on fears of racial degeneration. If, as scientific racialists of the turn of the century believed, only fit races thrive, then the health of the race or nation must be constantly safeguarded and scientifically improved. Such ideas formed the base of broad eugenics movements in Europe, the United States, and soon after in the colonies. **Eugenics** was constructed as a practical, nationalist science intended to keep the race or nation "fit." Among its most important ideas was the fear of contamination by "inferior" races and a view that any inter-mixing weakened the positive characteristics of the race.[2] This was an enormously important factor in shaping policy and action in the colonies, where people of different pigments and origins were in close contact.

This is not to suggest, however, that race was the only means employed by colonizers of categorizing the populations of the world. We have seen, in chapter 12, how conceptions of gender and technology helped to shape the connections between metropole and colony. Within the colonies, these conceptions also played an important role. References to the "primitiveness" of African and South-East Asian tools were useful,

---

[2] Ann L. Stoler, *Carnal Knowledge and Imperial Power: Race and the Intimate in Colonial Rule* (Berkeley: University of California Press, 2002).

for example, for justifying the seizure of land and mineral wealth from populations that weren't "using" them fully.[3] Meanwhile, colonialism was also explained in gendered terms. The role of male colonizers was often taken to be paternalistic: they were to be fathers to the child-like colonial subjects.[4] At the same time, European and U.S. women after about 1914 were often seen as having an additional role of "civilizing" female colonial subjects, an idea especially propounded by French pro-colonial groups.

At least one author has argued that class was also an important scheme by which at least the British classified people in their empire. David Cannadine, in his book *Ornamentalism*, suggests that race could at times be overcome by class, and that upper-class British inhabitants of colonies often felt an affinity to chiefs, princes, sheiks, and other ruling figures. This, he suggests, led the British to make allies with these individuals first and foremost.[5]

As we have seen, the liberal ideas that were at the heart of many of these societies (Japan to a lesser degree) placed an emphasis on the duty of the imperialist power to civilize and improve colonial societies. At the same time, however, racialism and eugenics suggested that colonial subjects could not reach the conqueror's levels of civilization, and that in fact these societies should be allowed to decline or stagnate as was only natural. Colonizers often engaged in wide-ranging debates over which task was more important—humanitarian civilizing or controlling and dominating. Frequently, however, the two urges were allied. For example, the abolition of slavery, of

human sacrifice, or even of religious rituals could serve both the urge to control and to reshape colonial societies. Sometimes, however, civilizing and dominating missions were at odds. In southern Africa and in the Caribbean, missionaries sometimes aided or armed converted indigenous populations against settlers trying to take over their land, for example.

These divisions illustrate a very important point about colonialism. Even though there was by the beginning of the twentieth century a somewhat shared model of the world among colonizers (and especially among colonizers from one metropole), people saw their relationship to this model in different ways. Missionaries, for example, often saw their task as sharing the superiority that eugenics and religion told them they had. Settlers might more often have seen themselves as carrying out the natural or God-given task of taming wild land and putting it to use for civilization. Administrators had to serve all of these needs, but focused most on the task of controlling and categorizing populations. Of course profit was also an ever-present motive.

The diversity of objectives and worldviews among colonizers is important to note: even within each of these groups perspectives might vary widely. Nevertheless, the colonial setting had the curious effect of creating a siege mentality among colonizers that drew them together by exacerbating their status as "whites." Policing the boundaries and keeping the distance between citizens (of the metropole) and colonial subjects became an obsession in this period, and the boundaries came to be drawn largely upon racial lines. In the European and U.S. empires, generally all "whites"—even from rival states—were accepted on the privileged side of the race barrier.

Meanwhile, relations with "non-whites" were impaired by a eugenics-driven fear of contamination. This fear was reflected in two particular trends. The first was the rather rapid decline of strategies that had earlier been developed to allow Africans, Asians, and Pacific Islanders to assimilate into the society of the conquerors. In the mid and late nineteenth century, policies or processes had existed in many colonies whereby locals could acquire the citizenship of the metropole or at least

---

[3] Michael Adas, *Machines as the Measure of Men: Science, Technology, and Ideologies of Western Dominance* (Ithaca, NY: Cornell University Press, 1990).

[4] For an important depiction of paternalism and U.S. imperialism, see Mary A. Renda, *Taking Haiti: Military Occupation and the Culture of U.S. Imperialism 1915–1914* (Chapel Hill: University of North Carolina Press, 2001). For more on Victorian British depictions of the role of women in empire, see Anna Davin, "Imperialism and Motherhood," in *Tensions of Empire: Colonial Cultures in a Bourgeois World*, edited by Frederick Cooper and Ann Stoler (Berkeley: University of California Press, 1997), 87–101.

[5] David Cannadine, *Ornamentalism: How the British Saw Their Empire* (Oxford: Oxford University Press, 2002).

equal legal status with Europeans. In the Dutch colonies of South-East Asia, for example, rules in place in 1884 allowed such status to be conferred on locals who were Christian, could speak and write Dutch, had a European education, and were considered "suitable" in dress and behavior.[6] In French West Africa, Africans who learned French were loyal to the administration, and consented to French law could be granted French citizenship.[7] In German colonies of the same period, because of German male-centered laws of inheritance, the sons of a German father and an African or Pacific Islander mother were automatically granted German citizenship.[8] By the 1910s, however, this had largely changed. Race (and particularly skin color) had come to determine French citizenship in West Africa, colonial authorities were challenging the right of mixed-heritage children to claim German citizenship, and even in the Netherland Indies the color line was being more firmly enforced.

This change was mirrored by strategies to separate the space occupied by colonizers and colonized. In many colonies, these took the form of divided cities built with a white-dominated area (in the British Empire known often as the *cantonments*) and with larger and segregated districts for locals. This type of policy was often justified by science as a way to slow the spread of disease. It was sometimes justified by racial notions of culture as a way to serve the different needs of white Europeans on the one hand and Africans or Asians on the other. The practice reached its apogee in South Africa, where huge settlements outside white-dominated cities were built, entire populations forced to relocate to new areas, and mixed-race districts like District Six in Cape Town were razed to the ground. In the houses of the colonizers, as well, space was divided between servants' or public areas accessible to locals and private areas reserved only for the colonizers. In reality, of course, these borders were often permeable—the need for laborers and for servants meant that both city lines and domestic lines were often crossed.

Maintaining the empire was wrapped up, therefore, in maintaining the frontiers of distinctiveness between the colonizer and the colonized. In addition, the systematic categorization of humans led to colonizers making distinctions *among* the colonized. This was a useful facet of colonial ideology because it allowed colonizers to divide and conquer. As we have seen and as shall be further discussed later, the empire was affordable and controllable only because of the assistance of some members of the local population. In the process of selecting (or being selected by) these groups and individuals, rigid categorization helped. The physical creation of distinct "tribal" groups ruled by an appointed chief, prince, or shayk helped colonial administrators to manage local populations in a way that was familiar to them of the rigidity of national identity back in the metropole. By playing these groups and their leaders against each other, the colonizers also divided potential opposition and placed themselves at the center of local power dynamics. By restricting the rights of local women, they made alliances with powerful men. They also created allies by recognizing the so-called *traditional* rights of landlords and elders, even when these were newly invented. In this way, schemes of categorization that managed power in the colonies were rapidly created.

HIERARCHY AND COLONIAL PROJECTS IN THE ERA OF HIGH IMPERIALISM

To what degree was this new model a uniform, shared culture among and within the great imperial metropoles? Was imperialism in fact so widely shared and commonly understood among the inhabitants of industrialized societies as to constitute a single, unified body of thought and culture?

---

[6] Stoler, *Carnal Knowledge*, 39.
[7] Alice R. Conklin, "Redefining 'Frenchness': Citizenship, Race Regeneration, and Imperial Motherhood in France and West Africa, 1914–1940," in *Domesticating the Empire: Race, Gender, and Family Life in French and Dutch Colonialism*, edited by Julia Clancy-Smith and Frances Gouda (Charlottesville: University Press of Virginia, 1998), 65–83.
[8] Lora Wildenthal, "Race, Gender, and Citizenship in the German Colonial Empire," in Cooper and Stoler, *Tensions of Empire*, 263–283.

The idea of a widespread culture of imperialism in this period is accepted by many leading scholars who study this period, but others warn against accepting too readily the idea of a uniform imperial blueprint across metropoles and even among classes and groups within the imperial citizenry of a single empire. They argue, instead, that different groups and even individuals within metropoles had very different ideas of what their rule of the colonies would look like, and that they brought these diverse plans and ideas with them to the colonies. Some historians and anthropologists also suggest that once within the physical space of the colony, most imperial blueprints had to be abandoned in the face of the unexpected actions and attitudes of the inhabitants of the colonies. Thus, one of the leading historians of colonialism, Frederick Cooper, warns us not to see colonialism as a single blueprint, but rather as "a series of hegemonic projects" that the colonizers sought to implement.[9]

What do we mean by "projects"? In order to understand Cooper's assertion, we need to put ourselves in the shoes of citizens of the metropole (and in some cases, other industrialized societies) who set out for the colonies. On one level, their motivations and intentions were obvious. Missionaries intended to spread the word of God. Settlers primarily intended to establish businesses or plantations. Civil servants were on a career path as teachers, administrators, or policemen. Women often followed their husbands or went to the colonies looking for jobs or potential husbands among the colonial officials. As we discussed in chapters 8 and 10, these individual and group motivations were all influenced by a widely shared sense of a national or racial mission to bring civilization to barbarism, to tame the savage landscape and peoples of the colonies, and to spread their dominion over the world.

These broad imperialist ideologies, however, masked much more complex and personal aspirations and objectives. In other words, while cultures of imperialism created shared ideologies and worldviews across and among metropoles, different groups of western European, U.S., and Japanese citizens each related to these imperialist notions in their own particular ways based on their own experiences and places within their societies. When they relocated to the colonial periphery, they often brought with them plans to recreate the local populations and territory that were not just "imperial" but also tailored to their specific visions of their colonial mission.

Good examples of this complexity can be found by looking at missionaries, whose goal of propagating the word of God and creating havens of holiness in savage lands entailed more than merely preaching. Mission stations had to be built, schools to be implemented, assistants to be trained. Because commerce was believed to help concentrate civilize people, mission stations undertook economic projects, which had the added benefit of helping to pay for the endeavor. Often, missionaries intended to create their own vision of what God's paradise might look like, trying to reproduce aspects of their homelands that they admired, but escape those they did not. Along the way, they sought to reshape the roles of women and men in society to fit an idealized notion of a Christian community. This was a truly hegemonic project, one that involved their acting as fathers and mothers to shape who they perceived to be their spiritual children.

Such personal as well as culturally informed motives were evident in the actions of missionaries of the Dutch Missionary Society who worked with women of the Karo ethnic group in Sumatra in the early twentieth century. These missionaries were largely middle-class Dutch citizens who believed strongly in their own values of hard work, Protestantism, and the nuclear family with the husband as chief breadwinner. However, unlike some other colonizers, they brought with them a favorable view of women playing a public role in the capitalist economy as nurses and earning their own money by working from the home. Viewing Karo society through the lenses of their imperial imaginations, the missionaries arrived with the preconception that women were the

---

[9] Frederick Cooper, "The Dialectics of Decolonization," in Cooper and Stoler, *Tensions of Empire*, 406–435.

most backward element in Karo society, and were therefore holding back both the religious and economic development of the society. Based on their own perceptions, they saw Karo women as being of low status because of the practice of polygyny and bride-price and because women did most of the agricultural labor. They failed to perceive the ways in which women could exercise power within these frameworks, and thus they rather rapidly came to the conclusion that in order to transform the local society into a civilized, Christian community, they would have to reverse all of these facets of local culture. This they attempted through mission schools, but especially through the training of girls in western-style baby care and nursing, and also by trying to entice girls to become entrepreneurs by learning to sew, which also suited their belief in capitalism as a civilizing force. Together, these ventures constituted a whole project to "civilize" the Karo through their society's women.[10]

Similarly, while settlers may have come to the colonies largely with economic projects of self-improvement, they were also seeking to escape pressures back home and to create for themselves a place that existed only in their imagination. As we saw in chapter 8 for an earlier period, settlers' motivations in the early twentieth century were diverse. Many settlers came from among the ranks of the disenchanted poor who were no longer wanted in the metropole. In the twentieth century, however, a large proportion of settlers who set out to build plantations and farms in Africa and South-East Asia came from among the ranks of the aristocracy, men and women of title if sometimes not much wealth. These individuals were often fleeing their industrialized, increasingly democratic societies in search of a world of the past.[11] They hoped to be able to recapture in the colonies the large estates and unquestioned power their ancestors wielded.

Thus when they arrived in Kenya, Indochina, or elsewhere, they set about transforming the region to suit these conceptualizations. They expelled local populations from the land, partly to force them to become workers or servants. They then tried to socially engineer these workers' lives, to tie them to a European daily and monthly clock, and to force them to live in nuclear family households on the land. They transformed the very landscape of the colonies, building not only their vast agricultural plantations but also hunting parks and pleasure gardens. Many of these upper-class settlers quickly came to prefer Africa or South-East Asia to the metropole, not least because they were allowed to control and discipline the population in ways they would not have been allowed at home.

Aristocratic settlers saw in the colonies a place to recreate their one-time privileges. During the depressions of the 1870s and 1920s–1930s, many newly impoverished middle-class Europeans also turned to the colonies as a place to escape the economic and social pressure of the metropole. Usually, these emigrations were underpinned by a sense of moral advantages as well. In Germany, for example, a number of writers in the 1870s had begun to argue that taming the savage environments of the colonies could strengthen the German people morally, culturally, and physically. They argued that industrialization was sapping the strength of the strong, proud German farmer *volk* (folk). As economic depression descended on Europe after 1873, many middle-class Germans blamed their troubles on industrialization, and accepted the idea that the colonies could be a place for them to rebuild "traditional" German culture and nationalism. This idea did not conflict with their economic goals. Indeed, the two were mutually reinforcing as part of the same colonial project.[12]

Even scholarly undertakings like the writing of history were colonial projects. In South Asia, for example, British historians undertook a "scientific" study of the Indian past, but they did so with

[10]Rita Smith Kipp, "Emancipating Each Other: Dutch Colonial Missionaries' Encounter with Karo Women in Sumatra, 1900–1942," in Clancy-Smith and Gouda, *Domesticating the Empire*, 211–235.
[11]Cannadine, *Ornamentalism*, 39–40.

[12]Woodruff D. Smith, "The Ideology of German Colonialism, 1840–1906," *Journal of Modern History*, 46 (1974), 641–662.

specific purposes in mind. In the first place, knowing Indian history was considered a useful tool for helping the administration with the very real task of ruling hundreds of millions of Indian subjects.[13] In addition, British historians' histories of India suggested that the region had historically developed only very slowly and in certain directions, legitimizing the claim that Britain's rule was necessary for India to "advance." Finally, the British used history to support the colonial categorization of Indians not only into separate races (light "Aryans" and dark "Dravidians") but also into numerous castes, or rigid classes. In their histories, British scholars argued that such caste divisions had existed largely unchanged for thousands of years. In fact, as we saw in chapter 9, the rigid division of society into castes had sharply increased under colonialism. The new science of anthropology, too, played its role. Colonial anthropologists investigated and stored knowledge of local societies to put at the disposal of the administration. They also used that knowledge to legitimize colonial rule, by presenting colonial societies as unchanging, better suited for rural life than the city, and in need of guidance. In Africa, anthropologists legitimized the division of African peoples into "tribes" by defining the customs and practices of different groups as if there were no intermixing or overlap. Their scholarship served to support and justify this categorization, and to confirm it as colonial policy.

For social scientists as well as scientists, the colonies were potential laboratories for experimenting with human subjects. Baron Shimpei Goto, the first Japanese Chief of Civil Affairs (governor) of Formosa, wrote that "I wish to find Formosa on scientific principles." He read widely the writing of European colonial officials, and attempted to distill a scientific colonialism from among them.[14] He then used Formosa as a site of experimentation with techniques of social control and industrial development. This idea of the colony as a laboratory, and colonial subjects as acceptable subjects of experimentation, was not restricted to the Japanese empire. In many colonies, officials found that they could try out policies and practices that would not have been acceptable at home. This extended even to experimenting with medicines and anti-insect chemicals without the kind of governmental oversight they would have had to endure at home.

Colonial urban planning, too, was an experiment in the dualistic goals of civilizing and separating. The rebuilding of Moroccan cities by French architects in the first half of the twentieth century is an important example. Their plans called for a zone, or *sanitary corridor*, separating the old Arab city (the medinas) from the new French city. The new part of the city was to retain only a few Moroccan ornamental motifs and several architectural features particularly useful in the hot climate. Moroccans were to be allowed to live in the new parts of their cities, so long as they agreed to keep their houses like their neighbors', and thus to at least outwardly adopt French cultural practices. Later, special districts were built to house the increasing Arab population of cities like Casablanca. The houses in these districts were modeled on those of the old medinas, but with wider streets and better draining and water supplies. It was hoped that these amenities would help to civilize their Arab inhabitants, even while their decoration acknowledged Arabs as exotic and different from Europeans.[15]

The work of scholars like Frederick Cooper in identifying the many different colonial projects has done a great deal to help reveal the complexity and depth of colonialism in the era of the New Imperialism. However, it should be kept in mind that despite their differences, these projects and models were linked by a number of dominant ideas and by the connections among the imperial

---

[13] Michael Gottlob, "India's Connection to History: The Discipline and the Relation Between Center and Periphery," in *Across Cultural Borders: Historiography in Global Perspective*, edited by Eckhardt Fuchs and Benedikt Stuchtey (Lanham: Rowman & Littlefield, 2002), 75–98.

[14] Hyman Kublin, "The Evolution of Japanese Colonialism," *Comparative Studies in Society and History*, 1 (1959), 67–84.

[15] Gwendolyn Wright, "Tradition in the Service of Modernity: Architecture and Urbanism in French Colonial Policy, 1900–1930," in Cooper and Stoler, *Tensions of Empire*, 322–335.

powers. Thus, researchers continue to disagree about the degree to which it's possible to describe a single "imperial paradigm" in this period.

THE PROCONSULAR STATE AND THE REALITIES OF COLONIAL RULE

If colonialism was made up of many projects, however, one could argue that the project that made all the others possible was the creation of a colonial state. It was the creation of a state structure with sufficient force and power to compel local resources and impose its will on local populations that made possible the diverse projects of settlers, missionaries, administrators, and other colonial agents. Because of the enormous distances involved and the difficulties of controlling vast empires, each colony rather rapidly developed into what we call a **proconsular state**. The term *proconsul* refers to the fact that the governors wielded *imperium* (imperial authority) like the proconsuls of imperial Rome, and that they were effectively independent in exercising day-to-day rule over the colony. Thus while technically reporting to some secretariat of the imperial government, colonial administrations nevertheless developed all of their own institutions paralleling those of the metropole. By the early twentieth century, most colonies had their own police, health services, infrastructure, executive decision-making bodies, and judiciaries—all under the control of a governor who had almost total day-to-day power. In the case of the French Empire, several colonies were often lumped together in super-colonies such as French West Africa or the Indochinese Union under a single governor-general, but the principle remained the same. In the case of protectorates such as Morocco, the British, German, or French "advisor" remained behind the scenes, but nevertheless largely manipulated the institutions of the state. In general, colonial administrations were autocratic, except where large numbers of settlers from the metropole were involved. In these instances, and where groups of locals had been assimilated as citizens in a previous era, some democratic institutions crept in.

The localization of imperial authority within the colonial administration was made necessary in part because of the extreme distances and relative difficulty of communications between the metropole and the colony even after industrial transportation became widely available. In addition, localization also reflected the fact that in order to be successful, colonialism had to be more responsive to conditions in the colonies than those in the metropole. Colonial administrations were involved in many projects, but two always remained central: stability and profitability. Administering the colony was a dynamic process that did not proceed according to any plan and could never be entirely completed. Instead, it was a homespun and wobbly effort by administrators to balance the needs of many different groups and manage the tensions among them. In other words, colonial administration was a cobbled-together response to what colonizers found in the colonies: not the compliant, inferior populations they had imagined but rather vibrant and diverse communities who challenged their foreign rulers in a myriad of ways.

This reality forced administrators to abandon any blueprints written in the metropole and to engage with local conditions and populations. It also points the way to a real colonial conundrum from the perspective of the administrators. Simply put, the personal success of an administrator was contingent upon his ability to please the many colonial stakeholders—not only the government back home, but also missionaries, corporations, settlers, and others. This meant providing ongoing security and stability to the colony, which in turn required both firm control over the indigenous and transient population and the differentiation and exceptional status of Europeans from them. However, colonial rule could not profitably or securely be run by force alone, but rather required the colonial administrators to rely upon the assistance or at least compliance of portions of the local population. This was the underlying force behind "indirect" rule that there simply wasn't enough money and weren't enough colonizers to run the colonies.

In the past, historians have often viewed the colonies of the New Imperialism as being of two sorts: those experiencing direct rule and those experiencing indirect rule. As we saw in chapter 9, in direct rule, such as was practiced in the Japanese Empire or in the early years of French West Africa, authority was exercised at even very local levels by Europeans or Japanese soldiers and administrators. In indirect rule, by contrast, the administration relied heavily on local elites and rulers to administer local government and even dispense justice. This was very much the case in British colonies in Africa, where indirect rule imitated that which had been practiced in India for more than a century by Britain, and by the Mughals before. But it was quickly copied by other empires that were equally thinly stretched. In reality, all colonies relied to some degree on indirect rule by locals who proved willing to ally with the state, although this was the least true in colonies with many settlers who could be relied upon to support the administration and who jealously guarded their prerogatives. But even in highly colonized regions such as Kenya and Algeria, chiefs and sheiks were apportioned some power and funding by the administration. In the most rapacious colonial states, like the Belgian Congo, indirect rule was simply given over to thugs and soldiers rather than to secular or religious rulers.

In most colonial situations, indirect rule was the very heart of colonial administration, and only the cooperation of local allies kept the colony profitable and stable.[16] This was not new, of course. As we have seen, Hernando Cortes in Meso-America, the Mughals in the Deccan, and the French administrators of Indochina as well as all other previous imperial powers had relied to varying degrees on the cooperation and assistance of some local groups to maintain their authority and power. To a degree that often surpassed earlier empires, the thinly spread colonial

rulers of the High Imperial era relied heavily on local allies, who in return were often able to make demands upon the administration. This was especially true in regions where there were few colonial officials or settlers from the metropole. Frequently, the demands made by specific local allies conflicted with those of other local groups, and even with those of metropolitan concerns. The principal task of the governor and his administrators, therefore, was balancing the needs of all of these groups sufficiently to avoid unrest, work interruptions, and the breakdown of law and order. This process had the effect, over time, of enabling some groups of locals to establish themselves higher in the colonial hierarchy than others. Such hierarchies followed certain patterns. Because almost all colonial administrators were men who arrived in the colonies with strong ideas about women's roles, for example, colonized women had very little luck in asserting their rights. In fact, in almost all colonies, women *lost* status and rights during the colonial period.

STRATEGIES OF COLONIAL SUBJECTS: NEGOTIATION, ACCOMMODATION, AND PETITION

The colonialism of the twentieth century reshaped colonial societies more rapidly and completely than in previous periods. It eliminated old hierarchies, old orders, and old rituals among colonial societies, and replaced them with a new system of power that placed metropolitan citizens at the top. The race line that held Europeans, white citizens of the United States, and Japanese citizens apart from colonial subjects in their respective empires became largely uncrossable in this period. Yet because of the diffuseness of colonial military force, many subjects were able to negotiate with, subvert, petition, and even infiltrate the colonial system and its projects to varying degrees.

In chapter 11, we looked with nuance at the labels of *collaborator* and *resister* that have been too loosely applied by scholars and laypeople alike to the inhabitants of colonies in earlier eras.

---

[16] See Jürgen Osterhammel, *Colonialism: A Theoretical Overview* (Princeton, NJ: Markus Wiener, 1997), 51–68.

We concluded that these categories missed the real stories of human experiences among colonial subjects: that they tried to survive and to thrive, that they employed a variety of strategies during the course of their lives, and that they made decisions based on many factors other than colonialism. Nevertheless, we cannot ignore the fact that modern colonialism was in many cases so invasive in its attempts to control individuals and the wider population that it influenced the day-to-day experiences of millions of people around the world. Certainly, subjects sometimes overtly resisted or collaborated with the state, but the use of these terms as rigid categories obscures the fact that the inhabitants of the imperial periphery employed a wide range of strategies in dealing with the colonial state beyond outright resistance and total cooperation. Among the most important of these were negotiation, accommodation, and petition. While these may seem to be "minor" strategies to us compared to more dramatic episodes of armed or organized massed resistance, they were in fact far more common and were ultimately enormously significant in shaping colonial experiences.

In the context of colonialism, **negotiation** is the somewhat formal process by which local populations and groups met with colonial administrators and other authority figures in order to shape the policies and practices of the state to better suit their own interests. Very often, negotiation took place following the implementation of a new law, often created by some agency in the metropole. Colonial administrators were frequently called upon to implement empire-wide ordinances or laws created by the colonial office, metropolitan parliament, or emperor. In many cases, these ordinances could not feasibly be implemented in the colony, however, without causing enormous disruptions. The decision to abolish slavery in the Gold Coast Colony and Protectorate in 1874 was a case in point.[17] The 1873–1874 war against Asante (described in chapter 11) had brought to the

attention of the British press the existence of slavery in the region, and abolitionists demanded that it be outlawed in the new colony. However, the governor of the new colony, George Strahan, was well aware that among the biggest supporters of British rule in the region were the palm oil growers, merchants, and chiefly officeholders of the southern states, many of whom owned slaves. He therefore consulted with a number of these men who served on his Executive Council. Together, they sought a way to implement the laws that would satisfy the abolitionists back home without disrupting commerce and the livelihoods of important locals. Their solution was to outlaw slavery, but without creating any mechanism for liberating slaves. Slaves who came to the courts could claim their freedom, but the administration would not go to them. The burden of liberation was placed on the slave, and absolutely no resources were provided either to help liberate slaves or to provide a livelihood or a pathway home following emancipation. This solution was a success, so far as Strahan was concerned: he could point to the abolition of slavery as a major achievement, but without threatening the stability and profitability of the colony.[18] It was a victory for the slave owners, as well, for relatively few slaves were able to liberate themselves.

The example of abolition in the Gold Coast points out an important relationship between actual power and negotiating clout. Simply put, the ability of a group or individual colonial subject to influence policy formation was proportional to their ability to cause or reduce trouble in the colony. Men like the members of Strahan's Executive Council—chiefly officeholders and big merchants—were often able to influence policy. Other groups were not: the enslaved population of the Gold Coast, for example, or often the poor, children, and women. But the correlation was not perfect, because it was influenced by the preconceptions of the administration. For example, until the early twentieth century,

---

[17] See chapter 11.

[18] Trevor Getz, *Slavery and Reform in West Africa* (Athens: Ohio University Press, 2004), 96–117.

western-educated people of mixed heritage (**metis**) were often quite influential in colonial policy within the European empires because of their ability to claim European ancestry and to act and talk like Europeans. However, as racism became more pronounced and the colonial obsession with racial boundaries emerged, settlers and administrators began to turn their backs on people of mixed heritage because they were living representations of the permeability of racial boundaries. They similarly began to revile colonial subjects who "acted like white people." Instead, they preferred to rely even more on "traditional" and "exotic" rulers like chiefly officeholders, princes, and sheiks. As we will see in chapter 14, this increased the frustration of the western-educated classes, eventually with enormous consequences.

Aside from formal negotiation, colonial subjects also practiced policies of **accommodation**. In other words, they adjusted to the circumstances of colonial rule and interference without entirely accepting subordination. Accommodation is even more difficult to see in the colonial record than the kinds of petty, unorganized resistance discussed in chapter 11, largely because it often wasn't a strategy that entailed *action*. More often, accommodation was an almost invisible strategy, having more to do with how people thought than how they acted. Individuals engaged in accommodation might even appear outwardly as collaborators, engaged in supporting roles as paid chiefs, or clerks, or policemen. Inwardly, however, they understood themselves as psychologically, spiritually, or culturally independent. This can be seen as a kind of spiritual resistance. It can alternately be seen as more of an intentional or even unconscious method strategy for survival. In either case, accommodation was a way of living under colonial oppression while refusing to be defined by the colonizers.

As an act of resistance, accommodation can be seen as the process by which colonial subjects came to define their relationship to the colonial state in terms that acknowledged the realities of the conquerors' power while also subverting them. The venerable West African historian David Robinson has explored just such a process among the Muridiyya Muslim order in French West Africa, especially Senegal. In the early years of French rule, this Murid brotherhood formed around a pious scholar, Amadu Bamba Mbacké. Amadu Bamba was an important figure in the resistance to French conquest in the 1880s, and developed a large following even after its completion. Eventually, his power in some areas grew so strong that he threatened the authority of chiefs cooperating with the administration. He was arrested in 1895 and deported from the region for 16 years. However, his reputation only grew greater in exile, and he was gradually transferred closer and closer back to his hometown.

During his years in exile, Amadu Bamba came to the conclusion that since French military power was too great to be resisted, it had to be accommodated so long as it did not interfere with Islamic spiritual matters and the right of his followers to work and to learn. As Amadu Bamba and his successors and followers became outwardly reconciled to colonial rule, the French administrators began to see them as surrogate chiefs and allies. Murid communities were especially engaged in agriculture, and their contribution to the vital peanut crop was also appreciated by the administration. By the 1920s, the Murids were seen as model subjects, contributing vital links in the chain of government, agricultural wealth, and soldiers to the state. In return, they received government tolerance for their preaching and teaching and support for their pioneering agricultural communities.[19] However, the teachings of Amadu Bamba helped his followers to create an alternate psychological and spiritual space within the brotherhood and within Islam, a separate place that wasn't ruled by the French, and an independent identity that wasn't defined by them. In this way, outward cooperation concealed inward independence.

Such space could also be created through physical avoidance. Literally, inhabitants of the colonies found ways to create both secret and obvious societies and activities that allowed them to be

---

[19]David Robinson, "Beyond Resistance and Collaboration: Amadu Bamba and the Murids of Senegal," *Journal of Religion in Africa*, 21 (1991), 149–171.

away from the gaze of the colonizers. These might be geographic spaces such as private back rooms in the home or places of worship. They might also be social spaces such as secret or even public organizations such as religious brotherhoods and sisterhoods, intellectual groups such as reading clubs, initiation societies, or even trade unions. Many of these organizations were relatively new, or had been greatly altered, but they nevertheless were expressed as *traditional*. This creation of tradition was an important act of accommodation. While not obviously an act of resistance, inventing or referencing shared traditions allowed large groups of people to create and define their own identities. At the same time, it kept away the colonizers who defined themselves as being modern rather than traditional. Even when colonial anthropologists did try to enter these societies and activities, most often they did not have the cultural frame of reference to understand them.

Yet total avoidance was not usually possible. Populations in the colonies did have to interface with the colonizers, often on a day-to-day basis. Because of the realities of power, these colonizers often held the keys to economic wealth, position, or even survival. Thus, colonial subjects had to develop strategies to obtain what they wanted from authority figures, whether white *memsahibs* or powerful officials. One important tool for doing so was the petition.

Petitions were an accommodative and negotiated strategy that not only acknowledged the overwhelming power of the colonial system but also recognized the ability of colonial subjects to disrupt its functioning. Unlike rebellion, petitioning took place within an accepted framework. Often, the colonial administration or large colonial corporations created a system of appeals and official complaint forms in order to direct angry workers or subjects away from more damaging forms of resistance. Petitions were seen as a useful means of control because in order to submit them, individuals and groups not only had to accept the power of the officials that received them but also to mimic the language and forms of colonial authority. The petitioners could not appeal to

the government to judge their complaints on their own merit, but had to fit them in to the conceptual schemes of the colonizers. Petitioners in early twentieth-century Nigeria opposed to corporal punishment, for example, had to argue that whipping went against British notions of morality, civilization, and law. It can be argued, therefore, that by submitting petitions workers were accommodating or even cooperating with the system.

Yet petitions were also a form of resistance on several levels. Most obviously, petitions were a way for colonial subjects to bypass their immediate superiors and administrators and appeal to higher authorities. If they knew and understood colonial and imperial law, or company rules, they could use those rules against colonial agents who mistreated them. On example emerged following widespread strikes in 1929 among Eastern Indian Railway workers in India. The strike was large enough to threaten the functioning of the colonial state, and therefore the government stepped in and created a system that allowed workers to seek redress by submitting petitions. Because the strikers' main complaint had been harsh treatment by European railway officials, the petition process was designed specifically to hear complaints of abuse. As the historical anthropologist Laura Bear notes, these petitions were a form of accommodation, in which the railroad agreed to consider the appeal, and in return the employee agree to use respectful language and to play by the rules of the appeal process. The employees hoped by this process that higher authorities would find that their particular supervisor was unnecessarily abusive.

This process seems to indicate that Indian employees of the Eastern Indian Railway were implicitly accepting the authority of the company and the state even as they complained about individual supervisors. Yet the Eastern Railway petitions were forms of resistance on another level as well. While encoded as complaints against single agents, the petitions in fact indicted the whole company and system. When employees wrote that their supervisors took bribes, betrayed their honor, slept with prostitutes, and beat them, they were in fact attacking the notions of European racial superiority and of the benevolence of colonial "civilization." Sometimes this condemnation was hidden behind flattering language, but some petitioners explicitly threatened violence. One wrote, "To see justice done I am determined [*sic*] if not by EIR then by the Viceroy and *perhaps by myself*" and a group petition warned that "there will be a day of retribution."[20]

Generally, however, petitions were part of a process by which colonial subjects sought to reform rather than to overthrow the state. Between the implementation of the New Imperialism and the beginning of the Second World War, armed attempts to overthrow colonial rule were relatively infrequent and always unsuccessful. Thus, groups such as the Indian National Congress and African National Congress instead tried to work within the system to change laws in their favor. Often, these movements were made up largely of western-educated individuals, who believed that they had proven themselves able to act as civilized as Europeans or North Americans of European descent, and thus that they deserved the same rights. They petitioned for voting rights, the right to own land and serve on juries, and the kinds of legal protections available to citizens of the metropole. These were rights that in most previous colonial regimes had been available to those who culturally assimilated. By the early twentieth century, however, the racialization of colonialism had closed off this route to colonial subjects. Eventually, frustrated, these individuals would turn from reformers to resisters, and would form the core of the anti-colonial nationalist movements.

Conclusion

In the context of the development of the New Imperialism, certain ideas and practices came to be shared widely in the twentieth century.[21] Among the most important was the emergence of the systematized ranking and categorizing of populations according to race, technology, and cultural conventions that was assumed to be somewhat "scientific" and "modern" (although it had religious aspects as well). The first of two key arguments in this chapter rests on the emergence of this modern system of categorization, which came to be widely circulated across at least industrialized societies, even if the exact criteria and relative rankings employed varied. It formed a worldview that was so powerful and so all-encompassing that it made twentieth-century colonialism substantively more exclusive than the earlier, more assimilative forms of colonialism from which it had descended. Practiced in some way by all imperial cultures of this period, this process of categorization not only defined modern imperialism but also modern colonialism, since it imposed a shared experience across colonized populations as well.

Yet the actual *experience* of colonialism continued to differ by locality and even by individual. This is the second of the key arguments of this chapter: that despite the existence of the colonizers' model of the world, local environments and local populations vastly impacted colonial rule. The projects and policies developed by representatives of the metropole almost always proved unworkable at first because their authors paid little attention to these realities. In almost all cases, their plans had to be modified before they could become workable. Thus, imperial blueprints underwent complex and often long processes of development in the colonies. These processes provided a place for colonial subjects to manipulate, transform, and even subvert colonial rule. Often they did so by negotiating with and accommodating colonial rule, or by petitioning for reforms. Yet in reality, they could not do so with impunity, because they were

---

[20]Laura Bear, "An Economy of Suffering: Addressing the Violence of Discipline in Railway Workers' Petitions to the Agent of the East Indian Railway, 1930–1947," in *Discipline and the Other Body*, edited by Steven Pierce and Anupama Rao (Raleigh: Duke University Press, 2006), 243–272.

[21]See, for example, James M. Blaut, *The Colonizer's Model of the World: Geographical Diffusionism and Eurocentric History* (New York: Guilford Press), 1993. In the section heading in this chapter, we have moved the apostrophe.

constrained in many cases by the structures of colonialism that sought to segregate, classify, and control them.

Questions

1. Describe the "colonizers' model of the world" as a culture of imperialism in this period. In what way does it seem to have been similar to those of earlier periods? In what ways is it unique? How do you account for these similarities and differences?
2. The missionaries of the Dutch Missionary Society brought their own particular perspectives to their projects among the Karo people. Based on what you read in this chapter, what part of their project was based on the shared culture of imperialism among industrialized societies at this time, and what part was particular to them? Would you consider their project among the Karo women to be "colonialism," and why or why not?
3. Define negotiation, accommodation, and petition as strategies of colonial subjects. How are they related and different from each other? In what circumstances could each be useful? How does identifying these strategies help to enrich the discussion of "collaboration" and "resistance" in the late nineteenth and twentieth centuries that was begun in chapter 11?

CHAPTER 14

Empire: Imperial World Wars and the Slow March toward Decolonization

The period 1914–1965 represents the apex of High Imperialism. During this period, colonial penetration of Africa, Asia, and Oceania was completed. In almost every colony, the colonizers during this period intensified their control over economic, political, social, and cultural aspects of daily life. During this period, also, two great wars were fought on pretexts that were often unabashedly imperial. Yet during these same years, anti-colonial movements emerged around the world that were subsequently able to break down the great formal empires. These processes of construction and destruction seem contradictory, yet they occurred simultaneously, and cannot be separated from each other. In fact, although most colonies only achieved their political independence following the conclusion of the Second World War, the movements that won this fight had their roots in the early years of the century, at the very moment in which High Imperialism seemed undefeatable. It is for this reason that we look at both High Imperialism and decolonization in the same set of three contemporaneous chapters. In the previous chapter, we focused on the operation of colonialism during this period. In this chapter and the next, we will explore how this colonialism both intensified and began to break down at the same time. In this chapter, we will establish the global setting in which these movements emerged, while chapter 15 will focus mostly on the rise of nationalist and international anti-colonial movements led by colonial subjects.

Specifically, this chapter explores the First and Second World Wars as imperial and colonial wars. In it we make five principal arguments. First, we assert that the origins of the First World War were inseparable from the imperial ambitions of the principle antagonists. Second, once war was engaged, the imperial powers drew heavily on the populations and resources of their colonies during the war, with grave long-term implications. Third, the Second World War was also an imperial war with global as well as European causes. Fourth, the Second World War like the one that preceded it resulted in serious dislocations to the lives of colonial subjects and to the colonial system. Finally, the end of the Second World War created an environment that facilitated a great global shift away from large formal empires and toward a sort of informal imperialism in which Japan and the western European states would play a much smaller role than the massive powers of the United States, the Soviet Union, and (much later) China.

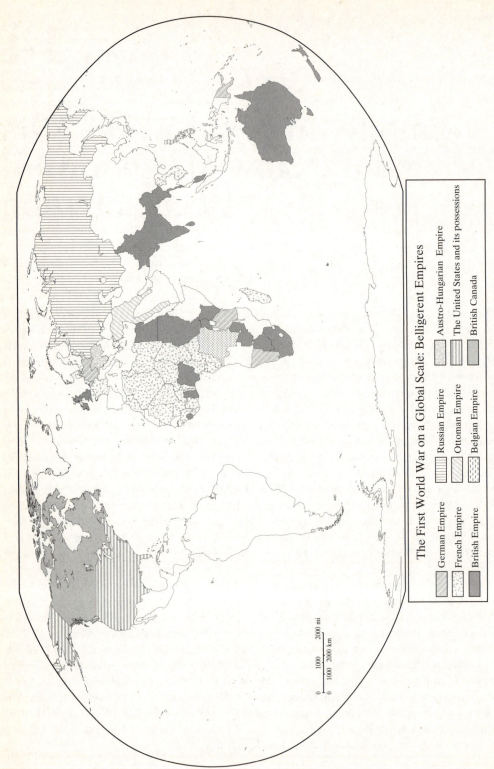

The First World War on a Global Scale: Belligerent Empires

Scholars tend to call this shift **decolonization**, and we all recognize its global origins. In reading this chapter, however, it is important to note that the two world wars and the events between (such as the influenza epidemic of 1919–1920 and the Great Depression) are not alone sufficient explanations for the breakdown of the great European and Japanese empires. Important elements of this story lie in the actions and attitudes of colonial subjects and in many local narratives that are discussed in the next chapter of this volume.

IMPERIAL AMBITIONS AND THE FIRST WORLD WAR

The First World War unmistakably marked the climax of the cultures of imperialism that characterized the New Imperialism. The nationalist and racialist sentiments that we explored in the previous three chapters had culminated in the early twentieth century in ideologies that embraced extreme racism, jingoism, chauvinism, and militarism. Politicians frequently manipulated this popular sentiment by blaming rival states for domestic crises such as economic depression and the plight of industrial workers. Such attempts to divert popular anger had helped to fuel the scramble for colonies, and they also increased friction across borders within Europe. The "scientific" basis for colonial racism—the notion of survival of the fittest—similarly promoted nationalist aggression among the populations of the great powers.

The First World War can also be seen as the apex of the global, competitive climate stirred up in the New Imperialism. In the years leading up to the First World War, nationalist and racialist sentiment within the major states of Europe fed this competition in ways that were unique to each state but were also broadly shared. In France, it was focused on anti-German sentiment and the yearning to reclaim the territories of Alsace and Lorraine, lost in the 1871 Franco-Prussian War. The Ottoman Turks hoped to reclaim their place in the Balkans, lost successively to Austro-Hungary and to independent and nationalist Balkan states. Germany, a relatively new state,

hoped to claim a "place in the sun" alongside older powers like Britain in order to become Europe's great "middle" power. The Habsburg emperors of Austro-Hungary strove to cling to power by replacing the ethnic sentiment of their empire's many different groups with imperial loyalty. Italy, also a new state, aimed to build nationalism by claiming the mantle of the Roman Empire. Finally, Russia's czars hoped to rebuild national pride lost in their defeat to Japan in 1905, and to claim access to the Mediterranean through the Ottoman-controlled Straits of Dardanelles. In pursuit of these imperial and national objectives, the antagonists slowly coalesced in the late nineteenth century into two alliances. The first was the Austro-Hungarian and German Triple Alliance, with Italy as a junior partner, in 1882. Although Italy switched sides in 1914, the alliance between Austro-Hungary and Germany established them as the Central Powers of the First World War, so termed because of their location at the center of Europe. This alliance directly threatened France and Russia, who signed the Franco-Russian Entente in 1894, thus forming a rival coalition within Europe.

But the First World War was destined to be a global imperial war rather than a strictly European one. As British Prime Minister Lloyd George himself concluded quite early in the war, "it is not one continent that is engaged—every continent is affected."[1] The participation of the continent-spanning land empires of Russia and the Ottomans guaranteed this, as did the later entry of Japan and the United States. Furthermore, the economies of all of the antagonists relied more heavily than ever before on strategic raw materials and funds from around the world.

Perhaps most significant in globalizing the conflict, however, was the position of the British Empire. Still acknowledged in 1900 as the greatest power in the world, Great Britain remained aloof from the two alliances in "splendid isolation" as long as it could. France, Germany, and Russia competed to win Britain over to their

---

[1] Richard Rathbone, "World War I and Africa: Introduction," *Journal of African History*, 19 (1978), 4.

side—to shift the balance of power in their favor—but as an island nation with no territorial aims in Europe, Britain was vulnerable and had ambitions only in its connection to its empire in Africa, Asia, and the Americas. Britain's economy was especially reliant on its commerce with India, the crown jewel of colonies. Admittedly, British military planners at times feared a German or French invasion, but as history has shown such an enterprise was massively difficult to undertake. Thus short of outright warfare and a military disaster, the only way in which the two alliances could blackmail, threaten, or cajole Britain into joining them was by playing the imperial card.

It was these imperial considerations that shaped much of the diplomatic and military interplay of the Great Powers in the last stages of colonial acquisition in the early twentieth century. We have seen in chapter 10, for example, how Germany, Italy, and France threatened Britain's vital Suez Canal in Egypt by racing to annex colonies along the upper Nile. Germany also tried to create a crisis by threatening to create a naval base in Morocco that could threaten British control over the western Mediterranean and thus the sea route to India. Their main attempt at this was the famous Agadir crisis of 1911—in which a German gunboat intervened in a civil conflict in Morocco and German diplomats negotiated to force France to make concessions to her in return for full control over the country. This attempt at blackmail ultimately backfired and drove Britain, Russia, and France closer to each other. The Entente powers capitalized on this trend by making concessions to Britain in both North Africa and Asia. France acknowledged British rule in Egypt, and in 1907 Russia settled their rivalries with Britain in Persia, Afghanistan, and Tibet. These relationships were strengthened by Germany's decision to increase the size of their ocean-going navy and thus raise both the threat to British imperial shipping and the possibility of a future invasion of the British Isles. Thus in 1907, Britain joined the Franco-Russian coalition, transforming it into the Triple Entente. Eventually, the Dutch, Italians, and Belgians were

also driven into joining the Entente by German war decisions and their own calculations.

Of the great empires, the Ottomans were the last to choose sides in the war. In part this had to do with the rise to power of the Young Turks (CUP), a broad reformist party that espoused Turkish nationalism and sought to rebuild the empire while modernizing it. The CUP hoped to restore to the empire territory that had been lost in the Balkans and Egypt as well as to Russia and Persia in Central Asia. They also pledged to eliminate the *capitulations*, concessions won by the European empires that allowed them to escape taxes, to be free of prosecution by Ottoman courts, and to generally exploit the Ottoman economy. They were also plagued by the question of *millets* (see chapter 2), or semi-autonomous groups of non-Muslim subjects.[2] In the event of war, while most of the Arab population and other Muslims could be relied upon to remain largely loyal, at least initially, the non-Muslim populations were likely to be more divided. This was especially true because the capitulations (see chapter 8) had established foreign powers as the protectors of these groups. The French had established themselves as patrons of the Ottoman Empire's Catholics and Maronite Christians, the Russians had linked themselves to the Orthodox Christian community, and the British had established ties with Protestants and later Jews.

Initially, the CUP had seen Britain as their logical ally, and had eschewed links with the Triple Alliance since Austro-Hungary was their greatest enemy in the Balkans. However, their failure to win British support during the Balkan War of 1912–1913 helped push them toward Germany, with whom they eventually signed an alliance just as the war began. For the CUP, the First World War represented an opportunity to abolish the capitulations, which they did on September 9, 1915, and to reclaim lost territory from Russia.[3]

---

[2] Feroz Ahmad, "The Late Ottoman Empire," in *The Great Powers and the End of the Ottoman Empire*, edited by Marian Kent (London: George Allen & Unwin, 1984), 5–30.
[3] Ibid., 13–16, 18.

But if the First World War was an opportunity for the new Ottoman leadership, it was also a great threat to the empire. Britain, France, and Russia all had designs on Ottoman territory, and individually and collectively carried out their campaigns against the Ottomans in pursuit of new colonies and influence in the region. Soon after the Ottoman Empire entered the war, the Entente powers began to squabble over the territory each would claim in the event of its defeat. Russia's demands were for Constantinople and the Dardanelle Straits, which would give their navy access to the Mediterranean. Czar Nicholas II also hoped to claim new regions of Central Asia. Russia's French allies were largely still opposed to breaking up the Ottoman Empire, although influential colonial lobbies such as the Comité de l' Asie Française and the Lyon and Marseilles Chamber of Commerce proposed annexing the Ottoman provinces of Cilicia and Syria, which had large Maronite and Catholic populations.[4] Britain, meanwhile, responded with a proposal that would give the Russians what they wanted in return for major territorial concessions in Central Asia, which would enlarge Britain's Indian holdings. Much of this British policy was made by one of the few members of government who had traveled substantially in the Middle East, Sir Mark Sykes. Sykes was instrumental in trying to provoke an anti-Ottoman uprising among the Arab population, and also in negotiating an agreement with his French counterpart François Georges Picot. The secret accord, which came to be known as the Sykes-Picot Agreement, spelled out British and French ambitions in the region. By its terms, France obtained British agreement to conquer and rule Lebanon and to exert "influence" over Syria, while Britain obtained French acceptance of their claim to the provinces of Basra and Baghdad. The states in between were to be ruled by Arab chieftains, each of whom would fall within a British and French sphere of influence.[5]

Britain's empire-building ambition in the Middle East unfolded in 1916 and 1917. The fall of the czar's government in 1917 had released them from having to consider Russian claims in the region. In the same year, David Lloyd George became prime minister of Great Britain. Lloyd George possessed a sense of a Christian mission to retake the Holy Lands that went back as far as the crusaders. This conviction made him an object of lobbying by Zionists—mostly European Jewish groups—who for several decades had been arguing for the creation of a Jewish state in the Ottoman province of Palestine. Leading Zionists managed to convince Lloyd George that returning the Jewish population of Europe to Palestine was a holy as well as a politically astute act. Thus in November 1917, his government issued the Balfour Declaration, which acknowledged the need for a Jewish homeland (but not necessarily a Jewish state) in Palestine. In return, Jewish leaders agreed to the establishment of British "protection" over the region. Ironically, at the same time British generals were sponsoring an Arab revolt in the region by promising them British support for an Arab homeland that included Palestine. On this basis, both Arab and Jewish auxiliaries supported the British army's invasion of Ottoman Mesopotamia in December 1916. By the following March, it was in Baghdad. In September 1917, another army invaded Palestine and drove deep into Syria. In possession of much of the territory it claimed at war's end, Britain was able to largely implement the territorial dismemberment of the Ottoman Empire on its own terms, although France was able to insist on the spoils guaranteed to them by the Sykes-Picot Agreement.

If Britain was the big winner in the Mediterranean, it was Japan that profited from the war by expanding its empire in East Asia. Entering the war opportunistically on the side of the Triple Entente, Japan first invaded Germany's Pacific Island colonies and then the German concession in China's Shantung province. Even though China had entered the war on the side of the Entente as well, the Chinese received no benefits in the 1919 Peace Treaty signed at the end of the war. Instead,

[4] L. Bruce Fulton, "France and the End of the Ottoman Empire," in Kent, *The Great Powers*, 140–171.
[5] David Fromkin, *A Peace to End All Peace: The Fall of the Ottoman Empire and the Creation of the Modern Middle East* (New York: Owl, 1989), 188–199.

Japan was allowed to keep the Shantung territory, which it began to expand to China's cost soon after war's end. In disgust, the Chinese delegation refused to sign the Peace Treaty.[6]

In Africa, meanwhile, Germany's colonies were conquered in a series of campaigns launched by French, British, and Belgian forces largely made up of settlers and colonial subjects. Cut off from home by the British navy, German commanders fought with local troops as well. Togoland and Cameroon were rapidly captured by combined British and French colonial forces, while South African columns invaded German South-West Africa in 1915, although only after putting down a rebellion among Afrikaners sympathetic to the German cause. In German East Africa, meanwhile, a multi-national force including large South African and Indian contingents campaigned against German forces that held out until the end of the war.

At war's end, the victorious allies had to decide how to dispose of the territory of their vanquished opponents. Both the original members of the Triple Entente and later their U.S. allies had cast their struggle as being against Austro-Hungarian, Ottoman, and German despotism and in support of self-determination for its victims—like Serbia and Belgium. At the Peace Treaty negotiations in Paris and Versailles in 1919, this rhetoric was repeated. Such language gave hope to anti-colonial activists, including delegates meeting at the First Pan-African Congress in Paris. They placed much of their hope in U.S. President Woodrow Wilson, who seemed genuinely dedicated to a progressive and internationalist agenda and who opposed the annexation of the colonies of the defeated powers.

Wilson was in fact committed to what he saw as a humanitarian and internationalist agenda. Indeed, he approached the Paris and Versailles peace conferences with the hope of creating a new and democratic world order based on "capitalist economic development, free trade, and the rule of law."[7] Wilson believed that the Europeans and the Americans should act toward Africans, Latin Americans, and Asians as stern but fair fathers raising unruly children, rather than as rulers. While still espousing the paternalistic racism of his day, he largely saw formal colonialism as too despotic to be valuable, and opposed the transfer of the territories of the vanquished to the empires of the victors. This stance placed him in opposition to many of his counterparts at the conference, however. The French delegates hoped to have their country's control of the former Ottoman territory of Syria and of German colonies in Africa ratified, and Japan laid its claim on the table to Kiaochow in Shantung Province and several Pacific Islands. Meanwhile, the various British dominions staked their claims as well: South Africa to German South-West Africa, New Zealand to German Samoa, and Australia to New Guinea. Britain itself claimed large swathes of the Middle East and part of Cameroon and German East Africa. But Wilson, who wielded a great deal of clout, opposed all of these territorial claims.

The job of overcoming Wilson's objections fell to one of the great imperialists of the age, South African Prime Minister Jan Smuts. An Afrikaner who had once fought the British in the Anglo-Boer War a decade and a half earlier, Smuts was a leading supporter of the British Empire's war efforts in 1914–1918. He believed strongly in the racial destiny of white South Africans to control the southern third of the African continent. A key step in this process was the acquisition of South-West Africa with its German settler population, whom he felt would add to the strength of South Africa.[8] Smuts was also aware that public opinion in South Africa was heavily in favor of annexing the territory, and that failing to do so would endanger his political standing. Thus, Smuts was keenly in favor of the transfer of German colonies. However, he was close to Wilson on other issues—among

[6]C.P. Fitzgerald, *The Birth of Communist China* (Baltimore: Penguin, 1964), 54.

[7]Mary A. Renda, *Taking Haiti: Military Occupation and the Culture of U.S. Imperialism 1915–1914* (Chapel Hill: University of North Carolina Press, 2001), 113.

[8]Trevor Getz, "Smuts and the Politics of Colonial Expansion: South African Strategy in Regard to South-West Africa [Namibia] and the League of Nations Mandate: c.1914–1924," unpublished MA Thesis, University of Cape Town, 1997, 128–142.

them opposition to demanding reparations from Germany and the project for a League of Nations—and thus won the president's trust. In late 1918, he wrote an important treatise, entitled *The League of Nations: A Practical Suggestion*, that Wilson read avidly.[9] Wilson's subsequent proposals for the League followed many of his suggestions, including a proposal that the states such as France and British dominions such as South Africa administer the territories taken from the defeated powers not as colonies but as **mandates**.[10] In other words, the League would jointly assume sovereignty over these territories, and allow the states and dominions to run them only so long as they improved and "civilized" them.

The idea of mandates faced opposition initially from the delegates of Japan, France, and British Empire, who were concerned that they would not be able to sufficiently exercise authority over their conquests under these conditions. Smuts broke the deadlock by proposing language that differed from Wilson's in two ways. First, it gave sovereignty over the mandates not to the new League of Nations as a body, but rather to the victorious powers. This tiny difference in language rendered the League powerless to manage the mandatory system, especially after the United States failed to join. Second, Smuts' revisions divided the conquered territories into three classes of mandates. "A" mandates (largely in the Middle East) were in many ways supposed to be on track to self-rule, but "B" and "C" mandates (largely in Africa and the Pacific) were considered more "primitive," and thus could be ruled with relative impunity. In this decision, not only technological but also racial considerations played a role. The only restrictions for "C" mandates were that the mandatory power (like South Africa in South-West Africa or Japan in the South Pacific) was supposed to eliminate slavery and guard against arms and liquor entering the

territories. Wilson accepted this compromise, which went into effect on April 28, 1919. Its ratification meant that the race line and imperial ambitions had won over liberal ideals, and the British, Japanese, and French empires were consequently free to treat many of their new acquisitions as de facto colonies.

As this narrative shows, the origins and unfolding of the First World War were both highly influenced by both cultures of imperialism and economic and political concerns of the imperial powers. While it is also important to consider other topics like local rivalry within Europe and the effects of industry upon war planning, the war cannot be understood without consideration of empire and imperialism as contributing factors.

THE COLONIAL EXPERIENCE AND THE FIRST WORLD WAR

If the First World War was fought with imperial ambitions firmly in mind, it was also partly paid for by imperial contributions of gold, blood, and raw materials. Among the most important of these were strategic resources: metals for weapons production, saltpeter to make gunpowder, energy sources such as coal and petroleum, and even strategic foodstuffs. Arguably, it was Britain's ability to blockade the Central Powers from access to resources and markets outside of Europe, and the conversant failure of Germany's U-boats to isolate Britain and France from their empires, that finally led to the economic collapse of the German home front, effectively ending the war.[11]

Of similar significance were the empires' manpower contributions, especially in the case of the French and British imperial war efforts. The colonies and dominions of the British Empire made the largest contribution, approximately 2.5 million men. Of these India was far and away the largest contributor. Even at the beginning of the war, two Indian divisions were already in Europe, and by late 1914 contingents were serving in

---

[9] J.C. Smuts, *The League of Nations: A Practical Suggestion* (London: Hodder and Stoughton, 1919).

[10] Thomas J. Knock, *To End All Wars: Woodrow Wilson and the Quest for a New World Order* (Princeton, NJ: Princeton University Press, 1992), 202–213.

[11] See, for example, John Keegan, *The First World War* (New York: Vintage, 2000), 265–266, 318.

East Africa, Egypt, and Mesopotamia as well. Approximately 1.2 million Indian troops eventually served, and the colonial Indian government paid to supply all of the troops in Palestine and Mesopotamia, a task that employed millions more Indian subjects of the empire.[12] The dominions also made massive contributions of up to 20% of the adult male white population. This number included 464,000 Canadians and Newfoundlanders, 332,000 Australians, 112,000 New Zealanders, and 76,000 South Africans serving overseas. Of Rhodesia's 30,000 white settlers, 6,800 served. So too did thousands of Africans from Rhodesia. Nigeria contributed 17,000 soldiers and 37,000 carriers for the campaign in neighboring Cameroons. More than 15,000 West Indians served in Mesopotamia, Africa, and Europe. It is estimated that the forces raised in the colonies lost over 205,000 dead during the war.

The French, facing a manpower deficit vis-à-vis Germany on the Western Front, also relied heavily on colonial troops. More than 475,000 colonial troops served on that front alone. Approximately 335,000 were African, including 120,000 from West Africa who formed the divisions of the *tirailleurs sénégalais* and an equal number of Algerians. Moroccan troops were mainly retained in their homeland, which had not yet been completely pacified. Africa also provided 135,000 wartime workers for industry in France itself.[13] In Asia, the French mobilized almost 50,000 Indochinese troops, who served mainly in the eastern theaters. Belgium and Germany also mobilized African troops, although they served mainly in the colonies. General Paul Emil von Lettow-Vorbeck defended German East Africa throughout the war with 11,000 African *askaris* (soldiers) against a British-led force made up of more than 50,000 African, Indian, and European troops.

Colonial recruitment was a necessity for the British and French empires, but both the method of recruitment and the soldiers' experiences were defined by the realities of colonial categorization. As always, the most important category was race. Colonial contingents usually included both European settler (white) enlistees on the one hand and non-white or mixed-heritage enlistees on the other. This division corresponded pretty well to the division between citizens and subjects, although in French West Africa and a few other regions small numbers of assimilated Africans had been granted citizenship. European settlers, whose identity as citizens of the metropole had been magnified by their settlement in the colonies, often embraced the national cause eagerly. This was true, for example, in Australia and New Zealand, whose settler populations saw themselves as Britons strengthened by their time on the frontier.[14]

In general, however, pro-empire sentiment was weaker among colonial subjects. In Jamaica, for example, the black leadership was divided as to whether service would prove that Jamaicans were ready for self-rule or would be a futile sacrifice.[15] In South Africa, many African leaders saw military service as a way to forward Africans' claims to citizenship.[16] In neighboring Rhodesia as well, many Africans and especially appointed chiefs supported the war effort and assisted in recruitment. But in both colonies, there was a great deal of debate about the war. In some districts, for example, Africans speculated that if the Germans won, they would eliminate hated cattle-dipping regulations and restrictive pass laws.[17] There were even anti-colonial rebellions during the war, mostly in protest at recruitment efforts. Some of these efforts became coercive, with local leaders required to provide a certain number of troops and kidnapping or forced enlistment used

---

[12] Keith Jeffrey, " 'An English Barrack in the Oriental Seas'? India in the Aftermath of the First World War," *Modern Asian Studies*, 15 (1981), 369–386.

[13] C.M. Andrew and A.S. Kanya-Forstner, "France, Africa and the First World War," *Journal of African History*, 19 (1978), 14.

[14] Christopher Pugsley, *The Anzac Experience: New Zealand, Australia and Empire in the First World War* (Auckland: Reed Publishing, 2004), 300–313.

[15] Glenford Howe, *Race, War and Nationalism: A Social History of West Indians in the First World War* (Oxford: James Currey, 2002), 20–30.

[16] Bill Nasson, "War Opinion in South Africa, 1914," *Journal of Imperial and Commonwealth Studies*, 223 (1995), 257.

[17] Timothy Stapleton, *No Insignificant Part: The Rhodesia Native Regiment and the East Africa Campaign of the First World War* (Waterloo: Wilfrid Laurier, 2006), 25–29.

as a tool. These policies occasionally provoked uprisings such as those in French West Africa and among the Kwale Ibo of Nigeria.

Initially, many settlers and colonial officials in the European overseas empires also opposed the recruitment of colonial subjects and other non-citizens on the basis that they would make inferior troops, and also due to fear that recruitment would disrupt colonial economies, cause rebellion, or just empower Africans, Asians, and Oceanians by providing them with military training. As the need for huge numbers of conscripts to began to overcome these fears, colonial administrators depended heavily on their already-developed racialized notions as to which ethnic and identity groups were "martial" or "warriors" (see chapter 12). In the Caribbean, for example, Hondurans, Jamaican Maroons, and Caribs were targeted for recruitment because their ability to carry out long anti-colonial campaigns convinced the British that they were natural warriors. In Rhodesia, Ndebele men were seen as being more warlike than those of the MaShona. In North Africa, a French army saying developed that "the Algerian is a man, the Tunisian a woman, and the Moroccan a warrior." As a result of this perspective, few Tunisians were recruited, while Moroccans were in high demand.[18] In India, 40% of recruits to the British Indian army came from the Punjab, whose Sikhs and Muslims were considered by the British to be the most martial Indian groups.

Ironically, once in Europe, even white colonial settlers often adopted the dress of these groups in an attempt to capture their "primitive" military spirit. South African troops dressed as Zulus before going into combat, and New Zealanders as Maoris. Even U.S. soldiers often put on stylized Native American war paint.

The methods by which these colonial troops were recruited were often complex. In the British Caribbean islands of Barbados and Jamaica, methods included newspaper propaganda, preaching in churches that the war was a struggle against Satan, posters advertising the economic and moral

advantages of service, and offers of release for prisoners. Recruiters also targeted women for their potential to use shame to convince men to fight. Propaganda encouraged young women and old grannies alike to turn their backs on shirkers and embrace enlistees.[19] In much of Africa and South-East Asia, the onus of recruitment was put on allied chiefly officeholders and other elites, who were paid bounties or coerced into providing recruits from their communities. In some cases, recruitment methods almost resembled the slave raids of previous generations, in which men were snatched off the street to become soldiers, sailors, and carriers.[20] Coercion often wasn't enough, however, and both the French and British empires made promises as well. Both held out the prospect of good pay and of pensions following the war, but only France pledged, in 1915, to allow veterans the rights to eventual citizenship. This law was opposed by settlers but embraced by African leaders like the Senegalese politician Blaise Diagne, who henceforth supported French recruiting drives.

Once overseas, colonial troops were often treated quite badly. This wasn't merely a matter of race—even Anzacs (settler-soldiers from Australia or New Zealand) were subject to greater discipline and placed in dangerous situations more frequently than British metropolitan regiments. However, conditions were often exacerbated by racism. Military justice was heavily weighted against black servicemen in Europe, who suffered very high levels of imprisonment and execution. Workers in France, most of whom were North African, were segregated from the local population by a policy called **encadrement**, ostensibly to protect them but really to stop them from "corrupting" the local population (and especially women).[21] But it is hard to generalize the experience of colonial soldiers in Europe. For

---

[18] Andrew and Kanya-Forstner, "France, Africa and the First World War," 14.

[19] Howe, *Race, War, and Nationalism*, 43–53.

[20] Joe Lunn, *Memoirs of the Maelstrom: A Senegalese Oral History of the First World War* (Portsmouth: Heinemann, 1999), 39–43.

[21] Tyler Stovall, "Colour-Blind France? Colonial Workers during the First World War," *Race and Class,* 35 (1993), 35–55.

example, while some regiments were pressed into high casualty situations, other officers eschewed non-white troops and turned the African and Asian outfits on their front into laborers, effectively sparing them the high casualty rates of metropolitan units.

What is clear, however, is that after the war, the promised benefits of service did not appear. Non-white soldiers were often not paid their promised pensions or compensated for wounds. The pathway to citizenship established for African soldiers in the French army never really materialized—fewer than 300 Algerians gained French citizenship between 1918 and 1923, and some had not been soldiers. In French West Africa, meanwhile, the colonial administration after the war managed not only to halt the extension of citizenship, but also to restrict the rights of "assimilated" Africans in the 1920s. Meanwhile, colonial officials struggled to deal with the demands of veterans who were potentially still important allies, but who also became increasingly disgruntled as they failed to receive veterans' services.[22] In Nigeria, returning veterans who received neither back pay nor pensions challenged the power of the chiefs who had helped to recruit and conscript them.[23]

The link between First World War veterans and the growth of anti-colonialism should not be exaggerated. Arguably, African, Caribbean, and Asian soldiers were empowered by their experiences to claim new rights. Their victories against European soldiers led them to question the myth of white superiority. Their service in regional or cross-colonial regiments helped to break down the ethnic divisions instilled by colonialism. Equally, as veterans they were deeply affected by

their exclusion from pensions and other benefits. Nevertheless, in many cases ex-soldiers remained among the most loyal colonial subjects, and in general they did not return to organize widespread anti-colonial activities.

Yet the experiences and suffering of colonial soldiers and conscripted laborers must be seen in the wider context of the misery that the war brought to the wider colonial setting. In regions where the war was fought, destruction and chaos brought the colonial system home even to populations that had previously been largely untouched. This was true, for example, in East Africa, where for more than three years armies tore across the countryside, largely subsisting on food appropriated from local communities. Even where outright conflict was absent, the war was devastating to local economies. Under colonialism, economic policy had specifically been oriented toward extracting raw materials for factories in the metropole to turn into finished goods, which were in turn sold back to consumers in the colonies. With the disruptions of submarine warfare and blockade, colonies were suddenly cut off from both the factories they supplied and the supplies they needed. In West Africa, shortages of kerosene, cloth, matches, and metal goods were exceeded only by food shortages that led to major price hikes.[24] This was especially a hardship for women in urban areas whose husbands had been recruited for the war and who had to survive on their own resources. In the German colonies, conditions were often even worse.

Nor did conditions radically improve at war's end. Immediately following the armistice, a global influenza pandemic broke out. Its effects were horrendous in many colonies. In some parts of India, British army records suggest that 21.9% of Indian troops died. In the Fiji colony, up to 14% of the entire population may have been wiped out.[25] In British West Africa, rates

[22] See Andrew and Kanya-Forstner, "France, Africa and the First World War," 16; Alice Conklin, *A Mission to Civilize: The Republican Idea of Empire in France and West Africa, 1895–1930* (Stanford: Stanford University Press, 1997), 151–173; and Gregory Mann, *Native Sons: West African Veterans and France in the Twentieth Century* (Durham, NC: Duke University Press, 2006), 105–107.

[23] James K. Matthews, "World War I and the Rise of African Nationalism: Nigerian Veterans as Catalysts of Change," *Journal of Modern African Studies*, 20 (1982), 502.

[24] Rathbone, "World War I and Africa," 7–8.

[25] Stacey L. Knobler, Alison Mack, Adel Mahmoud, and Stanley M. Lemons, eds., *The Threat of Pandemic Influenza: Are We Ready?* (Washington, DC: The National Academies Press, 2005), 61.

may have risen as high as 5%. Following on its heels were a series of rinderpest epidemics that killed cattle around the world as well. Economic improvements were also slow in the colonies. The French, British, and Belgian governments attempted to rebuild their own infrastructure by exacerbating their exploitation of the colonies. Ironically, the French called this process the *mise en valeur*, or "adding value," although little benefit accrued to colonial populations. The final straw was the Great Depression that began in 1929, further undermining global economies and local livelihoods in colonies around the world.

THE ARMENIAN GENOCIDE AS A COLONIAL EVENT

One of the most dramatic episodes of the First World War was the relocation and genocide of the Armenian population of the Ottoman Empire. This process had its roots in the systems of millets and capitulations that made the Armenians and some other non-Muslim inhabitants of the empire into a differentiated, subjugated population. Often persecuted and at times rebellious under the late Ottoman Sultans, the Armenian population found itself equally at odds with the CUP on the eve of the war. Following the entry of the Ottomans into the war, the CUP administration abolished the capitulations that tied the Armenians to Russian protection and, in early 1915, began to disarm Armenian soldiers serving in the army and later to execute many of them. Portraying the Armenians as potential traitors, the Ottoman government then began to deport them from the border with Russia. The caravans of Armenian civilians were forced to travel across the country in great thirst and hunger, often attacked by local civilians and Ottoman troops, and concentrated for eventual deportation. Although the exact facts are still in dispute, it seems likely that at least some of the senior government ministers were involved in both the deportation and the attacks, and that as many as 1.5 million Armenian subjects of the Ottoman Empire died.

There are numerous interpretations of the origins and causes of the Armenian genocide.[26] However, it can be argued at least in part that it was one episode in a long history of modern colonial violence stretching through brutal events like the massacre of the Herero in German South-West Africa (chapter 12) and the European Holocaust (later in this chapter). The Armenians, after all, had a distinct status in the Ottoman Empire as *dhimmi* (non-believers but "people-of-the-book") and hence subjects rather than citizens of the state. Ottoman treatment of the Armenians was frequently quite benign, but they were nevertheless seen as a colonial "other" and subject to special conditions such as irregular taxes. They also enjoyed fewer rights than Muslims, such as their exclusion from serving as witnesses in Islamic courts.[27] It also seems that the Armenians experienced a type of racial stereotyping that was not entirely dissimilar to that of subjugated populations in other empires. Of course, it could be argued that at least until 1908 the Armenians still enjoyed greater rights and protections than colonial subjects of other empires. For example, in the early twentieth century they were allowed to elect legislators to represent them. Yet this changed with the rise of Turkish nationalism and the CUP, which was accompanied by a distinction between Turkish citizens and non-Turkish (including other Muslim) subjects of the empire.[28] The combination of this ideology, the inferior status of the Armenians, and the stresses of the First World War were the fertile ground from which the genocide sprang.

[26] Donald Bloxham, "The Armenian Genocide of 1915–1916: Cumulative Radicalization and the Development of a Destruction Policy," *Past and Present*, 181 (2003), 141–192; Gwynne Dyer, "Turkish 'Falsifiers' and Armenian 'Deceivers': Historiography and the Armenian Massacres," *Middle Eastern Studies*, 12 (1976), 99–107; and Stephan Astourian, "The Armenian Genocide: An Interpretation," *History Teacher*, 23 (1990), 111–160.
[27] Bat Ye'or, *The Dhimmi: Jews and Christians Under Islam* (Madison, WI: Farleigh Dickinson University Press, 1985), 51–80.
[28] David Kushner, *The Rise of Turkish Nationalism: 1876–1908* (London: Frank Cass, 1977).

IMPERIAL AMBITIONS AND THE SECOND WORLD WAR

The Great Depression also helped to create the conditions for the rise of the totalitarian empires of Fascist Italy, Nazi Germany, and to a degree imperial Japan. Together, these states formed the so-called Axis powers who initiated the Second World War. In a story similar to that of the depression of the 1870s, the depression that began in 1929 was blamed by these governments on internal minorities and global competitors, thus diverting popular anger away from the government. The solution proposed by each state was intensely imperialist, and involved occupying and dominating neighboring or overseas markets and territory. Each government sold their solution as the natural outcome of racial struggle and as the right of a superior people. Admittedly, the scientific racism that they embraced was not laden with the sense of a "civilizing" mission espoused by the liberal empires of an earlier generation, but it nevertheless had its roots in a shared racialized worldview. Seen in this way, the ideologies of the governing parties in the three Axis powers were highly developed cultures of imperialism not unrelated to those that had built the empires of the states they were soon to be fighting against—especially Britain, France, and the United States. As a result, one possible view of the Holocaust is as the culmination of decades of imperial ideology and colonial violence.

All three of the Axis powers had come as relatively late players to great power imperialism. Italy and Germany were only formed as modern states in the early 1870s, while the Japanese state had been comparatively insular before the Meiji Restoration of the 1860s. To a large degree, therefore, the pro-imperial sentiment in all three states centered around the need to "catch up" with the larger empires of France, Britain, and to a lesser degree Russia and the United States. The governments of all three states also established their legitimacy through recreating or inventing an imperial past, especially as militarists and fascists came to dominate them in the 1920s. For the Fascist party in Italy, this meant invoking the glory of the Roman Empire. Japanese propaganda

focused on the divinity of the emperor. The rhetoric of the National Socialist (Nazi) party of Germany not only recalled the struggles of the Teutonic knights against Asiatics, but also invented the idea of an Aryan racial superiority that linked them even to the supposed "white" conquerors of India 3.5 millennia earlier.

The totalitarian ideology of all three states promoted a worldview of competition between states and races that, while radical, was an adaptation of the racialism and nationalism that had characterized the New Imperialism in "liberal" states such as France and Britain. Just as the pro-empire social Darwinists in these countries had applied Darwin's concept of the survival of the fittest to human nations (**social Darwinism**), so the fascists argued that in order to compete societies must practice total obedience to the state. They believed that successful "nations" must increase in population, and that this process required the occupation of **lebensraum** (living room) and the acquisition of resources from less-competitive peoples. Such ideas, with variation, can be found in Italian Fascist leader Benito Mussolini's "Definition of Fascism" (1923), in German Nazi party leader Adolf Hitler's autobiography *Mein Kampf* (1925), and the Japanese government publication "The Way of Subjects" (1943).[29]

In the 1920s, these ideologies drove Italy, Germany, and Japan to renewed attempts at colonial acquisition; a mini-scramble for colonies. Italy already possessed a small empire in Libya and coastal East Africa, and was able to concentrate on two hinterlands: the weaker Balkan states such as Albania just across the Adriatic Sea and the still-independent African state of Abyssinia (Ethiopia) that had defeated Italian armies several decades earlier. Because Italy had been on the winning side in the First World War, its initial

---

[29] Benito Mussolini, "Definition of Fascism," in *The Social and Political Doctrines of Contemporary Europe*, edited and translated by Michael Oakenshott (Cambridge: Cambridge University Press, 1939), 168–179; Adolf Hitler, *Mein Kampf* (Germany: Secker and Warburg, 1925); and "The Way of Subjects," in *Tokyo Record*, translated by Otto D. Tolischus (New York: Reynal and Hitchcock, 1943), 405–427.

expansion in this period went relatively unchallenged. In 1926, Italy declared Albania a protectorate. In 1935, Mussolini successfully invaded Abyssinia, following which he declared Italian King Victor Emmanuel II an emperor.[30] With the start of the European front of the Second World War in 1939, Mussolini was able to pursue a greater empire in the Balkans and in the British North African colonies.

Like the Italian Empire, Japanese territorial acquisitions in the era between the two world wars built on an existing empire that by 1918 included Formosa, Korea, the Liaodong and Shantung provinces in China, as well as the former German colonies of the Mariana, Caroline, and Marshall Islands and German New Guinea. Even before the formerly German territories could be fully integrated into the empire, however, pro-expansionist groups began to call for further annexations. There were several reasons for this. Some were economic—not only were Japanese corporations worried about the lack of raw materials (especially minerals and petroleum) held by the empire, but they also expressed concern about the development of industries in China and other Asian states that could compete with Japanese industry.[31] Moreover, some politicians and military men saw parts of China such as Manchuria as a fitting place for settlement of the overcrowded population of the home islands.[32] Both domestic politics and foreign policy concerns also promoted expansionism. The increasingly powerful army generals saw empire-building both as a way to increase Japan's national prestige globally and to boost their own domestic political influence. Their culminating moment was the 1931 Japanese invasion of the Chinese province of Manchuria, which arguably was the moment at

which the Second World War really began. Having occupied Manchuria, the Japanese renewed their invasion of China in 1937, capturing much of its northern and central provinces. Following the eruption of general warfare in Europe, Japan also occupied many of the former European and U.S. colonies in South-East Asia, including Burma, the Netherlands East Indies (Indonesia), the Philippines, Malaya, and French Indochina.

Both the Japanese and Italian empires were largely built in familiar spheres of colonialism— Africa, East and South-East Asia, and to a lesser degree the Balkans. Germany, however, was poorly positioned to exploit these regions, sandwiched as it was between France, Italy, Denmark, Poland, and Czechoslovakia. Also, while Japan and Italy had been on the winning side in the First World War and therefore retained their earliest colonies, Germany had lost its overseas empire in 1918. To a certain extent therefore, Adolf Hitler's Nazi party was initially forced to find domestic enemies against whom to direct the people's anger—Germany's Jews, Gypsies, and other ethnic minorities. From the beginning of his rise to power, however, Hitler saw Germany's logical zone of expansion in the territories of the East. Mobilizing language that would have seemed familiar to British and French imperialists, he wrote in 1928 that "When a people has too restricted a living space . . . that leads to a certain crisis. . . . Poverty, social sickness, finally bodily sickness."[33] In his autobiography and elsewhere, he wrote and spoke of eastern Europe including Poland and Soviet Byelorussia as Germany's natural lebensraum. He made no secret of the fact that he planned to expel the populations of these territories and replace them with German farmers in the form of a settler empire to be known as Greater Germany.

THE COLONIAL EXPERIENCE AND THE SECOND WORLD WAR

From an imperial perspective, one of the major goals of each of the Axis powers in the Second World War was to build an empire that rivaled

[30]Christopher Seton-Watson, "Italy's Imperial Hangover," *Journal of Contemporary History*, 15 (1980), 169–179.

[31]Kaoru Sugihara, "The Economic Motivations Behind Japanese Aggression in the Late 1930s: Perspectives of Freda Utley and Nawa Toichi," *Journal of Contemporary History*, 32 (1997), 259–280.

[32]Louise Young, *Japan's Total Empire: Manchuria and the Culture of Wartime Imperialism* (Berkeley: University of California Press, 1998), 307–399.

[33]Adolf Hitler, speech of September 18, 1928.

those that had been established in earlier eras. For their opponents, conversely, the war was fought partly to protect existing empires, which once again contributed mightily to the war effort. Ironically, during the war the populations of most of the British, French, Belgian, Dutch, and U.S. colonies remained relatively and sometimes enthusiastically loyal, although there were important exceptions. Nevertheless, the contributions they made, the privations they suffered, and the changes they experienced led directly to their successful attempts to re-establish their political independence in the period following the war.

Throughout the Second World War, empires both old and new depended on contributions from their colonial peripheries to stay in the fight. This was true of the very newest empire, that of Nazi Germany, which recruited divisions from among colonized populations that they deemed sufficiently Aryan, as in Denmark and Lithuania, and stripped resources from those they did not, whether wheat from the Ukraine or oil from Moldavia. It was also true of the older empires, like Russia, whose Soviet government relied heavily on Siberian and Muslim troops and on raw materials from the distant ends of the empire following the loss of much of the Slav heartland to German forces. The Japanese, similarly, intensely exploited the resources of their colonies and the human power necessary to produce them. They also tried to recruit local auxiliaries as soldiers in some regions by presenting themselves as anti-colonial liberators. This effort culminated in a propaganda campaign depicting the Japanese empire as the Great East Asia Co-Prosperity Sphere. German propaganda similarly depicted their invasion of the Soviet Union as a campaign to liberate Europeans from the Bolsheviks, an argument that at least temporarily won them the support of some ethnic minorities who had been under Soviet control. On the other side, the allies encouraged anti-Japanese activists in mainland South-East Asia with promises of independence, even while consistently planning to re-colonize it after the war.

As a total, industrial war, the Second World War required the mobilization of imperial resources from all of the combatants. Once again, however, the most efficient and extensive mobilization campaign belonged to the British. Imperial and Dominion (now Commonwealth) troops made enormous contributions in terms of actual combatants. The Australasian colonies (New Zealand and Australia) contributed 700,000 troops, and Canada another 500,000. Some 166,500 sub-Saharan African troops fought against the Japanese, and tens of thousands more in North Africa and Italy. They fought alongside more than 2.5 million Indian soldiers, as well as Burmese and Malayan troops. Meanwhile, hundreds of thousands of colonial subjects were recruited into the merchant marine and other support roles from Asian, Caribbean, and African colonies.[34]

The human power contributions of the French colonies were in a way even more impressive. In 1939, as France entered the war, 10 out of 80 French divisions on the border were colonial units. Seven of these were African. Following the surrender by metropolitan France to German forces in 1940, almost all effective resistance continued in the colonies. For most of the war, the vast majority of the anti-Nazi free French army was actually made up of Africans, and 20% of the French soldiers who landed in Normandy and southern France in 1944 to liberate their "homeland" were Africans. Meanwhile, more than 100,000 Africans were mobilized by the French administrators of North Africa, who actively collaborated with the Nazis. Thus, historian Myron Echenberg estimates that 200,000 Africans from French colonies fought in the Second World War.[35]

These numbers, of course, include only combatants and non-combatants sent overseas. They say nothing of the conscription of laborers for resource production, infrastructure development,

---

[34] For more on the contributions of the British colonies and Commonwealth, see Marika Sherwood, "Colonies, Colonials, and World War Two," http://www.bbc.co.uk/history/worldwars/wwtwo/colonies_colonials; and F.W. Perry, *The Commonwealth Armies: Manpower and Organisation in Two World Wars* (Manchester: Manchester University Press, 1988).

[35] Myron Echenberg, "'Morts Pour la France': The African Soldier in France During the Second World War," *Journal of African History*, 26 (1985), 363–380.

and transportation within the colonies. The war effort demanded enormous increases in mining and food production, and much of the labor that produced these goods in the colonies was forced. Even on farms, peasants were compelled to produce strategic crops rather than subsistence foodstuffs.[36] Meanwhile, the expansion of mining operations, alongside other recruitment efforts, removed many young men from rural communities. As a result, women were left alone to provide for their families. This "feminization" of subsistence labor caused immense suffering for many communities. At the same time, the finished industrial goods on which colonial populations had began to rely dried up due to the production switch to war materials and the effects of submarine warfare. The result was, in many cases, an even more intense economic and social crisis than had occurred during the First World War.

The misery of the war was of course even more pronounced in regions of the colonial periphery where actual combat took place. The Second World War was truly global to a degree even greater than that of its predecessor. The physical conflict spread across much of the territory conquered in the era of the New Imperialism. The struggle between the Japanese and allied forces led by the United States and the British Commonwealth territories of Australia and New Zealand encompassed much of the Pacific and included colonies of Japan, the United States, Britain, the Netherlands, and France. Campaigns pitting German and Italian forces against those of the British Empire and the United States crisscrossed every colony and protectorate in North Africa. This is to say nothing of immense regions of China, Europe, and the Soviet Union. In many of these regions, civilian casualties from disease, poverty, and violence reached enormous levels. Often, it was this kind of privation rather than ideological conviction that most drove the development of guerila forces of resistance. These groups found ready support in one set of combatants or another. Sometimes, as in Indochina, rival guerila groups were sponsored by both sides.

THE HOLOCAUST AS A COLONIAL EVENT

In the years prior to the Second World War, Hitler's Nazis managed to add to Germany the new territories of Czech Sudetenland and Austria, but these heartlands of the Habsburg Empire were largely peopled with ethnic Germans and thus provided little additional land for German settlers. However, the territories acquired in eastern Europe following the September 1939 invasion of Poland were different. Poland, Yugoslavia, and the former provinces of Soviet Russia (labeled *Ostland* by the Nazis) were placed under the control of *Gauleiters*, pro-consuls with enormous powers beyond even those of the governors of other empires' African and Asian colonies.[37] To them Hitler assigned the tasks of "liberating" Germans living in these territories and eliminating or subjugating the rest of the population.[38] In reality, German settlement of these territories was small, and the Nazi administrators had to learn to accommodate some portions of the local populations.[39] This was even more true in their conquests in the west, such as France and Belgium. The Nazi version of modern imperial ideology allowed that most northern Europeans were racially similar enough to Germans to be allowed to exist in some manner. However, those lower on the racial hierarchy created by Nazi ideology were persecuted haphazardly at first, and then systematically eliminated.

---

[36] Michael Crowder has pointed out that insufficient research had been done on this in 1985. This is still largely true. Michael Crowder, "World War II and Africa: Introduction," *Journal of African History*, 26 (1985), 287–288.

[37] Jonathon Steinberg, "The Third Reich Reflected: German Civil Administration in the Occupied Soviet Union, 1941–4," *English Historical Review*, 110 (1995), 620–651.

[38] This idea wasn't totally new. During the First World War, the German commander of the Eastern Front, Erich Ludendorff, had imagined a similar project for expelling non-Germans from the occupied Baltic states and ruling them as colonies of settlement.

[39] See, for example, Wendy Lower, "A New Ordering of Space and Race: Nazi Colonial Dreams in Zhytomyr, Ukrain, 1941–1944," *German Studies Review*, 25 (2002), 227–254.

The methodical murder of more than 12 million people—ethnic groups such as Jews and Gypsies as well as political opponents and the disabled—by the Nazis and their accomplices is known to us today as the Holocaust. Long viewed as a particularly German crime, the Holocaust in reality represents the very height of imperial ideology and colonial violence. While perhaps the most systematized of colonial genocides, it can appropriately be discussed together with crimes such as the Japanese atrocities in Nanjing in 1937–1938, the Ottoman genocide of Armenians during the First World War, and all of the dispossession and murder that accompanied the New Imperialism in Africa, Asia, Caribbean, and the Pacific Islands.

Until recently, few researchers have focused on the connections between colonialism and the Holocaust, although they were made soon after the end of the Second World War by the political theorist and journalist Hannah Arendt.[40] In the last decade or so, this situation has reversed. In one especially compelling recent work, Jürgen Zimmerer has placed Nazi ideology in the context of pre-existing colonial worldviews. Like earlier colonizers, the Nazis saw their new conquests as blank slates, primitive regions populated by stagnant populations that could be developed and transformed to German needs. The Nazis were aware of these connections, and even planned to model their colonial office—the *Ostministerium* (Ministry for the East) on the British India Office.[41] Nor did the Nazis learn colonial techniques only from the British Empire. A number of German former colonial officials, including General von Lettow-Vorbeck, worked as propagandists or even as administrators for the Nazis. The German experience in South-West Africa was a particularly important precedent, in that it involved both warfare against guerilla partisans and the genocide of two large populations, the Nama and Herero. It was during these events especially that the propaganda of lebensraum and the racialized justification for genocide had entered the German mainstream.[42]

THE AFTERMATH OF THE SECOND WORLD WAR AND POLITICAL DECOLONIZATION

In their abilities to mobilize resources and human power from around the world, the imperial powers of the Second World War reached the apex of formal empire. Nor did their decline seem imminent when the war ended in 1945. Indeed, the metropoles on the winning side put together plans not only to rebuild their imperial authority and colonial presence but to augment and expand them. Britain still straddled the world. France proposed to impose themselves once more in their Asian, Caribbean, and African colonies and even claimed bits of the now-defunct Italian Empire. The Belgian government tightened its control over the Congo, and the Dutch sent troops to reassert their authority in the Netherlands East Indies.[43] Nor did the Portuguese or Spanish governments relax their grips over their scattered colonies. Yet this outward picture of imperial serenity hid serious rot at the core of the system of formal empires. In a short three decades after 1945, these vast empires collapsed as their colonies, dominions, and protectorates largely claimed their independence. Was the Second World War the great watershed of decolonization? Did it "cause" empires to fall? In the next chapter, we will look at these questions from localized perspectives in colonies around the world. It is equally important, however, to be able to take a

---

[40] Hannah Arendt, *The Origins of Totalitarianism* (New York: Shocken, 1951).

[41] Jürgen Zimmerer, "The Birth of the *Ostland* Out of the Spirit of Colonialism: A Postcolonial Perspective on the Nazi Policy of Conquest and Extermination," *Patterns of Prejudice*, 39 (2005), 197–219.

[42] Benjamin Madley, "From Africa to Auschwitz: How German South West Africa Incubated Ideas and Methods Adopted and Developed by the Nazis in Eastern Europe," *European History Quarterly*, 35 (2005), 429–464.

[43] For a straightforward account of European attempts to re-pacify post-Japanese South-East Asia, see John Springhall, *Decolonization Since 1945: The Collapse of European Overseas Empires* (New York: Palgrave, 2001), 31–65.

global view of the impact of the Second World War in terms of imperialism and colonialism. This is the task of this section.

It can be argued that, even more than its predecessor, the Second World War damaged the capacity of the imperial powers to manage their widespread empires. During the war, the flow of men and materials vital to maintaining both economic and political domination of the colonies was impeded. The administrations of those colonies and protectorates near battlefields often suffered logistical and infrastructural breakdowns, while those further away had to operate on reduced funding and with smaller staffs. Equally important in many regions was the damage to European prestige and to the racialized hierarchy of colonialism. This was especially true in East and South-East Asia, where the ease of Japan's victories over European colonial armies early in the war exposed white superiority as a lie. In Indochina, the French administration's meek acceptance of Japanese rule following the defeat of the French metropole by the Nazis left only indigenous resistance forces to oppose the armies of Japan. As a result, it was these forces—especially the communist-oriented nationalist movement of the Vietminh—which gained experience and both internal and international recognition during the war.[44] Their resistance to the Japanese formed a pillar of their claims for independence in 1945. Throughout much of the French Empire, local movements were able to use the weakness of the metropole to assert themselves—not just in Indochina, but in Syria and the North Africa protectorates of Tunisia and Morocco as well.

The very first former colonies to gain independence following the 1945 armistice belong to the losing imperial powers. Italy's empire was dismembered. The French government of General Charles de Gaulle hoped that Libya might be handed over to them, but in the end all of the Italian colonies became independent states again—not only Libya, but also Ethiopia and Albania. Meanwhile, most of Japan's South-East Asian conquests were handed back to the victorious allies that had colonized them, and their Chinese territories were returned to China, which began a long road toward superpower status. This reconstitution of China was supported both by the Soviet Union and by the United States.

Even in territories that had not been battlefields, the very threat of Axis attack had weakened the colonial state. This was especially true in the most prized colony of them all—British India. We have seen how during the war India provided the British with more than 2 million soldiers. The strategic and economic contribution of the Raj was equally extensive. But the Japanese advance toward India in the early years of the war and British military disasters at their hands also stirred up the anti-colonial movement. In response, British Prime Minister Winston Churchill in 1942 sent a liberal politician, Sir Stafford Cripps, to negotiate with Indian leaders. Although no agreement was signed, the Cripps mission was just one sign that Indian independence was around the corner. The huge mobilization of Indians for the war effort, their enormous losses in battle, and their continued mobilization after the war to help keep South-East and Central Asia in the empire also slowly turned the Indian army from loyal collaborators to a potentially revolutionary body.[45] It was this transition that most convinced the post-war British government that Indian self-rule could not be opposed, but rather had to be managed so that power was handed over to as friendly an independent government as was possible. For many British planners, this meant pro-British moderates in urban areas and princely rulers in rural regions. In the event, the British lost control of the process partly because they did not realize either the massive dislocations suffered by their Indian colonial subjects during the war or how radically their experiences had changed their view of British rule. Without the approval of the British, it was nationalists led by Mohandas K. Gandhi and Jawaharlal Nehru who ushered Britain's South Asian colonial subjects into independence, although British interference

---

[44]Franz Ansprenger, *The Dissolution of the Colonial Empires* (New York: Routledge, 1981), 147–151.

[45]Springhall, *Decolonization Since 1945*, 66–75.

was enough to help fracture the former colony into two parts as India and Pakistan.

Britain's retreat from South Asia, like many subsequent decisions by European metropoles to back away from their colonies, was based partly on a changing imperial economic situation. Immediately following the end of the war, Britain and the European metropoles had at first calculated that the best way to rebuild from the devastation of the war was to increase their investment in and exploitation of their colonies. Two factors changed this calculation, however. The first was the growth of the European Economic Community, which in the 1950s began to provide huge investment opportunities within Europe. The second was the growing cost of empire, especially as independence movements grew (see chapter 15). These costs weighed heavily in the British decision to abandon India in 1947, and became increasingly important in the 1950s. In 1955–1956, the British Chancellor of the Exchequer Harold Macmillan carried out an extensive analysis of the costs and benefits of empire, and found that many colonies were more expensive than they were beneficial to Britain. When Macmillan became prime minister in 1957, he gradually began to manage Britain's retreat from Africa, partly on the grounds of cost. In the end, economic pressure was one of the most successful strategies of anti-colonial movements. Often, rebels found that the immense financial cost of putting down dissidence were more significant than casualties in driving out the imperialists. Such expenses were key in forcing decisions like the one made by French President de Gaulle to retreat from Algeria in 1958.

Empires could go broke fighting insurgencies, as the Portuguese did trying to suppress three separate African independence movements in the 1970s. However, most of the other imperial powers recognized this danger, and the inevitability of decolonization, in time. They generally refined their strategies from resisting decolonization to trying to manage it so that "friendly" governments were left in place. The British embraced this approach first, but the French recognized it by the late 1950s as well. The term *friendly*, however, needs to be understood in the context of the

largest power shift exposed by the Second World War—the rise of the United States and the Soviet Union as superpowers. By as early as 1948, these two states were engaging in Cold War maneuvering in the context of decolonization. Both were broadly anti-colonial for several reasons. For the United States, the monopolistic domination of colonies by their metropoles meant that U.S. companies were excluded from doing business in much of the world. These North American corporations hoped that decolonization would therefore open new markets to them. The Soviets had pragmatic reasons to oppose colonialism as well, not only because the empires in question were held by capitalist, western metropoles but also because the anti-colonial movements often possessed a flavor or communism. In addition, both American liberalism and Soviet socialism were at least outwardly ideologically supportive of self-determination. However, in both cases, these intentions had limits: the Soviets were busy building an empire in eastern Europe, while the United States had economic designs on the former colonies.

As tensions between the two superpowers heated up, their conflict began to shape the process by which decolonization occurred. In South-East Asia, for example, the United States alternately promoted and opposed independence movements depending on their political–global orientation. In the Philippines, the United States handed over power to a local government under Manuel Roxas in 1946. In return, the Roxas administration granted the U.S. military bases and extended to North American firms the same rights enjoyed by Philippine companies.[46] Similarly, the United States vetoed Dutch attempts to re-annex Indonesia because they saw the nationalist movement led by Sukarno as a moderate force that could better head off communist insurgents than the Dutch could. On the other hand, the United States supported both the French actions against

---

[46] John Bastin and Harry J. Benda, *A History of Modern Southeast Asia: Colonialism, Nationalism, and Decolonization*, 2nd edition, (Sydney: Prentice Hall, 1977), 154–157.

the Vietminh and the British re-occupation of Malaya because they viewed the dominant anti-colonial parties there as communists.

The Cold War was an important global context for shaping the strategies of anti-colonial forces as well. Movements for independence around the world recognized the United States and the Soviet Union as potential allies and sponsors, and courted their support. It was largely for this reason, for example, that Vietminh leader Ho Chi Minh referenced the American Declaration of Independence in the 1946 Vietnamese document declaring independence.[47] Anti-colonial leaders were also inspired by their peers around the world. Libya's successful independence, for example, inspired nationalist leaders in neighboring Egypt. Often, when a state became independent, its neighbors quickly ramped up their efforts, as in West Africa, where every colony except one became self-governing within five years of Ghana's successful decolonization in 1957. Nor were these effects limited geographically to one region. The successful decolonization of Ghana in 1957 inspired both other Africans and Caribbean leaders. The Vietminh victory over French forces at Dien Bien Phu in 1954 inspired the creation of a unified nationalist movement in Algeria. This so-called *demonstration effect* had both spiritual and very concrete elements.[48] Independent states could lend military and economic aid to insurgencies or political parties across the border and could provide refuge for their leaders. Moreover, the geo-politics of decolonization often led to a sort of domino effect. The loss of India in 1948 removed, for Britain, much of the justification for its retention of Arabian and East African colonies. Egypt's successful assertion of its independence in 1952 further weakened the links between these colonies and the metropole.

This was especially made clear when Egyptian President Gamal Abdel Nasser nationalized the Suez Canal in 1954. The result was a British retreat from its Indian Ocean colonies, although only as U.S. informal influence moved in.[49]

One of the most effective venues for former colonies to aid their still-colonized compatriots was the United Nations (UN). The UN had not initially been formulated to facilitate decolonization. Rather, both U.S. President Franklin Roosevelt and British Prime Minister Winston Churchill had initially seen it as a way to maintain the balance of power in post-war Europe and hopefully to avoid future wars. But while Roosevelt had hoped that it would be an instrument guaranteeing self-determination on an American model, Churchill had hoped that it would preserve the imperial status quo. His vision triumphed at first, largely because most prominent founding members of the UN were the imperial metropoles. However, the United States had insisted on a leading role for China from the beginning, and India quickly became a leading member state following independence. After the Communist victory in China in 1949–1950, these two powers began to use the UN as a forum to promote independence movements around the world. They were able to do so partly by embarrassing or otherwise forcing the United States and the Soviet Union to side with them. Perhaps the most skillful diplomat in this respect was the Indian representative V.K. Krishna Menon, who was instrumental in pushing the United States to support Indonesian and later Laotian and Cambodian independence. He did so largely by forcing the U.S. representatives to take a stance in forum of the UN.[50] By 1960, the number of former colonies in the UN had reached a critical enough mass to pass a resolution in the General Assembly calling for global decolonization.

[47] "Declaration of Independence of the Democratic Republic of Viet Nam (September 2, 1945)," in *Ho Chi Minh: Selected Writings 1920–1969* (Hanoi: Foreign Languages Publishing House, 1977), 53–56.

[48] See David B. Abernethy, *The Dynamics of Global Dominance: European Overseas Empires, 1415–1980* (New Haven, CT: Yale University Press, 2000), 358.

[49] For more on the retreat from "East-of-Suez," see W. David McIntyre, *British Decolonization, 1946–1997: When, Why and How Did the British Empire Fall?* (New York: St. Martin's Press, 1998), 58–67.

[50] Alistair M. Taylor, *Indonesian Independence and the United Nations* (Westport, CT: Greenwood Press, 1975).

The UN was a useful tool for anti-colonial movements not least because, in the post-war world, international public opinion had largely turned against colonialism. Some of this had to do with the rhetoric of anti-fascism and freedom used by the allies as propaganda during the Second World War. Among the most important documents in this respect was the Anglo-American Atlantic Charter, largely forced on Churchill by Roosevelt, which declared that all peoples had the right to self-determination.[51] Such promises were picked up by opponents of colonialism in the imperial metropoles, in the colonies, and around the world. As the United States became the dominant partner among the western allies, anti-colonial leaders in the French, British, and Dutch empires began to appeal to U.S. public opinion. They included the Sultan of Morocco and Algerian nationalists as well as Ho Chi Minh.[52] After the war, U.S. public opinion was especially influential in British, Dutch, and Belgian calculations because of the power of the U.S. dollars being given to these states under the Marshall Plan. Many of Britain's African colonies won their independence more quickly because of pressure from the U.S. government and public. However, public opinion in other regions was important as well. The British government was aware, for example, of the significance of Arab public opinion, especially following the discovery of large oil deposits in the region. This helped guide both their decisions not to support French attempts to reclaim Syria in 1945–1946 and not to unilaterally create a Jewish state of Israel in Palestine. The latter issue was especially difficult, because although the creation of Israel was opposed by Arab opinion, it enjoyed quite a bit of support in the United States. Eventually, the British handed the issue over to the UN to resolve.

Even within the imperial metropoles themselves, public opinion began to switch against empire in the post-war era, especially as newspapers became more efficient at revealing colonial atrocities. One such atrocity was the British treatment of Kenyans accused of having joined the Mau Mau anti-colonial movement, who suffered detention, privation, and abuse in hastily erected detention camps in the late 1950s. The revelation of these camps caused outrage in Britain, which helped to spur Prime Minister Macmillan to grant independence to several Central and East African colonies.

Conclusion

The crumbling of the great European and Japanese formal empires followed so rapidly on the end of the Second World War that the connection between them seems inescapable. Indeed, the two world wars had together seen the liquidation of five empires on the losing sides—German, Austrian Habsburg, Ottoman, Italian, and Japanese. At the end of the first war, however, the victors had managed to simply transfer most of the territories of the defeated into their own empires. At the end of the Second World War, by contrast, the dissolution of the Japanese, Nazi German, and Italian empires only began the process by which empires collapsed. By 1975, only a few scattered colonies still existed, although arguably new types of empires were on the rise.

The obvious chronological links between these events is backed up by the measurable impact of the two world wars on both metropole and colony. Two lengthy wars drained the great metropoles of men, money, and resources. The contributions and suffering of the populations of the colonies and dominions helped to drive them toward independence.

But the significance of the two world wars as a cause of decolonization shouldn't be overemphasized. There were precedents for the sort of controlled decolonization practiced by Britain, especially, in the self-rule granted to Australia, New Zealand, and Canada in the late nineteenth century. At the same time, focusing on global events obscures the fact that independence was not granted by imperial fiat, but won by the struggles of colonial subjects for the freedom. These

---

[51] See Douglas Brinkley and David R. Facey-Crowther, eds., *The Atlantic Charter* (New York: Palgrave, 1994).

[52] Ansprenger, *The Dissolution of the Colonial Empires*, 152–154.

movements didn't suddenly spring into existence in the 1940s, but rather had been slowly coalescing for decades—arguably ever since the formal colonies had come into existence. Their story forms the subject of the next chapter.

Questions

1. How was the First World War an "imperial" war? Can it be compared to earlier imperial wars like the Seven Years' War, and why or why not? How was it the specific result of the kinds of imperialisms and the context of the early twentieth century?

2. How did the First and Second World Wars affect life in the overseas colonies of the belligerent powers? How did this contribute to the shaping of anti-colonial movements?

3. To what degree can Nazi Germany be considered an "empire" and the territories conquered during the Second World War "colonies"? Justify your answer.

4. To what degree was the Second World War the "great watershed of decolonization"? In other words, to what degree was it responsible for the rapid independence of formerly colonized societies in the decades following 1945? Defend your answer.

CHAPTER 15

Imperialism and Colonialism: Nationalism and Independence

The many nationalist parties and mass movements that emerged from among the colonies and protectorates of the imperial periphery in the mid-twentieth century are often studied separately, as if each were the unique flowering of a purely localized national consciousness. Yet while it is necessary to properly contextualize each movement within its local environment, such an approach misleadingly obscures the connections between nationalist movements around the world. The evidence of these connections is not only their simultaneity, or that they often adopted similar models of liberation, but also the result of archival research that shows that their leaders attended conferences together, wrote letters to each other, and even often shared books and pamphlets.

In this chapter, we will focus on the rise of nationalist parties in colonies, protectorates, and other dependencies around the world, and in their struggle for political independence. We will focus on the period 1945–1997. These dates embrace a global trend of decolonization—the flood of colonized peoples toward independence bracketed by Jordan and the Philippines in 1946 and Hong Kong in 1997. In the decades between these dates, approximately one-third of the world's population went from living under imperial rule to living in nation-states. In some cases and in some ways, the real change they experienced was very small, and in others very large, but overall it marked a shift in power, identity, and agency with global implications.

Probably the most significant story in the process of decolonization was the fusing of anti-colonial sentiment and feelings among disparate groups and individuals into unified *nationalist* parties that through violence and by passive resistance managed to oust their imperial rulers. But exactly what "nationalism" was and why it emerged as the most significant force against colonialism in this period is still often poorly understood. In the first three sections of this chapter, we attempt to address these questions. In the first two, we look at the debate as to how emancipatory (or anti-colonial) nationalism emerged as the leading ideology and structure of political liberation movements in the colonies. In the third section, we explore how these movements recruited the general populations of the colonies. The fourth section takes the form of a narrative that seeks to explain the ways in which nationalism grew and functioned on a global scale. In the fifth section, we explore the alternatives to nationalism explored but largely discarded by anti-colonial leaders: these included organization on racial, religious, and "civilizational" bases. In the sixth and final section, we consider settler nationalism as a variation on the development of emancipatory nationalism in the colonies.

THE CHALLENGE FACING ANTI-COLONIAL MOVEMENTS AND THE SEARCH FOR UNIFYING IDEOLOGIES

Colonialism thrived on the disunity of colonial subjects. At its heart was indirect rule (see chapters 11 and 13), a set of policies and practices by which colonial subjects were sub-divided by religion, locality, or "ethnicity" and then ruled by chieftains and princes allied to the colonial state. Indirect rule and the divide-and-conquer strategy were political necessities in colonies of exploitation. They allowed small numbers of administrators and settlers to rule over huge numbers of locals. But they were also more than just conveniences. The categorization and division of people was at the very heart of modern colonialism, because only by ranking people and by arguing that some were unable to rule themselves could colonial rulers justify both their occupation of the colonies and the fact that colonial subjects were not invited to become full citizens.[1]

So long as colonialism succeeded in dividing the populations of each of their colonies—whether in Africa, Asia, the Caribbean, the Pacific, and other parts of the globe—the great empires were able to hold on to their colonies and dependencies. By contrast, whenever a great mass of people in a colony or group of colonies overcame their divisions and united to overthrow colonial rule, they succeeded. In some cases, as occurred often in the British Empire, the metropole recognized this fact and retreated rather quickly. In other cases, as with the Portuguese, they fought long wars to hold their empires. Eventually, however, colonies whose populations managed to unite against colonial rule won their independence.[2]

The divisive nature of colonialism, of course, was precisely engineered to make it difficult for colonial societies to achieve this kind of unity. Nor were colonial categories the only divisions within the colonies; some divisions pre-dated colonialism, and colonial societies managed to create others themselves. For decades, these cross-cutting lines of "tribe," religion, class, ethnicity, chieftaincy, and principality worked well to maintain the colonial state. Thus the challenge, for anti-colonial leaders, was to develop a tool to cross these boundaries and bind people together. In the post-war era, that tool was nationalism.

In order to understand the way nationalism is used as a term to describe decolonization movements, we will define it here as an ideology whose adherents believe that the political unit (the state) and the unit of belonging (the nation) should be identical.[3] In the context of decolonization, this generally meant that nationalists believed that all of the people living in a single colony were co-nationalists, and that they deserved to be sovereign over the territory of the colony. Local conditions, of course, caused some variations of this ideology to emerge. In India, for example, religion was such a powerful force that many nationalists nevertheless accepted that the territory of India, once independent, should be partitioned into several states whose citizenship would be defined by religion. In West Africa and among some Arab anti-colonial leaders, as we will see later in this chapter, nationalists sometimes saw the boundaries of their "nation" as being larger than the colonial borders of their state. Generally, however, nationalists accepted the borders established by the colonizers, and concentrated on unifying the people living within those boundaries.

The nationalists' main problem in creating a national sentiment within the borders of their colonies was, of course, to overcome the mutual distrust of different segments of their populations. Consider, for example, the problems of the pioneering Convention People's Party (CPP), the nationalist political party of Kwame Nkrumah that led the Gold Coast to independence in 1957.

---

[1] This is the central argument made by Mahmood Mamdani in *Citizen and Subject: Contemporary Africa and the Legacy of Late Colonialism* (Princeton, NJ: Princeton University Press, 1996).

[2] See chapter 14. Or, for a brief narrative history, M.E. Chamberlain, *Decolonization: The Fall of the European Empires* (Oxford: Basil Blackwell, 1985).

[3] This definition, which is contested, is adapted from the work of Ernest Gellner, *Nations and Nationalism* (Ithaca, NY: Cornell University Press, 1983).

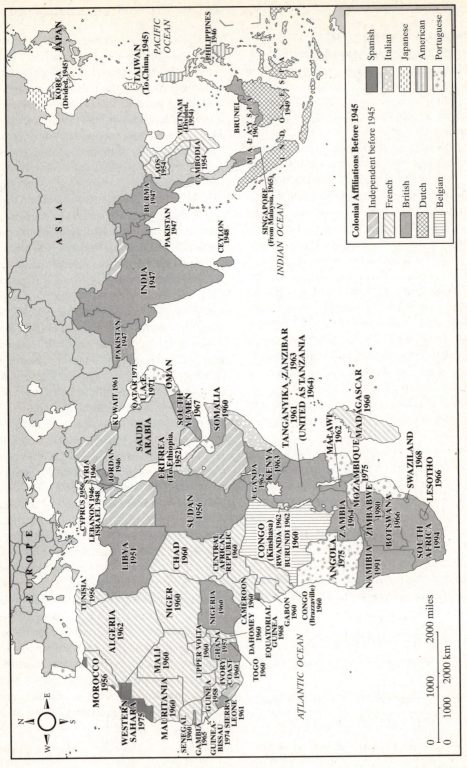

Global Political Decolonization, 1945–1997

Colonial Affiliations Before 1945

- Spanish
- Italian
- Japanese
- American
- Portuguese
- Independent before 1945
- French
- British
- Dutch
- Belgian

JAPAN

KOREA (Divided, 1945)

TAIWAN (To China, 1945)

PACIFIC OCEAN

PHILIPPINES 1946

VIETNAM (Divided, 1954)

LAOS 1954

CAMBODIA 1954

BRUNEI 1963

M A L A Y S I A

BURMA 1947

PAKISTAN 1947

A S I A

I N D O N E S I A 1949

SINGAPORE (From Malaysia, 1965)

INDIA 1947

CEYLON 1948

INDIAN OCEAN

PAKISTAN 1947

E U R O P E

CYPRUS 1956
SYRIA 1946
LEBANON 1946
ISRAEL 1948

JORDAN 1946

KUWAIT 1961
QATAR 1971
U.A.E. 1971
OMAN

SAUDI ARABIA

ERITREA (To Ethiopia, 1952)

SOUTH YEMEN 1967

SOMALIA 1960

TUNISIA 1956

LIBYA 1951

SUDAN 1956

UGANDA 1962

KENYA 1963

TANGANYIKA–ZANZIBAR 1961 (UNITED AS TANZANIA 1964)

MALAWI 1962

MOZAMBIQUE 1975

MADAGASCAR 1960

SWAZILAND 1968

LESOTHO 1966

MOROCCO 1956

ALGERIA 1962

WESTERN SAHARA 1975

NIGER 1960

CHAD 1960

CENTRAL AFRICAN REPUBLIC 1960

CONGO (Kinshasa) 1962

RWANDA 1962
BURUNDI 1960

ZAMBIA 1964

ZIMBABWE 1980

BOTSWANA 1966

NAMIBIA 1991

SOUTH AFRICA 1994

ANGOLA 1975

MAURITANIA 1960

MALI 1960

UPPER VOLTA

NIGERIA 1960

CAMEROON 1960

EQUATORIAL GUINEA 1968

GABON 1960

CONGO (Brazzaville) 1960

TOGO 1960

DAHOMEY 1960

GHANA 1957

IVORY COAST 1960

GUINEA 1958

SIERRA LEONE 1961

GUINEA-BISSAU 1974

GAMBIA 1965

SENEGAL 1960

ATLANTIC OCEAN

N
W E
S

0   1000   2000 miles

0   1000   2000 km

308

Throughout the early 1950s, the CPP's ideology of a unified identity for the population of the Gold Coast had to compete with British rhetoric that claimed the local population was best served by remaining in the empire. In addition, Nkrumah's party had to contend with a movement led by chiefs who ruled portions of former Asante to reconstitute an independent Asante state. Their calls for national unity were also challenged by separatists among the Ewe ethnic group, who hoped to build a separate ethnic state along with the Ewe living in neighboring (French) Togo. In addition, the CPP was distrusted by many Muslim leaders from the north, who opposed it because it was dominated both by southerners and by Christians. Even rural dwellers were suspicious of the CPP because it was led largely by urban elites.[4] In essence, these organizations represented **sub-nationalisms**, or alternative ideas of the nation among specific portions of the population that were based on ethnicity, religion, or some other organization sense of belonging. Each of these sub-nationalist groups had complex motives of their own, but they were also often useful for the colonial administration, which saw them as tools to deny the kind of unity that could bring about decolonization. Nkrumah overcame this challenge quite effectively, but many nationalist movements did not do as well. In nearby Nigeria, the power of ethnic and religious division was so strong that the anti-colonial movement could only establish a veneer of unity by proposing a federal plan that would give each part of the country broad autonomy. After independence, the plan soon broke down and civil war broke out.

THE DEVELOPMENT OF EMANCIPATORY NATIONALISM

In the process of fighting for independence, Nkrumah and other leaders of nationalist liberation movements quickly discerned a strategy to overcome internal divisions by convincing the populace to embrace a "national" identity over their ethnic, religious, class, and other identities. The key to creating this sentiment was to convince them not only that nationalism was the best means to defeat colonialism, but also that they truly had a lot in common with their co-nationalists who were of different ethnicities, classes, or religions. But to what degree did this shared experience really exist, and to what degree did the nationalists have to invent this sentiment from out of nowhere? This forms the first of three key debates about the nature of **emancipatory nationalism**.

The theory that nationalist sentiment was invented is often called *imagining the community*. Benedict Anderson is the historical sociologist who perhaps first effectively framed this theory, which states that nationhood is not the result of people living together in continuous histories over thousands of years, but rather is created when people across a wide area begin to believe (or imagine) that they are all members of a single nation.[5] Because the nation is larger than the family, blood ties do not suffice to bind people together. Instead, members of the nation have to be able to recognize each other and acknowledge each other as having a shared past and a shared national identity. Thus when French citizens imagine themselves as members of the French nation, they don't just do so abstractly. They recognize the importance of the French Revolution, perhaps, and think about French contributions to civilization. They identify themselves culturally and linguistically as French. Their co-nationalists are other people not only carrying a French passport, but also speaking French and enjoying the same TV shows on Canal+, or reading the same French newspapers such as *Le Monde*. Skin color is probably less important, but it may still play a role in their determination as to who is French and who is not.

For nationalists seeking to create an anti-colonial national consciousness in the colonies, a logical starting point was the shared oppression of

---

[4] See Jean Allman, *The Quills of the Porcupine: Asante Nationalism in an Emergent Ghana* (Madison: University of Wisconsin Press, 1993); and Richard Rathbone, *Nkrumah and the Chiefs: The Politics of Chieftaincy in Ghana, 1951–1960* (Athens: Ohio University Press, 2000).

[5] Benedict Anderson, *Imagined Communities*, revised edition (New York: Verso, 1991).

most (if not all) of the inhabitants of the colony under colonial rule. The importance of this point cannot be overstated. In the words of Edward Said:

> To become aware of one's self as belonging to a subject people is the founding insight of anti-imperialist nationalism. From that insight came literatures, innumerable political parties, a host of other struggles for minority and women's rights, and, much of the time, newly independent states.[6]

However, negative experience with colonialism could not create a national consciousness alone. Instead, people had to also be given a positive sense of the history and identity of the nation. Specifically, nationalists found that they had to establish their own legitimacy as leaders of the anti-colonial struggle. One way to do this was to depict themselves as the heirs to a long history of anti-colonial resistance. In Ghana, for example, Kwame Nkrumah's speeches frequently referred to leaders of military resistance such as Yaa Asantewaa as well as abortive nationalists such as the leaders of the Fante Confederation (see chapter 11) in order to associate themselves with these earlier resisters. In reality, however, these links were often fictional, and earlier movements had had little real impact on the efforts of the new nationalists.

The task of constructing a continuous history of oppression and resistance was just part of the methods by which the nationalists built a sense of nationhood. In India, nationalist leaders espoused several discourses of nationalism and used numerous tools to build a sense of an Indian "nation" that would have broad appeal. One of the most clearly enunciated nationalist visions was that of Indian National Congress leader Jawaharlal Nehru, who called upon a secular vision of a unified Indian nation-state similar to those of Europe. For Nehru, Indians had historically already achieved this national unity under the broadly tolerant rule of the Mughal Emperor Akbar (see chapters 1 and 2), and only needed to re-claim it. Nehru argued that the role of the emperors had been to support all of the religious communities of India equally, and to unite the region's cultural diversity in the hands of the state, and that a new Indian government could play a similar unifying role.[7]

While Nehru stressed the historical continuity of the secular Indian state, others focused on spirituality as the center of Indian national identity. The nationalist philosopher Sri Aurobindo, for example, suggested that Hindu spirituality was what separated India from the more materialistic "west." His ideas influenced Mohandas Gandhi, who led India to independence. Gandhi took a somewhat "civilizationist" approach to nationalism, seeing India as a great civilization with its own special and specific features, many of which were of Hindu derivation. However, this conceptualization was problematic, because in stressing India's Hindu roots, it threatened to exclude Muslims and other non-Hindus.[8] This religious division was a problem that Gandhi struggled to overcome during much of his life.

While Indian intellectuals and religious leaders debated the form the nation would take, Gandhi's approach to nationalism was most successful in mobilizing the mass of the population to the message of the Indian National Congress. He did so by outwardly expressing his "Indianness" through his rejection of western dress in favor of homespun Indian cloth robes. Then he turned this seemingly personal choice into a nationalist issue by promoting a boycott of British factory-made cloth, both as a way to put pressure on British politicians and as a self-conscious rejection of the industrialized West in favor of "Indian" domesticity and simplicity. It was a message that was not lost on India's poor, who were most likely to spin their own cloth and who embraced Congress's choice of the spinning wheel as a symbol of their movement. Nor was this Gandhi's last effort to reach the impoverished

---

[6] Edward Said, *Culture and Imperialism* (New York: Vintage Books, 1994), 214.

[7] Jawaharlal Nehru, *The Discovery of India* (New York: Anchor Books, 1960), 121–130.

[8] Prasenjit Duara, "On Theories of Nationalism for India and China," in *In the Footsteps of Xuanzang: Tan Yun-Shan and India*, edited by Tan Chung (Delhi: Gyan Publishing, 2002).

masses of the Indian population. After being selected in 1942 as the head of the Congress movement, Gandhi reached out to the poor as well as other groups not previously embraced by the liberal, largely Hindu intellectuals who had spearheaded the nationalist movement. These included women, non-Hindus, and low-status members of society. Under his leadership, Congress lowered its dues to enable poor Indians to join, and also began to publish its literature in Indian languages rather than merely in English.[9] Allied to these policies, Gandhi built a conception of Indian nationhood that, while arguing that there was a place for all religions in India, was based largely on Hindu concepts. Among these were national tolerance and non-violence (*ahimsa*) and the rejection of force in favor of *satyagraha*, or passive resistance to colonialism. In this way, Gandhi tried to establish a contrast between western (colonial) violence and the spirituality that he placed at the core of Indian nationhood.

How successful were all of these efforts to invent a national past and present? In India, the success of Congress in unifying a broad mass of society—including important allies of the colonial state in the military and among the land-owning classes—was perhaps the central factor in winning an early independence for India. Yet despite his many successes, Gandhi was never able to fully win many Muslims over to the Indian nationhood he had helped to invent. Indeed, many Muslims had imagined for themselves a different, and separate, Muslim nation. Thus, British India was partitioned upon independence into two and later three separate states—Hindu-dominated India and Muslim-dominated Pakistan and Bangladesh. Gandhi's failure in this respect may point to the conflict between two "imagined nations"—that of India, and that of Islam. As we have seen, nationalist leaders in this period were often in conflict with activists for alternate "sub-nationalisms," whether ethnic, religious, or organized along some other lines. However, it may also point to what historian

Carolyn Hamilton has called the *limits of historical invention*. In a rebuttal to Benedict Anderson and other scholars, Hamilton has written that the sense of nationhood that arises in periods like the one discussed in this chapter is not entirely invented. Instead, it often relies on very real historical or contemporary issues and events. For example, Hamilton has shown how the depictions of the first Zulu king—Shaka kaSenzangakhona—by South Africa's principal anti-colonial nationalists were drawn from oral traditions and written sources from the time of his life and that were already widely embraced by large groups of people.[10] These included stories both of his successes as fighter against the British and of his oppression of those he came to rule. These deeply ingrained stories led as many people to reject him as a hero as to embrace him. The lesson is that anti-colonial nationalism had real limits, because the inhabitants of the colonies chose what national identities to accept or reject based on their real experiences and knowledge of the past and the world around them. At the same time, this also suggests that the embracing of nationalism by the populations of many colonial societies was not merely because they bought into a false history or a constructed idea of a shared heritage. Modern colonialism truly had become widely and deeply oppressive in the era of the High Imperialism, and few members of colonial societies did not feel themselves to be negatively impacted by it. Moreover, historian Terence Ranger has argued that nationalists who claimed the legacy of earlier independence movements may not have been wrong. Previous methods and ideologies of resistance, he writes, helped to create "types of political organization and inspiration . . . which looked in important ways to the future, which in some cases are directly and in others indirectly linked with later manifestations of . . . opposition."[11]

---

[9] One useful intellectual biography of Gandhi is Anthony J. Parel, *Gandhi's Philosophy and the Quest for Harmony* (Cambridge: Cambridge University Press, 2006).

[10] Carolyn Hamilton, *Terrific Majesty: The Powers of Shaka Zulu and the Limits of Historical Invention* (Cape Town: David Philip, 1998).

[11] Terence Ranger, "Connexions between 'Primary Resistance' Movements and Modern Mass Nationalism in East and Central Africa," *Journal of African History*, 9 (1968), 631.

ORGANIZING RESISTANCE AMONG THE PEOPLE

Constructing a national identity was not the only task in the building of a united anti-colonial movement. Anti-colonial nationalists also had to undertake the everyday tasks of disseminating their ideas and mobilizing the people to support them through strikes, boycotts, and in many cases military conflict with the colonizers or separatists. This process required not just an ideology, but also a structure. An important structure for underground movements in oppressive colonial situations was the guerilla cell pioneered by communist insurgents in East Asia and south-eastern Europe. In most cases, however, political parties were able to function relatively openly, and these became the central organization of the nationalist movement. Parties such as the Indian National Congress or Nkrumah's CPP were far more highly organized after the Second World War than they had been before. Successful political parties were run by full-time salaried staffers, were equipped with presses and equipment, and stretched across the entire colony. In the case of the *Rassemblement Démocratique Africain* (African Democratic Rally), the party for some time stretched across all of the colonies of French West Africa.[12]

Perhaps most importantly, these parties were able to exploit the inherent weakness in the colonial system—indirect rule. Admittedly, indirect rule was the strategy that enabled modern colonialism to function despite the massive disparity between the large populations of colonial subjects and the thin line of colonizers. But it did so only by relying heavily on the assistance of local groups. Some of these could be chiefs and aristocrats, who could be rewarded by giving power over rural populations. At least some, however, had to be western-educated (at least to some degree) clerks, sergeants, and assistants. These individuals, the heirs to the

nineteenth-century modernizers (see chapter 11), were encouraged to wear western dress, to speak the languages of the colonizer, and often to become Christian. However, no matter how "rational" or "modern" they acted, they could not be granted equal status with imperial (or in this case white) citizens, as assimilated populations had been in some earlier empires. Such recognition of equality would have threatened the categorization and differentiation that had become the very substance of colonialism.[13]

The result was that these western-educated elites generally became very frustrated. Many of them were just as well read in the classics as their colonizers. They dressed in the fashion of middle-class or upper-class westerners, and spoke European languages as well or better than many metropolitan citizens. They actively conformed to the culture of the colonizers, but were still kept from both socio-economic and legal equality by their race and status as subjects. Ironically, due to the structure of indirect rule and the proconsular state (see chapter 12), these individuals tended to be employed in positions that were well placed not only to sabotage the working of the state but to take it over and run it themselves. If they were lawyers, they could become judges. If they were clerks, they could run departments of the colonial state. Thus although they could be accused of being collaborators, they had also become the prime infiltrators. It was mainly these men (and a few women in similar positions) who led the nationalist liberation movements of the post-war era.[14]

The second great question about emancipatory nationalism must be why the great mass of people in the many colonies chose to follow these western-educated classes, who had previously generally held themselves aloof from other colonized

---

[12] See Jean Suret-Canale and A. Adu Boahen, "West Africa 1945–1960," in *UNESCO General History of Africa*, vol. VIII, *Africa Since 1935*, edited by Ali Mazrui (Berkeley: University of California Press, 1999), 165–169. Originally published 1993.

[13] This idea is underlined repeatedly by the Indian historical anthropologist Partha Chatterjee in *The Nation and Its Fragments* (Princeton, NJ: Princeton University Press), 1993; and *Nationalist Thought and the Colonial World* (Minneapolis: University of Minnesota Press, 1993).

[14] For a political view of this process, see David B. Abernethy, "Colonialism as a Self-Defeating Enterprise," in *The Dynamics of Global Dominance: European Overseas Empires, 1415–1980* (New Haven, CT: Yale University Press, 2000), 325–344.

subjects. One proposed answer has to do with the real shared suffering of colonialism. Nationalists were able, by and large, to point to colonialism as the cause of all type of problems. They could argue to urban women that colonial tariffs raised prices in the marketplace. They could appeal to farmers by pointing to unpopular agricultural policies, and could promise the landless the return of land confiscated by settlers and the state. They could build on the anger of veterans who had not received their promised pensions. Among the most important of their potential supporters were urban workers, who were often dissatisfied with both pay and working conditions. Here, however, they faced an important challenge in the post-war era from labor unions, who claimed to represent workers as a *class*, rather than as part of the nation. In order to win the worker's support, the nationalists had to both co-opt the unions and promise the laborers that the new government would give them the benefits and wages for which they were agitating.[15] In total, the nationalists had to present the nation as a cure-all for the ills of colonialism.

The nationalists also found it useful to co-opt religious leaders and movements. As we saw in chapter 13, colonized peoples had often found that religion and spirituality were areas in which they could create independent spaces for themselves. This was true of both pre-existing religions such as Buddhism in Indochina and Christian churches such as the independent Zionist churches of Africa. Sometimes, these religions became the focus of subversive sentiments for liberation. The National Church of Nigeria and the Cameroons, for example, worshiped a "God of Africa" and sang hymns asking to be delivered from colonialism.[16] In colonial Nyasaland, local independent churches were the main means of organizing uprisings during the First World War.

Nationalists, of course, readily saw the potential value of these religious organizations to their cause, both because they were already highly organized and because they embodied liberation ideologies. This is not to say that they only used them opportunistically; many nationalists were true believers and quite serious members of churches, mosques, shrines, and temples. Others were more secular. Whatever their motives, they worked hard to capture these organizations and their members for the nationalist cause. Often they were successful. In South Africa, for example, the South African Council of Churches became one of the principal organizations against settler rule quite early in the struggle and maintained its prominence right up to the 1994 transfer of power.

There are two broad views on the motives of the nationalists themselves. One view, espoused in many of the biographies of nationalist leaders written in the 1960s and 1970s, sees them as benevolent liberators who put the needs of their countrymen before themselves. An opposing, more critical, view depicts the nationalists as largely serving their own needs. This view occurred, for example, in the Caribbean-Algerian psychiatrist and political philosopher Franz Fanon. In his 1961 book *The Wretched of the Earth*, which focused on the psychological effects of colonialism, Fanon warned that nationalist movements of western-educated "clerk" classes might find themselves merely replicating the colonial ruling classes because that was the only political system they knew. Thus, while expelling the colonizers, they could generally fail to serve the needs of the great mass of the people.[17]

THE DIFFUSION OF EMANCIPATORY NATIONALISM: A GLOBAL PERSPECTIVE

A third central question asked by scholars about emancipatory nationalism is whether it should be seen as having primarily local roots and influences

---

[15] For a case study from French West Africa, see Frederick Cooper, "The Dialectics of Decolonization: Nationalism and Labor Movements in Postwar French Africa," in *Tensions of Empire: Colonial Cultures in a Bourgeois World*, edited by Frederick Cooper and Ann Stoler (Berkeley: University of California Press, 1997), 406–434.

[16] Thomas Hodgkin, *Nationalism in Colonial Africa* (New York: New York University Press, 1957).

[17] Franz Fanon, *The Wretched of the Earth* (Paris: François Maspero, 1961). Originally published as *Les Damnés de la Terre*.

or whether its main inspirations were global, and especially in either the liberalism of the "west" or the Marxism espoused by the leaders of the Soviet Union and their allies.

The task that anti-colonial nationalists took on was, almost universally, to create new nations within the spaces of the colonies. Certainly, they did so in the context of unique local conditions. As Edward Said points out, no analysis of its origins can overlook "the reserves in Indian and Arab culture that *always* resisted imperialism."[18] Nevertheless, while conceding the distinctiveness of each nationalist struggle, we must also acknowledge that the spread of anti-colonial or emancipatory nationalism in the post-war era was a truly global story. We must take this worldwide perspective because global events such as the Second World War and the Cold War were so influential in weakening imperialism around the world, because the language and strategies of anti-imperial nationalists drew on precedents from the "west," and perhaps most importantly because the individual nationalist movements were inspired by, and linked to, each other. These links were intellectual and physical, economic and political, communal and personal. In many ways, historians are only just beginning to recognize their depth and significance.

This is not to say that scholars have historically ignored the international context of decolonization. However, their narratives have, until recently, focused on a model that placed at its center the industrialized world and Europe more specifically. Most obviously, the leaders of resistance movements across the colonial world had close ties to Europe, the United States, and perhaps less ironically the Soviet Union. Many had studied in the imperial metropole. For example, many of the future leaders of nationalist movements in the Portuguese colonies met in the Portuguese capital of Lisbon in the 1940s. These included Amilcar Cabral of Portuguese Guinea and Agostinho Neto of Angola. Similarly, Mohandas Gandhi was a student in Britain and later a lawyer admitted to the British bar. Kwame Nkrumah studied in the United States, while Léopold Senghor studied in France. In some cases, they met together at large conferences that took place in Europe and the United States (such as the pan-African conferences) and the Soviet Union (such as the Third International of 1919 and the Congress of Oppressed Peoples of 1920). Even those nationalists who did not study in Europe or the United States read the work of British liberals and French enlightenment philosophers as well as communists and socialists from Germany, the Soviet Union, and later China.

There is no arguing that the cultures of the imperial metropoles contributed to and figured into the strategies of nationalist leaders in the colonial periphery. The Indian National Congress initially conducted all of its business in English. The 1945 Vietnamese Declaration of Independence cites as its precedents both the U.S. Declaration of Independence and the French Declaration of the Rights of Man. Tanganyikan nationalist leader Julius Nyerere translated Shakespeare's plays into Kiswahili both for their political messages and to prove that Tanganyika had become globally significant. Meanwhile, metropolitan support for liberation movements was a significant factor in their success. The Indian National Congress was in fact started by a Briton, Allen Octavian Hume, alongside several anglicized Indians. Labor unions in France supported strikers in West Africa. Liberals in the United States and Britain supported "moderate" nationalist movements around the world, and especially the independence of the settler-dominated colonies of Australia, New Zealand, and Canada. African-Americans strongly supported movements for national liberation in Africa beginning with Ethiopia in the 1930s and continuing to South Africa in the 1980s. The Soviet government lent financial and even military support to armed revolutions against colonial regimes after the late 1940s. All of these connections helped to inspire and support nationalist movements against colonial rule.

Nevertheless, the traditional Europe-centered narratives of the post-war spread of emancipatory nationalism miss much of the story. They fail to

---

[18] Said, *Culture and Imperialism*, 199.

perceive the connections among nationalists in different colonies and former colonies, who supported and inspired each other both before and following the Second World War. For example, two of the most important anti-colonial centers were communist Cuba and China, which followed up on their own national revolutions by rapidly extending their support to movements abroad. Similarly, the nationalists of Ireland served as important inspirations for anti-colonialists in India and other large British colonies. The violence that punctuated Ireland's relationship with Britain especially inspired Indian anti-colonialists in the province of Bengal, whose revolutionary strategies contrasted with the non-violent approach of Gandhian philosophy. The success of Ireland's 1916 Easter Uprising, and the continuing guerilla warfare that culminated in 1921 with the British acceptance of the creation of the independent Irish Free State, proved that armed revolt could be successful despite the might of the British Empire. The Indian press, especially in Bengal, wrote extensively on these events, and Indian nationalists had extensive contacts with Irish leaders.[19] Egyptian nationalist Said Zaghlul also admired the Irish, and modeled his Egyptian *Waft* party partly after the Irish Sinn Féin.[20]

Many of the long-distance connections among nationalists in this period have been little investigated. In the 1950s, for example, Israel and Ghana formed a special relationship that began with a personal interaction between Israeli Prime Minister David Ben-Gurion and Ghanaian Prime Minister Kwame Nkrumah. Israel's goal was to find allies among the other post-colonial states, a difficult task given the animosity of many influential newly independent Muslim countries. Meanwhile, Ghana sought the expertise of engineers and other professionals to help replace the British experts who were leaving the country. Thus as Ghana moved to independence, Nkrumah both accepted Israeli

agricultural and health experts and established economic ties with Israel. Yet within just a few years, the two countries found themselves in opposition as Israel aligned with the United States and Ghana began a relationship with the Warsaw Pact countries. At the same time, Nkrumah's allies among the independent states of North Africa began to pressure Ghana to commit to the anti-Israeli Arab–Africa bloc. Thus, their relationship ended in 1961, a victim both of Arab–Israeli and Cold War tensions.[21]

As we have seen in chapter 14, the diffusion of both the ideology and strategies of emancipatory nationalism was heavily influenced by the "demonstration effect" of early independent states upon latecomers. After Ghana's successful decolonization in 1957, for example, Kwame Nkrumah brought together nationalist leaders from many parts of Africa for discussions about the continent's future. Correspondence between Caribbean leaders was also significant, although language was sometimes a barrier. In North Africa, Algerian nationalists in their long struggle for independence leaned heavily on Moroccan, Tunisian, and even Libyan and Egyptian colleagues for inspiration and support.

PAN-MOVEMENTS

Nationalist movements that spanned the territory and population of a colonial state were the most widely embraced anti-colonial strategy and ideology. However, anti-colonial leaders made use of other philosophies and intellectual movements in the post-war era as well. For example, we have seen that sub-nationalisms based on ethnic, religious, or regional identity within colonial borders also flourished during this period. Ideologies that called on colonial subjects to unite *across* colonial boundaries also emerged contemporaneously. These were usually based on their members' identities as members of a class (communism), a race (pan-Africanism and Arab nationalism), a religion

[19] Michael Silvestri, "'The Sinn Fein of India': Irish Nationalism and the Policing of Revolutionary Terrorism in Bengal," *Journal of British Studies*, 39 (2000), 454–486.
[20] John Gallagher, "Nationalisms and the Crisis of Empire, 1919–1922," *Modern Asian Studies*, 15 (1981), 355–368.

[21] Zach Levey, "The Rise and Decline of a Special Relationship: Israel and Ghana, 1957–1966," *African Studies Review*, 46 (2003), 155–177.

(pan-Islamism), or a colonial subject (the **Non-Aligned Movement** [NAM] and Afro-Asian solidarity).

Many liberation movements of the late twentieth century borrowed from or even explicitly espoused communist philosophy and doctrine with the support of the Soviet Union and China. The communist leaderships in these states supported decolonization for both ideological and pragmatic reasons. Ideologically, international class struggle was the key to global revolution and thus was at the heart of communist ideology even following the Soviet Union's spat with China in the 1960s. Pragmatically, supporting anti-colonial insurgency was a way for the Soviets especially to weaken its Cold War enemies and to strike back at the powers that had supported anti-communist forces during the Russian Civil War of 1917–1922.[22] Meanwhile, anti-colonial forces embraced communism for several reasons of their own. In areas where militant struggle was required, the revolutionary ideology of communism and the long experience of communist guerilla struggles made it a suitable vehicle for anti-colonialist sentiment. In addition, embracing communism attracted financial and material support first from the Soviet Union and its satellites, and later from China and Cuba. Communism also increased the nationalists' appeal to urban workers and the poor because it promised relief from poverty. In most cases, however, their allegiance to communism was secondary to their struggle for national liberation. Thus although both the French and the United States insisted on seeing the Vietminh/Vietcong as communists first and foremost, Ho Chi Minh's soldiers were in fact more inspired to be fighting a war of national liberation than to be part of an episode in a global, communist class struggle.[23]

Many nationalist leaders, in fact, were wary of communism for several reasons. First, it often did not match their own aspirations to achieve wealth and personal success. In addition, in the long term state communism was not attractive to the bulk of the rural peasantry who wanted land of their own rather than to work on collective state farms. Finally, the price of Soviet support was often too high. Soviet military advisors frequently took control of insurgents' forces, and of course committing to the Soviets' side attracted the animosity of the United States.

Many nationalists both before and after independence therefore leaned toward the NAM, which generally stayed neutral in the Cold War.[24] Joining the NAM was a useful position for several reasons. First, it allowed formerly colonized states to constitute a powerful voting bloc in the United Nations. By threatening to vote as a group against the interests of either of the Cold War powers, the newly independent states could bring international pressure to bear for the first time. In this way, the NAM could often protect its members from the large powers' attempts to influence or subvert their politics. Additionally, joining the NAM helped some newly independent states to calm their own domestic squabbles between Marxists on the one hand and conservatives on the other.

In the 1960s, the NAM managed to lend some support to liberation movements through the United Nations, and was significant for placing the anti-colonial struggles and Latin American revolutionary movements in the same frame of reference. Otherwise, however, it played little role in physically supporting liberation movements and represented a real step down from the optimism for pan-colonial unity that had flourished in the 1950s. These hopes had been promoted by the Bandung Conference (or Asian-African Conference) of 1955. The conference had been initiated by many of the world's most important anti-colonial leaders, including Jawaharlal Nehru

---

[22] One vehicle for promoting communism as a response to colonialism before the Second World War was the Communist International (ComIntern), which was founded in Moscow in 1919. After the war, however, the international organization withered away.

[23] For the origins of Vietnamese communism in the context of nationalism, see William J. Duiker, *The Rise of Nationalism in Vietnam, 1900–1941* (Ithaca, NY: Cornell University Press, 1976).

[24] Hans Köchler, ed., *The Principles of Non-Alignment. The Non-Aligned Countries in the Eighties—Results and Perspectives* (London: Third World Centre, 1982). Note that Cuba and some other members of the NAM leaned heavily toward the Soviet side.

of India, Achmed Sukarno of Indonesia, and Gamal Abdel Nasser of Egypt. Nevertheless, the unity promised by this early conference dissipated in the 1950s due both to conflicts among members (such as that between India and Pakistan) and rifts created by the Cold War, and the NAM was no real replacement.[25] Perhaps the most pressing reason for the failure of both attempts had been the lack of popular support among the populations of both former colonies and those still struggling for their independence.

While the NAM neither succeeded in building a popular following nor in taking unified action, somewhat more significant links were forged at the level of "civilizational" and racial identities. Two important examples were **pan-Africanism** and **pan-Arabism**. These movements attracted a number of important anti-colonial activists, who established intellectual frameworks and even attracted popular support. Both played a significant role in the struggle against formal colonialism. Pan-Africanism as a political movement for achieving the liberation of peoples of African descent from racialized oppression in the Americas, Europe, and Africa had coalesced around the beginning of the twentieth century, although it had deeper roots as a philosophical movement. Pan-African meetings, or congresses, were organized largely by Afro-European and African-American leaders in 1919, 1921, 1923, and 1927. At the Fifth Pan-African Congress in 1945, African students and activists took the fore, including the future prime minister of Kenya, Jomo Kenyatta, and of Ghana, Kwame Nkrumah. Some interpretations of this conference have suggested that a split developed at this time between African leaders focusing on decolonization, and African-American and Afro-Caribbean leaders focused on civil rights struggles.[26]

Nevertheless, significant connections were sustained across the ocean. The Trinidadian intellectual George Padmore became a major advisor to Kwame Nkrumah. Aimé Césaire of Martinique and Léopold Senghor, the future leader of an independent Senegal, worked closely on the development of the concept of *negritude,* a philosophy that extolled an explicit quality of "blackness" that they argued was positive, rather than negative.[27] At the level of intellectual activities, scholars from both Africa and across the Atlantic worked together to challenge the western scholarly community. In 1969, a large joint group of scholars from Africa and African-American communities disassociated itself from the African Studies Association based in the United States, for example, in order to press for the reinterpretation of the histories of peoples of African descent from their own perspective.[28]

Within Africa, however, pan-Africanist leaders became most concerned with supporting each other across the continent. Unlike in the case of the NAM, these links had very real results. Nkrumah, one of the greatest advocates of continental integration, lent significant financial aid to the struggle of Sekou Touré and the insurrectionist leadership in the French colony of Guinea. Upon independence, plans were even put into place for a union between the two states that later included Mali as well. This plan eventually failed largely due to the opposition of other nationalist leaders in West Africa, but important connections had nevertheless been forged. Beneath the level of state politics, pan-Africanism as a force for regional and continental unity also survived in the West African Press Union and West African Student Union and publications such as the *Présence africaine*. Pan-Africanist sentiment also helped lead to the development of the Organization of African Unity, now known as the African Union, by which African states coordinate both economic and political policy.

[25] An early commentary on the collapse of unity between postcolonial states was Guy J. Pauker, "The Rise and Fall of Afro-Asian Solidarity," *Asian Survey,* 5 (1965), 425–432. For an approachable narrative, see Peter Willetts, *The Non-Aligned Movement: The Origins of a Third World Alliance* (London: Pinter, 1983).

[26] For an analysis, see Alexandre Mboukou, "The Pan African Movement, 1900–1945: A Study in Leadership Conflicts Among the Disciples of Pan Africanism," *Journal of Black Studies,* 13 (1983), 275–288.

[27] Aimé Césaire, *Discourse on Colonialism* (New York: Monthly Review Press, 2000). Originally published 1950. Léopold Senghor, "The Spirit of Civilization, or the Laws of African Negro Culture," *Présence Africaine* (1956), 51–64.

[28] Joseph E. Harris, in collaboration with Simane Zeghidour, "Africa and Its Diaspora Since 1935," in Mazrui, *Africa Since 1935,* 715–716.

Similar to pan-Africanism, pan-Arabism as an ideology and strategy called for liberation from colonialism through the creation of a state that united all of the Arab peoples of the world. In essence, it promoted an Arab nationalism, and thus its proponents such as Abdul Rahman al-Kawakabi and Shakib Arslan imagined and wrote of a unified Arab culture and history that was only partly based on fact.[29] Interestingly, one of the intellectual roots of this concept of a single Arab people was the racializing doctrine of British colonialism that developed in support of Arabian revolts against the Ottomans during the First World War. By the 1940s, however, pan-Arabism had been turned against the British as a force for liberation. It later came to be a rallying ideology against the state of Israel as well. One of its most vociferous supporters was Egyptian leader Gamal Abdel Nasser who saw Egypt as being at the junction of the pan-African and pan-Arab worlds. In 1958, Nasser's Egypt even briefly entered a federation with Syria as the United Arab Republic, which was conceptualized as a core from which a truly united Arab state could be built. As the concept of the Arab nation developed, pan-Arabism came to encompass not just the Arabian Peninsula and Egypt but Arabic speakers across northern Africa and Asia. The Arab League, founded in 1945, embraced this linguistic definition of the nation by including states as far away from Arabia as Morocco, which was admitted in 1958.

Popular support for pan-Arabism flourished in the late 1940s and 1950s as a liberation ideology. In Syria and Iraq, this was expressed mostly by the development of the Arab Renaissance or Baath parties. These two parties, because they were largely secular, built on Arab rather than Islamic identities for the nation. In the long run, however, the two parties both came to work *within*

the borders of their respective states and became antagonistic toward each other.[30] Even the United Arab Republic failed to work out, as the antagonisms of Arab leaders overcame the sense of unity that prevailed among much of the public.

Pan-Arabism, of course, had never embraced all Muslims, many of whom were not Arabs. However, the alternate sense of a nation of all Muslims, or pan-Islamism, was espoused by many Arabs and non-Arab Muslims alike. In Algeria, for example, French settler colonialism had discriminated against the local population not as Arabs but as Muslims. This helped to promote Islam as a unifying identity for the FLN (*Front de Libération Nationale* or National Liberation Front) of Algeria, which depicted its 1954 uprising against the French partly in religious terms. Appeals to Islam were common among anticolonial movements in the Islamic world, of course, but this did not necessarily lead to frequent calls for the revival of a united Islamic caliphate. Instead, pan-Islamism was more often subsumed by local nationalisms, whether in the form of Baath parties as in the Middle East or nationalist movements that sought unity across religions as in Indonesia. Thus pan-Islamic movements such as the Muslim Brotherhood, although influential in fighting for liberation in Egypt and elsewhere, did not come to power themselves in this era.

SETTLERS AND SETTLER NATIONALISM

A final variant on and reaction to emancipatory nationalism during the second half of the twentieth century was the emergence of settler nationalism within the colonies of the European empires. **Settler nationalism** was a variant on emancipatory nationalism because it too imagined a nation within the colony, although only settlers of European descent (or whites) were considered eligible for citizenship. It was a reaction to emancipatory nationalism because in many cases it

---

[29] A perhaps unbalanced reading that asserts this point is Barry Rubin, "Pan-Arab Nationalism: The Ideological Dream as Compelling Force," *Journal of Contemporary History*, 26 (1991), 535–551. More supportive accounts are Bassam Tibi, *Arab Nationalism: Between Islam and the Nation-State* (London: Palgrave, 1997); and C. Ernest Dawn, "The Formation of Pan-Arab Ideology in the Inter-War Years," *International Journal of Middle East Studies*, 2 (1988), 67–91.

[30] John F. Devlin, "The Baath Party: Rise and Metamorphosis," *American Historical Review*, 96 (1991), 1396–1407.

emerged in response to the political agitation of the indigenous population.

In Africa, settler nationalism emerged most often as a rejection of metropolitan attempts to appease demands for independence by colonial subjects. In southern and central Africa, for example, British settlers became increasingly anxious in the 1960s as Harold MacMillan's administration began to negotiate with "moderate" African nationalists. Macmillan's Colonial Secretary, Iain Macleod, had called for African majority rule in Kenya in the first year of that decade, aggravating the 60,000 Europeans there. He also began negotiations with the increasingly effective nationalist leaderships in Northern Rhodesia and Nyasaland.[31] Kenya became independent in 1964, as did Nyasaland (as Malawi) and Northern Rhodesia (as Zambia). None of these regions had had a large enough settler population to oppose this devolution, but Southern Rhodesia did. Fearing that they too would soon be forced to agree to the same sort of handover, the white settler leadership of Rhodesia in 1965 declared independence from the British Empire. A similar crisis catalyzed a settler rebellion in Algeria, where French President de Gaulle faced a potent combination of nationalist uprising in the colony and popular exhaustion in France with the effort to put it down. Thus in 1961, the French electorate voted to allow Algerians to vote on their own future. In response, French troops in Algeria (especially the Foreign Paratroop Regiment) and settlers, or *pieds-noirs* (black feet) rose up in rebellion and tried to form a settler-led state.

In both of these cases, the rise of settler nationalism exposed the settlers' ambivalent situations. On the one hand, as colonizers they generally sought to separate themselves both culturally and physically from colonial subjects (see chapter 12). They did this in part by clinging closely to their status as metropolitan citizens, which they demonstrated by extreme loyalty to the empire and by rituals that they identified with

the homeland—for example, afternoon tea was a key ornament of settler culture in the British colonies. At the same time, settlers often rejected the liberal attitudes of the metropole and saw themselves as both hardier and more capable than the metropolitan government of managing "inferior" indigenous populations. In 1960s Rhodesia, this worldview manifested itself in a kind of "populism" among white farm owners who looked down on both the local population and the "corrupt" corporations and financiers in Britain whom they resented.[32] In South Africa, the settler nationalism that was built first by Afrikaners but then later embraced by some English speakers exalted the individualism of frontier life and white South Africans' practicality and willingness to work hard.[33] European settlers in Africa often saw Europe as being too soft in defense of civilization against the assault of African barbarism and communism. These sentiments helped to justify the South African government's decision to declare itself an independent republic under white rule in 1961. Similarly, while anti-British sentiment in Australia and New Zealand was stirred up by tragic losses during the First World War, inhabitants of both dependencies had already begun to see themselves as special and different frontier-dwellers in the years leading up to it. In some cases, this led them to describe themselves with the types of qualities they ascribed to the local population of Aborigines or Maori: hardiness, frontier spirituality, an affiliation with the land.

Settlers, of course, were able to seize the structure of the colonial state far more easily than were colonial subjects. In some colonies, they already ran much of the state and even served as members of colonial parliaments of legislative councils. In addition, these colonizers controlled

---

[31] W. David McIntyre, *British Decolonization, 1946–1997: When, Why and How Did the British Empire Fall?* (New York: St. Martin's Press, 1998), 45–52.

[32] Ian Henderson, "White Populism in Southern Rhodesia," *Comparative Studies in Society and History*, 14 (1972), 387–399.

[33] Benedikt Stuchtey, "In Search of Lost Identity: South Africa Between Great Trek and Colonial Nationalism, 1830–1910," in *Across Cultural Borders: Historiography in Global Perspective*, edited by Eckhardt Fuchs and Benedikt Stuchtey (Lanham: Rowman & Littlefield, 2002), 53–74.

much of the local religious and economic institutions and were allowed to carry weapons both as private citizens and as members of the colonial army or militia.[34] On the other hand, while they sought to control their own circumstances and maintain their economic, social, and political control over the colony, settlers often could not shake their cultural and national-racial affiliation with the metropole. Therefore, they sought not so much legal sovereignty as effective control over their colonies in all but the most threatening conditions. Thus while Australia, New Zealand, and Canada effectively achieved their independence with the 1931 Statute of Westminster, passed by the British parliament, their new governments avoided describing this separation as "independence." New Zealand and Canada didn't even ratify this act until the mid-1940s.

In the long term, the success of settler nationalism in maintaining the colonizers' hold on political power within the colony was a function of demography. In regions where the population of peoples of European descent was higher than that of the former colonial subjects, settler nationalism resulted in the creation of an independent state dominated by the settlers. This was true, for example, in Canada, New Zealand, some Caribbean islands, and Australia. In regions where settlers were in a minority, however, settler rule was eventually overturned. This was the case in Rhodesia (which became Zimbabwe in 1980) and in South Africa (1994).

THE MESSY REALITY OF THE ROAD TO INDEPENDENCE

In this chapter, we have sought to define general trends rather than immerse ourselves in specific stories. Yet there is a danger in doing this that readers will gain the impression that decolonization was a simple, linear pathway from colonial rule to independence. In fact, the process was convoluted, fragmented, and often occurred in fits and starts. Moreover, in some cases it became extraordinarily violent. In the process, nationalisms, sub-nationalisms, pan-movements,

settler nationalisms, and public opinion in the metropole and abroad interacted in often unexpected ways. Two examples serve to illustrate this: decolonization in Kenya and in Algeria.

Kenya was a British with a small but well-entrenched European settler class largely living in the cool highlands of the interior, a significant number of Indians who served largely as a mid-level professional and trading class, and a large multi-ethnic population of Africans of whom the Kikuyu were the largest group. Perhaps more than any other colonial subjects in Kenya, the Kikuyu socio-economy had been devastated by the appropriation of land for settler-owned plantations. In the period prior to the Second World War, various reform movements based on ethnic or labor affiliations emerged, many of which attempted to address the land issue, but their ineffectiveness in winning reforms led to the rise of the Kikuyu Central Association (KCA), which represented landless rural Kikuyu. By the end of the Second World War, this organization had become militant, and it was banned in the 1940s. However, it continued to exist in secret. Meanwhile, the East African Trades Union Congress emerged to represent urban Kikuyu speakers who had fled to the cities in search of jobs. This organization was banned by the British administration following a 1950 strike, and also went underground. This left only the more moderate Kenya African Union (KAU), which presented demands for reform to the British Colonial Secretary in May 1951. Under pressure from European settlers, however, the Colonial Secretary failed to meet these demands.

Thus by 1951, Kenyans, and especially the Kikuyu, had become much more militantly anti-colonial. Landless squatters, unemployed urban workers, and poorly paid laborers were all disgruntled. The introduction of a forced-labor program in the highlands and the transition to mechanized farm labor were probably the final straw for many of them.[35] The result was an

---

[34] Abernethy, *The Dynamics of Global Dominance*, 318–320.

[35] Kinuthia Macharia, *The Social Context of the Mau Mau Movement in Kenya (1952–1960)* (Lanham: University Press of America, 2006).

armed uprising that included quite large forces in the forested interior and guerilla groups in the urban areas. This movement is memorialized as the Mau Mau uprising, although its members called themselves the Land and Freedom Army. Between 1952 and 1954, they carried out quite an aggressive campaign against the British, who responded with brutal force and the establishment of vast prison camps. The Mau Mau have often been called a *nationalist* group, yet this is disputed since they largely (although not exclusively) drew their membership from among the Kikuyu.[36]

It could be said that the British won the battles of the Mau Mau conflict only to lose the war. Although the rebellion was checked, by 1956 the massive expense of the campaign against the Mau Mau together with the bad publicity generated by the evidence of terrible crimes committed by soldiers and settlers against incarcerated Africans began to turn public opinion in Britain against continued colonial rule in Kenya. World events also played a role—the nationalization of the Suez Canal by Egypt in 1956 made Britain's rule of East Africa much more difficult. Thus by the early 1960s, the British government began to negotiate with "moderate" African leaders including many imprisoned early in the campaign. Despite settler protests, they gradually reached an agreement to hand over power. The process, which took several years, brought to the fore the Kenya African National Union (KANU) led by Jomo Kenyatta. Although he had been imprisoned early in the conflict, Kenyatta was less radical than many of those who fought during the war and managed to placate both those white settlers who remained and the Kikuyu-speaking population, some of whom were now taking over former plantations.[37] His main opponents were some radical former combatants and ethnic minorities. Kenyatta was able to overcome these groups, although they formed an

opposition, and to peacefully take power from the British on December 12, 1963.

Neither the Land and Freedom Army nor KANU could be said to have been truly "nationalist" before the 1960s. At times, both sought to be broadly inclusive, but they generally wavered between representing nationalist and sub-nationalist interests. Nevertheless, they were able to muster enough of a consensus and force the British administration's hand enough to bring the pressure for decolonization to a tipping point. Helped somewhat by world events, they strained the ties between the settlers and the British public and eventually made continual colonial rule too politically and monetarily costly for the British government.

A not entirely dissimilar process characterized the struggle for independence in Algeria. There, as in much of North Africa, the Second World War ended with high expectations, especially following the independence of the former Italian colony of Libya. Yet the strength of the very large settler population and the close ties to France—which still considered Algeria to technically be a province—meant that the nascent nationalist movement could gain little traction. These early nationalists were largely Francophone members of the middle classes. In the 1920s–1930s, they had formed reform-minded groups such as the Étoile (Star) and the PPA (*Parti du Peuple Algérien* or Algerian People's Party). Their leaders were tied to various ideologies, including both pan-Arabism and socialism/communism. They were, however, largely urban and excluded the Berber population of the interior. The PPA was largely inactive during the Second World War. Immediately upon the end of that conflict, however, rioting and revenge attacks took place between settlers and Muslim Algerians. Following a government crackdown, many of these groups organized underground as the FLN, partly inspired by the Vietnamese defeat of French forces that year at the Battle of Dien Bien Phu.[38]

---

[36] Bruce J. Berman, "Nationalism, Ethnicity, and Modernity: The Paradox of Mau Mau," *Canadian Journal of African Studies*, 25 (1991), 181–206.

[37] David Birmingham, *The Decolonization of Africa* (Athens: Ohio University Press, 1995), 45–46.

[38] Charles-Robert Ageron, *De l'Algérie française à l'Algérie algérienne* (Saint Denis: Bouchène, 2005).

Starting in November 1954, the FLN's armed wing (the ALN [*Armée de Libération Nationale*]) unleashed a guerrilla war against the French army and the settler population in Algeria. After 1956, they were assisted by aid from many independent states that was smuggled through Tunisia and Morocco. Over the next few years, this campaign was successful in scaring many European farmers away from the interior, although it was largely quashed in the city of Algiers itself. By 1956, the French government had committed approximately 400,000 soldiers in Algeria. However, their inability to successfully end conflict brought down the French government, and ushered into power the former General Charles de Gaulle, whom the military hoped would prosecute the war vigorously.[39]

Yet at the same time, French public opinion was shifting slowly against the continuation of the conflict, especially among the political center.[40] In part, this was because of the prospect of the creation of a European Economic Community that shifted French economic attention from North Africa to Europe. Equally important was evidence of torture and brutality by French troops in Algeria. Thus despite having achieved some military success, by late 1959 de Gaulle called for "self-determination" in Algeria. The transfer of power was eventually set for July 5, 1962, but was almost derailed by an uprising among French military hardliners and settlers. Yet this group, known as the OAS (*Organisation de l'armée secrete*) was quashed by loyal French troops. In the event, power was successfully handed over to the FLN, which immediately took over as a "national" leadership. All other organized groups in the country, including those who called for a pan-Muslim national identity and those claiming to represent the minority Berber population, were declaimed as "factionalists" and suppressed. Unlike KANU in Kenya, the FLN was unable and unwilling to convince many settlers to stay following the transfer of power.

Three conclusions stand out from these two stories. The first is that nationalist movements and parties were not always entirely inclusive, even when they claimed a national mandate. The second is that decolonization was often not the result of military or electoral victories, but rather the gradual shifting of public opinion in the metropole due to the rising moral, economic, and political cost of imperial rule. Settlers could slow this process down, but could not ultimately arrest it. Finally, the story of decolonization in a single colony is not only local but also involves the metropole, other colonies, and the changing global situation.

Conclusion

The story told in this chapter focuses on political decolonization; that is, the transfer of sovereignty from empire to nation-state. This process took place at an accelerated rate in the 1950s and 1960s, with almost all former colonies and dependencies achieving independence by 1980. Arguably, however, this transfer did not end the power of empires to intervene in the former colonies and dependencies. Decolonization did not guarantee to the newly independent states the wealth necessary to place their economies on an equal footing with those of the early industrializers. Nor did it rid them of the stigma and psychological effects of colonialism, or the damage it had done to their social organizations and cultures. The same might be said of the metropoles, which perhaps escaped the economic repercussions of imperialism, but nevertheless still today cannot escape the rebounding ill-effects of the racist and totalitarian systems they created. Finally, even the gradual demise of the formal empires arguably only created space for new imperial systems, ones that (as in the early and mid-nineteenth century) were informal but not irrelevant. It is these realities that help to shape the current, post-colonial era of world history.

---

[39] Birmingham, *The Decolonization of Africa*, 19–22.
[40] Christopher Harrison, "French Attitudes to Empire and the Algerian War," *African Affairs*, 82 (1983), 75–95.

Questions

1. To what degree do you agree with Benedict Anderson that national identities were "invented" during the struggle for independence, and to what degree do you agree with Carolyn Hamilton that there were limits to this invention and that nationalist sentiments were based on real shared experiences and histories?

2. How did the leaders of the Congress Party construct a sense of an Indian "nation" as part of the struggle for independence? How successful were they in doing so?

3. How and why did settlers impact the speed and course of struggles for decolonization in colonies in which they were numerous?

4. How do you account for the fact that pan-movements were largely unsuccessful compared to nationalists who created new states within the borders of former colonies?

CHAPTER **16**

Imperialism and Colonialism: A Post-Colonial World?

Did the end of the great formal European empires signal the beginning of a post-imperial and post-colonial world? Are empires now merely the domain of historians, or do they function in the contemporary world? Are the former colonial subjects of these empires now "free" of the effects *imperialism* and *colonialism*? These are the questions underlying our investigation in this chapter of three controversies beginning with the period of decolonization and beyond. The first controversy is the problem of whether the Cold War can be described as an era of imperialism and its chief belligerents—the United States and its allies on the one hand and the Soviet Union and its associated states on the other—imperial powers. Second, we ask whether there is a form of economic neo-imperialism operating in the world today through international corporations and institutions. Third, we look at the debate over how the cultures of imperialism and colonialism created in earlier ages continue to impact the lives of people today.

In the wake of the political decolonizations of the late 1940s through the mid-1970s, many commentators and scholars seemed to think the age of empires was over. Building partly on the predictions of mid-century figures such as British Prime Minister Winston Churchill, a series of writers has over the past half-century predicted the replacement of global empires with a system of democratic, parliamentary nation-states. Perhaps the best-known contemporary contributor to this theory is Johns Hopkins professor Francis Fukuyama. In a 1989 article read and debated widely in both scholarly and political circles, Fukuyama famously argued that: "The triumph of the West, of the Western idea, is evident first of all in the total exhaustion of viable systematic alternatives to Western liberalism."[1] As such, he concluded that empires had become obsolete, and that all over the world people were moving instead toward a nation-state form of government that looked like "western" liberal democracies.

While Fukuyama wrote of North American-style nation-states as the successors to the age of empires, other scholars such as historian Bernard Lewis and political scientist Samuel P. Huntington had visions of the world crystallizing into a system of loosely bound civilizations, rather than empires. Lewis, specifically, saw the politicization of Islam as heralding "no less than a clash of civilizations—the perhaps irrational but surely historic reactions of an ancient rival

---

[1]Francis Fukuyama, "The End of History?" *National Interest* (Summer 1989), 3. See also *The End of History and the Last Man* (New York: Penguin Books, 1992).

against our Judeo-Christian heritage, our secular present, and the worldwide expansion of both."[2] Similarly, Huntington predicted that "the principal conflicts of global politics will occur between nations and groups of different civilizations. The clash of civilizations will dominate global politics. The fault lines between civilizations will be the battle lines of the future."[3] Such theories gained strength with the events of September 11, 2001, which seemed to some proof that culturally integrated "civilizations" rather than centralized empires had become the fundamental political institutions of the day.

However, not everyone was quite sure that colonialism and imperialism could be thrown into the dustbin of history. As early as the 1950s, leaders of the newly emerging nations understood that the global Cold War, and its related alliances and ideologies, might lead to the rise of new empires that could have direct implications for their future sovereignty. By the 1970s and 1980s, these leaders also frequently called attention to the survival of imperial domination in the form of new global economic systems and institutions spearheaded by western powers, especially the United States. Beginning in these same decades, scholars and intellectuals tracked what they believed was an emerging "cultural" imperialism emanating from the west. This form of imperialism, they argued, perpetuates the racial, psychological, and intellectual legacies of earlier colonial eras through the continued subjugation of the world's peoples to western language, hierarchies, and notions of "difference." Most recently, the behavior of the United States in its global War on Terror since 2001 has convinced a wide variety of people around the world— including state leaders, intellectuals, and ordinary citizens in Europe, North America, Latin America, the Middle East, Africa, and Asia—that imperialism is alive and well a half-century after decolonization. For many of the world's peoples, then, self-determination, freedom, and sovereignty on a global scale has still seemed elusive even after the collapse of most empires following the Second World War.

Over the course of this book, we have explored the concept of imperialism and colonialism from the fifteenth through the twentieth century. During these five centuries, the practices and experiences of imperial expansion and colonialism did not remain constant. Players changed, as did motivations, scope and extent, technologies, and strategies. At the same time, there were enough continuities between the actions of the states involved to locate them over this *longue durée* as imperial, and the regions of their expansion as colonial. One question for the post-colonial period may be whether these years finally represent a clear break with the long global trend of empire, or if instead they should best be viewed as some new phase of imperial activity. In the following, we use the definitions and constructions with which the book began to explore if and how the Cold War, global economic institutions, the phenomenon of cultural imperialism, and U.S. military intervention after 2001 fit with the past half-millennium of imperialist and colonialist activity.

COLD WAR IMPERIALISM?

In the introduction to this book, we argued that empire "is an agglomeration of multiple polities and diverse populations bound together in an uneven relationship in which one polity exercises significant control over the others and, in many cases, claims sole sovereignty over all of the polities." As we have seen, the claim to sole sovereignty was not definitive: empires often included territories controlled not only by formal rule but also by informal means, including unequal legal and institutional arrangements, political interference, and the threat of violence.[4] Imperialism, by contrast, we characterized as "an ideology or

[2] Bernard Lewis, "The Roots of Muslim Rage," *Atlantic Monthly* (September 1990), 9, http://www.theatlantic.com/doc/print/199009/muslim-rage.

[3] Samuel P. Huntington, "The Clash of Civilizations?" *Foreign Affairs*, 72 (Summer 1993), 22–36.

[4] Jürgen Osterhammel, "Britain and China," in *The Oxford History of the British Empire*, vol. III, *The Nineteenth Century*, edited by Andrew Porter (Oxford: Oxford University Press, 1999), 148–149.

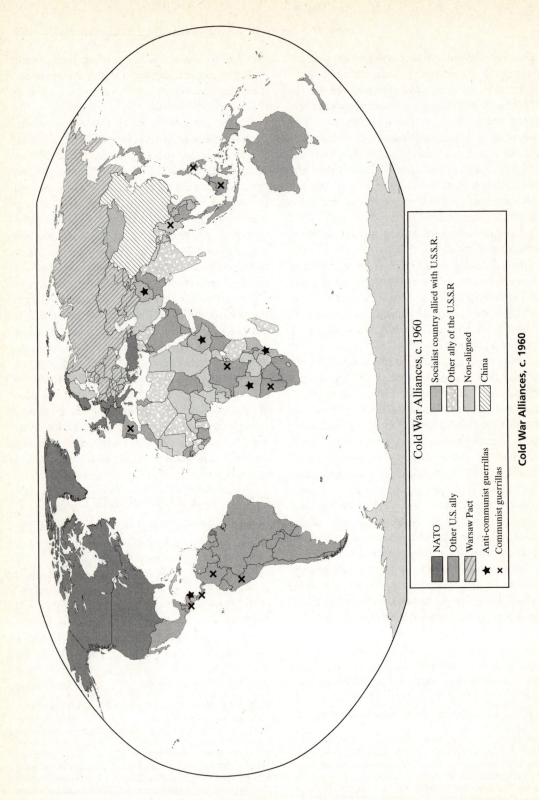

Cold War Alliances, c. 1960

	NATO
	Other U.S. ally
	Warsaw Pact
★	Anti-communist guerrillas
✗	Communist guerrillas

	Socialist country allied with U.S.S.R.
	Other ally of the U.S.S.R
	Non-aligned
	China

Cold War Alliances, c. 1960

doctrine in support of the creation and maintenance of empire" that, when translated into action, is "expressed as an aggressive set of policies culminating variously in formal dominion or informal control over external polities or peoples . . . as well as being characterized by belligerence toward rival expansionist powers." Finally, we argued that colonialism "refers to the set of practices and policies implemented by imperial agents to obtain and maintain control, stability, economic objectives, and social engineering in the constituent polities of the imperial periphery." In light of these definitions, to what extent is it possible to argue that the Cold War represented not just an ideological struggle but also a conflict between two very powerful twentieth-century empires?

The Cold War was a mammoth confrontation between the United States and its allies on the one hand and the Soviet Union and its allies on the other that took shape in the years immediately following the end of the Second World War. The conflict between the two sides did not appear instantaneously, but rather came on "like a rolling fog" between the Yalta and Potsdam conferences of 1945 and the outbreak of hostilities in Korea in 1950.[5] Indeed, at the end of the war, it appeared that all parties of the Grand Alliance between the United States, Britain, and the Soviet Union were committed to maintaining an alliance during peacetime.[6] Instead, especially after Harry Truman succeeded Franklin Roosevelt in the White House, in the five years between 1945 and 1950 the United States and the Soviet Union grew to believe that their respective social, political, and economic systems were mutually incompatible, and that each represented a dire threat to the survival of the other.[7] In this period, both sides began to use their considerable economic and military might to divide Europe, and then the world, between them.

At immediate issue following the war was the fate of war-torn Europe. Given their enormous suffering as a result of German aggression, the Soviets insisted on establishing dominance over eastern Europe—many of whose states fought on the German side during the war, and others of whom had been antagonistic to Soviet aims in earlier periods. From the Soviet point of view, Soviet security required "friendly," pro-communist regimes in all of the buffer states between Germany and the Soviet Union. The United States and Britain, however, were wary about the implications of Soviet domination in eastern Europe, and feared that Soviet influence could spread to the devastated and fragile countries of western Europe as well.[8] As a result of this and other conflicts within Europe, both sides quickly developed doctrines and policies that explicitly pitted them against one another. In particular, 1947 was critical. In March of that year, President Harry Truman of the United States articulated what became known as the Truman Doctrine, in which the United States pledged to assist any democratic nation threatened by either internal or external authoritarian (that is, Communist) forces. Henceforth, the goal of the United States would be to "contain" communism in the Soviet Union and its eastern European neighbors.[9] The Truman Doctrine was followed by the establishment, in June, of a massive U.S. aid policy for the reconstruction of Europe that came to be known as the Marshall Plan. The Soviet Union's Josef Stalin rightly interpreted the Marshall Plan as a U.S. effort to undermine communist movements throughout Europe, and announced the withdrawal of both the

---

[5] A.J. Stockwell, "Southeast Asia in War and Peace: The End of the European Colonial Empires," in *The Cambridge History of Southeast Asia*, vol. II, part II, edited by Nicholas Tarling (Cambridge: Cambridge University Press, 1999), 33.

[6] Henry Heller, *The Cold War and the New Imperialism: A Global History, 1945–2005* (New York: Monthly Review Press, 2006), 29.

[7] Melvyn Leffler describes the animosities that developed between the United States and the Soviet Union just after the war partly in terms of the personalities of Truman and Stalin, both of whom were deeply suspicious of the other's motives. See Leffler, *For the Soul of Mankind: The United States, the Soviet Union, and the Cold War* (New York: Hill and Wang, 2007), 79–82.

---

[8] Geoffrey Roberts, "Stalin and Soviet Policy," in *Origins of the Cold War: An International History*, 2nd edition, edited by Melvyn P. Leffler and David S. Painter (New York: Routledge, 1994), 43–44.

[9] The possibility that Greece would fall prey to a socialist movement and then be dominated by Soviet influence was one of the key events that moved Truman to articulate his famous doctrine. For a detailed account of these motives, see Elizabeth Edwards Spalding, *The First Cold Warrior: Harry Truman, Containment, and the Remaking of Liberal Internationalism* (Lexington: University Press of Kentucky, 2006), chapter 3.

Soviet Union and the states of eastern Europe from all negotiations for aid.[10] In September, Soviet hostility to the United States over both the Truman Doctrine and the Marshall Plan was made explicit when Politburo member Andrei Zhdanov declared an open conflict between the two powers, in which the Soviet goal would be to resist "the threat of new wars and imperialist expansion" represented by the United States.[11]

In 1950, the conflict spilled over from Europe to the rest of the world when North Korean forces invaded South Korea on June 25. Because the Soviets and the Americans had not been able to agree on a plan for the future government of Korea at the end of the Second World War, they had divided the peninsula between a Soviet-supported north and a U.S.-supported south at the thirty-eighth parallel. Both sides armed their respective client-states, and then in 1948 both withdrew.[12] The invasion by the North Koreans into the South proved to be the first test of Truman's policy of "containment" outside of Europe. Given that communists in China had just succeeded in gaining control over that country a year earlier, and that Chinese and Soviet communists now seemed to be working in conjunction with one another, from the perspective of the United States the situation was urgent. As a result, the United States—backed by the United Nations (UN)—responded by sending troops to push the North Koreans out of the South. This effort proved successful until forces fighting for the South crossed the thirty-eighth parallel into North Korea—a move that led the Chinese to send its own army into North Korea to block the advance of the UN troops.[13] Following Chinese participation in the war, the conflict settled into a bloody three-year stalemate in which over 3 million Koreans died. In 1953, when both sides realized a decisive win did not seem likely, they signed a cease-fire that effectively ended the war and left the two Koreas intact.

Stalemate notwithstanding, the Korean War proved to be a critical moment in the Cold War, as the United States and its allies committed itself to fighting the spread of communism all over the world, while the Soviet Union (in an increasingly uneasy alliance with China) sought to aid communist movements wherever possible. Eisenhower made this commitment explicit in 1954, when he argued that allowing one state to fall to communism would result in a "domino effect," in which the establishment of communism in one country would cause neighboring countries to follow like a series of dominos.[14]

From Korea until the end of the Cold War in 1989, the United States and the Soviet Union battled each other for global dominance, allies, and access to critical resources on nearly every continent. In addition to attempting to marshal as many allies to their respective sides as possible—and in doing so to protect their own security and global political goals—they also sought to secure areas that would provide access to critical resources necessary to waging the struggle, especially oil. Their methods for effecting their goals, moreover, were unabashedly interventionist: both sides sought to influence the political and ideological commitments of other states through promises of economic aid, diplomatic pressure, covert operations geared toward regime change, and by providing both military training and arms to local allies. To bolster their powers of persuasion and influence, Cold War adversaries built huge military complexes capable of extending their land, air, and sea power to locations all over the

---

[10] Truman did, in fact, see the Marshall Plan in terms of the policy of containment. Ibid., chapter 4.

[11] Geoffrey Roberts, "Starting the Cold War," *History Review* 38 (December 2000), 9–14.

[12] Peter Preston, *Pacific Asia in the Global System* (Malden, MA: Blackwell, 1998), 97.

[13] For an account of the lead-up to the Chinese decision to join the war effort on behalf of the North Koreans, as well as Stalin's role in requesting such action, see Korea Institute of Military History, *The Korean War*, vol. II (Lincoln, NE: Bison Books, 2001), chapter 3. Originally published by South Korean Institute of Military History, 1998).

[14] Eisenhower's exact words were "You have a row of dominos set up, you knock over the first one, and . . . the last one . . . will go over very quickly." John Lewis Gaddis, *The Cold War: A New History* (New York: Penguin Group, 2005), 123.

world. Thus, when persuasion and covert influence proved ineffective, Cold War adversaries sometimes used their military capabilities to participate directly in "hot" wars by invading or occupying strategically important territories. They also created vast military alliances in order to serve as counterweights to one another: the North Atlantic Treaty Organization (NATO) for the United States and its allies in 1949, and the Warsaw Pact alliance for the Soviets and their allies in 1955.

In both the United States and the Soviet Union, the mutual struggle between the two superpowers manifested in rhetorical belligerence toward one another, which political leaders in both nations sought to manipulate into cultures of conformity among their own populations. This trend reached its apogee in the United States during the 1950s, when senator Joseph McCarthy used the communist threat to expose, humiliate, and in many cases ruin Americans with ties to radical or leftist groups.[15] This "witch-hunt" atmosphere whipped up public support for anti-communist activities both inside and outside the United States, and simultaneously silenced many citizens who might otherwise have been critical of its foreign policy. While the extremes of the McCarthy era did not outlast the 1950s, fears about communist threats in the rest of the world did: as late as 1983, President Ronald Reagan reminded the American public that the Cold War was a "struggle between right and wrong and good and evil."[16] Until the end of the Cold War, politicians were able to use such constructions to justify highly interventionist foreign policies. In the Soviet Union, state propaganda about the evils and decadence of capitalism partnered with deep censorship of individual

expression: writers, artists, politicians, and workers were expected to tow the communist ideological line or else suffer persecution or imprisonment.[17] Soviet citizens, moreover, were directed to devote themselves to fighting capitalism as practiced by the United States and its allies, which Soviet leaders characterized as not only bourgeois and decadent but also imperialist.

Whether or not they could be classified as cultures of imperialism, these cultures of mutual antagonism both supported and justified a wide variety of interventions into the affairs of sovereign states on the pretext of safeguarding either U.S. or Soviet national security. Such interventions were frequently justified in areas that the United States, the Soviet Union, or China regarded as within their respective spheres of influence. This reasoning had, in fact, driven China to send 300,000 troops to defend North Korea when U.S. forces pushed invading North Korean forces north of the thirty-eighth parallel in 1950. Concern over spheres of interest likewise drove Soviet foreign intervention. We have already seen that Soviet desires to protect its borders from invading forces were behind its insistence on ensuring the establishment of friendly regimes in states such as Poland, eastern Germany, Romania, Bulgaria, Hungary, and Czechoslovakia. In practice, this meant that the states surrounding the Soviet Union had little choice but to adopt socialist governments on the Soviet model, and to accept direction from the Soviet capital in Moscow on matters of both internal and foreign policy. When Soviet satellite states sought to exert a measure of independence, as they did in Hungary in 1956 and Czechoslovakia in 1968, Moscow responded with military action. Following the suppression of the Czechoslovakian movement in 1968, Soviet premier Leonid

---

[15] The new medium of television was critical to the spread of McCarthyism, even as anti-communists targeted television and film personalities as among the most strident leftists. See Thomas Patrick Doherty, *Cold War, Cool Medium: Television, McCarthyism, and American Culture* (New York: Columbia University Press, 2003).

[16] James Mann, *The Rebellion of Ronald Reagan: A History of the End of the Cold War* (New York: Viking Penguin, 2009), 29.

[17] This policy of internal censorship and persecution became known as Zhdanovshchina, for Andrei Zhdanov's role in creating it. For a more detailed account of Zhdanovshchina, see Geoffrey Roberts, *Stalin's Wars: From World War to Cold War, 1939–1953* (New Haven, CT: Yale University Press, 2006), 333–346.

Brezhnev justified the action with the Doctrine of Limited Sovereignty, which held that Moscow had the right to invade any surrounding socialist country that was under threat by elements "hostile to socialism."[18]

The United States also insisted on its right to safeguard areas within its sphere of influence, which since the nineteenth century had included all of Latin America and the Caribbean. Thus, when in 1959 the Cuban nationalist and socialist Fidel Castro overthrew the U.S.-oriented government of Fulgencio Batista y Zaldivar, the U.S. government retaliated by imposing an embargo on all Cuban goods—the export of which had been crucial to Cuba's economy—and also by planning a secret invasion of the island. This plan culminated in 1961, during the presidency of John F. Kennedy, in the Bay of Pigs invasion. Although the goal had been to storm the island with CIA (Central Intelligence Agency) operatives and anti-socialist Cubans and then overthrow Castro, the invasion was instead a complete failure.[19] In fact, it probably strengthened Castro's growing commitment to communism, and certainly influenced his decision to allow the Soviets to place nuclear missiles on the island in 1962.

When the missiles were discovered by U.S. surveillance missions, the two superpowers came frighteningly close to engaging in outright hostilities. On October 22, 1962, Kennedy told a shocked American public about the missiles, and justified the government's plan to intercept any and all nuclear arms being shipped to Cuba by arguing that the placement of missiles in Cuba represented an unacceptable threat to national security. Moreover, he famously proclaimed that "any nuclear missile launched from Cuba against any nation in the Western Hemisphere" would be interpreted "as an attack by the Soviet Union

against the United States, requiring a full retaliatory response on the Soviet Union."[20] Although the crisis ebbed six days later when Soviet premier Nikita Khrushchev agreed to disassemble the missiles, the Cuban Missile Crisis revealed not only the real dangers of the possibility of nuclear war, but also the lengths to which leaders of the United States were prepared to go to protect their "sphere of influence."

This determination to protect the Americas from the threat of communism spread far beyond Cuba, and—especially during the administration of John F. Kennedy (1961–1963)—increasingly included Central and South America as well. Indeed, following the Cuban Revolution of 1959 Kennedy's administration grew far more concerned about communist movements in Latin America, vowing to fight such movements at any cost. In a speech to Latin American diplomats in March 1961, Kennedy announced his Americas-wide "Alliance for Progress," which affirmed the U.S. commitment to come to the aid of any government threatened by communism.[21] In 1963, the United States backed this commitment by transforming the School for the Americas (SOA)—which had, since 1946, been a training center for professionalizing Latin American armies—into a school for training Latin American military leaders in counter-insurgency and military intelligence techniques, with the aim of rooting out or dislodging communist-inspired movements.[22] This training facility complemented other anti-communist actions that pre-dated the Kennedy administration,

---

[18] Matthew J. Ouimet, *The Rise and Fall of the Brezhnev Doctrine in Soviet Foreign Policy* (Chapel Hill: University of North Carolina Press, 2001), 4.

[19] For the complex development of the plan as well as its outcome, see A.A. Fursenko and Timothy J. Naftali, *One Hell of a Gamble: Khrushchev, Castro, and Kennedy, 1958–1964* (New York: W.W. Norton, 1997), chapter 5.

[20] For details on the crisis itself, see ibid., chapter 13; the full text of Kennedy's speech is available online in many locations, including http://www.historyplace.com/speeches/jfk-cuban.htm.

[21] Walter LaFeber, *Inevitable Revolutions: The United States in Central America* (New York: W.W. Norton, 1993), 151.

[22] The School for the Americas was located in the Panama Canal Zone until 1984, when it was transferred to Georgia. The SOA has been widely criticized for its role in training conservative, but anti-communist, oligarchs in Latin America how to use sophisticated weaponry, tactics, and torture to maintain their hold on power. See, for example, Lesley Gill, *The School of the Americas: Military Training and Political Violence in the Americas* (Durham, NC: Duke University Press, 2004).

such as the CIA-directed coup that overthrew a government sympathetic to communism in Guatemala in 1954.[23] In places such as Nicaragua, from the 1960s through the 1970s the U.S. government sanctioned massive interference and financial assistance to prevent the leftist Sandinistas from gaining power over its longtime ally and pro-U.S. Somoza government. Even after the Sandinistas finally won power in 1979, the United States did not leave the issue alone for long. When the staunch anti-communist Ronald Reagan came into power in 1981, his administration began to fund the Contras, an opposition group that wanted to bring the Sandinistas down. In 1986, it also became clear that the Reagan administration had gone outside the law to secretly funnel money to the Contras with money gained from selling armaments to the government of Iran.[24]

In addition to safeguarding areas within their respective spheres of influence, both the United States and the Soviet Union pursued active policies of intervention in locations where nationalist communist groups battled for power with non-communist groups. Following the articulation of the Truman Doctrine and Eisenhower's "domino theory," such intervention could be justified anywhere in the world. The motivation to combat the spread of communism in Asia was, in fact, behind the United States' decision to intervene in Vietnam after the communist Ho Chi Minh's forces defeated the French in 1954. Following the French defeat, the peace conference in Geneva dictated that Vietnam should be divided between a communist North and a non-communist South until free elections could be held. Fearing that free elections would lead to the extension of communism to the whole of Vietnam, the United States intervened with military aid to help a non-communist South Vietnamese leadership avoid the elections. This blatant interference contributed to the creation, in 1960, of a National Liberation Front in South Vietnam, dedicated to opposing the corrupt South Vietnamese government as well as U.S. meddling in Vietnamese

affairs. Meanwhile, the government in North Vietnam received Chinese and Soviet aid and assistance to achieve the same objective.[25] The result, as in Korea, was a massive military buildup, fierce and brutal fighting and, ultimately, stalemate: in 1975, the United States finally withdrew from Vietnam after admitting it could not win the war. The next year, the communist government in the north conquered South Vietnam and created a united, independent country.

The governments of the United States and the Soviet Union sanctioned interventions in many other locations throughout the four decades of the Cold War. Examples include the Congo in 1961, where CIA operatives cooperated with the anti-communist Mobutu Sese Seko to murder Patrice Lumumba, a popular Maoist Marxist who had just been elected prime minister of the newly independent state.[26] In Angola, a ferocious war that ended in the state's independence from Portugal in 1975 nevertheless left three warring factions in the country to decide who would rule it. One of those groups, the MPLA, was Marxist in orientation, while another—UNITA—was non-communist.[27] These ideological differences attracted the attention of the United States and its allies as well as the Soviet Union and its allies. Both sides sent money and arms to its favored group, which resulted in a long, drawn out civil war that lasted for over a quarter century.[28] Afghanistan provides yet another example of interference. There, the Soviet government became deeply involved when a pro-Soviet coup in 1978 was threatened by massive resistance by anti-Soviet Afghans. When it seemed that the

---

[25] Stockwell, "Southeast Asia in War and Peace," 39; for an excellent set of essays that set up the Cold War context of the Vietnam War, see Mark Atwood Lawrence and Fredrick Logevall, *The First Vietnam War: Colonial Conflict and Cold War Crisis* (Cambridge: Harvard University Press, 2007).

[26] Carole Collins, "The Cold War Comes to Africa: Cordier and the 1960 Congo Crisis," in *The Cold War: Hot Wars of the Cold War*, edited by Lori Lyn Bogle (New York: Routledge, 2001).

[27] MPLA stands for Movimento Popular de Libertação de Angola; UNITA stands for União Nacional para a Independência Total de Angola.

[28] Joseph Smith, *The Cold War, 1945–1991*, 2nd edition (Oxford: Blackwell, 2000), 118.

---

[23] LaFeber, *Inevitable Revolutions*, 113.

[24] Mann, *The Rebellion of Ronald Reagan*, 56.

resistance would topple the pro-Soviet government, the Soviets intervened and installed their
own handpicked leader. This action, however, was
countered not only by intense Afghan resistance
but also by aid and arms provided by the United
States, nearby Islamic states, and China, none of
which wished to see Soviet influence extended in
the region.[29] The result was nine years of brutal
warfare and millions of deaths, after which the
Soviet Union was forced to withdraw.

The Cold War adversaries also battled for
influence in, and dominance over, the Middle East.
Indeed, neither side could ignore this critical region
because of its vast supply of oil—a fuel that was
necessary for the functioning of the industrial
economies and military expansion of both superpowers. U.S. fears about Soviet designs on the
region began to take shape as early as 1946, when
the Soviet Union temporarily occupied Iran's northern province of Azerbaijan.[30] Fears about Soviet
influence were, in fact, behind the admittance of
Turkey to NATO in 1952. Just one year later, the
British government—which had dominated Iran's
economy for decades—finally convinced U.S. leadership that the newly elected, reformist Iranian
president Mohammad Mossadegh had communist
sympathies. Although this was blatantly untrue, the
British needed a way to spur U.S. sympathies, especially since Mossadegh had recently nationalized
the oil industry in Iran that had long been under
British control. To counter this action, British Prime
Minister Winston Churchill had tried to tackle the
problem himself by ordering British operatives to
stage a coup in Iran. However, Mossadegh discovered the plot, closed the British embassy in Tehran,
and ejected all British subjects from the country.
Churchill then turned to the United States, but found
he could get no help until Dwight Eisenhower succeeded Harry Truman in 1953. As it turned out,
Eisenhower was ready to listen to allegations of

Mossadegh's communist leanings. As a result, in
that year CIA operatives arranged a coup that drove
Mossadegh's democratically elected government
from power, and brought the autocratic Mohammed
Reza Shah back from exile and into power.
Thereafter, until the Iranian Revolution of 1979,
Iran proved to be a staunch anti-communist ally in
the region.[31]

To bolster its interests in the Middle East even
further, in 1955 the United States backed the creation of the Baghdad Pact, which was intended to
serve as a military alliance between pro-western,
anti-communist states in the region. The original
members were Turkey and Iraq, although Iran,
Pakistan, and Britain joined a year later.[32] In the
aftermath of the Suez Crisis of 1956, which led to
a dramatic decline of British and French prestige
and diplomatic presence in the region, the United
States increasingly feared that the power vacuum
left by their retreat might allow the Soviets to
increase their influence in a variety of states. The
result was a major new policy initiative by
President Eisenhower in 1957, which became
known as the Eisenhower Doctrine. Its goal, like
the Truman Doctrine before it and Kennedy's
Alliance for Progress a few years later, was to
promise aid and support for any country in the
Middle East threatened by communism.[33] In the
same year, the United States planned to use CIA
operatives to stage a coup in Syria, although the
plan was unsuccessful. In 1958, the United States
responded to the Lebanese president's call for help
to rid him of opposition groups with leftist sympathies by sending troops to quell the opposition.
And, from the 1960s forward, the United States
increasingly lent its military and financial might to
the state of Israel, while the Soviet Union sought
to champion rival Arab states.[34]

[29] See Hassan Kakar, *Afghanistan: The Soviet Invasion and
the Afghan Response* (Berkeley: University of California
Press, 1995).

[30] Mehran Kamrava, *The Modern Middle East: A Political
History Since the First World War* (Berkeley: University of
California Press, 2005), 109.

[31] For a readable summary of these events, see Stephen
Kinzer, *All the Shah's Men: An American Coup and the Roots
of Middle East Terror* (Hoboken, NJ: Wiley and Sons, 2008).

[32] Kamrava, *The Modern Middle East*, 109.

[33] Ibid., 110.

[34] Heller, *The Cold War and the New Imperialism*, 118, 198; and
Rashid Khalidi, *Sowing Crisis: The Cold War and American
Dominance in the Middle East* (Boston: Beacon Press, 2009).

What this all boils down to is that few states in the post–Second World War world had the option of remaining uninvolved in global Cold War rivalries. This was especially the case because the European empires that had dominated the late nineteenth and first half of the twentieth centuries were disintegrating in precisely the same decades that Cold War tensions were heating up. As a result, the diminishing authority of imperial metropoles created space for both the United States and the Soviet Union to attempt to actively win the allegiance of the many new states that were forming in this period. In states where both communist and western-oriented sympathies co-existed, as in Vietnam and Angola, the result could be prolonged war, along with a long delay in independence and considerable destruction to state infrastructure. In the aftermath of the Truman Doctrine of 1947, the Eisenhower Doctrine of 1957, and Kennedy's Alliance for Progress in 1961, moreover, it became progressively more dangerous for groups in any part of the world to pursue a communist revolution, since doing so almost guaranteed either overt or covert interference from the United States. At the same time, the Brezhnev Doctrine of 1968 simply confirmed what states in eastern Europe and parts of Central Asia already knew: that it was impossible to choose their own political course outside of subordination to Soviet control.

We now return to our original question about the extent to which the actions and policies of the United States and the Soviet Union can be classified as imperial, or whether they represent a clear break with the 500 years that preceded it. Let us begin with the term *empire*, which we posited "is an agglomeration of multiple polities and diverse populations bound together in an uneven relationship in which one polity exercises significant control over the others and, in many cases, claims sole sovereignty over all of the polities." In the case of the Cold War superpowers, it is clear that uneven relationships were a hallmark of the era on both sides. Not only did the United States and the Soviet Union dominate their respective military and economic blocs with respect to their acknowledged allies, but both sides also used their economic and military resources to impose their will on a wide variety of states much weaker than themselves. While neither side claimed sole sovereignty over the polities they sought to influence (although the Soviets did claim "limited sovereignty" in eastern Europe), they nevertheless clearly exerted significant control over them through direct military action, economic aid or sanctions, covert operations geared toward regime change, and control over foreign policy. In many respects, then, the Soviet Union and the United States during the Cold War could be construed as empires marked by similar types of informal commitments that were common during the nineteenth century.

As we have seen, the existence of empire is not always accompanied by cultures of imperialism, which we argued are characterized by "an ideology or doctrine in support of the creation and maintenance of empire" that, when translated into action, is "expressed as an aggressive set of policies culminating variously in formal dominion or informal control over external polities or peoples . . . as well as being characterized by belligerence toward rival expansionist powers." Yet during the Cold War, we have seen how both sides formulated an explicit ideology—whether anti-capitalist or anti-communist—that justified interference on a global scale. Moreover, both sides translated their respective ideologies into a highly aggressive set of policies designed not only to exert control but, even more importantly, to thwart one another. If one accepts these arguments, it becomes possible to view Cold War ideologies as cultures of imperialism that justified both interference and expansion on a global scale. And what of colonialism? Earlier, we argued that colonialism "refers to the set of practices and policies implemented by imperial agents to obtain and maintain control, stability, economic objectives, and social engineering in the constituent polities of the imperial periphery." Although the actions and policies of the Cold War superpowers did not involve the settlement of colonists or the wholesale transfer of colonial administrations to the states under their domination, we have seen that there was no shortage of agents trying to implement U.S. and Soviet policies "on the ground" in many zones of interference. In many cases, the Cold War powers used a variety of types of agents that had been used in past eras of colonialism, including soldiers, diplomats, and covert operatives.

Clearly, the era of the Cold War was not the same as the era of High Imperialism that preceded it. The global struggle between capitalism and its representatives and communism and its representatives was a new development made possible by the Russian Revolution of 1917 and the historically specific circumstances of the Second World War and the immediate post-war period. The dominant players, too, had shifted from western Europe to the United States and the Soviet Union. Moreover, the closing of the arms gap—that is, the ability of weaker powers to gain access to modern weaponry and tactics—also ensured that the efforts of the superpowers to intervene in global affairs did not meet with as much success as earlier interventions during the era of informal empire. At times, indeed, both powers were forced to withdraw from the hot wars they had helped to ignite.

At the same time, these shifts in power and ideologies also shared deep continuities with the past. First, both the United States and the Soviet Union had been players in earlier imperial expansions of the nineteenth and twentieth centuries, and were thus hardly divorced from the ideologies justifying intervention that had characterized earlier eras. Moreover, although Cold War ideologies were new to the post-war period, international rivalry between great powers was not: as we have seen, these rivalries provided one of the most consistent features of imperial expansion from the early modern period through to the world wars. As a result, for many of the world's peoples, the policies and actions of the two superpowers during the Cold War looked less like a break with the past than the substitution of interference by one set of powers for another.

ECONOMIC NEO-IMPERIALISM?

It was not only Cold War policies that increasingly began to look like imperialism under a new name to many of the world's peoples. Indeed, just as decolonization was beginning to reshape the world into a series of new nations during the 1960s and 1970s, people in what are now called *developing countries* began to criticize the United States and its allies in western Europe for its control over institutions that governed the accelerating integration of global markets and financial institutions.[35] These criticisms grew louder and more frequent during the 1980s and 1990s, and increasingly included not only voices from the developing world but from academics and policymakers in the industrialized world as well. Especially after the collapse of the Soviet Union in 1989, antagonists of what was believed to be a U.S.-led policy of globalization argued that virtually nothing could stand in the way of the obtrusive economic policies of the industrialized world. Moreover, these critics explicitly associated such economic policies with imperialism. Representative of this viewpoint is the following quotation from 2005:

> The current historical bloc led by the United States maintains a widely shared worldview and imposes corresponding global practices and forms of state control and domination through the World Bank, the International Monetary Fund, neoliberal politics, and military superiority.[36]

In this section, we explore the reasons behind such perceptions, and once again apply our own definitions of empire, imperialism, and colonialism to determine whether or not the perceived phenomenon of economic neo-imperialism shares

---

[35] This phenomenon has often been referred to as *globalization*. For a careful review of globalization and its definitions, see Jürgen Osterhammel and Nils Peterson, *Globalization: A Short History* (Princeton, NJ: Princeton University Press, 2003).
[36] Peter McLaren and Ramin Farahmandpur, *Teaching Against Global Capitalism and the New Imperialism: A Critical Pedagogy* (Oxford: Rowman & Littlefield, 2005), 47.

continuities with earlier imperial eras. Although this issue is extremely complicated and involves many players, we have chosen here to focus on two institutions at the center of the controversy over economic neo-imperialism: the World Bank and the **International Monetary Fund** (IMF).

Both the World Bank and the IMF were conceived in July 1944, during the UN Monetary and Financial Conference at Bretton Woods, New Hampshire. The purpose of the conference was to finance the reconstruction of Europe after the Second World War—in fact, the actual name for the World Bank is the International Bank for Reconstruction and Development—and to prevent future economic crisis such as the Great Depression. The **World Bank** was charged with the first task, which included financing a variety of development and infrastructure project in order to aid reconstruction. The IMF was charged with the second: based on the experiences of the Depression, its task was to help prevent its member economies from going into a slump, either by encouraging the adoption of particular monetary policies or by loans intended to stimulate demand.[37]

Given the origins of the two institutions, it cannot be said that they were created for the purpose of forwarding an imperial agenda. At their founding, the process of decolonization that marked the next three decades had not even begun, and indirect instruments such as the World Bank and the IMF were not needed to manipulate economies in the global south that were under the direct control of the great empires. At the same time, it may well be significant that the United Kingdom, France, and the United States—three of the most powerful imperial nations in the world—were all signatories to the first Articles of Agreement establishing membership in the institutions. In other words, while the World Bank and the IMF were not created to service imperial expansion or control, they were created by nations with significant stakes in the imperial system as it existed at the end of the Second World War.

Moreover, since their founding both institutions have been headquartered in Washington, DC, and their administrations have been headed by an American (World Bank) and a European (IMF).[38]

Membership in the IMF is voluntary, although nations cannot qualify for loans from the World Bank unless they are also members of the IMF.[39] When nations become members of the IMF, they must agree to expose their financial and economic policies to the scrutiny of IMF directors, which includes—among other things—information on government budgets, exchange rates, credit, spending, banking, gross domestic product, and inflation.[40] Governance of the IMF is conducted by a managing director, a board of executives, and a board of governors of member countries. Voting in the IMF is weighted toward those who contribute the most money to the fund. Therefore, the larger a state's contribution, the more voice it has.[41] Additionally, the United States is the only member country to hold effective veto power in the IMF. The World Bank is governed on similar principles: its organizational structure includes a president, a board of directors in Washington, DC, that is composed of appointed members by its largest shareholders and 19 elected members, and a board of governors made up of member countries.[42]

---

[37] Joseph Stiglitz, *Globalization and Its Discontents* (New York: W.W. Norton, 2003), 12.

[38] Ibid., 19.

[39] IMF Home Website, "What is the IMF?" Box 2, accessed at http://www.imf.org/external/pubs/ft/exrp/what.htm#lending. The websites for both the IMF and the World Bank provide a wealth of information on their internal organization, founding, histories, and missions.

[40] "The IMF's Main Business: Macroeconomic and Financial Sector Policies," Box 5, accessed at http://www.imf.org/external/pubs/ft/exrp/what.htm#box5.

[41] "Who Runs the IMF?" accessed at http://www.imf.org/external/pubs/ft/exrp/what.htm#runs. For example, the United States—which holds the most voting power in the IMF because of its financial contribution to its funds—has 371,743 votes, compared to the United Kingdom's substantial 107,635, and Uruguay's 3,315. "IMF Members' Quotas and Voting Power, and IMF Board of Governors," accessed at http://www.imf.org/external/np/sec/memdir/members.htm.

[42] The appointed members of the World Bank are chosen from the United States, the United Kingdom, France, Germany, and Japan. "Organization," World Bank Official Website, accessed at http://web.worldbank.org/WBSITE/EXTERNAL/EXTABOUTUS/0,,contentMDK:20040580~menuPK:1696997~pagePK:51123644~piPK:329829~theSitePK:29708,00.html.

In 1945, member states of the IMF and the World Bank consisted of 29 countries, mostly but not exclusively from the Americas and Europe. In the 1960s, however, membership exploded to include many of the newly independent states created in the process of decolonization. In the early 1990s, membership expanded again to include most of the newly independent states of the former Soviet Union, including Russia itself. As of 2008, membership had been extended to 186 states: an extraordinary number given that the UN recognizes only 193 states around the world.[43] What this means is that 50 years after the creation of these institutions, their membership has grown to include almost every country in the world. For proponents of these institutions, this means that most of the world is now working together to reduce poverty and to maintain economic stability. To their critics, it suggests that two institutions dominated by the wealthiest countries in the world now have almost unlimited reach to pursue economic policies that benefit those countries.

At the World Bank, these policies have shifted over the decades away from European reconstruction (which was largely successful)to the relief of poverty in developing nations. Especially since the era of decolonization brought in so many poor member states desperately in need of infrastructure, the World Bank has focused on providing monies for projects such as road building, education, and financial sector reform.[44] The economic policies of the IMF, in contrast to the World Bank, do not involve financing projects. Rather, the IMF provides three types of services to its member countries. First, the IMF collects economic data about its members, and then advises them annually about IMF recommendations for maintaining economic stability and efficiency. This surveillance, however, does not automatically require action by member states, and can be ignored if member states have not taken out loans from the IMF.[45] The second function of the IMF is to provide currency to those states who have difficulty making their international payments or who cannot achieve stable economic growth. The third function of the IMF is to provide technical assistance to countries who request help with matters of banking, taxation, statistics, and exchange rates.[46]

Notwithstanding the lofty goals of the World Bank and the IMF, the theory and assumption behind many of their policies have been rife with problems. These problems, according to many of their critics, have had a drastic effect on their effectiveness. For example, leaders of World Bank policies often had an imperfect understanding of the countries they were trying to help, and as a result frequently made misplaced assumptions about their needs. Moreover, World Bank policy-makers were frequently reluctant to accept guidance or advice from those in the country who were supposedly being helped. The result, in many cases, was a colossal waste of money and a wide variety of ineffective projects.[47] IMF policy-makers, too, have often failed to understand the internal dynamics of the states to which they are giving aid. Indeed, the head of the IMF has never been required to have prior experience in dealing with the economics of the developing world, and most IMF agents have not been expected to live in the countries for which they make policy.[48]

A deeper problem with the IMF is that the policies it has tended to recommend also clearly benefit the industrial nations that dominate it. For example, IMF policies insist that developing countries open their markets to the goods of industrialized countries, even when industrial

---

[43] The World Bank maintains an extensive and thorough chronology of its history. See "Chronology," accessed at http://web.worldbank.org/WBSITE/EXTERNAL/EXTABOUTUS/EXTARCHIVES/0,,contentMDK:20035653~menuPK:56305~pagePK:36726~piPK:36092~theSitePK:29506,00.html.
[44] "The IMF and the World Bank Have Different Mandates," accessed at http://www.imf.org/external/pubs/ft/exrp/what.htm#box2.

[45] Stiglitz, *Globalization and Its Discontents*, 48.
[46] "How Does the IMF Serve Its Member Countries," accessed at http://www.imf.org/external/pubs/ft/exrp/what.htm#member.
[47] Interview with Malcolm Gillis, former head of Harvard Institute for International Development, September 6, 2009.
[48] The mistakes of the IMF with regard to its policies is the main theme of Stiglitz's *Globalization and Its Discontents*. However, as the former president of the World Bank, his criticisms of that institution have been somewhat muted.

countries do not allow the free flow of goods into their own markets. In addition, IMF policies frequently insist that developing countries stop subsidizing their agricultural sectors, even while industrial countries subsidize their own agricultural sectors to keep them competitive.[49] In fact, most aid from the industrialized nations through the IMF is "tied": that is to say it comes with stipulations that benefit the donor in some way. For example, such aid might require that the country being "aided" buy tools or materials from the donor country. Because this is often very inefficient, the aid actually often ends up helping the recipient country very little while imposing strict conditions upon it.

Moreover, since the 1980s the IMF has become more committed than ever to the ideas of neo-liberalism, or the idea that markets function best with the least amount of government interference.[50] Thus, hallmarks of IMF policy since that time have been the insistence on the elimination of subsidies, the elimination of capital controls, the elimination of trade restrictions and tariffs on foreign goods, the liberalization of restrictions on foreign investment, fiscal discipline with regard to government spending, privatization, and deregulation of anything that impedes market function. Moreover, critics argue that these policies have dominated IMF approaches to client countries without much regard to the differences between them or to their specific needs.[51]

These same critics argue that this kind of market liberalization can actually make client-states' economies more unstable—and their people poorer—than when they applied for help in the first place. They point to numerous examples in which rapid market liberalization, privatization, and the influx of foreign capital investment have caused severe economic disruption, because the sudden influx of foreign goods and foreign companies into weak economies often meant that local products and enterprises could not compete with products and services from the industrialized

world.[52] The result has been, in many cases, the loss of jobs and the destruction of local businesses. To people in developing countries, then, the consequences of market liberalization often smack of unfair foreign domination.

This perception is not altogether inaccurate. Indeed, when member nations apply for IMF loans, they must submit themselves to IMF policies and recommendations, even if national leaders believe the recommendations will be detrimental to the economic health of their countries. Moreover, if countries that have accepted money from the IMF fail to comply with its regulations and recommendations, they risk having their loans suspended. When this happens, foreign companies and agencies that are unaffiliated with the IMF tend to grow uneasy, and withhold monies and investment as well. In some cases, as in the Asian Crisis of 1997, IMF recommendations have required loan recipients to pay off foreign transnational companies who lost money first, before the internal economic needs of the country were met.[53] Such policies, along with the vast authority allocated to IMF policy-makers, have encouraged many people around the world to see the actions of the IMF as impinging on the sovereignty of its loaner nations as well as politically motivated to benefit western transnational companies.

This brings us back to our question about the extent to which it can be said that the United States and other western nations have exercised a kind of economic neo-imperialism over an increasing portion of the world since the break-up of the great formal empires. Certainly an uneven relationship now exists between the United States, western Europe, and, to a lesser extent, Japan on the one hand and developing countries on the other. And, it can be said that these powerful nations can exert their economic will on those countries through an aggressive set of policies through financial institutions such as the IMF, the World Bank, and their links with transnational companies. In addition, it is certainly true that these financial institutions maintain agents within many developing countries

[49] Ibid., 7.
[50] Heller, *The Cold War and the New Imperialism*, 241–242.
[51] Stiglitz, *Globalization and Its Discontents*, 34.
[52] Ibid., chapter 3.
[53] Heller, *The Cold War and the New Imperialism*, 292–293.

to ensure that their policies are being followed as precisely as possible. It also seems clear that the policies of the World Bank, and especially the IMF, have served to benefit western industrialized states far more than they benefit developing countries. Moreover, the players involved in exerting their economic will in the United States and western Europe were also among the most important in establishing informal empires in an earlier period. For these reasons, on the surface it appears that the policies of the World Bank and especially the IMF share strong continuities with the informal imperialism that so marked the middle of the nineteenth century.

Yet there are also several distinctive features of the relationship between western industrialized countries and the developing world—many of whose nations were once colonies—that do not fit neatly into the definitions we forwarded at the beginning of this book. First, even though the IMF and the World Bank can be said to be dominated by the United States in terms of location, voting power, and control of administration, these are not simply the agencies of one powerful nation. Rather, their governance is also disproportionately shared by other industrial countries in western Europe and Japan, and they are advised by boards of governors that are made up of all member nations. Even if we allow that small, economically weak member nations might have little voice in shaping the direction of policy, or that the chosen representatives might not represent the interests of their countries as a whole, these are nevertheless multi-state entities. In the long period of imperialism covered by this book, examples of shared responsibilities for imperial domination were extremely rare—although the informal domination of the Ottoman Empire and China during the nineteenth century offer examples (see chapter 8).

Perhaps most importantly, neither the World Bank nor the IMF can develop authority over economic affairs in a sovereign country unless those countries request intervention themselves. In other words, member nations must ask for IMF loans and World Bank projects, and only then do IMF economic conditions begin to apply. Even if

we allow for the fact that many of the nations that asked for help after the 1960s were once colonies and thus found themselves in dire economic circumstances as a result of their colonial past, is it still possible to classify a relationship as *imperial* when intervention has intentionally been sought by the weaker party? While we do not claim to be able to answer this complex question fully, it is important to note a basic inconsistency with earlier cases of informal and formal colonial rule, in which foreign domination was almost always forced. In spite of this, many people in both the developing world have focused their dissatisfaction with the inequalities in global economic relations around opposition to domination by financial institutions such as the IMF and the World Bank. In recent years, some of these former colonies have begun to turn increasingly to China as an alternate donor, and a debate has begun to rage as to whether China is a collaborative partner or an imperial power in wait.[54]

CULTURAL IMPERIALISM AND POSTCOLONIALISM

This chapter is designed around the problem of whether or not we are living in a post-colonial world. In this formulation, the term *post-colonial* (with a hyphen) refers to a period *after* colonialism, and thus we have been asking whether the age of empires has conclusively ended. This question is related to the one asked by postcolonial (usually written without a hyphen) scholars, but with a subtle distinction. Postcolonial scholars are not generally concerned with exploring the similarities and differences between the era of formal empires and the period we live in. Rather, they explore connections between the two periods so as to look at the impact of the former era on the contemporary world. Like many of the contributors to theories surrounding Cold War imperialism and neo-imperialism, scholars in the postcolonial camp tend to espouse a negative view of imperialism

---

[54] Barry Sautman and Yan Hairong, "Friends and Interests: China's Distinctive Links with Africa," *Africa*, 50 (2007), 75–114.

and colonialism and to see its ongoing impact as detrimental to the world today. As a body of knowledge, therefore, **postcolonialism** revolves around the exploration of the cultural, economic, and political legacies of colonialism today. As a philosophy, it also involves attempts to unravel its impact in the present.[55] It is perhaps unfortunate that the relatively straightforward ideas and methods employed by postcolonialists often get wrapped up in such dense language and theory that they cease to make sense to the uninitiated. Unfortunate, because the work of postcolonial scholars is important and innovative enough that it deserves attention from anyone seeking to understand empires and their impact on human lives.

In order to adequately explore the main strands of postcolonial thought, we need first to historicize it—to understand when and where it comes from. Because a truly comprehensive historicization would take more space than we have here, we will limit ourselves to making four points. First, postcolonialism gradually coalesced as a body of thought and a community of practitioners over the period from the 1960s to the present, but it also drew on the work of scholars and anti-colonial resisters who had written earlier in the century and even in the nineteenth century. Second, postcolonialism is part of a wider movement toward the study of culture that includes postmodernism and what is often called *cultural studies* in the academy today, although these are not the same thing. Third, despite this relationship to other approaches and movements, postcolonialism is unique in that it largely emerged from the work of scholars and activists from the formerly colonized states, not only in the Middle East and South Asia, but also in other parts of Asia, Africa, the Caribbean, and Latin America. Often, these have been men and women who have moved around quite a bit among these regions and between them and the West. The result has been a particularly rich body of work fusing together ideas from many different places. Finally, the coalescing of postcolonialism as an interlinked body of scholarship and work arguably was made possible only by the break-up of formal European-centered empires. The way in which this transition happened resulted both in new opportunities and freedoms and in lingering disappointments and dissatisfactions in the former colonies, all of which helped to form the context for postcolonial work.

Postcolonial scholars are, of course, deeply concerned with the colonial past. Even when they write about the present, postcolonialists do so through an interpretation of the lasting changes wrought by the colonialism, capitalism, and liberalism of the recent past. Central to their work is an appreciation that over the era in which the grand empires were built, the many different, multi-faceted cultural systems that had characterized the diverse societies of the world came to be replaced or dominated by a monopolistic colonial system. In other words, postcolonialism begins with the assertion that colonialism fundamentally re-ordered the world. What some scholars call *modernity* or *globalization* refers, in the minds of many postcolonial scholars, to the process of the conquest and domination of much of the world by the forces of colonialism and imperialism. Most of them would agree that through this process, European people and western ideals and culture came to be widely held as superior and central, while ideas and people emanating from elsewhere were depicted as inferior and peripheral.[56] Two results of this process were the creation of a new, widely imposed set of hierarchies and the segregation of peoples, genders, cultures, and ideas under this hierarchical system.[57] Another, at times contradictory, trend was the imposition of "western" ideals of gender, race, and culture upon

[55] For some guide texts to postcolonialism used repeatedly in this chapter, see John McLeod, *Beginning Postcolonialism* (Manchester: Manchester University Press, 2000); Barbara Bush, *Imperialism and Postcolonialism* (Harrow: Pearson Longman, 2006); and Robert J.C. Young, *Postcolonialism: A Very Short Introduction* (Oxford: Oxford University Press, 2003).

[56] See, for example, Achille Mbembe, *On the Postcolony* (Berkeley: University of California Press, 2001).
[57] Partha Chatterjee, *The Nation and Its Fragments: Colonial and Postcolonial Histories* (Princeton, NJ: Princeton University Press, 1993).

the colonized. Some postcolonial scholars also point out that by putting themselves on top of this hierarchy, the colonizers claimed the right to "gaze" at colonized people: to describe them, to know them, and to speak for them without allowing them to speak back.[58] Some go further, to argue that one of the places where this powerful gaze was (and remains) most concentrated is the "academy" and its universities. Finally, many postcolonial scholars argue that these cultures of colonialism and imperialism were key to the development of uneven distributions of economic and political power around the world in the past few centuries.

A subsequent key contention within postcolonial thought is that despite the demise of the formal empires, we are not yet free of the colonial re-ordering of the world.[59] Postcolonial scholars point to evidence for existence of colonialism today in the continued global dominance of the ideas and structures that it introduced to the world: for example, capitalism, centralized European-style forms of governance, "scientific" notions of race and the tribe, European languages, and the formal university. Postcolonial scholars also assert that certain symbols and hierarchies introduced by colonialism are still powerful today: for example, it is easy to find in movies, books, magazines, and other forms of popular and scholarly communication categories such as the African savage, the inscrutable Asian, and the cultured and rational European. Some postcolonial scholars even see the colonial-era ideology of the "civilizing mission" as the root of contemporary European and North American claims to be defenders of "human rights" around the world. Finally, many find it ironic that formal colonialism was only defeated by European-style nationalist parties. They believe that the current "nationalist" rulers of the former colonies, despite being locals, have merely stepped into the shoes of the former colonizers

without implementing any real changes or reversing the effects of colonialism.[60]

It ensures that many contributors to postcolonialism can be said to be activists who are fighting to "free" the former colonies from the ongoing effects of cultural, political, and economic imperialism and colonialism today. They see themselves as not unlike previous generations of anti-colonial resisters, even if their weapons are words rather than swords or guns. The leading South Asian postcolonial scholar Dipesh Chakrabarty, for example, has called on academics in universities to "play the role of public intellectuals with the aim of furthering the causes of social justice and democracy."[61] Their mission is to reverse or overturn the colonial order, possibly by finding a way to return to the cultural plurality of the pre-colonial era or by presenting alternatives to totalizing colonial tools such as capitalism and the nation-state. For example, the Committee for Cultural Choices and Global Futures (CCCGF), a leading postcolonial organization based in India, declares as its mission "an intellectual concern for the ecology of plural knowledge, a normative concern for cultural survival, and a potential concern with the search for humane futures for the victims of history."[62]

The phrase *victims of history* deserves something of a deeper examination, especially in a history text like this one. As expressed by the CCCGF's mission statement, it refers to the postcolonial objective of convincing or forcing the world to listen to the voices of those rendered powerless or objectified by past and present colonialism. Within this context, many postcolonial scholars are somewhat wary of History as an academic discipline, not least because they see it as having been originally enacted by the colonizers

---

[58] The classic study is Edward W. Said, *Orientalism* (New York: Vintage Books, 1978).

[59] To paraphrase Simon Gikandi, *Maps of Englishness: Writing Identity in the Culture of Colonialism* (New York: Columbia University Press, 1996), 14.

[60] Partha Chatterjee, *Nationalist Thought and the Colonial World: A Derivative Discourse* (London: Zed Books, 1986); and Mahmood Mamdani, *Citizen and Subject; Contemporary Africa and the Legacy of Late Colonialism* (Princeton, NJ: Princeton University Press, 1996).

[61] Dipesh Chakrabarty, "Where Is the Now?" *Critical Enquiry*, 30 (2003–2004), 459.

[62] Vinay Lal, UCLA web description, http://www.history.ucla.edu/people/faculty?lid=51.

to forcibly replace pre-colonial forms of histori-cal analysis in Africa, Asia, and elsewhere—oral tradition, memory, and religious rituals, for example—and then used to justify colonial rule.[63] For example, we have seen in earlier chapters how colonial curricula and teachers frequently taught Africans, Asians, and other colonial subjects that they had no history or only a barbaric past. Thus, it is no surprise that in places such as South Africa and India, some students and scholars have rejected History as it had been taught in colonial universities and sought new ways of relating to the past.[64] This includes seeking to create an appreciation for popu-lar memory and other ways in which people outside the academy have sought to understand the past. It also includes attempts to write "radical histories from below" that seek to understand past events from the perspectives of colonial subjects whose views have often been excluded in the past. Postcolonial scholars are often engaged in these tasks, although not everyone believes that the views of the colonized "everyman" can be adequately rep-resented by any university-trained scholars, no mat-ter how postcolonial. These critics, like Gayatri Chakravorty Spivak, have suggested instead that the role of academics should be to expose how colonialism has sought to portray its subjects in ways that take power away from them.[65]

In sum, postcolonialists seek to undo colo-nialism by forcing us to confront its effects. They strive to expose the horrors of colonialism in order to force us to question assumptions about who is civilized and what is modern. They attempt to reveal the flaws in colonial hierarchies and categories and to help us to see the world in messier, more plural terms. They turn the "colo-nial gaze" back on the colonizer by listening to the perspectives of colonial subjects and their

descendants. Finally, they attempt to confront what they argue is the reality of colonialism's continued existence and to challenge it with alter-nate systems of knowledge.

But postcolonialism has its skeptics as well. There are those who argue that colonialism ended with the death of colonies. They suggest that whatever defines the modern world, it is not imperialism or colonialism. Some of these schol-ars are from former colonies, and believe that the postcolonial perspective excuses corrupt or crimi-nal leaders who can merely point to "colonial-ism" as the cause of poverty in their countries. They also suggest that postcolonialism merely portrays them as *victims*, rather than real people. Others critics suggest that postcolonialism is just complex academic posturing and not really rele-vant to real, material crises such as poverty, envi-ronmental degradation, and AIDS.[66] Still others suggest that postcolonialism was in the past use-ful in revealing the powerful legacy of colonial-ism, but that it has already done so to such a degree that colonial power has been broken. Consequently, they argue, postcolonialism is a victim of its own success and no longer really necessary.[67] Postcolonial scholars, however, respond by citing what they feel is the very real and ongoing nature of colonialism and the need to undo its legacy and to restore power to the former subjects of empires, many of whom still languish in poverty and powerlessness.

THE PERSISTENCE OF EMPIRE?

As we have seen in this chapter, many of the world's peoples remained unconvinced that the era of global imperialism ended with the decolo-nization of the great European empires after the Second World War. In fact, the practices and poli-cies of the two Cold War superpowers in the decades immediately following the War shared a

---

[63] See Ranajit Guha, *Dominance Without Hegemony: History and Power in Colonial India* (Cambridge: Harvard University Press, 1997).

[64] An important South African work in this regard is Premesh Lalu, *The Deaths of Hintsa: Postapartheid South Africa and the Shape of Recurring Pasts* (Cape Town: HSRC Press, 2009).

[65] Gayatri C. Spivak, "Can the Subaltern Speak?" in *Marxism and the Interpretation of Culture,* edited by C. Nelson and L. Grossberg (Champaign: University of Illinois Press, 1988).

[66] For a discussion from the perspectives of African studies, see Rita Abrahamsen, "African Studies and the Postcolonial Challenge," *African Affairs*, 102 (2003), 189–210.

[67] Vijay Mishra and Bob Hodge, "What Was Postcolonialism?" *New Literary History*, 36 (2005), 375–402.

great many continuities with past imperial practice in the nineteenth and early twentieth centuries. Meanwhile, the economic power exerted by western industrialized nations through institutions such as the IMF and World Bank has not always worked to the benefit of people in developing or economically weak countries, and has led many people to believe that the United States and its economic allies are intentionally attempting to recreate the economic dependencies that so characterized the era of informal imperialism. Finally, scholars led by those who hail from the former colonized world point out the many ways that the psychological, cultural, and linguistic legacies of imperialism are still with us in the present.

This is not all. Since the beginning of the United States' War on Terror following the attacks on the World Trade Center and the Pentagon on September 11, 2001, critics from all over the world—including from within the United States—have warned of the dawn of a new imperial era. Pointing to the invasions of Iraq and Afghanistan in 2001 and 2003, they argue that the United States represents a new form of belligerent empire-building unfettered by competition from rival superpowers.[68] Depicting it as drunk on its own power, empowered by its economic domination of the world, and sustained by 725 military bases on foreign soil, these critics argue that the United States must be viewed in the same way as the imperial powers of earlier eras.[69] Opposition to such formulations, however, are loud and plentiful: its champions argue that the invasion of Afghanistan was a matter of self-defense, and the invasion of Iraq was an attempt to free the world of a brutal dictator. Moreover, they claim that U.S. military bases and economic policies offer protection for many of the world's peoples as well as an avenue for future economic growth. For our purposes here, while it is certainly true that U.S. policies in the early twenty-first century grew out of a long tradition of global imperialism and colonialism—in which the United States was a direct participant—it is perhaps too early to evaluate their long-term significance in the history of empires. Similarly, we cannot yet evaluate the suggestion that China is turning into an imperial metropole with a world-spanning informal empire. One thing, however, seems certain: many of the world's peoples view the current global political situation in terms of an imperial past. If nothing else, this justifies a deeper understanding of that past, for the legacies of imperialism and colonialism have cast long shadows over the present.

---

[68] G. John Ikenberry, "America's Imperial Ambition," *Foreign Affairs* (September/October 2002); Eric Hobsbawm, "America's Imperial Delusion," *Guardian*, June 15, 2003; Noam Chomsky, *Imperial Ambitions: Conversations on the Post 9-11 World* (New York: Metropolitan Books, 2005); and Gedilaghine Igor, "Iranian FM Blasts US 'imperialism' as He Visits Russia," *Agence France Presse*, April 4, 2002.

[69] For the number of military bases on foreign soil and their relationship to this conception of American imperialism, see Chalmers Johnson, *The Sorrows of Empire: Militarism, Secrecy, and the End of the Republic* (New York: Metropolitan Books, 2004), 4.

GLOSSARY

accommodation in terms of colonialism, accommodation suggests the process by which colonial subjects acceded to imperial rule and colonial projects but found ways to avoid some of its effects.

acculturation modifications in culture, beliefs, or values as a result of borrowing from or adapting to other cultures.

ayans a term applied collectively to various merchants, officials, and representatives of subordinated peoples in the Ottoman Empire who in the eighteenth century played a leading role in commerce and often supported reformist movements.

capitulations agreements made between the Ottoman Empire and various European imperial states, often under threat of force, that recognized special rights for Europeans and sometimes their status as "protectors" of non-Muslim populations within the empire.

civilizing mission the idea of a duty or mission to colonize and thus culturally or economically "raise" colonial subjects, various concepts of a civilizing mission were often used to prop up cultures of imperialism in the metropole as well as shaping colonialism in the periphery.

collaboration a problematic term describing the process by which some colonial subjects aided or worked with colonizers and agents of colonialism. Often used as a pejorative.

colonialism the set of practices and policies implemented by imperial agents to obtain and maintain control, stability, economic objectives, and social engineering in the constituent polities of the imperial periphery. These projects may be formulated by metropolitan agencies, colonial officials, or in rare cases local groups. In every case, however, the manner in which they unfold is heavily influenced by decisions undertaken by locally stationed agents of the imperial power and by the actions of the inhabitants of these overseas regions. Thus, while colonialism is related to imperialism, it is tied much more closely to events within the colonized regions and among colonized peoples and becomes therefore somewhat different in practice. The study of colonialism by necessity takes into consideration the manner by which populations, groups, and individuals accommodated, negotiated,

resisted, infiltrated, cooperated, and tried to manage colonial rule.

colonization as distinct from colonialism, the act of settling metropolitan citizens overseas while maintaining their identity as distinct from that of the local colonial subjects.

colony derived from a Greek term specifically relating to overseas settlements of Greek-speaking peoples, *colony* in the modern world has come to refer to a wide range of polities in a subordinate position to an imperial metropole.

Columbian Exchange a label given to the exchange of species, goods, people, diseases, and ideas following Columbus's arrival in St. Domingue and the flourishing of trade routes between Afro-Eurasia and the Americas.

concubinage the supposedly informal association of male colonizers or colonial officials and female colonial subjects, concubinage in fact was often a long-term arrangement and females designated as concubines often played important roles as cultural brokers.

creole a term that connotes mixed or complicated identity. In the Spanish colonies in the Americas, creole usually suggested people of European ancestry but born in the Americas. In the French Caribbean, by contrast, it referred to peoples of mixed ancestry.

creolization the process by which individuals and groups in a new place come together to form new, hybrid identities and cultural expressions of those identities.

decolonization as usually used to describe a process of the twentieth century, decolonization refers only to the transfer of sovereignty from imperial metropole to local authorities.

dependency in describing relationships within empires, a dependency is a semi-autonomous state in a subordinate position to an imperial metropole but without formally having lost its sovereignty.

dominion in describing relationships within the twentieth-century British Empire, a dominion was a colonial possession heavily settled by British emigrants and with some degree of self-rule.

economienda a system implemented in several regions of the Americas that gave Spanish settlers control over the labor and to some extent the entire lives of local colonial subjects. This system mutated into the *rapartimiento* and *mita* systems of forced labor in Mexico and Peru.

emancipatory nationalism a type of nationalism that takes the form of a struggle against an "outside" or imperial power. Emancipatory nationalism usually functions to bring together a population with many different identities and its proponents struggle to impose a national identity over all of them.

empire an agglomeration of multiple polities and diverse populations bound together in an uneven relationship in which one polity exercises significant control over the others and, in many cases, claims sole sovereignty over all of the polities. This relationship is characterized by an intricate network of political, economic, cultural, legal, communication, and demographic ties. An empire is born when disparate polities or peoples become subordinated to a dominant polity. It can be said to have ceased to exist when the constituent polities re-establish sovereignty over themselves or become so integrated into the dominant polity that there is no longer any significant difference between them either by law or in practice. In many cases, however, one empire segues into another, a process that is denoted by the transfer of the imperial metropole to a new location.

encadrement a French policy put in place during the First World War that segregated soldiers drawn from among colonial subject populations from the French population.

eugenics the scientific or pseudo-scientific pursuit of improved "racial qualities" through selective breeding and sometimes the elimination or sterilization of supposedly inferior peoples. Eugenics was harnessed to imperialism in some cases in the late nineteenth and early twentieth centuries.

free trade a set of theories and/or political and economic policies supporting the lowering of protectionism and restrictions to international capitalist trade. It characterized the dominant British ideology and policy during much of the nineteenth century while the British enjoyed an advantage in producing finished products cheaply and rapidly due to the advances of the Industrial Revolution.

High Imperialism a term that usually describes the cultures of imperialism and colonialism of the period following the First World War and up to decolonization, both of which were more invasive and extensive than in previous periods.

imperialism an ideology or doctrine in support of the creation and maintenance of empire. When held by significant and opinion-forming segments of society, often

within the context of tension between great powers, it can become inextricably intertwined with other economic, social, cultural, demographic, environmental, gendered, and political aspects of society so that it is relevant both to domestic politics and to foreign affairs. When political decision-making bodies translate imperialist sentiments into action, it is expressed as an aggressive set of policies culminating variously in formal dominion or informal control over external polities or peoples (that is, empire), as well as being characterized by belligerence toward rival expansionist powers.

informal empire a situation characterized by cultures of imperialism and overseas spheres of influence but without formal transfers of sovereignty or authority from subordinated states to the imperial metropole. Informal empire can co-exist with formal empire, and often does. The term is most commonly associated with the mid-nineteenth century and especially during the British Empire during this period.

International Monetary Fund an international organization formed in 1945 that helps to formulate and control global monetary policy through macroeconomic manipulation, often accused of being a neo-imperial institution.

invention of tradition the notion that traditions do not necessarily result from long histories, but are instead created or produced to suit contemporary needs.

lebensraum the German imperial notion of a need for "room to live" that justified Nazi imperial expansion in eastern Europe.

legitimacy the acceptance of a group's, dynasty's, or individual's "right" to hold power by significant portions of the population and/or important elite groups.

mandate the sovereignty of territories surrendered by one of the losing powers in the First World War was in many cases technically placed with the League of Nations, but real authority was transferred to winning powers who were given mandates by the League to administer them. In reality, this often meant they were treated as colonies.

mandsabdar feudal, land-administrating military commanders within the Mughal Empire who often had close personal relationships with the empire and served as important props to the imperial system.

mercantilism an economic theory and system that preached economic competition among states and the need to conserve capital within a state or empire, mercantilism thrived during the seventeenth and eighteenth centuries.

mestizo   a term applied in the Spanish empire in the Americas referring to people of mixed racial background.

metis   a French term for people of mixed heritage.

metropole   a term that is normally applied to define and delimit the ruling polity and/or mass of imperial citizenry within an empire, as distinct from the periphery and colonial subjects.

millets   communities outside of Sharî'a law within the Ottoman Empire and in a subordinate (colonial) yet often semi-autonomous and even privileged position.

missionism   the driving force behind religious missionaries as well as their objectives, missionism is especially applied to evangelical Christians in the nineteenth and twentieth centuries who in the imperial context traveled to colonies to convert colonial subjects and attempt to re-shape their lives.

mita system   a colonial labor system modified by the Spanish in Peru, whereby all taxpayers had to work a prescribed number of days annually for the colonial power.

negotiation   in terms of colonialism, negotiation connotes formal or semi-formal processes by which certain colonial subjects and colonizers or agents of the metropole came to terms that enabled the implementation of colonial projects, although often modified by the process.

New Imperialism   a label applied to the late nineteenth and early twentieth centuries by British economist John A. Hobson. The New Imperialism refers to the increase in imperial competition and the sudden rush for formal colonies on the part of a number of European powers including Britain, France, Germany, and later Italy as well as Japan and to some degree the United States.

Non-Aligned Movement   an international organization of states that emerged during the post–Second World War era that refused to align with either side in the Cold War struggle but that took a strong stance in favor of decolonization.

pacification   a term that ironically technically means *making peaceful*, but which during the New Imperialism was applied to the conquest and often violent subjugation of colonies and their populations.

pan-Africanize   in the context of decolonization, an anti-colonial movement that sought to unite all Africans or peoples of African descent in struggle against colonialism and discrimination.

pan-Arabism   a movement for the unification of Arabs, defined linguistically and in terms of heritage and heredity.

periphery   a contested but still useful term describing the whole of an empire outside of the metropole(s).

postcolonialism   a widely applied term that mostly relates to scholarly or intellectual attempts to reverse the "colonial gaze" and thus to understand history and the contemporary world through the eyes of people living under colonial rule or in the shadow of its legacies.

privateer   a privately owned warship commissioned to prey on the commercial shipping or warships of an enemy nation.

proconsular state   in describing colonialism, the term *proconsular* refers to the need to build an almost complete state structure and bureaucracy within the colony in order to administer it.

protectorate   in describing relationships within empires, protectorates were possessions that were subordinate to an imperial metropole but retained some sovereignty through the reality or fiction of a treaty between the local rulers and the imperial power.

rationalization   in describing state formation, the process by which the state becomes more highly organized, usually through the development of infrastructure and bureaucracy.

reconquista   the process by which the Christian monarchies of Portugal and Spain came to dominate the Iberian Peninsula by ejecting, dominating, or defeating rival Islamic states.

resistance   a blanket term describing the processes by which colonial subjects opposed colonial rule and colonial projects either by violent or by non-violent means.

sectoral alliances   informal or formal partnerships between the state and elements of business, aristocracy, religious hierarchy, and/or political factions that facilitated the rise of empires.

settler nationalism   a type of nationalism that emerged in the post-war period during which empires were in retreat. In some cases, imperial citizens living in the colonies sought to replace imperial rule with their own authority and power while maintaining the structures of colonialism in place.

sipâhî   feudal landowners within the Ottoman Empire who promised service to the Sultan in return for military and administrative service.

social Darwinism   the application of evolutionary theory to human situations, social Darwinism promotes competition among nations or "races" on the idea that the fittest will naturally survive and supposedly inferior peoples dwindle.

sub-nationalism a social and/or political movement based that seeks to define and promote a nation based on ethnic, religious, or other identity but not encompassing the entire population of a state.

tributary a term sometimes used to describe the relationship between a conquered population or state and an imperial metropole, in which day-to-day political authority remains in the hands of local leaders but the conquered (or tributary) state repeatedly pays an agreed sum or sends a certain amount of goods or people to the metropole.

World Bank an international financial institution set up in 1946 mainly to assist in European reconstruction. Since the 1960s, it has provided project-based and technical assistance mainly to developing countries.

zamindar within the Mughal Empire and later under the British, a class of rural gentry who controlled land and to some degree the people working on it.

INDEX